Foundations of Bilingual Education and Bilingualism

BILINGUAL EDUCATION AND BILINGUALISM
Series Editors: Professor Nancy H. Hornberger, *University of Pennsylvania, Philadelphia, USA*
and Professor Colin Baker, *University of Wales, Bangor, Wales, UK*

Other Books in the Series
At War With Diversity: US Language Policy in an Age of Anxiety
  James Crawford
Bilingual Education and Social Change
  Rebecca Freeman
Curriculum Related Assessment, Cummins and Bilingual Children
  Tony Cline and Norah Frederickson (eds)
English in Europe: The Acquisition of a Third Language
  Jasone Cenoz and Ulrike Jessner (eds)
Japanese Children Abroad: Cultural, Educational and Language Issues
  Asako Yamada-Yamamoto and Brian Richards (eds)
Language Minority Students in the Mainstream Classroom
  Angela L. Carrasquillo and Vivian Rodriguez
Languages in America: A Pluralist View
  Susan J. Dicker
Learning English at School: Identity, Social Relations and Classroom Practice
  Kelleen Toohey
Language, Power and Pedagogy: Bilingual Children in the Crossfire
  Jim Cummins
Language Revitalization Processes and Prospects
  Kendall A. King
The Languages of Israel: Policy, Ideology and Practice
  Bernard Spolsky and Elana Shohamy
Reflections on Multiliterate Lives
  Diane Belcher and Ulla Connor (eds)
The Sociopolitics of English Language Teaching
  Joan Kelly Hall and William G. Eggington (eds)
Studies in Japanese Bilingualism
  Mary Goebel Noguchi and Sandra Fotos (eds)
Teaching and Learning in Multicultural Schools
  Elizabeth Coelho
Teaching Science to Language Minority Students
  Judith W. Rosenthal
Working with Bilingual Children
  M.K. Verma, K.P. Corrigan and S. Firth (eds)
Young Bilingual Children in Nursery School
  Linda Thompson

Other Books of Interest
Beyond Bilingualism: Multilingualism and Multilingual Education
  Jasone Cenoz and Fred Genesee (eds)
The Care and Education of Young Bilinguals
  Colin Baker
Encyclopedia of Bilingualism and Bilingual Education
  Colin Baker and Sylvia Prys Jones

Please contact us for the latest book information:
Multilingual Matters, Frankfurt Lodge, Clevedon Hall,
Victoria Road, Clevedon, BS21 7HH, England
http://www.multilingual-matters.com

BILINGUAL EDUCATION AND BILINGUALISM 27
Series Editors: Nancy Hornberger and Colin Baker

Foundations of Bilingual Education and Bilingualism

Third Edition

Colin Baker

MULTILINGUAL MATTERS LTD
Clevedon • Buffalo • Toronto • Sydney

Library of Congress Cataloging in Publication Data
Baker, Colin.
Foundations of Bilingual Education and Bilingualism/Colin Baker, 3rd edn.
Bilingual Education and Bilingualism: 27.
Includes bibliographical references and index.
1. Education, Bilingual. 2. Education, Bilingual–Great Britain. 3. Bilingualism.
4. Bilingualism–Great Britain. I. Title. II. Series.
LC3715.B35 2001
370.117–dc21   00-050072

British Library Cataloguing in Publication Data
A CIP catalogue record for this book is available from the British Library.

ISBN 1-85359-524-1 (hbk)
ISBN 1-85359-523-3 (pbk)

Multilingual Matters Ltd
UK: Frankfurt Lodge, Clevedon Hall, Victoria Road, Clevedon BS21 7HH.
USA: UTP, 2250 Military Road, Tonawanda, NY 14150, USA.
Canada: UTP, 5201 Dufferin Street, North York, Ontario M3H 5T8, Canada.
Australia: Footprint Books, PO Box 418, Church Point, NSW 2103, Australia.

Copyright © 2001 Colin Baker. Reprinted 2002, 2003.

Printed and bound in Great Britain by Biddles Ltd (www.biddles.co.uk).

Contents

Introduction vii
Acknowledgements. xi
Chapter 1   Bilingualism: Definitions and Distinctions 1
Chapter 2   The Measurement of Bilingualism 17
Chapter 3   Languages in Society 42
Chapter 4   Language Revival and Revitalization. 67
Chapter 5   The Development of Bilingualism 85
Chapter 6   Second Language Acquisition and Learning 109
Chapter 7   Bilingualism and Cognition 134
Chapter 8   Cognitive Theories of Bilingualism and the Curriculum 162
Chapter 9   An Introduction to Bilingual Education. 181
Chapter 10   Bilingual Education for Bilingualism and Biliteracy. 203
Chapter 11   The Effectiveness of Bilingual Education 228
Chapter 12   The Effectiveness of Bilingual Education: The United
               States Debate. 244
Chapter 13   Language Development and Language Allocation in
               Bilingual Education 268
Chapter 14   Bilingual Schooling Issues: Underachievement, Assessment
               and Special Needs 295
Chapter 15   Literacy in Minority Language and Multicultural Societies . . 318
Chapter 16   Literacy and Biliteracy in the Classroom 341
Chapter 17   Immersion Classrooms 356
Chapter 18   The Politics of Bilingualism. 366
Chapter 19   Multiculturalism and Anti-Racism 401
Chapter 20   Bilingualism in the Modern World 416
Conceptual Map. 438
Bibliography 439
Index   474

Introduction

This book is intended as an introduction to bilingual education and bilingualism. Written from a cross-disciplinary perspective, the book covers a wide range of topics: individual and societal concepts in minority and majority languages; childhood developmental perspectives; general bilingual education issues, bilingual and second language classrooms, and political and multicultural perspectives. Bilingualism relates to, for example, use of two communication systems, identity and personality, thinking, social organization and culture. All of these are encapsulated in this book.

In compiling the second and third editions, increasingly tough decisions had to be made as to what to include and exclude, what to present in detail and what to summarize, what assumptions to explore and what to take 'as read'. I have often been asked: 'Why don't you put Chapter X earlier?' I agree, everything should be earlier. The Introductions to the two sections explain the order of the book. Other frequently asked questions are 'Why don't you expand on Y?'; Why don't you leave out Z because it is irrelevant to me?' and Why can't we have an edition just for our region?'. What follows are some explanations of the nature of the third edition.

An attempt is made to balance the psychological and the sociological, the macro education issues and the micro classroom issues, the linguistic and the sociopolitical, and to balance discussion at individual and societal levels. An attempt is made to be inclusive of the major international concerns in bilingualism and bilingual education. Faced with the social and political problems that surround bilinguals, students will find in this book an attempt to analyze constructively those problems and recognize the positive values and virtues in a future bilingual and multicultural world.

This book starts with wide, macro issues, and then funnels down to specific, micro issues. Definitional, sociological and psychological issues provide the foundation. Discussions of bilingual education and bilingual classrooms are built on that essential foundation. However, the book is more than a cross-disciplinary foundation with a series of education layers built on top. Within the boundaries of clarity in writing style and readable structuring, explicit inter-connections are made between chapters. A simple **concept map** of these inter-connections is given in an Appendix. This conceptual map will, for most, only make sense after reading the whole book. The map also provides the instructor with a simplified but integrated plan of the book. It is an attempt to avoid the compartmentalization that sometimes results from reading discrete chapters, to show how themes link together into an integrated whole.

In writing the book, a constant challenge has been 'From whose perspective?' There are majority mainstream viewpoints, relatively advantaged minority language viewpoints and various disadvantaged minority language viewpoints. There are left-wing and right-wing politics, activist and constructivist ideas. The book attempts to represent a variety of viewpoints and beliefs. Where possible, multiple perspectives are shared. Readers and reviewers have kindly pointed out some of the hidden and implicit assumptions made, and kindly provided alternative viewpoints that I have tried to represent faithfully in the text. Where there are conclusions and dominating perspectives, I alone stand responsible.

Another issue has concerned generalization and contextualization. The book was written for an international audience to reflect ideas that transcend national boundaries. The book attempts to locate issues of international generalizability. Unfortunately, space limits discussion of a variety of regional and national language situations. There are other writings that will provide necessary contextualization (e.g. Baker & Jones, 1998). Where particular situations have been discussed (e.g. US debates), it is often because of the thoroughness of documentation and the depth of analysis in the surrounding literature. Where bilingual situations are discussed, by inference this will usually include multilingual situations. In this book, multilinguals are often implied in the use of the term 'bilinguals'.

In an attempt to make the contents of this book relevant to a variety of contexts and regions, various chapters focus on **integrating theories**. From one individual research study, it is usually impossible to generalize. A study from Europe may say little about North America. Results on six-year-olds may say nothing about sixteen- or sixty-year-olds. Research on middle-class children speaking French and English in a dual language school may say little or nothing about children from a lower social class in a 'subtractive' bilingual environment (where the second language is likely to replace the first language). Therefore, an overview and integration of major areas of bilingual research is required. From a gray mass of research and sometimes from a paucity of research, a theoretical framework will attempt to outline the crucial parameters and processes. Thus a theoretical framework on a particular area of bilingualism may attempt to do one or more of the following: attempt to explain phenomena; integrate a diversity of (apparently contradictory) findings; locate the key parameters and interactions operating; be able to predict outcomes and patterns of bilingual behavior; be capable of testing for falsification or refinement; express the various conditions that will allow the theory to be appropriate in a variety of contexts.

However, in providing a relatively comprehensive synthesis of bilingualism and bilingual education, the danger lies in suggesting that there is a systematic coherence to the subject. While some teachers and many students want 'recipes' and clear assertions, the current state of our knowledge and understanding rarely provides that clarity. The book therefore attempts to represent differences, contested positions, varied viewpoints and the limitations of research and theory.

Instructors, in particular, will wish to know what are the specific changes in the third edition. First, there are many minor changes. For example, references have been updated, research findings added and corrections made. Second, and importantly, there are new or more thoroughly covered topics: recent changes in bilingual education in the United States, Dual Language schools, California and Proposition 227, the recent politics of bilingual education, the economic advantages of bilingual education, language loss in the world and endangered languages, debates on effective bilingual education, bilingualism in the economy, bilingualism and the Information Communications Technology revolution, language censuses, fractional and holistic views of bilingualism, a critical approach to the politics of language testing, translanguaging in the classroom, immersion experiences outside Canada, early bilingualism in children, trilingualism and codeswitching.

The third edition does not go into great detail on classroom methodology because there is a **Reader** to accompany this book entitled: *Policy and Practice in Bilingual Education: Extending the Foundations* (1995) and published by Multilingual Matters Ltd. This Reader contains a selection of the most important and influential contributions on bilingualism and bilingual education and is edited by Ofelia García (New York) and myself. Each is a 'classic' or a pivotal paper. The Reader provides an introduction to recent fundamental and formative ideas on Bilingualism and Bilingual Education in four sections: Section 1, Policy and Legislation on Bilingualism in Schools and Bilingual Education; Section 2, Implementation of Bilingual Policy in Schools: Structuring Schools; Section 3, Using Bilingualism in Instruction: Structuring Classrooms; Section 4, Using the Bilingualism of the School Community: Teachers and Parents. The hope is that the third edition will have retained the strengths of the first and second editions, eradicated perceived weaknesses, and added new text to provide a comprehensive, international introduction to this ever-expanding and flourishing area of study.

ORGANIZATION OF THE BOOK

The starting point of the book is an introduction to the language used in discussing bilingual education and bilingualism. Not only are important terms introduced, but also key concepts, distinctions and debates which underpin later chapters are presented. There are important dualisms and paradoxes throughout the study of bilingualism: the individual bilingual person as different from groups and societies where bilinguals live; the linguistic view compared with the sociocultural view; preservation and revivalist viewpoints; language skills and language competences; subtractive and additive forms of bilingualism. The opening chapters (1 to 8) present foundational issues that precede and influence discussions about bilingual education. Before we can sensibly talk about bilingual education we need to tackle questions such as:

- Who are bilinguals?
- How does bilingual education fit into minority language maintenance, language decay and language revival?
- How does a child become bilingual?
- What effect does the home and the neighborhood play in developing bilingualism?

- Does bilingualism have a positive or negative effect on thinking?

Chapters 9 to 17 focus on the many aspects of bilingual education. We commence with a broad discussion of different types of bilingual education, followed by an examination of the effectiveness of those types. After a focus on systems of bilingual education, the book proceeds to examine bilingual classrooms, biliteracy and dual language classroom strategies. The underlying questions are:

- What forms of bilingual education are more successful?
- What are the aims and outcomes of different types of bilingual education?
- What are the essential features and approaches of a classroom fostering bilingualism?
- What are the key problems and issues of bilingual classrooms?

Chapter 18 is central to understanding bilingualism and bilingual education. It considers the political and cultural dimensions that surround bilingualism in society (and bilingual education in particular). Different views of the overall value and purpose of bilingualism join together many of the threads of the book, and lead also in a consideration of the nature of multiculturalism in society, in school and the classroom (Chapter 19). The finale of the book (Chapter 20) takes a look at the present and future with themes of bilingualism and the Internet, employment, mass media, economy and tourism.

Thus the concluding issues of the book include:

- Why are there different viewpoints about language minorities and bilingual education?
- Why do some people prefer the assimilation of language minorities and others prefer linguistic diversity?
- Can schools play a role in a more multicultural and less racist society?
- Will globalization mean the demise of minority languages in the world?

STUDY ACTIVITIES

Study activities are placed at the end of each chapter. These are designed for students wishing to extend their learning by engaging in various practical activities. Such activities are flexible and adaptable. Instructors and students will be able to vary them according to local circumstances. Many more study activities are found in the Reader that accompanies this text.

FINALE

To end the beginning. The motivating force behind this book is to introduce students to a positive world of bilingualism and bilingual education. The book has been written for minority language students seeking to understand and preserve, and for majority language students seeking to become more sensitized. The book is an attempt to contribute to the preservation and celebration of a linguistically and culturally diverse world. Bilinguals help preserve the variety and therefore the 'beauty in diversity' of our world. Bilinguals are environmentally friendly people.

Acknowledgements

The idea of this introductory text derived from a fellow Essex gentleman, Mike Grover. He wrote one simple sentence in the early 1990s that has affected my academic life ever since: 'Consider writing THE textbook on Bilingual Education'. My thanks to Mike of Multilingual Matters for not only trusting me with this responsibility, but also for his continual encouragement and friendly, facilitative style. The ever-friendly and always helpful, highly efficient team at MLM makes an author's life a pleasure.

Multilingual Matters perceptively appointed Ofelia García as Academic Consultant when this project began. I have always received detailed, sensitive, wise and judicious advice from her. Achilles' heels have been quickly spotted, detailed polishing recommended, and cultural assumptions gently revealed. A large debt is owed to Ofelia who has helped to shape much of the book.

In the first and second editions, I recorded my grateful thanks to those who helped in the construction of those editions. I wish to repeat my sincere gratitude to: Andrew Cohen, Nancy Dorian, Viv Edwards, John Eggleston, Peter Garrett, Ann Illsley, Sharon Lapkin, Hilaire Lemoine, Dilys Parry, Gwenllïan Rowlinson, Bernard Spolsky, Merrill Swain and Iolo Williams.

For the third edition, various outstanding scholars constructively gave expert advice on improvements and needed developments: Jasone Cenoz, Jim Cummins, Tony Cline, Jim Crawford, Annick de Houwer, Nancy Hornberger, Christer Laurén, Karita Mard, Stephen May, Steve Walter and Terry Wiley. Sandra Pucci and Howard Smith combined their skills as scholars and expert teachers to provide the detailed feedback on pedagogy and presentation that helped ensure the book is student-oriented. Sylvia Prys Jones wrote the *Encyclopedia of Bilingualism and Bilingual Education* (1998) with me, and during three years of cooperation, I learnt much from such a brilliant intellect. The new chapter on 'Bilingualism in the Modern World', and the discussion on one-parent bilingual families owes much to Sylvia's superlative contribution to the *Encyclopedia*. Continuous dialogue with Cen Williams (Bangor University) and Meirion Prys Jones, Head of Education in the Welsh Language Board, has been a constant source of encouragement and enlightenment.

Working in this area has always been inspired by my Welsh wife, Anwen, and three bilingual offspring (Sara, Rhodri and Arwel) who still daily teach me the beauty of bilingualism. Their loving support is always appreciated. *Diolch yn fawr iawn am bopeth.*

The help and support given me by all those mentioned above has been extremely generous and far more than is deserved. However, the responsibility for all that is not as fair or just as it should be is totally mine.

Colin Baker

CHAPTER 1

Bilingualism: Definitions and Distinctions

Introduction

Terminology
Dimensions of Bilingualism

Bilingual Ability
The Four Language Abilities
Labels and Distinctions
A Fifth Language Competence?
Minimal and Maximal Bilingualism
Balanced Bilinguals
Two Views of Bilinguals
'Semilingualism'/'Double Semilingualism'
Conversational Fluency and Academic
Language Competence

An Individual's Use of Bilingualism
Language Choice

Conclusion

CHAPTER 1

Bilingualism:
Definitions and Distinctions

INTRODUCTION

Since a bicycle has two wheels and binoculars are for two eyes, it would seem that bilingualism is simply about two languages. The aim of this chapter is to show that the ownership of two languages is not so simple as having two wheels or two eyes. Ask someone if they are bilingual. Is someone bilingual if they are fluent in one language but less than fluent in their other language? Is someone bilingual if they rarely or never use one of their languages? Such questions need addressing before other topics in this book can be sensibly discussed.

To understand the answers to these questions, we should make an **initial distinction between bilingualism as an individual characteristic and bilingualism in a social group, community, region or country.** Bilingualism and multilingualism can be examined as the possession of the individual. Various themes in this book start with bilingualism as experienced by individual people. For example, a discussion of whether or not bilingualism affects thinking requires research on individual monolinguals and bilinguals. From sociology, sociolinguistics, politics, geography, education and social psychology comes a different perspective. Bilinguals and multilinguals are usually found in groups. Such groups may be located in a particular region (e.g. Basques in Spain), or may be scattered across communities (e.g. the Chinese in the US). Bilinguals may form a distinct language group as a majority or a minority. Bilinguals and multilinguals within a country may be analyzed as a distinct group. For example, linguists study how the vocabulary of bilingual groups change across time. Geographers plot the density of bilinguals in a country. Educationalists examine bilingual educational policy and provision for minority language groups.

The first distinction is therefore between bilingualism as an individual possession and as a group possession. This is usually termed **individual bilingualism and societal bilingualism**. Like most distinctions, there are important links between the two parts. For example, the attitudes of individuals towards a particular minority language may affect language maintenance, language restoration, language shift or language death in society. In order to understand the term 'bilingualism', some important further distinctions at the **individual** level are discussed in this chapter. An introduction to bilingualism as a group possession (societal bilingualism) is provided in Chapter 3.

If a person is asked whether he or she speaks two languages, the question is ambiguous. A person may be **able** to speak two languages, but tends to speak only one language in practice. Alternatively, the individual may regularly speak two languages, but competence in one language may be limited. Another person will use one language for conversation and another for writing and reading. The essential distinction is therefore between **language ability** and **language use**. This is sometimes referred to as the difference between **degree** and **function**. This chapter continues by examining bilinguals' language abilities. Language use is discussed later.

TERMINOLOGY

Before discussing the nature of language abilities, a note about **terminology**. Entry into the many areas of bilingualism and bilingual education is helped by understanding often-used terms and distinctions. There exists a range of terms in this area: language ability, language achievement, language competence, language performance, language proficiency and language skills. Do they all refer to the same entity, or are there subtle distinctions between the terms? To add to the problem, different authors and researchers sometimes tend to adopt their own specific meanings and distinctions. There is no standardized use of these terms (Stern, 1992).

Dimensions of Bilingualism

Valdés and Figueroa (1994) suggest that bilinguals are classified by:

(1) Age (simultaneous/sequential/late – see Chapter 5).
(2) Ability (incipient/receptive/productive).
(3) Balance of two languages.
(4) Development (ascendant – second language is developing; recessive – one language is decreasing).
(5) Contexts where each language is acquired and used (e.g. home, school).

To this they add a sixth dimension: circumstantial and elective bilingualism. **Elective bilingualism** is a characteristic of individuals who choose to learn a language, for example in the classroom. Elective bilinguals come from majority language groups (e.g. English-speaking Americans who learn Spanish or French). They add a second-language without losing their first language.

Circumstantial bilinguals learn another language to survive. Because of their circumstances (e.g. as immigrants), they need another language to function effectively (for example, Latinos in the United States). Consequently, their first language is in danger of being replaced by the second language. Their first language is insufficient to meet the educational, political and employment demands and communicative needs of the society in which they are placed. Circumstantial bilinguals are groups of individuals who must become bilingual to operate in the majority language society that surrounds them.

Elective bilingualism is about choice. Circumstantial bilingualism is often about survival with little or no choice. The difference between elective and circumstantial bilingualism is thus valuable because it immediately raises differences of prestige and status, politics and power among bilinguals.

Labels and Distinctions

- **Language skills** tend to refer to highly specific, observable, clearly definable components such as handwriting.
- **Language competence** is a broad and general term, used particularly to describe an inner, mental representation of language, something latent rather than overt. Such competence refers usually to an underlying system inferred from language performance.
- **Language performance** hence becomes the outward evidence for language competence. By observing general language comprehension and production, language competence may be implied.
- **Language ability** and **language proficiency** tend to be used more as 'umbrella' terms and therefore they are used somewhat ambiguously. For some, language ability is a general, latent disposition, a determinant of eventual language success. For others, it tends to be used as an outcome, similar but less specific than language skills, providing an indication of current language level. Similarly, language proficiency is sometimes used synonymously with language competence (e.g. Ellis, 1985); and other times as a specific, measurable outcome from language testing. However, both language proficiency and language ability are distinct from language achievement.
- **Language achievement (attainment)**. Language achievement is usually seen as the outcome of formal instruction. Language proficiency and language ability are, in contrast, viewed as the product of a variety of mechanisms: formal learning, informal uncontrived language acquisition (e.g. on the street) and of individual characteristics such as 'intelligence'.

BILINGUAL ABILITY

The Four Language Abilities

If we confine the question 'Are you bilingual?' to ability in two languages, the issue becomes 'what ability'? There are four basic language abilities: **listening, speaking,**

reading and writing. These four abilities fit into two dimensions: receptive and productive skills; oracy and literacy. The following table illustrates:

	Oracy	Literacy
Receptive skills	Listening	Reading
Productive skills	Speaking	Writing

The table suggests avoiding a simple classification of who is, or is not, bilingual. Some speak a language, but do not read or write in a language. Some listen with understanding and read a language (passive bilingualism) but do not speak or write that language. Some understand a spoken language but do not themselves speak that language. To classify people as either bilinguals or monolinguals is thus too simplistic. Or, to return to the opening analogies, the two wheels of bilingualism exist in different sizes and styles. The two lenses of bilingualism will vary in strength and size.

The four basic language abilities do not exist in black and white terms. Between black and white are not only many shades of gray; there also exist a wide variety of colors. The multi-colored landscape of bilingual abilities suggests that each language ability can be more or less developed. Reading ability can range from simple and basic to fluent and accomplished. Someone may listen with understanding in one context (e.g. shops) but not in another context (e.g. an academic lecture). These examples show that the four basic abilities can be further refined into sub-scales and dimensions. There are **skills within skills**, traditionally listed as: pronunciation, extent of vocabulary, correctness of grammar, the ability to convey exact meanings in different situations and variations in style. However, these skills tend to be viewed from an academic or classroom perspective. Using a language on the street and in a shop require a greater accent on social competence with language (e.g. the idioms and 'lingo' of the street).

If language abilities are multicolored, and if bilinguals have a range of colors in both languages, then positive terms are needed to portray the variety. Calling bilinguals LEP (Limited English Proficiency) students in the US seems negative and pejorative. Such a label can accentuate children's perceived deficiency rather than their proficiencies, children's perceived 'deprivation' rather than their accomplishments, their lower, marginalized, minority status through majority eyes rather than their bilingual potentiality. Such a label highlights past and present performance rather than potentialities and the possibility of functioning well in two or more languages.

The range and type of sub-skills that can be measured is large and debated (Lado, 1961; Mackey, 1965; Macnamara, 1969; Oller, 1979; Carroll, 1980; Baetens Beardsmore, 1986). Language abilities such as speaking or reading can be divided into increasingly microscopic parts. What in practice is tested and measured to portray an individual's bilingual performance is considered later in the book. What has emerged so far is that a person's ability in two languages are multidimensional and will tend to evade simple categorization.

A Fifth Language Competence?

The four basic language abilities are commonly regarded as speaking, listening, reading and writing. However, there are times when a person is not speaking, listening, reading or writing but is still using language. As Skutnabb-Kangas (1981) proposed, the language used for **inner thinking** may be a fifth area of language competence. This may be simply termed inner speech and placed under the umbrella title of 'speaking'. It may alternatively be worth differentiating from actual speaking as it raises the dimension of the extent of the ability of bilinguals to use both languages as thinking tools. Cummins (1984b) expresses this notion as academic competence in a language. That is, the ability to use one or both languages for reasoning and reflection, outside education as well as inside.

Minimal and Maximal Bilingualism

So far, it has been suggested that deciding who is or is not bilingual is difficult. Simple categorization is arbitrary and requires a value judgment about the minimal competence needed to achieve a label of 'bilingual'. Therefore, a classic definition of bilingualism such as 'the native-like control of two or more languages' (Bloomfield, 1933) appears too extreme and maximalist ('native like'). The definition is also ambiguous (what is meant by 'control' and who forms the 'native' reference group?). At the other end is a minimalist definition, as in Diebold's (1964) concept of *incipient bilingualism*. The term *incipient bilingualism* allows people with minimal competence in a second language to squeeze into the bilingual category. Tourists with a few phrases and business people with a few greetings in a second language would be incipient bilinguals. The danger of being too exclusive is not overcome by being too inclusive. Trawling with too wide a fishing net will catch too much variety and therefore make discussion about bilinguals ambiguous and imprecise. Trawling with narrow criteria may be too insensitive and restrictive.

Who is or is not categorized as a bilingual will depend on the purpose of the categorization. At different times, governments, for example, may wish to include or exclude language minorities. Where a single indigenous language exists (e.g. Irish in Ireland), a government may wish to maximize its count of bilinguals. A high count may indicate government success in language planning. In comparison, in a suppressive, assimilationist approach, immigrant minority languages and bilinguals may be minimized (e.g. Asian languages in the UK in the Census – see Chapter 2).

Is there a middle ground in-between maximal and minimal definitions? The danger is in making arbitrary cut-off points about who is bilingual or not along the competence dimensions. Differences in classification will continue to exist.

One alternative is to move away from the multi-colored canvas of proficiency levels to a portrait of the everyday use of the two languages by individuals. Categorization of bilinguals by their use of language is considered later in the chapter. Before such consideration, important labels and distinctions in terms of language ability are discussed.

Balanced Bilinguals

The literature on bilingualism frequently spotlights one particular group of bilinguals whose competences in both languages are well developed. Someone who is approximately equally fluent in two languages across various contexts may be termed an equilingual or ambilingual or, more commonly, **a balanced bilingual**. As will be considered in Chapter 7, balanced bilinguals are important when discussing the possible thinking advantages of bilingualism.

Balanced bilingualism is sometimes used as an idealized concept. Fishman (1971) has argued that rarely will anyone be equally competent across all situations. Most bilinguals will use their two languages for different purposes and with different people. For example, a person may use one language at work; the other language at home and in the local community.

Balanced bilingualism is also a problematic concept for other reasons. The balance may exist at a low level of competence in the two languages. Someone may have two relatively undeveloped languages which are nevertheless approximately equal in proficiency. While this is within the literal interpretation of 'balanced' bilingual, it is not the sense employed by many researchers on bilingualism. The implicit idea of balanced bilingualism has often been of 'reasonable' or 'appropriate' competence in both languages. A child who can understand the delivery of the curriculum in school in either language, and operate in classroom activity in either language would be an example of a balanced bilingual.

Is 'balanced bilingualism' of use as a term? While it has limitations of definition and measurement, it has proved to be of value in research and theory (see Chapter 7). However, categorizing individuals into such groups raises the issue of comparisons. Who is judged normal, proficient, skilled, fluent or competent? Who judges? The danger may be in using monolinguals as the point of reference as will now be considered.

Two Views of Bilinguals

An argument advanced by François Grosjean (1985, 1994) is that there are two contrasting views of individual bilinguals. First, there is a fractional view of bilinguals, which evaluates the bilingual as 'two monolinguals in one person'. There is a second, holistic view which argues that the bilingual is not the sum of two complete or incomplete monolinguals, but that he or she has a unique linguistic profile.

The Monolingual or Fractional View of Bilingualism

Many teachers, administrators, politicians and researchers look at the bilingual as two monolinguals in one person. For example, if English is a bilingual's second language, scores on an English reading or English attainment test will normally be compared against monolingual scores and averages. A bilingual's English language competence is often measured against that of a native monolingual English speaker (e.g. in the US and the UK). This is unfair because it derives from a myopic monolingual view of people. It is also unfair because bilinguals will typically use their two languages in different situations and with different people. Thus bilinguals may be stronger in each language in different domains.

One expectation from this fractional viewpoint will be for bilinguals to show a proficiency comparable to that of a monolingual in both their two languages. If that proficiency does not exist in both languages, especially in the majority language, then bilinguals may be denigrated and classified ed as inferior. In the United States, for example, children of immigrant families, or of other language minority families, are often officially federally categorized as LEP (Limited English Proficient). In northern Europe, bilinguals who appear to exhibit a lack of proficiency in both languages may be described as 'semilingual'.

While areas such as Africa, India, Scandinavia and parts of Asia see bilingualism as the norm, in countries such as the United States and England, the dominant view of the world is monolingual. Although between a half and two-thirds of the world's population is bilingual to some degree, the monolingual is often seen as normal in these two countries, and the bilingual as an exception, if not an oddity.

The Holistic View of Bilingualism
François Grosjean (1985, 1994) presents a more positive alternative view of bilinguals. Grosjean uses an analogy from the world of athletics, and asks whether we can fairly judge a sprinter or a high jumper against a hurdler. The sprinter and high jumper concentrate on one event and may excel in it. The hurdler concentrates on two different skills, trying to combine a high standard in both. With only a few exceptions, the hurdler will be unable to sprint as fast as the sprinter or jump as high as the high jumper. This is not to say that the hurdler is a worse athlete than the other two. Any comparison of who is the best athlete makes little sense. This analogy suggests that comparing the language proficiency of a monolingual with a bilingual's dual language or multilingual proficiency is similarly unjust.

However, this raises the question, should bilinguals only be measured and compared by reference to other bilinguals? When for example, someone learns English as a second language, should that competency in English-only be measured against other bilinguals? In countries like Wales for instance, where first-language Welsh-speaking children compete in a largely English-language job market against monolingual English speakers, the dominant view is that they should be given the same English assessments at school. However, Grosjean (1985, 1994) stresses that any assessment of a bilingual's language proficiency should ideally move away from the traditional language tests with their emphasis on form and correctness, and to an evaluation of the bilingual's general communicative competence. This appraisal would be based on a totality of the bilingual's language usage in all domains, whether this involves the choice of one language in a particular domain, or a mixing of the two languages.

There is sometimes a political reality that deters a holistic view of the bilingual from developing. In Australia, much of Canada, the United States and the United Kingdom, the dominant English-speaking monolingual politicians and administrators will not accept a different approach or standard of assessment (one for monolinguals, another for bilinguals).

Yet the bilingual is a complete linguistic entity, an integrated whole. Bilinguals use their two languages with different people, in different contexts and for different purposes. Levels of proficiency in a language may depend on which contexts (e.g. street and home) and how often that language is used. Communicative competence in one of a bilingual's two languages may be stronger in some domains than in others. This is natural and to be expected. Any assessment of a bilingual's competence in two languages needs to be sensitive to such differences of when, where and with whom bilinguals use either of their languages. Such an assessment should reveal the multi-competences of bilinguals (Cook, 1992).

'Semilingualism'/'Double Semilingualism'

Bilinguals tend to be dominant in one of their languages in all or some of their language abilities. This may vary with context and change over time. Dominance in one language may change over time with geographical or social mobility. For others, the dominance may be relatively stable across time and place. The topic of dominance will be considered in Chapter 2 when tests are discussed. For the present, a further group has been proposed, one which is distinct from balanced and dominant bilinguals. Sometimes termed pejoratively as semilinguals or double semilinguals, the group is regarded as not having 'sufficient' competence in either language. This section will suggest that such a label is more politically motivated than genuine or accurate.

Hansegård (1975; see Skutnabb-Kangas, 1981) described semilingualism in terms of deficiencies when compared with monolinguals in six language competences. A **'semilingual'** is considered to exhibit the following profile in both their languages: displays a small vocabulary and incorrect grammar, consciously thinks about language production, is stilted and uncreative with each language, and finds it difficult to think and express emotions in either language.

The notion of semilingualism, or **double semilingualism**, has received much criticism (e.g. Skutnabb-Kangas, 1981; Wiley, 1996a; MacSwan, 2000). There are **six major problems**. **First**, the term took on disparaging and belittling overtones, particularly in Scandinavia and with **immigrant** groups in the US. Semilingualism may be used as a negative label which invokes expectations of underachievement which may evoke a self-fulfilling prophecy.

Second, if languages are relatively undeveloped, the origins may not be in bilingualism *per se*, but in the economic, political and social conditions that evoke under-development. This is a theme considered in detail in later chapters. The danger of the term semilingualism is that it locates the origins of under-development in the internal, individual possession of bilingualism, rather than in external, societal factors that co-exist with bilingualism. Thus the term may be a political rather than a linguistic concept.

Third, most bilinguals use their two languages for different purposes and events. Language may be specific to a context. A person may be competent in some contexts but not in others. Some children are competent in the school context, but are less competent in the vernacular of the street. Some are competent in a language for religious purposes, but less so in the home.

Fourth, the educational tests that are most often used to measure language proficiencies and differentiate between people may be insensitive to the qualitative aspects of languages and to the great range of language competences. Language tests may measure a small, unrepresentative sample of a person's daily language behavior (see Chapter 2). Thus 'deficiencies' are an artifact of narrow academic tests. Standardized tests of language proficiency fail to measure the discourse patterns that children from different cultures use with considerable competence.

> 'Test scores [are] based on specific language and literacy tests of the school. These tests, in turn, reflect particular literacy practices and social expectations favoring groups that control institutions. Also, because school tests are based on 'standard' academic language, there is an implicit bias against language variation within L1 (i.e., there is a bias against speakers of non-standard and creolized varieties of L1. In interpreting results based on standardized tests, practitioners sometimes claim that students have 'no language', meaning that they have no standard academic language. (Wiley, 1996a, pp. 167–168).

Fifth, there is dispute regarding the frequency of double semilingualism, for example among Finnish–Swedish speakers. How many or how few fit into a semilingual category will be disputed. Establishing a cut-off point for who is or is not a double semilingual will be arbitrary and value laden. There is a lack of sound objective empirical evidence on such a categorization.

Sixth, the comparison with monolinguals may not be fair. It is important to distinguish whether bilinguals are 'naturally' qualitatively and quantitatively different from monolinguals in their use of their two languages (as a function of being bilingual). An apparent deficiency may be due to unfair comparisons with monolinguals.

The criticisms raise serious doubts about the value of the term 'semilingualism'. However, this does not detract from the fact that there are language abilities on which people do differ, with some people being at the earlier stages of development. Being at an early stage may not be the result of being bilingual. Economic and social factors or educational provision may, for example, be the cause. Rather than highlight the apparent 'deficit' in language development, the more equitable and positive approach is to emphasize that, when suitable conditions are provided, competence in language is capable of development to high levels. When a 'language deficit' is perceived, a more proper approach is to locate the causes in, for example, the type of tests used, material deprivation, in the quality of treatment in schooling and not in language itself (see Chapters 14 and 18).

Conversational Fluency and Academic Language Competence

So far, the chapter has centered on the variety of language abilities and the danger of categorization using a small or biased selection of language sub-skills. The question is whether the variety of sub-skills can be reduced to a small number of important dimensions. Hernández-Chávez *et al.* (1978), for example, suggest there are 64 separate components to language proficiency. In comparison, tests abound which purport to measure reading ability as a single entity. Many reading tests tacitly assume that reading can be reduced to one dimension.

Is it the case that children who perform well on a spelling test also do well on an oral comprehension test? Oller's (1982) research suggested that different language skills do tend to correlate moderately well. If a variety of measures of speaking, reading and writing are analyzed, the claim was for one underlying, global language dimension. This overlap between different academic language tests was sufficient for Oller and Perkins (1980) to suggest that there exists a single factor of **global language proficiency**. This global factor is seen as co-existing with other specific language factors which measure relatively minor language skills.

The idea of a global language factor is contentious as Oller (1982) admits. 'The evidence now shows that there are both global and specific aspects of language proficiencies. The perfect theory of the right mix of general and specific components, however, has not been found — and probably will never be agreed on' (Oller, 1982, p. 710). Oller's (1982) idea of a global language factor is based on quantitative testing. As will be considered later in the book, such tests leave qualitative differences between people unexplored. There is also an emphasis on language in an academic context. This leaves the out-of-school communicative profile of people relatively ignored.

Oller's (1982) much disputed claim for one global language factor provides a starting point for a distinction between two different language abilities. Oller's (1982) language proficiency factor has been allied to the language abilities needed to cope in the classroom. Most (but not all) language tests are closely linked to the cognitive, academic language skills of the classroom. Reading and writing tests are obvious examples. The notion of a curriculum based language competence led various authors to make an important distinction. Apart from **academically related language competence**, it has been proposed that there is a conceptually distinct category of **conversational competence** (Cummins, 2000b). Skutnabb-Kangas and Toukomaa (1976) proposed a difference between **surface fluency** and **academically related aspects of language competence**. Surface fluency would include the ability to hold a simple conversation in the shop or street and may be acquired fairly quickly (e.g. in two or three years) by second language learning. To cope in the curriculum, conversational language competence may not be enough. Academically related language competence in a second language may take from five to eight years or longer to acquire. This theme is considered in detail later in the book when a distinction is made between basic interpersonal communicative skills and cognitive/academic language proficiency (see Chapter 8). Such a distinction between two levels of language competence is important as it involves disputing Oller's (1982) 'single factor' language skill.

The chapter now moves to focusing on language use as opposed to language ability.

AN INDIVIDUAL'S USE OF BILINGUALISM

Language cannot be divorced from the context in which it is used. Language is not produced in a vacuum; it is enacted in changing dramas. As props and scenery, audience, co-actors and actresses, the play and the role change, so does language. A pure linguistic or psychological approach to two language competences is not sufficient. Communication includes not only the structure of language (e.g. grammar, vocabulary) but also who is saying what, to whom, in which circumstances. One person may have limited linguistic skills but, in certain situations, be successful in communication. Another person may have relative linguistic mastery, but through undeveloped social interaction skills or in a strange circumstance, be relatively unsuccessful in communication. The social environment where the two languages function is crucial to understanding bilingual usage. This section considers the **use** and **function** of an individual's two languages.

An individual's **use** of their bilingual ability (**functional bilingualism**) moves away from the complex arguments about language proficiency that tend to be based around school success and academic performance. Functional bilingualism moves into language production across an encyclopedia of everyday events. Functional bilingualism concerns when, where, and with whom people use their two languages (Fishman, 1965). The table below provides examples of the different targets (people) and contexts (often called **domains**) where functional bilingualism is enacted in different role relationships.

Examples of Language Targets	Examples of Language Contexts (Domains)
1. Nuclear Family	1. Shopping
2. Extended Family	2. Visual and Auditory Media (e.g. TV, Radio, Records, Cassettes, CDs, Video)
3. Work Colleagues	3. Printed Media (e.g. Newspapers, Books)
4. Friends	4. Cinema/Discos/Theater/Concerts
5. Neighbors	5. Work
6. Religious Leaders	6. Correspondence/Telephone/Official Communication
7. Teachers	7. Clubs, Societies, Organizations, Sporting Activities
8. Presidents, Principals, Other Leaders	8. Leisure & Hobbies
9. Bureaucrats	9. Religious Meetings
10. Local Community	10. Information Technology (e.g. computers)

A distinction needs to be made between functional bilingualism and language background (Baker & Hinde, 1984; Baker, 1985). Language background is a wider concept, referring to both the participative and non-participative experience of language. Non-participative language background is indirect, bystander experience, and measured by questions such as 'What language does your mother speak to your father when you are present?'. Functional bilingualism is a narrower concept, concerning direct involvement in a language domain. Functional bilingualism is therefore restricted to the personal production and reception of language (i.e. speaking, writing, reading and direct listening in various domains). When functional bilingualism is studied as real speech events, Hymes (1972b) suggests that there are eight interrelated categories, mnemonically represented by the word 'SPEAKING':

(S) **Setting** includes the time, place and physical appearance of the context of the speech event such as the arrangement of furniture and equipment in a classroom.
(P) **Participant** identity, for example personal characteristics such as age, ethnicity, gender, social status, and relationships with each other.
(E) **End** includes the purpose of the speech event as well as the individual goals of the participants.
(A) **Act** sequence refers to the order and organization of the interaction and what topics are discussed.
(K) **Key** or the tone and manner in which something is said or written.
(I) **Instrumentalities** or the linguistic code, for example the language used and whether the form is speech or literacy.
(N) **Norm** or the standard social and cultural rules of the interaction relationship.
(G) **Genre** or type of event such as sermon, lecture, poetry or letter.

Language Choice

As one or more of these eight factors changes, so may the particular language used. This suggests that **language choice** – who will speak what language, when and to whom (Fishman, 1965) – can be the result of a large and interacting set of factors.

Not all bilinguals have the opportunity to use both their languages on a regular basis. Where a bilingual lives in a largely monolingual community there may be little choice about language use from day-to-day. However, in communities where two or more languages are widely spoken, bilinguals may use both their languages on a daily or frequent basis. Some bilinguals will not have mastery of both languages, yet still use both languages successfully for communication in varying circumstances.

When bilinguals use both their languages on a day-to-day basis, language use is not haphazard or arbitrary. If the other person is already known to the bilingual, as a family member, friend or colleague, a relationship has usually been established through one language. If both are bilingual they have the option of changing to the other language (e.g. to include others in the conversation).

If the other person is not known, a bilingual may quickly pick up clues as to which language to use. Clues such as dress, appearance, age, accent and command of a language may suggest to the bilingual which language it would be appropriate to use. In bilingual areas of Canada and the United States for example, employees dealing with the general public may glance at a person's name on their records to help them decide which language to use. A person called Pierre Rouleau or Maria García might be addressed first in French or Spanish, rather than English.

An individual's own attitudes and preferences will influence their choice of language. In a minority/majority language situation, older people may prefer to speak the minority language. Younger folk (e.g. second-generation immigrants) may reject the minority language in favour of the majority language because of its higher status and more fashionable image. In situations where the native language is perceived to be under threat, some bilinguals may avoid speaking the majority or dominant language to assert and reinforce the status of the other language. French-Canadians in Quebec sometimes refuse to speak English in shops and offices to emphasize the status of French.

Li Wei *et al.* (1992), in a study of a Chinese community in northern England, indicate that the degree of contact with the majority language community can be a factor in language choice. Their research shows that Chinese speakers who were employed outside the Chinese community were more likely to choose to speak English with other Chinese speakers. In contrast, those Chinese immigrants who worked in family businesses, mainly catering, and had less daily contact with English speakers, were more likely to use Chinese with other Chinese–English bilinguals.

Some minority languages are mostly confined to a private and domestic role. This happens when a minority language has historically been disparaged and deprived of status. In Western Brittany in France, for example, many Breton speakers only use their Breton in the family and with close friends. They can be offended if addressed by a stranger in Breton, believing that such a stranger is implying they are uneducated and cannot speak French (Baker & Jones, 1998).

An individual may also change languages, either deliberately or unconsciously, to accommodate the perceived preference of the other participant in the conversation. The perception of which language is regarded as more prestigious or as more accommodating may depend on the nature of the listener. To gain acceptance or status, a person may deliberately and consciously use the majority language. Alternatively, a person may use a minority language as a form of affiliation or belonging to a group. (Code switching is discussed in Chapter 5.)

A consideration of distinctions and classifications about bilingual ability and function often moves to measurement. To what extent can we measure someone's performance in their two languages? How can we portray when, where and with whom people use their two languages? What are the problems and dangers in measuring bilinguals? These questions provide the themes for the next chapter.

CONCLUSION

Defining exactly who is or is not bilingual is essentially elusive and ultimately impossible. Some categorization, however, is often necessary and helpful to make sense of the world. Therefore categorizations and approximations may be required. Definitions in a phrase (e.g. Bloomfield's (1933) 'native-like control of two languages' offer little help. Intrinsically arbitrary and ambiguous in nature, they can be easily criticized and are difficult to defend.

A more helpful approach may be to locate important distinctions and dimensions surrounding the term 'bilingualism' that refine thinking about bilingualism. The fundamental distinction is between bilingual ability and bilingual usage. Some bilinguals may be fluent in two languages but rarely use both. Others may be much less fluent but use their two languages regularly in different contexts. Many other patterns are possible. This distinction leads naturally into dimensions. In terms of proficiency in two languages, the four basic dimensions are listening, speaking, reading and writing. Thinking in those languages may be a fifth language proficiency. With each of these proficiency dimensions, it is possible to fragment into more and more microscopic and detailed dimensions (e.g. pronunciation, vocabulary, grammar, meaning and style). Those sub-dimensions can subsequently be further dissected and divided.

Creating a multidimensional, elaborate structure of bilingual proficiency may make for sensitivity and precision. However, ease of conceptualization requires simplicity rather than complexity. Therefore simple categorization is the paradoxical partner of complex amplification. This chapter has focussed on the categories of balanced bilingualism, semilingualism, and one-factor ideas of language ability. These categories have received some depth of discussion and critical response in the research literature. As will be revealed in later chapters, these categories also relate to central research on bilingualism and bilingual education.

Separate from bilingual ability is a person's use of their two languages. That is, what use is made of two languages by the individual; when, where and with whom? This highlights the importance of considering domain or context. As a bilingual moves from one situation to another, so may the language being used in terms of type (e.g. Spanish or English), content (e.g. vocabulary) and style. Over time and place, an individual's two languages are never static but ever changing and evolving.

KEY POINTS IN THIS CHAPTER

- There is a difference between bilingualism as an individual possession and two or more languages operating within a group, community, region or country.
- At an individual level, there is a distinction between a person's ability in two languages and use of those languages.

- Language abilities are listening, speaking, reading and writing. Thinking in a language is sometimes seen as a fifth language ability.
- Balanced bilinguals with equal and strong competence in their two languages are rare.
- There is a difference between a monolingual or fractional view of bilinguals and a holistic view. The fractional view sees bilinguals as two monolinguals inside one person. The holistic view sees bilinguals as a complete linguistic entity, an integrated whole.
- The term 'semilingual' or 'double semilingualism' has been used to describe those whose languages are both under-developed. However, the label has tended to take on negative, political and personally pejorative connotations.
- A distinction is made between the kind of language required for conversational fluency and the type of language required for academic, classroom operations.
- Bilinguals typically use their two languages with different people, in different contexts and for different purposes.

SUGGESTED FURTHER READING

BAETENS BEARDSMORE, H., 1986, *Bilingualism: Basic Principles*. Clevedon: Multilingual Matters.
BAKER, C. and JONES, S.P., 1998, *Encyclopedia of Bilingualism and Bilingual Education*. Clevedon: Multilingual Matters.
HOFFMANN, C., 1991, *An Introduction to Bilingualism*. London: Longman.
ROMAINE, S., 1995, *Bilingualism*. (Second Edition). Oxford: Basil Blackwell.
SKUTNABB-KANGAS, T., 2000, *Linguistic Genocide in Education – Or Worldwide Diversity and Human Rights?* Mahwah, NJ: Erlbaum.

STUDY ACTIVITIES

(1) Do you consider yourself and/or people known to you as 'bilingual'? Would you describe yourself, or someone known to you, as 'balanced' in their languages? Which language or languages do you think in? Does this change in different contexts? In which language or languages do you dream, count numbers, pray and think aloud?

(2) This activity can be based on self-reflection or you may wish to interview someone who is bilingual. Make a table or diagram to illustrate how one person's dual or multilingual ability and language usage has changed and developed since birth. Write down how different contexts have affected that change and development. The diagram or table should illustrate the life history of someone's bilingualism indicating changes over time and over different contexts.

CHAPTER 2

The Measurement of Bilingualism

Introduction

The Purposes of the Measurement
of Bilinguals

Examples of the Measurement
of Bilinguals

Limitations of Language Censuses

A Critical View of Language Testing

The Structure of Language Competence

Conclusion

CHAPTER 2

The Measurement of Bilingualism

INTRODUCTION

Having discussed definitions, dimensions and distinctions, the topic of measuring bilinguals both elaborates and illuminates that discussion. Problems of categorizing 'bilinguals' makes further sense when we attempt to measure and categorize. The chapter therefore begins by clarifying the different reasons for measuring bilinguals. This occurs not only in education but also in society (e.g. censuses). Illustrations are then given of such measurement with ways of profiling the language ability and use of individuals and whole language minorities. It is important to develop a critical awareness of language measurement, both in the internal limitations of measurement and the politics surrounding language testing. The chapter finishes with an overview of language models which is helpful for understanding debates about bilingualism in later chapters (especially Chapters 7, 8, 11 and 12).

We start by returning to the paradox of the last chapter. It is natural and meaningful to try to categorize the complexity of individual differences in bilingualism. We make sense of our world by continual classification. People are constantly compared and contrasted. Yet the simplification of categorization often hides the complexity of reality. Sorting often simplifies unsympathetically. Individual differences are reduced to similarities. Yet over-complexity can be unwelcome and confusing. Complications can confound those needing order and pattern. The measurement of bilinguals attempts to locate similarities, order and pattern.

THE PURPOSES OF THE MEASUREMENT OF BILINGUALS

Measurement of bilinguals can take place for a variety of purposes, and it is valuable to differentiate between some of these overlapping aims.

Distribution

An example of the measurement of bilinguals is found in census questions, requesting information about ability or usage in two or more languages (e.g. in US, Canada, Ireland). Such census data allow a researcher to estimate the size and distribution of bilinguals in a particular area. For example, geographers map the proportion and location of minority language groups within a state or region (see, for example, the Ethnologue WWW site:

http://www.sil.org/ethnologue/ethnologue.html).

Selection

Bilinguals may be distinguished as a 'separate' group for selection purposes. For example, a school may wish to allocate children to classes, groups or tracks based on their degree of bilingual proficiency or language background. A different example is measuring bilinguals at the outset of research. An investigation may require the initial formation of two or more groups (e.g. 'balanced' bilinguals, 'partial' bilinguals and monolinguals).

Summative

Summative means 'totaling up' to indicate the destination a person has reached in their language learning journey. **Summing up** someone's language proficiency may occur, for example, at the end of a semester or a school year. When measuring the current performance level of a person, a wide variety of language proficiency and achievement tests are available (e.g. reading comprehension, reading vocabulary, spelling, grammar). Such tests may be used in schools to measure the four basic language abilities. In a minority language context, emphasis is often on measuring proficiency in both the minority language and the majority language.

In the United States, emphasis on minority language groups becoming proficient in English has been a dominant issue in the testing of bilinguals (see Chapter 18). Thus in most US schools, language testing is solely in English, with second language competence ignored.

With proficiency testing, the measurement of bilinguals becomes fused with second language testing and the general area of language testing. Apart from general language tests, there are measures of the relative dominance of a person's two languages and the mixing of a person's two languages (sometimes pejoratively termed 'interference' — see Chapters 5 and 6). Such tests spotlight the particular characteristics of bilinguals as different from second language learners and first language development. Examples are provided later in this chapter.

Formative

Language proficiency tests are often used for summative judgments. In comparison, a test or assessment device that gives feedback during learning, and to aid further development is **formative assessment**. A student may be profiled on a precise breakdown of language skills to provide facilitative feedback to the teacher that directly leads to action. This is the notion of formative testing. If the test reveals areas where a child's language needs developing, there can be immediate intervention and remedial help. A diagnosis of a problem in language may lead to the formation of a plan to effect a remedy. The assessment of bilinguals is considered in Chapter 14.

EXAMPLES OF THE MEASUREMENT OF BILINGUALS

A full inventory of bilingual measurement devices would be immense and is not provided (see Hornberger & Corson (1997) and Clapham & Corson (1997) for comprehensive surveys of this area). The examples given below help to make some essential points and tend to represent the styles most often used in research.

Language Background Scales

Language background or functional bilingualism scales are self-rating scales. They endeavor to measure actual **use** of two languages as opposed to proficiency. An example for schoolchildren is now presented (adapted from Baker, 1992):

Here are some questions about the language in which you talk to different people, and the language in which certain people speak to you. Please answer as honestly as possible. There are no right or wrong answers. Leave an empty space if a question does not fit your position.

In which language do YOU speak to the following people? Choose one of these answers

	Always in Spanish	In Spanish more often than English	In Spanish and English equally	In English more often than Spanish	Always in English
Father					
Mother					
Brothers/Sisters					
Friends in the Classroom					
Friends on the Playground					
Teachers					
Neighbors					
Grandparents					
Other relatives					
Friends outside School					

In which language do the following people speak TO YOU?

	Always in Spanish	In Spanish more often than English	In Spanish and English equally	In English more often than Spanish	Always in English
Father					
Mother					
Brothers/Sisters					
Friends in the Classroom					
Friends on the Playground					
Teachers					
Neighbors					
Grandparents					
Other relatives					

Which language do YOU use with the following?

	Always in Spanish	In Spanish more often than English	In Spanish and English equally	In English more often than Spanish	Always in English
Watching TV/Videos/DVDs					
Religion					
Newspapers/Comics					
Records/Cassettes/CDs					
Listening to Radio					
Shopping					
Playing Sport					
On the Telephone					
Reading Books					
Earning Money					
Clubs/Societies					
Other Leisure Activities					

This scale has **limitations** besides the problems of ambiguity and 'social desirability' considered later. It is not exhaustive of targets (people) or of domains (contexts). Language activity with uncles and aunts, discos, correspondence, organizations, clubs, societies, leisure, hobbies and travel are not included, for example. The choice of items included in such a scale is somewhere between an all-inclusive scale and a more narrow sample of major domains. At first glance, it may appear that the more inclusive a scale is the better. There is a problem, illustrated by Baker and Hinde (1984: 46):

> 'A person who says she speaks Welsh to her father (mostly away at sea), her grandparents (seen once a year), her friends (but tends to be an isolate), reads Welsh books and newspapers (only occasionally), attends Welsh Chapel (marriages and funerals only) but spends most of her time with an English speaking mother and in an English speaking school might gain a fairly high "Welsh" score.'

This example suggests that the 'to whom' question is insufficient. Frequency of usage in such contexts and with certain targets needs adding. Besides 'to whom and where', a 'how often' question is necessary. Also, such scales do not indicate networking or status and power in relationships which are important in language shift and language attitudes. Further problems of language background and functional bilingualism scales are discussed by Baker and Hinde (1984) and Baker (1985).

The language background of **a language group** needs to include many different contextual dimensions. Listed below are some of the contexts that need to be included in such a language use or language census survey (adapted from the European Commission, 1996):

(1) Preferred categorization of the language (e.g. minority, lesser used, community, heritage, indigenous, autochthonous).
(2) Recent history of the language; major changes in the last decade.
(3) Geographical (areal) extent of the language.
(4) Number of users (e.g. from a census).
(5) Legal status of language. Existence and effect of any language legislation. Use of language in courts.
(6) Dominant language(s) of the territory.
(7) Recent and past immigration and emigration affecting the language.
(8) Relations with neighboring language groups and with the dominant language.
(9) (a) Use of language in education in primary and secondary education:
       (i) as a medium of instruction;
       (ii) as a subject itself;
       (iii) the history and culture surrounding the language;
       (iv) provision of teachers, schools and curriculum materials.
     (b) Use of language in Further, Vocational, Technical, Adult, Continuing and Higher Education.

(10) Literacy and biliteracy of the language group.
(11) Provision of language learning classes for immigrants.
(12) Effect of retirement patterns on the language.
(13) Use of language in media (e.g. TV, radio, books, newspapers, periodicals, magazines, telephone, satellite).
(14) Subsidization.
(15) Unemployment in the language group. Types of employment among language group (e.g. socioeconomic status, industrialization, technologization). Whether language is a requirement or advantage in finding a job.
(16) Use of the language in bureaucracy, forms, with regional and local authorities, with services (e.g. water, electricity, post office, railways, buses, police).
(17) Effect of travel on language group (e.g. road access, train systems, air travel, shipping).
(18) Effect of tourism on language group.
(19) Effect of local and central government on the language. Attitude of government to the language.
(20) Amount of language activism among the language group.
(21) Cultural vitality of the language group; institutions dedicated to supporting the language and culture; cultural festivals.
(22) Effect of urbanization and suburbanization on the language.
(23) Use of language in computing (e.g. in schools, adapted keyboards and fonts).
(24) Use of language in music: traditional, pop and rock, folk, classical.
(25) Use of language in theater, cinema.
(26) Use of translation, dubbing, subtitling of foreign language media.
(27) Promotion of translation, terminological research, standardization of language.
(28) Use of the language in advertising on TV, radio, in the press.
(29) Use of language in public speech and literacy events.
(30) Use of the language on goods labels and instructions.
(31) Use of the language in financial transactions (e.g. bills, banking).
(32) Use of the language on signposts (e.g. streets, major roads, in hospitals, schools, religious buildings, government offices).
(33) Use of the language in hospitals, care of elderly, homes and hostels.
(34) Use of the language by parents with their children.
(35) Use of the language in new and existing marriages.
(36) Use of the language in religious events and among religious leaders.
(37) Gender differences in the use of the language.
(38) Social status of the language and language speakers.
(39) Attitudes of speakers and non speakers to the language. Optimism or pessimism surrounding the language.
(40) Promotion of research activity on the language.

Language Censuses

The Belgium census of 1846 was one of the first national censuses to ask language questions. Other countries were soon to follow Belgium's lead: Switzerland in 1850, Ireland in 1851, Hungary in 1857, Italy in 1861, Canada in 1871, Austria and Finland in 1880, India and Scotland in 1881, the United States in 1890, Wales in 1891 and Russia in 1897 (Ó Gliasáin, 1996). Other countries such as Venezuela, Bolivia and Australia have more recently asked language questions in a census. Such censuses are often perceived by governments as providing relatively accurate measures of the number of language speakers in local communities, regions and countries.

Languages in the United States' Census

The United States census was instituted at the beginning of the United States political system in Article 1 Section 2 which stated that political representation in the House of Representatives was to be based on a population census. The census has been taken every ten years since 1790, when Secretary of State, Thomas Jefferson, supervised the first census. A question on race was included in that first 1790 census. The first time a question was asked about 'languages spoken at home' was in 1890 (with a question on Hispanic origin being introduced in 1970 and 'ancestry' in 1980, see Macías, 2000). Increasingly, census data are used to help states and localities 'benchmark' and measure progress in meeting their objectives and legislatively mandated targets.

Two examples are given below of census questions on language from two different US censuses, the first from 1910 and the second from 1990. These examples illustrate how **census questions** are constructed in a way that does not always give accurate and comprehensive information about use of languages, and also reveals implicit official attitudes towards the use and maintenance of minority languages.

The United States Census of 1910

In the 1910 United States census, advice was given to enumerators when asking respondents about the mother tongue of members of the household. Three extracts are given below illustrating notions from a bygone era. The following points should be noted.

- The question of mother tongue excluded those born in the United States. This indicates an assumption that all those born in the United States would be able to speak English, and that the maintenance of minority languages or bilingualism in English and a minority language was not considered.
- A person's ability in languages other than English was ignored if they were able to speak English.
- Ability in a heritage language was counted only if a person was unable to speak English.
- The language of the under-10-year-olds was ignored.

Extracts from Advice to Enumerators in the United States 1910 Census

'127. The question of mother tongue should not be asked of any person born in the United States'

'133. Column 17. Whether able to speak English; or, if not, give language spoken. This question applies to all persons age 10 and over. If such a person is able to speak English, write English [on the form]. If he is not able to speak English – and in such cases only – write the language which he does speak, as French, German, Italian.'

The United States Census of 2000

In 2000, a Census of the population was taken throughout the United States. Starting in January 2000 with visits to very remote areas and in March with postal delivery, Census 2000 questionnaires were made available in six languages – English, Spanish, Chinese, Tagalog, Vietnamese, and Korean. Language Assistance Guides were produced in 49 languages apart from English. Two questionnaires were used. A short questionnaire was sent to every household in the US, requesting information on individuals (e.g. gender, race, Hispanic origin, home ownership and age). A longer questionnaire was sent to about one in six of all US households. The longer questionnaire asked about ancestry, residence five years ago (migration), income and education. It also included a question about home languages. Question 11 on the 2000 Census form was phrased as follows:

Question 11

(a) **Does this person speak a language other than English at home?**

☐ Yes
☐ No *Skip to 12*

(b) **What is this language?**
(*For example: Korean, Italian, Spanish, Vietnamese*)

(c) **How well does this person speak English?**

☐ Very well
☐ Well
☐ Not well
☐ Not at all

This question is more comprehensive than the 1910 language question. It asks about the use of a minority language in the home irrespective of command of English. It also asks a more searching question about the level of ability in English.

The 1992 Census of Venezuela

One of the most comprehensive set of questions in a language census comes from Venezuela. The South American country of Venezuela has a population of about 20 million. The official and majority language of the country is Spanish. Just over 1.5% of the population are indigenous Indians, and about 37 native languages are spoken. Bilingualism and multilingualism are common among the indigenous Indians. Most speak Spanish as well as their own mother tongue and some speak more than one indigenous language. About half the indigenous Indian population belong to the Wayuu ethnic group. The following questions from the 1992 Venezuelan census aim to give a comprehensive picture of an individual's use of languages. The following points should be noted.

- The census asks about competence in more than one indigenous language, as well as competence in a non-indigenous language.
- The census distinguishes between language ability and language use.
- The census distinguishes between oracy and literacy in both indigenous languages and Spanish.

Solo Para Personas De 5 Años o Mas
For People over 5 Years Old

20. ¿Habla algun idioma indigena?
     Do you speak any indigenous language?

     Si *Yes* ❐   No *No* ❐

     ¿Cuál o cuáles?
     Which one or which ones?

21. ¿Habla algun idioma no indigena?
     (Puedi marcar más de una respuesta)
     Do you speak any non-indigenous language?
     (you may choose more than one answer)

     Si *Yes* ❐   No *No* ❐

     Castellano *Spanish*
     Portugués *Portuguese*
     Inglés *English*

22.   ¿En que idioma se comunica usualmente con los demas habitantes de la comunidad?
     Which language do you normally use to communicate with other members of the community?

23. Save escriber en:
     (Pueda marcar más de una respuesta)
     Can you write in:
     (You may choose more than one answer)

     Castellano Spanish Si *Yes* ❐   No *No* ❐
     Idioma indigena *Indigenous language* Si *Yes* ❐   No *No* ❐

24. Sabe leer en:
     Can you read in:
     Castellano *Spanish* Si *Yes* ❐   No *No* ❐
     Idoma indigena *Indigenous language* Si *Yes* ❐   No *No* ❐

LIMITATIONS OF LANGUAGE CENSUSES

Language census data contain a set of limitations, even when there is a long tradition of census compilation.

- Census questions about home language, mother tongue and first language are often **ambiguous**. In the 1986 Canadian Census, one of the three language questions was 'Can you speak English or French well enough to conduct a conversation?' This reveals the ambiguity of Census questions. The term 'speak well enough' may be interpreted in different ways by different people. What one person considers 'well enough' may be at a different level of fluency to another. A brief conversation in the shop can be at a different level from a conversation in the classroom or in a President's office. Sometimes the questions do not distinguish between language use and language ability (see Chapter 1). Thus a question, 'Do you speak English?' does not specify whether the question is about everyday use of language, ability to speak the language irrespective of regular use, or both use and ability. Some can but don't. Others do but with difficulty.

- Questions on census forms do not usually include the **four language abilities**: understanding a language, speaking, reading and writing. Thus oracy may be evaluated and not literacy.

- There are not usually questions about contexts or **domains** of language use (e.g. home, school, religion, street, shopping). Therefore a response is very generalized across many domains and insensitive to where languages are used.

- Census data may rapidly become **out of date** when factors such as migration, social upheaval, war or a high birthrate mean that the language situation is rapidly changing.

- Language questions can be **politically inflammatory**. For example, in the 1846 Belgium census the language question was restricted to asking what language was usually spoken by respondents. Soon after, language censuses in Belgium began asking questions about knowledge of the official languages of Belgium. Since there was a mixture of official and unofficial (autochthonous) languages in use in Belgium, the restriction of such questions to official languages provoked argument and debate. In such Belgium language census questionnaires, all those over 14 years of age had to complete and sign the questionnaire. This also provoked contention and controversy. The outcome was that, in 1961, the majority of parliamentarians in Belgium decided to suspend the language censuses in Belgium to avoid further dispute.

- Not all censuses include questions on language. Some censuses ask about **ethnic groups**, which may not correspond to language groups. In the former Soviet state of Georgia, for instance, 70% of the population were recorded on the last census as being ethnic 'Georgians'. However, this group includes not only first language speakers of Georgian, but also first language speakers of two closely related languages, most of whom also speak Georgian. A question about ethnic groups is sometimes wrongly used to estimate the size of a language group. This tends to occur in England where there is no language census question but a question on ethnic origins.
- Conversely, a language question in a census may be treated by respondents as if it refers to **identity**. For example, in Ireland, a non-Irish speaker may wish to be seen as Irish and therefore answer the Irish language question affirmatively. Thus a census language question may be interpreted as an attitude question. People from a particular ethnic group may feel they ought to say that they speak the indigenous or heritage language even if they do not. It may be regarded as socially desirable to say one speaks a language, and speaks it well. The opposite may also occur. If a minority language is disparaged and of low status, a speaker of that language may claim not to speak the language. Answers to questions about language on a census form may thus reflect 'a pose', a socially desirable answer and not everyday behavior.
- Censuses do not usually cover all of the **population** of a country despite considerable efforts to be inclusive. Some of the population may refuse to respond through the mail system, or to answer census personnel calling at their dwelling. Other people are out of reach or difficult to track down. Itinerants, illegal immigrants and the homeless, for example, may be missed by the census.

Self-rating on Proficiency

Students may be asked to assess their language strengths and weaknesses. An example to illustrate self-rating on language proficiency comes from a survey by the Linguistic Minorities Project (1985: 349). Children in London were asked to rate themselves on the four basic dimensions of language competency (see the table on the following page).

Limitations in Measurement

The self-rating covers the basic four language abilities across two languages (e.g. Spanish and English). The answers are possibly too broad (e.g. there are many graduations possible in between 'yes', 'quite well' and 'only a little'. Apart from this problem of scaling, there are other problems frequently encountered with measuring language competence. These may be listed as:

(1) **Ambiguity.** Words such as 'speak', 'understand', 'read' and 'write' include a wide variety of levels of proficiency. The range is from those with minimal proficiency to Bloomfield's (1933) maximum notion of 'native-like control of

Tick one box for each question for each language		
	One Language	**Another Language**
Can you **understand** this language if it is spoken to you now?	Yes, quite well	
	A little	
	No, not now	
Can you **speak** this language now?	Yes, quite well	
	A little	
	No, not now	
Can you **read** this language now?	Yes, quite well	
	A little	
	No, not now	
	Never could	
Can you **write** this language now?	Yes, quite well	
	A little	
	No, not now	
	Never could	

two languages'. Tests also often contain only a small and unrepresentative sample of the totality of language proficiencies.

(2) **Context.** A bilingual may be able to understand a language in one context (e.g. a shop) and not in another context (e.g. academic lecture). Another bilingual may be able to read newspapers but not textbooks. Proficiency and usage will vary with changing environments. A response summated across contexts is required. This may not be sensitive to different levels of proficiency across different contexts.

(3) **Social desirability.** Respondents may consciously or unconsciously give a 'halo' version of themselves. Self-ratings are vulnerable to exaggeration or understatement. People may say they are fluent in a second language (when in reality they are not) for self-esteem or status reasons. Others may indicate they do not speak a language when they can. This may occur, for example, in a low prestige, 'subtractive' (see Chapters 4 and 6) minority language environment where the introduction of the second language may replace the first language. Questions about proficiency can be interpreted as political referendum or attitudinal questions (Baker, 1985; Baetens Beardsmore, 1986).

(4) **Acquiescent response.** There is a slight tendency of respondents to answer 'yes' rather than 'no' in self-rating questions. It appears preferable to be posi-

tive rather than negative (Kline, 1983). This also tends to hold with a preference for 'Agree' rather than 'Disagree' and 'Like Me' rather than 'Not Like Me'.

(5) **Self-awareness.** A self-rating depends on accuracy of knowledge about oneself. For one person, the frame of reference may be other neighborhood children who are not so fluent. When compared to children in another community, apparent fluency may be less. What is competent in one environment may seem less competent in another. The age, nature and location of the reference group may cause self-assessment not to be strictly comparable across a representative sample of people. A child may also self-rate on surface fluency and not be aware of much less fluency in cognitively demanding language tasks (Skutnabb-Kangas, 1981).

(6) **Point of reference.** There is a danger of using monolingual proficiency and performance as the point of comparison (see Chapter 1).

(7) **Test aura.** Another danger is of raising language measurement to the level of scientific measurement with an accompanying exaggerated mystique. More 'natural' forms of language sampling may be given lower status (e.g. recording natural conversation) as they rarely carry the mystique of educational and psychological (psychometric) measurement.

(8) **Narrow sampling of dimensions of language.** Language measurement may unwittingly be perceived as something tangible and concrete (as when measuring height and weight). Rather, language tests mostly contain a specification of language skills that is debatable.

(9) **Insensitivity to change.** It is customary and seen as good practice to produce measurement which is reliable over time and across occasions (give consistent scores for the same individual over weeks or months). However the paradox is that such measurement may be insensitive to change within individuals. Test scores need an expiry date (e.g. not valid after two years).

(10) **Labeling.** Test scores are apt to create labels for individuals (e.g. someone is seen as having low performance) which create expectations (e.g. of further underachievement) that may lead to a self-fulfilling prophecy.

Language Balance and Dominance Measures

Various tests have been devised to gauge the relative dominance or balance of a bilingual's two languages. While such measures have been used in research, they have also been important in US education. Because in many areas in the United States instruction for language minority children was mandated to take place in the child's dominant language, some measure of language dominance was needed. This may be through, for example, English language and Spanish language proficiency tests.

Five examples of psychometric tests are given below:

- **Speed of reaction in a word association task.** This seeks to measure whether a bilingual can give an association to stimulus words more quickly in one language than the other. No particular difference would seem to indicate a balanced bilingual. An example is presenting a word such as 'house', then measuring the time taken to produce an association (e.g. window). When a person is consistently quicker in giving associations in one language than another, the likelihood is that one language is dominant. However, dominance is different from competence. A person may be competent in two or more languages while being dominant in one. Similarly, there could be equal dominance and a low level of competence in both languages.

- **Quantity of reactions to a word association task.** Bilinguals are measured for the number of associations given within one minute when a stimulus word (e.g. 'color') is presented. An approximately equal number of responses might indicate a balance between the two languages.
- **Detection of words using both languages.** Words in both languages are extracted from a nonsense word such as DANSONODEND. The letters in the nonsense words must be equally representative of both languages. This is not easily achievable, and depends on relatively similar alphabets and scripts.
- **Time taken to read** a set of words in the respondent's two languages.
- **Amount of mixing** the two languages, the quantity of borrowing and switching from one language to another.

A major **problem** with such balance and dominance tests lies in the representativeness of the measure of language proficiency and performance. In this respect, such tests would appear to tap only a small part of a much larger and more complex whole (language ability or language use). The tests cover a small sample of language sub-skills that might be tested. Dominance will vary by domain and across time, being a constantly changing personal characteristic. It is possible to be approximately equally proficient in two languages, yet one may be dominant. Speed of processing may provide evidence about balance but not about dominance in actual language use, in different sociocultural contexts and over time (Valdés & Figueroa, 1994).

Communicative Language Testing

In attempting to assess a bilingual's competence in two languages, there is a danger of using a simple paper and pencil test believing the test will provide a faithful estimation of everyday language life. Multiple choice language tests, dictation, reading comprehension tests and spelling tests are all well worn paths in the testing of academic language skills (see Clapham & Corson, 1997). Reducing everyday language competence to tests of specific skills is like measuring Michelangelo's art solely by its range of colors.

A radical alternative is seeing how bilinguals perform in both languages in a range of **real communicative situations**. Observing a bilingual in a shop, at home, at work and during leisure activity might seem the ideal way of measuring bilingual competence. This idea is time-consuming and may be biased by the researcher. Such an observation situation is affected by the presence of the tester and being a 'research' situation, sometimes intrusive into individual privacy and may be unrepresentative across time and place.

However, the greater danger lies in only viewing languages inside an academic context. The classroom is one language domain where language minority students from different cultural contexts may not reveal their wealth of language talents. Such academic testing is often more suited to elective bilinguals (see Chapter 1) whereas circumstantial bilinguals require their language abilities and uses to be portrayed across out-of-school domains to be realistic and representative.

In order to collect data that are *realistic and representative*, we need to know how situations (domains) relate to one another. We also need to know the sample of language performance that relates adequately to all round language competence. This demands an overall model or theory of language competence, a subject considered later in the chapter.

A particular emphasis in language testing is on **communicative competence** (Hart *et al.*, 1987). While tests of spelling, grammar, written comprehension and reading abound, the importance of using languages in realistic, everyday settings is reflected in current testing movements. The ideal is expressed by Skehan (1988, p. 125).

> 'Genuine communication is interaction-based, with more than one participant; unpredictable and creative, i.e. genuine communication may take the participants in unforeseen directions; is situated in a context which is both linguistic/discoursal and also sociocultural; has a purpose, in that participants will be trying to achieve something by use of language, e.g. to persuade, to deceive, etc.; uses authentic stimulus materials, and avoids contrived, specially produced materials; is based on real psychological conditions, such as time pressure; and is outcome evaluated, in that successful performance is judged in terms of whether communicative purposes have been achieved.'

A test of language proficiency which meets Skehan's (1988) criteria is probably impossible to achieve. A test that truly measures purposeful communication across sufficient contexts without tester effects is improbable. For some, the answer is simply not to test. For others, a best approximation is accepted. A test may therefore be used that measures the more limited notion of performance rather than the wider idea of competence.

A test that attempts to approximate the conditions outlined by Skehan (1988) is the **oral interview**. An example is the US Foreign Service oral interview which is in four stages (Lowe, 1983; Shohamy, 1983). Following a warm-up period, there is a check on the level of language proficiency, a deeper probe of that level, finishing with a wind-down period. The interview takes about half an hour. The two middle stages check that a person can perform consistently at a level across varying themes and in various language functions. The session is jointly conducted by two interviewers.

By training, the interviewers avoid narrow, predetermined checklists and attempt to make the interview sensitive to the candidate. The interviewers judge and score using prescribed criterion. A person is assigned to a level ranging from 0 (no competence) to 5 (Educated Native Speaker competence). This assumes a distinction between educated native speakers and other native speakers in their language competence. The levels 1 to 5 also have the possibility of a '+' rating, thus giving an 11-point rating scale.

Such interview procedures may not reflect reality. Does genuine communication take place between strangers, in a contrived, artificial context? Is the language repertoire of a person truly elicited? Is 'interview language' representative of a person's everyday language functioning? Can we generalize from oral communicative tests based on a single type of test, given on a single occasion, based on a test interview which is not a typical event in real life? There are doubts about whether such interview procedures can validly imitate and investigate real communicative competence. At the same time, they are a compromise between artificial pencil and paper tests and the impracticality of the detailed observation of individuals.

Criterion Referenced Language Tests: A Curriculum Approach to Language Testing

A recent shift in testing has been away from norm referenced tests to criterion referenced tests (UNESCO, World Education Report, 1991). This is partly due to the movement in language education towards communicative skills, curriculum objectives and mastery learning. What is the distinction between norm referenced and criterion referenced tests?

Language proficiency tests are usually classified into Norm Referenced and Criterion Referenced tests; the former usually being summative tests, the latter mostly being formative tests. Standardized norm referenced tests essentially compare one individual with others, as in an IQ test. A norm referenced test of reading ability, for example, may enable the teacher to compare one student with a national or regional average (norm). The student can then be exactly placed in an ordered list (e.g. in the top 16%). A **criterion referenced test** moves away from comparing one person with another. Instead it profiles an individual child on a particular language skill. The profile will test what a child can and cannot do on a precise breakdown of language skills. The parallel is with a car driving test. There are a variety of components to driving (e.g. backing around a corner, three-point turn, starting on a steep hill). Proficiency in driving often requires being able to satisfy an examiner on these sub-skills. Comparisons with other drivers are unimportant. An individual's mastery of specific tasks is the criterion for passing or failing.

Specifying driving criteria is easier than identifying language criteria, hence the analogy is not exact. The sub-components of language proficiency will be contested, and may not be easily definable or measurable. Apart from language skills, there are the qualitative aspects of language which are not simply reducible for testing (e.g. the emotive, status and poetic functions of languages).

One advantage for bilinguals of criterion referenced testing over norm referenced testing is the point of comparison. Norm referenced testing may compare bilinguals with monolinguals. Various authors (e.g. Frederickson & Cline, 1996; Grosjean, 1985, 1994) regard such comparison as unfair and invalid (see Chapter 1).

In criterion referenced testing the bilingual will be profiled on specific language skills. In theory, **unfair comparisons** between bilingual and monolingual may then be avoided. In practice, however, criterion referenced tests *can* be used to create comparisons between children, between groups of children and between schools. An advantage of criterion referenced language tests is that they may facilitate feedback to the teacher that directly leads to action. This is the notion of formative testing. If the test reveals areas where a child's language needs developing, further action can be taken.

Listening Objectives	Speaking Objectives
1. Sound discrimination	1. Pronunciation
2. Listening vocabulary	2. Speaking vocabulary
3. General comprehension of speech	3. Fluency of oral description
4. Understanding morphology of verbs	4. Control of morphology of verbs
5. Understanding morphology of prepositions	5. Control of morphology of prepositions
6. Understanding morphology of qualifiers	6. Control of morphology of qualifiers
7. Understanding morphology of nouns	7. Control of morphology of nouns
8. Understanding syntax of statements	8. Control of syntax of statements
9. Understanding syntax of questions	9. Control of syntax of questions

One illustration of testing language proficiency by criterion referenced tests is given by Harris (1984, see also Harris & Murtagh, 1999). Focusing on the attainment of Irish listening and speaking objectives, the above table specifies the test items.

The number of items to measure each objective ranged from three (control of syntax of questions) to 25 items (general comprehension of speech). Fourth grade children were assessed for their mastery of 140 separate items. While Harris' (1984) language tests are based on linguistic theory, in contrast the next example is based on a communicative approach to language testing.

A broad set of language goals, for which assessment **tasks** were developed, was part of the National Curriculum in England and Wales from 1990 to 1995. The basic premise was that teaching and testing should not be separate but integrated. Examples of requirements (language goals) for speaking in Welsh are given below as an illustration of language testing directly related to the curriculum (Department of Education and Science and The Welsh Office,1990). An example indicates the general kind of criterion referenced **tasks** that are created to indicate an individual's level of attainment.

Such test tasks are important because they tend to accent what a child can do, rather than typical classroom tests which focus on what cannot be done. Communi-

LEVEL ONE (Approximate Age 5)

Example of a Language Goal:	Participate as a speaker and listener in group activities including imaginative play.
Example of Assessment Task:	Play the role of shopkeeper or a customer in a classroom shop. The teacher observes and records speaking proficiency with provided guidelines.

LEVEL TWO (Approximate Age 7)

Example of a Language Goal:	Respond appropriately to complex instructions by the teacher, and give simple instructions.
Example of Assessment Task:	Follow three consecutive actions such as: list three places where a flower will grow best in the classroom; find out the views of others in the classroom, and reach a consensus viewpoint.

LEVEL THREE (Approximate Age 9)

Example of a Language Goal:	Give, receive and follow accurately precise instructions when pursuing a task as an individual or as a member of a group.
Example of Assessment Task:	Plan a wall display or arrange an outing together in a group.

LEVEL FOUR (Approximate Age 11)

Example of a Language Goal:	Give a detailed oral account of an event or explain with reasons why a particular course of action has been taken.
Example of Assessment Task:	Report orally on a scientific investigation.

Criterion referenced language tests should provide direct feedback into the following areas:

- teaching decisions (e.g. diagnosis of curriculum areas not mastered by an individual student);
- reporting to, and discussing achievement with parents;
- locating children in need of special support and the type of curriculum support they need;
- identifying children for accelerated learning;
- informing about standards in the class in terms of curriculum development through a subject. (Baker, 1995)

cative skills, knowledge and understanding are profiled rather than marks, percentages or grades. **Competence** is highlighted rather than errors and deficiencies. Such tasks compare the child with a scheme of language development, rather than comparing the child with other children. Such tests are formative, giving direct feedback and 'feedforward' to enable curriculum decisions about individual children.

A CRITICAL VIEW OF LANGUAGE TESTING

Language testing is not a neutral activity. It relates to cultural, social, political, educational and ideological agendas that shape the lives of all students and teachers. Such language tests are deeply embedded in cultural, educational and political debates where different ideologies are in contest. Elana Shohamy (1997, 2000) therefore proposes a perspective she terms '**critical language testing**' which views test-takers as **political subjects in a political context**.

Critical language testing asks questions about whose formal and hidden agendas tests relate to, and what sort of political and educational policies are delivered through tests. Critical language testing argues that language testers must ask themselves what sort of vision of society language tests create, and for what vision of society tests are used? For example, are language tests intended to fulfill pre-defined curricular or proficiency objectives, or are there other hidden aims, manoeuvres or manipulations?

Critical language testing asks questions about **whose knowledge** the tests are based on? What is the intended or assumed status of that knowledge (e.g. 'truth' or something that can be negotiated and challenged)? What is the meaning of language test scores, and to what degree are they prescriptive, final and absolute, or to what extent are they open to discussion and interpretation?

Critical language testing thus widens the field of language testing by relating it to political and social debates. 'This debate is surrounded by the roles that tests play and have been assigned to play, about competing ideologies, the discourses that are constructed and the roles of language testers. This debate draws language testers towards areas of social processes and power struggles embedded in the discourses on learning and democracy.' (Shohamy, 1997, p. 4).

The chapter now continues by considering various language structure theories. Theories about the structure of language competence provide an integrating consideration of the themes of the definition and measurement of bilingualism.

THE STRUCTURE OF LANGUAGE COMPETENCE

The language theories of the 1960s (e.g. Lado, 1961; Carroll, 1968) tended to center on language skills and components. The skills comprise listening, speaking, reading and writing and the components of knowledge comprise grammar, vocabulary, phonology and graphology. These earlier models did not indicate how skills and knowledge were integrated (Bachman, 1990). For example, how does listening differ from speaking? How does reading differ from writing? It has also been suggested that such skill and knowledge models tend to ignore the sociocultural and sociolinguistic context of language (Hymes, 1972a,b). Earlier models fail to probe the competence of 'other' people in a conversation. In a conversation, there is negotiation of meaning between two or more people. Real communication involves anticipating a listener's response, understandings and misunderstandings, sometimes clarifying one's own language to ensure joint understanding and relationships of similar and different status and power (Paulston, 1992a).

Earlier models also tended to be purely linguistic and ignore the settings and social contexts where language is used. A more sociolinguistic approach will examine actual content and context of communication called 'speech acts' or the 'ethnography of communication'. This approach includes looking at the rules of dual language usage among bilinguals, their shared knowledge in conversation, and the culturally, socially and politically determined language norms and values of bilingual speech events.

Various models of language competence have been developed. Two major examples will be briefly outlined; both have implications for the definition and measurement of bilingual proficiency, and both illustrate relatively comprehensive considerations of language competence.

Canale and Swain's Model of Language Competence

Canale and Swain (1980) and Canale (1983, 1984) suggest that language competence has four components: a **linguistic** component (e.g. syntax and vocabulary); a **sociolinguistic** component (e.g. use of appropriate language in different situations); a **discourse** component (e.g. ability to initiate and participate in sustained conversations and read sizable written texts); and a **strategic** component (e.g. improvisation with language when there is difficulty in communication).

Just as Oller's (1979) 'one factor' proposal has been criticized for not recognizing specific language areas, so Canale and Swain (1980) have been criticized for not showing whether or how the four components are inter-related, even if they can be subsumed into one overall global factor. Also, the description of a structure for language competence does not always relate easily to tests. Testing sociolinguistic and strategic competence is, of essence, likely to be difficult, contested and elusive, although not impossible, as Bachman (1990) reveals.

Bachman's Model of Language Competence

A second major model of language competence has been proposed by Bachman (1990). Bachman's model is valuable in that it considers both **language competence and language performance**. The model includes not only grammatical knowledge but also knowledge of how to use language in a particular communicative context. 'Communicative Language Ability can be described as consisting of both knowledge, or competence, and the capacity for implementing, or executing that competence in appropriate, contextualized communicative language use' (Bachman, 1990, p. 84).

To fully define, refine and enable the testing of communicative competence, Bachman (1990) has proposed a model that is summarized in the following table.

Language Competence

(1) Organizational Competence
    (i) Grammatical (e.g. Syntax, Vocabulary)
    (ii) Textual (e.g. Written and oral cohesion)
(2) Pragmatic Competence
    (i) Illocutionary Competence (e.g. speech strategies, language functions)
    (ii) Sociolinguistic Competence (e.g. sensitivity to register, dialect, cultural figures of speech)

To explain the table: for Bachman (1990), communicative competence is composed of two major components: organizational competence and pragmatic competence. **Organizational competence** is broken down into two parts, grammatical competence and textual competence. Grammatical competence comprises knowledge of vocabulary, syntax, morphology and phonology/graphology. For example, a person needs to arrange words in a correct order in a sentence with appropriate endings (e.g. high, higher, highest).

Textual competence involves 'the knowledge of the conventions for joining utterances together to form a text, which is essentially a unit of language — *spoken or written* — consisting of two or more utterances or sentences' (Bachman, 1990, p. 88).

Pragmatic competence is composed of two sub-parts: illocutionary competence and sociolinguistic competence. Following Halliday (1973), Bachman (1990) lists four language functions as part of illocutionary competence: ideational (the way we convey meanings and experiences), manipulative (using language in an instrumental way to achieve ends), heuristic (the use of language to discover new things about our world and solving problems), and the imaginative function (using language beyond the 'here and now' (e.g. for humor or fantasy).

The second part of pragmatic competence is sociolinguistic competence. Sociolinguistic competence is sensitivity to the context where language is used, ensuring that language is appropriate to the person or the situation. This may entail sensitivity to differences in local geographical dialect, sensitivity to differences in register (e.g. the register of boardroom, baseball, bar and bedroom). Sociolinguistic competence also refers to sensitivity to speaking in a native-like or natural way. This will include cultural variations in grammar and vocabulary (e.g. Black English). Another part of sociolinguistic competence is the ability to interpret cultural references and figures of speech. Sometimes, to understand a particular conversation, one needs inner cultural understanding of a specific language. A Welsh figure of speech such as 'to go round the Orme' (meaning 'to be long-winded') is only fully understandable within local northern Welsh cultural idioms.

In order to represent language as a dynamic process, Bachman (1990) argues that the listed components given in the table above interact with each other. He therefore adds to the model the notion of **strategic competence** where individuals constantly plan, execute and assess their communication strategies and delivery.

Since competence in a language is viewed as an integral part of language performance and not abstracted from it, tests of language competence cannot just use pencil and paper tests, but also need to investigate the language of genuine communication. Instead of tests that are artificial and stilted (e.g. language dictation tests), communicative performance testing involves creative, unpredictable, contextualized conversation.

This suggests that it will be difficult to measure communicative proficiency in an unbiased, comprehensive, valid and reliable way. Simple classroom tests are likely to be but a partial measure of the bilinguals' everyday performance. In testing communicative competence, Bachman (1990) adds a list of features that influence measured communicative competence in an academic context. Such external influences are likely to affect the language competence profile of the person tested, often in a negative way. This list includes:

(1)   Test Environment (e.g. effect of the tester; the scheduling and place of the test).
(2)   Test Rubric (e.g. layout of the test, time allocation, language of the instructions, details as to what constitutes an appropriate response).
(3)   Format of the Test (e.g. written, 'taped', 'live' testing).
(4)   Nature of the Test Language (e.g. chosen topic, context embedded or context reduced communication).
(5)   Nature of the Test Response (e.g. multiple choice or self-created; written or spoken; concrete or abstract; allowing non-verbal communication or not).

CONCLUSION

The topic of measurement often follows from a discussion of definitions, distinctions, dimensions and categorizations. Just as dimensions and categorizations can never capture the full flavor of the global nature of bilingualism, so measurement usually fails to capture fully various conceptual dimensions and categorizations. Just as the statistics of a football or an ice hockey game do not convey the richness of the event, so language tests and measurements are unlikely to fully represent an idea or theoretical concept. Complex and rich descriptions are the indispensable partner of measurement and testing. The stark statistics of the football or ice hockey game and the colorful commentary are complementary, not incompatible.

Language background scales to measure language usage and a plethora of tests to measure language proficiency exist. The latter includes norm and criterion referenced language tests, self-rating scales and language dominance tests. Particular attention in this chapter has been given to criterion referenced tests measuring mastery of specific language objectives. Suitable for both first and second languages, sometimes based on theoretical principles, sometimes eclectic, such tests tend to relate directly to the process of teaching and learning.

The chapter considered theories of the structure of language competence. Such theories join the first two chapters, integrating issues of definition with ideas about measurement. In particular, the focus has been on linking a linguistic view of language competence with a communicative view. Language can be decomposed into its linguistic constituents (e.g. grammar, vocabulary). It is also important to consider language as a means of making relationships and communicating information. This important dualism will follow us through the book: ability and use; the linguistic and the social; competence and communication.

KEY POINTS IN THE CHAPTER

- Bilinguals are measured both for their proficiency and use of their languages. Examples include census surveys of languages in a population, selection for different classes in school according to language ability, assessment of competency following second language learning.
- Language Background scales measure a person's use of their languages in different domains and in different relationships.
- Language balance and dominance measures seek to gauge the relative strength of each language of a bilingual.
- Communicative language testing attempts to measure a person's use of language in authentic situations
- Criterion referenced language tests seek to provide a profile of language sub-skills whereas norm referenced tests compare a person with other people.
- 'Critical language testing' examines whose knowledge the tests are based on, and for what political purposes the tests will used. It regards test-takers as political subjects in a political context.
- Language competence includes not only linguistic competence (e.g. vocabulary, grammar) but also competence in different social and cultural situations with different people.

SUGGESTED FURTHER READING

BACHMAN, L.F., 1990, *Fundamental Considerations in Language Testing.* Oxford: Oxford University Press.
CLAPHAM, C. and CORSON, D. (eds), 1997, *Language Testing and Assessment.* Volume 7 of the *Encyclopedia of Language and Education.* Dordrecht: Kluwer.
HORNBERGER, N. and CORSON, D. (eds), 1997, *Research Methods in Language and Education.* Volume 8 of the *Encyclopedia of Language and Education.* Dordrecht: Kluwer.
SHOHAMY, E., 2000, *The Power of Tests: A Critical Perspective on the Uses and Consequences of Language Tests.* London: Longman.
VALDES, G. and FIGUEROA, R.A., 1994, *Bilingualism and Testing: A Special Case of Bias.* Norwood, NJ: Ablex.

STUDY ACTIVITIES

(1) Use the Language Background Scale (modified to suit your context) on yourself or someone you know. This may also be used with a class of students. Examine the answers given and sum up in words or in numbers the balance and use of languages. If used with a group of students, are there groups or clus-

ters of students? Are there those dominant in one language, those dominant in another language and those with a balance between the two?

(2) Using a local school(s), find out what tests are used to measure language achievement in the classroom. These may be listening, speaking, reading, writing or language development tests. Find out whether these are norm referenced or criterion referenced tests. For what purposes are these tests being used? How fair are these to bilingual children?

(3) Using the library or the Internet, gather detailed information about one country's language census. Baker and Jones (1998) provide some references and World Wide Web addresses to help. What were the major findings? What problems are there in the wording of the question(s)? What other limitations do you find in the survey?

CHAPTER 3
Languages in Society

Introduction

Diglossia

Endangered Languages

Language Planning

Language Shift and Language
Maintenance

Language Decline and Death

Conclusion

CHAPTER 3
Languages in Society

INTRODUCTION

Bilinguals are present in every country of the world, in every social class and in all age groups. Numerically, bilinguals and multilinguals are in the majority in the world, with estimates of their size being between half and two thirds of the world's population. The bilingual population of the world is growing as international travel, communications and mass media, emigration and a planetary economy create the global village.

Bilingual individuals do not exist as separated islands. Rather, people who speak two or more languages usually exist in **networks, communities and sometimes in regions**. People who speak a minority language within a majority language context may be said to form a speech community or language community.

Bilingualism at the individual level is half the story. The other essential half is to analyze how **groups** of language speakers behave and change. Such an examination particularly focuses on the movement and development in language use across decades. Such movement in a minority language is often downwards. A language minority is rarely stable in its size, strength or safety. Therefore, examining the politics and power situation in which minority languages are situated becomes important (see Chapter 18).

This chapter focuses on the idea that there is no language without a language community. Since language communities do not usually exist in isolation from other communities, it becomes important to examine the **contact** between different language communities. The rapid growth of information (e.g. across the World Wide Web) and inter-continental travel has meant that language communities are rarely if ever stable. Some languages become stronger (e.g. English); other languages tending to decline, even die. Some languages thought to be dead, may occasionally be revived (e.g. Manx in the Isle of Man). This chapter therefore seeks to examine **language communities, language contact, language change and language conflict**. This will reveal that decisions about bilingual education are part of a much wider whole. That is, bilingual education can only be properly understood by examining the circumstances of language communities in which such education is placed.

This chapter takes a **sociolinguistic perspective**. Sociolinguistics is the study of language in relation to social groups, social class, ethnicity and other interpersonal factors in communication. The chapter examines central sociolinguistic concepts such as diglossia, language shift, language maintenance, language death, language revitalization and language spread. There is also a linguistic view of these topics (e.g. change in syntax, semantics and lexicon) that is not covered in this or the following chapter on language revival (see Aitchison, 1991; McMahon, 1994; Romaine, 1995, 2000; Dixon, 1997 for a linguistic discussion of these topics). The sociolinguistic perspective begins by examining a central idea in sociolinguistics, that of diglossia.

DIGLOSSIA

The term bilingualism is typically used to describe the two languages of an individual. When the focus changes to two languages in society, the term often used is **diglossia** (Ferguson, 1959; Fishman, 1972, 1980). While the term **diglossia** has recently become broadened and refined, it was originally a Greek word for two languages. In practice, a language community is unlikely to use both languages for the same purpose. A language community is more likely to use one language in certain situations and for certain functions, the other language in different circumstances and for different functions. For example, a language community may use a minority language in the home, for religious purposes and in social activity, but use the majority language at work, in education and when experiencing the mass media.

Ferguson (1959) first described **diglossia** in terms of two varieties of the same language (dialects). Fishman (1972, 1980) extended the idea of diglossia to two languages existing side by side within a geographical area. Ferguson's (1959) original description distinguishes between a high language variety (called H) and a low variety (called L). This distinction can also be between a majority (H) and minority

Context		Majority Language (H)	Minority Language (L)
1.	The home and family		✔
2.	Schooling	✔	
3.	Mass Media	✔	
4.	Business and commerce	✔	
5.	Social and cultural activity in the community		✔
6.	Correspondence with relatives and friends		✔
7.	Correspondence with government departments	✔	
8.	Religious activity		✔

(L) language within a country, which is a rather non-neutral and discriminatory distinction. In both situations, different languages or varieties may be used for different purposes as the table above illustrates.

The example shows that languages may be used in different situations, with the low variety more likely to be used in informal, personal situations; the high or majority language being more used in formal, official communication contexts. It is typically embarrassing or belittling to use the low variety of language in a situation where the high variety is expected.

The table opposite suggests that the different language situations usually make one language more **prestigious** than the other. The majority language will often be perceived as the more eminent, elegant and educative language. The high variety is usually seen as the door to both educational and economic success.

The concept of diglossia can be usefully examined alongside the concept of bilingualism. Fishman (1980) combines the terms **bilingualism** and **diglossia** to portray four language situations where bilingualism and diglossia may exist with or without each other. The following table, based on Fishman (1980; see Glyn Williams, 1992, for a critique) portrays this relationship.

		DIGLOSSIA	
		+	−
INDIVIDUAL BILINGUALISM	+	1. Diglossia and Bilingualism together	3. Bilingualism without Diglossia
	−	2. Diglossia without Bilingualism	4. Neither Bilingualism nor Diglossia

The **first** situation is a language community containing **both individual bilingualism and diglossia**. In such a community, almost everyone will be able to use both the high language (or variety) and the low language (or variety). The high language is used for one set of functions, the low language for a separate set of functions. For example. the high language is used for education and government; the low language is used in the family and local neighborhood.

The **second** situation outlined by Fishman (1972, 1980) is **diglossia without bilingualism**. In such a context there will be two languages within a particular geographical area. One group of inhabitants will speak one language, another group a different language. One example is Switzerland where, to a large extent, different language groups (German, French, Italian, Romansch) are located in different areas. The official status of the different languages may be theoretically equal. Fluent bilingual speakers of both languages may be the exception rather than the rule (Andres, 1990).

In some cases, the ruling power group will typically speak the high language, with the larger less powerful group speaking only the low language. For example, in a colonial situation, English (e.g. in India) or French (e.g. in Haiti) was spoken by the ruling elite, with the indigenous language(s) spoken by the masses.

The **third** situation is **bilingualism without diglossia**. In this situation, most people will be bilingual and will not restrict one language to a specific set of purposes. Either language may be used for almost any function. Fishman (1972, 1980) regards such communities as unstable and in a state of change. Where bilingualism exists without diglossia, the prediction is that the majority language will become even more powerful and extend its use. The other language may decrease in its functions and decay in status and usage.

However, this is not the only outcome. In Wales, for example, an attempt is being made for the minority language (Welsh) to be increasingly available in hitherto English language domains (e.g. in education, television, pop music) giving bilinguals a choice. It is believed in Wales that allowing separate functions for Welsh will relegate the language to low status and subordinate uses only. Welsh would have sentimental and not instrumental (e.g. economic) value. Thus the Welsh view is that diglossia in Wales leads to language decline (except where the minority language has prestigious uses such as for religious purposes). This is similar to Sridhar (1996) who suggests that rather than compartmentalisation of languages in a diglossic situation, the reality is an overlapping and intermeshing use of languages.

Fishman (1972, 1980) disagrees believing that keeping up with the prestige and power of a world-wide language such as English is impossible, impractical and not realizable. 'All functions for the minority language' sets the wrong goal for that language. Instead, the minority language must be safeguarded in the home and community. Also, Humanities and Social Sciences may be a target for a 'High' use of Welsh or Basque, for example, plus power functions in local and regional government. However, the Natural Sciences and Technology may be a preserve for English or Spanish in these examples.

The **fourth** situation is where there is **neither bilingualism nor diglossia**. One example is where a linguistically diverse society has been forcibly changed to a relatively monolingual society. In Cuba and the Dominican Republic, the native languages have been exterminated. A different example would be a small speech community using its minority language for all functions and insisting on having no relationship with the neighboring majority language.

Boyd and Latomaa (1999) empirically tested this four-fold typology among nine language groups (e.g. Turkish, Vietnamese, Finnish and English speakers in the Nordic region in places such as Helsinki, Copenhagen, Göteborg and East Finnmark). By rating parents' and children's degree of bilingualism and type of diglossia, they found the typology to have only limited predictive value. Part of the problem was that language groups could not be easily allocated to the four 'cells' as there are underlying continuous dimensions in both bilingualism and diglossia. Also, when elements such as language stability and maintenance were examined in each of the language groups, the typology did not always fit the data. For example, Boyd and Latomaa (1999, p. 320) found that 'For the Americans in Göteborg and

Copenhagen, high levels of bilingualism and low levels of diglossia do not seem to have led to instability and language shift in the younger generation.'

Fishman (1980) argues that diglossia with and without bilingualism tends to provide a relatively stable, enduring language arrangement. Yet such stability may be increasingly rare. With increasing ease of travel and communication, increased social and vocational mobility, a more global economy and more urbanization, there tends to be more contact between language communities. As we shall see later in this chapter, language shift tends to be more typical than language stability. Changes in the fate and fortune of a minority language occur because the separate purposes of the two languages tend to change across generations. The **boundaries** that separate one language from another are never permanent. Neither a minority language community nor the uses that community makes of its low/minority language can be permanently compartmentalized. Even with the **territorial principle** (a language being given official status in a specific geographical area), the political and power base of the two languages changes over time. However, keeping boundaries between the languages and compartmentalizing their use in society is regarded as important for the weaker or lower variety to survive.

The **territorial principle** occurs when language rights or laws apply to a specific region. For example, in Belgium there are three designated regions where Flemish, French and German speakers have language rights inside their regions, but not outside those regions in the remainder of Belgium (Nelde, Labrie & Williams, 1992). Switzerland is another example. In contrast, the **personality principle** applies when status to the language is given to individuals or groups wherever they travel in a country (Paulston, 1997). For example, in Canada francophones have the right to use French wherever they travel across Canada. The 'personality' refers to the linguistic status of the person.

An attempted merging of the territorial and personality principles when applied to language rights has been termed the '**asymmetrical principle**' or 'asymmetrical bilingualism' (Reid, 1993). As conceived by its Canadian advocates (e.g. in Quebec), the principle gives full rights to minority language speakers and less rights to the speakers of a majority language. This is a form of positive discrimination, seeking to discriminate in favor of those who are usually discriminated against. Some of the functions of a minority language may be legislated for, so as to preserve that language in a proactive manner. We return to the question of language rights in Chapter 18.

An argument for the maintenance and spread of a language is often based on its historic existence within a defined boundary (e.g. Welsh in Wales; Basque in the Basque Country). As the indigenous language of the region, language rights may be enshrined in law. For example, Welsh speakers have certain language rights in Wales (e.g. 1993 Welsh Language Act allowing, among other things, the use of Welsh in courts of law) but not when they cross into England or mainland Europe. But what status has immigrant languages that cannot claim either territorial or personality rights?

Such a geographical argument for an indigenous language has unfortunate implications for **immigrant language minorities** (Stubbs, 1991). Do languages belong to regions and territories and not to the speakers of those languages, or to groups of speakers of those languages wherever they may be found? Do immigrant languages in the United States, Canada, United Kingdom and Germany not 'belong' as they are not indigenous languages? Do such immigrant languages only belong in the home country (e.g. Korean in Korea, Turkish in Turkey)? Should immigrant language minorities either speak the language of the territory or return to the home country? In Europe, there are many indigenous (or autochthonous) languages that are seeking preservation status in the European Community. Almost no status is accorded the immigrant languages of Europe (e.g. the various Asian languages such as Panjabi, Urdu, Bengali, Vietnamese, Korean, Hindi and Gujerati).

An immigrant language retains distinctive attributes (e.g. as revealed in its uses and functions, customs and rituals, culture and shared meanings, communication styles and literature; see Allardt, 1979). One example is the **Pennsylvania Amish** who decided to ensure the continuity of their heritage language by reserving an exclusive place for that language at home, and reserving English for school and for contacts with the outside secular world. One language was reserved for particular societal functions; another language for distinctly separate functions. This compartmentalization ideally exists in a relatively stable arrangement.

In language communities, the functions and boundaries of the two languages will both affect and be reflected in bilingual education policy and practice. In a diglossic situation, is the high or low variety of language used in the different stages of schooling, from kindergarten to university? If the low variety is used in the school, in which curriculum areas does it function? Is the low variety just used for oral communication or is biliteracy a goal of the school's curriculum? Are science, technology and computing taught in the high or low variety? Is the low variety just allowed for a year or two in the elementary school with the higher variety taking over thereafter (e.g. transitional bilingual education in the U.S., see Chapter 9)? Does the school deliberately exclude the low variety as a medium for classroom learning? The purposes and functions of each language in a diglossic situation are both symbolized and enacted in the school situation. This links with Chapter 9 where different forms of bilingual education are examined.

ENDANGERED LANGUAGES

How would you feel if you were the last speaker of your language? Marie Smith, the last speaker of the Alaskan Eyak language, gave her answer (Nettle & Romaine, 2000, p. 14): 'I don't know why it's me, why I'm the one. I tell you, it hurts. It really hurts.'

Richard Littlebear (1999), a Native American Cheyenne member, tells of his meeting with Marie Smith. 'I felt that I was sitting in the presence of a whole universe of knowledge that could be gone in one last breath. That's how fragile that linguistic universe seemed.'

To be told that a loved one is dying or dead is one of the most unpleasant experiences of life. To talk about a dead language or a dying language sounds academic and without much sentiment. Yet languages have no existence without people. A language dies with the last speaker of that language. For humanity, that is a great loss. Three further examples will illustrate.

- In Cameron in 1994/95, a researcher, Bruce Connell, visited the last speaker of a language called Kasabe (or Luo). In 1996, he returned to research that moribund language. He was too late. The last speaker of Kasabe had died on 5th November 1995 taking the language and culture with him. Connell reports that the last speaker was survived by a sister who could understand but not speak Kasabe, and whose children and grandchildren did not understand the language (Crystal, 2000). Simply stated, on 4th November 1995 Kasabe existed. On 5th November it did not.
- On the 8th October 1992 a northwestern Caucasian language called Ubykh died. A linguist, Ole Andersen arrived in the Turkish village of Haci to interview the last speaker, Tefvik Esenc, only to learn that he had died just a couple of hours earlier (Crystal, 2000; Nettle & Romaine, 2000). His three sons were unable to talk to their father in Ubykh as they had become Turkish speakers. Tefvik Esenc had composed his own gravestone eight years earlier: 'This is the grave of Tefvik Esenc – the last person able to speak the language they called Ubykh.'
- The last native speaker of Cupeño died in California in 1987, of Catawba Sioux in 1980, of Wappo in 1990, and of Manx in 1974 (Nettle & Romaine, 2000).

There is no exact agreement as to the **number of living languages** in the world. There is, however, growing agreement that many or most are dying languages (Nettle & Romaine, 2000).

Grimes (1996) lists 6703 living languages in the world, while Mackey (1991) suggests 6170 living languages. Moseley and Asher's (1994) *Atlas of the World's Languages* specifies close to 5900 discrete languages, while Bright (1992) lists 6300 living languages. A UNESCO 'Atlas of the World's Languages in Danger of Disappearing (Wurm, 1996) estimates 5000 to 6000 languages in existence. The variation in estimate is due, for example, to the difficulty in defining a language (e.g. as different from a dialect), and problems of gathering reliable, valid and comprehensive information about languages in large expanses such as Africa, South America and parts of Asia.

There are thus approximately 6000 languages in the world today. Such living languages are found in under 200 sovereign states. Around 120 states have adopted either English, French, Spanish or Arabic as their official languages. Another 50 states have their own indigenous official language. Mackey (1991) suggests that there are around 45 regional languages with official status in the world. If we add together these international and 'official' languages, they only account for around 1.5% of the total languages in the world. Or more dramatically, 98.5% of the languages of the world have no formal recognition. Williams (1996b, p. 47) suggests that 'only 1% of the world's languages have more than half a million speakers and only 10% have more than 100,000. Hundreds of languages have no adolescent speakers'.

According to Michael Krauss (1992) of the Alaska Native Research Center, between 20% to 50% of the world's existing languages are likely to die or become perilously close to death in the next 100 years. Wurm (1996) estimates that 50% of the world's languages are endangered. The US Summer Institute of Linguistics (see: http://www.sil.org/ethnologue/ethnologue.html) calculated that in 1999, 51 languages in the world only had one speaker, and 500 languages had fewer than 100 speakers.

In the long term: 'It is a very realistic possibility that 90% of mankind's languages will become extinct or doomed to extinction' (Krauss, 1995, p. 4). This estimated 90% death:10% safe ratio is based on the following argument:

- 50% of the world's languages are no longer being reproduced among children. Thus many of these 50% of languages could die in the next 100 years unless there are conservation measures.
- An additional 40% are threatened or endangered. Economic, social and political change is one such threat. For example, such a threat is found in countries where there are a large number of languages and where centralization, economic and social development for example, will take priority over language survival. Nine countries have more than 200 languages: Australia, Brazil, Cameroon, India, Indonesia, Mexico, Nigeria, Papua New Guinea and Zaire. These nine countries account for about 3300 of the world's 6000 languages. Another dozen countries have more than 100 languages each (e.g. Burma, Chad, Ethiopia). Many of these countries have relatively small numbers of speakers of the different languages. Assimilation, urbanization, centralization, uniformity and economic pressures will make future generations prefer majority languages.
- As few as 600 languages (10%) may survive, although Krauss (1995, p. 4) believes this is too optimistic and suggests that 'it does not seem unrealistic to guess on these bases that 300 languages may be deemed safe'.
- Officially, 7.5% of mammals and 2.7% of birds are listed as 'endangered' or 'threatened', although this may be an underestimate. There are consequently enthusiastic conservation measures. If 90% of the world's languages are vulnerable, **language planning** measures to maintain linguistic and cultural diversity are urgently required (Grenoble & Whaley, 1998).

However, a 'preservation of species' approach to language survival is different from evolution of species in mechanisms and politics (May, 2001). The biological evolutionary metaphor may suggest to some that language loss is about survival of the fittest. If a language fails to adapt to the modern world, it deserves to die. Natural selection (Social Darwinism) suggests the inevitability of weaker forms dying. But this ignores the human-made reasons why languages die – often due to political and economic policies.

Social and political factors, and not just 'evolution', are at work in language loss. Power, prejudice, discrimination, marginalization and subordination are some of the causes of language decline and death. The history of Native American languages in the United States is an example of language genocide and eradication rather than suicide or natural change (see Chapter 10). Language loss is thus not 'evolutionary' but determined by politicians, policy-makers and peoples. Thus an evolutionary metaphor can understate and undervalue why languages die (May, 2001).

David Crystal (2000) suggests that there are five basic arguments why retaining **language diversity** is essential:

(1) It is widely agreed to that ecological **diversity is essential**. The concept of an ecosystem is that all living organisms, plants, animals, bacteria and humans survive and prosper through a network of complex and delicate relationships. Damaging one of the elements in the ecosystem will result in unforeseen consequences for the whole of the system. Nettle and Romaine (2000) argue that cultural diversity and biological diversity are inseparable. Where biodiversity and rich ecosystems exist, so do linguistic and cultural diversity. Evolution has been aided by genetic diversity, with species genetically adapting in order to survive in different environments. Diversity contains the potential for adaptation. Uniformity holds dangers for the long-term survival of the species. Uniformity can endanger a species by providing inflexibility and unadaptability. The range of cross fertilization becomes less as languages and cultures die and the testimony of human intellectual achievement is lessened. In the language of ecology, the strongest ecosystems are those that are the most diverse. That is, diversity is directly related to stability; variety is important for long-term survival. Our success on this planet has been due to an ability to adapt to different kinds of environment over thousands of years (atmospheric as well as cultural). Such an ability is born out of diversity.

(2) **Languages express identity**. Identity concerns the shared characteristics of members of a group, community or region. Identity provides the security and status of a shared existence. Sometimes identity is via dress, religious beliefs, rituals, but language is almost always present in identity formation and identity display. Language is an index, symbol and marker of identity.

(3) **Languages are repositories of history**. Languages provide a link to a personalized past, a means to reach the archive of knowledge, ideas and beliefs from the past. 'Every language is a living museum, a monument to every culture it has been vehicle to' (Nettle & Romaine, 2000, p. 14).

(4) **Languages contribute to the sum of human knowledge**. Inside each language is a vision of the past, present and future so that when a language dies its vision of the world dies with it. If the world is a mosaic of visions, one part of that mosaic is lost. Language not only transmits visions of the past but also expressions of social relationships, individual friendships with local landscapes, a wealth of organizing experiences, rules about social relationships as well as

ideas about art, craft, science, poetry, song, life, death and language itself. Language lies at the heart of human education, culture and identity. When a language dies so does culture, identity and knowledge that has been passed down from generation to generation through and within that language. A language contains a way of thinking and being, acting and doing. Each language contains a view of the universe, a particular understanding of the world. If there are 6000 living languages, then there are 6000 overlapping ways to describe the world. That variety provides a rich mosaic. Different languages contain different understandings of people as individuals and communities, different values and ways of expressing the purpose of life, different visions of past humanity, present priorities and our future existence.

(5) **Languages are interesting in themselves**. David Crystal (2000) argues that language itself is important, each language having different sounds, grammar and vocabulary that reveal something different about linguistic organization and structure. The more languages there are to study, the more our understanding about the beauty of language grows.

Crystal (2000) suggests that there are a number of solutions to avoid language death (see Chapter 4). While the solutions will be different for languages at different stages of survival and revitalization, he suggests that an endangered language will progress if its speakers:

- increase their prestige within the dominant community;
- increase their wealth relative to the dominant community;
- have access to a stable economic base;
- increase their legitimate power in the eyes of the dominant community;
- increase the number of domains in which their language is used;
- have a critical mass in communities and regions;
- have a strong presence in the educational system;
- have a literacy in that language;
- make use of electronic technology;
- have a strong sense of ethnic identity;
- have internal and external recognition as a group with unique unity;
- resist the influence of the dominant culture or are protected and formally recognized by that dominant culture.

The solution to avoiding language death involves language planning, a deliberate intervention to arrest the decline of a language. Ofelia García (1992b), uses an analogy to introduce the need for language planning and language preservation. Her **Language Garden Analogy** commences with the idea that if we traveled through the countries of the world and found field after field, garden after garden of the same, one-color flower, without variety of shape, size or color, how dull and boring the world would be. Fortunately, there is a wide variety of flowers throughout the world of all shapes and sizes, all tints and textures, all hues and shades. A garden full of different colored flowers enhances the beauty of that garden and enriches our visual and aesthetic experience.

If just a few of the majority languages of the world solely existed, how tedious and uninteresting it would be. Rather, for the moment we have a language garden full of variety and color. The initial conclusion is simply that language diversity in the garden of the world makes for a richer, more interesting world with a depth of experience gained from a breadth of cultures.

However, language diversity makes the garden more difficult to tend. In a garden, some flowers and shrubs spread quickly. Some majority languages, particularly English, have expanded considerably during the last century. When the garden is neglected, a few strong species of flower may take over, and small minority flowers may be in danger of extinction. Therefore some delicate flowers need extra care and protection. This leads to the second part of García's (1992b) analogy. A free language economy will mean the extinction of many languages. **Language planning** is essential to avoid such trends (Cooper, 1989). When a gardener wishes to create a beautiful garden, there will be both careful planning and continued care and protection. Sometimes radical action may be taken to preserve and protect. The analogy suggests that language diversity requires planning and care.

This analogy suggests that a *laissez-faire* situation is less desirable than deliberate, rational language planning. Gardeners are needed (e.g. teachers in schools) to plant, water, fertilize and reseed the different minority language flowers in the garden to ensure an enriching world language garden. While there are gardeners (e.g. teachers) tending the language garden, there are landscape engineers who plan and control the overall shape of the language garden. The view of language landscape engineers (e.g. politicians, policy-makers) is often to regard the language garden as just one part of a wider control of the environment. The dominant power groups who determine the social, economic and cultural environment may see language as just one element in an overall landscape design. For example, the type of school program that is allowed in a region (submersion, transitional, immersion or supportive of the minority community language — see Chapter 9) is but part of a design for the total landscape in which the languages are located.

A language policy-maker who is concerned only for majority languages will regard protecting rare languages as expensive and unnecessary, and will wish to standardize the variety of language in the country. In the USA, for example, many politicians prefer monolingualism rather than bilingualism. The preference is for the assimilation of minority language communities into a more standardized, monochrome garden.

It is important to note **variations in attitude** to the language environment. Williams (1991a) sums up differing 'environmental' attitudes to the survival and spread of minority languages. First, the **evolutionist** will follow Darwin's idea of the survival of the fittest. Those languages that are strong will survive. The weaker languages will either have to adapt themselves to their environment, or die. A different way of expressing this is in terms of a free, *laissez-faire* language economy.

Languages must survive on their own merits without the support of language planning.

However, survival of the fittest is too simplistic a view of evolution. It only accents the negative side of evolution: killing, exploitation and suppression. A more positive view of evolution is **interdependence** rather than constant competition. Cooperation for mutually beneficial outcomes can be just as possible as exploitation (Williams, 1991a; Williams, 1999). An evolutionist argument about language shift also fails to realize that it is not a simple, spontaneous or impulsive process. Rather, the fate of languages is often related to the manipulated politics and power bases of different groups in society. **Language shift** (in terms of numbers of speakers and uses) occurs through deliberate decisions that directly or indirectly affect languages and reflects economic, political, cultural, social and technological change. It is therefore possible to analyze and determine what causes language shift rather than simply believing language shift occurs by accident. Thus, those who support an evolutionary perspective on languages will typically be supporting the spread of majority languages and the replacement of minority languages. Those who advocate monolingualism often feel that their particular culture and perspectives are the only legitimate varieties – all others are inferior and less worth preserving. Evolutionists who argue for an economic, cost–benefit approach to languages, with the domination of a few majority languages for international communication, hold a myopic view of the function of languages. Languages are not purely for economic communication. They are also concerned with human culture, human heritage, the value of a garden full of different languages rather than the one variety.

The second approach to languages is that of **conservationists** (Williams, 1991a). Conservationists will argue for the maintenance (and increasingly the enrichment) of variety in the language garden. For conservationists, language planning must care for and cherish minority languages, revitalizing and invigorating. Just as certain animal species are now deliberately preserved within particular territorial areas, so conservationists will argue that threatened languages should receive special status in heartland regions (or on reservations). Native Indian languages in North America and the Celtic languages in Britain and France have invoked the conservationist argument. In Ireland, certain areas called Gaeltachta are officially designated for Irish conservation.

The third attitude to languages is that of **preservationists** (Williams, 1991a). Preservationists are different from conservationists by being more conservative and seeking to maintain the status quo rather than to develop the language. Preservationists are concerned that any change, not just language change, will damage the chances of their language surviving. Such a group is therefore traditionalist, anti-modern in outlook. Whereas conservationists may think globally and act locally, preservationists will tend to think locally and act locally.

One example of language preservation may be when language is closely tied in with religion. The historical survival of Pennsylvania German within the **Amish** community in the USA has been a classic illustration of a preservationist approach to language. The Pennsylvania Germans, sometimes called the Pennsylvania

Dutch, came to the USA from Germany in the early 18th century. They originally settled in farming communities in southeastern and central Pennsylvania. The language is a German dialect related to that spoken in the German Palatinate along the Rhine river. Distinctive in dress, these Protestant Old Order Amish and Old Order Mennonite sectarians speak Pennsylvania German (a German dialect) at home and in the community. English is learnt at school since it is the language of instruction. English is also increasingly spoken with outsiders (Huffines, 1991). Archaic forms of German are used in Protestant religious worship. The language of the community has thus been preserved within the established boundaries of that community. However, particularly among the non-sectarian Pennsylvania Germans, the language is dying (Huffines, 1991). As English replaces the High German used in religious worship, the *raison d'être* for the use of Pennsylvania German in the home and community disappears. Religion has preserved the language. As religious practices change, preservation changes to transformation.

LANGUAGE PLANNING

Language planning, also called language engineering, refers to 'deliberate efforts to influence the behavior of others with respect to the acquisition, structure, or functional allocation of their language codes' (Cooper, 1989, p. 45). Traditionally, such language planning involves three goals in terms of policy and cultivation (Hornberger, 1994; Wiley, 1996b; Kaplan & Baldauf, 1997; Dogancay-Aktuna, 1997): **status planning** (e.g. raising the status of a language within society across as many language-domain institutions as possible), **corpus planning** (e.g modernizing terminology, standardization of grammar and spelling) and **acquisition planning** (creating language spread by increasing the number of speakers and uses by, for example, interventions with parents, health visitors, midwives (Welsh Language Board, 1998; Evans, 2000), language learning in school, adult language classes, literacy). The inter-generational transmission of a language (parents passing their language(s) onto their children) is one essential if insufficient foundation for language survival and maintenance.

Status planning is found in a variety of policies: political movements seeking recognition or official status for a language (both minority languages like Maori and Welsh, and majority languages like English in the United States), as well as religious and nationalist movements seeking revitalization of a language such as Hebrew in Israel. Status planning is political by nature, attempting to gain more recognition, functions and capacity for a language. By maintaining use in, and sometimes spreading into new language domains, a language may hopefully be secured and revitalized (e.g. official use of that language in courts of law, local (regional) and central government, education, mass media and as many public, private and voluntary institutions as possible). Through laws, rights (see Chapter 18) and constitutions, but also by persuasion and precedent, status planning attempts to conserve, revitalize or spread a language. Special attention is often given to modernization – to ensure that the language is used in modern, influential spheres (e.g. computers, Internet, television, radio, advertising, newspapers and magazines).

However, while individuals may be influenced by such changes in status of a language, such actions are not guaranteed to maintain a language. Status planning has to affect everyday usage in the home and street, family and work relationships, and not just official usage, to influence language change (Welsh Language Board, 1999).

Corpus planning is a typical part of language planning where languages are precarious and when they are resurgent. A common process for all languages, majority and minority, is to modernize vocabulary. Science and Information Communications Technology (ICT) are just two examples where standardized terminology is created and spread. An alternative is the increasing use of 'loan words' (e.g. English words used in Spanish, possibly leading eventually to 'Spanglish' or preference for English). Schools, books and magazines, television and radio all help to standardize a language and hence new concepts have to have an agreed term. The Catalans, Basques, Welsh and Irish are examples of countries who formally engage in corpus planning through centrally funded and coordinated initiatives. Another example is France which, since the establishment of the Académie Française, has tried to maintain the purity of French and halt the influence of English as in '*le weekend*' (see Baker & Jones, 1998).

Being prescriptive about 'correctness' in a language and insisting on the purity of spoken or written language (e.g. US politicians insisting on standard English and not Ebonics or Black English in schools), relates to prestige speech styles. In the UK, speaking 'Queen's English' (Received Pronunciation) with a 'high class' accent connects with power and position, upward mobility and affluence. To speak non-standard or dialect English in the US and UK often relates to being seen as less intelligent, inferior, less educated and cultured, and less trustworthy. Teachers' judgments of students' intelligence and personality are affected by such students' languages and accents. Listening to the language variety of a person evokes social stereotypes and expectations, coloring the behavior of the listener toward the speaker. Thus when corpus planning is about purity and normalization, there is a danger that linguistic policy becomes political, with power and status going to those with the purity of language (Spolsky, 1998).

Acquisition planning is particularly concerned with language reproduction in the family and language production at school. In all minority languages, there are families who use the majority language with their children. In Wales, where both parents are Welsh speaking, 8% speak only English to their children. Due to perceived economic or educational advantages of speaking English, or status in the neighborhood, is a principal and direct cause of language shift. Where there is a shortfall in language maintenance in families, education becomes the principal means of producing more language speakers. Through bilingual education, language learning but also adult classes (e.g. Ulpan), the potential numbers of minority language speakers can be increased (e.g. French speakers in Canada, Quechua (Quichua) speakers in Peru).

It is possible to plan for the status, corpus and acquisition of a language and yet not intervene directly in the daily usage of ordinary people. Languages decline when speakers drop in number and their daily usage diminishes. Therefore language planning has to relate to everyday language life as enacted in homes, streets, communities, workplaces and leisure activities. In Wales, such planning involves interventions in the economy so that minority language speakers can function in Welsh in employment (Welsh Language Board, 1999). Such planning also involves targeting key local cultural, leisure, social and community institutions where minority languages speakers will use their language, form relationships and networks using that language. Planning also needs to empower local communities directly, enabling everyday language life to be enacted through a minority language.

Cooper (1989: 98) provides a classic scheme for understanding language planning by asking a series of key questions:

- **Which actors** (e.g. elites, influential people, counter-elites, non-elite policy implementers)
- **attempt to influence which behaviors** (e.g. the purposes or functions for which the language is to be used)
- **of which people** (e.g. of which individuals or organizations)
- **for what ends** (e.g. overt (language related behaviors) or latent (non-language-related behaviors, the satisfaction of interests)
- **under what conditions** (e.g. political, economic, social, demographic, ecological, cultural)
- **by what means** (e.g. authority, force, promotion, persuasion)
- **through what decision-making processes and means**
- **with what effect or outcome?**

This relatively comprehensive set of questions makes some important points. First, language planning may be generated by different groups. For example, poets, linguists, lexicographers, missionaries, soldiers as well as administrators, legislators and politicians may become involved in language planning. Cooper (1989) argues, however, that language planning is more likely to succeed when it is embraced or promoted by elite groups or counter-elites. Such **elites** tend to work primarily from their own self-interests. Language planning is motivated by efforts to secure or reinforce the interests of particular people. However, language planning may positively affect the masses by adding to their self-identity, self-esteem, social connectedness and economic and employment opportunities.

A consideration of language planning runs the danger of over-emphasizing its importance in overall political planning. Language planning is rarely high priority for governments. **First**, there is often piecemeal pragmatism rather than planning. The revival of Hebrew is often quoted as one triumphant and successful example of language planning. Yet the rapid advance of Hebrew in Israel appears to have occurred by improvization and diverse ventures rather than by carefully structured, systematic and sequenced language planning (Spolsky & Shohamy, 1999). **Second**, as Heath (1986) has shown, political and economic decisions usually govern language decisions. Language decisions are subsidiary and minor concerns of those in power, whose pervading interests are more frequently about power and purse. Language is usually an outcome from other decisions rather than a determinant of social, political or economic policies. Yet, as the European Commission has increasingly stressed, minority language issues and the need for bilingualism and multilingualism in a future Europe are relevant to European cultural and economic development, to peacefulness and equality in society. Bilingualism is one part of interconnected politics.

Language status and corpus planning require full consideration of bilingualism and not just planning for the minority language. Where minority languages exist, there is usually the need to be bilingual if not multilingual. Minority language monolingualism is usually impracticable and unfavorable to individuals (e.g. for employment). To create blockades and barricades between languages is almost impossible in the 20th century. Cross-cultural communication is the reality; a bunker approach to a minority language and culture may be tantamount to language death. This returns us to the concept of diglossia, highlighting the importance of different functions for the minority and majority language. Where different languages have different functions, then an **additive** rather than a **subtractive** bilingual situation may exist.

An **additive** bilingual situation is where the addition of a second language and culture is unlikely to replace or displace the first language and culture (Lambert, 1980). For example, English-speaking North Americans who learn a second language (e.g. French, Spanish) will not lose their English but gain another language and some of its attendant culture. The 'value added' benefits may not only be linguistic and cultural, but social and economic as well. Positive attitudes to diglossia and bilingualism may also result. In contrast, the learning of a majority second language may undermine a person's minority first language and culture, thus creating a **subtractive** situation. For example, an immigrant may find pressure to use the dominant language and feel embarrassment in using the home language.

When the second language is prestigious and powerful, used in education and in the jobs market, and when the minority language is perceived as of low status and value, stable diglossia and bilingualism may be threatened. Instead of addition, there is subtraction; division instead of multiplication. Additive and subtractive bilingualism are further discussed in the next chapter.

LANGUAGE SHIFT AND LANGUAGE MAINTENANCE

With changes of season and weather comes growth and death, blossoming and weakening. Minority language communities are similarly in a constant state of change. Such language shift may be fast or slow, upwards or downwards, but never absent.

Generally, **language shift** is used in the language planning literature to refer to a downwards language movement. That is, there is a reduction in the number of speakers of a language, a decreasing saturation of language speakers in the population, a loss in language proficiency, or a decreasing use of that language in different domains. The last stages of language shift are called language death. **Language maintenance** usually refers to relative language stability in number and distribution of its speakers, its proficient usage by children and adults, and its retention in specific domains (e.g. home, school, religion). **Language spread** concerns an increase – numerically, geographically or functionally – in language users, networks and use (Cooper, 1989).

However, there is a **danger** in the ways these terms are used. First, the terms are ambiguous and may refer to the numerical size of the language minority, their saturation in a region, their proficiency in the language or the use of the language in different domains. Second, these are predominantly sociolinguistic concepts. Linguists have their own use of these terms (e.g. referring to changes in grammar and vocabulary over time — see Aitchison, 1991; McMahon, 1994; Romaine, 1995, 2000; Dixon, 1997).

A variety of factors create **language shift**. For example, out-migration from a region may be vital to secure employment, a higher salary or promotion. In-migration can be forced (e.g. the capture of slaves) or voluntary (e.g. guest workers). Sometimes this movement of minority language groups occurs within a particular geographical area. Within a country, marriage may also cause a shift in bilingualism. For example, a bilingual person from a minority language community may marry a majority language monolingual. The result may be majority language monolingual children. Increasing industrialization and urbanization in the 20th century has led to increased movement of labor. With the growth of mass communications, information technology, tourism, road, sea and air links, minority languages seem more at risk. Bilingual education, or its absence, will also be a factor in the ebb and flow of minority and majority languages.

A relatively comprehensive list of factors that may create **language maintenance and shift** was given by Conklin and Lourie (1983) (see also Gaarder, 1977, pp. 141f). This list (tabulated on the following pages) essentially refers to immigrants rather than indigenous minorities, but many factors are common to both groups. What is missing from this list is the power dimension (such as being in subordinate status — e.g. the Puerto Ricans in New York City — see Zentella, 1988).

This concludes the initial consideration of important factors in language shift. It has been shown that such shifts are particularly related to economic and social change, to politics and power, to the availability of local social communication networks between minority language speakers and to the legislative and institutional support supplied for the conservation of a minority language. While such factors help clarify what affects language shift, the relative importance of these factors is debatable and unclear. There are various levels of establishing **causes** of language shift, levels such as the political, the economic, the psychological (e.g. at the individual or home level) and at the sociolinguistic level. A list of the relative

FACTORS ENCOURAGING LANGUAGE MAINTENANCE	FACTORS ENCOURAGING LANGUAGE LOSS
A. Political, Social and Demographic Factors	
1. Large number of speakers living closely together.	Small number of speakers well dispersed.
2. Recent and/or continuing in-migration.	Long and stable residence.
3. Close proximity to the homeland and ease of travel to homeland.	Homeland remote or inaccessible.
4. Preference to return to homeland with many actually returning.	Low rate of return to homeland and/or little intention to return and/or impossible to return.
5. Homeland language community intact.	Homeland language community decaying in vitality.
6. Stability in occupation.	Occupational shift, especially from rural to urban areas.
7. Employment available where home language is spoken daily.	Employment requires use of the majority language.
8. Low social and economic mobility in main occupations.	High social and economic mobility in main occupations.
9. Low level of education to restrict social and economic mobility, but educated and articulate community leaders loyal to their language community.	High levels of education giving social and economic mobility. Potential community leaders are alienated from their language community by education.
10. Ethnic group identity rather than identity with majority language community via nativism, racism and ethnic discrimination.	Ethnic identity is denied to achieve social and vocational mobility; this is forced by nativism, racism and ethnic discrimination.

importance of these factors is simplistic because the factors interact and inter-
mingle in a complicated equation. Such a list does not distinguish the more
important factors in language shift. Nor does it reveal the processes and mechanisms of language shift. It is thus difficult to predict which minority languages are
more or less likely to decline, and which languages are more or less likely to be
revived. A frequent, if generalized, **scenario for immigrants** is given by García
and Diaz (1992, p. 14):

'Most US immigrant groups have experienced a language shift to English as a
consequence of assimilation into American life. The first generation immigrants sustain their native or first language while learning English. The second
generation, intent upon assimilation into a largely English-speaking community, begin the shift towards English by using the native language with first

FACTORS ENCOURAGING LANGUAGE MAINTENANCE	FACTORS ENCOURAGING LANGUAGE LOSS
B. Cultural Factors	
1. Mother-tongue institutions (e.g. schools, community organizations, mass media, leisure activities).	Lack of mother-tongue institutions.
2. Cultural and religious ceremonies in the home language.	Cultural and religious activity in the majority language.
3. Ethnic identity strongly tied to home language.	Ethnic identity defined by factors other than language.
4. Nationalistic aspirations as a language group.	Few nationalistic aspirations.
5. Mother tongue the homeland national language.	Mother tongue not the only homeland national language, or mother tongue spans several nations
6. Emotional attachment to mother tongue giving self-identity and ethnicity.	Self-identity derived from factors other than shared home language.
7. Emphasis on family ties and community cohesion.	Low emphasis on family and community ties. High emphasis on individual achievement.
8. Emphasis on education in mother tongue schools to enhance ethnic awareness.	Emphasis on education in majority language.
9. Low emphasis on education if in majority language.	Acceptance of majority language education.
10. Culture unlike majority language culture.	Culture and religion similar to that of the majority language.

generation speakers (parents, grandparents, others) and English in more formal settings. By slow degrees, English is used in contexts once reserved for the first language. Encroachment of English into the domain of the first language serves to destabilize the native language.

Eventually, third generation speakers discontinue the use of the native language entirely. The shift completes when most of the third generation are monolingual English speakers'.

However, a '**three generation shift**' is not the only possible pattern. Paulston (1994) cites the Greeks in Pittsburgh as experiencing a four generation shift. She attributes this slower shift to the use of a standardized, prestigious written language; access to an institution teaching Greek language and literacy (i.e. Greek churches in Pittsburgh); and arranged marriages with one partner being a monolingual Greek speaker from Greece. In contrast, the three generation shift among

FACTORS ENCOURAGING LANGUAGE MAINTENANCE	FACTORS ENCOURAGING LANGUAGE LOSS
C. Linguistic Factors	
1. Mother tongue is standardized and exists in a written form.	Mother tongue is non-standard and/or not in written form.
2. Use of an alphabet which makes printing and literacy relatively easy.	Use of writing system which is expensive to reproduce and relatively difficult to learn.
3. Home language has international status.	Home language of little or no international importance.
4. Home language literacy used in community and with homeland.	Illiteracy (or aliteracy) in the home language.
5. Flexibility in the development of the home language (e.g. limited use of new terms from the majority language).	No tolerance of new terms from majority language; or too much tolerance of loan words leading to mixing and eventual language loss.

(Adapted from Conklin & Lourie, 1983).

Italians in Pittsburgh is attributed to their speaking a non-standard, non-written dialect of Italian with little prestige; no religious institutional support as they shared English language Roman Catholic services with, for example, Irish priests, nuns and laity; and marriage to Roman Catholics with religious compatibility being more important than language compatibility.

A five stage shift from minority language monolingualism to majority language monolingualism was found by Von Gleich and Wölck (1994) in Peru: (1) monolingualism in Quechua (Quichua), (2) bilingualism but Quechua stronger than Spanish, (3) bilingualism with Quechua and Spanish approximately balanced, (4) bilingualism but Spanish dominant over Quechua, (5) monolingualism in Spanish.

Amongst Panjabi, Italian, Gaelic and Welsh communities in Britain, there are occasional 'fourth generation' individuals who sometimes wish to revive the language of their ethnic origins. For some, assimilation into the majority language and culture does not give self-fulfillment. Rather, such revivalists seek a return to their roots by recovering the language and culture of their ethnic heritage. In Europe, with increasing pressure towards a European identity, language minority members seem increasingly aware of the benefits of a more distinctive and intimate local identity. The pressure to become part of a larger whole seems to result in a counter-balancing need to have secure roots within a smaller and more domestic community. A local language is valuable in this more particular identity. Bilingualism provides the means to be international and local.

LANGUAGE DECLINE AND DEATH

Another way of identifying the causes of language shift is to examine a dying language within a particular region (Dorian, 1989, 1998; Grenoble & Whaley, 1998).

Susan Gal (1979) studied in detail the replacement of Hungarian by German in the town of Oberwart in eastern Austria. After 400 years of relatively stable Hungarian–German bilingualism, economic, social and family life became more German language based. Using an anthropological style, Gal (1979) studied the process of language decline. For Gal (1979) the issue was not the correlates of language shift, but the process. For example, while industrialization was related to language decline in Oberwart, the crucial question became:

> 'By what intervening processes does industrialization, or any other social change, effect changes in the uses to which speakers put their languages in everyday interactions?' (p. 3)

Gal (1979) showed how **social changes** (e.g. industrialization and urbanization) change social networks, relationships between people, and patterns in language use in communities. As new environments arise with new speakers, languages take on new forms, new meanings and create new patterns of social interaction.

Another celebrated study is by Nancy Dorian (1981). Dorian carried out a detailed case study of the decline of Gaelic in east Sutherland, a region in the north-east Highlands of Scotland. In the history of the region, English and Gaelic co-existed with English generally being the ruling language and the 'civilized' language. Gaelic was regarded more as the 'savage' language of lower prestige. In this region of east Sutherland, the last two groups to speak Gaelic were the 'crofters' (farmers of a small amount of land) and the fishing community. Dorian (1981) studied the fishing community who had become a separate and distinct group of people in a small geographical area. Surrounded by English speaking communities, these fisher-people originally spoke only Gaelic and later became bilingual in English and Gaelic. The fisher-folk thought of themselves, and were thought of by their neighbors, as of lower social status. They tended to marry within their own group. When the fishing industry began to decline, the Gaelic speaking fishing-folk began to find other jobs. The **boundaries** between the Gaelic speakers and the English speakers began to crumble. Inter-marriage replaced in-group marriage, and 'outside' people migrated to the east Sutherland area. Over time, the community gave up its fisher identity and the Gaelic language tended to decline with it:

> 'Since Gaelic had become one of the behaviors which allowed the labeling of individuals as fishers there was a tendency to abandon Gaelic along with other "fisher" behaviors.' (Dorian, 1981, p. 67)

Across generations in the 20th century, Gaelic in east Sutherland declined. Whereas grandparents, and were spoken to, only in Gaelic, parents would speak Gaelic to other people but use English with their children and expect their children to speak English in reply. The children were able to understand Gaelic from hearing their parents speak it, but were not used to speaking it themselves:

> 'The home is the last bastion of a subordinate language in competition with a dominant official language of wider currency … speakers have failed to transmit the language to their children so that no replacement generation is available when the parent generation dies away.' (Dorian, 1981, p. 105)

A different and controversial perspective is given by John Edwards (1985). When languages die, Edwards asks, are they murdered or do they commit suicide? In the histories of the native Indian languages of Canada and the USA, and particularly in the histories of the African languages of those who became slaves, there is evidence of murder. In histories of the Irish, Gaelic and the Welsh language it is typically argued that the language has been murdered by English and England's dominant rule over the peripheries of Britain. However, it is debated whether the 'destruction' of Celtic languages has been deliberate and conscious, or through negligence and indifference.

When minority language speakers become bilingual and prefer the majority language, the penalty for the minority language may be decline, even death. Yet, where people are determined to keep a language alive, it may be impossible to destroy a language. Language activists, pressure groups, affirmative action and language conservationists may fight for the survival of the threatened language. In Puerto Rico, the government introduced English into schools to attempt bilingualization of the island. Over three-quarters of the population remain functionally monolingual in Spanish. Resnick (1993) has shown that nationalism, political uncertainty and the relationship between language and identity have made some groups of Puerto Ricans resistant to language change and the use of English.

For Edwards (1985, 1994a), **language shift** often reflects a pragmatic desire for social and vocational mobility, an improved standard of living, a personal cost–benefit analysis. This provides a different slant on the language garden analogy. One answer to the environmentalist who wishes to preserve a garden of great beauty is that, when the priority is food in the stomach and clothes upon the back, 'you can't eat the view'. Sometimes, there may be a gap between the rhetoric of language preservation and harsh reality. This is illustrated in a story from Bernard Spolsky (1989b, p. 451):

> 'A Navajo student of mine once put the problem quite starkly: if I have to choose, she said, between living in a hogan a mile from the nearest water where my son will grow up speaking Navajo or moving to a house in the city with indoor plumbing where he will speak English with the neighbors, I'll pick English and a bathroom!'

However, where there are oppressed language minorities who are forced to live in segregated societies, there is often little choice of where to live and work. In the quote, the Navajo may have had the choice. In actuality, many language minorities have little or no real choice. Thus, electing for language suicide is misleading. Attribution of suicide is a way of 'blaming the victim' and diverting a focus on the determination of real causes of language shift. Freedom of choice is more apparent than real. There is often no viable choice among language minority speakers.

CONCLUSION

This chapter has focused on languages at the group, social and community level. Two languages within a region is termed diglossia. Majority and minority languages are frequently in contact, sometimes in conflict. The relationship between the two languages tends to shift constantly as a consequence of a variety of changeable cultural, economic, linguistic, social, demographic and political factors.

The argument for preserving language minority communities sometimes relates to the existence of an indigenous language in a defined territory. Also, language minorities may lay claim to the personality principle; or their language group (e.g. immigrants) having unifying ethnic characteristics and identity. One 'preservationist' argument uses a gardening analogy. There is a need to maintain colorful diversity in the language garden of the world. Language planning by adding and protecting, controlling and propagating is required to avoid monochrome gardens of majority-only languages. Conscious language planning to conserve and preserve may be preferred to the narrow view of evolutionists. Language planning may seek to create language vitality by attending to the economic, social and symbolic status, geographical distribution and institutional support accorded to a minority language. Not to plan for language maintenance and spread may be to court language death. Preserving language diversity requires the optimism of resurrection rather than the pessimism of decline and death. It is to a positive accent of construction rather than destruction that we turn in the next chapter.

KEY POINTS IN THIS CHAPTER

- Diglossia is used to describe and analyze two languages existing together in a society in a relatively stable arrangement through different uses attached to each language.
- The territorial principle is a claim to the right to a language within a geographical area while the personality principle is a claim to the right to use a language based on an individual's ownership of a language that belongs to them wherever they travel within their country (e.g. Canada).
- The languages of the world are rapidly declining in number with predictions of 50–90% of the world's languages dying or near death in the next century. The world's language and cultural diversity is thus endangered.
- Language planning is needed for language maintenance, revitalization and reversing language shift. Language planning includes acquisition planning (home and education), status planning (e.g. in key institutions) and corpus planning (e.g. standardization and modernization).

SUGGESTED FURTHER READING

COULMAS, F., 1997, *The Handbook of Sociolinguistics*. Oxford: Blackwell.

EDWARDS, J., 1994, *Multilingualism*. London: Routledge.

FISHMAN, J.A. 1989, *Language and Ethnicity in Minority Sociolinguistic Perspective*. Clevedon: Multilingual Matters.

McKAY, S. L. and HORNBERGER, N.H. (eds), 1996, *Sociolinguistics and Language Teaching*. Cambridge: Cambridge University Press.

NETTLE, D. and ROMAINE, S., 2000, Vanishing Voices: The Extinction of the World's Languages. Oxford: Oxford University Press.

PAULSTON, C.B., 1994, *Linguistic Minorities in Multilingual Settings*. Amsterdam / Philadelphia: John Benjamins.

ROMAINE, S., 1995, *Bilingualism* (2nd edition). Oxford: Basil Blackwell.

ROMAINE, S., 2000, *Language in Society: an Introduction to Sociolinguistics* (2nd edition). Oxford: Oxford University Press.

SKUTNABB-KANGAS, T., 2000, *Linguistic Genocide in Education – Or Worldwide Diversity and Human Rights?* Mahwah, NJ: Erlbaum.

SPOLSKY, B., 1998, *Sociolinguistics*. Oxford: Oxford University Press.

STUDY ACTIVITIES

(1) As a group activity or with a partner, make an abbreviated list of the factors of language shift from Conklin and Lourie (1983). On a five-point scale (5 = very important, 4 = fairly important, 3 = neither important or unimportant, 2 = fairly unimportant, 1 = unimportant), rate your perception of the strength of these factors in language shift.

(2) Using the list of factors in language shift from Conklin and Lourie (1983), compare the prospects for maintenance or shift in two different language communities.

(3) Create a poster or a chart using the language garden analogy. This may be a chart to convey a large amount of information about the language garden. Alternatively it may be a simple poster advertising the importance of language variety in the world.

(4) Find out how many different languages are spoken in your area (local or regional). List the names of these languages and in which regions they are spoken as an indigenous language. Through interviews with language minority members, or through a library search, provide a brief example of that language (on paper or on tape).

(5) Are the languages in your list 'native' or 'immigrant' languages in your area? Are they spoken by different generations or more by older generations? Is there preservation and maintenance of the language, or is the language declining?

CHAPTER 4

Language Revival
and Revitalization

Introduction

A Model of Language Shift and Vitality
Status Factors
Demographic Factors
Institutional Support Factors

Language Revival and Reversal
Assumptions of Reversing Language Shift
Steps in Reversing Language Shift
Limits and Critics

Conclusion

CHAPTER 4

Language Revival and Revitalization

INTRODUCTION

Just as rain forests and whales have become the subject of environmental protection, so there are increasing pleas for dying languages to be protected and for endangered languages to be revived and revitalized. This chapter focuses on the possibilities of language maintenance, and on optimistic attempts to encourage the growth and **revitalization** of a minority language. To achieve this, major theoretical contributions are considered. The first contribution seeks to answer the question 'How is **language vitality** achieved? Building on one part of this theory, the chapter examines the importance of economics in the maintenance and revitalization of a minority language. The next contribution considers 'How can a language be revived and reversed?' We start with Giles, Bourhis and Taylor's (1977) consideration of language vitality.

A MODEL OF LANGUAGE SHIFT AND VITALITY

In an attempt to create a model rather than a list of the many factors involved in **language vitality**, Giles, Bourhis and Taylor (1977) propose a three factor model: status factors, demographic factors and institutional support factors, which combine to give more or less minority **language vitality** (see also the International Journal of the Sociology of Language (1994, Vol. 108). Consideration of this model gives some explanatory flesh to the framework of Conklin and Lourie (1983), presented in the previous chapter.

Status Factors

A key issue in language status is whether the language minority is in the ascendancy (superordinate) or is subordinate. The survival of Swedish in Finland is partly explained by the high status of Swedish speakers in Finland. Language minorities are more often in subordinate status to a language majority (e.g. Asian languages in Canada and England; Spanish in the USA). However, a more refined analysis requires a breakdown into different types of language status.

The **economic status** of a minority language is likely to be a key element in language vitality. Where, for example, a minority language community experiences considerable unemployment or widespread low income, the pressure may be to shift towards the majority language. A minority language may be sacrificed on the altar of economic progress. A language of the poor and of the peasant is not the language of prosperity and power. Guest workers, immigrants and refugees looking for social and vocational mobility may place a high value on education in the majority language. The importance of an economic dimension to a minority language is explored in detail in Chapter 20.

The **social status** of a language — its prestige value — will be closely related to the economic status of a language and will also be a powerful factor in language vitality. When a majority language is seen as giving higher social status and more political power, a shift towards the majority language may occur. Where language minorities exist, there is often a preponderance of lower socioeconomic class families. Where a minority language is seen to co-exist with unemployment, poverty, social deprivation and few amenities, the social status of the language may be negatively affected.

A language's **symbolic status** is also important in language vitality. A heritage language may be an important symbol of ethnic identity, of roots in 'the glorious past'. The symbolic importance of a language is exemplified in the Celtic countries. In Ireland, for example, the Irish language is often regarded as a mark of nationhood, a symbol of cultural heritage and identity. There tends to be a positive public attitude to Irish, but a private skepticism. Interest in the survival of the minority language exists, but not always personal involvement in that language. As a symbol of ethnic history, of heritage and national culture, the Celtic languages are sometimes valued by the public. As a tool of widespread personal communication, as a medium of mass education, the languages are less valued. When the personal balance sheet includes employment, educational and vocational success and interpersonal communication, the credit of positive attitudes towards language as a cultural and ethnic symbol is diminished by the costs of perceived prior needs and motives. Goodwill towards the language stops when the personal pay-off is limited.

Is there a paradox beginning to emerge in the relationship between majority and minority languages? Majority languages such as English have high status as languages of international communication. At the same time, internationalism (e.g. the increasing Europeanization) appears to awaken a basic need for rootedness, for an anchor in a local language and a local cultural community. Becoming European can revive and reawaken the need to belong to one's local heritage and historical groups. In becoming part of a larger whole, a **local identity is essential and fundamental**. The push to become a member of the global village seems to lead to a strong pull towards primary roots.

Demographic Factors

The second of Giles, Bourhis and Taylor's (1977) factors concerns the **geographical distribution** of a language minority group. One part of this is the territorial principle: two languages having their own rights in different areas within a country (see Chapter 3); or, in Ireland, there being designated heartland areas where some protection and maintenance of the Irish language is encouraged (the Gaeltachta). A second part of this factor is the **number of speakers** of a certain language and their saturation within a particular area. The high numbers of Spanish speakers in Miami has been a component of Latino vitality, both economic and cultural, within that area.

Research in Wales, using census data, indicates that saturation of speakers within a particular area is important in language maintenance (Baker, 1985). For example, in communities where over 70% of the people speak Welsh, there appears to be more chance of the language surviving. Also important in the language maintenance equation is the demographics of biliteracy. Analysis of the Welsh language census data shows that where bilingualism exists without biliteracy, there is an increased likelihood of language decay. When someone can speak a minority language but not write in that language, the number of functions and uses of that language is diminished. Bilingualism without biliteracy also means a decrease in the status of that language, and less chance of a linguistically stable language.

At the same time, it is possible for a small language minority to survive when surrounded by the majority language. Three examples will illustrate that small numbers of minority language speakers can still provide a lively language community, even when surrounded by a majority language community. **First**, in a large city or in border areas, a small number of minority language speakers may be socially and culturally active in their minority language. Such speakers may interact regularly and create a strong language cell. The language of children in the home and street may be important for continuation over time. **Second**, when some language groups have strong religious beliefs, they may prefer not to interact with majority language speakers. Such is the case of the Old Order Amish, Pennsylvania Germans. They continued to speak Pennsylvania German at home and in the community. Such a minority has historically created strong boundaries in their language usage. **Third**, when minority language speakers can travel easily between the homeland and their current area of residence, the minority language may be invigorated and strengthened (e.g. Puerto Ricans in New York; Mexicans in Texas and California; the Turkish minority in northern Greece).

The idea of demographic factors relates to mixed, **inter-language marriages**. In such marriages, the higher status language will usually have the best chance of survival as the home language. With inter-language marriages specifically, and with language minority communities in general, there is likely to be movement across generations. For example, immigrants may lose their heritage language by the second or third or fourth generation. This highlights the vital importance of languages in the home as a major direct cause in the decline, revival or maintenance of a minority language. Language reproduction in the young is a crucial part of language vitality.

As a generalization with exceptions, a minority language is more likely to be preserved in a **rural** than an **urban** area. Once the migration of rural people to urban areas occurs, there is an increased chance of the minority language losing its work function. In the office and in the factory, the dominant language is likely to be the majority language with a decrease in the minority language. In rural areas, the language of work and cultural activity is relatively more likely to be the historical language of that area (Robinson, 1996). The language of the farm or of the fishing boat, of religion and of rustic culture is more likely to be the minority language. There will be important exceptions (e.g. where an urban ethnic group generates its own industries, or is sited in a particular part of a city, or congregates regularly for religious purposes).

Institutional Support Factors

Language vitality is affected by the extent and nature of a minority language's use in a wide variety of institutions in a region. Such institutions will include national, regional and local government, religious and cultural organizations, mass media, commerce and industry, and not least education. The absence or presence of a minority language in the **mass media** (television, radio, newspapers, magazines, World Wide Web and computer software) at the very least affects the prestige of a language. The use of a minority language in books and magazines, for example, is also important for biliteracy. Strong representation in the mass media also gives a minority language both status and a feeling of being modern. The perceived quality of television programs (compared to majority language programs) will be important (Baetens Beardsmore & van Beeck, 1984). However, it is possible to exaggerate the importance of television and radio in its effect on the communicative use of a minority language. Television and radio provide only a passive medium for language. Research from Wales (see Baker, 1985, 1992) suggests that it is majority language mass media that is the destroyer of a minority language and culture, rather than minority language television and radio being the salvation of the language. The glossy, high quality of TV English language programs provides fierce competition for minority languages. Media attractiveness has resulted in the invasion of Hollywood productions in countries where English is not prevalent. Active participation in a minority language is required for language survival; an event that mass media by its receptive nature does not provide.

Religion can be a strong and important vehicle for the maintenance of a majority and a minority language. The use of classical Arabic in Islam, Hebrew in Judaism, and German among the Protestant Old Order Amish in Pennsylvania all illustrate that religion can be a preserver of language. The revitalization of Hebrew among Jews both in Israel and elsewhere has strong connections with historic religious identity (Spolsky & Shohamy, 1999). Religion may help standardize a language. Through its holy books, tracts and pamphlets, traveling missionaries and teachers, a relatively standard form of a language may evolve.

Providing **administrative services** in a minority language also serves to give status to that language. It also increases the usefulness of that minority language for communication. The use of languages within educational institutions is probably an essential but not sufficient condition for language maintenance. Where **schooling** in a minority language does not exist, the chances of the long-term survival of that language in a modern society may be severely diminished. Where the minority language is used in the school situation, the chances of survival are greatly increased but not guaranteed. Nancy Hornberger's (1988) anthropological study of language planning, language shift and bilingual education in the Quechua speaking highlands of southern Peru suggested that:

> 'Schools cannot be agents for language maintenance if their communities, for whatever reason, do not want them to be.' (p. 229)

Community support for bilingual education in the minority language and culture outside school are important. Education by itself cannot enable a minority language to become revitalized. Other supports are essential, particularly regeneration of the language within the family and an economic basis for the language. The importance of the family in language maintenance is considered in the next chapter.

Giles, Bourhis and Taylor's (1977) theory of language vitality has been **criticized** by Husband and Khan (1982). **First**, they suggest that the dimensions and factors are not separate and independent of each other. In reality, these elements interact, inter-relate and are often mutually dependent on each other. While presented as comprehensive and wide-ranging, a critique that the factors are 'something of an untheorized *pot pourri*' (p. 195) relates to a consensus rather than a conflict perspective (see Chapter 18), with no means of 'sifting and weighing the many variables that are listed' (p. 195). These authors doubt whether a list of the variables that constitute language vitality is any greater than the sum of its parts or creates an integrated whole.

Second, different language contexts have widely differing processes and recipes that affect language vitality. The historical, social, economic, cultural and political processes that operate in any language community vary considerably (e.g. compare US immigrant communities with Native Americans; or colonial India, francophone Quebec and the indigenous language minority of Ireland). We need a historical and sociological perspective, for example, to help explain patterns of interaction that relate to language vitality. Change and variability across time is seemingly not catered for in this theory. **Third**, the theory is not easy to operationalize in research. Many of the factors may not be easily or unambiguously measured. Thus the theory is difficult to test although ethnographic approaches to language revitalization research have lent some support (see King (2000) for such an approach).

LANGUAGE REVIVAL AND REVERSAL

A major contribution to the theory of attempting the reversal of language shift is by Joshua **Fishman** (1991, 1993, 2000c). Fishman (1991) notes a changing perspective in the topic of language shift. The premise has been that minority languages, like patients in a hospital or doctor's surgery, will ultimately die. Therefore all one can do is to understand the causes of death and illness, and attempt to overcome those causes for as long as possible. Instead, Fishman (1991) argues that language shift needs to take the jump of modern medicine by attempting 'not only to combat illness, but to cultivate "wellness"' (p. xii).

Fishman (1991, 2000a) seeks to answer the question 'what are the priorities in planning language shift?' For example, what is the point of pouring money into minority language mass media and bilingual bureaucracy when home, family, neighborhood and face-to-face community use of the minority language is lacking? It is like blowing air into a punctured balloon. Blowing minority language air in through the mass media and legislation does not make a usable balloon, because of the unmended hole.

Fishman (1991) provides a list of **priorities** to halt language decline and attempt to reverse language shift. This plan also shows why many efforts to reverse minority language situations have often resulted in failure rather than success. Before we examine this plan, Fishman (1991) provides a basic philosophy and set of assumptions that are required before establishing priorities in reversing language shift.

Assumptions of Reversing Language Shift

First, when a society or community is losing its language and culture, it is likely to feel pain. This hurt may be symptomatic of the social injustice towards that community. Although it may not be a cancer but more like a toothache, to those who experience it, there is real rather than imaginary suffering. Such suffering needs remedying. **Second**, the basis of reversing language shift is that a more global village, a world more unified by mass communication and speedy travel, a more integrated eastern and western Europe, does not bury the need for local language and local culture. Indeed, a more centrally organized and uniform world may increase rather than decrease the need for language and cultural identity at a local level. Having local cultural and linguistic roots may be a necessary precondition before integrating into a global village. **Third**, and most importantly for Fishman (1991), the political basis of the plan is to support **cultural pluralism and cultural self-determination**. The destruction of minority languages is the destruction of intimacy, family and community, often involving oppression of the weak by the strong, subjugating the unique and traditional by the uniform and central. Thus, Fishman (1991) argues for 'greater sociocultural self-sufficiency, self-help, self-regulation and initiative' (p. 4) among linguistic communities.

Fourth, an ethnic or culture group that has lost its language is different from a group that retains their minority language. Fishman (1991) cites the case of Jews who, not speaking Hebrew, tend to have a different daily life-pattern, a different kind of sub-culture. Language shift accompanies cultural change. This suggests that language shift is not just about language; it is about the attendant culture as well. The argument for language restoration and resurrection must therefore involve a call for cultural change and greater cultural self-determination. Fishman (1991) warns of the danger of language as the sole focus for shift. The danger is that minority language activists will:

> 'become so accustomed to speaking only to each other that they forget how to speak effectively to others. What activists no longer need to explain to each other they often no longer know how to explain to others. They often need to remind themselves and to make themselves more conscious of their own RLS [Reversing Language Shift] 'basic principles', so that they can then make others more conscious of these principles as well.' (pp. 18/19)

A different warning is given to those who believe that reversing language shift is purely about the accumulation of **power and money** (e.g. as has been said about the use of Hebrew and Welsh). Believing that language minorities who are attempting language reversal and resurrection are concerned with achieving power and increasing wealth is simplistic and misguided. Fishman (1991) argues that human values, feelings, loyalties and basic life-philosophies are present in the complex reasons for language change. Language activists often have ideals, commitments, even altruism that makes their motives more than just power and money. Minority languages and cultures, in their desire for a healthy existence, may be sometimes irrational or super-rational. This is similar to religion, love, art and music where there are personal elements that transcend conscious rationality, and transcend self-interest in power and money.

Fifth, to help understand language shift, Fishman (1991) clarifies the relationship between language and culture in terms of three links:

(1) **A language indexes its culture.** A language and its attendant culture will have grown up together over a long period of history, and be in harmony with each other. Thus the language that has grown up round a culture best expresses that culture. Its vocabulary, idioms, metaphors are the ones that best explain at a cognitive and emotive level that culture.

(2) **A language symbolizes its culture.** To speak German in the USA, during World War I, and in France and Britain during World War II was not appropriate nor acceptable. Not that the allies were at war with the German language. Rather, the German language symbolized the enemy. Therefore, that language was inappropriate in allied countries. A language tends to symbolize the status of the culture with which it is associated. For example, to speak English in Kuwait following the victory against Saddam Hussein of Iraq was to be symbolically associated with status, power and victory. Speaking English often symbolizes money and modernity, affluence and achievement. English may also symbolize colonial subjugation. A language that is apparently dying may symbolize low status and low income. In certain parts of Ireland and Wales, the indigenous language is sometimes perceived as a symbol of the past rather than the present, of disadvantage rather than advantage.

(3) **Culture is partly created from its language.** Much of a culture is enacted and transmitted verbally. The songs, hymns, prayers of a culture, its folk tales and shrewd sayings, its appropriate forms of greeting and leaving, its history, wisdom and ideals are all wrapped up in its language. The taste and flavor of a culture is given through its language; its memories and traditions are stored in its language. An example is a saying or a figure of speech in a minority language that requires a long explanation in another language. Even then that pithy saying may sacrifice some of its meaning and feeling in translation. At the same time, culture is derived from many more sources than language. For example, there are many different cultures which all use the Spanish language.

Sixth, Fishman (1991) makes an argument for **language planning** (see Chapter 3). Just as there is economic planning, educational planning and family planning, so there can and should be language planning. Such planning has as its base 're-establishing local options, local control, local hope, and local meaning to life. It reveals a humanistic and positive outlook *vis-à-vis* intergroup life, rather than a mechanistic and fatalistic one. It espouses the right and the ability of small cultures to live and to inform life for their own members as well as to contribute thereby to the enrichment of human kind as a whole' (p. 35).

Steps in Reversing Language Shift

Fishman's (1990, 1991, 1993, 2000c) Graded Intergenerational Disruption Scale (GIDS) is an aid to understanding language planning and attempted **language reversal** from an international perspective. Just as the Richter scale measures intensity of earthquakes, so Fishman's scale gives a guide to how far a minority language is threatened and disrupted in international terms. The higher the number on the scale, the more a language is threatened. The idea of stages is that it is little good attempting later stages if earlier stages are not at least partly achieved. Various foundations are needed before building the upper levels. The value of the scale is not just in its eight sequenced steps or stages. Rather it provides a sense of prioritization for reversing languages in decline. The eight stages are briefly summarized (see following page), and then considered one by one.

Stage 8

Stage 8 represents the 'worst case' for a language. A few of the older generation will still be able to speak the language but probably not to each other because they are socially isolated. The few remaining speakers of a language are so scattered that minority language interaction is rarely possible. At this stage it is seen as important that folklorists and linguists collect as much information as they can from these few survivors of the language community. The folk-tales and sayings, grammar and vocabulary, need to be collected on tape and paper as a permanent record of that language. Since the language building is in ruins and the foundations have crumbled, can anything be done to save the language? The one ray of hope is that the records of the language can be used by a younger generation to revive the language. With Australian Aboriginal languages and Cornish in England, this has been

Fishman's (1990, 1991) Graded Intergenerational Disruption Scale for Threatened Languages

Stage 8   Social isolation of the few remaining speakers of the minority language. Need to record the language for later possible reconstruction.

Stage 7   Minority language used by older and not younger generation. Need to multiply the language in the younger generation.

Stage 6   Minority language is passed on from generation to generation and used in the community. Need to support the family in intergenerational continuity (e.g. provision of minority language nursery schools).

Stage 5   Literacy in the minority language. Need to support literacy movements in the minority language, particularly when there is no government support.

Stage 4   Formal, compulsory education available in the minority language. May need to be financially supported by the minority language community.

Stage 3   Use of the minority language in less specialized work areas involving interaction with majority language speakers.

Stage 2   Lower government services and mass media available in the minority language.

Stage 1   Some use of minority language available in higher education, central government and national media.

attempted. Thus the remnants of the foundations can be reused to start to reconstruct the language.

Stage 7

A language in Stage 7 will be used on a daily communication basis, but by more mature-age speakers beyond child-bearing. A language used by the older rather than the younger generation is likely to die as that older generation disappears. The language is unlikely to be reproduced in the younger generation as mothers and fathers speak the majority language with their children. While the aim of Stage 8 is to reassemble the language, the aim of Stage 7 is to spread the language amongst the young. Mothers and fathers are encouraged to bring up their children in the minority language. It is essential to reproduce that dying language in children who may later bring up their children in that language to ensure language continuity.

Fishman (1991) is clear about well-intentioned but, in the long-term future of a language, less important events. The danger in Stage 7 includes positive attitudes towards the language without positive action: 'the road to societal language death is paved with the good intentions called "positive attitudes"' (p. 91). The danger also lies in exaggerating the value of symbolic events in the minority language, on the stage and the written page, in the gathering of the clans and at ceremonies.

These events are relatively unimportant in the long-term salvation of the language compared with the raising of children in that minority language. However, this is not to argue that such language events are valueless. Their value ultimately lies in indirectly encouraging language life at the daily participative level.

When a language is passed on from generation to generation through child-rearing practices, then a language has some chance of long-term success. In child development and particularly in the teenage years, using rather losing a minority language becomes crucial. When the popular majority language culture becomes attractive to teenagers, minority language youth activities with youth participating and interacting in their minority language becomes critical (Baker, 1992).

The crucial importance of ensuring that a minority language is passed from one generation to another is summed up by Fishman (1991):

> 'The road to societal death is paved by language activity that is not focused on intergenerational continuity, i.e. that is diverted into efforts that do not involve and influence the socialization behaviors of families of child-bearing age.' (p. 91)

Performances and publications, ceremonies and cultural meetings need to be seen as a means to an end, and not as an end in themselves. Such formal language events, however carefully arranged, do not intrinsically lead to the passing of a language from generation to generation. Such events are valuable to the extent they foster the passing of a language across generations. Such events must not just be for the elite, the firm disciples or the converts, but have missionary aims to secure the language in the younger generation. Such events are important to the extent to which they encourage everyday activity, at family and community level, in that language. One-off events (e.g. eisteddfodau in Wales), may produce the feeling of a strong language and an emotional lift for the individual.

Fishman's (1991) argument is that unless such events link into usual, daily, family socialization, the language in the long term is not being promoted.

Stage 6

Stage 6 is seen as the crucial, pivotal stage for the survival of a language. In Stage 6, a language will be passed to the next generation. At this sixth stage, the minority language will be used between grandparents, parents and children. This is regarded as quintessential in the fate of a language. If the minority language is used in the family, it may also be used in the street, in shops, with neighbors and friends. The language will more probably be spoken in the neighborhood and in community life, in religious and cultural events, in leisure and local informal commercial activity. At Stage 6, there will be a language community of a varying proportion.

This stage essentially concerns the informal use of a language in the home and the community. As such, the language may be supported and encouraged, but it may be outside the realms of formal language planning. The focus of this stage is the family, and the family within its community. As an institution, the family creates and maintains boundaries from the outside that may prevent the majority language from over-intrusion. However, Fishman (1991) points out that the more urbanized 20th century family does not live in a strong enough castle to prevent considerable outside influence from other languages. With the increase in one-parent families and both parents going out to work, the idea of mother and father as sole transmitters of the minority language is less strong. The alternative is that agencies and institutions supporting the home also create a minority language and minority cultural environment (e.g. the availability of minority language nursery schools). What is crucial is that early childhood and teenage socialization is enacted in the minority language and culture. The danger is in believing that other institutions such as the school, the mass media, the economy and government legislation will reverse language shift in themselves. Rather, language reversal is pivotal on Stage 6. Fishman (1991) argues that Stage 6 cannot be dispensed with.

Unless a language is transmitted across the generations, other activities may have short-term success and long-term failure:

> 'If this stage is not satisfied, all else can amount to little more than biding time ... Attaining Stage 6 is a necessary, even if not a sufficient, desideratum of RLS [Reversing Language Shift].' (p. 399)

Stage 5

Stage 5 occurs when a minority language in the home, school and community goes beyond oracy to literacy. First, literacy in the minority language is seen to be important because it facilitates alternative means of communication, especially across distance and time. Second, the image and status of a minority language is raised when it is present in print. Such status is not merely symbolic. Literacy in the minority language means that a person is not just subject to majority language print media. Majority language media will contain dominant and powerful viewpoints, the attitudes of the center, the values and the beliefs of the majority language. Minority language literacies allow the possibility of minority language culture, political and ideological viewpoints to be presented. Third, literacy ensures a much wider variety of functions for a language. Such literacy may open more doors to employment, increase the chance of social and vocational mobility. However, at Stage 5, literacy in the majority language or biliteracy may be more important than literacy purely in the minority language if such mobility is desired. Also, access to print and providing an effective print environment in a minority language can be difficult. Insufficient resources, poor quality materials and a lack of funding may each turn the best of intentions into the most difficult of interventions. Establishing and maintaining a print environment for minority languages has been difficult to achieve, even in well established bilingual education programs for Latinos in the United States (Pucci, 1994, 2000).

Where education is through the majority language, then literacy in the minority language may be achieved through local community effort. Via Saturday and Sunday schools, in evening classes and through religious institutions, a literacy program in the minority language may be established. While such local efforts may

be costly in money, they have the advantage of giving control in such literacy education to the community rather than to the central majority-language government.
With such control, local institutions can determine the appropriate means of
literacy and cultural acquisition. While creating a financial burden, such activities
may give a language community a focus, a shared commitment and a further *raison
d'être*. While self-sacrifice is often hard and unfair, it can result in vitality, commitment, enthusiasm and a sense of unifying purpose.

For Fishman (1991), Stages 8 to 5 constitute the minimum basis of reversing
language shift. The activities at these stages rely solely on the efforts of the language
community itself. Such stages reflect a diglossic situation where the minority
language has separate functions from the majority language. Given that bilingualism rather than minority language monolingualism will exist, such a minority
language group may not be disadvantaged. They will usually have access to mainstream education from elementary to university levels. The full range of
government services also will be available, including educational and welfare
services. After Stage 5 comes the attempt to capture the formal functions so far
reserved for the majority language (e.g. mass media, compulsory education, political self-determination). It is at this point that the minority language may come out
of its enclave and seek to challenge majority language castles.

Stage 4

One of the first approaches into the majority language castle may be through education. Schools may be created and supported by the minority language community
itself, not funded by the central purse. Such private schools may be outside the
budgets of many relatively poor minority language communities. Therefore,
minority language medium education paid for by central government may be
sought. Central government will often still require some control over the curriculum of such schools. That is, minority language medium education may only
partly be under the control of the local minority language community. Such schools
may need to prove that they are as effective and as successful as neighboring
majority language schools; those attending them not being at a disadvantage but an
advantage.

Stage 3

In previous stages, some people will use their minority language in a place of work
at the 'lower work' (local and less specialized work) level. In previous stages, a few
such workers will function economically in a relatively isolated way in the local
neighborhood or as a self-contained group. Few bridges will exist with the majority
language community. At Stage 3, creating a wider economic base for the minority
language becomes important.

Such economic activity will involve the establishment of minority language
staffed enterprises and services, not just for the local market but for national and
international markets as well. Such minority language enterprise will, at times,
require communication in the majority language. However, the on-the-floor

activity and in-house communication may all be through the minority language (see Chapter 20).

However, success by language minority enterprise in international and national economic activity may not be without danger to the minority language. The economic value of majority languages, and the arrival of immigrants should there be economic success, are just two possible after-effects. As economic independence and self-regulation evolve, the temptation may be to increase profit by switching to international majority languages.

Such minority language economic activity nevertheless aids increasing affluence, vocational mobility and social status. Young minority language speakers may be more willing to stay in an area rather than migrate to majority language pastures when there is economic opportunity. When there are jobs and money in the local community, the minority language has firmer roots and resources.

Stage 2

The penultimate stage is extending lower government services and mass media into the minority language. Local government institutions may offer their services through the minority language; health and postal services, courts and the police service for example. Telephone and banking services, energy providing bodies and supermarkets may also become willing to use the minority language in their service and communication with the public.

Central government may wish to control its services to language minority regions to influence attitudes and opinions, information and ideology. The more the decision-making processes (educational, economic and political) are released to such regions, the more power that local language has to capture the minds of the minority. In Stage 2, national radio and television may be asked to provide a set number of hours in the minority language.

Alternatively, as in Wales, a particular channel may be mostly dedicated to minority language use. Not only does the use of minority language television and radio help to disseminate the attendant culture. It will also provide primary and secondary employment for minority language speakers.

The particular dangers of this stage may be in creaming off the most able and ambitious professionals into majority language positions. Minority language media also face severe viewing competition from Anglo-American, high-budget programs. The mass media provide status for a minority language, a channel for the minority cultural message, but no salvation for the language in and by itself.

Stage 1

In this final stage, the pinnacle of achievement in language shift, the minority language will be used at university level and will be strongly represented in mass media output, governmental services and throughout occupations. Alongside some degree of economic autonomy there will also be cultural autonomy. At this stage the language will be officially recognized in central government legislation or a Language Act. An example is the 1993 Constitution of South Africa that raised nine languages (Ndebele, North Sotho (Pedi), South Sotho (Sesotho), Siswati,

Tsonga, Tswana, Venda, Xhosa and Zulu) to national official status alongside English and Afrikaans. Other examples include the Welsh Language Act of 1993 and Norway's Sámi Language Act of 1992.

Throughout the four latter stages, Fishman (1991) is keen to point out that Stage 6 is still pre-eminent. When mass communications, economic rewards and vocational opportunities exist through the minority language, it is still the family, the neighborhood and community language life that is vital to the long-term success of the language. All the trappings of language status (e.g. mass media), all the power of legislation, all the success in economic self-determination does not assure the future of a language. Important as Stages 4 to 1 are, a language is ultimately lost and won inside the minds and hearts of individuals. While such individuals will doubtless be affected by economic, political and media factors, there is a personal cost–benefit analysis that ultimately determines whether one language is passed on to the next generation or not.

Limits and Critics

While Fishman (1991) is careful to point out that one stage is not necessarily dependent on a previous stage, there are priorities. The more advanced stages cannot usually be secured unless the fundamental stages are either first built or repaired. The danger is in advancing on all fronts. Attempting to win individual battles without having a strategy for the whole war does not champion success. There is also a danger in working solely for tangible, newsworthy, easily recognized victories (Fishman, 1993). Changing the language of road signs, tax forms and gaining minority language presence on television are battles that have been fought and won in some minority language regions. It is more difficult, but more important, to support and encourage the minority language for communication in daily family and community life. For Fishman (1991, 1993), it is the informal and intimate spoken language **reproduced across generations** that is the ultimate pivot of language shift.

Initial activity to reverse language shift will usually derive solely from the minority language community. The language community needs to be awoken and **mobilized** to support its language, especially at a family and community participative level. However, there may come a time when the majority language government will support that community's efforts to survive. Through the provision of bilingual education, government services and a minority language television service, the central government may come to support its minority languages.

Fishman (1991) is particularly guarded about how much **bilingual education** can achieve in reversing language shift. There is sometimes the belief that, where families do not transmit the minority language, the school is there to do it instead. Where parents do not bring up their children in the minority language, the school is expected to be the substitute minority language parent. The school may initiate second language acquisition in the minority language. But few rather than many may use the school-learnt language throughout life, particularly in parenting their children. Even when a child successfully learns minority language oracy and literacy skills in school, unless there is considerable support in the community and the economy outside school, that language may wither and die. A classroom-learnt second language may become a school-only language.

For that language to survive inside the individual, a person needs to become bonded in the **language community** while at school, and particularly after leaving school. There needs to be pre-school, out-of-school and after-school support and reward systems for using the minority language. The minority language needs to be embedded in the family–neighborhood–community experience and in the economics of the family. Unless this happens, it is unlikely that bilingually educated children will pass on the minority language to the next generation. Thus, for Fishman (1991, 1993), each stage needs examining for how it can be used to feed into Stage 6 — the inter-generational transmission of the minority language.

Fishman's (1991, 2000c) eight stages must be seen as overlapping and interacting. In language revival, it is not the case of going one step or stage at a time. The myriad of factors in language reversal link together in complex patterns. A language at Stage 2 may still be securing elements of previous stages. A language at Stage 6 may be engaged in long-term planning to secure higher stages. Also, different communities and different geographical areas may be at different stages within the same nation. One area may have secured bilingual education provision, a neighboring area may have undeveloped bilingual education provision. Minority language literacy may be strong in some communities, weak in others. The use of the minority language in business and the local economy may vary considerably from rural to urban areas, and according to closeness of access to airports, roads, railways and sea links. In some villages, language death may be close. In other villages within the same region, most community life may be in the minority language.

Glyn Williams (1992), in a **critique** of Fishman, has argued that the presupposition is that change is gradual, mechanical, evolutionary and cumulative. Williams (1992) suggests that the viewpoint of Fishman tends to be of a consensus nature, concerned with integration, equilibrium, order and cohesion. Williams (1992) regards the work of Fishman as politically conservative with a consequent limited discussion of deviance, power, struggle and conflict. The preference is to play down the conflict while ignoring power relationships, thereby not expressing the anger, discrimination and frustration felt by language minority groups and their members. This theme is returned to when considering Paulston's (1980) equilibrium and conflict paradigms in Chapter 18.

Ó Riagáin (2000) also argues that Reversing Language Shift does not indicate the economic interventions that are so important for language revival. For parents to raise their children in the minority language, for schools to have a strong reason for content teaching through the minority language, economic and employment incentives and rewards are crucial to language revival, but not sufficient in themselves (Fishman, 2000a). Economic prescriptions are needed to provide a strong rational for intergenerational transmission. Integrative motives and cultural sentiment may not be enough to persuade parents, educators and students to use the minority language. The economic base of the language community can be a vital safeguard to the maintenance of a threatened language. The state, and not just the local language community is thus important (e.g. in economic regeneration of a language minority area). Material dimensions of success (individual and societal) and economic advancement have grown in importance in a consumerist society. Because these areas area often controlled by majority language groups, a power struggle becomes vital. As Pierre Bourdieu (1991, p. 57) declared: 'those who seek to defend a threatened language, – are obliged to wage a total struggle. One cannot save the value of a competence unless one saves the market, in other words, the whole set of political and social conditions of production of the producers/consumers.'

Fishman (2000b) indicates that globalization is a constructive, unifying phenomenon but also one which is destructive of cultures, languages and identities. Economic, communications, technological and political and globalization is the current largest threat to languages. Reversing Language Shift is thus both highly essential but very formidable. It is the weak against the strong, the few against the many, the poor and dependent against the rich, the powerless against the powerful (Fishman, 2000b). Return to the 'glorious past' is impractical. The new aim of language minorities has to be self-regulation within globalization. Such a paradox leads some to be pessimistic of the future of most languages and cultures; others try to ensure that global unification and the threat of the neighboring Big Brother language is counterbalanced by some degree of local autonomy and celebration of diversity. The ambitious agenda is to avoid parochialism, seclusion and detachment, combining globalism with some aspects of local autonomy.

The usefulness and status of the majority language for bilinguals means an uneasy and difficult separation of the different uses of the threatened and majority language. Some uses may be reserved for the minority language (e.g. religion), some shared (e.g. in the school curriculum), with an inherent struggle at the personal and societal level.

Finally, typologies and graded scales are helpful in organizing thinking and create a general guide rather than a comprehensive map. They represent, in outline form, a highly complex interaction of a variety of phenomena. The GIDS scale is a valuable attempt at sequencing and prioritizing action where there is downward language shift and upward ambitions.

CONCLUSION

This chapter has focused on language vitality and language reversal. Languages do not just exist inside individuals; they exist inside groups varying in size and strength. Sometimes such language groups shift to insignificance even death. Other times they attempt to spread and not just survive. One argument for the survival of languages has been that as languages die, so does part of the totality of human history and culture. Just as species of animals and plants are threatened, so are many minority languages. In the current century, preservation of the environment is a dominant issue. Maintaining the diversity of nature has developed as part of 21st century thinking. Preserving language diversity may also be environmentally friendly.

KEY POINTS IN THE CHAPTER

- Language vitality concerns three factors: (1) economic, social and symbolic status; (2) geographical density and distribution of language minority speakers; (3) institutional support factors (e.g. religion, administration, mass media, education and community).
- Fishman's model of Reversing Language shift has eight stages that reflect different conditions in the health of a language and steps needed to revive a language.
- The transmission of a minority language in a family is an essential foundation for the re-building of that language.

SUGGESTED FURTHER READING

COULMAS, F., 1997, The Handbook of Sociolinguistics. Oxford: Blackwell.
CRYSTAL, D., 2000, *Language Death*. Cambridge: Cambridge University Press.
FISHMAN, J.A., 1991, *Reversing Language Shift*. Clevedon: Multilingual Matters.
FISHMAN, J.A. (ed.), 2000, *Can Threatened Languages be Saved?* Clevedon: Multilingual Matters.
GILES, H. and COUPLAND, N., 1991, *Language: Contexts and Consequences*. Milton Keynes: Open University Press.
NETTLE, D. and ROMAINE, S., 2000, *Vanishing Voices: The Extinction of the World's Languages*. Oxford: Oxford University Press.
PAULSTON, C.B., 1994, *Linguistic Minorities in Multilingual Settings*. Philadelphia: John Benjamins.

STUDY ACTIVITIES

(1) Draw a diagram, chart or poster of Fishman's eight RLS (Reversing Language Shift) stages. This may be a simple poster with an immediate effect or a chart giving the crucial factors in each stage.
(2) Using language minority groups or communities known to you, where do you think they may be placed on Fishman's RLS scale? Do you find any difficulties in placement of groups on that scale?

CHAPTER 5

The Development of Bilingualism

Introduction

Types of Childhood Bilingualism

The Simultaneous Acquisition
of Bilingualism

One-Parent Families and Bilingualism

Stages of Development?

The Sequential Acquisition
of Bilingualism

Conclusion

CHAPTER 5
The Development of Bilingualism

INTRODUCTION

This chapter looks at the various ways in which children and adults become bilingual. There are various routes to bilingualism. Such **routes** include: learning two languages early on in the home; acquiring a second language in the street, in the wider community, in the nursery school, elementary or high school; and, after childhood, learning a second or foreign language by adult language classes and courses. This chapter outlines different major routes to becoming bilingual and examines some of the central issues involved.

As the previous chapters of this book have illustrated, a discussion of bilingualism has to take in psychological, linguistic, social and educational factors. Later in the book, it will be shown that political factors are also crucial in understanding bilingualism and bilingual education. While psychologists and linguists have studied the development of children's two languages, it is important to examine simultaneously the **social context** in which children acquire their languages. Being a member of an immigrant community, an elite group, a counter-elite, a majority or minority language group are important 'macro' influences in the acquisition of bilingualism. There are also 'micro' social contexts of the street, the nursery, the school, and the local community that similarly foster functional bilingualism. Such contexts tend to make bilingualism a constantly shifting rather than a stable phenomenon.

The variety of individual differences and social contexts makes simple generalizations about the development of bilingualism difficult and dangerous. The chapter therefore commences with a basic typology of the development of childhood bilingualism.

TYPES OF CHILDHOOD BILINGUALISM

An initial distinction is between **simultaneous and sequential childhood bilingualism**. This separates children who are exposed to two languages from birth from those who acquire a second language later. Simultaneous childhood bilingualism refers to a child acquiring two languages at the same time early in life, sometimes called infant bilingualism. For example, where one parent speaks one language to the child, and the other parent speaks a different language, the child may learn both languages simultaneously. An example of sequential childhood bilingualism is when a child learns the language of the home, then goes to a nursery or elementary school and learns a second language (Thompson, 2000).

Nursery and kindergarten education often encourages a child to acquire a second language without formal instruction in that language (Baker & Jones, 1998; Thompson, 2000). In the pre-school education context, language development may be supported through sessions that emphasize meaning-making over grammatical accuracy. Winsler *et al.* (1999) found that Spanish-speaking Mexican-American children, for example, who attended a bilingual (Spanish–English) pre-school when compared with those who stayed at home gained linguistically. Such children developed in their Spanish language proficiency as much as home-based children, as well as developing greater English proficiency. Such early bilingual education did not lead to native language loss.

In contrast, second language classes for children and adults foster bilingualism through direct instruction. This provides a distinction between informal **language acquisition** and more formal **language learning** (Krashen, 1977, 1981, 1982, 1985). However, the boundary between acquisition and learning is not distinct and separate (e.g. informal language acquisition can occur in a second language class). As has been indicated in Chapter 1, there is a movement towards making second language acquisition more naturalistic in an educational setting, developing communicative competence in a less formal way. Thus, the distinction between naturally becoming bilingual and being taught to become bilingual may have imprecise borders.

THE SIMULTANEOUS ACQUISITION OF BILINGUALISM

There are four basic dimensions along which the simultaneous acquisition of bilingualism in childhood varies. These four dimensions may be translated into four questions.

(1) **What language(s) is each parent ABLE to speak?** In some family situations, the parents or guardians may both be bilingual. That is, both parents may be able to speak both the languages of the particular society. For example in the USA, the parents may both be able to speak English and Spanish fluently. Alternatively, both parents may be monolingual with the child acquiring the second language from relatives, neighbors and the local community. In other families, one parent may be practically bilingual, the other monolingual. It is

important when asking the question of what language or languages each parent is able to speak, that consideration is given to whether those languages are minority or majority languages. Does the context concern additive or subtractive bilingualism?

(2) **What language(s) does each parent speak to the child IN PRACTICE?** While parents have the ability to speak both languages to their children, there is often a conscious decision or a latent understanding about which language to use with the child from birth upwards. A bilingual parent may choose to use both the languages with the child. A mother, for example, may use both English and Spanish with the child. A different situation is when one parent speaks one language to the child, the other parent speaks a different language. For example, the mother may speak Spanish to the child and the father will speak English. A third circumstance is when bilingual parents both speak the minority language to their children, leaving the child to learn the majority language outside the home.

(3) **What language(s) do other family members speak to the child?** There are families where both parents use the same language in speaking to their children, but where the children speak to each other in the 'outside' language (Baker, 2000b). For example, with recent immigrants, the parents speak the heritage language; the children speak to each other in the language of the street, school and television. Playing with neighborhood children, making friends in and out of school with majority language speakers and use of the mass-media may create bilingualism in the child. An alternative scenario is when the grandparents and other relations use a different language with the child than the home language. For example, Chinese children in the USA may speak English at home and at school, but acquire at least a passive understanding of Cantonese or Mandarin through regular visits to extended family members.

(4) **What language(s) does the child experience in the community?** Even before the age of three, the language experience with neighbors, networks of friends, local community and the nursery school may be a particularly important part of becoming bilingual (Cummins, 1991b). Sometimes a child may experience both the languages of home in the outside world. Alternatively, the child raised monolingually might pick up a second language outside the home. For example, children whose parents speak Spanish to them in the home may attend an English medium nursery school and become bilingual in that way. The chapter continues by focusing on the more typical and better documented routes to childhood bilingualism.

Case Studies of Simultaneous Childhood Bilingual Acquisition

Some of the earliest research on bilingualism concerns detailed case studies of children becoming bilingual. For example, Ronjat (1913) described a case of the mother speaking German and the father speaking French in a French community. Ronjat's (1913) case study introduced the principle of '**one person, one language**'. That is, the case study announced the idea that a very effective method of raising children bilingually was for each parent to speak a separate language to the child.

While there have been a number of case studies of children growing up bilingually since Ronjat's first study, the most detailed case study is still Leopold's (1939 to 1949). Leopold's classic study of his daughter Hildegard was based on the father speaking German in the home and the mother speaking English.

Leopold was a phonetician by training and made a comprehensive record of the development of Hildegard's speech. The results were published in four books which Hakuta (1986, p. 48) described as 'a masterpiece of devotion to detailed description'. Leopold analyzed the development of vocabulary, the sound system, word combinations and sentences.

One important aspect of Leopold's studies is the **shifting balance** of the two languages in childhood. When Hildegard went to Germany, her German became stronger. When back in the United States and attending school, Hildegard's English became the dominant language. Many bilingual situations are changeable, where, at an individual level (and not just at a societal level), the languages shift in dominance. Hildegard, for example was reluctant to speak German during her mid-teens, with German becoming the weaker language. Leopold's second daughter understood German but spoke very little German to her father. In childhood, the second daughter, Karla, was a passive bilingual. Yet at the age of 19, Karla visited Germany where she was able to change from receptive German to productive German, managing to converse relatively fluently in German. Other examples of shifting bilingualism in childhood are given by Fantini (1985) who details a child's shift between English, Italian and Spanish and Yukawa (1997) who examines three cases of first language Japanese loss and re-acquisition.

Apart from the 'one person/one language' method of raising children bilingually, there are other case studies showing **different approaches** (see Schinke-Llano, 1989; Romaine, 1995). Romaine (1995) provides a six-fold typology of early childhood bilingualism in terms of the language spoken by mother and father, the language of the community and the strategy of the parents. Each of the six patterns reveal different approaches that can be successful in bringing up children bilingually. Two of these approaches have already been mentioned: each parent speaking a different language to the child; and parents speaking a minority language to the child who acquires a second language in the community or extended family. A third approach also deserves mentioning.

There is the case where both parents (and the community) are bilingual and constantly **mix** their languages. Romaine (1995) considers this 'a more common category than it might seem on the basis of its representation in the literature' (p. 186). For example, along the USA–Mexico border there are many communities where English and Spanish is mixed. This is supported by Lyon (1996) who found that, in families in Wales, mixed language input with little apparent self-monitoring or consciousness was quite typical. García (1983) showed that a parental mixing of languages can still lead to a child communicating effectively in two languages.

ONE-PARENT FAMILIES AND BILINGUALISM

Almost all case-studies of bilingual children have been based on two-parent families. Books dealing with raising children bilingually tend to assume the presence of two parents in the family home. By accident rather than design, this implies that a one-parent family has little or no chance of raising a child bilingually. This is not true. Two examples will illustrate this.

(1) A second language is often acquired outside the home. In parts of Africa, children acquire one language at home or in the neighborhood and another language (or even two or three) at school, in inter-ethnic communication and in urban areas. Children of immigrant USA communities may acquire Spanish in the home and neighborhood, and learn English at school. A single parent who speaks French but resides in the USA may decide to make French the family language so that the children may have the opportunity of bilingualism. In cases like these, the absence of a parent does not necessarily hinder a child's bilingual development.

(2) In some cases, the maintenance of a family's bilingualism may be challenged by the absence of a parent. In cases such as those in (1) above, where one parent speaks the dominant language of the community to the children, and the other parent uses a minority language with them, the death or departure of the second parent may mean that the family is in danger of becoming monolingual. However, if the remaining parent is committed to the maintenance of the family's bilingualism, it could be accomplished in various ways (see Baker & Jones, 1998).

The disruption of a family by death or divorce is typically traumatic for both parents and children. At times of great mental and emotional stress, when many practical difficulties and changes have to be faced, bilingualism may seem low on the list of priorities. However, single-parent families are often adept at meeting challenges and may look for ways of maintaining a child's bilingualism without causing further disruption to the child's life. In addition, where a child has undergone such stress, it may be wise, if possible, to avoid the added trauma of losing a language, a culture and an intrinsic part of the child's identity.

STAGES OF DEVELOPMENT?

One early formulation of the language development of bilingual children envisaged discrete stages of development. For example, Volterra and Taeschner (1978) suggested a three stage model moving from mixing languages to partial separation to fuller separation. This three stage model is not now regarded as wholly accurate (De Houwer, 1995). However, the issue of mixing and separation continues to be important in a debate about whether a young bilingual child develops two separate linguistic systems or just one overall integrated system (De Houwer, 1995; Lanza, 1997; Nicoladis, 1998). Language mixing is said to be evidence of one linguistic system in infant bilinguals. Lack of separation, it is claimed, shows that an infant lacks awareness that there are two different language systems early on.

Recent research has found that bilingual children (around two years old) know which language to speak 'to whom' and in 'what situation' (Quay, 1994; De Houwer, 1995; Lanza, 1997; Nicoladis & Genesee, 1997; Nicoladis, 1998; Deuchar & Quay, 1999). Very young children easily switch languages and **differentiate their two languages**, but there is much individual variation. For example, Deuchar and Quay (1999) found that bilingual children as young as, and younger than, two years of age use their two languages in contextually sensitive ways. In the last five months of a child's second year (1:7 to 2:0), utterances were beginning to be matched to the context (e.g. which language to use with each parent).

Current research suggests that 'in terms of phonology, lexicon and syntax, children seem to produce their two languages differentially from very early in development' (Nicoladis, 1998, p. 106). The old idea that children use their two languages as a single system (Unitary Language System) is not supported. The ability to use the appropriate language with a particular person (pragmatic differentiation) also occurs very early. In Nicoladis' (1998) case study of a Portuguese-English child from 12 to 18 months of age, pragmatic differentiation occurred about three weeks before lexical differentiation. This hints that the child's understanding that he should address each parent in a different language may have affected his understanding that words belonged to two different and distinct languages. Social awareness of the one parent–one language routine seemed to have encouraged an awareness of translation equivalents and two separate language systems. 'Children's understanding of the appropriate social use of their two languages may lead to an understanding that the translation equivalents in their vocabulary belong to two distinct input languages' (Nicoladis, 1998, p. 105).

Genesee *et al.* (1996) established that **'appropriate language matching'** is witnessed in two year olds from bilingual homes when talking to strangers. Children rapidly and accurately accommodated the monolingualism of a stranger and talked in the appropriate language. A study of a Dutch and English bilingual aged three showed that the child would accurately choose the appropriate language when speaking with a monolingual person (De Houwer, 1990). However, with people the child knew to be fluent bilinguals, she was much more ready to use both languages (i.e. codeswitching) in her contributions to the conversation. The study suggests that many bilingual children tend not to mix languages when addressing monolinguals, but are aware enough of bilinguals to move between both languages when addressing them.

De Houwer (1995, p. 248) neatly sums up this area:

> '... more and more evidence suggests that bilingual children do not differ much from monolingual children in their approach to the language learning task. Like monolingual children, bilingual children pay a lot of attention to the input they receive. They soon notice that this input differs depending on who is talking or where and in what situation someone is talking. Just like monolin-

gual children, bilingual children attempt to talk like the people around them. Because of the bilingual situation, however, the bilingual child has more options than the monolingual one: … at a very young age bilingual children are skilled conversationalists who easily switch languages.'

The age at which a child differentiates the two language systems and rarely mixes the two will differ considerably from child to child according to **child socialization practices** (Lanza, 1997; Nicoladis & Genesee, 1997). Codemixing is affected by the language model provided by parents. If parents codeswitch regularly, then their children may imitate. If parents discourage codeswitching (e.g. by clear language separation), then less mixing may occur. What is culturally appropriate, the norm of the community, and what is valued by parents and significant others will have an important influence.

Thus a variety of factors may affect the point at which a child separates the two languages: exposure to the two languages in different domains, the attitudes of parents to the two languages and to mixing the languages, the language abilities and metalinguistic abilities of the child, personality, peer interaction, exposure to different forms of language education, as well as sociolinguistic influences such as the norms, values and beliefs of the community (Nicoladis & Genesee, 1997).

Nicoladis and Secco (2000) found that when very young children (under two years) do codemix, about 90% could be accounted for by **lexical gaps** in one language. Gaps in vocabulary are filled by appropriate elements from the other language. If a translation equivalent was missing, the accessible equivalent in the other language will be used – a pragmatic choice. Thus, a lack of differentiation between languages is not supported by recent research.

Language Loss in Children

Before considering the sequential acquisition of bilingualism, it is important to mention **language loss** in bilingual children. In particular, children from language minorities (indigenous and particularly immigrant children) are sometimes at risk of losing their minority language. With a higher status majority language ever present on the screen, in the street, at school and in shops, children quickly learn which language has prestige, power and preference. They quickly learn that they are different in language, behavior, ethnicity and culture, and some children, and particularly teenagers, may come to perceive their language and cultural differences as undesirable. Students quickly perceive what helps them belong and become accepted in mainstream society.

Language loss in children is a reality in the United States. Research by Hakuta and D'Andrea (1992) and Wong Fillmore (1991a) indicates the strength of the dominance of English in US society that places considerable pressure on language minority students not only to acquire English at a young age, but also to replace their minority language with English. In such subtractive situations, the ideal of early bilingualism meets a challenge due to a societal ethos that does not favor bilingualism. Hakuta and D'Andrea (1992) found in the United States that early exposure to English (e.g. in the home) not only may mean for some children a shift from Spanish to English but also the potential loss of Spanish. Such early exposure to English in the USA may also decrease the chances of placement in a dual education program where Spanish is used.

This is not a criticism of early bilingualism, but rather a warning that the minority language needs care and attention, status and much usage in the young child. This is not a limitation of early bilingualism, but rather a caution that minority language development needs particular nurturing in political situations where another language is ever-dominant. For example, when **English** is introduced very early and dominantly into a US language minority child's life, the minority language may be insufficiently stable and developed, and may therefore be replaced by the majority language. A loss of the minority language may have social, emotional, cognitive and educational consequences for the child, as later chapters (e.g. Chapter 18) will examine. As Wong Fillmore (1991a, p. 343) argues: 'What is lost is no less than the means by which parents socialize their children: When parents are unable to talk to their children, they cannot easily convey to them their values, beliefs, understandings, or wisdom about how to cope with their experiences'.

The dialogue that takes place between parents and children is an important contributor to the child's cognitive development. As children interact with parents, they are introduced to new features of language (e.g. syntax, semantics). When the child loses the home language, the parent can no longer offer this language education to the child. The necessary cognitive scaffolding is stifled.

Thus minority language loss is an issue not just of geographical regions and language communities but also for individual children. **Family language planning** is needed to ensure relatively stable and enduring bilingualism.

THE SEQUENTIAL ACQUISITION OF BILINGUALISM

Sequential acquisition of bilingualism refers to the situation where a child acquires a first language, and later becomes proficient in the second language. The sequential acquisition of bilingualism takes us into the field of **second language acquisition**. Such acquisition may be through formal or informal means; informally through street, nursery school and community, or formally through school, adult classes and language courses. There is no single 'best' route by which learners, young or old, become competent in a second language. There are a variety of informal and formal educational means of acquiring proficiency in a second language.

Background Issues

Many children become competent bilinguals through the process of simultaneous bilingualism. The evidence of bilingualism through foreign language learning is not always so positive. In the US and Britain, despite extensive foreign language learning in school (and the extensive research on second language acquisition), only a small proportion of children learning a foreign language become functionally and fluently bilingual. In the US, fewer than one in 20 children become bilingual following foreign language instruction. There are various popular reasons for such **failure**: the emphasis on reading and writing rather than on authentic communication; having a low aptitude to learn a second language; a lack of motivation and interest, and a lack of opportunity to practice second language skills. Another popular explanation is attempting to learn a language too late; that is, believing that it is easier to learn a language when someone is younger rather than older. The issue of age in learning a language is considered later.

In certain western countries (e.g. Netherlands, Finland, Sweden, Belgium) and eastern countries (e.g. Israel, Singapore), foreign language learning has been relatively more successful. Such international comparisons highlight the need to bring political, cultural and economic factors into second language learning discussions. No language learner is an island. Surrounding the shores of the individual psychology of effective second language acquisition lie the seas of social, cultural and political context. Any map of sequential bilingualism needs to include all these features.

Informal Second Language Learning

Bilingualism is often achieved through the informal acquisition processes of the street and screen, neighborhood and newspaper. A child sometimes rapidly acquires a second or third language in addition to that of the home without planning or intent by parents. Peers in the street, cartoons and shows on television are two examples of language influences that may informally lead to bilingualism in the child and teenager. Little researched, the almost incidental addition of a second or third language via the street and screen may be as influential as formal education, and sometimes more potent than language classes. This particularly tends to be the case with acquiring the majority language of the neighborhood (circumstantial bilinguals – see Chapter 1).

Formal Second Language Learning

Where a second language is not acquired in the community (natural second language acquisition), **the school** has been the major institution expected to produce second language learning (for both elective and circumstantial bilinguals but for different reasons – see Chapter 1). Through second language and foreign language lessons, via language laboratories and computer-assisted language learning, drill and practice routines, immersion classes, drama and dance, the initial stages of monolingualism to bilingualism may occur.

The routes to bilingualism are not solely in early childhood and in formal education. **Voluntary language classes** sometimes exist for school-age children. When the school does not support immigrant languages, reproduction of those languages in the family may be not enough for language maintenance. Therefore, local community groups have developed extra schooling for their children. In England and Canada, for example, evening classes, vacation classes, Saturday schools and Sunday schools are organized by various communities for children to learn the heritage language of their parents and grandparents. Children of second, third or fourth generation immigrants may have learnt English as their first or dominant language. If parents have chosen to speak English to their children, even if their own first language is not English, the heritage language may be learnt in voluntary classes. Where English is the dominant language of the community and the only language of the school, such voluntary classes may be important in attaining bilingualism rather than moving children towards majority language monolingualism (Viv Edwards, 1995a, 1996; Ghuman, 1993; Dosanjh & Ghuman, 1996).

Such **voluntary provision** may be for religious, cultural, social, integrative and ethnic minority vitality reasons. Thus the providers are often religious institutions such as synagogues, mosques, temples and Orthodox churches. Jewish families attending a local synagogue are often enthusiastic for Hebrew to be taught to their children to maintain a Jewish identity and for religious observance. Moslems have often been keen for Qur'anic Arabic to be transmitted for worship in the mosque, just as *gurdwaras* have been instrumental in the acquisition of Panjabi. The Roman Catholic Church also has promoted the community language teaching of Polish, Ukrainian and Lithuanian.

In the United Kingdom, there has been such **community language classes** in Spanish, Italian, Portuguese, Greek, Turkish, Urdu, Hindi, Panjabi and Bengali, for example. In the case of European languages, High Commissions and Embassies in London have often lent support. In other communities, particularly among the British Asians, the providers are groups of enthusiastic parents and local community organizations who rent premises such as schools and halls to teach a heritage language. Another example comes from Belgium where the Polish government supports accredited Polish classes that pupils attend in addition to their classes in mainstream Belgium schools.

Apart from voluntary classes for children, another well traveled route to second language acquisition is **adult provision** (see Baker & Jones, 1998; Spolsky & Shohamy, 1999). Such provision takes varying forms in different geographical areas:

- **Evening classes**. Sometimes called night schools or classes, a second or foreign language is taught on a once or twice a week basis for several weeks to several years. Such classes have often traditionally aimed at securing formal qualifications in the language (e.g. passing exams in a second majority language) or at gaining proficiency in the majority language. One example is 'English as a Second Language' classes established for immigrants into the USA and England. Recently, the growth has also been in acquiring communicative competence in a heritage language (e.g. Hebrew, Basque, Welsh).

- **Ulpan courses**. Perhaps the most notable example of a mass movement of adult language learning has been the case of Hebrew in Israel. After the establishment of the State of Israel in 1948, the steady flow of immigration became a flood. Emergency measures were needed to teach Hebrew in a short time to large numbers of people as a living, spoken language. The idea of creating an intensive Hebrew language course was born and called an *Ulpan*. The word

'*Ulpan*' is derived from an Aramaic root meaning 'custom, training, instruction, law'. There were originally about 25 students in the class, and they met for six hours each day apart from the Sabbath. From the beginning, the emphasis was on equipping the learners for everyday communication in the spoken language. Cultural activities such as singing and field trips were part of the course. Over the years different kinds of *Ulpanim* have been established in Israel.

- Intensive courses for new immigrants at the '*merkaz klita*' (residential absorption centers for new immigrants), usually 30 hours a week for five months.
- Less intensive *ulpanim*, called *ulpaniyot*. These are non-residential *ulpanim*, held perhaps a couple of mornings or evenings a week, to fit in with the needs of professional people or those with home responsibilities.
- *Ulpanim* at Kibbutzim. The learners have lessons and also work on the kibbutz.
- Military *Ulpanim*. These are very intensive in order to bring the students' language to the high level of Hebrew required by the Israeli military. These courses place emphasis on technical vocabulary and reading skills (maps, plans, written instructions etc.)
- Specialized courses for advanced learners in various vocational fields.

A typical *Ulpan course* for beginners will include pronunciation practice, dialogues, pair work, with emphasis on authentic communication. Many courses include singing and other cultural activities, trips to places of interest and living for a short time with Hebrew speaking families (Spolsky & Shohamy, 1999).

Like their models in Israel, the Basque and Welsh *Ulpanim* vary in intensity from five days a week courses to two mornings or two evenings a week (Baker & Jones, 1998). Some vocational courses are held for teachers, hospital workers, administrators and workers in industry. Other courses have a bias towards the needs of particular groups like parents. As in Israel, the emphasis is on developing competence in the spoken language.

- **Distance learning methods**. A variety of media-based courses for learning a second language are often available to adults. Radio and television series, use of satellite television, cassette tapes, records, compact discs, videos, video discs, magazines and self-teach books, computer programs (Computer-assisted language learning) and correspondence courses are all well tried approaches in second language acquisition. Evaluation studies of the relative effectiveness of these different approaches tend to be lacking.

In early childhood, becoming bilingual is often an unconscious event, as natural as learning to walk or to ride a bicycle. In a school situation, a child is not usually the one who has made a decision about the language(s) of the classroom. Second language acquisition at school is often imposed by teachers and a local or national educational policy. For migrant workers, refugees and immigrants, adult language learning also may be essential for work and adaptation to new institutions and bureaucracy. However, for other adults, second language acquisition sometimes becomes more voluntary, more open to choice. This raises the issue of whether it is preferable to learn a new language as a child or as an adult?

The Age Factor

A much debated theme in second language acquisition is the relationship of **age in learning a second language** and success in gaining language proficiency (Harley, 1986). One argument is that the lower the age at which a second language is learnt, the greater the long-term proficiency gained in that language is. According to this viewpoint, young children learn a language more easily and successfully. Others tend to argue that older children and young adults learn a language more efficiently and quickly than young children do. For example, a 14-year-old learning Spanish as a second language has superior intellectual processing skills than the five-year-old learning Spanish. Therefore, less time is required in the teenage years to learn a second language than in the younger years.

A comprehensive and balanced review of this area is provided by Singleton (1989). Singleton's analysis may be briefly summarized as follows:

(1) Younger second language learners are neither globally more nor less efficient and successful than older learners in second language acquisition. There are many factors that intervene and make simple statements about age and language learning simplistic and untenable.

(2) Children who learn a second language in childhood do tend to achieve higher levels of proficiency than those who begin after childhood. Such a finding does not contradict the idea that someone can become proficient in learning a second language after childhood. This tendency may be related to social contexts in which language is acquired and maintained or lost, as well as to the psychology of individual learning. Younger children appear to pick up the sound systems of a new language more easily than adults.

(3) In a formal classroom language learning situation, older learners tend initially to learn quicker than younger learners. However, the length of exposure (e.g. the number of years of second language instruction) is an important factor in second language success. Those children who begin to learn a second language in the elementary school and continue throughout schooling, tend to show higher proficiency than those who start to learn the second language later in their schooling. In absolute rather than comparative terms, this still includes the possibility of late learners becoming highly proficient, particularly when they are highly motivated.

(4) Support for foreign language instruction at an early age in school needs to find its rationale and support from areas other than second language research. For example, teaching a foreign language early in the elementary school needs to be defended in terms of general intellectual stimulation, the general curriculum value of teaching a modern language, the benefits of biculturalism and

the benefits of learning a language for as long as possible rather than as quickly as possible. Second language instruction in the elementary school rests on the suitable provision of language teachers, suitable materials and resources, favorable attitudes of the teachers and parents, and the need to make the learning experience enjoyable.

(5)   In the United States, one pressure is for immigrant children to learn English as soon as possible. Some claim, without justification from research, that the optimal time to learn a language is from age three to seven, and because of supposed biological constraints, certainly before the onset of puberty. In a status review of this area, Hakuta (1999, pp. 11–12) argues that:

> 'The evidence for a critical period for second language acquisition is scanty, especially when analyzed in terms of its key assumptions. There is no empirically definable end point, there are no qualitative differences between child and adult learners, and there are large environmental effects on the outcomes. … The view of a biologically constrained and specialized language acquisition device that is turned off at puberty is not correct.'

While there are no critical periods of language learning, there are advantageous periods. Early childhood and school days seem two advantageous periods.

How **successful** have adults been in becoming bilingual? There is a distinction between answering this question in an absolute and a relative manner. The 'absolute' answer simply is that adults do learn a second language to varying degrees of fluency. Some fall by the wayside, others reach a basic, simple level of communication, yet others become functionally bilingual. In Israel, Wales and the Basque country, the adult route to bilingualism has many success stories.

The 'relative' answer involves comparing children and adults of varying ages. In this sense, the question becomes 'Who is more likely to become proficient in a second language, children or adults?' A specific example of adult success provides an illustration of a typical pattern. This example focuses on language usage rather than acquisition.

From 1950s Israeli census data, it is possible to examine whether older or younger adults become functional in **Hebrew**. For example, do young immigrants become more or less functional in Hebrew as a second language compared with older immigrants? The results follow a clear pattern (Bachi, 1956; Braine, 1987). As the figure on the following page illustrates (based on Bachi, 1956), the extent of the everyday use of Hebrew varies with age of in-migration. The younger the child, the more likely he or she will be to use Hebrew. Between 30 and 40 years of age, a notable drop occurs. Is this due to a loss of learning ability, less exposure to Hebrew, less motivation or decreasing social pressure? From age 40 onwards, the likelihood of being functional in Hebrew falls again.

Trilingualism

While this book is about bilingualism and bilingual education, it is important to recognize that many people are multilingual. For example, many Swedish people

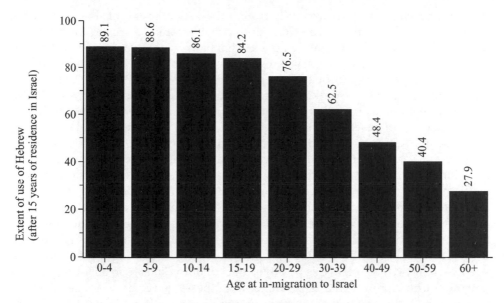

are fluent in Swedish, German and English. Many individuals in the African and Indian continents speak a local, regional and official or international language. In Zaire, for example, children may learn a local vernacular at home, a regional language such as Lingala or Kikongo in the community or at school, and French as they proceed through schooling. Clyne (1997) provides Australian examples (e.g. Italian, Spanish, English) that explore trilingual linguistic issues.

One documented route to **trilingualism** is parents speaking two different languages to their children at home. The children then take their education through a third language. The majority language of the community will influence the relative strengths of the three languages and relative proficiency in each of the three languages may also change over time. Stable trilingualism seems less likely than stable bilingualism.

One case study (Hoffmann, 1985) concerns Spanish (acquired mostly from the father and *au pairs*), German (acquired mostly from the mother and visits), and English (acquired mostly among peers and in school). The one-parent/one language 'rule' was followed. English came to be dominant as the school experience and peer relationships developed.

A similar case study (Jean-Marc DeWaele, 2000) follows Livia, a girl raised in Dutch by her mother, French by her father, with English acquired in the London neighborhood. The mother and father use Dutch when speaking together, making Dutch the dominant language of the family. English quickly became her 'default language' when meeting new children in London. From five months to two and a half years, Livia learnt Urdu from a childminder, thus becoming quadralingual at an early age. By one year and two months she had a passive knowledge of some 150 French, Dutch, Urdu and English words. Multiword utterances in Dutch and

French appeared at two years two months. Awareness of her languages (metalinguistic awareness – see Chapter 7) came before her second birthday, for example, in relaying that the mother duck in her bath was Dutch-speaking. Thus the concept of different languages was present very early – in this case before the second birthday. The **value of multilingualism** was also understood at a very early age: 'If she doesn't get the cookie she ordered in one language, she code-switches to the other, just to make sure we understand her request' (DeWaele, 2000, p. 5).

In a review of **research on trilingualism**, Cenoz and Genesee (1998, p. 20) conclude that 'bilingualism does not hinder the acquisition of an additional language and, to the contrary, in most cases bilingualism favors the acquisition of a third language'. Cenoz (2000, p. 46) also suggests that 'studies on the effect of bilingualism on third language acquisition conducted in different contexts tend to associate bilingualism with advantages in third language acquisition.' Where advantages are not present, the context is typically subtractive. The cognitive advantages of bilingualism such as cognitive flexibility and metalinguistic awareness (see Chapter 7) and the development of enhanced linguistic processing strategies may help explain this positive effect of bilingualism on acquiring a third language. The linguistic interdependence hypothesis (see Chapter 8) also suggests that positive influences may occur from bilingualism to trilingualism (Cenoz, 2000).

Trilingualism has become a key growth area in research that has sociolinguistic, psycholinguistic, political and educational dimensions (see Cenoz & Jessner, 2000). Many recent studies of trilingualism analyze the current and future place of English as the most important language of wider communication, not only in science and commerce but also in travel and technology (e.g. World Wide Web). Early trilingualism, when a child is exposed to three languages from birth, is more rare than trilingualism achieved through schooling (e.g. two languages learnt at school). Particular examples of this are found in the Basque Country (Basque, Spanish, English – see Lasagabaster, 2000), Catalonia (Catalan, Spanish, English – see Muñoz, 2000), Finland (Finnish, Swedish, English – see Björklund & Suni, 2000), Friesland (Frisian, Dutch, English – see Ytsma, 2000) and Romania (Romanian, Hungarian and English – see Iatcu, 2000).

Codeswitching

One issue that frequently occurs for parents and teachers of children of differing ages is when one language is mixed with another. Terms such as Hinglish, Spanglish, Tex-Mex and Wenglish (respectively for Hindi-English, Spanish-English, Texan-Mexican and Welsh-English) are often used in derogatory fashion to describe what may have become accepted language borrowing within a particular community. However, in other bilingual communities, strict separation of languages may be the acceptable norm for political, social or cultural reasons. If a power conflict exists between different ethnic groups, then language may be perceived as a prime marker of a separate identity, and codeswitching may be less acceptable.

Monolinguals who hear bilinguals codeswitch may have negative attitudes to codeswitching, believing that it shows a deficit, or a lack of mastery of both languages. Bilinguals themselves may be defensive or apologetic about their codeswitching and attribute it to laziness or sloppy language habits. However, codeswitching is a valuable linguistic tool. It does not happen at random. There is usually purpose and logic in changing languages.

Very few bilinguals keep their two languages completely separate, and the ways in which they mix them are complex and varied. Grosjean (1992) distinguishes between the 'monolingual mode' (when bilinguals use one of their languages with monolingual speakers of that language) and the 'bilingual mode' when bilinguals are in the company of other bilinguals and have the option of switching languages. Even in the 'monolingual mode', bilinguals occasionally mix their languages.

Various terms have been used to describe switches between languages in conversation. The term '**codemixing**' has sometimes been used to describe changes at the word level (e.g. when one word or a few words in a sentence change). A mixed language sentence such as '*Leo un magazine*' (I read a magazine) might be called codemixing. In contrast, '*Come to the table. Bwyd yn barod*' (food is ready) might be called codeswitching. The first phrase is in English; the second in Welsh. However, codeswitching is now the term generally used to describe any switch within the course of a single conversation, whether at word or sentence level or at the level of blocks of speech.

Language borrowing has been the term used to indicate foreign loan words or phrases that have become an integral and permanent part of the recipient language. Examples are '*le weekend*' from English into the French language and '*der computer*' from English into the German language. All languages borrow words or phrases from other languages with which they come into contact. Codeswitching may often be the first step in this process. Myers-Scotton (1992) argues against trying to establish criteria to distinguish between codeswitches and loans. Codeswitches and loans are not two distinct and separate entities. Rather, they form a continuum. As Eastman (1992, p. 1) suggested: 'efforts to distinguish codeswitching, codemixing and borrowing are doomed.'

'**Language interference**' was a term that was once used when people acquiring two languages mixed their languages. When a child seems to have a temporary difficulty in separating out two languages, 'interference' has been the ascribed term. Many bilinguals regard this as a negative and pejorative term, revealing a monolingual's perspective. For the child, switching between languages may be to convey thoughts and ideas in the most personally efficient manner. The child may also realize that the listener understands such switching. When such interference is temporary in a child's bilingual development, the more neutral terms '**transfer**' and '**crosslinguistic influence**' (see Sharwood Smith, 1989) are preferable.

The discussion of codeswitching will now be considered from a sociolinguistic perspective. Those interested in a linguistic perspective (e.g. 'where in a sentence can a speaker change languages?') may consult Myers-Scotton (1993, 1997), Poplack and Meechan (1998) and Romaine (1995).

Codeswitches have a variety of purposes and aims. Codeswitching will vary according to who is in the conversation, what is the topic, and in what kind of context the conversation occurs. The languages used may be negotiated and may change with the topic of conversation. Also, social and political factors can influence codeswitching (Heller, 1992; Treffers-Daller, 1992, 1994; Poplack *et al.*, 1988). For example, competition among language groups, the relationships between the language majority and language minority, the norms of the community and inter-group relations in a community may have a major effect on use of codeswitching.

Twelve over-lapping **purposes of codeswitching** will now be considered.

(1) Codeswitches may be used to **emphasize** a particular point in a conversation. If one word needs stressing or is central in a sentence, a switch may be made.

(2) If a person does not know a word or a phrase in a language, that person may **substitute** a word in another language. This often happens because bilinguals use different languages in different domains of their lives. A young person may, for instance, switch from the home language to the language used in school to talk about a subject such as mathematics or computers. Myers-Scotton (1972) describes how a Kikuyu university student in Nairobi, Kenya, switched constantly from Kikuyu to English to discuss geometry with his younger brother.

> *'Atiriri angle niati has ina degree eighty; nayo this one ina mirongo itatu.'*

Similarly, an adult may codeswitch when talking about work, because the technical terms associated with work are only known in that language.

(3) Words or phrases in two languages may not correspond exactly and the bilingual may switch to one language to **express a concept that has no equivalent** in the culture of the other language. For example, a French–English bilingual living in Britain may use words like 'pub' or 'bingo hall' when speaking French, because there are no exact French equivalents for these words.

(4) Codeswitching may be used to **reinforce** a request. For example, a teacher may repeat a command to accent and underline it (e.g. *'Taisez-vous les enfants!* Be quiet, children!') In a majority/minority language situation, the majority language may be used to underline authority. In a study conducted at a hospital in Mid-Wales (Roberts, 1994), it was found that nurses repeat or amplify commands to patients in English in order to emphasize their authority (e.g. *'Peidiwch a chanu'r gloch Mrs Jones* – don't ring the bell if you don't need anything!'). A Spanish-speaking mother in New York may use English with her children for short commands like 'Stop it! Don't do that!' and then switch back to Spanish.

(5) Repetition of a phrase or passage in another language may also be used to **clarify** a point. Some teachers in classrooms explain a concept in one language, and then explain it again in another language, believing that repetition adds reinforcement and completeness of understanding.

(6) Codeswitching may be used to **communicate friendship** or family bonding. For example, moving from the common majority language to the home language or minority language both the listener and speaker understand well

may communicate friendship and common identity. Similarly, a person may deliberately use codeswitching to indicate the need to be accepted by a peer group. Someone with a rudimentary knowledge of a language may inject words of that new language into sentences to indicate a desire to identify and affiliate. The use of the listener's stronger language in part of the conversation may indicate deference, wanting to belong or to be accepted.

(7) In **relating a conversation** held previously, the person may report the conversation in the language or languages used. For example, two people may be speaking Spanish together. When one reports a previous conversation with an English monolingual, that conversation is reported authentically – for example, in English – as it occurred.

(8) Codeswitching is sometimes used as a way of **interjecting** into a conversation. A person attempting to break into a conversation may introduce a different language. Interrupting a conversation may be signaled by changing language. The message to the speakers from the listener is that 'I would like to become involved in this conversation'.

(9) Codeswitching may be used to **ease tension and inject humor** into a conversation. If discussions are becoming tense in a committee, the use of a second language may signal a change in the 'tune being played'. Just as in an orchestra, different instruments may be brought in during a composition to signal a change of mood and pace, so a switch in language may indicate a need to change mood within the conversation.

(10) Codeswitching often relates to a **change of attitude or relationship**. For example, when two people meet, they may use the common majority language (e.g. Swahili or English in Kenya). As the conversation proceeds and roles, status and ethnic identity are revealed, a change to a regional language may indicate that boundaries are being broken down. A codeswitch signals there is less social distance, with expressions of solidarity and growing rapport indicated by the switch. A study of Italian immigrants into the United States at the turn of the 20th century (Di Pietro, 1977) showed that the immigrants would tell a joke in English and give the punch line in Italian, not only because it was better expressed in that language, but also to emphasize the shared values and experiences of the minority group. This is a common feature across many languages and cultures, East and West.

Conversely, a **change** from a minority language or dialect to a majority language may indicate the speakers' wish to elevate their own status, create a distance between themselves and the listener, or establish a more formal, business relationship. Myers-Scotton and Ury (1977) describe a conversation between a Kenyan shop keeper and his sister, who had come in to buy some salt. After exchanging greetings in their own Luyia dialect, the brother switches to Swahili in front of the other customers and says: '*Dada, sasa leo unahitaji nini?*' (Sister, what do you need today?) For the rest of the conversation, the brother speaks in Swahili and the sister in the Luyia dialect. The brother's codeswitch to Swahili, the business language of Kenya, indicates to his sister that, although they are closely related, he must maintain a business relationship with her. She should not expect any favors or to receive anything for free.

(11) Codeswitching can also be used to **exclude** people from a conversation. For example, when traveling on the metro (subway, underground), two people speaking English may switch to their minority language to talk about private matters, thus excluding others from the conversation. Bilingual parents may use one language together to exclude their monolingual children from a private discussion. A doctor at a hospital may make a brief aside to a colleague in a language not understood by the patient.

(12) In some bilingual situations, codeswitching occurs regularly when certain topics are introduced (e.g. money). Spanish–English bilinguals in the South West United States often switch to English to discuss money. For example, a person may say '*La consulta era* (the visit cost) twenty dollars' (Valdés-Fallis, 1976). This reflects that English is the language of commerce, and often the dominant language of the mathematics curriculum.

Familiarity, projected status, the ethos of the context and the perceived linguistic skills of the listeners affect the nature and process of codeswitching (Martin-Jones, 2000). This suggests that codeswitching is not just linguistic; it indicates important social and power relationships.

A variety of **factors** may affect the extent to which children and adults switch between their languages (Romaine, 1995). The perceived status of the listeners, familiarity with those persons, atmosphere of the setting and perceived linguistic skills of the listeners are examples of variables that may foster or prevent code-switching. Such factors operate as young as two years of age. Whereas a two-year-old's mixing of language has tended to be seen as 'interference' or a lack of differentiation between languages, research has shown that codeswitching by two-year-olds can be context-sensitive (e.g. according to which parent is being addressed), as discussed earlier in this chapter.

The chapter concludes by examining a topic related to codeswitching: children acting as interpreters for their parents and others (Kaur & Mills, 1993). Bilingual children (and adults) are frequently expected to act as go-betweens by interpreting from one language to another. Such an interpreter's role also illustrates how bilingual development impacts on other aspects of child development such as personality and family relationships.

Children as Language Brokers

In language minority families, children often act as **interpreters** or **language brokers** for their parents and others. For example, in first and second generation immigrant families, parents may have little or no competency in the majority language. Therefore, their children act as interpreters in a variety of contexts. Rather than just transmit information, children act as information and communication brokers (Tse, 1995, 1996a, 1996b), often ensuring the messages are 'culturally translated as in the following example:

Father to daughter in Italian: '*Digli che è un imbecille!*' (Tell him he is an idiot!)

Daughter to trader: 'My father won't accept your offer.'

Language minority students can be important language brokers between the home and the school (McQuillan & Tse, 1995). Also, when there are visitors to the house, such as sellers and traders, religious persuasionists and local officials, a parent may call a child to the door to help translate what is being said. The child interprets for both parties (e.g. the parent and the caller). Similarly, at hospitals, the doctor's, dentist's, optician's, school and many other places where parents visit, the child may be taken to help interpret. Interpretation may be needed in more informal places: on the street, when a parent is watching the television or listening to the radio, reading a local newspaper or working on the computer.

Pressure is placed on children in language brokering: linguistic, emotional, social and attitudinal pressure. First, children may find an exact translation difficult to achieve as their language is still developing. Second, children may be hearing information (e.g. medical troubles, financial problems, arguments and conflicts) that is the preserve of adults rather than children. Third, children may be expected to be adult-like when interpreting and child-like at all other times; to mix with adults when interpreting and 'be seen and not heard' with adults on other occasions. Fourth, seeing their parents in an inferior position may lead to children despising their minority language. Children may quickly realize when language brokering that the language of power, prestige and purse is the majority language. Negative attitudes to the minority language may result. Fifth, bilinguals are not necessarily good interpreters. Interpretation assumes an identical vocabulary in both languages. Since bilinguals tend to use their two languages in different places with different people, an identical lexicon is often not present. Also, proficiency in two or more languages is not enough. Some reflection on language (in Chapter 7 discussed as metalinguistic awareness), an awareness of the linguistic nature of the message, reflecting on the structural features of languages is also required (Malakoff, 1992).

Language brokering also has many **positive outcomes**. **First**, it can bring parental praise, reward and status within the family for playing a valuable role. The research of Malakoff (1992) found that this ability is widely distributed among bilingual children who are quite expert as early as the third or fourth grade. Such ability may gain both esteem from others and raise self-esteem. **Second**, the child learns adult information quickly and learns to act with some authority and trust. Early maturity has its own rewards in the teenage peer group. **Third**, Kaur and Mills (1993) found that children accustomed to acting as interpreters learned to take the initiative. For example, a child may give the answer to a question rather than relaying the question to the parent. This puts children in a position of some power, even of language censorship.

Fourth, when parents become dependent on their children for language brokering, it may make the family more close, trusting and integrated. Such language brokering is a lifeline for the many parents who have to hand over much power to their children. Yet it may make parents aware of their own language inadequacies, resulting in feelings of frustration and resentment, particularly in language minority cultures where children are expected to stay in a subordinate position for a long time.

Fifth, the cognitive outcomes for child language brokers may be valuable. Children who are regular interpreters for their parents may realize early on the problems and possibilities of translation of words, figures of speech and ideas. For example, such children may learn early on that one language never fully parallels another, and that it is hard to translate exactly the inner meaning of words and metaphors. This may lead such children to be more introspective about their languages. This is termed metalinguistic awareness and is considered in Chapter 7. Thus, interpretation may both require and stimulate metalinguistic awareness (Tse, 1996a).

Sixth, another advantage for the child language broker is in character formation, for example, possibly gaining more empathy. The children are negotiating between two different social and cultural worlds, trying to understand both, and provide bridges between these two worlds. Their understanding of different cultures may be deepened by the responsibility. This handling of dialogue may lead to increased maturity, astuteness, independence and higher self-esteem. Being expected to carry an adult role early on may lead to a positive self-concept, and feeling responsible like an adult.

CONCLUSION

This chapter has discussed two routes to bilingualism: simultaneous and sequential. The former route is when two languages are acquired consecutively from birth. The latter route, sequential bilingualism, may be through formal educational avenues or informal paths (e.g. street, neighborhood and nursery schools). Language learning in classes and courses, as well as acquisition in informal domains (e.g. playing on the street, at work) allow individuals of all ages to become bilingual and multilingual. One-parent families can also be as successful as other nuclear and extended family situations. However, language loss can occur when political contexts are particularly unfavorable to minority language maintenance.

Codeswitching is a frequent behavior among bilinguals with a variety of valuable purposes and benefits. Interpreting is a similarly frequent expectation of bilinguals — including young children in immigrant families.

Another route to bilingualism is via formal second language learning in school, or using a second language in school as the medium of learning. Bilingualism can also be reached by avenues outside of school. The vehicles of voluntary classes and adult courses provide the opportunity for a second or foreign language to be learnt and developed. The street and screen can also be vehicles to childhood bilingualism. Having introduced simultaneous and sequential bilingualism, the next chapter takes a global look at some of the key issues and current ideas in second language acquisition.

KEY POINTS IN THE CHAPTER

- There is a difference between simultaneous (acquire two language together) and sequential (acquire one language later than the other) childhood bilingualism.
- There is a distinction between informal language acquisition and formal language learning.
- Early studies of bilingual children revealed that if each parent speaks a different language to the child, relatively balanced bilingualism occurs although the balance shifts throughout an individual's language history.
- The 'one person, one language' parental approach in a family is a well documented and successful route to bilingualism. Many other routes may be equally successful.
- Voluntary language learning classes, community classes, Saturday schools, classes in the mosque, synagogue, temple or church and Ulpan adult language learning schemes are routes to sequential bilingualism and minority language maintenance in individuals.
- While there are no critical periods of language learning, there are advantageous periods. Early childhood and school days are two advantageous periods. But many successful adult second language learners show that increasing age is not a disadvantage. Older learners will show a similar development sequence in learning a second language.
- Codeswitching is typical in bilinguals having many valuable purposes in relationships and relaying messages, as well as expressing roles, norms and values.
- Codeswitching varies according to who is in the conversation, what is the topic, and in what kind of context the conversation occurs.
- Very young children easily switch languages and differentiate their two languages, but there is much individual variation due to different socialization practices and life experiences.
- Children may act as language brokers for parents when their proficiency in the majority language is ahead of their parents. This has many advantages and disadvantages for the child.
- Bilingualism does not hinder the acquisition of a third language and typically bilingualism favors the acquisition of a further language.

SUGGESTED FURTHER READING

BAKER, C., 2000, *A Parents' and Teachers' Guide to Bilingualism* (2nd edition). Clevedon: Multilingual Matters.

DE HOUWER, A., 1995, Bilingual language acquisition. In P. FLETCHER and B. MACWHINNEY (eds), *The Handbook of Child Language*. Oxford: Blackwell.

NICOLADIS, E. and GENESEE, F., 1997, Language development in preschool bilingual children. *Journal of Speech-Language Pathology and Audiology* 21, 4, 258–270.

ROMAINE, S., 1995, *Bilingualism* (2nd edition). Oxford: Basil Blackwell.

STUDY ACTIVITIES

(1) Create a case study of one person's bilingual development. This may be yourself or someone you know. By interviewing that person, or self-reflection, make a cassette tape or a video or a written case study of the factors which seem personally important to that person in their bilingual development. This may be developed as a project. A project may include the following stages. First, look in the library for case studies of bilinguals. Books by Arnberg (1987), Döpke (1992), Fantini (1985), Harding and Riley (1987), Lanza (1997), Lyon (1996) and Saunders (1988) provide examples. Second, prepare an interview guide. Write down (as an aide memoire) the topics and kinds of questions you would like to ask in an interview. Third, try to use a tape recorder, or write down when the respondent is talking to record the interview. If you make a tape, transcribe the key quotes or all of the interview. Fourth, write out a case study of the bilingual development of that person. Are there particular stages or periods in the development? Or was the development more smooth with gradual changes?

(2) Interview a mother or father who is learning a second language at the same time as their child. Ask about the progress each is making. What differences are there? Ask about why there are qualitative and quantitative differences in progress? What attitudes and motivations do the language learners have? If there are differences of attitude, try to work out an explanation.

(3) By observation or tape-recording, gather samples of codeswitching. Try to find illustrations of different purposes of codeswitching. Ask the people in your sample (after completing the observation/recording) how conscious they are of codeswitching. What are their explanations for codeswitching? What particular purposes for codeswitching were most found in your samples? How regular was codeswitching in the conversation? What was the personal history of those you observed or recorded that helps explain such codeswitching?

(4) Examine between three and six of the 120 'questions about bilingualism most asked by parents' in Baker (2000a). Discuss in a group whether the advice given in the answers (a) matches the group's experience and (b) seems relevant. Compose a poster presentation giving the group's advice to any one question selected from that book.

CHAPTER 6
Second Language Acquisition and Learning

Introduction

Rationales for Second Language
Acquisition

Contexts and Situations in
Language Learning

Language Inputs

The Individual Learner

Learner Processes

Second Language Outcomes

Conclusions

Second Language Acquisition and Learning

INTRODUCTION

This chapter examines the foundations of second language acquisition and learning. The topic is a broad one, and is one important segment of the question 'How do you become bilingual?' This chapter synthesizes a variety of theories of a psychological, socio-psychological and pedagogic nature that highlight the major features of becoming bilingual via second language learning. Six components are considered: rationales for second language learning, contexts that affect such learning, learner inputs and development, individual learner differences, learning processes and outcomes from second language learning.

RATIONALES FOR SECOND LANGUAGE ACQUISITION

The various overlapping purposes why children or adults acquire a second or third language can be clustered under three headings: **ideological, international and individual.**

Ideological Reasons

For language minority children, the aim of second language instruction may be **assimilationist** and subtractive. For example, the teaching of English as a second language in the United States and in England often aims at rapidly integrating minority language groups into mainstream society. Assimilationist ideology (see Chapter 18) tends to work for the dominance of the second language, even the repression of the home, minority language. In contrast, when children learn a minority language as their second language, maintenance and **preservation** of that minority language may be the societal aim. For example, when English speaking children are taught in school language lessons to speak Irish in Ireland or Maori in New Zealand, the aim is to preserve and strengthen the indigenous minority language. Such maintenance may not only exist in indigenous language 'territory'. Where first language English children in the US learn to speak Spanish as a second language (e.g. in dual language schools), there may be an attempt to preserve the language community within a particular area. This provides an additive situation: a second language is added at no cost to the first language.

A different societal reason for second language acquisition other than assimilationist or preservationist is to obtain increased **harmony** between language groups through bilingualism. In Canada, French speaking children learning English, and English speaking children learning French may help parents and politicians produce a more dual language, integrated Canadian society. For example, the promotional video by the Canadian Official Languages Board entitled '*One Country Two Languages*' enthusiastically conveys the idea that integration into Canadian society is best achieved through widespread bilingualism and biculturalism.

The assimilationist, preservationist and harmony viewpoints all argue for the importance of a second language for careers, access to further and higher education, access to information and communications technology and for travel. However, it is important to distinguish whether the second language is to replace the first language or to be added to that first language. Rather than multiplying experience, second language teaching may be for divisive reasons, impoverishing the language minority child.

While teachers may be relatively powerless to change the basic societal aims and reasons in second language teaching, understanding the role they play in such teaching is important. Second language teaching does not exist in a political vacuum. Nor is language teaching a neutral, value-free activity. Therefore, second language teachers need to be aware of their goals at a conscious level, and, for example, make the second language experience more additive than subtractive.

International Reasons

Apart from the political and social reasons for second language acquisition and learning, there are international reasons given by second language educationalists for second language learning. Second and third language learning is often encouraged for **economic and trade** reasons (e.g. in Singapore, Basque Country, Finland). Given notions such as common markets, open access to trade, the free market economy, the importance of international trade to developing nations, then facility with languages is seen as opening doors to economic activity. Selling to the Japanese, for example, may be almost impossible through English or German. Speaking Japanese and having a sympathetic understanding of Japanese culture, manners, values and thinking may be the essential foundation for economic activity (see Chapter 18).

There is a growing realization that speaking foreign languages is important in increasingly competitive international **trade**. The California State Department of Education's (1989) 'Foreign Language Framework' suggested that, 'On a pragmatic level, schools in California as well as in other states need to develop more individuals with strong skills in a second language as a matter of long-range economic self-interest' (p. 4). The Report noted that two-thirds of translating jobs in the US Department of State are filled by foreign-born individuals because there are so few US students and adults who are proficient in the second languages required for such posts.

Second and third language learning is also encouraged for its value in **travel** across continents. For many mainland Europeans, for example, to speak two, three or four languages is not uncommon. Such language facility enables vacations to be spent in neighboring European countries or in North, Central or South America. In the attempted unification of Europe, traveling across frontiers is becoming more common, encouraging a person to acquire a repertoire of languages.

Third, languages provide access to **information and hence power**. Whether the information is in technical journals, on large computer databases, on the World Wide Web, on satellite television or in international e-mail lists, a repertoire of languages gives wider access to social, cultural, political, economic and educational information. For the business person and the bureaucrat, for the scholar and the sports person, access to multilingual international information opens doors to new knowledge, new skills and new understanding.

Individual Reasons

There are four reasons frequently given why the individual child or adult should acquire or learn a second or third language. One reason is for **cultural awareness**. To break down national, ethnic and language stereotypes, one motive in second language learning has become intercultural sensitivity and awareness. The Californian State Department Education's (1989) *Foreign Language Framework* regards one second-language-learning aim as being the civic and cultural benefits of foreign language teaching. Second language learning is important because 'the power language has to foster improved understanding between peoples of various cultural backgrounds. Culture is embedded in language' (p. 5). Increasing cultural sensitivity is seen as important as the world becomes more international, more of a global village, with more sharing of experience.

Cultural awareness in the classroom may be achieved at one level by discussing ethnic variations in eating and drinking, rituals of birth, death and marriage, comparing the greetings of New Zealand Maori, Arabs and Jews, or comparing shopping rituals in Malaysian markets, San Francisco superstores or all-purpose village stores in Venezuela (but see Chapter 19 for a critique of this approach). Such activity widens human understanding and attempts to encourage sensitivity towards other cultures and creeds. While cultural awareness may be conveyed in the first language, the inseparability of culture and language means that such awareness may best be achieved through simultaneous language learning.

The second 'individual' reason for second language learning has traditionally been for **cognitive development**. The learning of foreign languages has been for general educational and academic value. Just as history and geography, physics and chemistry, mathematics and music have traditionally been taught to increase intellectual fitness and stamina, so modern language learning has been defended as a way of sharpening the mind and developing the intellect. Given the memorization, analysis (e.g. of grammar and sentence structure) and the need to negotiate in communication, language learning has been regarded as a valuable academic activity in itself.

The third reason for an individual to acquire a language is for social, emotional and moral development, self-awareness, self-confidence, and social and ethical values (van Ek, 1986). Such **affective** goals include the possibility of incipient bilinguals being able to create a larger number and more effective relationships with target language speakers. Bilinguals can potentially build social bridges with those who speak the second language. Self-confidence and enhanced self-esteem may result from being able to operate socially or vocationally with those who speak the second or third language. The addition of a second language skill can boost an individual's self-confidence as a learner, a liaisor and a linguist.

The fourth 'individual' reason for acquiring a language is for **careers and employment**. For language minority and language majority children, being able to speak a second or third or fourth language may mean avoiding unemployment, opening up possibilities of a wider variety of careers or gaining promotion in a career (see Chapter 20). Potential individual careers include becoming translators and interpreters, buying and selling goods and services, exchanging information with local, regional, national and international organizations, migrating across national frontiers to find work, gaining promotion in neighboring countries, becoming part of an international team or company, as well as working from home or from the local village and using multilingual telecommunications to spread a product.

Such reasons for language learning and acquisition do not exist in a vacuum. There are micro and macro contexts that affect who is successful or not. This leads to considering the distinction between contexts where acquisition occurs informally as opposed to formal learning, and then to theories of second language acquisition that emphasize sociocultural and sociopolitical contexts. Becoming bilingual occurs partly due to helpful and harmful situations and environments surrounding the individual.

CONTEXTS AND SITUATIONS IN LANGUAGE LEARNING

Formal and Informal Contexts

Initially, it is helpful to distinguish between formal language learning contexts (e.g. school) and informal language acquisition contexts (e.g. street) (Krashen, 1981). Acquisition in informal contexts may be a more subconscious process where communication is a means and not a focus nor an end in itself. Learning in formal contexts occurs where the overt properties of a language are taught (e.g. grammar and vocabulary). Learning is thus a more conscious process that enables a learner to 'know about' the second language. With second language learning, the analysis and correction of errors is often formally and explicitly addressed.

Examples of formal contexts typically include language classrooms, language laboratories, computer-assisted language learning and audio visual methods. An informal language learning context or experience is when language learning is more incidental, accidental or uncontrived. For example, a person watches a Spanish film not primarily to widen vocabulary, but for the entertainment value of that film. In this example, a person's Spanish vocabulary may be extended, but it is an unintended outcome. Or, talking to a friend or relative in a second language may not intentionally be to practice the second language but to foster friendly relationships. While the person is practicing their second language skills this is an incidental outcome, not the prime reason for such conversation. There are also examples when the formal and informal experience merge. In the classroom there will be episodes where the teacher is having a friendly chat or giving simple instructions that are not primarily for language learning but have that effect.

Acquisition and learning are not defined by 'where' a second language occurs. Formal learning can occur in the street when a person asks questions about correct grammar, mistakes and difficulties. Acquisition can occur in the classroom when the focus is on content learning and second language acquisition is seemingly a by-product (see Chapter 10). Also, conscious thinking about language rules is said to occur in second language learning; unconscious feelings about what is correct and appropriate occurs in language acquisition.

When considering what effect different learning environments have on the acquisition or learning of a second language, we need to distinguish macro (e.g. sociopolitical contexts) and micro contexts (e.g. schools and classrooms). At the macro level, second language acquisition and learning occur against a context of politics and power (e.g. assimilation of immigrants), group relationships (e.g. at international, national and regional levels) and sociocultural climates and conflicts (see Chapter 18). At the micro level, styles and strategies of language learning, formal teacher-directed classrooms, flexible individual learning, adult classes (e.g. an Ulpan), acquisition in the street and community, correspondence courses, different forms of bilingual education (e.g. immersion and submersion — see Chapters 10 and 11) affect who learns how much of what language (Spolsky, 1989c).

Additive or Subtractive Bilingualism

Additive and Subtractive bilingualism have become important contextual concepts which help explain the kind of second language learning desired, particularly by politicians (e.g. the Unz 'initiative' in California in 1998 – see Chapter 12). When a second language and culture have been acquired with little or no pressure to replace or reduce the first language, an additive form of bilingualism may occur. When the second language and culture are acquired (e.g. immigrants) with pressure to replace or demote the first language, a subtractive form of bilingualism may occur. This may relate to a less positive self-concept, loss of cultural or ethnic identity, with possible alienation or marginalization.

Lambert's (1974) distinction between additive and subtractive bilingualism has been used in two different ways. First, additive bilingualism is used to refer to positive cognitive outcomes from being bilingual (see Chapter 7). Subtractive bilingualism hence refers to the negative affective and cognitive effects of bilingualism (e.g. where both languages are 'under developed'). Landry *et al.* (1991) suggest this first use is too narrow, with a second use of additive and subtractive bilingualism being more appropriate. This wider use of additive and subtractive bilingualism relates to the enrichment or loss of minority language, culture and ethnolinguistic identity at a **societal** level. In additive bilingualism, language minority members are proficient (or becoming proficient) in both languages, have positive attitudes to the first and second language, with ethnolinguistic vitality in the language community (Landry *et al., 1991).*

The **social and cultural background** of language learning indicates that children may be influenced by the beliefs, values and culture of the community in which they are placed (e.g. Gardner, 1985; Hamers & Blanc, 1982, 1983, 2000; Siguán & Mackey, 1987). For many people living in England, for example, the belief is that the 'universal' English language is all that is required; bilingualism is unnecessary. In contrast, in many language minority communities of Europe, bilingualism and biculturalism reflect the values of the home, neighborhood and wider networks in the language community.

Context Theories

Acculturation

The importance of the context of the language community is considered by Schumann (1978) who proposed an acculturation model of second language acquisition based on the **second language learner adapting to a new culture**. The model starts with the idea that language is one aspect of culture, and the relationship between the language community of the learner and the second language community is important in second language acquisition. The basic premise of the model is 'the degree to which a learner acculturates to the target language group will control the degree to which he acquires the second language' (Schumann, 1978, p. 34). Expressed in group rather than individual terms, these facilitating **social factors** include, for example, the extent to which the second language learner group expects to stay with the target language group for a longer rather than a short period (e.g. immigrants). Schumann's (1978) Acculturation Model (see also its extension in Andersen's (1983) Nativization Model), is one path to bringing in the politics and power of language in its societal contexts. It provides an explanation of why some children with aptitude and ability fail to learn or use a second language.

Accommodation

Such societal contexts are portrayed in Accommodation theory which derives from Giles and colleagues (e.g. Giles & Byrne, 1982). Like Schumann (1978), Giles & Byrne's theory seeks to explain **second language acquisition in a group or intergroup situation**. For Giles and Byrne (1982), the important factor is the perceived social difference between the ingroup (the language learner's social group) and the outgroup (the target language community). The **relationships between the**

ingroup and outgroup are seen as both fluid and constantly negotiated. There is a tendency in Schumann's Acculturation model for social and psychological distances to be seen as static or changing relatively slowly over time. For Giles and Byrne (1982), relationships between ingroup and outgroup are dynamic and constantly changing. One way of portraying Giles and Byrne's (1982) model is to profile a person from a subordinate group who is likely to acquire the language of the dominant group. The learner is likely to show the following characteristics (simplified from Giles & Coupland, 1991):

(1)   Have a relatively weak identification with their own ethnic group. That is, such learners do not see themselves as purely a member of their minority language group separate from the dominant language group. Alternatively, their first language is not important to membership of their ethnic group.
(2)   Do not regard their ethnic group as inferior to the dominant group. A good language learner makes 'quiescent' comparisons between their ethnic group and the dominant group, or is not concerned about a difference of status.
(3)   Perceive their ethnic group as having low vitality compared with the dominant group. Giles and Byrne (1982) talk of a perception of ethnolinguistic vitality which includes (see Chapter 4): (1) the economic, historic, social, political and language status of the ethnic group; (2) size and distribution of an ethnic group, mixed marriages, amount of in-migration and out-migration; and (3) institutional support for the ethnic group (e.g. mass-media, education, religion, industry, services, culture and government).
(4)   See their ethnic group boundaries as 'soft and open' and not 'hard and closed'.
(5)   Hold adequate status within their ethnic group (e.g. in terms of employment, gender, power and religion).

Thus for Giles and Byrne (1982), a person *less* likely to acquire a second language may have: a strong identification with their own group, makes 'insecure' comparisons with the outgroup; regard their own language community as having high vitality, good institutional support, being sizable and stable and of high status; perceive the boundaries between their own and the second language group as separate and rigid, and have inadequate status within their first language group. Further factors are considered in Giles and Coupland (1991).

Criticisms of Context Theories
Glyn Williams (1992) is **critical** in that Giles and Byrne may wrongly assume that language development is gradual and cumulative, of a consensus nature, concerned with order and cohesion with a consequent limited discussion of **power, struggle and conflict**. Of inter-group relationships, Williams (1992, p. 224) critically comments that the argument is merely 'couched in terms of individuals, rationally conditioned to behave in terms of optimization, with the quest for status and the associated positive identity being the motivating force of behavior'. This tends to play down conflict and power, thereby not expressing the anger, discrimination and frustration felt by language minority groups and their members. Tollefson

(1991) similarly criticizes Accommodation Theory for its ahistorical analysis and failure to account for domination and coercion in language shift.

Like the Acculturation Model, Accommodation Theory does not explain the internal mechanisms of how a child acquires a second language. It is essentially a socio-psychological model rather than a cognitive-processing model of second language acquisition. The individual approach is found when psychologists examine topics such as language inputs.

Also, context theories have developed from second language rather than foreign language considerations. Thus, the contexts discussed here often relate less well to foreign language learning.

LANGUAGE INPUTS

Linguistic input concerns the type of second language information received when learning or acquiring a second language. For example, how do teachers or native speakers adjust their language to the level of second language learners to make it comprehensible? What kind of differences are there in the input from natural settings compared with formal classroom settings? What kinds of input from a teacher most accelerates language learning?

Structured Input

In a behaviorist theory of language learning, precise and tight control of input from the teacher is regarded as very important. B.F. Skinner, in his book *Verbal Behavior* (1957), argued that all learning is a process of habit formation in which a stimulus creates a response and is reinforced to become a habit. This school of thought argued that language learning is no different from any other learning, and that good results could be achieved by intensive drills and repetition. Thus a second language has to be presented in small, highly sequenced doses with plenty of practice and reinforcement. Individual bricks (e.g. features of grammar) need to be carefully laid in a precise sequence to build second language skills and habits. Such a behaviorist theory of language learning became embodied in Audiolingualism.

According to **Audiolingualism**, second language learning is possible by the acquisition of a distinct set of speech habits. A habit is the ability to make a sound or say a word or use grammar correctly in an automatic, unconscious fashion. The teacher provides specific, well defined stimuli. The learner responds and is reinforced or corrected. Through repetition and drills it is hoped that the student will be able to use a second language automatically.

In the **Audiolingual approach**, language learning becomes the learning of structures, sounds and words to attempt to achieve native speaker-like pronunciation. Such a structural view sees language as a linguistic system, with the aim being to instill linguistic competence in the student. Because language teaching is based on linguistic structure, lessons should be carefully sequenced and graded. The sequencing is to be determined wholly by linguistic complexity (e.g. moving from simple grammar rules to more complex rules with their exceptions; practicing simple speaking patterns followed by ever increasing width of vocabulary and difficulty in sentence structure).

In the Audiolingual method, the focus is constantly on correct language. To achieve this, there is repetition of vocabulary phrases and sentences, imitative mimicry and memorization of short dialogues. The aim is for the learner to avoid making linguistic mistakes in sentence construction and gain an automatic, accurate control of basic sentence structures. Mastery of basic vocabulary and structures is required, by over-learning if necessary.

Part of the theory of **Audiolingualism** is that the learner's first language interferes with the acquisition of the second language. Such interference occurs because the learner is ensnared by the habits of the first language. Therefore, teachers are encouraged to focus on areas of difficulty posed by negative transfer from the first to the second language (e.g. Lado, 1964). A procedure called Contrastive Analysis was developed to show the areas of difficulty in transfer from first language to second language. Such analysis resulted in a list of features of the second language, different from the first language, which posed potential problems for the teacher.

In the late 1960s and 1970s, the assumptions of the Audiolingual Method were shown to be doubtful. When the Contrastive Analysis hypothesis was researched (e.g. Dulay & Burt, 1973, 1974), grammatical errors were found that could not be explained by negative transfer from the first to the second language. The Chomskyian revolution in linguistics also cast doubts on the behaviorist view of second language learning. Chomsky (1965) suggested that human beings have an inbuilt cognitive readiness for language. Instead of language being a series of surface patterns and habits, Chomsky emphasized the abstract, mentalist and universal nature of rules that underlie an individual's language competence. A child is endowed with a **language-acquisition** device (LAD) that comprises innate knowledge of grammatical principles.

The model for correct language in the **Structural Approach** is provided by the teacher, or via prepared tapes in the language laboratory or more recently through computer-assisted language learning programs. In contrast, Chomsky's mentalist view of language acquisition regards input as merely activating the learner's **internal language acquisition device**. Input from a teacher sets the wheels in motion rather than creating the wheels of language. While such structural viewpoints have tended to be criticized by language learning researchers and advisors, such a formal, teacher orchestrated style is to be found as a major component in many teachers' classroom repertoire as part of a number of eclectic approaches. For many language teachers, learning a language is not simply putting bricks in place nor pressing the button to start the machine. Efficient and effective second language learning does not occur purely by the building of stimulus–response links. Nor does second language learning occur by merely exposing a child or adult to the second language. Providing input which suits the stage of development of the second language learner becomes important.

Discourse analysis has shown that a second language learner and a native speaker work together to produce purposeful and efficient communication. That is, one needs to understand the interaction, particularly the negotiation of meaning to understand how input and output interact. There are strategies and tactics to make conversation appropriate and meaningful. For example, finding topics of conversation that can be mutually understood, speaking at a slow pace, repeating important phrases, stressing the key words in a sentence will help the input factor in second language acquisition. A learner will similarly give signals by verbal and non-verbal communication to indicate understanding, lack of understanding or to indicate the need to switch topics or level of language.

Meaningful Input

In the 1970s, there developed a major alternative approach to language teaching. Instead of regarding language as a linguistic system to be conveyed to the student, an alternative viewpoint was that language is essentially about conveying meaning. The focus since the 1970s has tended to shift partly away from teaching the formal nature of a language to socially appropriate forms of communication. For example, the sociolinguist Hymes (1972a) argued that language was essentially about communication. We use a language for a specific purpose. Language is a means rather than a structural end. Effective language does not mean grammatical accuracy nor articulate fluency, but the **competence to communicate** meaning effectively.

Criticisms of the audiolingual method led to a current emphasis on a more **communicative approach** in second language learning.

- Whereas in audiolingualism the teacher was regarded as crucial, the recent focus has changed to a selection and organization of second language input partly by the learner.
- A reconceptualization of language errors has occurred. Language errors and 'interference' or transfer are now regarded as a natural part of the learning process. Children spontaneously produce unique utterances and do not just imitate adult language as behaviorists would claim. For example, a child who says 'all finish food' (I've completely finished my food) reflects the use of some underlying implicit rules. The early incorrect production of sentences does not prevent a child from going on to produce correct, well formed sentences later. Corder (1967) suggested that second language learners need to discover their own errors rather than to be continuously corrected by the teacher. Therefore, the problem of interference becomes a problem of ignorance. The avoidance of interference between languages cannot be taught in the classroom; rather the avoidance of interference comes via observation of one's own language. Language development can thus be seen as the process of implicit rule formation rather than explicit habit formation.

Interdependence

In becoming functionally bilingual in the classroom and in the community, Cummins' (1984a) **interdependence** theory suggests that second language acquisition is influenced considerably by the extent to which the first language has developed. When a first language has developed sufficiently well to cope with decontextualized classroom learning (see Chapter 8), a second language may be relatively easily acquired. When the first language is less well developed, or where there is attempted replacement of the first language by the second language (e.g. in the classroom), the development of the second language may be relatively impeded.

Language Input in the Classroom

The **input** of language learning classrooms varies according to the type of second language learning occurring. While it is dangerous to over-generalize, the foreign language and the second language classroom may sometimes focus more on the form of the language (e.g. grammar) rather than on meaning. In contrast, in genuinely bilingual classrooms, where the second language may be a medium of teaching in the curriculum, the focus may be more on meaning than on form. While the aim in both situations is to ensure the comprehensible input of the second language, input is different from intake. The learner receives input of the second language from 'outside'. Intake refers to the inner assimilation of that second language. Input does not always result in intake; only when there is intake does second language acquisition occur.

In terms of what might comprise optimal **input in the classroom situation**, Wong Fillmore (1982) compared second language acquisition in United States kindergarten classrooms. She found that effective input differed according to the language composition of different classrooms. In classrooms where there were large numbers of second language learners, effective input comprised a teacher-directed rather than an open, informal classroom organization. In contrast, where the classes comprised second language learners *and* native speaking children, open classroom organization rather than teacher direction seemed to constitute the optimal learning environment. This may be explained as follows:

(1) In classes where there were large numbers of second language learners, the teacher was most effective by herself controlling the input. In such classes where there was more open organization, students tended to talk to each other in their **first** language, thus not obtaining practice in the second language.

(2) In classes of mixed second language learners and native speaking children, the optimal environment was a more open organization where second language learners received input from the teacher and from native speaking children. In such mixed classes, where the teacher tended to control the input, this tended to be at the level of **native** speakers and did not necessarily provide comprehensible input for second language learners.

Wong Fillmore (1982) thus shows the importance in second language input of the interaction between teaching style and the peer composition of different classes.

Comprehensible Language Input

To explain how language acquisition occurs, Krashen proposes that when learners are exposed to grammatical features a little beyond their current level, those features are 'acquired'. Krashen (1981, 1982, 1985) emphasizes that 'acquisition' is the result of comprehensible language input and not of language production. Input is made comprehensible because of the help provided by the context. If the language student receives understandable input, language structures will be, according to Krashen, naturally acquired. For Krashen, the ability to communicate in a second language 'emerges' rather than is directly put in place by teaching. Second language is said to be caused by the process of understanding second language input.

Krashen and Terrell (1983) argue that the goal of language teaching must be to supply understandable input in order for the child or adult to acquire language easily. A good teacher therefore is someone who continuously delivers at a level understandable by the second language speaker but also just very slightly beyond a learner's current competence (called moving from stage I to I+1). Just as father and mother talk (motherese) help the young child to acquire the first language by a simplified and comprehensible language (and non-verbal language), so an effective teacher is said to facilitate second language learning by ensuring a close match between the level of delivery and the level that is understandable, but at the same time, always pushing the language competence frontiers forward. Also, teaching must prepare the learner for real life communication situations. The classroom needs to provide conversational confidence so that, when in the outside world, the student can both linguistically cope and continue language learning.

However, occasionally a person learns a language without interpersonal communication (e.g. from a book). Also, meaningful input must not become over-simplification, over-elaboration or redundant repetition. Intake is therefore more important than intended input.

THE INDIVIDUAL LEARNER

Given the same contexts and same inputs, students still gain different levels of proficiency in the second language. Individual differences cannot be solely ascribed to differences of social, economic or political environment and input from class-room teaching methodologies. Individual differences also relate to personal characteristics. For example, the age at which somebody learns a second language, their aptitude for learning languages, cognitive style, motivation, attitude, previous knowledge, learning style, learning strategies and personality variables such as anxiety have variously been thought to influence second language acquisition.

It is possible to specify a *list* of factors that appear to be related to second language acquisition. Anxiety, self-esteem and self-concept, competitiveness in the classroom, anxiety that may be facilitative or interruptive, field independence as a cognitive style and social skills have each and all been related by research to second language acquisition. On the other hand, the separate and interacting size of influence of each of these ingredients in the overall recipe is not clear.

Ability and Aptitude

Second language learning in the classroom has often been connected to the **general ability** of a child ('intelligence') and to a specific language ability usually termed language aptitude. While the idea of a general academic ability or 'intelligence' has been criticized (see Baker, 1988), authors such as Oller and Perkins (1978) have argued that the general factor of intelligence is allied to a general factor of language ability. At its simplest, this means that a more 'intelligent' person is likely to learn a second language more easily. An overview would suggest that general academic ability can be substantially related to the acquisition of second language in a **formal** classroom setting. General ability may positively correlate with test scores on the formal aspects of language learning, (e.g. grammar, translation, parsing verbs).

However, as Cummins (1984b) has discussed, basic everyday language skills (see Chapter 8) may not be so related to general academic ability. That is, the skills required for 'street' conversation may be less dependent on general academic ability than the language required to operate in an academic environment — see Chapter 8. Genesee (1976) found that IQ was related to second language French reading, grammar and vocabulary but was relatively unconnected to oral skills. Naturalistic second language acquisition may be less connected to IQ than formal classroom acquisition. Also, as Ellis (1985) notes, general academic ability may affect the rate and success of classroom second language acquisition. There is 'no evidence that intelligence affects the route of acquisition' (p. 111).

In a similar way, tests of **language aptitude** have been connected with second language learning (Skehan, 1998). This connection may be largely due to the similarity of aptitude test and language proficiency test items. Aptitude tests have been related to second language learning in the classroom rather than second language proficiency in naturalistic, communicative contexts. Krashen (1981), for example, argues that aptitude relates to formal language learning but not to the subconscious internal acquisition of language that occurs naturally and spontaneously. Aptitude tests measure the ability of children to discriminate sounds in a language, to connect sounds with written symbols and the rote memorization of words of an artificial language. Such items tend to relate to formal, traditional approaches to language teaching. The items tend to relate less to the modern communicative approach in language teaching.

The concept of **aptitude** tends to be a popular explanation for failing to acquire a second language. An adult finding difficulty in learning a specific second language may place the blame on a lack of aptitude for language learning in general. This tends to indicate a belief that there is something in an individual's nature that cannot be nurtured. However, the concept of aptitude has recently come under attack. It is unclear how aptitude differs from general academic ability. If there is a difference between aptitude and general ability, it is unclear as to its constituent features. If we are unsure of its definition and structure, it is difficult to know precisely what is being tested in modern language aptitude tests.

While aptitude may affect the speed of second language acquisition in the formal classroom environment, it would not seem to affect the sequence or order of second language acquisition. There is also no evidence to show that aptitude affects the route which people take in second language acquisition.

Attitudes and Motivation

Another popular explanation of failure to learn a second language (or of success in learning) is attitudes and motivation (Baker, 1992). As Dörnyei (1998, p. 117) suggests:

> 'Motivation provides the primary impetus to initiate learning in the L2 and later the driving force to sustain the long and often tedious learning process … Without sufficient motivation, even individuals with the most remarkable abilities cannot accomplish long-term goals, and neither are appropriate curricula and good teaching enough on their own to ensure student achievement.'

What are the motives for learning a second language? Are the motives economic, cultural, social, vocational, integrative or for self-esteem and self-actualization? Reasons for learning a second (minority or majority) language tend to fall into two major groups:

Group 1: A wish to identify with or join another language group
Learners sometimes want to affiliate with a different language community. Such learners wish to join in and identify with the minority or majority language's cultural activities, and consequently find their roots or form friendships. This is termed **integrative motivation**.

Group 2: Learning a language for useful purposes
The second reason is utilitarian in nature. Learners may acquire a second language to find a job and earn money, further career prospects, pass exams, help fulfill the demands of their job, or assist their children in bilingual schooling. This is termed **instrumental motivation**.

Considerable research on this area has been conducted by Gardner and associates (see Gardner, 1985). Gardner argues that integrative and instrumental attitudes are independent of 'intelligence' and aptitude. Integrative motivation may be particularly strong in an additive bilingual environment.

Much of the research in this area, but certainly not all, links **integrative motivation** rather than **instrumental motivation** with the greater likelihood of achieving proficiency in the second language. Gardner and Lambert (1972) originally considered that integrative motivation was more powerful in language learning than instrumental motivation. The reason was that integrative motivation concerns personal relationships that may be long lasting. On the other hand, instrumental motivation may be purely self-oriented and short term. When employment has been obtained or financial gain has accrued, instrumental motivation may wane. An integrative motive was thought to be a more sustained motive than an instrumental motive due to the relative endurance of personal relationships.

Research has subsequently suggested that there may be occasions when the **instrumental motive** is stronger than the integrative motive in learning a language.

Lukmani (1972) found that Bombay female school students gave instrumental rather than integrative reasons for learning English. In the research by Yatim (1988), the language motivations of student teachers in Malaysia appeared to combine instrumental and integrative motives into an integrated entity. A person's motives may be a subtle mix of instrumental and integrative motives, without clear discrimination between the two. Such research relates motivation not only to the desire to learn a language but also to predicting language retention and language loss in individuals over time.

Another important strand in this research examines instrumental and integrative motivation within the **classroom**. One study is by Gliksman (1976, 1981). He classified 14–16-year-olds by their level of integrative motivation. Gliksman (1976) also systematically observed the number of times the students:

(1)   volunteered information by raising a hand;
(2)   were asked by teachers without volunteering;
(3)   answered correctly or incorrectly;
(4)   asked questions;
(5)   received positive, negative or no feedback from the teacher.

Gliksman (1976, 1981) found that students with a higher integrative motivation volunteered information more frequently, gave correct answers and received more positive feedback from the teacher than did less integratively motivated students. The two groups did not differ significantly on the number of questions they asked in class. Integratively motivated students were rated as more interested in their lessons. Gliksman found that such differences were consistent across a whole term and were not sporadic nor temporary.

An explanation lies in the functions that a second language plays in a particular society. Factors such as employment and career development can be stronger than integrative motivation. The social context will be one determinant of which kind of motivation is more powerful, and this does not preclude both motivations being equally and strongly operative in a particular context. It is clear that motivation is an important factor in second language acquisition, affecting the speed and final proficiency of the second language. It is unlikely to affect the sequence or order of acquisition.

Recently, a shift in thinking about language and motivation has occurred. Motivation is increasingly related to cognitive constructs, thoughts, values and beliefs (e.g. language learners' constructions of self-confidence, self-efficacy in a language task, appraisal of the language classroom, and their evaluation of the teacher, other learners in a group, and language learning resources). Such a view also examines motivation specific to particular tasks. Thus Williams and Burden (1997) provide a list of intrinsic (internal) and extrinsic (external) motivation factors that includes task-specific contexts (interest in a task, perceived value of the task, setting appropriate goals, and feelings of competence).

While there has been a recent movement to classroom-specific motives, it is at the level of understanding rather than action. Practitioners are still left with the question: 'How can I motivate learners?' What interventions and strategies are possible to motivate language learners? From a small number of research studies, Dörnyei (1998) offers the following motivational advice to teachers:

(1) Set a personal example with your own language behavior.
(2) Create a pleasant, relaxed atmosphere in the classroom, reduce anxiety.
(3) Present language tasks thoughtfully and carefully.
(4) Develop a friendly relationship with learners.
(5) Increase the second language self-confidence of the learner.
(6) Make language classes lively and interesting.
(7) Promote learner autonomy.
(8) Personalize the learning process.
(9) Increase each learner's goal-orientation.
(10) Familiarize learners with the culture attached to the language being learnt.

This is elaborated in the accompanying textboxes.

Dörnyei (1994) provides a list of overlapping and interacting strategies for teachers to use to motivate their students (see also Dörnyei & Scott, 1997; Dörnyei & Csizer, 1998).

Language
(1) Include a sociocultural component in the syllabus (e.g. television programs, inviting native speakers).
(2) Develop learners' cross-cultural awareness systematically, focusing on cross-cultural similarities rather than differences.
(3) Promote student contact with second language speakers (e.g. exchange programs, pen pals, trips).
(4) Develop learners' instrumental motivation by highlighting the usefulness of second language study

Learner
(1) Develop students' self-confidence in use of the language (e.g. realizable short-term goals, praise and encouragement, a regular experience of success, using confidence building tasks).
(2) Promote students' self-efficacy with regard to achieving learning goals (e.g. teaching useful communication strategies, developing realistic expectations).
(3) Promote favorable self-perceptions of competence in the second language (e.g. highlighting what students can do rather than what they cannot do, students not worrying about making mistakes).
(4) Decrease student anxiety in learning a second language.
(5) Promote motivation-enhancing attributions (e.g. students recognize the link between effort and outcome, attribute past failures to factors that can be changed).
(6) Encourage students to set attainable sub-goals for themselves (e.g. by a personal learning plan).

Situational
(1) Make the syllabus of the course relevant (e.g. based on a student 'needs analysis').
(2) Increase the attractiveness of course content (e.g. use of more authentic materials, audio-visual aids, multimedia technology).
(3) Discuss the choice of teaching materials with students (e.g. type of textbooks, computer-assisted language learning programs).
(4) Arouse and sustain curiosity and attention (e.g. introduce the unexpected and novel; break-up tedious or repetitious routines).
(5) Increase students' interest and involvement in language learning tasks (e.g. selecting varied and challenging activities, including students' interests, problem-solving, engaging students' emotions, personalizing tasks, using pair work and group activities).
(6) Match the difficulty of the students' language learning tasks with students' abilities.
(7) Increase student expectancy of task fulfillment (e.g. by creating realistic students' expectations, explanations of content and process, giving ongoing guidance about how to succeed, and making the criteria of success clear and transparent).
(8) Facilitate student satisfaction (e.g. allowing students to complete tasks that they can display or perform, celebrating student success).

Teachers
(1) Try to be empathic (sensitive to students' needs), congruent (behave in honest and true-to-self manner) and accepting of students' strengths and weaknesses.
(2) Adopt the role of a facilitator rather than that of an authority figure.
(3) Promote learner autonomy by allowing students real choices in learning, minimize external pressure, with students sharing tasks and responsibility for their own learning, using peer-teaching and project work.
(4) Act as a role model, sharing personal interests and perspectives, transmit personal positive values about second language, sharing personal commitment to the second language.
(5) Introduce language learning tasks to stimulate intrinsic motivation and help internalize *extrinsic* motivation, showing the purpose (and its integration into a whole) of each language learning task.
(6) Use motivating feedback, give feedback that is informative, and not over-react to errors.

Learning Group
(1) Establish goals with which the group agree and feel they own so as to establish a clear sense of direction.
(2) From the beginning, promote the internalization of classroom norms of behavior.
(3) Maintain classroom norms of acceptable behavior in a consistent manner, not letting violations going unnoticed, and maintaining unvarying professional standards of personal behavior.
(4) Minimize any detrimental effects of assessment on intrinsic motivation by focusing on improvement and progress, avoiding comparison of one student with another, making student assessment private rather than public, not encouraging a focus on competition in achievement outcomes, with personal interviews to consider the individual assessment of language proficiency.
(5) Promote the development of group cohesion and enhance inter-member relations by promoting friendships and effective working relationships, organizing outings and extra-curricular activities.
(6) Use cooperative learning techniques by plenty of groupwork where the evaluation of success is appropriate to the group rather than a focus on individual success.

Other Psychological Factors
There are other **individual psychological factors** that are important in second language learning. These include: possible language confusion when using the second language (language shock), the feeling of stress, anxiety or disorientation because of the differences between the learner's culture and the target language culture (culture shock), and the degree of inhibition or self-consciousness adolescent learners in particular may have in language learning (Schumann, 1978). Such factors provide dimensions that may determine the amount of contact a language learner will have with the target language. The amount of contact is defined both by social, external factors and by individual factors. When social and/or psychological distances are large, the learner may fail to progress very far in learning a second language. When the social and psychological factors are positive, second language acquisition may occur relatively painlessly. When psychological and social distances are great, then, at an individual and societal level, pidginization (the development of a simplified form of a language) may occur.

Affective Filter
An Affective Filter was proposed by Dulay and Burt (1977) with the idea that there is a filter that determines how much a person learns in a formal or informal language setting. The filter comprises affective factors such as attitudes to language, motivation, self-confidence and anxiety. Thus learners with favorable attitudes and self-confidence may have 'a low filter' with consequent efficient second language

learning. Those with unfavorable attitudes and/or high anxiety have 'high filters' and so the input of second language learning may be blocked or impeded. The affective filter influences the rate of development in second language learning and the level of success in becoming bilingual.

Krashen and Terrell (1983) suggest that teachers must ensure that learners do not become anxious or defensive in language learning. This relates to the Affective Filter hypothesis. The confidence of a language learner must be encouraged in a language acquisition process. When a learner is relaxed, confident and not anxious, then the input of the classroom situation will be more efficient and effective. If teachers insist on children conversing before they feel comfortable in doing so, or a teacher constantly corrects errors and makes negative remarks, the learner may feel inhibited in learning.

Learning Strategies and Learning Styles
When students learn a second language, there are various strategies that are favored by some students and not others (Chamot, 1999). The various strategies used by different students help explain differences in proficiency. Some students prefer much interaction with classmates. Other students favor learning from an audio tape, CD, DVD or video, independent of other students. Some people use plenty of gestures to aid communication in a second language and are happy to take risks. Other people only use phrases they know are correct with little adventure.

Early researchers tended to make lists of strategies that were the attributes of 'good language learners'. Rubin (1975) and Naiman *et al.* (1975) suggested that good second language learners are willing guessers, have a strong drive to communicate, are less anxious in trying out their second language, willing to make mistakes, look for patterns and analyze language, seek out chances to practice, and observe their own performance as well as the language of others. For O'Malley and Chamot (1990), learning strategies can be metacognitive (selective attention, planning, monitoring, evaluation), cognitive (rehearsal, organization, inferencing, summarizing, deducing, imagery, transfer, elaboration) and social/affective (cooperation, questioning for clarification and self-talk).

Research has shown the importance of using such learning strategies and that successful language learners often use strategies in an orchestrated fashion (e.g. Oxford, 1990, 1993, 1994). Successful language learners often select strategies that work well together. For example, translating, analyzing, planning and organizing strategies may be used in an integrated way. Particular strategies are used with particular tasks. For example, writing in a second language benefits from strategies of planning, self-monitoring, guessing and finding alternatives. Speaking in a second language is helped by risk-taking, summarizing and self-evaluation.

Factors considered to influence the choice of strategies used among students learning a second language include: motivation, gender, cultural background (e.g. preferred use of rote memory), attitudes, type of task, age, learning style, and tolerance of ambiguity (Chamot, 1999).

A consideration of learner strategies indicates the importance of understanding the social and affective aspects of learning along with the more cognitive aspects. Teachers thus need to use affective and social strategies, as well as intellectually related strategies, to promote effective second language learning. Helping individual students locate the particular strategies most relevant to their learning styles, and developing orchestrated strategies can facilitate second language learning.

LEARNER PROCESSES

The input that second language learners receive is sifted, processed and organized. Such processing cannot be easily observed; rather it has to be inferred mostly from cognitive strategies in language learning. Clarification of the processing strategies of the learner is important for the teacher to decide what comprises comprehensible input and facilitative situations. This was considered earlier as leaner differences.

One way of peering into the black box of the mind was proposed by Chomsky (1965). Chomsky departed from positing general cognitive strategy devices, claiming instead that there are mental mechanisms that are specifically linguistic. Chomsky describes this as the **language acquisition device** that contains an innate blueprint for a person to acquire a language. Chomsky thus proposed that in-between language input and language production is a linguistic process that involves the activation of universal principles of grammar with which the learner is endowed.

One recent approach to processing in second language acquisition draws on parallel distributed processing in computers and is called **connectionism**. The World Wide Web is an example. It posits that the brain has complex and extensive neural networks with links between information nodes. These links become strengthened when they are repetitively activated. They become weak and fossilized when rarely or never addressed. Thus language learning is effective when (1) repeated and plentiful associations are made (e.g. between word form and meaning) and (2) associations join with other associations and form larger and more central networks. When a student regularly processes particular associations in language, they become strengthened and have a higher probability of being 'online' (Ellis & Schmidt, 1997).

Another recent approach to second language processing derives from an **information processing approach** (e.g. McLaughlin, 1987; Anderson, 1995). Second language learning from this viewpoint requires language sub-skills to be practiced until they move from being controlled to automatic. As performance improves, cognitive restructuring occurs such that processing moves away from 'control' in the short-term memory to 'automation' in the long-term memory. Automated sequences can be made available immediately by the long-term memory with minimum attention from the person. Such automated processing is difficult to delete or change, being deeply embedded. However, such automated processing allows complex clusters of stored components to be activated.

SECOND LANGUAGE OUTCOMES

At what point is someone functionally bilingual? What is the yardstick for successful learning of a second language? This has been previously examined in Chapters 1 and 2. Therefore, only a few additional comments are added here. The language proficiency of any learner at any one point of time is best seen as evolutionary and not fixed. A language competence test as a measure of current language output should ideally reveal not just the current ceiling, but also the fittings and floors that need to be added and developed. Outputs in a second language must also be viewed according to varying contexts. A learner may appear relatively fluent in a restaurant or shop situation, yet much less fluent in a business or religious context.

Language Competence

Van Ek (1986, 1987) outlines six different forms of **language competence** to be acquired for communication purposes: linguistic, sociolinguistic, discourse, strategic, social-cultural and social competence. This essentially is a belief that there is something more than linguistic competence that needs to be acquired by the language student.

There exists **sociolinguistic competence** in a language that concerns the ability to communicate accurately in different contexts, with different people, and when there are different intentions in the communication. Sociolinguistic competence is the awareness of the language form required in different situations. Such competence arises when natural interaction occurs between students, without prompting by the teacher. **Discourse competence** is the ability to use appropriate strategies in constructing and interpreting different texts, the ability to contribute to the construction of a spoken discourse in communication. For example, discourse competence is found in the ability to use pronouns, transition words and insert progression into communication.

Strategic competence is the ability to use verbal and non-verbal communication strategies to compensate for gaps in the language user's knowledge. Strategic competence concerns the ability to use body language (gesturing, head nods, eye contact) to give meaning when verbal language is not at a level of competence to convey meaning. **Sociocultural competence** is the 'awareness of the sociocultural context in which the language concerned is used by native speakers and the ways in which this context affects the choice and the communicative effect of particular language forms' (van Ek, 1987, p. 8). Finally, **social competence** is the ability to use particular social strategies to achieve communicative goals. For example, social competence includes the ability to take the initiative in a conversation, to know when to interrupt someone else speaking without being ill-mannered. Social competence involves understanding the social conventions that govern communication within a culture.

Meaningful Output

An important contribution to the idea of language output is by Swain (1985, 1986). Swain argues that the opportunity to engage in meaningful oral exchanges (in the classroom or in the community) is a necessary component in second language acquisition. In conveying meaning, a person learns about the structure and form of a language. A person may understand a language (passive, receptive skills) but, through lack of meaningful practice, speak that second language less than fluently. People learn to read by reading, and learn to write by writing. To speak, and to be understood when speaking, requires meaningful and realistic conversations. We learn to speak a second language when given the opportunity to speak it. Such opportunities may be too infrequent in language classrooms.

The danger of the classroom is that students may learn to understand a second language (comprehensible input), but not to produce (**comprehensible output**). The classroom emphasis has traditionally been on written correctness and not on spoken language skills. When a student has opportunities to use his or her spoken language outside the classroom (e.g. in the street), language skills (e.g. grammar, syntax and communication of meaning) may be considerably enhanced (Housen & Baetens Beardsmore, 1987; Baetens Beardsmore & Swain, 1985).

Non-Linguistic Outcomes

There are important non-linguistic outcomes from second language learning such as change in attitudes, self-concept, cultural values and beliefs. For example, the learning of a second language and the act of becoming bilingual may change attitudes.

For Lambert (1974), becoming bilingual or being bilingual has effects on **self-esteem** and the ego. Having mastered a second language and being able to interact with a different language group may change one's self-concept and self-esteem. An English monolingual who has learnt Spanish may develop new reference groups and engage in new cultural activities that affect the self-concept. This suggests that bilingualism usually involves enculturation. Someone who is bicultural or multicultural may have different aspirations, world views, values and beliefs because of being bilingual or multilingual.

CONCLUSIONS

This chapter has discussed central ideas in the acquisition of a second language. The overarching question is 'Who learns how much of what language under what conditions?' This brings into play individual differences (e.g. in ability and attitude), the skills and competences being learnt (e.g. grammatical accuracy, conversational fluency and literacy), contextual and situational factors, linguistic inputs and learner processes.

To the highways and byways of bilingualism needs to be added the geography of the journey. The journey is affected by the psychology of the individual, the environment and conditions of language travel, the political and cultural weather surrounding acquisition, fellow travelers and map-makers. Becoming bilingual is a linguistic, social and psychological event. The chapter has sought to portray the main features of different routes, while indicating that no two journeys will be the same.

The individual and social aspects are necessarily fused; the linguistic, sociological and psychological cannot be realistically separated. Whether second language acquisition theories derived from psychology or linguistics have sufficient understanding of complex classrooms or sufficient power to provide a technology of teaching is doubtful. Such theories give ideas and insights, they do not always provide answers that are translatable into comprehensive procedures or recipes for classroom practice. 'Best' or 'perfect' recipes are as unlikely in teaching as they are in cordon bleu cooking.

An individual's internal conflicts, the complexity of competing multiple pressures and motives, the many and varied individual recipes of success and failure, the many individual exceptions, the complexity of contexts and effects of immediate and long-standing situations make second language learning a complex moving film and not a static snapshot.

Simple, clear guidelines for effective second language acquisition that suits all learners would be much welcomed. A 'best buy' will probably always be elusive. In the second language shop window, there are many alternative theories, many different teaching methods. Choosing the 'best' theory or the 'best' teaching method is as dangerous as choosing one garment for all occasions. The **complexity** of language acquisition makes the wearing of the same cloth unwise. Different learners, different environments, different teachers, different props (e.g. computer-assisted language learning) make theories and teaching methods contain 'part-truths'. There are implications rather than affirmations; propositions rather than prescriptions; insights rather than edicts.

KEY POINTS IN THE CHAPTER

- Reasons for second language learning include ideological (e.g. assimilation), international (e.g. trade) and individual (e.g. cultural awareness) ones.
- A distinction between language acquisition and language learning highlights a difference between informal and formal (e.g. school) situations where bilingualism is achieved.
- Additive Bilingualism occurs when a second language is learnt by an individual or a group without detracting from the maintenance and development of the first language. A context where a second language adds to, rather than replaces the first language is important for bilingualism to flourish.
- Subtractive Bilingualism occurs when a second language is learnt at the expense of the first language, and gradually replaces the first language (e.g. immigrants to a country or minority language pupils in submersion education).
- The importance of structured input was historically strong in the audiolingual method of language learning. Comprehensible, meaningful and authentic input is now preferred.
- Differences among individual learners include ability, aptitude for language learning, attitudes and motivation and strategies in learning (e.g. risk-taking).
- Language learning processes are effective when repeated and plentiful and

repeated associations are made (e.g. between word form and meaning), and when language sub-skills are practiced until they move from being controlled to becoming automatic.
* Language learning outcomes include several different forms of language competence: linguistic, sociolinguistic, discourse, strategic, social-cultural and social competence.

SUGGESTED FURTHER READING

ELLIS, R., 1997, *Second Language Acquisition.* Oxford: Oxford University Press.
ELLIS, R., 1997, *SLA Research and Language Teaching.* Oxford: Oxford University Press.
KRASHEN, S. and TERRELL, T. 1983, *The Natural Approach: Language Acquisition in the Classroom.* Oxford: Pergamon.
McLAUGHLIN, B., 1987, *Theories of Second-Language Learning.* London: Edward Arnold.
MITCHELL, R. and MYLES, F., 1998, *Second-Language Learning Theories.* London: Arnold.
SKEHAN, B., 1998, *A Cognitive Approach to Language Learning.* Oxford: Oxford University Press.
SPOLSKY, B., 1989, *Conditions for Second Language Learning.* Oxford: Oxford University Press.

STUDY ACTIVITIES

(1) Locate a teacher or a parent or a friend who has learnt a second language in school or in adult life. Ask them about the importance of school, classroom and learning factors in their second language acquisition. Discuss with them how they see their current ability, attitudes and usage of their second language.

(2) In a small group of students, discuss different experiences of learning a second language at school. From the experiences of the group, which dimensions seem most important? Which approaches in the classroom seem from the personal experiences of the group to be most effective?

(3) Visit a school where students are learning a foreign language. By interviewing the teachers and observing classroom sessions, describe the overt and latent reasons for second (or third) language acquisition. Ask the teachers and the students their purposes in learning a foreign language. If there are differences in aim between teachers and students, examine whether you think these can be made compatible or are in conflict.

(4) Observe a classroom in which a foreign language is being taught to the majority, and one in which a second language is being taught to a minority. Describe and explain the differences in approach.

(5) Imagine you are in a classroom 20 years hence. In that futuristic classroom, describe how language acquisition might take place. What kind of technology might be used? Will there be more or less emphasis on learning minority and majority languages? What motivations might the students have in the futuristic classroom? For what purposes are languages being learnt? What forms of assessment are being used?

CHAPTER 7

Bilingualism and Cognition

Introduction

Bilingualism and 'Intelligence'

Bilingualism and the Brain

Bilingualism and Divergent and Creative Thinking

Bilingualism and Metalinguistic Awareness: Initial Research

Bilingualism and Metalinguistic Awareness: Recent Trends

Bilingualism and Communicative Sensitivity

Field Dependency and Independency and Bilingualism

Other Explanations of Findings

Limitations of the Findings

Conclusion

CHAPTER 7

Bilingualism and Cognition

INTRODUCTION

There was one piece of advice that parents sometimes received from well-meaning teachers, doctors, speech therapists, school psychologists and other professionals: *Don't raise your child bilingually or problems will result*. Predicted problems ranged from bilingualism as a burden on the brain, mental confusion, inhibition of the acquisition of the majority language, identity conflicts, split loyalties, even a schizo-phrenia. Parents and teachers were sometimes advised to use only one language with individual children. When children persisted in speaking two languages in school, having their mouths washed with soap and water (Isaacs, 1976) and being beaten with a cane for speaking Welsh were once offered as a remedy.

A quotation from a professor at Cambridge University in 1890 portrays this historical deficit viewpoint:

> 'If it were possible for a child to live in two languages at once equally well, so much the worse. His intellectual and spiritual growth would not thereby be doubled, but halved. Unity of mind and character would have great difficulty in asserting itself in such circumstances'. (Laurie, 1890: 15).

There is almost no modern empirical research to indicate that bilingualism has a detrimental effect on cognition. Nevertheless, anxieties about bilingualism and thinking remain among some members of the public. The anxiety that two languages may have a negative effect on an individual's thinking skills tends to be expressed in two different ways. First, some tend to believe that the more someone learns and uses a second language, the less skill a person will have in their first language. Rather like weighing scales or a **balance**, the more one increases, the more the other decreases. Second, concern is sometimes expressed that the ability to speak two languages may be at the cost of **efficiency** in thinking. The intuitive belief is sometimes that two languages residing inside the thinking quarters will mean less room to store other areas of learning. In comparison, the monolingual is pictured as having one language in residence and therefore maximal storage space for other information.

Does the ownership of two languages interfere with efficient thinking? Do monolinguals have more effective thinking quarters? Is a bilingual less intelligent than a monolingual because of a dual language system? This chapter examines these typically negatively phrased questions and evaluates the evidence on bilingualism and thinking. We start by considering the relationship between intelligence and bilingualism. 'Intelligence' has been a major concept in psychology and sometimes related to bilingualism. It is also a term often used by members of the public in phrasing questions about bilingualism.

The chapter then moves on to consider recent research that tends not to compare monolingual and bilingual groups on an IQ test. Rather, the modern approach is to focus on a wider sample of products and processes of a bilingual's cognition. Do bilinguals and monolinguals differ in thinking styles? Are there differences in the processing of information? Does owning two languages create differences in thinking about language? These types of question are examined in this chapter.

BILINGUALISM AND 'INTELLIGENCE'

The Period of Detrimental Effects

From the early 19th century to approximately the 1960s, the dominant belief amongst academics was that bilingualism had a detrimental effect on thinking. For example, the quote from Professor Laurie (1890) suggested that a bilingual's intellectual growth would not be doubled by being bilingual. Rather both intellectual and spiritual growth would be halved. This view of Laurie (1890) tends to reflect a view commonly held amongst the UK and US populace right through the 20th century: that bilingualism has disadvantages rather than advantages in terms of thinking.

The early research on bilingualism and cognition tended to confirm this negative viewpoint, finding that monolinguals were superior to bilinguals on mental tests (Darcy, 1953; Náñez et al., 1992). Research up to the 1960s looked at this issue through one concept — 'intelligence'. A typical piece of research gave bilinguals and monolinguals an 'intelligence' test. When bilinguals and monolinguals were compared on their IQ scores, particularly on verbal IQ, the usual result was that bilinguals were behind monolinguals. An example of this early research is by a Welsh researcher, D.J. Saer (1923). He gathered a sample of 1400 children aged seven to fourteen from bilingual and monolingual backgrounds. A 10-point difference in IQ was found between bilinguals and monolingual English speakers from the rural areas of Wales.

Saer (1923) concluded that bilinguals were mentally confused and at a disadvantage in thinking compared with monolinguals. Further research by Saer et al. (1924) suggested that university student monolinguals were superior to bilinguals: 'the difference in mental ability as revealed by intelligence tests is of a permanent nature since it persists in students throughout their University career' (p. 53).

While it is possible that situations exist where bilinguals will perform on such tests at a lower level than monolinguals (this is considered in Chapter 8), the early research that pointed to detrimental effects has a series of weaknesses. Such weaknesses tend to invalidate the research in terms of individual studies and cumulatively across studies. These limitations may be listed as follows.

Definition

The concept of 'intelligence' and the use of intelligence tests is controversial and hotly debated. One part of the controversy lies in the **problems of defining and measuring intelligence**. The underlying questions are: What is intelligence and who is intelligent? A thief who cracks a bank vault? A famous football coach? Someone poor who becomes a billionaire? Don Juan? A chairperson who manipulates the members of a board? Is there social intelligence, musical intelligence, military intelligence, marketing intelligence, motoring intelligence, political intelligence? Are all or indeed any of these forms of intelligence measurable by a simple pencil and paper IQ test which requires a single, acceptable, correct solution to each question?

What is intelligent behavior or not requires a subjective value judgment as to the kind of behavior and the kind of person regarded as of more worth. This stance may affect how language minorities are seen. A simple view of intelligence can be comfortable for language majorities if they believe social inequalities are based on lack of 'intelligence' in an ethnic or linguistic minority. Such a view 'releases one from an obligation to entertain the uncomfortable view that inequalities are created by ourselves, and are neither natural nor inevitable' (Howe, 1997, p. 139).

There are three related controversies to that of the definition of 'intelligence':

- There is a fierce debate about the relative effects of heredity and environment on the development of intelligence. A strong hereditarian viewpoint tends to argue that intelligence is relatively fixed and unlikely to be affected by becoming bilingual. An environmental view of the origins of intelligence may be more appealing to supporters of bilingualism. The environmental view holds that intelligence is neither fixed nor static, but modifiable by experience (e.g. family, education, culture and sub-culture). The 'extra' experience of two languages may thus contribute to the nature and growth of intelligence.
- Does intelligence comprise one unitary factor, or can intelligence be divided into a wide variety of factors or components (e.g. Howard Gardner's (1984) logical-mathematical, linguistic, spatial, musical, bodily-kinesthetic, and personal 'multiple intelligences')? Is there one all-embracing general factor of intelligence (labeled 'g'), or is Guilford's (1982) 150 factor model of intelligence more valid? A multi-factor view of intelligence is more likely to reveal differences between monolinguals and bilinguals.
- IQ tests tend to relate to a middle class, white, Western view of intelligence. The cultural boundedness or relativity of IQ tests suggests that cross-cultural generalizations are dangerous and limited (Valdés & Figueroa, 1994).

To summarize: in the relationship between intelligence and bilingualism, the first problem is that IQ tests only measure a minute sample of everyday 'intelligence' that is culturally limited. Therefore, whatever pattern is found between IQ tests and bilingualism refers to 'pencil and paper' intelligence. Research does not investigate the relationship between dual language ownership and all the components that might go under the wide heading of 'intelligence'. To use an analogy: we cannot fully portray a football or basketball match simply from the number of passes. Similarly, with bilingualism and intelligence, the whole game has not been studied, just one small statistic.

Language of Testing

The second problem is the language of the IQ test given to bilinguals. It is preferable to test the IQ of bilinguals in their stronger language or in both languages. In the early research, many verbal IQ tests were administered in English only (Valdés & Figueroa, 1994). This tended to be to the disadvantage of bilinguals in that they were tested in their weaker language and thus under-performed in the IQ test.

Analysis

The early research tended to use simple averages when comparing monolingual and bilingual groups. Statistical tests were often not performed to see whether the differences between the average scores were real or due to chance factors. Thus, for example, when W.R. Jones (1966) re-analyzed Saer's (1923) research, he found that there was no statistically significant difference between the monolingual and bilingual groups.

Classification

As has been shown in Chapter 1, the classification of people into bilingual and monolingual groups is fraught with difficulty. It is too simplistic to place people into a monolingual or a bilingual group. We need to ask what language competences are being used for classification? Are all four basic language abilities being used? What is the degree of fluency in each language? Were bilinguals classified by their use of languages (functional bilingualism) or by their ability in language? As Chapter 1 revealed, who is or is not bilingual is a complex issue. The earlier research on bilingualism and cognition tended to regard classification as non-problematic. This means that the research results are simplistic and ambiguous, having classified bilinguals in an insensitive and imprecise manner.

Generalization

A fifth problem concerns sampling and the generalization of research results to the population of bilinguals. With all research, the findings should be restricted to the population that the sample exactly represents. In particular, research using a non-random sample of a population, merely a convenience sample, should theoretically have no generalization beyond that sample. Much of the research on bilingualism and cognition is based on convenience samples. Thus research on 11-year-olds cannot be generalized to other age groups. Findings in the US cannot be generalized to bilinguals in the rest of the world. In much of the early research on bilingualism and cognition, the sampling is both small and inadequate making generalization dangerous.

Context

The language and cultural environment of the research sample needs to be considered. This relates to the notion of subtractive and additive environments (see Chapter 6). Negative, detrimental cognitive findings may be more associated with minority language groups in subtractive environments. Subtractive environments are where the child's first language is in danger of being replaced by a more prestigious second language. Where bilingualism has high prestige in an additive environment, a different pattern of results may be more likely.

Also, IQ and similar tests are presented as context-free circumstances. In reality, 'intelligent' responses will be affected by the particular context in which a task is completed. 'Intelligent' responses are relative to situations (e.g. car driving, money-making, musical composition, classroom learning).

Matched Groups

The final problem is particularly important. To compare a group of bilingual children with monolinguals on IQ, or on any other measure of cognitive ability, requires that the two groups be equal in all other respects. The only difference between the two groups should be in their bilingualism and monolingualism. If such control does not occur, then the results of the research may be due to the other factor or factors on which the groups differ (rather than their monolingualism or bilingualism). Take the example of a monolingual group being mostly of higher socioeconomic status, and the bilingual group being mostly of a lower socioeconomic status. A result (e.g. showing monolinguals to be ahead of bilinguals) may be due to social class rather than, or as well as, bilingualism. The great majority of research on bilingualism and 'intelligence' failed to match the groups on other factors that might explain the results. It is necessary to match the groups on variables such as sociocultural class, gender, age, type of school attended and urban/rural and subtractive/additive environments.

Conclusion

The period of detrimental effects research lasted from approximately the 1920s to the 1960s. While the dominant result was that bilinguals were inferior to monolinguals, particularly on verbal IQ, these early studies share many serious methodological weaknesses. Singly and cumulatively, the early research on bilingualism and IQ has so many limitations and methodological flaws that its conclusion of detrimental effects cannot be accepted. While it is possible that, in some contexts, bilinguals may have cognitive disadvantages (see Chapter 8), the early research cannot be used to support this claim. Indeed, as will be seen later in this chapter, different conclusions may better reflect the current state of research.

The Period of Neutral Effects

There are a series of studies that reported **no difference** between bilinguals and monolinguals in IQ. For example, research in the United States by Pintner and Arsenian (1937) found a zero correlation (no relationship) between verbal (and non-verbal) IQ and Yiddish–English bilingualism/monolingualism. While the number of studies with a 'no difference' conclusion is small in number, the period of neutral effects is important because it highlighted the inadequacies of the early detrimental effect research. An example is the research by W.R. Jones (1959) in Wales. Using 2500 children aged 10 and 11, Jones (1959) initially found that bilinguals were inferior to monolinguals on IQ. A re-analysis showed that this conclusion was invalid. After taking into account the varying socioeconomic class of bilinguals and monolinguals, Jones (1959) concluded that monolinguals and bilinguals did not differ significantly in non-verbal IQ so long as parental occupation was taken into account. He also concluded that socioeconomic class largely accounted for previous research that had reported the inferiority of bilinguals on non-verbal IQ. Therefore, his conclusion was that bilingualism is not necessarily a source of intellectual disadvantage.

While the period of neutral effects overlaps chronologically with the detrimental and additive periods, there was a period when (in Wales, for example) such neutral effects were taught and publicized. Such a 'neutral' conclusion was historically important as it gave a boost to parents who wished to support bilingualism in the home and in the school. As a transitional period, it both helped to question a fashionable belief of bilingualism as a source of cerebral confusion, and became a herald for the additive effects period.

The Period of Additive Effects

A major turning point in the history of the relationship between bilingualism and cognition was reached in Canadian research by Peal and Lambert (1962). It is this piece of research that heralded the modern approach to bilingualism and cognitive functioning. This research broke new territory in three respects, each setting the pattern for future research.

First, the research overcame many of the methodological deficiencies of the period of detrimental effects. Second, the research found evidence that bilingualism need not have detrimental or even neutral consequences. Rather, there is the possibility that bilingualism leads to **cognitive advantages** over monolingualism. Peal and Lambert's (1962) finding has been widely quoted to support bilingual policies in various educational contexts. The political implication of the study was that bilingualism within a country was not a source of national intellectual inferiority (Reynolds, 1991). Third, the research by Peal and Lambert (1962), while using IQ tests, moved research towards a broader look at cognition (e.g. thinking styles and strategies). Other areas of mental activity apart from IQ were placed firmly on the agenda for research into bilingualism and cognitive functioning.

Peal and Lambert (1962) commenced with a sample of 364 children aged 10 years old drawn from middle-class French schools in Montreal, Canada. The original sample of 364 children was reduced to 110 children for two reasons. First, to create a group of balanced bilinguals (see Chapter 1) and a group of monolinguals. Second, to ensure that the bilingual and monolingual groups were matched on socioeconomic class.

Bilinguals performed significantly higher on 15 out of the 18 variables measuring IQ. On the other three variables, there was no difference between balanced bilinguals and monolinguals. Peal and Lambert (1962) concluded that bilingualism provides: greater mental flexibility; the ability to think more abstractly, more independently of words, providing superiority in concept formation; that a more enriched bilingual and bicultural environment benefits the development of IQ; and that there is a positive transfer between a bilingual's two languages facilitating the development of verbal IQ.

These conclusions are historically more important than the specific results concerning IQ. That is, it is analysis of the results rather than the details of the results that provided the stimulus for further research and debate.

The study by Peal and Lambert (1962), while being pivotal in research on bilingualism and cognitive functioning, has four basic methodological weaknesses that need to be briefly considered before accepting the research at its face value. **First**, the results concern 110 children 10 years of age and of middle-class, Montreal extraction. This is not a sample that can be generalized to the population of bilinguals either in Canada or throughout the world. This is particularly so since the results concern 110 children selected from an original sample of 364. An unanswered question is how the other 254 children performed across the broad range of tests given by Peal and Lambert (1962).

Second, children in the bilingual group were 'balanced' bilinguals (see Chapter 1). While the term 'bilingual' includes balanced bilinguals, there are many other groups of children 'less balanced'. We cannot assume that the results from this study apply to such 'less balanced' bilinguals. Are balanced bilinguals a special group with their own characteristics in terms of their motivation, aptitude for languages, cognitive abilities and attitudes? Are balanced bilinguals a special group of children who have a higher IQ that is due not only to owning two languages, but due to other factors as well (e.g. parental values and expectations)?

The **third** problem with Peal and Lambert's (1962) research is the chicken and egg problem — which comes first? What is the cause and what is the effect? Is it bilingualism that enhances IQ? Or does a higher IQ increase the chances of becoming bilingual? When research suggests that IQ and bilingualism are positively related, we cannot conclude the order of cause and effect. It may be that bilingualism enhances IQ. It may be that those with a higher IQ are more likely to become bilingual. The relationship may also be such that one is both the cause and the effect of the other. Research by Diaz (1985) suggests that, if there is a particular direction in the relationship, it is more likely to be bilingualism positively affecting 'intelligence', rather than 'intelligence' affecting bilingualism.

The **fourth** problem concerns socioeconomic status. While Peal and Lambert (1962) tried to equate their bilingual and monolingual groups for socioeconomic class by exclusion of some children, there are residual problems. As Cummins (1976, 1984a) and MacNab (1979) have suggested, equating socioeconomic class does not control for all the differences in a child's home environment. Socioeconomic class is only a rough, simple and very partial measure of a child's home and environmental background. This is true of monolingual children. It is even more so with children who are bilingual and bicultural where there may be an even more complicated home and family background regarding sociocultural factors. Parental occupation of bilingual children is likely to summarize differences between children very inadequately.

In the following example, notice how the sociocultural element is very different, yet the socioeconomic class is the same. Take two Latino children of the same age and gender living in the same street in New York. Their fathers both have the same job — taxi drivers. One family regularly attends church services in Spanish and belongs to a Latino/Latina organization with cultural activities in Spanish. This taxi driver and his wife send their children to a Spanish–English dual language school. The child is bilingual. In the second family, the child speaks English only. There is no interest in sending their children to a dual-language school. Neither does the family attend a church or another organization where Spanish is spoken and valued. The Latin-American roots are neither discussed nor appreciated. While the families are matched on socioeconomic status, the sociocultural differences between them are considerable. In this example, the first child is bilingual and the second child is monolingual, with the bilingual child having a higher IQ. The child's bilingualism may not be the only explanation of a higher IQ. Rather the alternative or additional explanation may be in the different social and cultural environment of these children. Thus, with Peal and Lambert's (1962) study, socioeconomic class may have been controlled, but not sociocultural class.

This completes the examination of Peal and Lambert's (1962) important and pivotal study. Since their research, the dominant approach to bilingualism and cognitive functioning has moved away from IQ testing to a multi-component view of intelligence and cognition. Although there has been research since Peal and Lambert (1962) that examine IQ and bilingualism, most recent studies look at bilingualism in terms of a range of thinking styles, strategies and skills.

Studies since the 1960s mostly confirm Peal and Lambert's (1962) positive findings. These research studies are reviewed later in this next chapter. Before such a review, a concept allied to IQ is considered. Just as members of the public ask basic questions about 'intelligence' and bilingualism, so questions often arise about bilinguals' brains. For example, is the storage of information different for bilinguals' and monolinguals' brains? Evidence on this topic will now be briefly considered.

BILINGUALISM AND THE BRAIN

A frequently asked question is whether a bilingual's brain functions differently compared with that of a monolingual's brain? The issue becomes whether language is differently organized and processed in the brain of a bilingual compared with that of the monolingual (Fabbro, 1999). This is not just an academic question but relates to how clinical diagnosis and rehabilitation (e.g. in a bilingual aphasic). As Paradis (2000) outlines, many 'neurolinguistics of bilingualism' questions remain unanswered (e.g. the role of cerebral structures in metalinguistic knowledge).

One topic in the study of bilingualism and the brain is **lateralization**. In the majority of right-handed adults, the left hemisphere of the brain is dominant for language processing. The question has naturally arisen as to whether bilinguals are different from monolinguals in this left lateralization? Vaid and Hall (1991) provide five **propositions**:

(1)   Balanced bilinguals will use the right hemisphere more than monolinguals for first and second language processing.

(2)   Second language acquisition will involve the right hemisphere in language processing more than first language acquisition.

(3)   As proficiency in a second language grows, right hemisphere involvement will decrease and left hemisphere involvement will increase. This assumes that the right hemisphere is concerned with the more immediate, pragmatic and emotive aspects of language; the left hemisphere with the more analytic aspects of language (e.g. syntax). That is, the core aspects of language processing are assumed to reside in the left hemisphere.

(4)   Those who acquire a second language naturally (e.g. on the street) will use their right hemisphere more for language processing than those who learn a second language formally (e.g. in the language classroom). Learning rules about grammar, spelling and irregular verbs will result in more left hemisphere involvement in second language learning. Picking up a language in a natural manner and using it for straightforward communication will involve more right hemisphere involvement.

(5)   Late bilinguals will be more likely to use the right hemisphere than early bilinguals. This proposition states that there might be a 'predominance of a left-hemisphere "semantic-type" strategy in early bilinguals and for a right hemisphere "acoustic-type" strategy in late bilinguals' (Vaid & Hall, 1991, p. 90).

Using a quantitative procedure called **meta-analysis** to review previous research in this area, Vaid and Hall (1991) found that the left hemisphere strongly dominated language processing for both monolinguals and bilinguals. However, differences between monolinguals and bilinguals were the exception rather than the rule. Bilinguals did not seem to vary from monolinguals in neurological processes; the lateralization of language of the two groups being relatively similar:

> 'The largely negative findings from the meta-analysis must be taken seriously as reflecting a general lack of support for the five hypotheses as they have been addressed in the literature to date' (Vaid & Hall, 1991, p. 104).

While the relationship between the brain and bilingualism is an important area, the present state of knowledge makes a simple generalization unsafe (Fabbro, 1999; Paradis, 2000).

A related area concerns the **mental representation** of a bilingual's two languages and the processing emanating from such representation (Fabbro, 1999). A principal issue has been the extent to which a bilingual's two languages function **independ-**

ently or interdependently. The early research attempted to show that early bilinguals (compound bilinguals) were more likely to show interconnections and inter-relatedness in their two languages than late (coordinate) bilinguals. In the 1960s, Kolers (1963) re-defined the issue in terms of memory storage. A **separate storage** hypothesis stated that bilinguals have two independent language storage and retrieval systems with the only channel of communication being a translation process between the two separate systems. A **shared storage** hypothesis stated that the two languages are kept in a single memory store with two different language input channels and two different language output channels. Evidence exists for both independence and interdependence requiring both hypotheses to be rejected. Rather, an integrated model involving both independence and interdependence needs to be produced (Grosjean, 1994).

Recent theories and research have therefore emphasized both the separate and connected aspects of bilingual's mental representations by integrating the topic with general cognitive processing theories (e.g. Matsumi, 1994) . For example, the bilingual dual coding systems model of Paivio and Desrochers (1980) (see following page) contains:

- two separate verbal language systems, one for each of a bilingual's two languages;
- a separate non-verbal imagery system, independent from the two language systems;
- the non-verbal imagery system functions as a shared conceptual system for the two languages;
- strong, direct interconnecting channels between each of these three separate systems;
- the interconnections between the two languages comprising association and translation systems; common images also being mediators. The model is given in the diagram below (adapted and simplified from Paivio & Desrochers, 1980; Paivio, 1991):

BILINGUALISM AND DIVERGENT AND CREATIVE THINKING

One problem with IQ tests is that they restrict children to finding the one correct answer to each question. This is often termed convergent thinking. Children have to converge onto the sole acceptable answer. An alternative style is called divergent or creative thinking. A child regarded as a diverger is more creative, imaginative, elastic, open ended and free in thinking. Instead of finding the one correct answer, divergent thinkers prefer to provide a variety of answers, all of which can be valid. In the British tradition, the term used for this area is divergent thinking (Hudson, 1966, 1968).

Divergent thinking is investigated by asking questions such as: 'How many uses can you think of for a brick?'; 'How many interesting and unusual uses can you think of for tin cans?'; 'How many different uses can you think of for car tires?'. On this kind of question, the student has to diverge and find as many answers as

BILINGUAL DUAL CODING MODEL

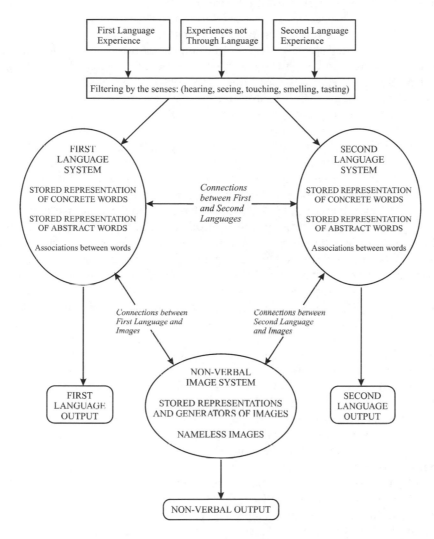

possible. For example, on the 'uses of a brick' question, a convergent thinker would tend to produce a few rather obvious answers to the question: to build a house, to build a barbecue, to build a wall. The divergent thinker will tend to produce not only many different answers, but also some that may be fairly original: for blocking up a rabbit hole, for propping up a wobbly table, as a foot wiper, breaking a window, making a bird bath.

In the North American tradition, it is more usual to talk about **Creative Thinking**. In this tradition, Torrance (1974a, 1974b) analyzes answers to the 'Uses of an Object' test (e.g. unusual uses of cardboard boxes, unusual uses of tin cans) by four categories. This test may be adapted into any language, with a culturally appropriate use of objects. Also, there are figural tests where a person is given a sheet of 40 circles or 40 squares and asked to draw pictures using these individual circles or squares, and subsequently place a label underneath.

A person's **fluency** score in creative thinking is the number of different acceptable answers that are given. A **flexibility** score is the number of different categories (listed in the Test Manual) into which answers can be placed. **Originality** is measured by reference to the Test Manual that gives scores of 0, 1, or 2 for the originality (statistical infrequency) of each response. **Elaboration** refers to the extent of the extra detail that a person gives beyond the basic use of an object.

The underlying hypothesis concerning creative thinking and bilingualism is that the ownership of two or more languages may increase fluency, flexibility, originality and elaboration in thinking. Bilinguals will have two or more words for a single object or idea. For example, in Welsh, the word *ysgol* not only means a school but also a ladder. Thus having the word '*ysgol*' in Welsh and 'school' in English may provide the bilingual with an added dimension — the idea of the school as a ladder. Similarly, having words for 'folk dancing' or 'square dancing' in different languages may give a **wider variety of associations** than having a label in just one language.

Does having two or more words for the one object or idea allow a person more freedom and richness of thought? Research has compared bilinguals and monolinguals on a variety of measures of divergent thinking (see Baker (1988) and Ricciardelli (1992) for reviews). The research is international and cross cultural: from Ireland, Malaysia, Eastern Europe, Canada, Singapore, Mexico and the US, sampling bilinguals using English plus Chinese, Bahasa Melayu, Tamil, Polish, German, Greek, Spanish, French, Ukrainian, Yorubo, Welsh, Italian or Kannada. As Laurén (1991) notes, such research has mostly occurred in additive bilingual contexts. The research findings largely suggest that bilinguals are superior to monolinguals on divergent thinking tests. An example will illustrate.

Cummins (1975, 1977) found that balanced bilinguals (see Chapter 1) were superior to 'matched' non-balanced bilinguals on the fluency and flexibility scales of verbal divergence, and marginally on originality. The 'matched' monolingual group obtained similar scores to the balanced bilingual group on verbal fluency and flexibility but scored substantially higher than the non-balanced group. On originality, monolinguals scored at a similar level to the non-balanced bilinguals and substantially lower than the balanced group. Probably due to the small numbers involved, the results did not quite attain customary levels of statistical significance. That there are differences between matched groups of balanced bilinguals and non-balanced bilinguals suggests that bilingualism and superior divergent thinking skills are not simply related. Cummins (1977) proposed that:

> 'there may be a threshold level of linguistic competence which a bilingual child must attain both in order to avoid cognitive deficits and allow the potentially beneficial aspects of becoming bilingual to influence his cognitive growth'. (p. 10)

The difference between balanced and non-balanced bilinguals is thus explained by a **threshold**. Once children have obtained a certain level of competence in their second language, positive cognitive consequences can result. However, competence in a second language below a certain threshold level may fail to give any cognitive benefits. Cognitive benefits may accrue when a child's second language competence is fairly similar to first language skills. This is the basic notion of the threshold theory which is examined further in Chapter 8.

The weight of the evidence suggests that balanced bilinguals have superior divergent thinking skills compared with unbalanced bilinguals and monolinguals. In a review of 24 studies, Ricciardelli (1992) found that in 20 of these bilinguals performed higher than monolinguals. Studies not supporting bilingual superiority sampled less proficient bilinguals, a result consistent with the Threshold Theory. However, some care must be taken in reaching too firm a conclusion. The research studies on this topic have limitations and deficiencies. To ensure a fair judgment, these problems need to be borne in mind.

The major **problems** may be listed as follows:

(1) Some studies fail to control adequately for differences between bilingual and monolingual groups (e.g. age and socioeconomic differences).
(2) Some studies have small samples such that generalization must be very restricted or non-existent.
(3) Some studies fail to define or describe the level or degree of bilingualism in their sample. As Cummins (1977) has shown, the extent of such competence is an important intermediate variable.
(4) Not all studies find a positive relationship between bilingualism and divergent thinking. Cummins and Gulutsan (1974), for example, found differences on only one of their five measures of divergent thinking. Laurén (1991) found that linguistic creativity differences were found in grades three, six and nine. Older bilinguals were ahead on only one of the four measures (use of compound nouns).
(5) The term 'creativity' is defined in different ways. As Laurén (1991) reveals, there are interpretations by psychologists (e.g. cognitive flexibility, fluency, originality and elaboration; tolerance of ambiguity); by linguists (e.g. the ability to create new meanings in different contexts); child development researchers (e.g. transforming the language input of parents and teachers); and creative writing proponents. Do bilinguals show advantages on psychological rather than the purely linguistic creativity measures?
(6) Does bilingualism bestow cognitive advantages of a permanent nature? If there are positive cognitive advantages linked with bilingualism, it is important to ask whether these are temporary, or cumulative and everlasting? Research studies tend to use children aged 4 to 17. What happens into the twenties or middle age or older age? Does bilingualism accelerate cognitive growth in the early years, with monolinguals catching up in later years? Balkan (1970) and Ben-Zeev (1977a) have suggested that such cognitive advantages

are predominant in younger rather than older children. Arnberg (1981) disagrees and argues that cognitive development is additive and cumulative, and that the further the child moves towards balanced bilingualism, the more there are cognitive advantages to be gained.

BILINGUALISM AND METALINGUISTIC AWARENESS: INITIAL RESEARCH

The research on bilingualism and divergent thinking suggests that bilinguals may have some advantage over matched monolinguals. For many bilingual children, the size of their total vocabulary across both languages is likely to be greater than that of a monolingual child in a single language (Swain, 1972). Does a larger overall vocabulary allow a bilingual to be more free and open, more flexible and original particularly in meanings attached to words? Is a bilingual person therefore less bound by words, more elastic in thinking due to owning two languages? For example, Doyle *et al.* (1978) found that bilinguals tend to be superior in their ability to relate stories and to express concepts within those stories when compared with monolinguals.

Leopold's (1939–1949) famous case study (see Chapter 5) of the German–English development of his daughter, Hildegard, noted the looseness of the link between word and meaning — an effect apparently due to bilingualism. Favorite stories were not repeated with stereotyped wording; vocabulary substitutions were made freely in memorized songs and rhymes. Word sound and word meaning were separated. The name of an object or concept was separated from the object or concept itself.

To illustrate: imagine that in a kindergarten a monolingual child and a bilingual child are taught the same nursery rhyme:

> Jack and Jill went up the hill
> To fetch a pail of water.
> Jack fell down and broke his crown
> And Jill came tumbling after.

The monolingual child may be relatively more likely to repeat the verse with little or no alteration. The focus is on the sound and the rhyme. The bilingual child may be more likely to center on the meaning than repeating the words parrot fashion. For example, the bilingual may offer the following version; the word substitutions suggesting that the nursery rhyme has been processed for meaning:

> Jack and Jill *climbed* a hill
> To fetch a *bucket* of water.
> Jack fell down and *banged* his *head*
> And Jill came *falling* after.

Hildegard is a single case and the nursery rhyme is merely an illustration. What has research revealed about samples of bilinguals?

Ianco-Worrall (1972) tested the sound and meaning separation idea on 30 Afrikaans–English bilinguals aged four to nine. The bilingual group was matched with monolinguals on IQ, age, sex, school grade and social class. In the first experiment, a typical question was: 'I have three words: CAP, CAN and HAT. Which is more like CAP: CAN or HAT?' A child who says that CAN is more like CAP would appear to be making a choice determined by the **sound** of the word. That is, CAP and CAN have two out of three letters in common. A child who chooses HAT would appear to be making a choice based on the **meaning** of the word. That is, HAT and CAP refer to similar objects.

Ianco-Worrall (1972) showed that, by seven years of age, there was no difference between bilinguals and monolinguals in their choices. Both groups chose HAT, their answer being governed by the meaning of the word. However, with four- to six-year-olds, she found that bilinguals tended to respond to word meaning, monolinguals more to the sound of the word. This led Ianco-Worrall (1972) to conclude that bilinguals:

> 'reach a stage of semantic development, as measured by our test, some two–three years earlier than their monolingual peers'. (p. 1398).

In a further experiment, Ianco-Worrall (1972) asked the following type of question: 'Suppose you were making up names for things, could you call a cow "dog" and a dog "cow"?' Bilinguals mostly felt that names could be interchangeable. Monolinguals, in comparison, more often said that names for objects such as cow and dog could not be interchanged. Another way of describing this is to say that monolinguals tend to be bound by words, bilinguals tend to believe that language is more arbitrary. For bilinguals, names and objects are separate. This seems to be a result of owning two languages, giving the bilingual child awareness of the free, non-fixed relationship between objects and their labels.

Other early research in this area, for example, by Ben-Zeev (1977a, 1977b), suggested that the ability of bilinguals to analyze and inspect their languages stems from the necessity of avoiding 'interference' between the two languages. That is, the process of separating two languages and avoiding code-mixing may give bilinguals superiority over monolinguals through an increased analytical orientation to language. One of Ben-Zeev's (1977a) tests, called the Symbol Substitution Test, asked children to substitute one word for another in a sentence. For example, they had to use the word 'macaroni' instead of 'I' in a sentence. The sentence to say becomes 'Macaroni am warm', thus avoiding saying 'I am warm'. Respondents have to ignore word meaning, avoid framing a correct sentence and evade the interference of word substitution in order to respond to the task correctly. Bilinguals were found by Ben-Zeev (1977a) to be superior on this kind of test, not only with regard to meaning, but also with regard to sentence construction.

Ben-Zeev (1977a), using Hebrew–English bilinguals from Israel and the United States aged 5–8, argued that bilinguals have advantages because they experience two language systems with two different sets of construction rules. Therefore bilinguals appear to be more flexible and analytical in language skills.

BILINGUALISM AND METALINGUISTIC AWARENESS: RECENT TRENDS

Much of the research on bilingualism and cognitive functioning has concentrated on cognitive style (e.g. divergent and creative thinking). The focus of research tends to be on the person and on the product. Such research has tended to focus on whether bilinguals are superior or inferior to monolinguals as people. It has attempted to locate dimensions of thinking where bilinguals perform better than monolinguals. The recent trend has been to look at the **process** of thinking rather than the **products** of thinking, working within the information processing, memorization and language processing approaches in psychology (e.g. Kardash *et al.*, 1988; Ransdell & Fischler, 1987, 1989; Bialystok, 1991; Harris, R., 1992; Keatley, 1992; Padilla & Sung, 1992; Hummel, 1993; Pavlenko, 1999). Not all such studies are 'favorable to bilinguals' (e.g. Ellis, N. (1992) and Geary *et al.*, (1993) on the processing of numbers). However, research on memorization, language recall, reaction times and processing times tends to use bilinguals to help describe and explain cognitive processing and language processing. Comparisons with monolinguals aim to aid psychological understanding of cognitive processes rather than to focus on bilinguals *per se*. However, Pavlenko (1999, 2000) provides a review that is both critical of research in this area, but places the bilingual at the forefront.

Process research which builds cumulatively on previous research on bilingualism and cognitive functioning has focused particularly on the metalinguistic awareness of bilingual children (Galambos & Hakuta, 1988; Bialystok & Ryan, 1985; Bialystok, 1987a, 1987b, 1997; Ricciardelli, 1993; Campbell & Sais, 1995; Bialystok & Codd, 1997; Cromdal, 1999; Carlisle *et al.*, 1999; Bialystok & Majumder, 1999). Metalinguistic awareness may loosely be defined as the ability to think about and reflect upon the nature and functions of language:

> 'As a first approximation, metalinguistic awareness may be defined as the ability to reflect upon and manipulate the structural features of spoken language, treating language itself as an object of thought, as opposed to simply using the language system to comprehend and produce sentences. To be metalinguistically aware is to begin to appreciate that the stream of speech, beginning with the acoustic signal and ending with the speaker's intended meaning, can be looked at with the mind's eye and taken apart' (Tunmer & Herriman, 1984, p. 12)

Such metalinguistic awareness is regarded by Donaldson (1978) and Bialystok (1997) as a key factor in the development of reading in young children. This hints that bilinguals may be ready slightly earlier than monolinguals to learn to read. In a review of this area, Bialystok and Herman (1999) analyze the effects that early bilingualism has on children's early literacy development but urge caution. Three areas of early literacy development are analyzed: experience with stories and book reading, concepts of print, and phonological awareness. These three areas cover the social, cognitive and linguistic aspects of literacy learning. The authors argue that each of these three areas of competence will have a different link to bilingualism.

However, there are many intervening variables that make simple statements currently impossible. The child's experience and level of proficiency in each language, the relationship between the two languages, and the type of writing systems employed by each language are examples of intervening factors that alters the nature of the bilingual experience. A similar cautious approach is taken by Green (1998) in a wide-ranging review of bilingualism and thought. He also suggests that current research is often simplistic in just connecting bilingualism and cognitive performance. A more on-line processing approach is needed (see later). Sociocultural performance in the context of each language group needs more attention and not just linguistic knowledge.

Bialystok and Codd (1997) found that four- and five-year-old bilinguals were ahead of monolinguals in developing concepts of number (cardinality of number) due to their higher levels of attentional control. Bilingual children need to be attentive to which language is being spoken, by whom, where and when. This attentiveness appears to give advantages in early number work, when attention to the symbolic nature of number is needed.

Early research suggested a relationship favoring bilinguals in terms of increased metalinguistic awareness (e.g. Ianco-Worrall, 1972; Ben-Zeev, 1977a, 1977b; see Tunmer & Myhill, 1984 for a review). It appears that bilingual children develop a more analytical orientation to language through organizing their two language systems. Phonological awareness and the cognitive skills of symbolic representation are needed to read and write. Letters are symbols without inherent meaning and do not resemble the sounds they represent. Bilinguals may comprehend such symbolic representation earlier than monolinguals as they see words written in two different ways.

In research that directly engages bilingualism and metalinguistic awareness, Bialystok (1987a, 1987b, 1997) found that bilingual children were superior to monolingual children on measures of the **cognitive control of linguistic processes**. Bialystok (1987a) conducted three studies each involving around 120 children aged five–nine. In the experiments, children were asked to judge or correct sentences for their syntactic acceptability irrespective of meaningfulness. Sentences could be meaningfully grammatical (e.g. why is the dog barking so loudly?); meaningful but not grammatical (e.g. why the dog is barking so loudly?); anomalous and grammatical (e.g. why is the cat barking so loudly?); or anomalous and ungrammatical (e.g. why the cat is barking so loudly?). These sentences test the level of analysis of a child's linguistic knowledge. The instructions requested that the children focus on whether a given sentence was grammatically correct or not. It did not matter that the sentence was silly or anomalous. Bialystok (1987a) found that bilingual children in all three studies consistently judged grammaticality more accurately than did monolingual children at all the ages tested.

Bialystok (1987b) also examined the difference between bilinguals and monolinguals in their processing of words and the development of the concept of a word. She found in three studies that bilingual children showed more advanced understanding of some aspects of the idea of words than did monolingual children. A procedure for testing children's awareness of 'What is a word?' is to ask children to determine the number of words in a sentence. It can be surprisingly difficult for young children to count how many words there are in a sentence. Until children are about six to seven years of age and learning to read, they do not appear to have this processing ability.

To be able to count how many words there are in a sentence depends on two things: first, a knowledge of the boundaries of words; second, a knowledge of the relationship between word meaning and sentence meaning. At around seven years of age, children learn that words can be isolated from the sentences in which they are contained, having their own individual meaning. Bialystok (1987b) found that bilingual children were ahead of monolingual children on counting words in sentences because (1) they were more clear about the criteria that determined the identity of words; and (2) they were more capable of attending to the units of speech they considered relevant.

> 'Bilingual children were most notably advanced when required to separate out individual words from meaningful sentences, focus on only the form or meaning of a word under highly distracting conditions, and re-assign a familiar name to a different object.' (Bialystok, 1987b, p. 138).

The **conclusion** can be summarized as follows. Relatively balanced bilinguals have increased metalinguistic abilities. This relates to two components (Bialystok, 1988; Ricciardelli, 1993): bilinguals' enhanced *analyzing* of their knowledge of language; and their greater *control* of internal language processing. Bilinguals appear to understand the symbolic representation of words in print earlier than monolinguals as they see words printed in two separate ways. In turn, this may facilitate earlier acquisition of reading.

The research of Galambos and Hakuta (1988) provides further refinement of the reasons for differences between bilinguals and monolinguals on cognitive processes. In two studies with low income Spanish–English bilingual children in the US, Galambos and Hakuta (1988) used a series of tests that examined children's ability to spot various errors in Spanish sentences. Such errors might be in terms of gender, word order, singular and plural, verb tense and time. For example, on a grammatically oriented test item, a child had to correct the following: '*La perro es grande*'. The correction would be '*El perro es grande*'. In a content oriented test item, '*La perro es grande*' would become '*El perro es pequeño*'. In the experiment, children were read the sentences, asked to judge whether it had been said in the right way, and then correct the error.

The effect of bilingualism on the processing of the test items was found to vary depending on the level of bilingualism and the difficulty level of the items. The more bilingual the child was, that is where both languages were relatively well developed, the better he or she performed on the test items:

> 'The information-processing approach successfully accounts for our findings that bilingualism by and large enhances the metalinguistic abilities to note

errors and correct errors… The bilingual experience requires that the form of the two languages being learned be attended to on a routine basis. Experience at attending to form would be predicted to facilitate any task that required the child to focus on form upon demand.' (Galambos & Hakuta, 1988, p. 153)

Galambos and Hakuta (1988) concluded that metalinguistic awareness is most developed when a child's two languages are developed to their highest level. Galambos and Hakuta (1988) agreed with Cummins (1976) that a certain level of proficiency in both languages must be attained before the positive effects of bilingualism on metalinguistic awareness can occur. This is usually termed the thresholds theory and is considered in Chapter 8.

Carlisle *et al.* (1999) also found that the degree of bilingualism constrains or enhances metalinguistic performance. Those in the early stages of bilingualism do not share the benefits until sufficient vocabulary development, in both languages, has occurred. Similarly, Bialystok and Majumder's (1999) research showed that balanced bilinguals in Grade 3 were superior to partial bilinguals on non-linguistic problem-solving tasks requiring selective attention. However, a reservation is expressed by Nicoladis and Genesee (1996) who did not find this effect with pre-literate children

The evidence of advantages for bilinguals in terms of metalinguistic awareness seems fairly strong. What is not apparent, as yet, is the extent of these effects. For example, are these effects temporary and located with certain younger children (e.g. those already embarked on the initial stages of reading)? Are the effects in any way permanent? Do they give a child an initial advantage that soon disappears with growing cognitive competence? Are these early benefits for bilinguals cumulative and additive? Apart from 'balanced bilinguals', which groups of bilinguals gain such advantages?

BILINGUALISM AND COMMUNICATIVE SENSITIVITY

In Ben-Zeev's research (1977b) on the comparative performance of bilingual and monolingual children on Piagetian tests, she found that bilinguals were more responsive to hints and clues given in the experimental situation (see Baker & Jones (1998) for a review of Piagetian research and bilingualism). That is, bilinguals seemed more sensitive in an experimental situation, and corrected their errors faster compared to monolinguals. Ben-Zeev's (1977b) research gave the first clue that bilinguals may have cognitive advantages regarding 'communicative sensitivity'.

What is **communicative sensitivity**? Bilinguals need to be aware of which language to speak in which situation. They need constantly to monitor the appropriate language in which to respond or to in which initiate a conversation (e.g. on the telephone, in a shop, speaking to a superior). Not only do bilinguals often attempt to avoid 'interference' between their two languages, they also have to pick up clues and cues when to switch languages. The literature suggests that this may give a bilingual increased sensitivity to the social nature and communicative functions of language.

An interesting experiment on sensitivity to communication, deserving replication, was undertaken by Genesee *et al.* (1975). They compared children in bilingual and monolingual education on their performance on a game. In this simple but ingenious research, students aged 5–8 were asked to explain a board and dice game to two listeners. One listener was blindfolded, the other not. The listeners were classmates and not allowed to ask any questions after the explanation. The classmates then attempted to play the game with a person giving the explanation. It was found that children in a bilingual education program (total immersion — see Chapter 10) were more sensitive to the needs of listeners. This bilingual education group gave more information to the blindfolded children than to the sighted listener compared with children in the monolingual education comparison group. The authors concluded that children in bilingual education 'may have been better able than the control children to take the role of others experiencing communicational difficulties, to perceive their needs, and consequently to respond appropriately to these needs' (p. 1013).

This implies that bilingual children may be more sensitive than monolingual children in a social situation that requires careful communication. A bilingual child may be more aware of the needs of the listener. In a variety of cognitive tests with bilingual and monolingual samples among the Konds (Kandhas) in Orissa, India, Mohanty (1994) found an increased sensitivity to messages among bilinguals. This links with sociolinguistic competence (see Chapter 1) and suggests a heightened social awareness among bilinguals of verbal and non-verbal message cues and clues in communication.

More research is needed to define precisely the characteristics and the extent of the sensitivity to communication that bilinguals may share. Research in this area is important because it connects cognition with interpersonal relationships. It moves from questions about skills of the bilingual mind to a bilingual's social skills.

FIELD DEPENDENCY AND INDEPENDENCY AND BILINGUALISM

One well researched dimension of cognitive style along which people vary is field dependence — field independence (Witkin *et al.*, 1971). An example from one of Witkin *et al.*'s (1971) tests helps illustrate this dimension. In the Embedded Figures Test, a child has to draw in the left hand figure over the right hand figure. Can the child recognize the cuboid in the right hand figure?

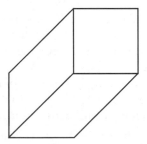 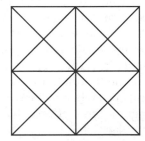

Children who are field independent will tend to see the object separate from the other lines in the right hand figure. Those who are field dependent will tend not to separate out the cuboid figure from the background. The simple shape is not identified in the more complex shape. Simply stated, some people tend to see in wholes, others in parts. Witkin *et al.* (1962) found that as children grow to maturity they become more field independent. While field dependence–independence may appear as a perceptual ability, Witkin and his co-workers regard it as a general ability to be aware of visual contexts, that relates particularly to problem solving ability and ease of cognitive restructuring.

One early study which examined whether bilinguals have a particular cognitive style compared with monolinguals was conducted in Switzerland by Balkan (1970). French–English balanced bilinguals aged 11 to 17 were matched with monolinguals on IQ, and compared on an adaptation of the **Embedded Figures Test**. Balkan (1970) found that bilinguals were more field independent and that those who learnt their second language before the age of four tended to be more field independent than late learners (who had learnt their second language between four and eight years). In Canada, students age 12 to 13 years in a bilingual education program were superior to control groups on the Embedded Figures Test (Bruck, Lambert & Tucker, quoted in Cummins, 1978). Although the comparison groups were different from those in Balkan (1970), the Canadian research provided further evidence for bilingualism being linked to greater field independence. However, Genesee and Hamayan (1980) found that those who were more field independent learnt a second language better. This highlights the cause–effect relationship. Does field independence cause bilingualism to occur more easily? Does bilingualism cause field independence? Or is one both the cause and the effect of the other?

Apart from the Swiss and Canadian research, a further confirmatory piece of evidence comes from English/Spanish bilinguals in the USA (Duncan & De Avila, 1979). Using the Children's Embedded Figures Test, the descending order of scores on field independence was:

(1)   proficient bilinguals;
(2)   partial bilinguals, monolinguals and limited bilinguals; and
(3)   late language learners.

The authors conclude that **proficient bilinguals** may have advantages in cognitive clarity and in analytical functioning. This theme, of more proficient bilinguals having cognitive advantages over monolinguals and less proficient bilinguals is returned to when considering the Thresholds Theory in the next chapter.

The Embedded Figures Test focuses on spatial ability. In contrast, metalinguistic awareness tests focus on linguistic domains. On the surface, they have little in common. Yet bilinguals do well on both tests compared with monolinguals. Are there any features in common between the tests that explain bilinguals' cognitive advantages. Bialystok (1992) argues that there is a commonality: **selective attention** that transfers across the spatial and linguistic domains. Bilingual children can reconstruct a situation (perceptual or linguistic), focus on the key parts of a problem and select the crucial parts of a solution. They can escape from perceptual seduction and overcome cues that are irrelevant. Their 'early experience with two languages may lead them to develop more sensitive means for controlling attention to linguistic input. They are used to hearing to things referred to in two different ways, and this can alert them earlier to the arbitrariness of referential forms' (Bialystok, 1992, p. 510). Bilinguals select which language to use with whom and avoid inappropriate language forms. They may need to attend to social conventions that occur in each language (e.g. different forms of politeness and deference to adults, different ways of greeting in Arabic and Spanish). Such selective attention may transfer across spatial, cognitive and linguistic domains. For Bialystok (1992), it is **selective attention** that is the explanation of bilinguals' advantages on divergent thinking, creative thinking, metalinguistic awareness, communicative sensitivity, Piagetian tests and on the Embedded Figures Test.

OTHER EXPLANATIONS OF FINDINGS

Cummins (1976) has suggested that there are three different ways one might explain a relationship between bilingualism and cognitive advantages. The first explanation is that bilinguals may have a wider and more varied range of **experiences** than monolinguals due to their operating in two languages and probably two or more cultures. The extra range of meanings that two languages provide, the added stream of experience that two languages may give, and the extra cultural values and modes of thinking embedded in two languages may be increased for the bilingual (see Chapter 19). Cummins (1976) believed that this was a hypothesis yet to be confirmed or rejected. This remains true at the present.

The second explanation of the cognitive advantages of bilingualism concerns a **switching** mechanism. Because bilingual children switch between their two languages, they may be more flexible in their thinking. Neufeld (1974) was critical of this hypothesis, suggesting that monolinguals also switch from one register to another. That is, in different situations and contexts, monolinguals and bilinguals have to know when and how to switch between different modes of speech. This second proposition may be a partial explanation only, — a small component in a wider and larger whole.

The third explanation is termed the process of **objectification** (Imedadze, 1960; Cummins & Gulutsan, 1974). Bilinguals may consciously and subconsciously compare and contrast their two languages. Comparing nuances of meaning, different grammatical forms, being constantly vigilant over their languages may be an intrinsic process due to being bilingual. Inspecting the two languages, resolving interference between languages may provide the bilingual with metalinguistic skills. Vygotsky (1962) suggested that bilingualism enables a child 'to see his language as one particular system among many, to view its phenomena under more general categories, and this leads to awareness of his linguistic operations' (p. 110). This third explanation is backed by the research on the metalinguistic advantages of bilingualism (Diaz & Klingler, 1991). However, as Nicoladis and Genesee (1996) suggest, automatic processing rather than controlled processing is the hallmark of higher cognitive functioning. Therefore, levels of awareness and automatic processing do not fit easily together unless there is 'subconscious awareness' in operation.

While objectification may be a component in explaining the cognitive advantages of bilingualism, it is unlikely to be a total explanation. Nor does objectification relate to a complete theory of intellectual functioning. A creative attempt to fit the disparate research on bilingualism and cognition into an overarching explanation is provided by Reynolds (1991). Reynolds (1991) commences with Sternberg's (1985, 1988) three part model of intelligence. This model of intelligence has three subtheories: contextual, experiential and componential.

In the **Contextual Subtheory**, intelligent behavior is regarded as adapting to the environment in which one is placed. Going to a party and meeting new people on one day, next day attending a religious institution and a family get-together, then attending school and leisure activities, each and all require a person to constantly adapt to changing contexts, sometimes selecting contexts, even altering the environment to suit oneself. Reynolds (1991) argues that bilinguals may be more capable at adapting to changing environments because of their experience of separate linguistic environments and their (sometimes) wider social and cultural environments. Evidence to support this comes from studies of bilinguals' increased communicative sensitivity.

In the **Experiential Subtheory**, intelligent behavior is seen as variable, depending on how much experience a person has of a situation. Acting intelligently is through effectively adapting to new situations. Effectiveness is when behaviors become automated and habitual earlier rather than later. 'Automatization' allows cognitive resources to be more sensibly allocated to the processing of new situations and challenges. According to Reynolds (1991), bilinguals' experience of two languages and switching between languages early in life allows easier automatization in dealing with language tasks and frees resources for less familiar linguistic demands.

The **Componential Subtheory** concerns the processes that underlie intelligent behavior. Such processes firstly involve *Metacomponents* which execute, control and monitor the processing of information. Because a bilingual has to control and monitor two language systems, the metacomponent system may be more evolved and efficient.

Secondly, there are *Performance components* which administer the schemes devised by the Metacomponents. Bilinguals may have advantages with performance components:

> 'Having command of two languages leads to greater use of verbal mediation and increased use of language as a cognitive regulatory tool. Having two interlocking performance systems for linguistic codes gives double the resources for executing verbal tasks… Also there is greater use of learning strategies when learning two languages.' (Reynolds, 1991, p. 167)

Thirdly, Sternberg's (1985, 1988) Componential Subtheory contains *KnowledgeAcquisition* components. Such components encode new information and match old, memorized information with incoming new information to enable intelligent functioning. Reynolds (1991) considers that a bilingual's dual language system may make the reception of new information more easy and fluent. New information can be assimilated via either or both the language systems of the bilingual. A bilingual may sometimes have a double chance of acquiring new information with two vocabularies and two verbal memories available.

LIMITATIONS OF THE FINDINGS

Research in the area of bilingualism and cognitive functioning often shares methodological problems. Before conclusions are presented, it is important to bear in mind the limitations of research in this area. First, research needs to match monolingual and bilingual groups on all variables other than language. This is in order for any difference between such groups to be explained by bilingualism rather than by any other factors. While some studies do attempt to **control for alternative explanations** by matching students in pairs or by the statistical technique of analysis of co-variance, there are factors that may provide alternative explanations that are missing from such research. These factors are the motivation of the children, socio-economic circumstances, parental attitude, school experience and the culture of the home and community. These may be alternative explanations of many of the findings rather than, or as well as, bilingualism.

A second criticism is in the nature of the bilinguals that are used in such research. Researchers who find cognitive advantages mostly focus on **balanced bilinguals**. Do balanced bilinguals represent all bilinguals? MacNab (1979) argued that bilinguals are a special, idiosyncratic group in society. Because they have learnt a second language and are often bicultural, bilinguals are different in major ways from monolinguals. For example, parents who want their children to be bicultural and bilingual may emphasize divergent thinking skills, encourage creative thinking in their children and foster metalinguistic skills. The parents of bilingual children may be the ones who want to accelerate their children's language skills. Such parents may give high priority to the development of languages within their children compared with monolingual parents. While this does not detract from the possibility that bilinguals do share some cognitive advantages, it does suggest a need to take care about a decision as to what are the determining factors. It may be that it is not only language that is important. Other non-language factors may be influential as well (e.g. the immigrant experience, political pressures, subtractive and additive contexts).

Third, the chicken and egg, **cause and effect relationship** must again be highlighted. What comes first? Most recent research in this area has assumed that bilingualism comes first and causes cognitive benefits. It is not impossible that the causal link may run from cognitive abilities to enhanced language learning. Or it may be that language learning and cognitive development work hand in hand. One both promotes and stimulates the other. It is unlikely that a simple cause–effect pattern exists. A more likely situation is a continuous process of interaction between language and cognition. However Diaz (1985), using sophisticated statistical techniques (structural equation modeling), suggested that bilingualism is more likely to be the cause of increased cognitive abilities than the reverse. From current studies, this seems a fair conclusion.

Fourth, we need to ask **which types of children have the benefits**? This concerns whether children of all abilities share the cognitive advantages of bilingualism. Is it just 'elective' bilinguals (see Chapter 1) upon whom much of the research is based, or do the results extend to circumstantial bilinguals (Valdés & Figueroa, 1994)? Do children below average in cognitive abilities also gain the advantages of bilingualism? There is certainly a tendency in research to use children from the middle classes, particularly those of above average ability. However Rueda (1983), using analytical orientation to language tests (see earlier in this chapter), found that bilingual, less able children (51–69 IQ level) tended to have cognitive advantages over 'matched' monolinguals. Rueda's (1983) research in Canada, which needs thorough replication, hints that cognitive advantages may be shared by below average ability children and not just the average and above average ability children.

Fifth, when reviewing research we need to consider the hopes and the ideologies of the researcher. Rosenthal (1966) has shown that **experimenters' expectations** can affect the outcomes and results of human and animal studies. As Hakuta (1986) suggests:

> 'a full account of the relationship between bilingualism and intelligence, of why negative effects suddenly turn in to positive effects, will have to examine the motivations of the researcher as well as more traditional considerations at the level of methodology.' (p. 43)

Have the assumptions and political preferences of authors crept unintentionally into their research and affected both the results and the interpretations of the results? In the choice of psychological tests and the choice of a sample, has there recently been a built-in bias towards finding positive results on bilingualism and cognitive functioning?

Finally, we must ask whether the positive benefits from bilingualism in terms of thinking are **temporary or permanent**? Most research studies tend to use children of school age. There is almost no research on the cognitive functioning of bilinguals and monolinguals after the age of 17. Does bilingualism accelerate cognitive growth in the early years of childhood with monolinguals catching up in later years? Are cognitive advantages predominant in younger rather than older children? Or are the advantages additive, cumulative and long lasting? It is possible that certain advantages (e.g. sensitivity to language, separation of word sound from word meaning) may be temporary. Age and experience may eventually give bilingual and monolingual similar cognitive skills. However, with the ideas of cognitive style (e.g. divergent and creative thinking) and communicative sensitivity, may go relatively more stable and lasting effects.

CONCLUSION

This chapter has reviewed the traditional expectation that bilingualism and intelligence are linked negatively. The conception has been that bilingualism leads to lower intelligence. Research from the 1920s to the 1960s supported that conception. Recent research has shown that a simple negative relationship as a misconception. The narrow view of intelligence contained in IQ tests and severe flaws in the design of early research combine with other limitations to cast doubts on this negative link.

Rather, the need is to specify the language ability levels of bilinguals (see Chapter 1) and to ensure like is compared with like. Since 1960, the indication has been that a more positive relationship between bilingualism and cognitive functioning can be expected, particularly in 'balanced' bilinguals.

A review of research on cognitive functioning and bilingualism suggests that two extreme conclusions may both be untenable. To conclude that bilingualism gives undoubted cognitive advantage fails to consider the various criticisms and limitations of research in this area. It also fails to recognize that there are studies (e.g. on memory), where bilinguals may sometimes be at a disadvantage compared with monolinguals (e.g. Ransdell & Fischler, 1987). However, to conclude that all the research is invalid fails to acknowledge that the judgment of the clear majority of researchers tends to be that there are positive links between bilingualism and cognitive functioning. While there is insufficient evidence to satisfy the skeptic, the evidence that currently exists does lead in the direction of bilinguals having some cognitive advantages over monolinguals.

KEY POINTS IN THE CHAPTER

- Historically, bilinguals were regarded as having a relatively lower IQ than monolinguals. Subsequent research showed the opposite.
- Research on the relationship between intelligence and bilingualism has moved from a period of investigating 'detrimental effects' to a current focus on the additive effects given by bilingualism.
- The ownership of two languages does not interfere with efficient thinking. On the contrary bilinguals who have two well developed languages share cognitive advantages.
- Bilinguals have advantages in thinking styles, particularly in divergent thinking, creativity, early metalinguistic awareness and communicative sensitivity.
- Research on the metalinguistic advantages of bilinguals is strong, and suggests bilinguals are aware of their languages at an early age, separating form from meaning, and having reading readiness earlier than monolinguals.

SUGGESTED FURTHER READING

BAKER, C. and JONES, S.P. 1998, *The Encyclopedia of Bilingualism and Bilingual Education.* Clevedon: Multilingual Matters.

BIALYSTOK, E. (ed.) 1991, *Language Processing in Bilingual Children*. Cambridge: Cambridge University Press.

BIALYSTOK, E. and HERMAN, J., 1997, Does bilingualism matter for early literacy? *Bilingualism: Language and Cognition* 2 (1), 35–44.

DE GROOT, A.M.B. and KROLL, J.F. (eds) 1997, *Tutorials in Bilingualism: Psycholinguistic Perspectives*. Mahwah, NJ: Erlbaum.

FABBRO, F., 1999, *The Neurolinguistics of Bilingualism: An Introduction*. Hove, East Sussex: Psychology Press.

PADILLA, R.V. and BENAVIDES, A.H. (eds.) 1992, *Critical Perspectives on Bilingual Education Research*. Tempe, AZ: Bilingual Press.

VALDÉS, G. and FIGUEROA, R.A. 1994, *Bilingualism and Testing: A Special Case of Bias*. Norwood, NJ: Ablex.

See also two journals for the most recent research in this area: (a) *International Journal of Bilingualism* and (b) *Bilingualism: Language and Cognition*.

STUDY ACTIVITIES

(1)   Find one or more examples of an IQ test. Examine the content of the test and locate any items which you think will be unfair to bilinguals in your region. Examine both the language and the cultural content of the IQ test.

(2)   Find a student or a teacher who you consider to be bilingual. Ask them to talk about the relationship between their bilingualism and thinking. Ask them if they feel it gives them any advantages and any disadvantages. Collect from them examples and illustrations.

(3)   Using one of the tests or experiments mentioned in this chapter, select a student (or a group of students) and give them that test. For example, ask them how many uses they can think of for a brick or for a cardboard box. Compare the answers of those who are more and less bilingual and see if there are differences in quality and quantity of answers.

Cognitive Theories of Bilingualism and the Curriculum

Introduction

The Balance Theory

The Iceberg Analogy

The Thresholds Theory

The Evolution of the Thresholds Theory

Curriculum Relevance

Criticisms

Conclusion

Cognitive Theories of Bilingualism and the Curriculum

INTRODUCTION

The previous chapter examined the relationship between bilingualism and IQ and that between bilingualism and cognition. The discussion was primarily based on research findings and culminated in explanations of the likely positive relationship between bilingualism and thinking processes and products. This chapter extends that discussion of explanations by firstly considering a 'naive' theory of language and cognitive functioning; then, secondly, examining the development of a major and dominating theory of bilingualism and cognition. The culmination of the chapter is a discussion of how this evolved theory has direct curriculum implications.

THE BALANCE THEORY

The previous chapter noted that initial research into bilingualism and cognitive functioning and into bilingualism and educational attainment often found bilinguals to be inferior to monolinguals. This connects with a naive theory of bilingualism which represents the two languages as existing together in **balance**. The picture is of weighing scales, with a second language increasing at the expense of the first language. An alternative naive picture-theory attached to the early research is of **two language balloons** inside the head. The picture on the following page portrays the monolingual as having one well filled balloon. The bilingual is pictured as having two less filled or half filled balloons. As the second language balloon is pumped higher (e.g. English in the US), so the first language balloon (e.g. Spanish) diminishes in size. As one language balloon increases, the other decreases.

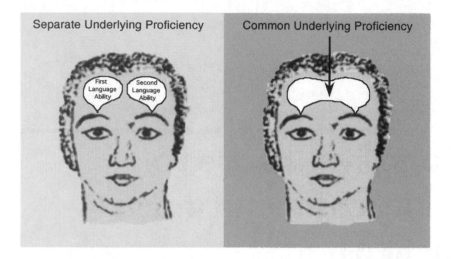

The balance and balloon picture theories of bilingualism and cognition appear to be held intuitively by many people. Many parents and teachers, politicians and large sections of the public appear to latently, subconsciously take the balloon picture as the one that best represents bilingual functioning. Cummins (1980a) refers to this as the **Separate Underlying Proficiency Model of Bilingualism**. This model conceives of the two languages operating separately without transfer and with a restricted amount of 'room' for languages.

What appears logical is not always psychologically valid. While both the balance or balloon ideas are plausible, neither fits the evidence. As the previous chapter concluded, when children become balanced bilinguals, the evidence suggests that there are cognitive advantages rather than disadvantages for being bilingual. Similarly, Chapter 11 will show that certain types of bilingual education (e.g. early total immersion and heritage language, bilingual education) appear to result in performance advantages (e.g. in two languages and in general curriculum performance) compared with submersion or monolingual education.

Research has also suggested that it is wrong to assume that the brain has only a limited amount of room for language skills, such that monolingualism is preferable (see Chapter 7). There appears to be enough cerebral living quarters not only for two languages, but for other languages as well. The picture of the weighing scales, of one language increasing at the expense the second language, does not fit the data. Other pictures, provided later in this chapter, better encapsulate research findings.

There is another fallacy with the balance or balloon theory. The assumption of the theory is that the first and second language are kept apart in two 'balloons' inside the head. The evidence suggests the opposite – that language attributes are not separated in the cognitive system, but transfer readily and are interactive. For example, when school lessons are through the medium of Spanish, they do not solely feed a Spanish part of the brain. Or when other lessons are in English, they do not only feed the English part of the brain. Rather lessons learnt in one language can readily transfer into the other language. Teaching a child to multiply numbers in Spanish or use a dictionary in English easily transfers to multiplication or dictionary use in the other language. A child does not have to be re-taught to multiply numbers in English. A mathematical concept can be easily and immediately used in English or Spanish if those languages are sufficiently well developed. Such easy exchange leads to an alternative idea called **Common Underlying Proficiency** (Cummins, 1980a, 1981a).

THE ICEBERG ANALOGY

Cummins' (1980a, 1981a) **Common Underlying Proficiency model** of bilingualism can be pictorially represented in the form of two icebergs (see below). The two icebergs are separate above the surface. That is, two languages are visibly different in outward conversation. Underneath the surface, the two icebergs are fused so that the two languages do not function separately. Both languages operate through the same central processing system.

A distinction can thus been made between the **Separate Underlying Proficiency (SUP) and Common Underlying Proficiency models of bilingualism (CUP)**. The former (SUP) relates to the 'two balloon' idea presented earlier in this chapter; the latter (CUP) relates to the iceberg idea. The **Common Underlying Proficiency** model of bilingualism may be summarized in six parts:

(1) Irrespective of the language in which a person is operating, the thoughts that accompany talking, reading, writing and listening come from the same central engine. When a person owns two or more languages, there is one integrated source of thought.

(2) Bilingualism and multilingualism are possible because people have the capacity to store easily two or more languages. People can also function in two or more languages with relative ease.

(3) Information processing skills and educational attainment may be developed through two languages as well as through one language. Cognitive functioning and school achievement may be fed through one monolingual channel or equally successfully through two well developed language channels. Both channels feed the same central processor.

(4) The language the child is using in the classroom needs to be sufficiently well developed to be able to process the cognitive challenges of the classroom.

(5) Speaking, listening, reading or writing in the first or the second language helps the whole cognitive system to develop. However, if children are made to operate in an insufficiently developed second language (e.g. in a 'submersion' classroom), the system will not function at its best. If children are made to operate in the classroom in a poorly developed second language, the quality and quantity of what they learn from complex curriculum materials and produce in oral and written form may be relatively weak and impoverished. This has been the experience of some Finns in Swedish schools who were forced to operate in Swedish (Skutnabb-Kangas & Toukomaa, 1976). Such children tended to perform poorly in the curriculum in both Finnish and Swedish because both languages were insufficiently developed to cope with given curriculum material.

(6) When one or both languages are not functioning fully (e.g. because of an unfavorable attitude to learning through the second language, pressure to replace the home language with the majority language) cognitive functioning and academic performance may be negatively affected.

The distinction between Separate Underlying Proficiency (SUP) and Common Underlying Proficiency models of bilingualism (CUP) does not fully sum up the findings from research on cognitive functioning and bilingualism. Therefore this chapter moves on to examining other more sophisticated theories.

THE THRESHOLDS THEORY

Several studies have suggested that the further the child moves towards balanced bilingualism, the greater the likelihood of cognitive advantages (e.g. Cummins & Mulcahy, 1978; Duncan & de Avila, 1979; Kessler & Quinn, 1982; Dawe, 1982, 1983; Clarkson, 1992; Cummins, 2000b). Thus the question has become 'Under what conditions does bilingualism have positive, neutral and negative effects on cognition?' How far does someone have to travel up the two language ladders to obtain cognitive advantages from bilingualism?

One theory that partially summarizes the relationship between cognition and degree of bilingualism is called the **Thresholds Theory**. This was first postulated by Toukomaa and Skutnabb-Kangas (1977) and by Cummins (1976). They suggest that the research on cognition and bilingualism is best explained by the idea of two thresholds. Each threshold is a level of language competence that has consequences for a child. The first threshold is a level for a child to reach to avoid the negative consequences of bilingualism. The second threshold is a level required to experience the possible positive benefits of bilingualism. Such a theory therefore limits which children will be likely to obtain cognitive benefits from bilingualism. It also suggests that there are children who may derive detrimental consequences from their bilingualism.

The Thresholds Theory may be portrayed in terms of a house with three floors (see following page). Up the sides of the house are placed two language ladders, indicating that a bilingual child will usually be moving upward and will not usually be stationary on a floor. On the **bottom floor** of the house will be those whose current competence in both their languages is insufficiently or relatively inadequately developed, especially compared with their age group. When there is a low level of competence in both languages, there may be negative or detrimental cognitive effects. For example, a child who is unable to cope in the classroom in either language may suffer when processing information. At the **middle level**, the second floor of the house, will be those with age-appropriate competence in one of their languages but not in both. For example, children who can operate in the classroom in one of their languages but not in their second language may reside in this second level. At this level, a partly-bilingual child will be little different in cognition from the monolingual child and is unlikely to have any significant positive or negative cognitive differences compared with a monolingual. At the top of the house, the **third floor**, there resides children who approximate 'balanced' bilinguals. At this level, children will have age-appropriate competence in two or more languages. For example, they can cope with curriculum material in either of their languages. It is at this level that the positive cognitive advantages of bilingualism may appear. When a child has age-appropriate ability in both their languages, they may have cognitive advantages over monolinguals.

Research support for the Thresholds Theory comes, for example, from Bialystok (1988), Clarkson and Galbraith (1992), Clarkson (1992), Dawe (1983) and Cummins (2000b). Dawe's (1983) study examined bilingual Panjabi, Mirpuri and Jamaican children aged 11 to 13. On tests of deductive mathematical reasoning, Dawe (1983) found evidence for both the lower and the higher threshold. As competency in two languages increased, so did deductive reasoning skills in mathematics. Limited competence in both languages appeared to result in negative cognitive outcomes. Bialystok (1988) examined two parts to metalinguistic awareness (analysis of linguistic knowledge and control of linguistic processing) in six- to seven-year-old monolingual, partial bilingual and fluently French–English children. She found that 'the level of bilingualism is decisive in determining the effect it will have on development' (p. 567).

The Thresholds Theory relates not only to cognition but also to education. With children in Immersion Education (e.g. in Canada – see Chapters 10 and 11), there is usually a temporary lag in achievement when the curriculum is taught through the second language. Until the second language (e.g. French) has developed well

Top Floor   Balanced Bilinguals

At this level, children have age-appropriate competence in both languages and there are likely to be positive cognitive advantages

SECOND THRESHOLD

Middle Floor   Less Balanced Bilinguals

At this level, children have age-appropriate competence in one but not two languages. There are unlikely to be positive or negative cognitive consequences

FIRST THRESHOLD

Lower Floor   Limited Bilinguals

At this level, children have low levels of competence in both languages, with likely negative cognitive effects

FIRST LANGUAGE

SECOND LANGUAGE

enough to cope with curriculum material, a temporary delay may be expected. Once French is developed sufficiently to cope with the conceptual tasks of the class-room, Immersion Education is unlikely to have detrimental achievement consequences for children. Indeed, such an immersion experience seems to enable children to reach the third floor of the house, with resulting positive cognitive advantages (Cummins, 2000b).

The Thresholds Theory also helps to summarize why minority language children taught through a second language (e.g. immigrants in the US) sometimes fail to develop sufficient competency in their second language (e.g. English) and fail to benefit from 'weak' forms of bilingual education. Their low level of proficiency in English, for example, limits their ability to cope in the curriculum. Therefore Maintenance Bilingual Education Programs, that allow a child to operate in their more developed home language, can result in superior performance compared with submersion and transitional bilingual education.

A **problem** with the Thresholds Theory is in precisely defining the level of language proficiency a child must obtain in order, firstly to avoid the negative effects of bilingualism, and secondly, to obtain the positive advantages of bilingualism. At what language 'height' the ceilings become floors is not clear. Indeed, the danger may be in constructing artificial 'critical stages' or levels, when transition is gradual and smooth. This point is returned to in the following section.

THE EVOLUTION OF THE THRESHOLDS THEORY

From out of the Thresholds Theory developed a succession of more refined theories of bilingualism. The first evolution of the Thresholds Theory considered the relationship between a bilingual's two languages. To this end, Cummins (1978, 2000b) outlined the Developmental Interdependence hypothesis.

This hypothesis suggested that a child's second language competence is partly dependent on the level of competence already achieved in the first language. The more developed the first language, the easier it will be to develop the second language. When the first language is at a low stage of evolution, the more difficult the achievement of bilingualism will be.

Alongside this, there developed a distinction between surface fluency and the more evolved language skills required to benefit from the education process (Cummins, 1984a). This was partly a reaction against Oller (1979) who was claiming that language proficiency differences between individuals were located on just one dimension (see Chapter 1). Cummins (1979) found that everyday conversational language could be acquired in two years while the more complex language abilities needed to cope with the curriculum could take five to seven or more years to develop. In California, Hakuta *et al.* (2000) found that oral proficiency takes three to five years to develop, while academic English proficiency can take four to seven years. This makes calls for English immersion schooling for immigrants (see Chapter 9 – where children are expected to acquire English just in one year) unrealistic and damaging).

Simple communication skills (e.g. holding a simple conversation with a shopkeeper) may hide a child's relative inadequacy in the language proficiency necessary to meet the cognitive and academic demands of the classroom. The language used when playing with a ball in the school playground is very different from 'calculate, using a protractor, the obtuse angle of the parallelogram and then construct a diagonal line between the two obtuse angles and investigate if this creates congruent triangles'.

Cummins (1984a, 1984b, 2000b) expressed this distinction in terms of **basic interpersonal communicative skills (BICS)** and **cognitive/academic language**

proficiency (CALP). BICS is said to occur when there are contextual supports and props for language delivery. Face-to-face '**context embedded**' situations provide, for example, non-verbal support to secure understanding. Actions with eyes and hands, instant feedback, cues and clues support verbal language. CALP, on the other hand, is said to occur in **context reduced** academic situations. Where higher order thinking skills (e.g. analysis, synthesis, evaluation) are required in the curriculum, language is '**disembedded**' from a meaningful, supportive context. Where language is 'disembedded', the situation is often referred to as '**context reduced**'.

The distinction between BICS and CALP is aided by an image of an iceberg (see Cummins, 1984b). Above the surface are language skills such as comprehension and speaking. Underneath the surface are the skills of analysis and synthesis. Above the surface are the language skills of pronunciation, vocabulary and grammar. Below the surface are the deeper, subtle language skills of meanings and creative composition.

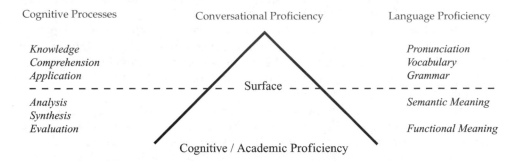

The distinction has been influential and valuable for policy and practice. It was never intended as contextually universal, a complete theory, or to indicate when second language reading (e.g. English in the US) or cognitively challenging content instruction in English should be introduced. Indeed, the conceptual distinction has been unfairly criticized for the absence of many components it was never intended to contain (see Cummins, 2000a; 2000b). However, before leaving this BICS/CALP distinction, it is important to declare its boundaries and limitations (see Wiley, 1996a).

(1) The distinction between BICS and CALP has intuitive appeal and does appear to fit the case of children who are seemingly fluent in their second language, yet cannot cope in the curriculum in that language. However, it only paints a two stage idea. The idea of a larger number of dimensions of language competences may be expressed more exactly. Children and adults may move forward on language dimensions in terms of sliding scales rather than in big jumps.

Such development is like gradually increasing in language competence analogous to increasing gradually the volume on a television set. Harley *et al.*'s (1987, 1990) research suggests that a bilingual's language competences are evolving, dynamic, interacting and intricate. They are not simple dichotomies, easily compartmentalized and static.

(2)   The BICS/CALP distinction enabled an understanding and explanation of previous research (e.g. Wong Fillmore, 1979; Snow & Hoefnagel-Höhle, 1978; Cummins, 1984b, 2000b). However, Martin-Jones and Romaine (1986) express doubts about it being possible to test the distinction. The distinction between BICS and CALP does not indicate how the two ideas may be precisely defined and accurately tested. Thus the distinction becomes difficult to operationalize in research.

(3)   Terms such as BICS and CALP tend to be imprecise, value-laden and become over-compartmentalized, simplified and misused. These hypothetical terms may unwittingly be regarded as real entities. Such terms may be used to label and stereotype students, especially if BICS is seen as inferior to CALP (Wiley, 1996a).

(4)   The relationship between language development and cognitive development is not unequivocal or simple. It is not simply a case of one growing as a direct result of the other. Cognitive and linguistic acquisition exist in a relationship that is influenced by various other factors (e.g. politics, power relationships, social practices, culture, context, motivation, school, home and community effects). Language proficiency relates to an individual's total environment, not just to cognitive skills.

(5)   The sequential nature of BICS first and then CALP is a typical route for immigrant children learning a second language. However, the order is not absolute. Occasionally there will be exceptions (e.g. a scholar who reads a language for research purposes but does not speak that language).

(6)   CALP is operationally about the ability to perform well on school tests (test-wiseness). This relates to specific, traditional, school-based literacy practices. Such practices favor the middle-class groups that control institutions. Such tests favor 'standard' academic language with a bias against speakers of dialects, Creoles and non-standard language (e.g. Black English).

(7)   Oral language and interpersonal communication is not necessarily less cognitively demanding than literate academic language. For example, careful logic, metaphor and other abstract aspects of language occur in face-to-face communication as often as in written language.

(8)   School-based academic/cognitive language does not represent universal higher-order cognitive skills nor all forms of literacy practice. Different sociocultural contexts have different expectations and perceived patterns of appropriateness in language and thinking such that a school is only one specific context for 'higher order' language production.

The distinction between BICS and CALP helps explain the relative failure within the educational system of many minority language children. For example, in the United States, transitional bilingual education programs aim to give students English language skills sufficient for them to be able to converse with peers and teachers in mainstream education and to operate in the curriculum. Having achieved surface fluency, they may be transferred to mainstream education. The transfer occurs because children appear to have sufficient language competence (BICS) to cope in mainstream education. Cummins' (1984a) distinction between BICS and CALP explains why such children tend to fail when mainstreamed. Their cognitive academic language proficiency is not developed enough to cope with the demands of the curriculum. What Cummins (1984a) regards as essential in the bilingual education of children is that the 'common underlying proficiency' be well developed. That is, a child's language-cognitive abilities need to be sufficiently well developed to cope with the curriculum processes of the classroom. This underlying ability could be developed in the first or the second language, but also in both languages simultaneously.

Cummins (2000a, 2000b) has extended the instructional implications of CALP in terms of three components : Cognitive, Academic and Language.

Cognitive: instruction should be cognitively challenging using higher order thinking skills such as evaluating, inferring, generalizing and classifying.

Academic: curriculum content should be integrated with language instruction so that students learn the language of specific academic areas.

Language: critical language awareness should be developed both linguistically (e.g. conventions of each language) and socioculturally/sociopolitically (e.g. different status and power with languages, language use).

A further development of this theory proposes two dimensions (Cummins, 1981b, 1983b, 1984b). This theory is represented in the diagram below:

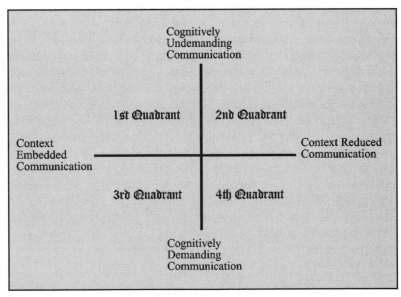

Both dimensions concern communicative proficiency. The **first dimension** refers to the amount of contextual support available to a student. **Context embedded communication** exists when there is a good degree of support in communication, particularly via body language. For example, by pointing to objects, using the eyes, head nods, hand gestures and intonation, people give and receive plenty of clues and cues to help the content of the message to be understood.

An example of context embedded communication would be when two children who are hardly able to use each other's languages seem able to communicate quite well by gestures, non-verbal reinforcements and bodily movements. It is not infrequent to see two young children of different languages playing together without difficulty. In **context reduced communication** there will be very few cues to the meaning that is being transmitted. The words of the sentence exist almost alone in conveying the meaning. An example of context reduced communication is often the classroom where the meaning is restricted to words, with a subtlety and precision of meanings in the vocabulary of the teacher or the book.

The **second dimension** is the level of cognitive demands required in communication. **Cognitively demanding communication** may occur in a classroom where much information at a challenging level needs processing quickly. **Cognitively undemanding communication** is where a person has the mastery of language skills sufficient to enable easy communication. An example would be having a conversation in the street, shop, or stadium, where the processing of information is relatively simple and straightforward.

Surface fluency or basic interpersonal communication skills will fit into the first quadrant (see diagram). That is, BICS (basic interpersonal communication skills) is context embedded, cognitively undemanding use of a language. Language that is cognitively and academically more advanced (CALP) fits into the fourth quadrant (context reduced and cognitively demanding). Cummins (1981b) theory suggests that second language competency in the first quadrant (surface fluency) develops relatively independently of *first* language surface fluency. In comparison, context reduced, cognitively demanding communication develops inter-dependently and can be promoted by either language or by both languages in an interactive way. Thus, the theory suggests that bilingual education will be successful when children have enough first or second language proficiency to work in the context reduced, cognitively demanding situation of the classroom.

The quadrants can act as a guide for instructional planning. A teacher valuably takes into account students' linguistic development and experience, as well as their understanding of the topic. Then the teacher can create activities or experiences that are cognitively challenging and contextually supported as needed. This will be exemplified in the next section of this chapter.

For Cummins (1981b, 2000b) it often takes one or two years for a child to acquire context-embedded second language fluency, but five to seven years or more to acquire context-reduced fluency. This is illustrated in the graphs on the following page. Research by Hakuta and D'Andrea (1992) with Mexican-Americans found that 'English proficiency reaches asymptotic performance after about eight years.

This corresponds quite well with the figures of five to seven years required for attainment of the full range of second language acquisition as estimated by Cummins (1984) based on a heterogeneous L1 population in Canada' (p. 96). In the San Francisco Bay Area, Hakuta *et al.* (2000) found that social English takes three to five years to develop, while academic English can take four to seven years. Shohamy (1999) found that seven to nine years are needed for heterogeneous immigrant students in Israel to catch-up with native speakers in Hebrew literacy. Such native-speakers are not standing still in language development. The immigrants are chasing a moving target.

Children with some conversational ability in their second language may falsely appear ready to be taught through their second language in a classroom. Cummins's (1981b) theory suggests that children operating at the context embedded level in the language of the classroom may fail to understand the content of the curriculum and fail to engage in the higher order cognitive processes of the classroom, such as synthesis, discussion, analysis, evaluation and interpretation.

This two-dimensional model helps explain various research findings:

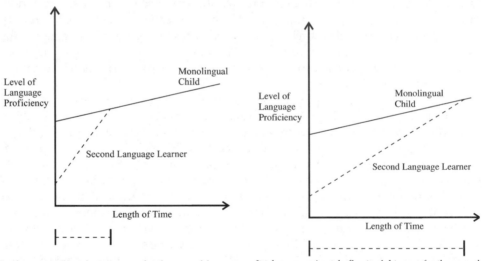

It takes approximately **two years** for the second language learner to reach the same level of proficiency as a monolingual in **context embedded** language proficiency

It takes approximately **five to eight years** for the second language learner to reach the same level of proficiency as the monolingual in **context reduced** language proficiency

(1) In the United States, minority language children may be transferred from transitional bilingual programs into English-only schooling when their conversational ability in English seems sufficient. Such students then frequently perform poorly in mainstream schooling. The theory suggests that this is due to their not having the developed ability in English (or their home language) to operate in an environment that is more cognitively and academically demanding.

(2)   Immersion students in Canada tend to lag behind their monolingual peers for a short period. Once they acquire second language proficiency sufficient to operate in a cognitively demanding and context reduced environment, they usually catch up with their peers.

(3)   Experiments in the United States, Canada and Europe with minority language children who are allowed to use their minority language for part or much of their elementary schooling show that such children do not experience retardation in school achievement or in majority language proficiency. Through their minority language, they develop the ability to be relatively successful in the cognitively demanding and context reduced classroom environment (Secada, 1991). This ability then transfers to the majority language when that language is sufficiently well developed. Children learning to read in their home language are not just developing home language skills. They are also developing higher order cognitive and linguistic skills that will help with the future development of reading in the majority language as well as with general intellectual development. As Cummins (1984a) noted, 'transfer is much more likely to occur from minority to majority language because of the greater exposure to literacy in the majority language and the strong social pressure to learn it' (p. 143).

CURRICULUM RELEVANCE

What a student brings to the classroom in terms of previous learning is a crucial starting point for the teacher. A student's reservoir of knowledge, understanding and experience can provide a meaningful context on which the teacher can build (Robson, 1995). For example, there will be occasions when a student will learn more from a story read by the teacher than listening to a language tape. When the teacher dramatizes a story by adding gestures, pictures, facial expressions and other acting skills, the story becomes more context-embedded than listening to a tape cassette. Getting a student to talk about something familiar will be cognitively less demanding than talking about something culturally or academically unfamiliar. This means that any curriculum task presented to the student needs considering for the following points:

- what the task requires of the child; the cognitive demands inherent in the task (as found by an individual child); the 'entry skills' that a task necessitates. This is illustrated in the table.
- form of presentation to the child (degree of context embeddedness or context reduction); what form of presentation will be meaningful to the child; use of visual aids, demonstration, modeling, computers, oral and written instructions; amount of teacher assistance;
- the child's language proficiencies;
- the child's previous cultural and educational experience and knowledge, individual learning style and learning strategies; expectations and attitudes, confidence and initiative; the child's familiarity with the type of task;

Cognitively undemanding

Greeting someone	Reciting nursery rhymes
Talking about the weather today	Listening to a story or poem on cassette
Make their own books based on their own spoken or written stories	Describe stories heard or seen on TV

Context embedded / **Context reduced**

Giving instructions about making a painting	Listening to the news
Use simple measuring skills	Reading a book and discussing the contents
Role play	Relate new information in a book to existing knowledge
Dramatic stories	Discuss ways that language is written; styles and conventions
Solution seeking	
Explaining and justifying	Reflecting on feelings

Cognitively demanding

- what is acceptable as evidence that learning has successfully occurred; what constitutes mastery or a sufficient approximation; an appropriate form of 'formative' and 'summative' assessment (see Chapters 2 and 14) that may be gestural, action (e.g. building a model), drawing, oral or written (Robson, 1995);

A simple example of using the two dimensions to produce an appropriate **teaching strategy** is now presented (see Frederickson & Cline, 1990; Cline & Frederickson, 1996).

A teacher wants a group to learn how to measure height and to understand the concept of height. Listed below are a few of the teaching strategies for teaching about height. Following the list is a diagram placing the four strategies on the two dimensions:

- One-to-one, individual teaching using various objects to measure height (1).
- A demonstration from the front of the room by the teacher using various objects (2).
- Teacher giving oral instructions without objects (3).
- Reading instructions from a work card without pictures (4).

As the following diagram indicates, the example of teaching height can be analyzed in terms of the two dimensions. One-to-one individual teaching will fit somewhere in the context embedded, cognitively undemanding quadrant. Using work cards may be closer to the context reduced, cognitively demanding area. Demonstrations and oral explanations appear on the diagonal from 'top

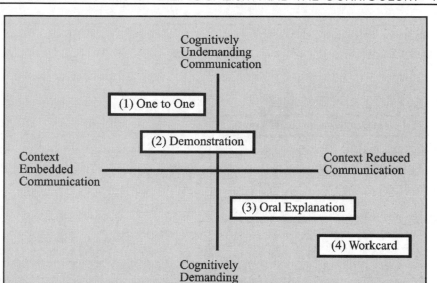

left' to 'bottom right', in-between individual teaching and work cards. The exact location of teaching approaches on the graph will vary according to teacher, topic, learner and lesson. The example illustrates that the two dimensions can be a valuable way of examining teaching approaches with bilingual children. The dimensions are also useful for analyzing appropriate methods of **classroom assessment**. The dimensions may help focus on task-related curriculum assessment that is more fair and appropriate to bilingual children than norm referenced testing. A teacher wanting to check progress on measuring height has a choice, for example:

- **observing** a child measure the height of a new object (1);
- asking the child to give a **commentary** while measuring a new object (2);
- asking the child to provide a **write-up** of the process (3);
- **discussing** in an abstract way the concept of height (4).

In plotting these four methods of assessment (see diagram on next page), placement on the graph will vary with different kinds of tasks and testing procedures. All four quadrants can be 'filled' depending on the student, teacher, topic and test. There is also value in comparing the two graphs presented here. The teaching and learning approach taken may well influence the form of assessment. That is, if a context embedded, cognitively undemanding learning strategy is used with a child, assessment may be on similar lines (e.g. observation of child activity). Equally, a context reduced, cognitively demanding learning strategy suggests a 'matched' method of assessment (e.g. discussion).

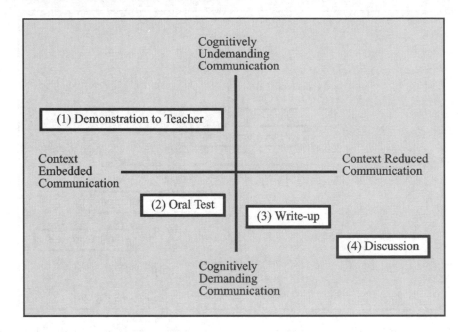

CRITICISMS

There are criticisms of Cummins' (1981b) theory of the relationship between language and cognition (Edelsky *et al.*, 1983; Edelsky, 1991; Martin-Jones & Romaine, 1986; Rivera, 1984; Frederickson & Cline, 1990; Robson, 1995; Wiley, 1996a). A detailed rebuttal can be found can be found in Cummins (2000a; 2000b). The criticisms can be briefly summarized as follows:

(1) Cummins' (1981b) early theory may artificially isolate certain ingredients in a bilingual's cognitive or classroom experience. The attainment of bilingualism or the relationship between bilingual education and school achievement rests on many other factors than are presented in this theory. The early theory was essentially individual and psychological. Bilingualism and bilingual education need to consider other variables; cultural, social, political, community, teacher expectations and home factors. Each and all of these variables help explain bilingualism as an individual and societal phenomenon. Cummins (1986b) addressed these issues in further theoretical formulations (see Chapter 18 and Cummins, 2000b).

(2) Cummins (1981b) criterion of educational success tended to center on dominant, middle-class indices of achievement. Thus language skills, literacy and formal educational achievement are highlighted. Alternative outcomes of schooling such as self-esteem, social and emotional development, divergent

and creative thinking, long-term attitude to learning, employment and moral development were not initially considered.

(3)   The theory has been produced as a *post hoc* explanation of a variety of research findings. The theoretical framework requires direct empirical investigation and confirmation with replication across culture and country, time and educational tradition.

(4)   The labels used tend to be vague, value-laden and in danger of creating an over-simplification and a stereotyping of individual functioning and classroom processes. Essentially hypothetical and abstract, the labels may be adopted as concrete and real (see earlier in this chapter).

(5)   The two dimensions are not necessarily distinct, and may not best be represented by two maximally separated (90 degrees apart) axes. When applying Cummins' two dimensions to curriculum tasks, Frederickson and Cline (1990) found it… 'difficult to disentangle the 'cognitive' from the 'contextual'. In some cases, movement along the contextual dimensions has actually been represented on the model as a diagonal shift [on the diagram from top left to bottom right], as it was found in practice that making tasks or instructions more context embedded also made them somewhat less cognitively demanding. Similarly, changes in cognitive demand may result in tasks actually being presented with greater context embeddedness' (p. 26).

(6)   When bilingual children appear to have learning difficulties, a teacher may decide to simplify tasks into smaller and more isolated steps. Such a strategy is part of the behavioral objectives approach or a task analysis approach to the curriculum. It may sometimes result in a non-meaningful context to a curriculum task. By making the task context-reduced, the learning may become more difficult rather than easier, as intended.

(7)   Attempting to achieve context embeddedness in any curriculum situation requires empathic understanding of a child's cultural background which itself is dynamic and ever evolving. A danger lies in the teacher developing self-defeating stereotyped assumptions about a child's ethnic experience which may transmit low expectations.

(8)   The theory does not make allowances for a child's cognitive strategies in learning, nor their learning style.

CONCLUSION

Early and now discredited ideas of two languages within an individual are represented by two pictures. First, two languages as a balance; second, two languages operating as two separate balloons in the head. Such misconceptions can be replaced by pictures such as the dual iceberg and the three tiered house. Depending on language development in both languages, the cognitive functioning of an individual can be viewed as integrated, with easy transfer of concepts and knowledge between languages. Understanding and thinking will be affected by the contextual support that exists and the degree of cognitive demands in a task. Successful cognitive operations in the classroom will depend on matching curriculum tasks with language competences. Sensitivity to the need for contextual support and the cognitive demands of a classroom are important if an individual is to maximize learning in the curriculum.

KEY POINTS IN THE CHAPTER

- Two languages acting like a balance in the thinking quarters of a bilingual is incorrect. Instead the Common Underlying Proficiency model suggests that languages operate from the same central operating system.
- The Thresholds Theory suggests that bilinguals who have age-appropriate competence in both languages share cognitive advantages over monolinguals.
- There is a distinction between Basic Interpersonal Communicative Skills (BICS) that concern everyday, straightforward communication skills that are helped by contextual supports, and Cognitive/Academic Language Proficiency (CALP). CALP is the level of language required to understand academically demanding subject matter in a classroom. Such language is often abstract, without contextual supports such as gestures and the viewing of objects.
- On average, it takes about two years for a new immigrant to acquire Basic Interpersonal Communicative Skills in a second language, but five to eight years to achieve Cognitive/Academic Language Proficiency in that second language.

SUGGESTED FURTHER READING

CLINE, T. and FREDERICKSON, N. (eds), 1996, *Curriculum Related Assessment, Cummins and Bilingual Children.* Clevedon: Multilingual Matters.
CUMMINS, J. 1984, *Bilingualism and Special Education: Issues in Assessment and Pedagogy.* Clevedon: Multilingual Matters.
CUMMINS, J., 2000, *Language, Power and Pedagogy: Bilingual Children in the Crossfire.* Clevedon: Multilingual Matters.
RIVERA, C. (ed.) 1984, *Language Proficiency and Academic Achievement.* Clevedon: Multilingual Matters.
WILEY, T.G., 1996, *Literacy and Language Diversity in the United States.* Center for Applied Linguistics and Delts Systems, McHenry, Illinois.

STUDY ACTIVITY

(1) Observe a classroom with bilingual children. Make a 10 minute cassette tape of the discourse between the teacher and various students, and/or between students themselves. Use the concepts and ideas of this chapter to describe and discuss the language used.

CHAPTER 9

An Introduction to Bilingual Education

Historical Introduction

A Short History of Bilingual Education in the United States

Varieties of Bilingual Education
Introduction
Submersion Education
Submersion with Pull-Out Classes
Segregationist Education
Transitional Bilingual Education
Mainstream Education (with
Foreign Language Teaching)
Separatist Education

Conclusion

CHAPTER 9

An Introduction to Bilingual Education

HISTORICAL INTRODUCTION

One of the **illusions** about bilingual education is that it is a 20th century phenomenon. In the USA it may appear that bilingual education was born in the 1960s. The Canadian bilingual education movement is often charted from an experimental kindergarten class set up in St Lambert, Montreal, in 1965. In Ireland, bilingual education is sometimes presented as a child of the Irish Free State of 1922. The story of bilingual education in Wales often starts in 1939 with the establishment of the first Welsh-medium primary school. Despite these 20th century events, the historical origins of bilingual education lie well before this century.

The illusion of bilingual education as a modern phenomenon is dangerous on two counts. **First**, it fails to recognize that bilingual education has existed in one form or another for 5000 years or more (Mackey, 1978). Bilingualism and multilingualism are 'a very early characteristic of human societies, and monolingualism a limitation induced by some forms of social change, cultural and ethnocentric developments' (Lewis, 1977, p. 22). Lewis (1977, 1981) discusses the history of bilingualism and bilingual education from the Ancient World through the Renaissance to the modern world.

Second, there is a danger in isolating current bilingualism and bilingual education from their **historical roots**. In many countries (e.g. the USA, Canada, England and Sweden), bilingual education must be linked to the historical context of immigration as well as political movements such as civil rights, equality of educational opportunity, affirmative action and melting pot (integrationist, assimilationist) policies. Bilingual education in Ireland and Wales can only be properly analyzed by the rise of nationalism and language rights movements, for example. In Japan, language education policy has to be examined through movements from monolingual ideology to internationalism (Maher, 1997).

Bilingual education relates to debates about the fundamental purposes and aims of education in general: for individuals, communities, regions and nations. Bilingual education, while isolated as a concept in this chapter, is one component inside a wider social, economic, educational, cultural and political framework. As Paulston (1992b, p. 80) observes: 'unless we try in some way to account for the socio-historical, cultural, and economic–political factors which lead to certain forms of bilingual education, we will never understand the consequences of that education'. The political context of bilingual education is considered in Chapter 18. The history of bilingual education in the United States is now considered, with a particular emphasis on the dynamic and ever developing nature of bilingual education policy.

A SHORT HISTORY OF BILINGUAL EDUCATION IN THE UNITED STATES

Introduction

In the United States, bilingual education has been determined partly by federal government and partly by state government, partly by local initiatives and partly by individuals (e.g. Proposition 227 in California – see Chapter 12). There has been neither total centralization nor devolution to states in bilingual education. Whilst states engage in much planning and policy-making, the federal government has exerted a powerful influence through funding, legislation and action in law. The federal government gives funds for education support services over and above state budgets.

Bilingual education in the United States has moved through considerable changes in the perspectives of politicians, administrators, educationalists and in school practice that indicate that shifts in ideology, preference and practice have occurred (Andersson & Boyer, 1971; Casanova, 1992; Casanova & Arias, 1993; Crawford, 1999; Fitzgerald, 1993; Kloss, 1977, 1998; Lyons, 1990; Malakoff & Hakuta, 1990; Perlmann, 1990; Schlossman, 1983; Schmidt, 2000).

Long before European immigrants arrived in the United States, the land contained a variety of **native** (indigenous) languages. When the Italian, German, Dutch, French, Polish, Czech, Irish, Welsh and other immigrant groups arrived, there were already around 300 separate (Native American) languages in the United States. [Crawford (1999) estimates this number as between 250 and 350 languages.] Immigrants brought with them a wide variety of languages. In the 18th and 19th centuries in the United States, up until the first World War, linguistic diversity was often accepted and the presence of different languages was frequently encouraged through religion, newspapers in different languages, and in both private and public schools.

There were exceptions to the acceptance of language diversity in this early period, such as Benjamin Franklin's anti-German stance in the 1750s, the Californian legislature mandating English-only instruction in 1855 and the ruthless language suppression policies of the Bureau of Indian Affairs in the 1880s (Crawford, 1999). Thus, a high-profile and much-debated US language policy was not present until recent years; the concepts of 'bilingualism' and 'language minorities' were not part of a major national consciousness about language in the 18th and 19th centuries.

However, there were early, pioneering examples of bilingual education in the United States as in the German–English schools. Set up by German communities in Ohio, Pennsylvania, Missouri, Minnesota, North and South Dakota and Wisconsin, bilingual as well as monolingual German education was accepted. Norwegian and Dutch were also languages of instruction within ethnic based schools. This **openness to immigrant languages** in the latter half of the 19th century was partly motivated by competition for students between public and private schools. Other factors such as benevolent (or uninterested) school administrators, the isolation of schools in rural areas, and ethnic homogeneity within an area also enabled a permissive attitude to mother tongue and bilingual education before World War I.

In most large cities in the latter half of the 19th century, English monolingual education was the dominant pattern. However, in cities such as Cincinnati, Baltimore, Denver and San Francisco, dual language education was present. In some schools in Cincinnati, for example, half the day was spent learning through German and the other half of the curriculum was delivered through English.

At the turn of the 20th century, Italian and Jewish immigrants were mostly placed in English-medium mainstream schools. However, examples of **bilingual education** existed and were permitted. For example, some Polish immigrants in Chicago attended Catholic schools where a small amount of teaching was through the mother tongue. So long as policy was within the jurisdiction of local towns and districts, the language of instruction did not become an issue in educational provision.

In the first two decades of the 20th century, a **change** in attitude to bilingualism and bilingual education occurred in the United States. A variety of factors are linked to this change and a subsequent restriction of bilingual education.

- The **number of immigrants** increased dramatically around the turn of the century. Classrooms in public schools were filled with immigrants. This gave rise to fears of new foreigners, and a call for the integration, harmonization and assimilation of immigrants. Immigrants' lack of English language and English literacy was a source of social, political and economic concern. The call for Americanization was sounded, with competence in English becoming associated with loyalty to the United States. The Nationality Act (1906) required immigrants to speak English to become naturalized Americans. The call for child literacy in English rather than child labor, socialization into a unified America rather than ethnic separation, along with increased centralized control, led to a belief in a common language for compulsory schooling.
- In 1919, the Americanization Department of the United States Bureau of Education adopted a resolution recommending 'all states to prescribe that all schools, private and public, be conducted in the English language and that instruction in the elementary classes of all schools be in English' (quoted in García, 1992c). By 1923, 34 states had decreed that **English** must be the sole language of instruction in all elementary schools, public and private.

- A major influence on bilingual education in the United States came with the entry of the United States into the First **World War** in 1917. Anti-German feeling in the United States spread, with a consequent extra pressure for English monolingualism and a melting pot policy achieved through monolingual education. The German language was portrayed as a threat to the unity of Americanization. Linguistic diversity was replaced by linguistic intolerance. Schools became the tool for the assimilation and integration of diverse languages and cultures. Socialization into being American meant the elimination of languages and cultures other than English from schools. An interest in learning foreign languages declined.

This period was not totally restrictive. In 1923, the US Supreme Court declared that a Nebraska state law prohibiting the teaching of a foreign language to elementary school students was unconstitutional under the Fourteenth Amendment. This case, known as *Meyer* v. *Nebraska* concerned a case against a teacher for teaching a Bible story in German to a 10-year-old child. The original Nebraska ruling was that such mother-tongue teaching cultivated ideas and affections foreign to the best interests of the country. The Supreme Court, in overturning the Nebraska ruling, found that proficiency in a foreign language was 'not injurious to the health, morals, or understanding of the ordinary child'.

This **Supreme Court** finding did not, in essence, support bilingualism or bilingual education. The Court observed that the desire of a state legislature to foster a homogeneous people was 'easy to appreciate'. This theme is considered further in Chapter 18 when integration and assimilation is considered.

In 1957, the Russians launched their Sputnik into space. For United States politicians and public, a period of soul-searching led to debates about the quality of US education, US scientific creativity and US competence to compete in an increasingly international world. Doubts arose about the hitherto over-riding concern with English as the melting-pot language, and a new consciousness was aroused about the need for foreign language instruction. In 1958, the **National Defense and Education Act** was passed, promoting foreign language learning in elementary schools, high schools and universities. This, in turn, helped to create a slightly more soul-searching attitude to languages other than English spoken among ethnic groups in the USA.

In the United States in the 1960s, various other factors allowed a few opportunities to bring back bilingual education, albeit in a disparate, semi-isolated manner. The 'opportunity' movement for bilingual schools to be re-established in the United States needs to be understood in the wider perspective of the **Civil Rights movement**, the struggle for the rights of African-Americans, and the call to establish general equality of opportunity (and equality of educational opportunity) for all people, irrespective of race, color or creed. The 1964 Civil Rights Act prohibited discrimination on the basis of color, race or national origin, and led to the establishment of the Office of Civil Rights. This Act is an important marker that symbolizes the beginning of a change in a less negative attitude to ethnic groups, and possibilities for increased tolerance of ethnic languages, at least at the Federal level.

The restoration of the practice of bilingual education in the USA is often regarded as starting in 1963, in one school in Florida. In 1963, **Cuban exiles** established a dual language school (Coral Way Elementary School) in Dade County in South Florida. Believing they were only in exile for a short period, the educated, middle-class Cubans set up this Spanish–English bilingual school. The need to maintain their mother tongue of Spanish was aided by (1) highly trained professional teachers being ready to work in such schools, (2) the Cubans' plight as victims of a harsh Communist state, and (3) their expected temporary stay in the United States. Their unquestioned loyalty to United States' policies and democratic politics gained sympathy for the Cubans. Bilingual education in Dade County received both political support and funding. More details of this movement are found in the section on dual language schools (see also Baker & Jones, 1998).

While the re-establishment of bilingual schools in the USA has benefited from the example and success of Coral Way Elementary School (Pellerano & Fradd, 1998), an understanding of bilingual education in the United States requires a grasp of legislation and lawsuits (Crawford, 1999; Hornberger *et al., 1999).*

In 1967, a Texas Senator, Ralph Yarborough, introduced a **Bilingual Education Act** as an **amendment** of the **1965 Elementary and Secondary Education Act**. The legislation was designed to help mother tongue Spanish speakers who were seen as failing in the school system. **Enacted in 1968** as **Title VII of the Elementary and Secondary Education Act**, the Bilingual Education Act indicated that bilingual education programs were to be seen as part of federal educational policy. It authorized the use of federal funds for the education of speakers of languages other than English. It also undermined the English-only legislation still lawful in many states. The 1968 Bilingual Education Act also allocated funds for such minority language speakers while they shifted to working through English in the classroom.

A landmark in United States' bilingual education was a lawsuit. A court case was brought on behalf of Chinese students against the San Francisco School District in 1970. The case concerned whether or not non-English speaking students received equal educational opportunities when instructed in a language they could not understand. The failure to provide bilingual education was alleged to violate both the equal protection clause of the 14th Amendment and Title VI of the Civil Rights Act of 1964. The case, known as *Lau versus Nichols*, was rejected by the federal district court and a court of appeals, but was accepted by the Supreme Court in 1974. The verdict outlawed English submersion programs for language minority children and resulted in nationwide 'Lau remedies'. The Supreme Court ruled that 'There is no equality of treatment merely by providing students with the same facilities, textbooks, teachers and curriculum; for students who do not understand English are effectively foreclosed from any meaningful education.'

The Lau remedies acknowledged that students not proficient in English needed help. Such remedies included English as a Second Language classes, English tutoring and some form of bilingual education. The Lau remedies created some expansion in the use of minority languages in schools although the accent nationally was still on a transitional use of the home language for English language learners.

The Lau court case is symbolic of the dynamic and continuing contest to establish language rights in the USA particularly through testing the law in the courtroom (Casanova, 1991; Crawford, 1999; Hakuta, 1986; Lyons, 1990; Schmidt, 2000). However, the kind of bilingual education needed to achieve equality of educational opportunity for language minority children was not defined although the right to equal opportunity for language minorities was asserted. The means of achieving that right was not declared. Nevertheless, during this era, there was a modest growth in **developmental maintenance bilingual education and ethnic community mother tongue schools**. These schools are considered later in this chapter.

Since the 1980s, there have been moves against an emergence of a strong version of bilingual education, particularly found in the rise of pressure groups such as English First and US English that seek to establish English monolingualism and cultural assimilation (consideration of such political movements is found in Chapter 18). In recent decades in the USA, bilingual education has become contentious, as will now be illustrated.

To understand the current period, it is helpful to examine the legislative changes with respect to bilingual education in the United States. We return to the 1968 Bilingual Education Act (Title VII and part of the Elementary and Secondary Education Act). This provided a compensatory 'poverty program' for the educationally disadvantaged among language minorities. It did not require schools to use a child's home language other than English. However, it did allow a few educators to bring 'home languages' into the classroom rather than exclude them. The **1974 amendments** to this **Bilingual Education Act** (see the chronology table) required schools receiving grants to include teaching in a student's home language and culture so as to allow the child to progress effectively through the educational system. Effective progress in student achievement could occur via the home language or via English. However, this gave rise to fierce debates about how much a student's native language should be used in school (Rhee, 1999). Some argued that it was essential to develop a child's speaking and literacy skills in their native language before English was introduced in a major way. Others argued that educational equality of opportunity could best be realized by teaching English as early as possible and assimilating language minority children into mainstream culture.

In **1978**, the United States Congress reauthorized Transitional Bilingual Education, allowing the native language to be used only to the extent necessary for a child to achieve competence in the English language. **Title VII funds** could not be used for Maintenance Bilingual Education programs. The **1984 and 1988 amendments** allowed increasing percentages of the funds available to be allocated to programs where a students' first language was not used.

The **Reagan administration** was generally hostile to bilingual education. In the *New York Times* on the 3rd March 1981, President Reagan is quoted as saying that 'It is absolutely wrong and against the American concept to have a bilingual education program that is now openly, admittedly, dedicated to preserving their native language and never getting them adequate in English so they can go out into the job market'. Reagan believed that preservation of the native language meant neglect of English language acquisition. Bilingual education programs were seen as serving to neglect English language competence in students. Reagan dismissed bilingual education in favor of submersion and transitional programs.

In 1985, **William Bennett**, the then Secretary of Education, suggested that there was no evidence that children from language minorities (whom the Bilingual Education Act had sought to help), had benefited from this Act. Some 25% of funds were made available for English monolingual, alternative instructional programs (e.g. Structured English programs; Sheltered English programs). This represented a further political dismissal of education through the minority language and a dismissal of 'strong' forms of bilingual education.

The Lau remedies were withdrawn by the Reagan government and do not have the force of law. The federal government left **local politicians** to create their own policies. Further changes in the rights to United States bilingual education are given in the table below. Legislation and litigation has often led to 'weak' forms of bilingual education (e.g. transitional bilingual education). Also, recent legislation has not tended to increase rights to a bilingual education. During the Reagan and Bush Presidencies in the United States, the accent was more on submersion and transitional bilingual education. The right to early education through a minority language failed to blossom in those years (Crawford, 1999).

In 1994, the 103rd Congress undertook a major reform of education through legislation entitled Goals 2000; Educate America Act, and also by the Improving America's Schools Act. This extensive reform included an acknowledgement that students for whom English was a second language ('Limited English Proficient' students) should be expected to achieve high academic standards. Such legislation aimed to provide children with an enriched educational program, improving instructional strategies and making the curriculum more challenging. The Improving America's Schools Act of 1994 reauthorized Title VII, strengthening the state role by requiring state educational authorities to review Title VII appropriations and provide additional funds for specific groups such as immigrants. Thus the reauthorization of Title VII in 1994 continued federal support for bilingual education programs.

Since Title VII of the Improving America's Schools Act of 1994, halting attempts have been made to move away from remedial, compensatory and deficiency models of bilingual education to more innovative models. For example, priority has been given to funding school reform where there is the clear aim to raise standards across the curriculum for all children. In doing this, bilingual children have the opportunity to reach high levels of skills to help develop the nation's human resources and improve US competitiveness in a global market. Thus school districts have been encouraged to create comprehensive school reform plans where bilingual instruction or English as a second language are incorporated into an overall holistic 'raising standards' school system. From 1994, the issue about bilingual education moved from being narrowly focused on the language of instruction to a

broader range of questions being asked about the quality and standards of education being given to language minority students.

Opponents of bilingual education in the United States do not generally oppose
foreign language programs for English speakers. Such programs are regarded as
important in educating students for the global economy. Some forms of bilingualism (e.g. English–Japanese, English–German) are seen to be of value for US
economic prosperity. One of the goals of the National Education Goals Panel of 1994
was thus that the percentage of students who are competent in more than one
language should substantially increase. The 1994 Amendments to the Bilingual
Education Act meant that proficient bilingualism became a desirable goal when it
brought economic benefits to individuals and particularly to the nation. Hence the
Amendments resulted in funding for a larger number of dual language programs.

However, the reauthorization of Title VII came under attack both by politicians
and the US Press. Congress considered legislation to repeal the law and eliminate its
funding. Whilst this did not succeed, it nevertheless pointed to a dominant political
and mass media – being against bilingual education. Title VII appropriations were
reduced by 38% between 1994 and 1996 leading to cuts in bilingual programs, in
teacher training and reducing the budgets for research, evaluation and support of
bilingual education in the United States.

The estimated number of school-age speakers of languages in addition to English
is around 6,670,000 or 13% of the school population (Waggoner, 1998). The number
of 'Limited English Proficient' (LEP) students is around three and a half million
forming approximately 22% of students in California, 13% in Texas, 12% in Florida,
11.5% in Arizona and 7.5% in New York (Macías *et al.*, 1998). Some three-quarters of
such 'LEP' students were reported as being enrolled in programs to meet their
English language needs. However, around 88% of such 'LEP' students are in Title I
(Compensatory Education Programs), Emergency Immigrant Education, Migrant
or Special Education programs. Only 0.4% are in transitional bilingual education
programs and 0.1% are in developmental bilingual education (Macías *et al.*, 1998;
Macías, 2000).

A summary of major events affecting the history of United States bilingual
education is given in the table on the following two pages.

Conclusion

Two conclusions. First, there is common perception that educational policy is often
static, always conservative and very slow to change. The history of bilingual education in the United States tends to falsify and contradict such beliefs. Such history
shows that there is constant change, a constant movement in ideas, ideology and
impetus. There is action and reaction, movement and contra-movement, assertion
and response. One conclusion is that change will always occur in bilingual education policy and provision. Nothing is static. While there will be periods when
bilingual education is criticized, forbidden and rejected, there will be reactions,
with the possibility of more positive, accepting periods ahead. There is no certainty
in the future history of bilingual education, only uncertainty and change. Yet uncer-

Year	United States, Legislation/Litigation affecting Bilingual Education.	Implication
1906	Nationality Act passed	First legislation requiring in-migrants to speak English to become naturalized.
1923	*Meyer* v. *Nebraska* ruling by the US Supreme Court	The ruling outlawed, as an unconstitutional infringement of individual liberties, arbitrary restrictions on the teaching of languages other than English. Proficiency in a foreign language was also constitutional.
1950	Amendments to the Nationality Act	English literacy required for naturalization.
1954	*Brown* v. *Board of Education*	Segregated education based on race made unconstitutional.
1958	National Defense and Education Act	The first federal legislation to promote foreign language learning.
1965	Immigration and Nationality Act	The Act eliminated racial criteria for admission which had hitherto largely barred immigration by, for example, Asians and Africans. Thus the effect was to expand immigration especially from Asia and Latin America. The Act also emphasized the goal of 'family unification' over occupational skills. This encouraged increased immigration by Mexicans in particular.
1965	Elementary and Secondary Education Act (ESEA)	Funds granted to meet the needs of 'educationally deprived children'.
1968	Elementary and Secondary Education Act (ESEA) amendment: The Bilingual Education Act, Title VII	Provided funding to establish bilingual programs for students who did not speak English and who were economically poor.
1974	*Lau* v. *Nichols*	Established that language programs for language minorities not proficient in English were necessary to provide equal educational opportunities.
1974	Equal Educational Opportunity Act (EEOA)	Codified the *Lau* v. *Nichols* decision, requiring every school district to take appropriate action to overcome language barriers that impede equal participation by its students in its instructional programs.
1974	Reauthorization of Bilingual Education Act Title VII of ESEA	Native-language instruction was required for the first time as a condition for receiving bilingual education grants. Bilingual Education was defined as transitional (TBE).
1975	Lau Remedies	Informal guidelines on schools' obligations toward LEP students. This required the provision of bilingual education in districts where the civil rights of such students had been violated.
1976	*Keyes* v. *School District no. 1*, Denver, Colorado	Established bilingual education as compatible with desegregation.

Year	United States, Legislation/Litigation affecting Bilingual Education.	Implication
1977	National Clearinghouse for Bilingual Education is established	To provide a national information center for bilingual education.
1978	Reauthorization of Bilingual Education Act Title VII of ESEA	A new restriction was introduced. Grants could support native-language instruction only to the extent necessary to allow a child to achieve competence in the English language. Funding was thus restricted to TBE; maintenance programs were now ineligible for funding. The term 'Limited English Proficient' (LEP) introduced, replacing LES (Limited English Speaking).
1980–81	Lau Regulations	The Carter Administration attempted to formalize the Lau Remedies, requiring bilingual instruction for LEP students where feasible. The Reagan Administration subsequently withdrew the proposal, leaving uncertainty about schools' obligations in this area.
1981	*Castañeda v. Pickard*	An Appeals court decision established a three-part test to determine whether schools were taking 'appropriate action' under the 1974 Equal Educational Opportunity Act. Programs for LEP students (bilingual or otherwise) must be: (1) based on sound educational theory, (2) implemented with adequate resources, and (3) evaluated and proven effective.
1983	US English Movement launched	Debates about the dominant place of English in law, society and education became more prominent.
1984	Reauthorization of Bilingual Education Act Title VII of ESEA	While most funding was reserved for TBE, monies for maintenance programs were once again permitted, along with 'special alternative' English-only programs.
1988	Reauthorization of Bilingual Education Act Title VII of ESEA	Same as in 1984, but 25% of funding given for English-only Special Alternative Instructional programs
1994	Reauthorization of Bilingual Education Act Title VII of ESEA	Full bilingual proficiency recognized as a lawful educational goal. Funded dual language programs that included English speakers and programs to support Native American languages.The quota for funding SAIP programs was lifted. The new law sought to bring LEP students into mainstream school reform efforts, making it more difficult for their particular needs to be ignored in policymaking.
1998	Proposition 227 passed in California	The 'Unz initiative' sought to impose severe restrictions on native-language instruction for English learners in California, the extent of which is still unresolved.

The author is extremely grateful to James Crawford for his assistance in constructing this table.

tainty and change provide occasional opportunities for bilingual education to progress.

Second, the conclusion must not be that bilingual education moves from more positive 'golden' times to being dismissed and rejected. The history of bilingual education in the Basque Country and Wales follows a different sequence. In these countries, bilingual education has moved from being dismissed and suppressed to considerable expansion. From a time when Welsh was banned in the classroom, there is currently a widespread acceptance and provision of bilingual education in Wales. No universal patterns of change can or should be deduced from either the United States or the Welsh experience. Such unpredictability provides a challenge to bilingual educators.

VARIETIES OF BILINGUAL EDUCATION

Introduction

So far in this chapter, the term bilingual education has been used as if its meaning is unambiguous and self-evident. The opposite is the case. Bilingual education is '**a simple label for a complex phenomenon**' (Cazden & Snow, 1990a). At the outset, a distinction is needed between education that uses and promotes two languages and education for language minority children. This is a difference between a classroom where formal instruction is to foster bilingualism and a classroom where bilingual children are present, but bilingualism is not fostered in the curriculum. The umbrella term, bilingual education, has been used to refer to both situations leaving the term ambiguous and imprecise. Precision can be attempted by specifying the major types of bilingual education.

One early and detailed classification of bilingual education is by Mackey (1970). This account of 90 different patterns of bilingual schooling considers: the languages of the home; the languages of the curriculum; the languages of the community in which the school is located and the international and regional status of the languages. A different approach to categorizing types of bilingual education is to examine the aims of such education. A frequent distinction in aims is between **transitional** and **maintenance** Bilingual Education (Fishman, 1976; Hornberger, 1991).

Transitional bilingual education aims to shift the child from the home, minority language to the dominant, majority language. Social and cultural **assimilation** into the language majority is the underlying aim. **Maintenance** bilingual education attempts to foster the minority language in the child, strengthening the child's sense of cultural identity and affirming the rights of an ethnic minority group in a nation. Otheguy and Otto (1980) make the distinction between the different aims of **static maintenance** and **developmental maintenance**. Static maintenance aims to maintain language skills at the level of the child entering a school. Developmental maintenance seeks to develop a student's home language skills to full proficiency and full biliteracy or literacy. This is sometimes referred to as **Enrichment Bilingual Education** for language minority children. (The term 'Enrichment Bilingual Education' is also used for language majority children who are adding a second language in school). Static maintenance attempts to prevent home language loss but not to increase skills in that first language. Developmental maintenance has a 'goal of proficiency and literacy in the home language equal to English' (Otheguy & Otto, 1980, p. 351). Enrichment bilingual education aims to extend the individual and group use of minority languages, leading to **cultural pluralism** and linguistic diversity (see Chapter 19).

Ferguson *et al.* (1977) widened these distinctions and provided ten examples of varying aims of bilingual education:

(1)   To assimilate individuals or groups into the mainstream of society; to socialize people for full participation in the community.
(2)   To unify a multilingual society; to bring unity to a multi-ethnic, multi-tribal, or multi-national linguistically diverse state.
(3)   To enable people to communicate with the outside world.
(4)   To provide language skills which are marketable, aiding employment and status.
(5)   To preserve ethnic and religious identity.
(6)   To reconcile and mediate between different linguistic and political communities.
(7)   To spread the use of a colonial language, socializing an entire population to a colonial existence.
(8)   To strengthen elite groups and preserve their position in society.
(9)   To give equal status in law to languages of unequal status in daily life.
(10) To deepen understanding of language and culture.

This list shows that bilingual education does not necessarily concern the balanced use of two languages in the classroom. Behind bilingual education are varying and conflicting philosophies and politics of what education is for. Sociocultural, political and economic issues are ever present in the debate over the provision of bilingual education. This will be addressed in Chapters 11 and 18.

The typology of education that is adopted in this chapter is presented in the table on the following page. Ten types of language education are portrayed. The ten different types of program have **multitudinous sub-varieties**, as Mackey's (1970) 90 varieties of bilingual education indicate. One of the intrinsic limitations of typologies is that not all real-life examples will fit easily into the classification. For example, elite 'finishing schools' in Switzerland, and classrooms in Wales where first language Welsh speakers are taught alongside 'immersion' English first language speakers make classification simplistic, although necessary for discussion and understanding. Thus typologies have value for conceptual clarity but they have **limitations**: (1) models suggest static systems whereas bilingual schools and classrooms constantly develop and evolve (as the short history of bilingual education in the USA revealed); (2): there are wide and numerous variations within a model; (3) models address 'inputs' and 'outputs' of the education system, but rarely address the classroom process; (4) models do not explain the success or failure or the relative effectiveness of bilingual education.

Each of ten broad types of program will now be briefly considered.

WEAK FORMS OF EDUCATION FOR BILINGUALISM

Type of Program	Typical Type of Child	Language of the Classroom	Societal and Educational Aim	Aim in Language Outcome
SUBMERSION (Structured Immersion)	Language Minority	Majority Language	Assimilation	Monolingualism
SUBMERSION with Withdrawal Classes / Sheltered English)	Language Minority	Majority Language with 'Pull-out' L2 Lessons	Assimilation	Monolingualism
SEGREGATIONIST	Language Minority	Minority Language (forced, no choice)	Apartheid	Monolingualism
TRANSITIONAL	Language Minority	Moves from Minority to Majority Language	Assimilation	Relative Monolingualism
MAINSTREAM with Foreign Language Teaching	Language Majority	Majority Language with L2/FL Lessons	Limited Enrichment	Limited Bilingualism
SEPARATIST	Language Minority	Minority Language (out of choice)	Detachment/ Autonomy	Limited Bilingualism

STRONG FORMS OF EDUCATION FOR BILINGUALISM AND BILITERACY

Type of Program	Typical Type of Child	Language of the Classroom	Societal and Educational Aim	Aim in Language Outcome
IMMERSION	Language Majority	Bilingual with Initial Emphasis on L2	Pluralism and Enrichment	Bilingualism & Biliteracy
MAINTENANCE/ HERITAGE LANGUAGE	Language Minority	Bilingual with Emphasis on L1	Maintenance, Pluralism and Enrichment	Bilingualism & Biliteracy
TWO-WAY/DUAL LANGUAGE	Mixed Language Minority & Majority	Minority and Majority	Maintenance, Pluralism and Enrichment	Bilingualism & Biliteracy
MAINSTREAM BILINGUAL	Language Majority	Two Majority Languages	Maintenance, Pluralism and Enrichment	Bilingualism & Biliteracy

Notes: (1) L2 = Second Language; L1 = First Language; FL = Foreign Language.
(2) Formulation of this table owes much to discussions with Professor Ofelia García. This typology is extended to 14 types of bilingual education in García (1997, p. 410).

Submersion Education

A swimming pool metaphor is present in the idea of submersion education. Rather than a quick dip into a second language in mainstream education, **submersion** contains the idea of a student thrown into the deep end and expected to learn to swim as quickly as possible without the help of floats or special swimming lessons. The language of the pool will be the majority language (e.g. English in the USA) and not the home language of the child (e.g. Spanish). The language minority student will be taught all day in the majority language typically alongside fluent speakers of the majority language. Both teachers and students will be expected to use only the majority language in the classroom, not the home language. Students may either sink, struggle or swim.

Submersion Education is the label to describe education for language minority children who are placed in mainstream education. In the USA, such a submersion experience is also found in '**Structured Immersion**' programs (Brisk, 1998). Structured Immersion programs contain only language minority children and no language majority children. As will be apparent later in this chapter, the language experience in a Structured Immersion program is 'submersion' rather than 'immersion'. Structured Immersion programs are thus for minority language speakers conducted in the majority language. The first language is not developed but is replaced by the majority language. **Different** from Submersion Education, the Structured Immersion teacher will use a simplified form of the majority language, and may initially accept contributions from children in their home language (Brisk, 1998; Hornberger, 1991). However, typically there is no native language support (August & Hakuta, 1997). In the USA, there are also '**Sheltered English**' programs, an alternative to ESL (English as a Second Language) programs. However, since such programs can be 'pull-out' with special content and curriculum materials, they are discussed in the next section.

Within submersion there will be ESL provision. Most ESL programs will be solely aimed at developing English language skills (grammar, vocabulary and communication). In Content-based ESL, students are taught parts of the curriculum through English and not just English as a language. Typically, such content instruction will be 'sheltered' by simplifying the language used (and often the content). 'Sheltered' or comprehensible input in English requires more non-verbal communication (e.g. visual aids, gestures), simple syntax, repetitions and summaries, speaking slowly and clearly, and checking often for understanding. Guadalupe Valdés (1998, p. 7) found that in such programs 'English-language learners interacted only with each other and with teachers who taught their classes' with few opportunities to hear English from native-speaking peers. She also found that questioning, critical thinking and collaboration became impossible in 'sheltered' classes. The students understood too little English to move to higher order thinking despite having the cognitive capacity. Frustration, non-participation, even dropping-out can be outcomes that educationally, economically and politically disempower children. There is a replication of the inequality and injustice that exists for many language minority children outside the classroom (Valdés, 1998).

There are various criticisms of a submersion form of education, including its variants. Language minority children, especially in their first months of schooling, often have little or no idea what the teacher is saying. Because the teacher is unlikely to have been trained in ESL methodology, such teachers may have little expertise in modifying instruction to accommodate such children.

In terms of the language garden analogy (see Chapter 3), one blossoming flower is displaced. The garden is re-seeded after the initial language plants have shown growth. One tender but healthy plant is simply replaced by the majority flower of the garden. The basic aim of submersion education is thus **assimilation** of language minority speakers, particularly where there has been immigration (e.g. USA, England). Also, where indigenous language minorities are perceived as working against the common good, submersion education becomes a tool of integration. The school becomes a melting pot to help create common social, political and economic ideals. As Theodore Roosevelt urged in 1917:

> 'We must have but one flag. We must have but one language. That must be the language of the Declaration of Independence, of Washington's Farewell Address, of Lincoln's Gettysburg Speech and Second Inaugural. We cannot tolerate any attempt to oppose or supplant the language and culture that has come down to us from the builders of the republic with the language and culture of any European country. The greatness of this nation depends on the swift assimilation of the aliens she welcomes to her shores. Any force which attempts to retard that assimilative process is a force hostile to the highest interests of our country.' (quoted in Wagner, 1980, p. 32)

Language diversity has often been discouraged in the USA so, it was argued, that harmony would hasten a healthy and homogeneous nation. A common language would provide, it was thought, common attitudes, aims and values. A common language and culture would cement society. A God-blest-English speaking America was preferable to the threat of Babel. Language uniformity was required for unity.

Considerable variations in student language ability in a classroom may often create **problems** in teaching and class management for the teacher. With students who range from fluent majority language speakers to those who can understand little classroom talk, the burden on the teacher may be great. In formal 'context-reduced' classrooms, there is no reason to assume that children will quickly and effortlessly acquire the majority language skills necessary to cope in the curriculum. The formal and complex language of the classroom typically takes five to seven or more years to develop.

Alongside problems of language, there are likely to be problems of social and emotional adjustment for language minority children in submersion education, which have connections with later drop-out rates from high school. It is not just the child's home language that is deprecated. The identity of the child, the parents, the home, community and culture appear to be deprecated, disparaged and discounted. It is not only the students' language that is denied. It also denies or denounces what they hold most sacred: their rootedness, relationships and often race. McKay (1988, p. 341) quotes from a student in a submersion classroom:

> 'School was a nightmare. I dreaded going to school and facing my classmates and teacher. Every activity the class engaged in meant another exhibition of my incompetence. Each activity was another incidence for my peers to laugh and ridicule me with and for my teacher to stare hopelessly disappointed at me. My self-image was a serious inferiority complex. I became frustrated at not being able to do anything right. I felt like giving up the entire mess.'

Skutnabb-Kangas (1981) indicates the **stresses** of learning through an undeveloped language as in submersion education. Listening to a new language demands high concentration, it is tiring, with a constant pressure to think about the form of the language and less time to think about curriculum content. A child has to take in information from different curriculum areas and learn a language at the same time. Stress, lack of self-confidence, 'opting-out', disaffection and alienation may occur. Where submersion is supported, it is when political ideology (e.g. assimilation of immigrants) is dominant over educational effectiveness (see Chapters 11 and 12).

However, the reality is that many mainstream schools in the USA contain children for whom English is a second language, and mainstream teachers are expected to provide effective and challenging education for such children. Such teachers are required both to develop the English language proficiency of their students and teach subject content (see Carrasquillo & Rodriguez (1996), Echevarría & Graves (1998), Echevarría *et al.* (2000) and Faltis (1997) for teaching approaches in such situations).

Submersion with Pull-Out Classes

Submersion education may occur with or without the addition of **withdrawal classes** or **'pull-out' classes** to teach the majority language. Language minority children in mainstream schools may be withdrawn for 'compensatory' lessons in the majority language (e.g. English as a second language (**ESL**) pull-out programs in the USA and England). Such **withdrawal classes** are provided as a way of keeping language minority children in mainstream schooling. However, 'withdrawn' children may fall behind on curriculum content delivered to others not in withdrawal classes. There may also be a stigma for absence. A withdrawal child may be seen by peers as 'remedial', 'disabled' or 'limited in English'. Withdrawal classes are administratively simple and require little or no additional expense.

A variation under this heading is **Sheltered English or Sheltered Content Instruction** or **SDAIE** (specially designed academic instruction in English), where minority language students are taught the curriculum with a simplified vocabulary but also purpose-made materials and methods (such as cooperative learning) — but in English only (Faltis, 1997; Faltis & Hudelson, 1998; Echevarría & Graves, 1998). In Sheltered English or Sheltered Content Instruction, content and curriculum materials are developed and pitched to match the English proficiency of the students. Sheltered English or Sheltered Content English is distinct from ESL (English as a

Second Language), as in ESL English is taught as a language, with a focus on learning that language (Faltis, 1997; Faltis & Hudelson, 1998; Echevarría & Graves, 1998; Echevarría *et al.*, 2000). In comparison, Sheltered Content Instruction has curriculum content knowledge, understanding and skills as the goals. Echevarría *et al.* (2000) present a model of sheltered instruction with the Sheltered Instruction Observation Protocol (SIOP), which provides a tool for observing and quantifying a teacher's implementation of quality sheltered instruction that teaches content material to English language learners.

Sheltered Content Teaching may involve temporary segregation from first language English speakers (Echevarria & Graves, 1998). Such segregation may produce: (1) greater opportunity for participation among students (they may be less inhibited due to no competition or comparisons with first language speakers of English); (2) greater sensitivity among teachers to the linguistic, cultural and educational needs of a homogeneous group of students; and (3) a collective identity among students in a similar situation (Faltis, 1993b). However, such language segregation removes first language role models; may produce a social isolation with overtones of stigmatization and reinforce negative stereotypes; may encourage the labeling of segregated students as linguistically and educationally inferior, deprived and in need of remedial attention; and may generate inequality in treatment (e.g. in curriculum materials and training of teachers).

Segregationist Education

A form of 'minority language only' education is segregationist language education (Skutnabb-Kangas, 1981). Segregationist education occurs where minority language speakers are denied access to those programs or schools attended by majority language speakers. Such separation can be through law (*de jure*) or practice (*de facto*).

Monolingual education through the medium of the minority language can be for apartheid (e.g. educating a colonial people only in their native language). The ruling elite prescribes education solely in the minority language to maintain subservience and segregation. Such language minorities 'do not learn enough of the power language to be able to influence the society or, especially, to acquire a common language with the other subordinated groups, a shared medium of communication and analysis' (Skutnabb-Kangas, 1981, p. 128). Segregationist education **forces** a monolingual language policy on the relatively powerless.

Transitional Bilingual Education

Transitional bilingual education is a common type of bilingual education in the United States and the form most supported by Title VII funds. The aim of transitional bilingual education is **assimilationist**. It differs from submersion education in that language minority students are temporarily allowed to use their home language, and they are often being taught through their home language, until they are thought to be proficient enough in the majority language to cope in mainstream education. Thus, transitional education is a brief, temporary swim in one pool until the child is perceived as capable of moving to the mainstream pool. The aim is to increase use of the majority language in the classroom while proportionately decreasing the use of the home language in the classroom.

The educational rationale is based on perceived priorities: children need to function in the majority language in society. The argument used is that if competency in the majority language is not quickly established, such children may fall behind their majority language peers (Mitchell *et al.*, 1999). Thus, arguments about equality of opportunity and maximizing student performance are used to justify such transitional programs. The extent to which such justifications are valid is considered later.

Transitional bilingual education (TBE) can be split into two major types: **early exit** and **late exit** (Ramírez & Merino, 1990). Early-exit TBE refers to two years maximum help using the mother tongue. Late-exit TBE often allows around 40% of classroom teaching in the mother tongue until the 6th grade.

While majority language monolingualism is the aim of transitional bilingual education, teachers or their assistants need to be bilingual. The temporary home language swim requires, for example, a Spanish speaking teacher who may be more sensitive and successful in teaching English to Spanish speaking children than English-only teachers. The former can switch from one language to another and be more sympathetic to the language of the children. For the government and school administrator, such bilingual teachers may become valuable allies or Trojan horses for the learning of the majority language. A **bilingual teacher** can become the unwitting promoter of transition from one language to another, and assimilation into the majority culture. Such teachers can promote the transition from home to school language from within their own cultural group. An Anglo teacher is thus not imposed on the Hispanic language minority; the conversion job is achieved by a bilingual teacher.

Similarly, in US schools with large transitional programs, there is sometimes a **hidden message** in the staffing. The people with power and prestige, such as principals and assistant principals, are often English monolinguals (García, 1993). The people with the least power and status are cooks, lunch monitors, cleaners and janitors, who, for example, speak a minority language such as Spanish. The language of formal announcements is English; the language used by those who serve may be Spanish. The language to learn is the language of power and prestige. The language to forget is the language of servitude, stigma and shame. This message is loudly proclaimed without words.

However, such Hispanic teachers may alternatively recognize the needs and wishes of their own communities. Such communities may desire their young to speak English early in schooling, but differ from administrators in wanting to preserve Spanish (García, 1991a). Hispanic teachers may continue to teach English in transitional bilingual education, but also try to preserve Spanish in the children, becoming allies of the community and not just allies of politicians and bureaucrats.

Mainstream Education (with Foreign Language Teaching)

In the USA, Australia, Canada and much of Europe, most language majority schoolchildren take their education through their home language. For example, a child whose parents are English speaking monolinguals attends school where English is the teaching medium (although some second (foreign) language teaching may occur). In Canada, this would be called a core program. In Wales and elsewhere, it is sometimes called a 'drip-feed' language program. The term 'drip-feed' highlights the kind of language element in mainstream schooling. Second (foreign) language lessons of half an hour per day may constitute the sole 'other' language diet. Drip-feeding French, German, Japanese or Spanish makes the language a subject in the curriculum similar to History, Science, Information Technology and Mathematics. This is distinct from teaching through the medium of a second language where curriculum content is the main focus rather than language learning (the latter is sometimes called embedding or content teaching).

The problem in some countries (e.g. USA, England) is that relatively few second language students blossom. Where children receive a half an hour second language lesson per day for between five and 12 years, few students become functionally fluent in the second language. LeBlanc (1992, p. 35) poses the critical question:

> 'We all know how much our country [Canada] invests in second-language training. We are talking in terms of millions and millions of dollars. All these students are taking second-language courses and, once they have finished, should normally be able to function in the second language. But what happens in reality?'

The Canadians found that after 12 years of French drip-feed language teaching, many English-background students were not fluent enough to communicate in French with French Canadians. Similarly in Britain, five years of French or German or Spanish in secondary school (age 11 to 16) results in only a few sufficiently competent to use that second language. For the great majority, the second language quickly shrivels and dies. **Mainstream** education rarely produces functionally bilingual children. A very limited form of fluency in a foreign language tends to be the typical outcome for the mass of the language majority.

This is not the only outcome of second and foreign language teaching. The learning of English in Scandinavia does not fit this pattern, with many learners becoming fluent in English. When motivation is high, when economic circumstances encourage the acquisition of a trading language, then foreign language teaching may be more fruitful.

Separatist Education

A more narrow view of language minority education would be to choose to foster monolingualism in the minority language. The aims are minority language monolingualism and monoculturalism in a context where such choice is self-determined. Schermerhorn (1970) called this a **secessionist** movement where a language minority aims to detach itself from the language majority to pursue an independent existence. As a way of trying to protect a minority language from being over-run by the language majority, or for political, religious or cultural reasons, separatist minority language education may be promoted. This type of education may be organized by the language community for its own survival and for self-protection.

It is unlikely that a school would formally state its aims in a linguistic separatist fashion. Rather, in the implicit functioning of isolationist religious schools and the political rhetoric of extreme language activists, the 'separatist' idea of such schools exists. Small in number, the importance of this category is that it highlights that language minority education is capable of moving from the goal of pluralism to separatism.

CONCLUSION

Having considered some of the history of bilingual education and 'weak' types of such education, the next chapter moves onto 'strong forms of bilingual education where bilingualism and biliteracy are part of the aims. What can then be examined (in Chapter 11) is the relative success and effectiveness of these different forms of 'weak' and 'strong' bilingual education.

KEY POINTS IN THE CHAPTER

- Bilingual education has a history spanning 5000 or more years and current movements need particularly understanding within the historical context of the last century.
- Bilingual education in the United States has a rapidly changing history where permissiveness towards bilingual education was initially present. In recent decades, a more dismissive and restrictive climate has been experienced. However, dual language schools currently provide a window of opportunity.
- Ten varieties of bilingual education are suggested with Submersion and Transitional Bilingual Education examined in this chapter as 'weak' forms of bilingual education. In these, bilingual pupils are present but bilingualism and biliteracy is rarely the outcome.
- The basic aim of 'weak' forms of bilingual education is assimilation of language minorities rather than maintenance of their home languages and cultural pluralism.

SUGGESTED FURTHER READING

CRAWFORD, J. 1999, *Bilingual Education: History, Politics, Theory and Practice* (4th edn). Los Angeles: Bilingual Education Services.
CRAWFORD, J. 2000, *At War With Diversity*. Clevedon: Multilingual Matters.
CUMMINS, J. and CORSON, D. (eds), 1997, *Bilingual Education. Volume 5 of the Encyclopedia of Language and Education*. Dordrecht: Kluwer.
GARCIA, O. and BAKER, C. (eds) 1995, *Policy and Practice in Bilingual Education: A Reader Extending the Foundations*. Clevedon: Multilingual Matters. (Sections 1 and 2).
GENESEE, F. (ed.), 1999, *Program Alternatives for Linguistically Diverse Students*. University of California, Santa Cruz: Center for Research on Education, Diversity and Excellence.
See also the *International Journal of Bilingualism and Bilingual Education* for the most recent articles on this topic.

STUDY ACTIVITIES

(1) Write a personal account of one type of bilingual education which you have experienced or with which you are most familiar. Describe your experience of the language dimensions of this form of education. Present this in a small group seminar to find out differences and similarities of experience.

(2) Visit one or more schools and ask about the history of a bilingual education program or language program within that school. What have been the aims of the school with regard to languages? Have these aims changed over the last 10 or 20 years? How do the teachers perceive the first and second language of children being ignored or used over the last decade or more?

(3) By using documents, interviews, visits to schools and visits to administrators, try to sketch the history of language and bilingual education within a specific community. Also observe what signs and symbols there are of language within the community. For example, on posters, in newspapers, mass media and community activity, is there more than one language in use?

CHAPTER 10

Bilingual Education
for Bilingualism and Biliteracy

Introduction

Immersion Bilingual Education

Developmental Maintenance and
Heritage Language Bilingual Education

Dual Language Bilingual Education

Bilingual Education in Majority
Languages

Conclusion

CHAPTER 10

Bilingual Education for Bilingualism and Biliteracy

INTRODUCTION

The previous chapter provided an historical background to bilingual education and an introduction to 'weak' forms of bilingual education. This chapter examines the 'strong' forms of bilingual education that were introduced in the ten-fold typology outlined in Chapter 9. Both US and European models are examined, with an initial consideration of immersion education that has been exported from Canada around the world.

IMMERSION BILINGUAL EDUCATION

Submersion, Withdrawal Classes and Transitional approaches are often given the title of bilingual education. This is because such schemes contain bilingual children. This counts as a '**weak**' use of the term bilingual education because bilingualism is not fostered in school. Such education does not, by aim, content or structure, have bilingualism as a defined outcome. The next form, immersion education, has bilingualism as an intended outcome, and therefore represents a 'strong' use of the term bilingual education.

Immersion bilingual education derives from Canadian educational experiments. The immersion movement started in St Lambert, Montreal, in 1965 (Lambert & Tucker, 1972; Rebuffot, 1993). Some concerned English speaking, middle-class parents persuaded school district administrators to set up an experimental kindergarten class of 26 children. The stated aims were for students (1) to become competent to speak, read and write in French; (2) to reach normal achievement levels throughout the curriculum including the English language; (3) to appreciate the traditions and culture of French speaking Canadians as well as English speaking Canadians. In short, the aims were for children to become bilingual and bicultural without loss of achievement. Typically bilingual education has more than 'effective education' aims, so subconsciously or consciously economic and employment advantages may also have been present (see later).

Types of Immersion Bilingual Education

Immersion education is an umbrella term. Within the concept of immersion experience are various programs (in Canada and countries such as Finland, Spain and Ireland see Chapter 17) differing in terms of the following aspects:

- Age at which a child commences the experience. This may be at the kindergarten or infant stage (**early** immersion); at nine to ten years old (delayed or **middle** immersion), or at secondary level (**late** immersion);
- amount of **time** spent in immersion. **Total** immersion usually commences with 100% immersion (e.g. per week) in the second language, reducing after two or three years to 80% per week for the next three or four years, finishing junior schooling with approximately 50% immersion in the second language per week. **Partial** immersion provides close to 50% immersion in the second language throughout infant and junior schooling.

Early Total Immersion has been the most popular entry level program in Canada, followed by late and then middle immersion (Canadian Education Association, 1992). The histograms on the following page illustrate several possibilities, with many other variations around these.

The **St Lambert experiment** suggested that the educational aims were met. Attitudes and achievement were not hindered by the immersion experience. Tucker and d'Anglejan (1972, p. 19), summarized the outcomes as follows:

'the experimental students appear to be able to read, write, speak, understand, and use English as well as youngsters instructed in English in the conventional manner. In addition and at no cost they can also read, write, speak and understand French in a way that English students who follow a traditional program of French as a second language never do.'

Since 1965, immersion bilingual education has spread rapidly in Canada (Rebuffot, 1993) and in parts of Europe. There are currently around 317,000 English speaking Canadian children in some 2115 French immersion schools. This represents some 6% of the total school population in Canada. What are the essential features of this speedy educational growth? **First**, immersion in Canada aims at bilingualism in two prestigious, majority languages (French and English). This relates to an additive bilingual situation. Such a situation is different from the incorrectly termed 'immersion' or 'structured immersion' of children from language minority backgrounds in the majority language (e.g. Spanish speakers in the USA). Use of the term 'immersion' in such a subtractive, assimilationist situation is best avoided. Submersion is a more appropriate term.

Second, immersion bilingual education has been optional not compulsory. Parents choose to send their children to such schools. The cultural and economic convictions of parents plus the commitment of the teachers may aid the motivation

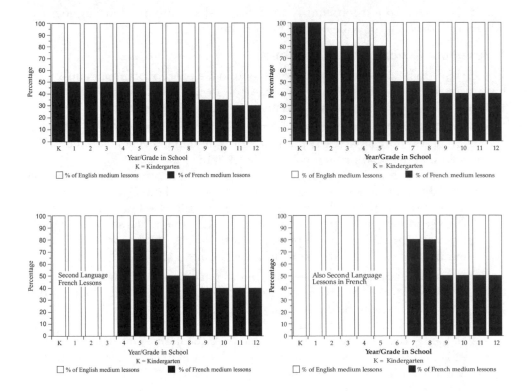

of students. Immersion thrives on conviction not on conformity. **Third**, children in early immersion are often allowed to use their home language for up to one and a half years for classroom communication. There is no compulsion to speak the second (school) language in the playground or dining hall. The child's home language is appreciated and not belittled. **Fourth**, the teachers are competent bilinguals. In Canada, for example, they initially appear to the children as able to speak French but only understand (and not speak) English.

Classroom language communication aims to be meaningful, authentic and relevant to the child's needs; not contrived, tightly controlled or repetitive. The content of the curriculum becomes the focus for the language. Perpetual insistence on correct communication is avoided. Learning a second language in early immersion becomes incidental and unconscious, similar to the way a first language is acquired. Emphasis is placed on understanding before speaking. Later on, formal instruction may occur (see Chapter 17).

Fifth, the students start immersion education with a similar lack of experience of the second language. Most are monolingual. Students commencing schooling with relatively homogeneous language skills not only simplifies the teacher's task, it also means that students' self-esteem and classroom motivation is not at risk due to

To summarize, Swain and Johnson (1997) provide a list of the core features and variable features of immersion programs

Core Features

(1)   The second language is the medium of instruction.
(2)   The immersion curriculum is the same as the local first language curriculum.
(3)   The school supports first language development.
(4)   Additive bilingualism occurs.
(5)   Exposure to the second language is largely confined to the classroom.
(6)   Students enter with similar (limited or nonexistent) levels of second language proficiency.
(7)   All the teachers are bilingual.
(8)   The classroom culture is that of the first language community.

Variable Features

(1)   The grade level of which immersion is introduced.
(2)   The extent of immersion, full or partial.
(3)   The ratio given to the first and second language in content-based teaching at different grade levels.
(4)   Whether there is continuity from elementary to secondary education, and occasionally from secondary to further and higher education.
(5)   The amount of language support given to students moving from their first to their second language, including the training that teachers need so as to give such bridging support.
(6)   The amount of resources that are available in the first and second language and the teacher training to use these.
(7)   The commitment of teachers and students, administrators and politicians to immersion.
(8)   The attitudes of students particularly towards the second language culture.
(9)   The status of the second language.
(10) What counts as success in an immersion program.

Some of the Differences between Immersion and Submersion Approaches

	Submersion	*Immersion*
Parental choice	Unlikely	Yes
Dual language enrichment	No	Yes
Cultural diversity valued	Unlikely	Yes
Use of first language in classroom	No	Yes
Bilingual (certified) teacher	No	Likely

some students being linguistically more expert. **Sixth**, students in immersion education experience the same curriculum as mainstream 'core' students.

With over a 1000 research studies, immersion bilingual education has been an educational experiment of unusual success and growth. It has influenced bilingual education throughout the world. For example, with variations to suit regional and national contexts, the **Catalans and Basques** (Artigal, 1991, 1993, 1997; Bel, 1993; Cenoz & Perales, 1997; Gardner, 2000) **Finnish** (Laurén, 1994; Manzer, 1993), **Japanese** (Oka, 1994; Maher, 1997), **Australians** (Berthold, 1992, 1995; Caldwell & Berthold, 1995), the Gaelic speakers in **Scotland** (MacNeil, 1994), **South Africans** (Brown, 1997; Martin, 1997), **Swiss** (Stotz & Andres, 1990) and the **Welsh and Irish** (Baker, 1988, 1993, 2000c; Reynolds *et al.*, 1998) have emulated the Canadian experiment with similar success. In Catalonia, research indicates that Spanish speaking children who follow an immersion program not only become fluent in Catalan, but also their Spanish does not suffer. Throughout the curriculum, such Catalan immersion children 'perform as well and sometimes better than their Hispanophone peers who do not' [follow an immersion program] (Artigal, 1993, pp. 40–41). Similarly, research studies in the Basque Country show that their Model B immersion program (50% Basque and 50% Spanish) has successful outcomes in bilingual proficiency (Sierra & Olaziregi, 1989; Gardner, 2000).

DEVELOPMENTAL MAINTENANCE AND HERITAGE LANGUAGE BILINGUAL EDUCATION

Alongside immersion education, there is another form of bilingual education that is a **'strong form'** of 'bilingual education'. This occurs where language minority children use their native, ethnic, home or heritage language in the school as a medium of instruction and the goal is full bilingualism. Examples include education through, or more often partly through, the medium of Navajo and Spanish in the USA (Krashen *et al.* (1998), Basque (Gardner, 2000), Welsh (Baker, 1993, 2000c). The native language is protected and developed alongside development in the majority language. In New Zealand, the Maori language has increasingly been promoted in schools (Spolsky, 1989a) with some indications of positive outcomes in achievement (Jacques & Hamlin, 1992). A similar promotion of Aboriginal languages is occurring in heritage language education in Australia (Caldwell & Berthold, 1995; Hartman & Henderson, 1994). In Ireland, Irish medium education is often available for children from Irish language backgrounds (Harris & Murtagh, 1999). Children become fluent in English and Irish and possibly other European languages. In China there are 55 ethnic minority groups plus the Han who are in a majority (92% of the 1.2 billion population). Since 1979, minority language education has been provided for over 20 minority groups, partly as a way of improving ethnic minority relationships with central government (Blachford, 1997; Lin, 1997). Similar movements are reported in Papua New Guinea and elsewhere in the South Pacific (Siegel, 1996; 1997) and for indigenous American Indians (Cantoni, 1996).

In the USA, there are schools that may be termed **'ethnic community mother**

tongue schools' (Fishman, 1989). Schools have existed using the mother tongue of the following varied communities: Arabs, Africans, Asians, French, German, Greek, Haitian, Jewish, Russian, Polish, Japanese, Latin American, Armenian, Dutch, Bulgarian, Irish, Rumanian, Serbian and Turkish. Maintained by communities who have lost or are losing their 'native' language, the schools mostly teach that native language and use it as a medium of instruction. Other schools are supported by foreign governments and religious organizations. 'These schools must be recognized as filling an important identity-forming and identity-providing function for millions of Americans' (Fishman, 1989, p. 454).

Since they are fee-paying private schools, the students tend to come from middle-class or the relatively more affluent working-class backgrounds and achieve biliteracy and biculturalism with some success (García, 1988). For example, there are around 130 Hebrew day schools in New York alone, 'successful in teaching children to read and write English, Hebrew, and many times Yiddish' (García, 1988, p. 22).

The 'public school' US example is called **maintenance bilingual education** or **developmental maintenance bilingual education**. These are relatively few in number with Navajo education being one major example (Holm & Holm, 1990, 1995; Reyhner & Tennant, 1995; McLaughlin & McLaughlin, 2000). In Canada, the term used to describe such education is **heritage language education**. However, in Canada, there is a distinction between heritage language lessons and heritage language bilingual education. (1) Heritage language programs give around two and a half hours per week language teaching, currently in more than 60 languages to about 100,000 students. These lessons often occur during dinner-hours, after school and at weekends. (2) In provinces such as Manitoba, British Columbia, Saskatchewan and Alberta, there are heritage language bilingual education programs (e.g. see Benyon & Toohey (1991) on programs in British Columbia; Feuerverger (1997) on Toronto). The heritage language is the **medium of instruction** for about 50% of the day (e.g. Ukrainian, Italian, German, Hebrew, Yiddish, Mandarin Chinese, Arabic and Polish; see Cummins, 1992a).

In essence, developmental maintenance language education refers to the education of **language minority** children through their minority and majority language. In most cases, the majority language will be present in the curriculum, ranging from second language lessons to a varying proportion (e.g. 10–50%) of the curriculum being taught in the majority language.

The term 'heritage language' may also be called 'native language', 'ethnic language', 'minority language', 'ancestral language', aboriginal language, or, in French, 'langues d'origine'. The **danger** of the term 'heritage' is that it points to the past and not to the future, to traditions rather than the contemporary. Partly for this reason, the UK term tends to be 'community language' or 'where English is an additional language'. The heritage language may or may not be an indigenous language. Both Navajo and Spanish can be perceived as heritage languages in the USA depending on an *individual's* perception of what constitutes their heritage language.

Heritage language programs in the USA (see Krashen *et al.*, 1998) and elsewhere vary in structure and content and overlap with the 90:10 model of dual language education (see later). Some of the likely features are as follows:

(1) Most, but not necessarily all of the children will come from language minority **homes**. At the same time, the minority language may be the majority language of a local community. In certain areas of the USA, Spanish speakers are in a majority in their neighborhood or community. In Gwynedd, North Wales, where the minority language (Welsh) is often the majority language of the community, developmental maintenance programs are prevalent. The children may be joined in most programs by a small number of majority language children.

(2) **Parents** will often have the choice of sending their children to mainstream schools or to developmental maintenance programs. Ukrainian, Jewish and Mohawkian heritage language programs in Canada, for example, gave parents freedom of choice in selecting schools.

(3) The language minority student's home language will often be used for approximately half or more of the **curriculum time**. The Ukrainian programs in Alberta and Manitoba allotted half the time to Ukrainian, half to English. Mathematics and science, for example, were taught in English; music, art and social studies in Ukrainian. There is a tendency to teach technological, scientific studies through the majority language. Other models use the student's home language for between 50% to almost 100% of curriculum time. Changes across grades usually move from much early use of the student's home language to approximately equal use of the two languages (e.g. by Grade 6).

(4) Where a minority language is used for a majority of classroom time (e.g. 80% to almost 100%), the justification is that children easily transfer ideas, concepts, skills and knowledge into the majority language. Having taught a child multiplication in Spanish, this mathematical concept does not have to be retaught in English. Classroom teaching **transfers** relatively easily between languages when such languages are sufficiently developed to cope with concepts, content and curriculum materials.

(5) The **justification** given for developmental maintenance programs is also that a minority language is easily lost, a majority language is easily gained. Children tend to be surrounded by the majority language. Television and train advertisements, shops and signs, videos and visits often provide or induce bilingual proficiency. Thus bilingualism is achieved by an initial concentration on the minority language at school. In the later stages of elementary schooling, increasing attention may be given to majority language development, ensuring that full bilingualism occurs. Developmental maintenance programs will quickly be seen to fail if students do not become fully competent in the majority language.

(6) Developmental maintenance **schools** are mostly elementary schools. This need not be the case. In Wales, for example, such schools are available to the end of secondary education and the heritage language can be used as a medium of vocational and academic study at College and University.

Native American Bilingual Education

An important example of developmental maintenance bilingual education is provision for **Native Americans**. McCarty and Watahomigie (1999) indicate that currently approximately two million American Indians, Alaska Natives and Native Hawaiians reside in the United State representing over 500 tribes and 175 distinct languages. As few as 20 of those languages are predicted to survive (e.g. Navajo, Ojibwa, Dakota, Choctaw, Apache, Cherokee, Tohono O'odham, Yupik are estimated to have over 10,000 speakers, while Coos, Kalapuya and Serrano have one remaining speaker). Only about 20 Native American languages are spoken in the home by younger generations – language transmission in the family being highly important for language survival (Crawford, 1995; Reyhner & Tennant, 1995). All of California's 31 Native American languages are dying as they are only spoken by small numbers of elders.

A history of Native American education shows that indigenous people in the United States share a record of attempts to eradicate their languages and cultures (Cantoni, 1996; Crawford, 1999; McLaughlin & McLaughlin, 2000). Forced assimilation has been prevalent for over a hundred years symbolized in phrases such as 'their barbarous dialects should be blotted out and the English language substituted' (McCarty & Watahomigie, 1999). One technique was to remove children from their tribes and send them to distant boarding schools. Stories abound of such children being kidnapped from their homes and taken on horseback to boarding schools particularly at military forts. Such children were given an English-only curriculum. There was severe punishment for speaking their Native language and a manual labor system which required them to work half days in kitchens and boiler rooms to minimize school costs. In the 1970s, Congress approved the Indian Education Act (1972) and the Indian Self-Determination and Educational Assistance Act (1975). This enabled bilingual education for American Indians, and for tribes and indigenous communities to work with the federal government to operate their own schools.

An example of such a language maintenance program is the Rock Point Community School in Arizona established in the mid-1930s and which has been famous since the early 1970s for its role in attempting to maintain the Native American language of Navajo (Holm & Holm, 1990, 1995). Rock Point is a reservation-interior community on the middle reaches of Chinle Wash. Containing 99% Navajo children, the languages used in this kindergarten to Grade 12 bilingual education program are Navajo and English. The three program aims are defined as: (1) students to become proficient speakers, readers, and writers of the Navajo and English languages; (2) students to acquire cultural knowledge of at least two cultures: Navajo and Anglo-American; (3) students to develop critical thinking skills in Navajo and English. In Kindergarten to Grade 5, Navajo is used for 50% of class time; in Grade 6 for 25%, and in Grades 7 to 12 for 15% of total class time. In Kindergarten to Grade 5, Reading, Language Arts, Math, Science, Social Studies and Health are taught through both Navajo and English, with separation of languages by differing blocks of time. In Grades 6 to 12, teaching through Navajo occurs for Literacy, Social Science, Electives and Science (one semester in Grade 6) with teaching in English for Reading, Language Arts, Math, Science, Social Studies, Health, Home Economics and Physical Education. The language of initial reading in instruction for Navajo speakers is Navajo and for English speakers it is English. All program teachers are proficient in both languages. Over 90% of the teaching staff are members of the Navajo ethnic group and provide bilingual role models (McCarty, 1997).

Such interventions show that bilingual education can be a success in raising language consciousness, raising standards of education, and preserving the indigenous languages of the United States. Such bilingual education gives a sense of identity and pride in their origins to Native American children, preserving not just their languages but also their rich cultures (Cantoni, 1996; McLaughlin & McLaughlin, 2000). This reflects the growing awareness among non-Native Americans of historical brutal assimilation and the current need to preserve the deep repository of history, customs, values, religions and oral traditions that belong to Native Americans but which can be valuably shared far beyond the Reservations to enrich all people.

Yet language rights and bilingual education programs have not guaranteed language maintenance for American Indians. Parents have sometimes made choices against language maintenance, sometimes based on their own indoctrination that 'white and English is best'. In 1990 with the passage of the Native American Languages Act, a further effort was made to preserve, protect and promote the rights and freedoms of Native Americans to use and develop their own indigenous languages.

DUAL LANGUAGE BILINGUAL EDUCATION

Dual language (or two way) bilingual education in the United States typically occurs when approximately equal numbers of language minority and language majority students are in the same classroom. For example, around half the children may be from Spanish speaking homes; the other half from English monolingual homes, working together in the classroom in harmony. Since both languages are used for instruction and learning, the aim is to produce relatively balanced bilinguals (Lindholm, 1991; Lindholm-Leary, 2001; Morison, 1990). Biliteracy is as much an aim as full bilingualism, with literacy being acquired in both languages (see Chapters 15 and 16).

There are a variety of **terms** used to describe such schools: two way schools, two way immersion, two way bilingual education, developmental bilingual education, dual language education, bilingual immersion, double immersion and interlocking education.

The **growth** of such programs has been considerable with the oldest dating back to 1963 in Dade County, Florida, and developed by a US Cuban community (see García & Otheguy, 1985, 1988; Baker & Jones, 1998). There are currently about 250 programs (see http://www.cal.org/cal/db/2way/) involving some 50,000 students (Genesee & Gándara, 1999). Dual language programs tend to share the following features:

(1)   A non-English language (i.e. the minority language) is used for at least 50% of instruction which lasts for up to six years.
(2)   In each period of instruction, only one language is used. Instruction must be adjusted to the student's language level but must also be challenging and intensifying, empowering and enabling. Language is learnt mostly via content.
(3)   Both English and non-English speakers are present in preferably balanced numbers. The English and non-English speakers are integrated in all lessons.

Dual language bilingual classrooms contain a mixture of language majority and language minority **students**. A **language balance** close to 50%–50% is attempted. If one language becomes dominant (e.g. due to much larger numbers of one language group), the aim of bilingualism and biliteracy may be at risk. The reality of such schools is often different, with an imbalance towards larger numbers of language minority students being more common.

An **imbalance** in the two languages among students may result in one language being used to the exclusion of the other (e.g. Spanish speaking children having to switch to English to work cooperatively). Alternatively, one language group may become sidelined (e.g. Spanish speakers become excluded from English speaking groups). Segregation rather than integration may occur. In the creation of a dual language school or classroom, careful student selection decisions have to be made to ensure a **language balance**.

When an **imbalance** does exist, it may be preferable to have slightly more language minority children. Where there is a preponderance of language majority children, the tendency is for language minority children to switch to the higher status, majority language. In most (but not all) language contexts, the majority language is well represented outside school (e.g. in the media and for employment). Therefore, the balance towards the majority language outside school can be complemented by a slight balance towards the minority language in school (among student in-take and in curriculum delivery). However, if the school contains a particularly high number of language minority children, the prestige of the school can sometimes suffer (both among language majority and language minority parents).

In **dual language magnet schools** in the USA, **students** may be drawn from a wide catchment area. For example, if a magnet school focuses on Environmental Arts and Sciences, parents throughout a district may be eager to gain a place for their children. Ensuring a language balance in each classroom then becomes a key **selection** feature.

There are situations where **attracting language majority students** to a dual language bilingual school is difficult. Where the monolingual mainstream school is as (or more) attractive to prospective parents, recruitment to dual language bilingual schools may initially be a challenge. For parents, allocation of their children to such dual language bilingual programs will be voluntary and not enforced. Hence, the good **reputation**, perceived effectiveness and curriculum success of such dual language bilingual schools becomes crucial to their continuation. Evidence from the USA suggests that language minority parents may be supportive of such a program (e.g. Hornberger, 1991). Majority language parents may need more persuading. Community backing and involvement in the school may also be important in long-term success.

The **development** of dual language bilingual schools often starts with the creation of a dual language kindergarten class rather than with implementation throughout a school. As the kindergarten students move through the grades, a new dual language class is created each year. Apart from elementary dual language bilingual schools, there is also dual language secondary education in the USA and, with different names, in many other countries of the world (e.g. Wales, Spain, India). A dual language bilingual school may be a whole school in itself. Also, there may be a dual language strand within a 'mainstream' school. For example, there may be one dual language classroom in each grade.

Dolson and Meyer (1992) list seven major **goals** in dual language programs:

(1) students should develop high levels of proficiency in their first language;
(2) students should achieve high levels of proficiency in their second language (e.g. English);
(3) academic performance should eventually be at or above grade level in both languages (e.g. by Grade 6);
(4) students should demonstrate positive cross-cultural attitudes and behaviors;
(5) students should show evidence of high levels of personal and social competence;
(6) schools should have programs of academic excellence for language majority and language minority students, and
(7) communities and society at large should benefit from having citizens who are bilingual and biliterate, who are more positive towards people of different cultural backgrounds, and, who can meet national needs for language competence and a more peaceful coexistence with peoples of other nations.

The **aim** of Dual Language bilingual schools is thus not just to produce bilingual and biliterate children. Genesee and Gándara (1999) suggest that such schools enhance inter-group communicative competence and cultural awareness. They produce children who, in terms of inter-group relations, are likely to be more tolerant, sensitive and equalized in status. 'Contact between members of different groups leads to increased liking and respect for members of the outgroup, including presumably reductions in stereotyping, prejudice, and discrimination' (Genesee & Gándara, 1999, p. 667).

To gain status and to flourish, such dual language schools need to show success throughout the curriculum (Lindholm-Leary, 2001). On standardized tests, on attainment compared with other schools in the locality, and in specialisms (e.g. music, sport, science), dual language bilingual schools will strive to show relative success. A narrow focus on proficiency in two languages will be insufficient in aim.

The **mission** of dual language bilingual schools may be couched in terms such as 'equality of educational opportunity for children from different language backgrounds', 'child-centered education building on the child's existing language competence', 'a positive self-image for each child', 'a community dedicated to the integration of all its children', 'enrichment not compensatory education', 'a family-like experience to produce multicultural children', and 'supporting Bilingual Proficiency not Limited English Proficiency'.

One of the special aims of dual language bilingual schools (e.g. compared with mainstream schools) is to produce **bilingual, biliterate and multicultural children**. Language minority students are expected to become literate in their native language as well as in the majority language. At the same time, majority language students should make 'normal' progress in their first language. To achieve these aims, a variety of practices are implemented in dual language bilingual schools (Christian *et al.*, 1997; Lindholm-Leary, 2001).

(1) The two **languages** of the school (e.g. Spanish and English, Japanese and English) have **equal status**. Both languages will be used as a medium of instruction. Math, Science and Social Studies, for example, may be taught in both languages. However, care has to be taken not to be repetitive, not to teach the same content in both languages. Strategies of separating, allocating and integrating two languages in the classroom are considered in Chapter 13.

(2) The **school ethos** will be bilingual. Such an ethos is created by classroom and corridor displays, notice boards, curriculum resources, cultural events, dinner-time and extra curricular activity using both languages in a relatively balanced way. Announcements across the school address system will be bilingual. Letters to parents will also be in two languages. While playground conversations and student-to-student talk in the classroom is difficult to influence or manipulate, the school environment aims to be transparently bilingual.

(3) In some dual language bilingual schools, the two **languages** are **taught** as languages (sometimes called Language Arts instruction). Here, aspects of spelling, grammar, metaphors and communicative skills may be directly taught. In other two way bilingual schools, use of both languages as media of instruction is regarded as sufficient to ensure bilingual development. In such schools, children are expected to **acquire proficiency** in language informally throughout the curriculum and through interaction with children who are effective first language role models. In both cases, reading and writing in both languages are likely to receive direct attention in the curriculum. Biliteracy is as much an aim as full bilingualism. Literacy will be acquired in both languages either simultaneously or with an initial emphasis on native language literacy.

(4) **Staff** in the dual language classrooms are often bilingual. Some **teachers** use both languages on different occasions with their students. Where this is difficult (e.g. due to teacher supply or selection), teachers may be paired and work together closely as a team. A teacher's aide, paraprofessionals, secretaries, custodial staff, parents offering or invited to help the teacher may also be bilin-

gual. Language minority **parents** can be valuable 'teacher auxiliaries' in the classroom. For example, when a wide variety of Spanish cultures from many regions is brought to the classroom, parents and grandparents may describe and provide the most authentic stories, dances, recipes, folklore and festivals. This underlines the importance of the culture of language minorities being shared in the classroom to create an additive bilingual and multicultural environment.

(5)   The **length of the dual language bilingual program** needs to be longer rather than shorter. Such a program for two or three grades is insufficient. A minimum of four years extending through the grades as far as possible is more defensible. Length of experience of a dual language bilingual program is important to ensure a fuller and deeper development of language skills, and biliteracy in particular. Where a US dual language bilingual program exists across more years, there is a tendency for the curriculum to be increasingly taught in the majority language — English.

A central idea in dual language bilingual schools is **language separation and compartmentalization**. In each period of instruction, only one language is used. **Language boundaries** are established in terms of time, curriculum content and teaching. These will each be briefly considered, and then extended in Chapter 13.

First, a decision is made about **when** to teach through each language. One frequent preference is for each language to be used on **alternate days**. On the door of the classroom may be a message about which language is to be used that day. For example, Spanish is used one day, English the next, in a strict sequence. Alternately, **different lessons** may use **different languages** with a regular change over to ensure both languages are used in all curricula areas. For example, Spanish may be used to teach Mathematics on Monday and Wednesday and Friday; English to teach Mathematics on Tuesday and Thursday. During the next week, the languages are reversed, with Mathematics taught in Spanish on Tuesday and Thursday. There are other possibilities. The division of time may be in half days, alternate weeks, alternate half semesters. The essential element is the distribution of time to achieve bilingual and biliterate students.

The amount of **time** spent learning through each language varies from school to school. Often, a 50%–50% balance in use of languages is attempted in early and later grades. In other classrooms, the minority language will be given more time (60%, 75%, 80% and particularly 90% is not uncommon), especially in the first two or three years. In the middle and later years of schooling, there is sometimes a preference for a 50%–50% balance, or more accent on the majority language.

Whatever the division of time, instruction in a dual language bilingual school will keep **boundaries** between the languages. Switching languages within a lesson is not considered helpful. If language mixing by the teacher occurs, students may wait until there is delivery in their stronger language, and become uninvolved at other times. When there is clear separation, the Spanish speakers, for example, may help the English-speakers on Spanish days, and the English speakers help the Spanish speakers on English days. Interdependence may stimulate cooperation and friendship, as well as learning and achievement. The potential problems of segregation and racial hostility may thus be considerably reduced.

However, the two languages will, in reality, sometimes be **switched** or mixed in the classroom (e.g. in private conversations, in further explanations by a teacher, and internal use of the dominant language). Use of languages by children, especially when young, is not usually consciously controlled. Switching language can be as natural as smiling.

Second, **bilingual teachers** ensure they do not switch languages. Children hear them using one language (during a lesson period or during a whole day) and are expected to respond in that same language. When, as in many forms of 'strong' bilingual education, there is a shortage of bilingual teachers, a pairing of teachers may ensure language separation. A teacher using Spanish only will work in close association with a teacher who only uses English with the same class. Such teamwork requires teachers to be committed to bilingualism and multiculturalism as important educational aims.

Third, language boundaries may be established in the **curriculum**. This may occur according to which 'language day' it is. Alternatively, in some schools, different parts of the curriculum are taught in different languages. For example, Social Studies and Environmental Studies may be taught in Spanish, Science and Math in English. Such a policy establishes separate occasions where each language is to be used, and keeps the two languages apart. Christian *et al.* (1997) found in research in two-way (dual language) schools that the separation of languages differed in the schools studied. Schools varied in how strict or flexible they were about language separation. For example, when a student did not understand curriculum content or instructions, a teacher might naturally move into the child's stronger language to explain. However, the danger is that students learn that they do not need to understand the second language because the teacher or peers will translate for them.

One danger in language separation is when the allocation of languages is by content. For example, the majority languages is used for science and technology and the minority language is used for social studies. In this example, the majority language becomes aligned with modern technology and science, while the minority language becomes associated with tradition and culture. This may affect the status of the language in the eyes of the child, parents and society. The relationship of languages to employment prospects, economic advantage and power thus need to be considered.

Such dual language bilingual schools differ from **transitional bilingual education** and **submersion/mainstream/ESL** approaches. US transitional bilingual education essentially aims to move children into English-only instruction within two or more years. In contrast, dual language bilingual schools aim to enable the child to achieve increasing proficiency in two languages (e.g. Spanish and English in the USA). Dual language bilingual schools differ from **immersion bilingual**

education in the language backgrounds of the students. Immersion schools usually contain only language majority children learning much or part of the curriculum through a second language (e.g. English speaking children learning through the medium of French in Canadian schools). Dual language bilingual schools aim to contain a balanced mixture of children from two (or more) different language backgrounds (e.g. from Spanish speaking and English speaking homes in the USA). Dual language bilingual schools differ from **developmental maintenance (heritage language)** schools in aiming for more of a balance of majority and minority language children. Developmental maintenance education is comparatively more concerned with preservation of the ethnic language, ethnic culture and, in many cases, has a large preponderance of language minority children. The type of school possible in a neighborhood is often determined by the sociolinguistic character of the school population (e.g. the size of one or more language minority groups, the presence of recent or more established immigrants, the numbers of majority language speakers).

Dual language bilingual schools in the USA date from 1963 in Dade County, Florida, and were developed by the US Cuban community in that area (see Lindholm, 1987; García & Otheguy, 1985, 1988; Baker & Jones, 1998). In September 1963, the **Coral Way Elementary School** started a bilingual program that embraced both Spanish and English speaking students. During the 1960s, another 14 such bilingual schools were set up in Dade County. This is related to the fact that many Cubans expected to return to Cuba, believing the Castro regime wouldn't survive. Local people supported the maintenance of Spanish among the soon-to-leave Cubans. Local English speaking children from middle class families were enrolled in the school. This reflected a wish among parents for foreign language instruction following Russia's initial triumph over the USA in the space race. (In 1958, the Russian Sputnik was launched.)

Since that era, there has been a steady **rise** in the number of Dual Language bilingual schools in the USA, particularly since 1989 — as the graph illustrates. Of around 250 schools in the United States, 23 states (and the District of Columbia) have dual language bilingual schools (e.g. Arizona, Illinois, Massachusetts, Oregon and Virginia). Approximately a half of such schools are located in Texas, California and New York. The languages of instruction in dual language bilingual programs in the USA are predominantly Spanish/English (in over 90% of such schools) but with the following combinations also represented: Chinese/English; French/English; Korean/English and Navajo/English.

Evaluations of the **effectiveness** of Dual language schools indicate relative success (Cazabon *et al.*, 1993; Lambert & Cazabon, 1994; Lindholm, 1991; Lindholm & Aclan, 1991; Lindholm, 1994, 1995; Lindholm-Leary, 2001; Thomas *et al.*, 1993). As Christian (1994, overview page) suggests:

> 'Emerging results of studies of two way bilingual programs point to their effectiveness in educating non-native English speaking students, their promise of expanding our nation's language resources by conserving the

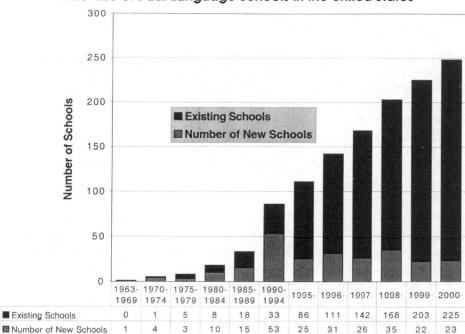

The Rise of Dual Language Schools in the United States

	1963-1969	1970-1974	1975-1979	1980-1984	1985-1989	1990-1994	1995-	1996-	1997-	1998-	1999-	2000-
Existing Schools	0	1	5	8	18	33	86	111	142	168	203	225
Number of New Schools	1	4	3	10	15	53	25	31	26	35	22	23

native language skills of minority students and developing second language skills in English speaking students, and their hope of improving relationships between majority and minority groups by enhancing cross-cultural under-standing and appreciation.'

One of the most detailed and comprehensive **evaluations** of dual language schools is by Kathryn Lindholm-Leary (2001). With wide-ranging and well documented data from 18 schools, she analyzed teacher attitudes and characteristics, teacher talk, parental involvement and satisfaction, as well as student outcomes (using 4854 students) in different program types. These programs included Transitional Bilingual Education, English-Only, the 90:10 Dual Language Model and the 50:50 Dual Language Model. The measured outcomes included Spanish and English language proficiency, academic achievement and attitudes of the students. socioeconomic background and other student characteristics were taken into account in reporting results. Among a wealth of findings, Lindholm-Leary (2001) found that:

- students who had 10% or 20% of their instruction in English scored as well on English proficiency as those in English-Only programs and as well as those in 50:50 Dual Language (DL) programs;
- Spanish proficiency was higher in 90:10 than 50:50 Dual Language (DL) programs. Students tended to develop higher levels of bilingual proficiency in the 90:10 than the 50:50 DL program;

- for Spanish-speaking students, no difference in English language proficiency was found between the 90:10 and 50:50 DL programs. However, DL students outperformed Transitional Bilingual Education (TBE) students in English by the Grade 6;
- students in both the 90:10 and 50:50 DL programs were performing about 10 points higher in reading achievement than the Californian state average for English-speaking students educated in English-Only programs;
- higher levels of bilingual proficiency were associated with higher levels of reading achievement;
- on Mathematics tests, DL students performed on average 10 points higher on Californian norms for English-speaking students educated only in English. There was a lack of difference in the scores of 90:10 and 50:50 DL students;
- DL students tended to reveal very positive attitudes towards their DL programs, teachers, classroom environment and the learning process.

Lindholm-Leary (2001) concludes that DL programs are effective in promoting high levels of language proficiency, academic achievement and positive attitudes to learning in students. Parents and teachers involved in such programs are both enthusiastic and recommend the expansion of such programs to raise the achievements of other majority and minority language children.

One **example** of a DL bilingual school is the James F. Oyster Bilingual Elementary School in Washington DC which has a two way program that commenced in 1971. The initiative was taken by the local community (by parents and local politicians) to produce a school that crossed language, cultural, ethnic and social class lines. Parents are very active in the running of the school. With students from kindergarten to 6th Grade, there is a ethnic mix of around 60% Hispanic, 20% White; 15% Black and 5% Asian and other language minorities (Freeman, 1995; 1998). Around two in every five children come from low-income families (e.g. are awarded a free lunch).

The Oyster program is distinctive because it has two teachers in each classroom: one teacher speaks only Spanish to the students; the other teacher speaks only English. The students experience Spanish and English medium instruction for approximately equal amounts of time. A strong multicultural dimension pervades the curriculum, with the contributions of different children encouraged and respected. The notion of equality permeates the ethos of the school (Freeman, 1995; 1998). This is reflected in the school's mission statement:

> 'Oyster Bilingual School's focus is on the development of bilingualism, biliteracy, and biculturalism for every student through the mastery of academic skills, the acquisition of language and communicative fluency, the appreciation of differences in racial and ethnic backgrounds, and the building of a positive self-concept and pride in one's heritage.'

Washington DC was also the site of an important speech that indicated a bright future for Dual Language schools. On 15th March, 2000, US Secretary of Education Richard W. Riley gave an address on exemplary language practices in school for

Latino youth, delivered at the Bell Multicultural High School, Washington, DC. As the following extract shows, emphasis was placed on a growth in dual language schools, particularly for economic purposes:

> *'It is high time we begin to treat language skills as the asset they are, particularly in this global economy. Anything that encourages a person to know more than one language is positive – and should be treated as such. Perhaps we should begin to call the learning of a second language what it truly is – 'bi-literacy.'*

> *Today, I want to spotlight the dual language approach, which is also sometimes referred to as two-way bilingual or dual immersion education.*

> *I am challenging our nation to increase the number of dual-language schools to at least 1,000 over the next five years, and with strong federal, state and local support we can have many more.*

> *Right now, we have about 260 dual-immersion schools and that is only a start. We need to invest in these kinds of programs and make sure they are in communities that can most benefit from them. In an international economy, knowledge – and knowledge of language – is power.*

> *Our nation can only grow stronger if all our children grow up learning two languages. The early school years are the best and easiest time for children to learn language.*

> *Unfortunately, too many teachers and administrators today treat a child's native language as a weakness if it is not English.*

> *I can assure you that when they enter the workforce in several years we will regret the inability of our children to speak two languages. Our global economy demands it; our children deserve it.'*

On 15th June, 2000, at the National Hispanic Education Meeting in Washington DC, Richard Riley went further by arguing that:

> *'in an international economy, knowledge of a second language is power. Those who speak English as well as another language will be wonderful assets for our nation in the coming years, so I am encouraging our schools to adopt an 'English plus one' approach. This approach challenges young people to meet high academic standards in two languages.' (http://www.ed.gov?Speeches/06-2000/hispaniceduc.html)*

BILINGUAL EDUCATION IN MAJORITY LANGUAGES

Bilingual education in majority languages comprises the joint use of two (or more) **majority languages** in a school. The aims of such schools usually include bilingualism or multilingualism, biliteracy and cultural pluralism. Such schools are in societies where much of the population is already bilingual or multilingual (e.g. Singapore, Luxembourg) or where there are significant numbers of natives or expatriates wanting to become bilingual (e.g. learning through English and Japanese in

Japan). **Asian** examples of Bilingual Education in Majority Languages include Arabic–English, Bahasa Melayu–English, Mandarin Chinese–English and Japanese–English. In Africa and India there are also schools where a 'majority' regional language and an international language coexist as teaching media in a school. Bilingualism in that regional language and an international language (e.g. French, English) is the aim and outcome of formal education. Generally, such schools will contain majority language children, with variations in the language heterogeneity or language homogeneity of the classes.

In the Asian examples, a country (e.g. Brunei, Taiwan) or a region may have one dominant indigenous language with a desire to introduce a second international language such as English into the school. The international language will be used as a medium of instruction alongside the native language. The aim is for fully bilingual and biliterate students through an enrichment bilingual education program. For example, the *Dwibahasa* (two language) school system in Brunei operates through Malay (Bahasa Melayu) and English (Jones *et al.*, 1993; Baetens Beardsmore, 1999). In Nigeria, bilingual education is present, particularly at the secondary school level, in English plus one of the national languages of Nigeria: Hausa, Ibo or Yoruba (Afolayan, 1995). In Singapore, English plus Mandarin, Malay or Tamil (the four official languages of the country) create bilingual education (Pakir, 1994). In Germany, German is paired with French, English, Spanish and Dutch to create a 'German model' of European multicultural and bilingual education (Mäsch, 1994).

Bilingual education in majority languages means that some curriculum content is learnt through a student's second language. Met (1998) provides the rationale for teaching and learning content through a second language. She argues that a **communicative approach** to second language teaching emphasizes authentic communication where the purpose of using language is to interpret, express and negotiate meaning. Thus integrating second language and content provides a purpose for using that second language reflecting real curriculum needs and purposeful learning for success in the curriculum.

Constructivist theory also stresses that learning best takes place in a holistic sense with the parts making a unified whole in a meaningful way. Traditional learning tends to rely on teachers transmitting small chunks of information which students are expected eventually to integrate into an understanding of the whole. Given that the brain stores information in networks, and the greater the number of connections and the stronger the connections among chunks of information the deeper and more powerful the learning, the more valuable it is to tie language and content together. Thus vocabulary and grammar should not be taught in isolation but in a context of authentic holistic learning. In content based second language instruction, meaning and understanding is the focus and second language learning a valuable by-product.

Two special examples of Bilingual education in majority languages will now be considered, commencing with the International School Movement and continuing with the European School Movement.

International Schools

International Schools are a diverse collection of schools throughout the world. Numbering over 830 schools, they are found in over 80 countries of the world, mostly in large cities (European Council of International Schools (ECIS), 1998; Sears, 1998). Mainly for the affluent, parents pay fees for mostly **private, selective, independent education** but there are also scholarships and bursaries. Children in these schools often have parents in the diplomatic service, multinational organizations, or in international businesses and who are geographically and vocationally mobile. Other children in an International school come from the locality, whose parents want their children to have an internationally flavored education (Sears, 1998). One **language** of the school is ordinarily English. International schools that have English as the sole medium of transmitting the curriculum could not be included under the heading of Bilingual Education in Majority Languages. Such schools become bilingual when a national or international language is incorporated in the curriculum. Sometimes the second language taught (for up to 12 years) is only taught as a language. In other schools, the second language is used as a medium to teach part of the curriculum. Some schools enable their students to acquire third and fourth languages. Generally, the languages of International schools are majority languages with international prestige. Minority languages are rarely found in such schools.

The primary and secondary **curriculum** of **International Schools** tends to reflect US, British as well as the local curriculum tradition. The teachers are from various countries, usually with a plentiful supply of British and American trained staff. Sometimes preparing children for the International Baccalaureate, United States tests or British examinations, most prepare their clientele for universities in Europe and North America. Sears (1998) in particular, but also Baker and Jones (1998) and Ochs (1993) provide illustrations and further discussion of the International Schools Movement.

European Schools Movement

Another European example of bilingual education in majority languages is the **European Schools movement** (Baetens Beardsmore, 1993; Baetens Beardsmore & Swain, 1985; Baker & Jones, 1998; Bulwer, 1995; Hoffmann, 1998; Housen & Baetens Beardsmore, 1987; Swan, 1996; Tosi, 1991). Mostly for the relatively elite workers of the European Community (EC), such schools are multilingual and cater for some 15,000 children from the different EC nations. The first school was opened in Luxembourg in 1953, with schools now sited in Belgium, Italy, Germany, the Netherlands and England (Swan, 1996). Such European Schools have up to 11 different language sections reflecting the first language of the students (and this may increase as other countries join the European Community). Younger children use their native language as the medium of learning but also receive second language instruction (English, French, or German) in the primary school years. Older children take part of their schooling in their native language and part through the medium of a **'vehicular'** or 'working' language. The 'vehicular' language will usually be a 'majority' second language for the child selected from English, French or German. This language will be taught by native speakers. Native student speakers of that language will also be present in the school as language models. The **vehicular language** is used to teach mixed language groups of students history, geography and economics from the third year of secondary education. In addition, students are taught a **third language** for a minimum of 360 hours.

The outcome of such schooling tends to be functionally bilingual and often multilingual students with a sense of cultural pluralism, European multiculturalism and European identity (Swan, 1996). Integration and harmonization of students from different nationalities is formally achieved in the '**European Hours**' lessons using the vehicular language. 'European Hours' are an important curriculum component from Grade 3 in primary education. In classes of 20 to 25 students for three lessons a week, children from different language backgrounds work cooperatively together. A small group project with a realistic, attainable goal (e.g. making puppets) provides the focus for a context embedded and cognitively undemanding 'European Hour'. Deliberately and explicitly, students are encouraged to respect each person's native language. Games and physical education are also occasions for a cooperative mixing of students from the different language sections. Students are linguistically mixed to avoid stereotypes and prejudices, and to build a supranational European identity (Baetens Beardsmore, 1993; Swan, 1996).

A major difference between the European schools movement and immersion programs is that the second language is taught as a subject before being used as a medium of instruction. That second language also continues to be taught as a subject, leading to a high level of grammatical accuracy (Baetens Beardsmore, 1993).

According to Housen and Baetens Beardsmore's (1987) **research** in one European School: 'This strong language commitment has no detrimental effects on academic achievement as can be gauged from results on the final European Baccalaureate examination, on which 90% of students have been successful' (p. 85). However, bilingualism, biliteracy and multiculturalism is not only due to the effects of schooling. The parents may also be bilingual or multilingual, and the children are more likely to come from literacy-oriented, middle class bureaucrat homes, with a positive view of bilingualism. Playgrounds are multilingual, satellite TV in Europe is multilingual and the growing notion of Europeanization creates privileged European schoolchildren who are 'educated bilinguals, equally at ease with two languages, with their own national culture and the supranational European identity' (Tosi, 1991, p. 33).

In **Europe**, there are other schools (apart from the European School Movement) that use two or more prestigious languages in the curriculum (Baetens Beardsmore, 1993; Cenoz, 1998; Genesee, 1998; Cenoz & Jessner, 2000). In the Basque Country, bilingual schools have effectively provided content teaching in Basque and Spanish (Gardner, 2000). A recent interest (e.g. by parents) in English language learning means that about 95% of Basque children now learn English starting at kindergarten or in Grade 3 (Cenoz, 1998; Lasagabaster, 2000). Early evaluations revealed that ' learning English from such an early age does not adversely affect the students'

The Stated **Objectives** of the European Schools Movement are (adapted from information from the Central Office of the Representative of the Board of Governors of the European Schools):

- to give students confidence in their own cultural identity — the bedrock for their development as European citizens;
- to give a sound education, based on a broad range of subjects, from nursery level to university entrance;
- to develop high standards in speaking and writing both the mother tongue and two or more foreign languages;
- to develop mathematical and scientific skills throughout the whole period of schooling;
- to encourage a European and global perspective in the study of history and geography, rather than a narrower, nationalistic one;
- to encourage creativity in music and the plastic arts and an appreciation of all that is best in a common European artistic heritage;
- to develop physical skills and instill in students an appreciation of the need for healthy living through participation in sporting and recreational activities;
- to offer students professional guidance in their choice of subjects and in career/university decisions in the later years of the secondary school;
- to foster tolerance, cooperation, communication and concern for others throughout the school community;
- to provide high-quality teaching through the recruitment of well qualified and experienced staff by the respective countries' Ministries of Education.

acquisition of Basque or Spanish or their overall cognitive development' (Cenoz, 1998, p. 181). **Trilingual education** is thus being evaluated.

In **Luxembourg**, children who speak Luxembourgish (Lëtzebuergesch) after birth become trilingual (Luxembourgish, French and German) through education (Hoffmann, 1998; Lebrun & Baetens Beardsmore, 1993). Children start their education at age five through the medium of Luxembourgish (a variety of Low German). German is initially a subject in the curriculum, then introduced as the main teaching medium. By the end of Grade 6, children function in much of the curriculum in German. French is introduced as a subject in Grade 2, and is increasingly used as a teaching medium in secondary education. Most students have a working knowledge of three languages by the conclusion of schooling (Hoffmann, 1998; Lebrun & Baetens Beardsmore, 1993). Through emphasis on the home tongue in the early years, emphasis on German in the primary school and emphasis on French in the secondary school, children become **trilingual and biliterate** (French and German literacy).

CONCLUSION

Having considered ten types of bilingual education in this and the previous chapter, the natural question to ask is whether one type is more effective than another. For Spanish speaking children in the USA, is it better for them to be placed in Submersion, Transitional, Maintenance or Two Way schooling? For a monolingual English speaker, is it detrimental to enter immersion schooling compared with mainstream schooling? Such questions will be examined in the next chapter by 'effectiveness' research.

KEY POINTS IN THE CHAPTER

- Ten varieties of bilingual education include different forms of 'strong' bilingual education where the use of both languages in the curriculum is fostered.
- Immersion, Developmental Maintenance and Dual Language education are the most well known forms of strong bilingual education. Immersion bilingual education started in Canada but is common in many countries of the world. It caters for majority language children learning through a second language. Dual Language education has grown in the United States mixing majority and minority language students.
- The varieties of 'strong' bilingual education differ in the amount of time given to the minority and majority languages in the classroom but full bilingualism and biliteracy is expected as outcomes. In Developmental Maintenance programs, the revitalization of home languages and cultures is a key aim.

SUGGESTED FURTHER READING

BAETENS BEARDSMORE, H. (ed.) 1993, *European Models of Bilingual Education.* Clevedon: Multilingual Matters.

CENOZ, J. and GENESEE, F. (eds), 1998, *Beyond Bilingualism: Multilingualism and Multilingual Education.* Clevedon: Multilingual Matters.

CRAWFORD, J. 1999, *Bilingual Education: History, Politics, Theory and Practice* (4th edn). Los Angeles: Bilingual Education Services.

CUMMINS, J. and CORSON, D. (eds), 1997, *Bilingual Education. Volume 5 of the Encyclopedia of Language and Education.* Dordrecht: Kluwer.

DANESI, M., McLEOD, K. and MORRIS, S. 1993, *Heritage Languages and Education: The Canadian Experience.* Oakville, Ontario: Mosaic Press.

GARCÍA, O. and BAKER, C. (eds) 1995, *Policy and Practice in Bilingual Education: A Reader Extending the Foundations.* Clevedon: Multilingual Matters. (Sections 1 and 2).

GENESEE, F. (ed.), 1999, *Program Alternatives for Linguistically Diverse Students.* University of California, Santa Cruz: Center for Research on Education, Diversity and Excellence.

JOHNSON, R.K. and SWAIN, M., 1997, *Immersion Education: International Perspectives.* Cambridge: Cambridge University Press.

LINDHOLM-LEARY, K.J., 2001, *Dual Language Education.* Clevedon: Multilingual Matters.

McCARTY, T.L. and WATAHOMIGIE, L.J., 1999, Indigenous Community-based Language Education in the USA. In S. MAY (ed.) *Indigenous Community-Based Education.* Clevedon: Multilingual Matters.

SEARS, C., 1998, *Second Language Students in Mainstream Classrooms.* Clevedon: Multilingual Matters.

SWAN, D., 1996, *A Singular Pluralism: The European Schools 1984–1994.* Dublin: Institute of Public Administration.

See also the *International Journal of Bilingualism and Bilingual Education* for the most recent articles on this topic.

STUDY ACTIVITIES

(1)   Imagine you are a parent or teacher and were required to make a public speech about changing a school from a 'weak' form of bilingual education to a 'strong' form. Prepare, and then deliver in front of the class, a speech of about five minutes to persuade the administration.

(2)   Visit a school, and by interview and observation decide the extent to which that school fits one or more of the types of bilingual education in this and the previous chapter.

(3)   Using some of the following World Wide Web addresses and search engines, create a short information pack or booklet on an aspect of bilingual education that is relevant in your district.

    1. ERIC Clearinghouse on Languages and Linguistics
    http://www.cal.org/ericcll/
    2. National Clearinghouse for Bilingual Education (US)
    http://www.ncbe.gwu.edu/
    3. Office of Bilingual Education and Minority Languages (US)
    http://www.ed.gov/offices/OBEMLA/
    4. Yahoo – Bilingual Education
    http://dir.yahoo.com/Education/Bilingual/
    5. Center for Applied Linguistics (US)
    http://www.cal.org/
    6. James Crawford's Language Policy Web Site and Emporium
    http://ourworld.compuserve.com/homepages/JWCRAWFORD/
    7. National Association for Bilingual Education
    http://www.nabe.org/
    8. Native American Languages
    http://www.mcn.net/~wleman/langlinks.htm
    9. OISE, University of Toronto, Second Language Education on the Web
    http://www.oise.utoronto.ca/~aweinrib/sle/
    10. CAIT (Canadian Association of Immersion Teachers)
    http://www.educ.sfu.ca/acpi/

CHAPTER 11

The Effectiveness of
Bilingual Education

Introduction

Evaluation Studies
The Sample of Children
Interacting Factors
Measures of Success
The Researchers

Reviews and Overviews of Research
Immersion Bilingual Education
Heritage Language Education/Developmental
Maintenance Education

Conclusion

CHAPTER 11

The Effectiveness of Bilingual Education

INTRODUCTION

Having considered ten types of bilingual education, this chapter turns to considering research on the major types of bilingual education. How effective are these major models for which types of children? What are the recorded successes and limitations? What makes a bilingual school more or less effective? These are the issues considered in this chapter and the next (which examines the debate in the United States).

EVALUATION STUDIES

We start with an historical perspective. From early research in the 1920s in Wales (Saer, 1922) and Malherbe's (1946) evaluation of bilingual education in South Africa, there have been many evaluations of bilingual projects and experiments, programs and interventions. The research is international; for example, Ireland (e.g. Harris, 1984) and England (e.g. Fitzpatrick, 1987); USA (e.g. Danoff *et al.*, 1977, 1978) and Canada (e.g. Swain & Lapkin, 1982); Peru (e.g. Hornberger, 1988, 1990a); Hong Kong (e.g. Boyle, 1990); Wales (e.g. Eurwen Price, 1985; Baker, 1995) and Spain (e.g. Sierra & Olaziregi, 1989; Artigal, 1997; Bel, 1993). A report from the World Bank (Dutcher, 1995) provides one of the few comparative international studies, covering bilingual education in the Philippines, Ireland, Canada, Mexico, Nigeria, Sweden and the United States.

It is possible to find historical **support** for most of the different forms of bilingual education by selecting and emphasizing a particular study. Some examples will illustrate. Criticism of Irish immersion education for children from English speaking homes was given by Macnamara (1966). He found such immersion children to be 11 months behind mainstream children on mechanical arithmetic. He suggested that it is 'probable that the use of Irish in teaching problem arithmetic hinders the progress of English speaking children' (Macnamara, 1966, p. 103). In comparison, support for immersion education comes from the Canadian research studies (e.g. Swain & Lapkin, 1982). Danoff *et al.* (1977, 1978) found submersion to be superior to transitional bilingual education with a large US sample of almost 9000 children. McConnell (1980) found US transitional bilingual education to be better than submersion, while Matthews (1979), also in the USA, found no difference between these two 'weak' forms of bilingual education.

Heritage language education has been evaluated as successful in Canada by Keyser and Brown (1981) and in England by Fitzpatrick (1987). In contrast, early research in Wales (e.g. Smith, 1923) questioned educational outcomes from heritage language programs for Welsh bilinguals.

Whether research finds a consensus in favor of one or some of the types of bilingual education is examined later in this chapter. For the moment, it is important to outline some reasons why studies vary in their findings.

The Sample of Children

The results of one study are limited to that sample of children at the time of the study. If there is some form of probability sampling (e.g. a random sample of a defined population is chosen), then these results may generalize to that specific population. Such **sampling** rarely occurs in bilingual education evaluations where instead, many studies have small and unrepresentative samples. It is usually ethically questionable and practically impossible to allocate children randomly into experimental and control groups that contain perfect mirrors of a large population of schoolchildren.

Given the wide variety of samples of children used in bilingual education effectiveness research, it is not surprising that differences in findings emerge. Samples of children include urban and rural schools, various socioeconomic class backgrounds, different ages and varying levels of motivation. The international research includes a mixture of bilingual groups: indigenous language minority groups, immigrants, and majority language children in minority language education. **Generalization** of results from one group to another is not valid. Such children may be in a subtractive or additive environment at home, school, community and nation.

Unlike the physical world, simple laws of behavior that govern large groups of people are not likely. The immense variety of individual differences and contextual differences makes clear cut, simple research results intrinsically elusive. Such results also say something about what has been, not what will always be. They do not guarantee that results will be stable across time as educational practice is always changing and developing.

Interacting Factors

Various factors, other than the sample of children, may have a variable effect on bilingual education. Parental interest, parental involvement in their children's education and parental cooperation with teachers is one intervening factor. Another factor is likely to be the enthusiasm and commitment of teachers to the education program. With a novel experiment in bilingual education, there may be extra enthusiasm and interest. The level of resource support (e.g. books, curriculum guidelines, computers, science equipment) may also produce variable outcomes (Gravelle, 1996).

There can be as much **variation** in outcomes (e.g. achievement in different curriculum areas) inside a particular bilingual education program (e.g. transitional, immersion or heritage language) as between different types of program. As Berliner (1988, p. 289) concluded about intervention programs, 'One of the major findings from studies of Follow-through programs, where competing theories and programs of early childhood education were purposefully funded, was that the variation across sites within the same program (whether it was behavioral, cognitive, requiring parent involvement, technology oriented, or whatever) was equal to the variation across the sites between the different programs.'

The crucial point is this. The language policy and language practice in schooling are only one element among many that make a school more or less successful. A recipe for success is unlikely to result from one ingredient (e.g. the language of the classroom). A great variety of factors act and interact to determine whether bilingual education is successful or not. As will be considered at the end of the chapter, it makes more sense to consider the wide variety of conditions which make bilingual education more or less successful. We need to specify all the ingredients in different recipes to fully understand the success or failure of forms of bilingual education. Bilingual education, whatever type or model, is no guarantee of effective schooling.

Measures of Success

An important question is: 'What tests or other sources of evidence are used to determine whether a form of bilingual education is successful?' Should the sole **outcomes** be competence in one or two languages? What aspects of language should be assessed (see Chapters 1 and 2)? Should the measure of success be performance across the whole curriculum? Whose version of the curriculum should be used (e.g. computational versus conceptual emphasis in Mathematics; religious knowledge versus moral development)? How important is it to include non-cognitive outcomes such as self-esteem, moral development, school attendance, social and emotional adjustment, integration into society, identity and gaining employment? What are the long-term effects of bilingual schooling (e.g. economic advantage, students later becoming parents who raise their children in the minority language)? The questions suggest that there will be debates and disputes over what are the valuable outcomes of schooling. Research on the effectiveness of bilingual education has varied in the choice of measures of outcome, as is illustrated later in the chapter. Such a choice reflects a particular emphasis, ideology or conviction.

A particular problem is that measures of success tend to be restricted to what is **measurable**. Quantitative outcomes (e.g. test scores) are used; qualitative evidence is rarely gathered. Can a play be judged only on an applause meter reading? Do a drama critic's notes add a vigorous, insightful interpretation to the performance?

While critics will differ in their evaluations, they may add flesh and life to the statistical bones of educational tests.

The Researchers

Research on bilingual education is rarely neutral. Often the researchers have hypotheses which hide their **expectations**. No educational research can be totally value-free, neutral or objective. The questions asked, the methodological tools chosen, decisions in analysis and manner of reporting usually reveal ideological and political preferences (August & Hakuta, 1997, 1998). Many researchers will be supporters of bilingual education, ethnic diversity, minority language rights and cultural pluralism. Such supporters may be convinced of the correctness of their beliefs. This is definitely not to argue that all evaluation research on bilingual education is invalid. Rather, it cannot be assumed that results are not affected by researchers, their beliefs, opinions and preferences. Some of the research on bilingual education is committed, prescriptive in nature, with interests, idealism and ideology mixed with investigation and intelligent discussion. 'Bilingual education is not merely a disinterested exercise in the application of theory and research to real-life situations. It is also an exercise in social policy and ideology' (Edwards, 1981, p. 27).

REVIEWS AND OVERVIEWS OF RESEARCH

After a substantial number of individual research studies on bilingual education had accumulated, various reviews and overviews appeared. A reviewer will assemble as many individual studies as possible and attempt to find a systematic pattern and an orderliness in the findings. Is there a **consensus** in the findings? Is it possible to make some generalizations about the effectiveness of different forms of bilingual education? Rarely, if ever, will all the evaluations agree. Therefore the reviewer's task is to detect reasons for variations. For example, different age groups, different socioeconomic class backgrounds and varying types of measurement device may explain variations in results.

The **early reviews** of bilingual education effectiveness were published in the late 1970s. Zappert and Cruz (1977), Troike (1978) and Dulay and Burt (1978, 1979) each concluded that bilingual education in the USA effectively promoted bilingualism with language minority children and was preferable to monolingual English programs. Since the late 1970s, many individual studies have been added and more recent reviews have emerged (e.g. Cummins & Corson, 1997; Dutcher, 1995; August & Hakuta, 1997, 1998). This chapter (and the following chapter) now examine recent reviews in three parts: (1) reviews of immersion education; (2) a review of Heritage Language education; (3) and major, influential and controversial reviews in the USA (in Chapter 12). Each has a relatively large collection of literature allowing some depth of treatment. (In comparison, there are relatively few and sufficiently rigorous evaluations of other types of bilingual education (e.g. Mainstream Bilingual Education) preventing consideration here.)

Immersion Bilingual Education

The various reviews of immersion tend to paint a relatively uniform picture. The 1980s overviews of Swain and Lapkin (1982), the California State Department of Education (1984), and Genesee (1983, 1984, 1987) highlighted four major outcomes of immersion bilingual education that are still found in recent reviews (Swain & Johnson, 1997; Swain, 1997; Jones, 1997; Laurén, 1997; Arnau, 1997; Genesee & Gándara, 1999). The vast majority of these studies concern Canadian immersion education, but there is a growing number of studies outside Canada (see Johnson & Swain, 1997; Hickey, 1997).

Second Language Learning

It is easy to predict that immersion students will surpass those in mainstream (core) programs given 'drip-feed' second language lessons for 30 minutes a day. Most students in **early total immersion** programs approach native-like performance in the second language around 11 years old in receptive language skills (listening and reading). Such levels are not so well attained in the productive skills of speaking and writing (Swain & Johnson, 1997).

The reviews confirm that one kind of bilingualism can be educationally engineered. Immersion students mostly succeed in gaining competence in two languages. However, as Chapter 1 revealed, bilingual ability is not the same as being functionally bilingual. One of the **limitations** of immersion bilingual education is that for many students, the second language can become a school-only phenomenon. Outside the school walls, immersion students tend not to use the second language any more than 'drip feed' students (Swain & Johnson, 1997). Such students are competent in a second language, but tend not to communicate in that language in the target community. Potential does not necessarily lead to production; skill does not ensure street speech. Lack of spontaneous or contrived second language opportunity and a dearth of cultural occasions to actively and purposefully use the second language may partly be the explanation. Other explanations will be considered later. Stern (1984) argued that the immersion programs were strong on language, but weak on widening students' cultural horizons and weak on sensitizing them to second language culture and values.

First Language Learning

If immersion education provides the route to near-native fluency in a second language, is it at the cost of attainment in the first language? Does bilingualism result in lesser achievement in the first language compared with 'mainstream' students? Like a balance, as one goes up, does the other go down?

For the first four years of **early total immersion**, students tend not to progress in the first language as do monolingual students in mainstream classes. This first language development relates more to school language measured by tests rather than a vernacular first language. Reading, spelling and punctuation, for example, are not so developed. Since such children are usually not given first language instruction for one, two or three years after starting school, these results are to be expected. However, the initial pattern does not last. After approximately six years of schooling, early total immersion children have caught up with their monolingual peers in first language skills. By the end of elementary schooling, the early total immersion experience has generally not affected first language speaking and writing development. Parents of these children tend to believe the same as the attainment tests reveal.

Indeed, when occasional differences in first language achievement between immersion and mainstream children have been located by research, it is often in favor of immersion students (Swain & Lapkin, 1982, 1991a). This finding links with Chapters 7 and 8 that discussed the possible cognitive advantages consequential from bilingualism. If bilingualism permits increased linguistic awareness, more flexibility in thought, more internal inspection of language, such cognitive advantages may help to explain the favorable first language progress of early immersion students.

Early partial immersion students also tend to lag behind for three or four years in their first language skills. Their performance is little different from that of total early immersion students, which is surprising since early partial immersion education has more first language content. By the end of elementary schooling, partial early immersion children typically catch up with mainstream peers in first language attainment. Unlike early total immersion students, partial immersion children do not tend to surpass mainstream comparison groups in first language achievement. Similarly, **late immersion** has no detrimental effect on first language skills (Genesee, 1983).

The evidence suggests that immersion children learn a second language at no cost to their first language. Rather than acting like a weighing balance, early total immersion, in particular, seems more analogous to cooking. The ingredients, when mixed and baked, react together in additive ways. The product becomes more than the sum of its parts.

Other Curriculum Areas

If immersion education results in children becoming bilingual, the question is whether this is at the cost of achievement in other curriculum areas. Compared with children in mainstream education how do immersion children progress in curriculum areas such as mathematics and science, history and geography? The reviews of research suggest that **early total immersion** students generally perform as well in these subjects as do mainstream children. That is, achievement in the curriculum is typically not adversely affected by early total immersion bilingual education.

The evaluations of **early partial immersion education** are not quite so positive. When children in early partial immersion learn mathematics and science through the medium of a second language, they tend to lag behind comparable mainstream children, at least initially. This may be because their second language skills are insufficiently developed to be able to think mathematically and scientifically in that second language.

The results for **late immersion** are similar. The important factor appears to be whether second language skills are sufficiently developed to cope with fairly complex curriculum material. Johnson and Swain (1994) argue that there is a gap in second language proficiency that needs bridging when students move from learning a language as a subject to learning through that second language. The more demanding the curriculum area, the higher the level of learning expected, and the later the switch to learning through a second language, the more important it is to provide 'bridging' programs. Such 'bridging programs' ease the discrepancy between second language proficiency and the language proficiency required to understand the curriculum. A 'bridging program' may require a language teacher and a content teacher (e.g. of mathematics) to operate together.

The results overall suggest that bilingual education by an immersion experience need not have negative effects on curriculum performance, particularly in early total immersion programs. Indeed, most children **gain** a second language without cost to their performance in the curriculum. However, the key factor seems to be whether their language skills have evolved sufficiently in order to work in the curriculum in their second language (see Chapter 8).

Attitudes and Social Adjustment

Apart from performance throughout the curriculum, evaluations of immersion education have examined whether immersion has positive or negative effects on students' motivation, attitude and study skills. The most positive results in this area have been found with **early total immersion students**. Parents of such students tend to express satisfaction with their offspring's learning as well as their personal and social behavior (e.g. Hickey (1997) in Ireland). Early immersion students also tend to have more positive attitudes towards themselves, their education and, in Canada to French Canadians (in comparison, for example, with late immersion students). However the danger here lies in attributing the positive attitudes to schooling. The cause may alternatively be parental values and beliefs, home culture and environment. This is further discussed in the next section.

Problems and Limitations

Various authors have recently highlighted possible limitations in immersion education that were not present in the early evaluations (e.g. Hammerly, 1988; reply by Allen *et al.*, 1989). **First**, Selinker *et al.* (1975) suggested that Canadian immersion students do not always become grammatically accurate in their French. Immersion students also tend to lack the social and stylistic sense of appropriate language use which the native speaker possesses. For example, the restricted use of verb tenses other than the present, and the sometimes incorrect use of 'tu' and 'vous', appear to be related to the functionally restricted language of the classroom. Certain forms of language do not naturally nor regularly occur in the classroom (e.g. because of the 'present' focus of learning and adult–student relationships). One solution is to investigate problematic areas of vocabulary and grammar, provide increased opportunities for receptive and particularly productive language in such weak areas, integrate a focus on the form of language used with meaningful content teaching, and give systematic and consistent feedback on language development to the student. Increasing group and collaborative learning is also seen as important in developing the productive language proficiency of students towards the standards of native French-Canadian speakers (Swain, 1993).

Second, surveys of graduates of Canadian immersion programs tend to find that relatively few students make much use of French after leaving school (Harley, 1994; Wesche, 1993). This partly reflects opportunity, partly a lack of confidence in their competence in speaking French, and partly a preference for English use. Also, immersion students do not tend to interact significantly more with francophones than students in mainstream (core) programs. Such students do not actively seek out situations where French is used (e.g. French language television). Their usage of French in out-of-school-contexts is relatively negligible compared with their use of English (Genesee & Gándara, 1999). Ability in French is not frequently translated into use of French outside the school gates, except, for example, where employment and personal economics become a focus. In most immersion programs, exposure to the second language is largely confined to the classroom.

Many immersion programs occur in geographical areas where the first language is dominant. While it is hoped that student will use the second language in the community, the reality is that the second language is used in the classroom, less so in playground, and very little in the wider community. Thus the culture of the classroom and school may aim to reflect the second language, but the latent peer culture is often that of the first language community (Swain and Johnson, 1997).

Third, there is difficulty in pinpointing the crucial interacting factors that create an effective immersion experience. There are, for example, intervening variables such as teaching techniques that may change the pattern of results. Genesee (1983) argued that individualized, activity based teaching techniques may be more effective than traditional whole class techniques. Genesee (1983) also argued that the intensity of language learning, for example, how many hours per day, is likely to be more important than the length of language learning (e.g. the number of years of second language learning). This is connected with the finding that older students tend to learn a second language more quickly than younger learners. Is it immersion as a system that leads to relatively successful outcomes or (or as well as) factors such as 'student motivation, teachers' preparation, home culture, parental attitude, ethnolinguistic vitality, amount of time studying different curricula' (Carey, 1991, p. 953).

Fourth, immersion programs can have effects on mainstream schools. For example, effects may include: a redistribution of classroom teachers and leaders, a change in the linguistic and ability profile of mainstream classes, discrepancies in class size with increasing numbers of mixed aged classes.

Fifth, Heller (1994, 1999) has argued that Canadian immersion schools provide anglophones with the linguistic and cultural capital for increased social and economic mobility and for political power. Immersion education is thus, in this perspective, about ulterior motives and vested interests. Such education is about gaining advantages in Canadian society: educational, cultural, linguistic, social, power, wealth and dominance advantages. Hence, immersion education may produce conflict with the minority francophone community (e.g. in Ontario) rather than the harmonious unity and 'bridge building' that bilingualism aims to achieve in Canadian society. This issue is considered further in Chapter 18.

Sixth, there is a danger in generalizing from the successful Canadian experience to elsewhere in the world. In Canada, immersion concerns two major high status international languages: French and English. In many countries where bilingualism is present or fostered, the situation is different. Often the context is one of a majority and a minority language (or languages) co-existing. This links with additive and subtractive bilingual situations. Canada is regarded as an additive bilingual context. Many countries across the world's continents contain subtractive bilingual contexts.

If immersion education is thought worthy of **generalizing from Canada to other countries**, there are certain conditions which need to be kept in mind:

(1) Immersion bilingual education as practiced in Canada is optional not enforced. The convictions of teachers and parents and of the children themselves affect the ethos of the school and the motivation and achievement of the children. Immersion education will work best when there is conviction and not enforced conformity.

(2) Immersion education in Canada starts with children who are at a similar level in their language skills. Such a homogeneous grouping of children may make the language classroom more efficient. Where there are wide variations in ability in a second language, teachers may have problems in providing an efficient and well-structured curriculum with equality of provision and opportunity.

(3) The Canadian immersion experience ensures there is respect for the child's home language and culture. This relates to the additive bilingual situation. Parents have generally been seen as partners in the immersion movement and some dialogue has existed with administrators, teachers and researchers (Hickey, 1999).

(4) Immersion teachers in Canada tend to be committed to such immersion education. Research in Wales has pointed to the crucial importance of teacher commitment to bilingual education in effecting achievement in school (Roberts, 1985).

(5) It is important not to view immersion education in Canada in purely educational terms. Behind immersion education is political, social and cultural ideology. Immersion education is not just immersion in a second language (French). Such bilingual education has aims and assumptions, beliefs and values that sometimes differ from and, at other times, are additional to mainstream education. It is important to see immersion education not just as a means to promote bilingualism, but also as a move to a different kind of society (see Chapter 18). By promoting bilingualism in English speakers, immersion education in Canada may support French language communities, increase the opportunities for francophones outside Quebec and help promote bilingualism in the public sector (and debatably in the private sector). However,

immersion education is seen as a Trojan horse of further English assimilation by some francophones. 'Francophones question whether an increase in bilingual anglophones will simply act to deprive them of their historical advantage in occupying bilingual jobs' (Lapkin *et al.*, 1990, p. 649). This is linked to the finding that children from higher socioeconomic backgrounds tend to be over-represented in immersion programs. Thus immersion education may act to reproduce elite groups, giving anglophone children with bilingual abilities an advantage in the jobs market (Heller, 1994, 1999).

Heritage Language Education/Developmental Maintenance Education

Major **reviews** of heritage language education are provided by Cummins (1983a, 1993), Cummins and Danesi (1990) and Dutcher (1995). Apart from looking at individual international educational interventions, the reviews also look at the pattern that can be found in the results of evaluations of heritage language education, thus attempting to derive international generalizations.

The results of such evaluations suggest that heritage language programs can be effective in four different ways. First, the students maintain their **home language**. This is especially in comparison with language minority children who are placed in mainstream or transitional education. Such mainstreamed children tend partly to lose and sometimes avoid using their heritage language. Second, such children tend to perform as well as comparable mainstream children in curriculum areas such as Mathematics, Science, History and Geography. That is, there is no loss in **curriculum performance** for such children taking their education in their home language. Indeed the evaluations suggest that they perform better than comparable children in mainstream education. To illustrate: take two 'equal' children from a language minority background. One attends a mainstream program, the other attends heritage language education. The chances are that the child in heritage language education will achieve more highly, all other factors being equal.

One 'cognitive' explanation is that heritage language education commences at the level of linguistic–cognitive competence reached on entry to school. (The cognitive reasons for this increased performance are considered in Chapter 8). In comparison, mainstreaming such language minority students has negative cognitive implications. It seemingly rejects a child's level of cognitive competence. It entails re-developing sufficient language capability in order for them to cope with the curriculum. If the analogy will stand, it is like someone with a basic level of skill in salmon fishing (with a fishing rod) who is made to learn big game sea fishing instead. The instructor ignores skills already attained with a rod. The student is made to practice casting on dry land, instead of building on existing skills with the fishing rod.

Third, studies suggest that children's **attitudes** are particularly positive when placed in heritage language education. When the home language is used in school, there is the possibility that a child's sense of identity, self-esteem and self-concept will be enhanced (Duquette, 1999). The child may perceive that the home language, the home and community culture, parents and relations are accepted by the school when the home language is used. In comparison, a language minority child who is mainstreamed is vulnerable to a loss of self-esteem and status. The home language and culture may seem disparaged. The school system and the teachers may seem latently or manifestly to be rejecting the child's home language and values. This may affect the child's motivation and interest in school work and thereby affect performance. A student whose skills are recognized and encouraged may feel encouraged and motivated; a student whose skills are ignored may feel discouraged and rejected.

The fourth finding of heritage language evaluations is perhaps the most unexpected. Indeed, it tends to go against 'common sense'. When testing children's **English language performance** (or whatever the second language is for that child), performance is generally comparable with mainstreamed children (see Cummins, 2000a). To explain this, take the previous example of two children from identical heritage language backgrounds with the same 'IQ', socioeconomic class and age. One is placed in heritage language education, the other in mainstream schooling. It might be expected that the child placed in mainstream English language education would perform far better in English language tests than the child in a heritage language education program. The prediction might be that the greater the exposure to English in mainstream education, the higher the English language test performance will be. Evaluations of heritage language education suggest something different. The child in heritage language education is likely to perform at least as well as the child in mainstream education. The explanation seems to lie in self-esteem being enhanced, and language and intellectual skills better promoted by education in the home language. Such skills appear to transfer easily into second language (majority language) areas, although some subject areas 'may lend themselves more easily to the transfer of knowledge across languages, depending on the structure of knowledge within the domain' (August & Hakuta, 1997, p. 52).

While evaluations of heritage language education are positive, the Canadian population are divided on the issue. For some, empowerment of heritage language groups is perceived as a major societal challenge — a challenge to existing power and political arrangements (Taylor *et al.*, 1993). Official Canadian policy has been supportive of multiculturalism, especially of the two 'solitudes' — French language and English language cultures. Extending multiculturalism to other 'heritage' languages has been more contentious (Cummins, 1992a). Ethnocultural communities (e.g. Ukrainian, German, Hebrew, Yiddish, Mandarin Chinese, Arabic and Polish) tend to support heritage language education. Anglophone and francophone Canadians tend to have a tolerance and goodwill towards such communities. Lukewarm support for heritage language communities tends to stop short if public monies are to be used to support heritage language education. The **anxieties** of sections of public opinion and of government include: the disruption of mainstream schools (e.g. falling rolls), problems of staffing, minimal communication between heritage language teachers and mainstream teachers, segregation of school communities, the financial costs of the absorption of immigrants into a bilingual education system, loss of time for core curriculum subjects, social tensions, and effects on the integration and stability of Canadian society (Cummins & Danesi, 1990; Cummins, 1992a; Edwards & Redfern, 1992).

Such **anxieties** have increased with the high levels of Canadian immigrants since the mid 1980s onwards. Due to low birth rates and a rapidly aging population in Canada, the population has been increased by in-migration policies. Hence language diversity in Canada has increased. In Toronto and Vancouver, for example, more than half the school population comes from a non-English speaking background (Cummins, 1992a). With increased in-migration and hence increased linguistic and cultural diversity, how does a government respond?

Gupta (1997) also voices concerns about heritage language education. She suggests that such education can be impractical when a child has multiple mother tongues, and is unprincipled when the maintenance of social cohesiveness in a multicultural, cosmopolitan environment is of more importance than mother tongue education. Sometimes ethnic privilege and socioeconomic status can be reproduced by heritage language education at the expense of other ethnic minority groups.

Cummins (1992a, p. 285) portrays the **debate** about the nature of Canadian identity, the debate about multiculturalism and the self-interest of public opinion thus:

'While the dominant anglophone and francophone groups generally are strongly in favor of learning the other official language, they see few benefits to promoting heritage languages for themselves, for Canadian society as a whole, or for children from ethnocultural backgrounds. The educational focus for such children should be on acquiring English and becoming Canadian rather than on erecting linguistic and cultural barriers between them and their Canadian peers. In short, whereas advocates of heritage language teaching stress the value of bilingual and multilingual skills for the individual and society as a whole, opponents see heritage languages as socially divisive, excessively costly, and educationally retrograde in view of minority children's need to succeed academically in the school language.'

If the focus switches from public political opinion to the educational opinion of teachers, parents and students, there is general satisfaction with Canadian Heritage Language programs. While such programs may present administrative challenges (e.g. shortage of teachers, availability of pre-service and in-service teacher education and a lack of curriculum materials), the **advantages** may be summarized as follows (Canadian Education Association, 1991):

- positive self-concept and pride in one's background;
- better integration of child into school and society;
- more tolerance of other people and different cultures;
- increased cognitive, social and emotional development;
- ease in learning of new languages;
- increased probability of employment;
- fostering stronger relationships between home and school;
- responding to the needs and wishes of community.

The overall **conclusions** from Cummins' (1983a, 1993) and Cummins and Danesi's (1990) review of heritage language education is that such education is not likely to have detrimental effects on a child's performance throughout the curriculum. Indeed, the indication from research is that language minority children tend to prosper more in such education than when placed in mainstream education. They maintain and enrich their home language and culture. Their performance throughout the curriculum does not suffer. This notably includes performance in the second language (majority language). Cognitive enhancement can also occur (Cummins, 1993; Danesi, 1991).

An important perspective comes from Dutcher (1995) who includes an **economic analysis** of developmental maintenance bilingual education. In a World Bank paper on the use of first and second languages in elementary education, she examines international evidence from Haiti, Nigeria, the Philippines, Guatemala, Canada, New Zealand, United States (Navajo), Fiji, the Solomon Islands, Vanuatu and Western Samoa. She concludes that development of the mother tongue is critical for cognitive development and as a foundation for learning the second language. That is, submersion and transitional models of bilingual education are internationally less effective in developing a child's thinking abilities. When such development is slowed considerably by learning in a second language (e.g. submersion), then the second language will in itself be learnt more slowly. Dutcher (1995) also found that parental support and community involvement were essential for successful bilingual education programs.

What is particularly important about Dutcher's (1995) review is the **economics of bilingual education**. She concludes that the recurrent costs for bilingual education are approximately the same as for traditional programs. Bilingual education is not an expensive option and has similar costs to mainstream programs. However, the most important conclusion is that strong forms of bilingual education create cost savings for the education system and for society. For example, such bilingual education provides higher levels of achievement in less years of study. Student progress is faster and higher achievement benefits society by less unemployment and a more skilled work force.

When there are weak forms of bilingual education, there may be costs to a national economy due to slower rates of progress at school, lower levels of final achievement, and sometimes the need for special or compensatory education. Higher drop-out rates means lower potential for the employment market, and the economy suffers with a lower level of skills among the work force and higher unemployment rates. In economic terms, students need to gain productive characteristics through education and Dutcher (1995) indicates that this is through early use of the native language.

For example, a World Bank **cost-effectiveness study** on Guatemala found that bilingual education was an economically prudent policy. Repetition and drop-out rates were decreased through a bilingual education intervention program, and standards of achievement rose (including in Spanish). It was estimated that education cost savings due to bilingual education were 5.6 million US dollars per year, while cost benefits were in the order of 33.8 million US dollars per year. Also, individual earnings rose by approximately 50%. In Guatemala, a strong form of bilingual education made economic sense as it produced a more skilled, highly trained and employable work force. Weak forms of bilingual education in comparison tend to have higher dropout rates and lower levels of achievement, and thus have less chance of serving and stimulating the economy through a skilled work force.

CONCLUSION

This chapter has examined the development of studies which have investigated whether bilingual education is more or less effective than monolingual education. It has also examined studies which look at the relative effectiveness of different forms of bilingual education. The initial studies examined individual programs and schools. A wide variety of different outcomes and conclusions resulted.

The evaluations of immersion bilingual education and developmental maintenance education tend to favor strong forms of bilingual education. Such studies indicate that such bilingual education not only results in bilingualism and biliteracy but also tends to heighten achievement across the curriculum. Strong forms of bilingual education tend to raise the standards and performance of children. However, these results do not stop at individual achievement. In societal terms, there are benefits for the economy in strong forms of bilingual education.

KEY POINTS IN THE CHAPTER

- Immersion, Developmental Maintenance and Dual Language bilingual education generally promotes both first and second languages for academic purposes with no lowering of performance elsewhere in the curriculum and typically increased achievement.
- Research generally supports 'strong' forms of bilingual education where a student's home language is cultivated by the school. 'Weak' forms of bilingual education where the student's second language is replaced for educational purposes by a second majority language tend to show less effectiveness.
- Strong forms of bilingual education can be an economically valuable policy. Repetition and drop-out rates are decreased, and a more skilled, highly trained and employable work force is produced.

SUGGESTED FURTHER READING

AUGUST, D. and HAKUTA, K., 1998, *Educating Language-Minority Children*. Washington, DC: National Academy Press.
BAETENS BEARDSMORE, H. (ed.) 1993, *European Models of Bilingual Education*. Clevedon: Multilingual Matters.
CUMMINS, J. and CORSON, D. (eds), 1997, *Bilingual Education. Volume 5 of the Encyclopedia of Language and Education*. Dordrecht: Kluwer.
CUMMINS, J. and DANESI, M. 1990, *Heritage Languages: The Development and Denial of Canada's*

Linguistic Resources. Toronto: Our Schools/Ourselves Education Foundation and Garamond Press.

DUTCHER, N., 1995, *The Use of First and Second Languages in Education: a Review of International Experience*. Washington, DC: World Bank.

GARCÍA, O. and BAKER, C. (eds) 1995, *Policy and Practice in Bilingual Education: A Reader Extending the Foundations*. Clevedon: Multilingual Matters. (Sections 1 & 2).

HELLER, M. 1994, *Crosswords: Language, Education and Ethnicity in French*. Ontario and New York: Mouton de Gruyter.

JOHNSON, R.K. and SWAIN, M., 1997, *Immersion Education: International Perspectives*. Cambridge: Cambridge University Press.

STUDY ACTIVITIES

(1) Collect together newspaper clippings about language in schools within your area. Try to find different attitudes in these clippings. Different newspapers may report the same story in different ways. Collect together these different interpretations and try to give an explanation of the variation.

(2) With a partner or in a small group, prepare a two minute television interview sequence on bilingual education. Locate questions which are important and likely to be of concern to the public. Prepare short punchy answers to these questions.

(3   Sit with a group of children or in a formal class of children, and attempt to measure the time the children and teacher spend using each language in the classroom. Try to work out over two or three sessions how much time is spent in either language. When recording, try to locate which language is being used for what purpose. For example, what language is used for classroom instructions, classroom management, discipline, questions, on-task and off-task talk among children, greetings, rewards and reinforcement.

The Effectiveness of Bilingual Education: The United States Debate

Introduction

The United States Debate
The Baker and de Kanter Review of Bilingual Education (1983)
Willig's (1985) Meta-analysis
The Ramírez Research
Greene's (1998) Meta-analysis
Public Opinion and the Effectiveness of Bilingual Education
California and Proposition 227
Expert Overviews of the Effectiveness of Bilingual Education
Explaining Opposition to Bilingual Education in the USA
Key Factors in Bilingual Schooling

Advancing the Effectiveness of Bilingual Education

Conclusion

CHAPTER 12

The Effectiveness of Bilingual Education: The United States Debate

INTRODUCTION

This chapter centers on the United States debate about the effectiveness of bilingual education. While in the 1960s and 1970s bilingual education slowly evolved in the United States, in the late 1970s, 1980s and 1990s public support for bilingual education tended not to favor such evolution. One branch of public opinion in the United States saw bilingual education as failing to foster integration. Rather, such opinion saw bilingual education as leading to social and economic divisions in society along language grounds. Minority language groups were sometimes portrayed as using bilingual education for political and economic self-interest, even separatism. In such a political context, a major and well publicized review of bilingual education was undertaken and published in the early 1980s.

The Baker and de Kanter Review of Bilingual Education (1983)

At the beginning of the 1980s, the United States Federal Government commissioned a **major review** of transitional bilingual education by Keith Baker and Adriana de Kanter (1983). Baker and de Kanter (1983) posed two questions to focus their review. These two questions were:

(1) Does Transitional Bilingual Education lead to better performance in English?
(2) Does Transitional Bilingual Education lead to better performance in non-language subject areas?

The review looked at bilingual education through 'transitional' eyes. It did not start from a neutral, comprehensive look at the various different forms of bilingual education. Notice also the **narrow range of expected outcomes** of bilingual educa-

245

tion in the questions. Only English language and non-language subject areas were regarded as the desirable outcome of schooling. Other outcomes such as self-esteem, employment, preservation of minority languages, and the value of different cultures were not considered. Nor were areas such as moral development, identity, social adjustment and personality development considered.

At the outset of their investigation, Baker and de Kanter (1981, 1983) located 300 pieces of bilingual education research from North America and the rest of the bilingual world. Of these 300, they rejected 261 studies. The 39 they considered in their review of bilingual education had to conform to six criteria. These may be listed as:

(1)   English and non-language subject area performance must have been measured in the research.
(2)   Comparisons between bilingual education and, for example, mainstream children must have ensured the groups were relatively matched at the commencement. This means that initial differences between the two comparison groups must have been taken into account. If not, the results may be explained by such initial differences (e.g. different socioeconomic grouping) rather than the form of education in which children were placed (Krashen, 1996).
(3)   Baker and de Kanter (1983) required the studies to be statistically valid. For example, appropriate statistical tests needed to have been performed.
(4)   Some studies were rejected because they compared the rate of progress of a bilingual education sample with national averages for a particular subject area. Such a comparison is invalid as the comparison would be between bilinguals and monolingual English speakers, rather than two different groups of bilinguals in different forms of schooling.
(5)   It was insufficient for chosen studies to show that a group of students had progressed over the year. Rather 'gain scores' needed to involve comparisons between different forms of schooling. That is, relative gain (one form of bilingual education program compared with another) rather than absolute gain (how much progress made in a specified time) was required.
(6)   Studies which solely used grade equivalent scores were rejected. There are problems of comparability and compatibility between students, schools and states when US grade scores are used.

The **conclusion** of Baker and de Kanter's (1983) review is that no particular education program should be legislated for or preferred by the US Federal Government:

'The common sense observation that children should be taught in a language they understand does not necessarily lead to the conclusion they should be taught in their home language. They can be taught successfully in a second language if the teaching is done right. The key to successful teaching in the second language seems to be to ensure that the second language and subject matter are taught simultaneously so that subject content never gets ahead of language. Given the American setting, where the language minority child must ultimately function in an English speaking society, carefully conducted second language instruction in all subjects may well be preferable to bilingual methods'. (p. 51)

The review therefore came out in support of the dominant government preference for English-only and transitional bilingual education. Functioning in the English language rather than bilingually was preferred. Assimilation and integration appear as the social and political preference that underlies the conclusions.

There was considerable **criticism** of the Baker and de Kanter (1983) review (e.g. Willig, 1981/82; American Psychological Association, 1982). The main criticisms may be summarized as follows: a narrow range of outcome measures was considered, although this is often the fault of the original research rather than the review; focusing on transitional bilingual education implicitly valued assimilation and integration and devalued aims such as the preservation of a child's home language and culture; and the criteria used for selecting only 39 out of 300 studies were narrow and rigid.

While the included studies may be relatively more sophisticated, this still meant studies with technical deficiencies (e.g. studies with small samples) were included in the review. It also excluded well-known and oft-quoted studies such as the Rock Point Navajo research (Rosier & Holm, 1980; see also Holm & Holm, 1990). The review therefore concentrated on a selective sample of technically superior research. It failed to look at patterns across the broadest range of research. This issue is returned to later in this chapter.

A further criticism of the Baker and de Kanter (1983) study provides a bridge with the next section. We have suggested in the previous chapter that single studies seldom provide a definitive answer. Therefore an overview strategy attempts to integrate the findings of a variety of studies. Baker and de Kanter's (1983) approach is **narrative integration**. This is essentially an intuitive process, and the methods of procedure tend to be variable from reviewer to reviewer. A comparison of the reviews of Baker and de Kanter (1983) with the earlier reviews by Zappert and Cruz (1977); Troike (1978) and Dulay and Burt (1978, 1979), shows that reviews of similar studies can result in differing conclusions. That is, different reviewers use the same research reports to support contrary conclusions.

An alternative and more rule-bound strategy is to use **meta-analysis**. This is a methodological technique which quantitatively integrates empirical research studies. The technique mathematically examines the amount of effect or differences in the research studies (Glass *et al.*, 1981; Hunter *et al.*, 1982). For example, how much difference is there in outcome between transitional and immersion bilingual education? There is no need to exclude studies from the meta-analysis which the reviewer finds marginal or doubtful in terms of methodology. The quality of the evaluations is something that is examined in the meta-analysis and can be allowed for statistically. Meta-analysis may show consistency of finding where narrative reviewers tend to highlight variation and disagreement in findings (McGaw, 1988).

Willig's (1985) Meta-analysis

Willig (1985) adopted a statistical meta-analysis approach to **reviewing bilingual education**. She selected 23 studies from the Baker and de Kanter (1981, 1983) review. All of her 23 studies concerned United States bilingual education evaluations and deliberately excluded Canadian immersion education evaluations. As a result of the meta-analysis, Willig (1985) concluded that bilingual education programs that supported the minority language were consistently superior in various outcomes. Bilingual education programs tend to produce higher performance in tests of achievement throughout the curriculum. Small to moderate advantages were found for bilingual education students in reading, language skills, mathematics and overall achievement when the tests were in the students' second language (English). Similar advantages were found for these curriculum areas and for writing, listening, social studies and self-concept when non-English language tests were used.

Willig's (1985) analysis also portrays the variety of bilingual education programs in existence that makes simple generalization difficult and dangerous. For example, the social and cultural ethos surrounding such programs is one major variation. Another variation is the nature of students in such programs and the variety of language intake within such programs. For example, some bilingual education programs start with children at a similar level of language skills. In other classrooms, there are various language and second language abilities, rendering classroom teaching more difficult.

A **criticism** of Willig's (1985) meta-analysis is that it only included 23 studies. An international review of the bilingual educational effectiveness studies could have included many more studies and provided more generalizable conclusions. Further criticisms of Willig (1985) are given by August and Hakuta (1997) and Keith Baker (1987). This latter critique includes a discussion of the relationship of meta-analysis to government policy regarding bilingual education. While there are disagreements about the various reviews of US evaluation studies of bilingual education, there is a consensus that more technically sophisticated and policy related research is required to make more rational decisions on educational policy, provision and practice for language minority children in the United States and beyond. One example follows.

The Ramírez Research

Some major US research is now described to exemplify the problems of limited focus evaluations of bilingual education, as well as to exemplify some recent trends in research findings. An eight-year, congressionally mandated, four and a half million dollar **longitudinal study of bilingual education** in the USA compared Structured English 'Immersion', Early Exit and Late Exit Bilingual Education Programs (Ramírez *et al.*, 1991; Ramírez, 1992). (The term 'Immersion' is not used in the original Canadian sense — English Submersion is more accurate.) Dual language or other forms of 'strong' bilingual education were not evaluated. The focus was only on 'weak' forms of bilingual education. The programs compared 'have the same instructional goals, the acquisition of English language skills so that the language-minority child can succeed in an English-only mainstream classroom' (Ramírez *et al*, 1991, p. 1).

Over 2300 Spanish speaking students from 554 Kindergarten to Sixth Grade classrooms in New York, New Jersey, Florida, Texas and California were studied. Ramírez and Merino (1990) examined the **processes** of bilingual education classrooms. The language of the classrooms were radically different in Grades 1 and 2:

- 'Structured Immersion' (Submersion) contained almost 100% English language.
- Early Exit Transitional Bilingual Education contained around two-thirds English and one-third Spanish.
- Late Exit Transitional Bilingual Education moved from three-quarters Spanish in Grade 1 to a little over half Spanish in Grade 2.

As a generalization, the outcomes were different for the three types of bilingual education. By the end of the third grade, Mathematics, Language and English reading skills were not particularly different between the three programs. By the Sixth Grade, **Late Exit Transitional Bilingual Education** students were performing higher at Mathematics, English Language and English reading than students on other programs. Parental involvement appears to be greatest in the late exit transitional programs. Although Spanish language achievement was measured in the research, these results were not included in the final statistical analyses.

One **conclusion** reached by Ramírez *et al.* (1991) was that Spanish speaking students 'can be provided with substantial amounts of primary language instruction without impeding their acquisition of English language and reading skills' (p. 39). When language minority students are given instruction in their home language, this

> 'does not interfere with or delay their acquisition of English language skills, but helps them to 'catch-up' to their English speaking peers in English language arts, English reading and math. In contrast, providing LEP students with almost exclusive instruction in English does not accelerate their acquisition of English language arts, reading or math, i.e., they do not appear to be 'catching-up.' The data suggest that by Grade 6, students provided with English-only instruction may actually fall further behind their English speaking peers. Data also document that learning a second language will take six or more years.' (Ramírez, 1992, p. 1)

This is evidence to support 'strong' forms of bilingual education and support for the use of the native language as a teaching medium. The results also showed little difference between early exit and the English Immersion (Submersion) students. Opponents of bilingual education have used this result to argue for the relative administrative ease and less expensive mainstreaming (Submersion) of language minority students and for the over-riding desirability of Transitional Bilingual education (e.g. K. Baker, 1992). Cziko (1992, p. 12) neatly sums up the **ambiguity** of the conclusions, suggesting that the research: 'provides evidence both for and against bilingual education, or rather, *against* what bilingual education normally *is* and *for* what it could be'.

A series of reviews and **criticisms** of the Ramírez *et al.* (1991) research followed (e.g. Cazden, 1992; Meyer & Fienberg, 1992; Thomas, 1992) with particular emphasis on the following:

- The benefits of 'strong' forms of bilingual education programs are not considered (e.g. Two Way bilingual education; Heritage Language education). This makes statements about bilingual education based on an incomplete range of possibilities (Cummins, 1992b). Mainstream classrooms with English Second Language (ESL) pull-out (withdrawal) classes — widely implemented in the USA — were also not included in the study (Rossell, 1992).
- The range of variables used to measure 'success' is narrow. For example, language minority parents may expect attitudinal, self-esteem, cultural and ethnic heritage goals to be examined as a measure of successful outcomes (Dolson & Meyer, 1992).
- The considerable differences that exist within bilingual education programs (let alone differing types of bilingual education program) makes comparisons and conclusions most difficult (Meyer & Fienberg, 1992). Also, the complexity of organization within a school, the ethos and varying classroom practices makes categorization of schools into watertight bilingual education programs formidable (Willig & Ramírez, 1993).
- The National Academy of Sciences reviewed this (and other) studies and concluded that the design of the study was ill-suited to answer key policy questions (Meyer & Fienberg, 1992; US Department of Education, 1992). More clarity in the aims and goals of bilingual education in the USA is needed before research can be appropriately focused. The goals for bilingual education in the USA are typically more implicit than explicit.
- There is a lack of data to support the long-term benefits of late exit transitional programs over other programs (K. Baker, 1992).

Greene's (1998) Meta-analysis

In 1996, Rossell and Baker reviewed 75 studies they regarded as methodologically acceptable. They concluded that there was no evidence to show that bilingual programs were superior to English-only options. Greene (1998) and Krashen (1996, 1999) strongly criticized this 'vote counting' review for its technically inadequate and an unsound approach (e.g. naiveness about experimental design, unavailability of some research studies quoted, simplicity of numerical analysis).

Greene (1998) re-analyzed the Rossell and Baker (1996) studies using a rigorous statistical technique – meta-analysis (echoing Willig's (1985) re-analysis of Baker and de Kanter (1983). Greene (1998) indicates that classification of 'weak' forms of bilingual education into transition bilingual education (TBE), ESL and developmental maintenance is fraught with difficulty. What is called TBE in one district could be ESL in the next. Crucially, Greene (1998) controlled for background characteristics between 'treatment' and control groups (e.g. socio-economic class, parents' level of education). Thus ruled out a third of the 75 research studies from analysis. (Other studies were excluded due to the need for legitimate control groups, unpublished and unavailable, duplicated reporting of the same program, and not being an evaluation study of bilingual education.) From the 11 remaining studies, it was found that the **use of native language instruction helps achievement in English**. That is, use of the home language in school tends to relate to higher achievement than English-only instruction. The numerical 'effect size' of home language programs on English reading, mathematics and a non-English language were almost an exact mirror of Willig's (1985) findings although only four studies were in common (Krashen, 1999).

Public Opinion and the Effectiveness of Bilingual Education

Apart from effectiveness studies, research on bilingual education research needs to include **public opinion** surveys (Krashen, 1996). The amount of parental and public support that exists for different forms of bilingual education is important in participative democratic societies as bilingual education is both an educational and political key topic.

Krashen (1999) provides a wide-ranging review of US public opinion polls regarding bilingual education. In polls that attempted to ask a representative sample of people, approximately two thirds of the public are in favor of bilingual education. However, considerable differences in public opinion polls occur because questions differ considerably. How bilingual education is defined differs widely. Leading questions which hint at the preferred or desirable answer, and the ambiguity of what respondents perceive as bilingual education, clearly has an effect on results.

Certainly there is little support in the United States for an extreme version of bilingual education in which only the home language is used. There is a high degree of support for English language proficiency for all children. When questions are phrased so that bilingual education includes proficiency in both languages, then generally there is a **consensus support for bilingual education** in the public. However, as the next section on California will show, this support is not guaranteed.

California and Proposition 227

Between 1978 and 2000, the number of students designated as limited English proficiency (LEP) in California rose from approximately a quarter of a million to 1.4 million. While Spanish is the language most often spoken by such bilingual students, there are also significant populations of Vietnamese. Hmong, Cantonese, Tagalog, Khmer, Korean, Armenian, Mandarin, Russian, Ukrainian, Serbo Croatian, Urdu, Hindi and Panjabi students, for example. With a multilingual population, California had become a state where both experimentation and experience with bilingual education had blossomed. A symbol of this is the California Association for Bilingual Education, drawing some ten thousand educationalists to its annual conference and with an established place both inside and outside the United States for being at the cutting edge of practice in bilingual schools.

In early 1996, the *Los Angeles Times* gave extensive coverage to the political activism of a small group of Spanish-speaking parents pulling their children out of the Ninth Street Elementary School. A Silicon Valley businessman called **Ron Unz** saw this as his political opportunity, having failed to win a Republican nomination three years earlier. Based on a personal philosophy of assimilation of immigrants, he denounced bilingual education, multiculturalism and ethnic separatism. But rather than talk about the English language and unifying American identity, his arguments were targeted at the educational ineffectiveness of bilingual schools in California. The press were delighted to add heat to the debate with mostly one-sided, personality based, template reporting that cultivated controversy (Crawford, 1999).

In July 1997, petitions for **Proposition 227** began circulating, requiring 433,000 signatures from registered voters to qualify as an initiative statute. The proposition was posed as an effort to improve English language instruction for children who needed to learn the language for economic and employment opportunities. In effect, Proposition 227 aimed at outlawing bilingual education in California, allowing temporary sheltered English immersion. 'Therefore' says the text of Proposition 227. 'it is resolved that: all children in California public schools shall be taught English as rapidly and effectively as possible' and such children 'shall be taught English by being taught in English'. Bilingual education was virtually eliminated; sheltered (or structured) English-immersion programs were put in their place (Quezada *et al.*, 1999).

Proposition 227 was passed on 2nd June 1998 in a public ballot by a margin of 61% to 39%. Analysis of the voting and subsequent surveys found that Latinos were clearly against the Proposition, but nevertheless, bilingual education had become virtually illegal (Attinasi, 1998). Implementation was diverse and sometimes disparate, but instruction became overwhelmingly in English. 'Many experienced bilingual teachers who were no longer in bilingual classrooms reported feeling frustrated by not being able to use the full range of skills they possessed to instruct their English learners' (Gándara *et al.*, 2000). With the sweet scent of victory in California, Ron Unz proceeded to Arizona and elsewhere across the United States (see James Crawford's WWW site: http://ourworld.compuserve.com/homepages/jwcrawford/home.htm).

On 28th April 1998, the **US Secretary of Education**, Richard W. Riley declared his non-support for Proposition 227. He stated that the Unz initiative 'would lead to fewer children learning English and would leave many children lagging behind in their academic studies'. In arguing that the initiative will be counter-productive, Secretary Riley (1998) asserted that a one-size-fits-all approach to learning English 'is not supported by years of research', deprofessionalizes teachers, 'is punitive and threatening' as it allows liability in litigation (see below), and is a direct attack on local control of education. Instead, he affirmed 'the economic, cultural, and political importance of being bilingual in our global culture'.

Those teachers and administrators who willfully and repeatedly violate Proposition 227 are left open to being sued by parents and personally liable for financial damages and legal fees. However, there is a minor provision for parental waivers and exceptions. This provision has been effective in preserving bilingual education in school districts where there is strong parental support and a history of effective bilingual programs. With limited state guidance in the first year of implementation, districts seemed to adopt their own interpretation of the new law. Some gave parents the right to choose from a range of options; others gave parents almost no rights of choice. Nearly 170,000 students remained in bilingual programs in 1998–99 (down from about 409,000 the previous year). In the second year, parents' right to decide whether children should get bilingual education was more firmly established, although some districts tried resisting this.

The attempted outlawing of bilingual education in California indicates:

(1)   the need to disseminate research backing strong forms of bilingual education. **Dissemination** of research is needed not just to teachers but also to parents and the public. The public image of bilingual education is preferably be based on fact rather than fiction, on evidence rather than on prejudice.

(2)   Bilingual education is not simply about provision, practice, and pedagogy but is unavoidably about **politics**. Despite the call for the depoliticizing of bilingual education (August & Hakuta, 1997), the reality is that opponents of bilingual education would win more ground if supporters stopped arguing for bilingual education. Claims for the advantages of bilingualism and bilingual education can valuably be part of a marketing campaign that reaches the mass media, parents, the public and particularly politicians.

(3)   Secure **evidence** is needed, not just from individual case studies, studies of outstanding schools or examples of effective practice. In a culture of monitoring and accountability, raising the standards of all students in all schools is needed. Bilingual education needs to provide evidence for high standards, high achievements and those outputs and outcomes of schooling that parents, public and politicians regard as important.

(4)   Evidence is not enough. There is a propaganda battle that goes beyond dissemination. The media (e.g. newspapers, magazines, television) are influential and can be utilized to support bilingual education. McQuillan and Tse (1996) found that in the period 1984 to 1994, 82% of research studies reported favorably on the effectiveness of bilingual education. However, only 45 percent of United States newspaper articles took a similar favorable position on bilingual education. Less than half of all newspaper articles made any mention of research findings, while nearly a third of such articles relied on personal or anecdotal accounts. This implies that research may need to become more accessible as well as disseminated through influential mass media channels. Promotion and marketing of research and reviews may be necessary in such a politicized climate, targeted at policy-makers and politicians, parents and the press. The alternative is that prejudice and ignorance will be dominant.

Expert Overviews of the Effectiveness of Bilingual Education

While public opinion surveys are infrequent, **expert opinion** is more likely to be privately or publicly sought. The United States Committee on Education and Labor asked the General Accounting Office (1987) to conduct a study on whether or not the research evidence on bilingual education supported the current government preference for assimilationist, transitional bilingual education. The General Accounting Office (1987) therefore decided to conduct a survey of experts on bilingual education. Ten experts were assembled, mostly professors of education, selected from prestigious institutions throughout the USA. Each expert was provided with a set of questions to answer in written form. The experts were asked to compare research findings with central political statements made about such research. The purpose was to verify the veracity of official statements.

In terms of learning English, eight out of ten experts favored using the native or heritage language in the classroom. They believed that progress in the native language aided children in learning English because it strengthened literacy skills which easily transferred to operating in the second language. On the learning of other subjects in the curriculum, six experts supported the use of heritage languages in such teaching. However, it was suggested that learning English is important in making academic progress (General Accounting Office, 1987).

That all the experts did not agree was to be expected. The group of ten had diverse research backgrounds and perspectives. Eight were knowledgeable about language learning and schooling for language minority children. Two were expert on social science accumulation and synthesis (meta-analysis).

Another high profile review was by an **expert panel of the US National Research Council** – The Committee on Developing a Research Agenda on the Education of Limited-English-Proficient and Bilingual Students. Chaired by Kenji Hakuta of Stanford University, it declared that (1) all children in the USA should be educated to be become fully functional in the English language; (2) the expectations of, and academic opportunities given to, such students must equal that of other students; and (3) 'in an increasingly global economic and political world, proficiency in language other than English and an understanding of different cultures are valuable in their own right, and should be among the major goals for schools' (August & Hakuta, 1997, p. 17).

This expert panel concluded that use of a child's native language in school does not impede the acquisition of English, but there is 'little value in conducting evaluations to determine which type of program is best. First, the key issue is not finding a program that works for all children and all localities, but rather finding a set of program components that works for the children in the community of interest, given the goals, demographics, and resources of that community' (August & Hakuta, 1997, p. 147). That is, a developmental maintenance program or a submersion program can both be successful in particular local contexts.

Also, many LEP children come from materially poor and disadvantaged homes, schools and communities. While bilingual programs academically benefit such children, the effect of these programs does not close the gap between disadvantaged and middle-class populations. There are many issues beyond language, at home and at school, that are faced by such bilingual students that affect their achievement (Valdés, 1997). Simply introducing bilingual programs will not by itself solve all the educational problems such children face – although they are one important part of the package.

Brisk (1998) provides a comprehensive examination of the **situational factors** that affect both the standards reached by bilingual students and the effectiveness of bilingual schools. Her model suggests that there are five situational areas that can promote or otherwise such effectiveness:

(1) **Linguistic**, e.g. amount of language use in the community, media, technology, home.
(2) **Cultural**, e.g. parental participation in classroom, curriculum content and the assumptions about background knowledge of students.
(3) **Economic**, e.g. the economic viability of the languages, career opportunities, educational costs.
(4) **Political**, e.g. the treatment of immigrants, attitudes to language diversity.
(5) **Social**, e.g. size and cohesiveness of the language community, race and gender relationships, attitudes to language and ethnic groups.

The expert panel of the US National Research Council complained of the extreme politicization of the evaluation of bilingual education and that consumers of such evaluations were advocates utterly convinced of the correctness of their opinions. Advocates of bilingual education lock onto studies supporting their position and criticize and discount studies against their position. Advocates of submersion and transitional bilingual education do the same. Research studies and their investigators are quickly labeled as being either for or against bilingual education.

The conclusion from the expert panel of the US National Research Council was that the effectiveness debate was too **simple and polarized** (August & Hakuta, 1997). All programs could be effective (e.g. transitional, submersion, dual language, developmental maintenance) depending on the subtle chemistry of interacting ingredients, environments and processes. Attempts to prove the superiority of a particular model are pointless and unproductive. Theory based research and interventions which predicted the effects of components on the 'growth' of children in different environments were needed.

As Crawford (1999) notes, being even-handed, wanting to depoliticize the issue and injecting scientific detachment into research is an academic vision that has little or no impact among journalists and politicians. The 487-page expert review was seized by opponents and proponents of bilingual education as justification of their position (Crawford, 1999). The report thus became a tool used by opposing political groups to support their position.

Nevertheless, the August and Hakuta (1997, 1998) report concludes that there is a fundamental divergence of opinion about the aims of education and bilingual education that research cannot resolve. Bilingual education is, and will continue to be, a political issue. For some pluralism, biculturalism and multilingualism are a

desirable outcome. For others the assimilation of minority languages, the integra-tion of minorities within the overall society are the important outcomes. This suggests that a definitive statement on whether bilingual education is more or less successful than, for example, mainstream education is impossible due to the variety of underlying values and beliefs that different interest groups have about education and the future society they envisage.

However, Cummins (1999a, 2000b) has argued that August and Hakuta (1997), Greene (1998), Rossell and Baker (1996), Willig (1985) and Baker and de Kanter make a wrong assumption. They all assume that research reviews can directly inform policy-making. Jim Cummins sees this as naive due to the 'myriad human, administrative, and political influences that impact the implementation of programs over time' (Cummins, 1999a, p. 26). There are hundreds of variables that affect program outcomes such that research cannot, by itself, directly advise policy, provision and practice. Rather, Cummins (1999a, 2000b) argues that it is tested theory that should drive policy-making. 'In complex educational and other human organizational contexts, data or 'facts' become relevant for policy purposes only in the context of a coherent theory. It is the *theory* rather than the individual research findings that permits the generation of predictions about program outcomes under different conditions' (Cummins, 1999a, p. 26).

That is, research should commence from theoretical propositions, testing, refining and sometimes refuting those propositions. When theory is firmly supported by research and if it accounts for findings from a variety of contexts, theory will explicitly inform policy-making. Thus Cummins (1999a, 2000b) is crit-ical of the US National Research Council report (August & Hakuta, 1997) as it comprehensively summarizes research but virtually ignores theories that address policy-relevant issues. Cummins (1999a, 2000b) asserts that theories such as Thresholds, Interdependence, Conversational and Academic Language Profi-ciency (see Chapter 8) are supported by research and answer a range of policy issues. Such theories are a more important focus than reviews of research.

Explaining Opposition to Bilingual Education in the USA

It has been suggested by Huddy and Sears (1995) that there are three theoretical explanations for opposition to bilingual education. First, **realistic interest theory** suggests that those in power wish to protect their own (and their group's) political and economic self-interests. Thus majority language groups may oppose bilingual education as such education does not benefit monolinguals (e.g. in the USA) or majority language speakers. Indeed, language majority groups may be subsidizing such bilingual education. If there is a feeling of threat among the majority language group, the threat may not be based on 'reality' but be narrowly subjective, constructed out of prejudice and stereotyping rather than realism.

Such majority language groups may endorse the principle of racial and ethnic equality and believe in the equality of all languages. However, a stronger motiva-tion and priority is language majority self-interest and hence the best of intentions can be killed by the strongest of motives.

This phenomenon is not confined to the USA. There is a belief in many countries where one language is dominant that bilingual education takes away resources from monolingual, majority language schools. However, a stronger concern among those in power may be that minority language bilingual education programs threaten majority language economic interests and political ascendancy.

A second theoretical explanation as to why there is opposition to bilingual education according to Huddy and Sears (1995) is that those in bilingual education are perceived as **undeserving of special treatment**. For example, in the USA, Huddy and Sears (1995) suggest that there is Anglo prejudice towards Latinos who are viewed as 'lazy' and as 'violators of the work ethic'. A new form of racism produces stereotypes of non-Whites not in terms of color but as 'unwilling to work', 'complaining', with an 'ethnic chip on their shoulder'. Therefore, language majority members may see bilingual education as giving undeserved government assistance to those who are perceived as unwilling to work, unwilling to assimilate and likely to be politically subversive.

A third explanation for opposition to bilingual education derives from **social identity theory**. Language majority members may oppose bilingual education because they view it as a threat to national, cultural and personal identity. Bilingual education becomes equated with the spread of foreign customs, foreign influences, challenging a sense of pride in nationality, national image and integration. From a language majority viewpoint, both individual rights and national solidarity may seem to be threatened by bilingual education. Bilingual education is seen to promote diversity rather than unity.

Key Factors in Bilingual Schooling

Collier (1995a) highlights particular factors that affect minority language students' success or failure in schooling in the United States. In particular, Collier is concerned with the length of time it takes for such students to acquire a second language to compete in the curriculum on an equal footing with native speakers of that language. Collier's (1995a) model has **four major components**: sociocultural, linguistic, academic and cognitive. These four factors are regarded as interdependent and interactive.

First, Collier (1995a) stresses the importance of **sociocultural** processes in acquiring a second language in school (e.g. in transitional bilingual education). The student may experience prejudice and discrimination, the subordinate status of their language minority group and assimilation influences. Such external influences may effect internal psychological workings such as self-esteem, anxiety, integration with peers and achievement in school. Thus Collier emphasizes the importance of a socioculturally supportive environment for language minority students.

Second, Collier (1995a) argues that academic success in the second language requires the **student's first language** to be developed to a high cognitive level. Her argument starts with the continuous development of the first language. She emphasizes that language development is a life-long process and cannot occur in a two-year period or even a five-year period. Throughout schooling, a student acquires more vocabulary, increased understanding of meaning, more complex syntax, more formal discourse patterns, increasingly complex aspects of pragmatics and subtle phonological distinctions in their first language. Students throughout schooling acquire increasingly complex skills in reading and writing, developing through to college when further vocabulary development, new subtleties in meaning and more complex writing skills evolve. Second language acquisition is an equally complex and evolving phenomenon. If a child is required to work through a second language in school, a deep level of language proficiency is required and this has to be developed throughout schooling and college.

How long does it take to develop academic second language proficiency? Collier (1995a) argues that it is difficult for second language students to develop proficiency levels in their second language to compete with native speakers. One reason is that native speakers are not sitting around waiting for non-native speakers to catch up. During the school years, native speakers' first language development continues at a rapid rate, such that the goal of proficiency equal to a native speaker is a moving target for the language learner.

Collier's (1995a) **longitudinal studies** suggest that, in US schools where all the instruction is given through the second language (submersion schooling), second language speakers of English with no schooling in their first language take between **seven and ten years** or more to reach the language proficiency of native English speaking peers. Some do not reach native levels of language proficiency at all. Where students have had two or three years of first language schooling in their home country before emigrating to the United States, they take between five and seven years to reach native speaker performance. Collier found this pattern among different home language groups, different ethnic groups and different socioeconomic groups of students.

The most significant variable in becoming proficient in the second language (English in the USA) is the amount of formal schooling students have received in their first language. Those students who are schooled solely in their second language, particularly from the Fourth Grade onwards, when the academic and cognitive demands of the curriculum increase rapidly, tend to progress slowly and show relatively less academic achievement. Thus one essential feature for students to develop academic language proficiency is that there is strong development through the first language of academic-cognitive thinking skills. Thinking abilities, literacy development, concept formation, subject knowledge and learning strategies developed in the first language transfer to the second language. As students expand their vocabulary and literacy skills in their first language, they can increasingly demonstrate the knowledge that they have gained in the second language.

The third part of Collier's (1995a) model is **academic development**. With each succeeding grade in school, the curriculum requires an ever-expanding vocabulary, higher cognitive levels and a more complex form of discourse. It is most efficient to develop academic work through a student's first language, while progress in the second language occurs through teaching meaningful academic content. Postponing or interrupting academic development to promote the second language tends to increase the probability of academic failure. Students cannot afford to lose time when the curriculum is both full and increasingly complex and demanding.

Thus Collier (1995a) argues for the importance of uninterrupted cognitive development in primary and secondary schooling for second language children. The key to understanding the role of the first language in the academic development of the second language is to ensure that there is uninterrupted cognitive development which best occurs through education in the first language. When students have to use an undeveloped second language at school (as in submersion schooling), they will be functioning at a lower cognitive level. Thus, cognitive maturity fails to occur, or occurs relatively slowly.

The fourth factor in Collier's (1995a) model is **cognitive development**. She argues that the teaching of a second language should avoid simplified, structured and artificially sequenced language work. The danger is in breaking down language into cognitively simple tasks. Rather, cognitive development occurs when there is development of the first language as the foundation for both cognitive development and second language proficiency.

Collier goes on to argue that all four components – sociocultural, academic, cognitive and linguistic – are interdependent. If one is developed at the neglect of the other, the student's overall growth and performance will suffer.

Collier's (1995a) conclusion is that **two-way bilingual education** at the elementary school level is the **optimal program** for the long-term academic success of language minority students. Such students maintain their first language skills and cognitive/academic development while developing in a second language. In such a model, students develop deep academic proficiency and cognitive understanding through their first language to compete successfully with native speakers of the second language. Evidence for this conclusion is given by Thomas and Collier (1995, 1997) who produced a growth pattern of language minority English language achievement in different types of bilingual education programs. This is summarized below (see also the graphs the following page).

- In kindergarten through to Grade 2, there is little difference between language minority children in ESL 'pull-out', transitional and two-way (dual language) programs in the United States. On a 'English language achievement' scale of 0–100 (with 50 as the average performance of native English language speakers), language minority children score around the 20 mark.
- ESL 'pull-out' children initially (Grades 1 and 2) progress faster in English language achievement than children in transitional and dual language programs. This might be expected as they have more intensive English-medium activity.
- By Grade 6, students in dual language programs and late-exit transitional programs are ahead on English language performance compared with

Student Achievement in English Language

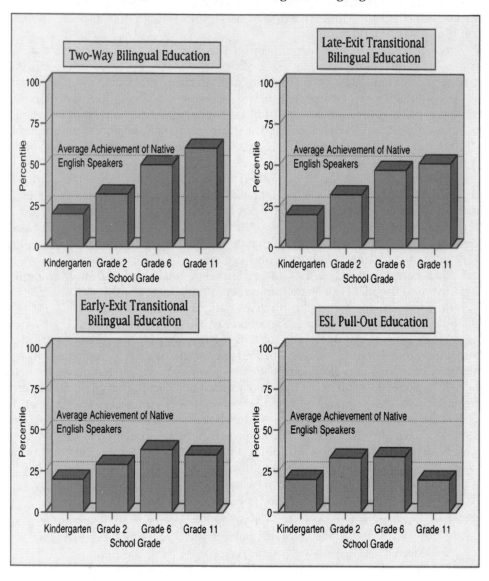

early-exit and ESL pull-out students. Dual language and late-exit transitional students achievements in English language tests are close to those of native English speakers (i.e. around the 50th percentile). Early-exit and ESL pull-out students tend to perform around the 30th percentile on such tests.
- By Grade 11, the order of performance is:
    (1) Two-way bilingual education (highest performance in English);
    (2) Late-exit transitional bilingual education;
    (3) Early-exit transitional bilingual education;
    (4) ESL pull-out programs (Lowest performance in English).
- By Grade 11, two-way bilingual education students are performing above the average levels of native English speakers on English language tests. On a 'English language achievement' scale of 0–100, two-Way bilingual education students average around 60, late-exit students about the same as native English speakers around 50, early-exit students around 30 to 40, and ESL pull-out students around 20.

Criticisms of Thomas and Collier's (1995, 1997) growth trajectories of language minority English language achievement in different types of bilingual education programs include:

(1) their aggregation is based on selective individual research studies and well-implemented and mature programs;
(2) little information is presented on how the growth trajectories were determined;
(3) the effects of student geographical mobility (e.g. leaving a district) are not clear and may produce biased results (e.g. when such students are excluded from longitudinal data);
(4) the effects of student background (e.g. socioeconomic) are not clear and will influence achievement levels;
(5) few details are provided about the 700,000 language minority students on which the growth trajectories are based and which dates from 1982–1996.

ADVANCING THE EFFECTIVENESS OF BILINGUAL EDUCATION

Articles by Carter and Chatfield (1986), Lucas *et al.* (1990), Baker (1990) and Cziko (1992) and overviews by August and Hakuta (1997, 1998) and Cummins (2000b) have suggested that the effectiveness of bilingual education can be addressed from a different perspective. Bilingual education research can look at effectiveness at four different levels. First, there is the effectiveness at the level of the **individual child**. Within the same classroom, children may respond and perform differently. Second, there is effectiveness at the **classroom** level. Within the same school and type of bilingual education program, classrooms may vary considerably. It is important to analyze the factors connected with varying effectiveness at classroom level. Third, effectiveness is often analyzed at the **school** level. What makes some schools more effective than others even within the same **type of bilingual education program** and with similar student characteristics? Fourth, beyond the school level there can be aggregations of schools into different types of **programs** (e.g. transitional compared with heritage language programs) or into different geographical regions.

It is possible to look at effective bilingual education at each and all of these levels, and at the inter-relationship between these four levels. For example, at the individual level we need to know how bilingual education can best be effective for cultural groups, and for children of different levels of ability and special needs. How do children with learning difficulties and specific language disorders fare in bilingual education? At the classroom level, we need to know what teaching methods and classroom characteristics create optimally effective bilingual education. At the school level, the characteristics of staffing, the size of groups and the language composition of the school all need to be taken into account to find out where and when bilingual education is successful.

Apart from individual classroom and school characteristics, the effectiveness of bilingual education can take into account the **social, economic, political and cultural context** in which such education is placed. For example, the differences between being in a subtractive or additive context may affect the outcomes of bilingual education. The willingness of teachers to involve parents, and good relationships between the school and its community may be important in effective bilingual education. Also, the local economics of schooling play an important part. Where the funding of schools is based on a local tax, then 'per student' expenditure in more affluent areas will be considerably greater than in the less affluent areas. In the USA for example, language minority students from an economically poor district will typically have considerably less expenditure on them (per student) than those in more wealthy suburbs. It is difficult to advance the effectiveness of bilingual education with very limited financial and material resources.

It is also important in bilingual education effectiveness research to examine a wide variety of **outcomes** from such education. Such outcomes may include examination results, tests of basic skills (e.g. oracy, literacy, numeracy), the broadest range of curriculum areas (e.g. science and technology, humanities, mathematics, languages, arts, physical, practical and theoretical pursuits, skills as well as knowledge). Non-cognitive outcomes are also important to include in an assessment of effectiveness. Such non-cognitive outcomes may include: attendance at school, attitudes, self-concept and self-esteem, social and emotional adjustment, employment and moral development.

For example, Stephen Krashen (1999) provides evidence to show that bilingual education is not the cause of **dropping-out** in United States schools – but it may be the cure. Latino students do have higher drop-out rates (e.g. 30% of Latino students classified as drop-outs compared to 8.6% of non-Latino whites and 12.1% of non-Latino Blacks). Krashen's (1999) review of the evidence suggests that those who had experienced bilingual education were significantly less likely to drop-out.

There are factors (other than bilingual education) related to dropping-out such as socioeconomic class, recency of immigration, family environment, and the presence of print at home. It is estimated that 40% of Latino children live in poverty compared with 15% of white non-Latino children. Latino children are more likely to have parents who did not complete High School. When these factors are controlled statistically, the drop-out rate among Latinos is the same (or virtually the same) as for other groups. Since 'strong' forms of bilingual schooling tend to produce higher standards of academic English and performance across the curriculum, then such schools become part of the cure.

The point behind such a comprehensive consideration of bilingual education is that effective bilingual education is not a simple or automatic consequence of using a child's home language in school (as in heritage language education) or a second language (as in immersion education). Various home and parental, community, teacher, school and society effects may act and interact to make bilingual education more or less effective. The relative importance of the differing ingredients and processes in various school and cultural contexts needs to be investigated to build a comprehensive and wide-ranging theory of when, where, how and why bilingual education can be effective.

This approach to studying effectiveness of bilingual education not only considers the infrastructure of such education but also what makes a school effective (August & Hakuta, 1997). For example, the following factors have been found to increase a school's effectiveness:

Staff: supportive but focused and purposeful leadership by the Principal/Headteacher and senior management, a high degree of commitment by (and coordination among) the teachers, staff with a shared vision, agreed goals, and staff development programs.

Curriculum: providing intellectually challenging, active and meaningful lessons, a curriculum that has coherence, balance, breadth, relevance, progression and continuity, a focus on basic skills but also on developing higher-order thinking skills, language and literacy development across the curriculum, smooth language transitions between grades, systematic, equitable and authentic assessment integrated with learning goals, a bilingual and bi/multicultural hidden curriculum and ethos throughout the school, a safe and orderly school environment, and a supportive, constructive classroom atmosphere.

Students: high expectations which are clearly communicated to students, the school needs to be responsive to a student's individual needs and to varying community profiles (e.g. culture, newcomers), providing opportunities for student-directed activities, involving students in decisions and building their trust and self-esteem, opportunities to practice which extend and elaborate, with positive and regular feedback based on careful monitoring.

Parents: plenty of parental involvement, with home–school collaboration that is reciprocal.

An example of research into **bilingual education effectiveness** is a case study by Lucas *et al.* (1990) in six schools in California and Arizona. This research revealed eight features seemingly important in promoting the success of language minority students.

(1) **Value and status were given to the language minority students' language and culture**. While English literacy was a major goal, native language skills were celebrated, encouraged inside and outside the formal curriculum and flagged as an advantage rather than a liability.

(2) **High expectations of language minority students were prevalent**. Apart from strategies to motivate students and recognize their achievement, individualized support of language minority students was available. The provision of counseling, cooperation with parents and the hiring of language minority staff in leadership positions to act as role models were some of the ploys to raise expectations of success at school.

(3) **School leaders gave the education of language minority students a relatively high priority**. This included good awareness of curriculum approaches to language minority children and communicating this to the staff. Strong leadership, the willingness to hire bilingual teachers and high expectations of such students were also part of the repertoire of such leaders.

(4) **Staff development was designed to help all the staff effectively serve language minority students**. For example, the teachers were provided with staff development programs which sensitized them to students' language and cultural backgrounds, increased their knowledge of second language acquisition and of effective curriculum approaches in teaching language minority students.

(5) **A variety of courses for language minority students was offered**. Such courses included English as a second language and first language courses. Small class sizes (e.g. 20–25) were created to maximize interaction.

(6) **A counseling program was available**. Counselors were able to speak the students' home language, could give post-secondary opportunity advice and monitored the success of the language minority students.

(7) **Parents of language minority children were encouraged to become involved in their children's education**. This included parents' meetings, contact with teachers and counselors, telephone contact and neighborhood meetings.

(8) **School staff were committed to the empowerment of language minority students through education**. Such commitment was realized through extra-curricular activities, participation in community activities, interest in developing their pedagogic skills and interest in the political process of improving the lot of language minority students.

CONCLUSION

This and the previous chapter has examined the development of studies which have investigated whether bilingual education is more or less effective than monolingual education. It has also examined studies which look at the relative effectiveness of different forms of bilingual education. The chapter has sought to portray how questions about the effectiveness of bilingual education have evolved. The initial studies (reviewed in the previous chapter) examined individual programs and schools. A wide variety of different outcomes and conclusions resulted. Following this first stage, the second stage reviewed the voluminous research. This stage continues to the present. Reviews of US research by government officials and by meta-analysis have produced differing conclusions. This reveals the political undertones of discussion about different forms of bilingual education.

The chapter has revealed a paradox. US research on bilingual education has clearly tended to favor more years rather than less in bilingual education. Yet there has been little US government support for bilingual education. Politics has proved stronger than research, selectively using the evidence, and marching on regardless. This is because there is a contest about whose definition of a US citizen is dominant. 'Blaming linguistic and cultural diversity is a smokescreen for the fact that the USA has not resolved fundamental inequalities. The root of the problem lies in an inability to accept an expanded definition of what it is to be a US American today' (Zentella, 1997, p. 286). Bilingual education, as practiced in the United States, has tended to be more about politics than pedagogy, 'mythology' more than effective methodology, and prejudice rather than preferable practice.

However, another of the conclusions that comes from this chapter is that simple questions give simplistic answers. We cannot expect a simple answer to the question of whether or not bilingual education is more (or less) effective than mainstream education. The question itself needs to be more refined. It needs to look at the conditions under which different forms of bilingual education become more or less successful. This means departing from simple studies and simple results to broad investigations that include a wide variety of conditions and situations. The scales of justice of bilingual education cannot give a simple verdict. The evidence is wide-ranging and complex; witnesses have complex accounts and arguments. There is no simple right or wrong, good or bad; no simple orthodoxy of approach that can guarantee success.

The effectiveness of bilingual education needs to consider children, teachers, the community, the school itself and the type of program. One particular factor cannot be isolated from another. We need to consider a whole variety of ingredients at the same time, all of which can make for a successful recipe. Children have a wide variety of characteristics which also need investigation. Children cannot be isolated from the classroom characteristics within which they work. Within the classroom there are a variety of factors which may make for effective education. Outside the classroom the different attributes of schools may, in their turn, interact with children and their classrooms to make education for language minority children more or less effective. Outside the school is the important role played by the community. The social, cultural and political environment in which a school works will affect the education of language minority children at all levels.

The key issue becomes 'what are the optimal conditions for children who are either bilingual, becoming bilingual or wish to be bilingual?' Answers may involve a complex set of conditions. Rather than a simple black and white sketch, a complex multi-colored canvas may need to be painted.

KEY POINTS IN THE CHAPTER

- Individual researches, meta-analyses, expert reviews and public opinion polls do not provide an agreed belief in the effectiveness of bilingual education. This is explained partly by the varying political aims of those who either support or oppose bilingual education.
- However, academic empirical research generally supports 'strong' forms of bilingual education where a student's home language is cultivated by the school. 'Weak' forms of bilingual education where the student's second language is replaced for educational purposes by a second majority language tend to be less effective.
- California's Proposition 227, virtually ending recent decades of bilingual education in California, shows that bilingual education is a key political issue as well as a pedagogical one.
- Experts fail to agree about the value of bilingual education because their political beliefs differ. Reliance on tested theory is one answer to differing opinions.

SUGGESTED FURTHER READING

ARIAS, M. and CASANOVA, U. (eds) 1993, *Bilingual Education: Politics, Practice, Research.* Chicago: National Society for the Study of Education/University of Chicago Press.
AUGUST, D. and HAKUTA, K., 1998, *Educating Language-Minority Children.* Washington, DC: National Academy Press.
CAZDEN, C.B. and SNOW, C.E., 1990, *English Plus: Issues in Bilingual Education.* (*The Annals of the American Academy of Political and Social Science 508, March 1990*). London: Sage.
CRAWFORD, J. 2000, *At War With Diversity.* Clevedon: Multilingual Matters.
GARCÍA, O. and BAKER, C. (eds) 1995, *Policy and Practice in Bilingual Education: A Reader Extending the Foundations.* Clevedon: Multilingual Matters. (Sections 1 and 2).
LINDHOLM-LEARY, K.J., 2001, *Dual Language Education.* Clevedon: Multilingual Matters.

STUDY ACTIVITIES

(1) Read the Lucas *et al.* (1990) article in the *Harvard Educational Review*. Write a summary in approximately 600 words of that article. List those effectiveness factors which you think are part of any form of education, and list separately those which you think are solely concerned with the language part of bilingual education. Are there other factors which you think are important in effective-

ness not mentioned in this article? Discuss in a group what are the priorities in producing bilingual children through formal education.

(2) Make a list of 'effectiveness factors' from your reading. Following observation in one or more classrooms, consider the effectiveness of these classrooms against this list. What factors seem, as the result of your classroom observation, to be more and less important?

(3) Using the same list of 'effectiveness factors', study one program in your area (e.g. transitional bilingual education). What features of that program are effective and which are less than effective due to the aims and nature of that program?

(4) Arrange a debate among students where two people support 'weak' forms of bilingual education, and two support 'strong' forms. Present the arguments for two major kinds of bilingual education, highlighting those which are most important in your region. Allow other students to ask questions of the four presenters.

Language Development and Language Allocation in Bilingual Education

Introduction

Language Development at School

Language Strategies in School

Third Language Acquisition

Language Allocation in
Bilingual Classrooms

Bilingualism, Deaf People
and Hearing Impaired People

Conclusion

CHAPTER 13

Language Development and Language Allocation in Bilingual Education

INTRODUCTION

This chapter begins by expressing the importance of schools in the first language development of bilinguals. Schools often play a major role in the maintenance and development of home language oracy, literacy and cultural awareness. When two languages are used in the school, boundaries between the majority and minority language may be valuable (e.g. as in dual language schools). The chapter therefore examines strategies for the separation of two languages in a school.

In contrast, a teaching and learning methodology that strategically uses both languages has recently been developed. Such a bilingual methodology gives different roles to each language in a session attempting to develop fully both languages and raise achievement through a more active processing of lesson content.

The chapter finishes with a special group of bilinguals who form their own language minority: deaf people. Often a neglected language minority, it will be demonstrated that many of the attributes of hearing bilinguals are shared by deaf bilinguals. Different views about deaf bilinguals are presented, followed by the debate about which kind of bilingual education is valuable for deaf students.

LANGUAGE DEVELOPMENT AT SCHOOL

For bilingual children, the **school** is usually an **essential agent** in developing the home language. When a child enters kindergarten or elementary school, first language development needs to be formally addressed, irrespective of whether or not that child has age-appropriate competency in the home language. While first language development throughout schooling is important for majority and minority language children, the minority context places extra reasons for careful nurturance of a minority language.

Two quotes from a historically influential and important report by **UNESCO** (1953) entitled '*The Use of Vernacular Languages in Education*' provide the basis for the use of the home language in school, where possible:

> 'It is axiomatic that the best medium for teaching a child is his mother tongue. Psychologically, it is the system of meaningful signs that in his mind works automatically for expression and understanding. Sociologically, it is a means of identification among the members of the community to which he belongs. Educationally, he learns more quickly through it than through an unfamiliar linguistic medium. But as was said earlier, it is not always possible to use the mother tongue in school and, even when possible, some factors may impede or condition its use.' (p. 11)

> 'It is important that every effort should be made to provide education in the mother tongue... On educational grounds we recommend that the use of the mother tongue be extended to as late a stage in education as possible. In particular, pupils should begin their schooling through the medium of the mother tongue, because they understand it best and because to begin their school life in the mother tongue will make the break between home and school as small as possible.' (pp. 47–48)

The typically lower status of the minority language, the anglophone nature of most mass media, and the dominance of 'common denominator' majority languages outside the school requires special attention to the continual evolution and progression of the minority language in school. A school can considerably develop the minority language learnt at home so that it has more uses and potentially can be used in more domains (e.g. reading, writing, preparation for employment). The school will widen vocabulary, teach conventional grammar, and help standardization of the minority language (e.g. new terminology in Information Technology). The school also gives the minority language status, esteem and market value to its students.

To preserve and reproduce the minority language in the young, a 'strong' form of bilingual education (one that supports the heritage language) needs to include a 'first language' program with explicit language development aims and goals. Such a program may involve lessons devoted to that language (e.g. Spanish listening, speaking, writing and reading development). It may also valuably involve a strategy for heritage **language development across the curriculum** through content based approaches (Met, 1998). Where children take lessons (e.g. Social Studies, Science) through the medium of their home language, language development in those curriculum areas can be overtly and consciously fostered. A child's home language develops when it is cultivated, encouraged and promoted in a purposeful way in many or all curriculum areas (e.g. Humanities, Sciences, Mathematics). The content areas taught shape the language that is learnt, although language proficiency constrains the content that can be learnt (Met, 1998).

LANGUAGE STRATEGIES IN SCHOOL

The learning methodologies and teaching strategies used to support language minority children in school are also important. Mainstream classrooms are often arranged in ways that do not fully support minority language children's linguistic and cultural development. Mainstream classrooms often prefer to assume a homogeneous student population, with similar linguistic and cultural characteristics, delivering a standardized 'transmission' or 'banking' curriculum with individual competition symbolized in regular standardized tests (Cummins, 2000a).

In contrast, language minority students thrive in an atmosphere where linguistic and cultural diversity is assumed, sharing a bicultural or multicultural curriculum with multiple perspectives and linguistic equality of opportunity (Freeman, 1995, 1998). Supportive and non-threatening cooperative learning techniques that stress interdependence, social interaction and teamwork have been successfully used with culturally and linguistically diverse students (Holt, 1993). Cummins (2000b) argues for a 'transformative pedagogy' that sees knowledge as fluid and not fixed, collaboratively constructed rather than memorized, where the sharing of experiences affirms students' identity, but essentially also involves critical enquiry to understand power, inequality, justice, and local social and economic realities (see the critical literacy approach, Chapter 15).

The benefits for a well developed home (minority) language spread to the learning of a second or third language. As Swain and Lapkin (1991a) found in research, those students **literate in their heritage language** progressed significantly more in written and oral French than those without such skills. First language literacy, in particular, enables relative ease of learning (and learning through) a second language by the transfer of knowledge, language abilities (e.g. literacy strategies, communication skills) and learning processes (see Chapters 8, 10 and 11).

THIRD LANGUAGE ACQUISITION

With respect to **learning a third language**, there is belief that bilinguals are relatively better at learning a new language than monolinguals. This belief is usually expressed as (1) bilinguals being more linguistically attuned to language learning and (2) that there is positive transfer from already having learnt a second language to learning another (e.g. in learning strategies, vocabulary, sensitivity to grammatical differences). The studies that exist mostly, but not universally, tend to support this belief (Bild & Swain, 1989; Cenoz & Valencia, 1994; Genesee & Lambert, 1983; Hurd, 1993; Klein, 1995; Mägiste, 1984; Ringbom, 1985; Saif & Sheldon, 1969; Swain et al., 1990; Thomas, 1988; Zobl, 1993).

Cenoz and Valencia's (1994) conducted a relatively sophisticated study in the Basque country of 320 17- to 19-year-old students. They found that the English language achievement of bilingual students (Spanish and Basque) was higher than monolingual Spanish speakers. This result was found when other influential factors (intelligence, motivation, age and length of exposure to English) were taken into account. Bilingualism, in and by itself, appears to give an advantage in learning a third language. One explanation for this result is the greater metalinguistic awareness of bilinguals and their possible greater sensitivity to communication (see Chapter 7). Another explanation may be in the transfer between languages of phonological (sound system) and pragmatic (communication) abilities (Verhoeven, 1994). This is predicted in Cummins' (1986b) interdependence hypothesis that suggests such a transfer between languages.

Cenoz and Genesee (1998, p. 20) provide a thorough review of research in this area and conclude that: 'bilingualism does not hinder the acquisition of an additional language and, to the contrary, in most cases bilingualism favors the acquisition of third languages.'

Cultural Awareness

'It is possible to become bilingual and not bicultural' is an oft repeated caution to teachers. A language divorced from its culture is like a body without a soul. Therefore, **developing heritage cultural awareness** alongside first language teaching is an important element in minority language education. Similarly, in two majority language bilingual education situations, developing bicultural (and intercultural) competence is important (Byram, 1998).

Classroom activities to foster minority culture awareness can include: enacting social conventions; cultural rituals and traditions using authentic visual and written materials; discussing cultural variations (e.g. the colorful kaleidoscope of Latin American dances, festivals, customs and traditions); identifying the varying experiences and perspectives of the particular language variety (e.g. of French Canadians, of the French majority in France, of bilinguals in France (e.g. Bretons, Provencal); classroom visits by native speakers of the language for 'question and answer' sessions (see Chapter 19).

In Wales, **developing a cultural awareness** about Wales is contained in the concept of the *'Curriculum Cymreig'* (the Welsh Cultural Curriculum) that endeavors to reflect the whole range of historical, social, economic, cultural, political and environmental influences that have shaped contemporary Wales. This involves giving students a sense of place and heritage, of belonging to the local and a wider community with its own traditions, a strong Welsh identity, access to the literature of Wales, differences and traditions in use of the Welsh and English languages in Wales, the distinctive nature of Welsh music, arts, crafts, technology, religious beliefs and practices (ACAC, 1993). There is a clear emphasis on developing heritage cultural awareness in Mathematics, Science and Technology and not just in Humanities and Aesthetic areas. For example, students study mathematicians William Jones (1675–1749), from Llanfihangel Tre'r' Beirdd who first used the 'pi (π) symbol and Robert Recorde (16th century) from Tenby, who devised the 'equals' (=) symbol. In Science, children discuss local soil samples and how they connect with local farming and agriculture, coal and slate mining that have been important to the Welsh economy, local small industries, and working from home via computer and communication networks. Some of this involves cross-curricular activity.

It is sometimes argued that a minority language must be fostered to **preserve the attendant culture**. The opposite is also tenable. The attendant culture must be fostered in the classroom to preserve the minority language. While separation of culture and language is false, minority language culture can be weakly or strongly represented in the classroom and in the whole atmosphere of the school. Such culture may be incidentally taught with little intent or rationale. Alternatively, such culture may be consciously included in language teaching and the overall physical and psychological environment of the school. This is particularly valuable in encouraging participation by children in their heritage culture. Language skills in the minority language are no guarantee of continued use of that language into teens and adulthood. Enculturation therefore becomes essential if that language is to be useful and used.

To foster a minority language in school without fostering its attendant culture may be to fund a costly life-support machine attached to a dying organism. To promote the attendant culture alongside minority language teaching may be to give a life-preserving injection to that language and culture.

When the minority language and culture is fostered in the school, the majority language is also usually developed. This raises an important question. How should these two languages be allocated in the curriculum? Can both languages be used to transmit content? What boundaries are needed between languages? These questions about bilingual methodology are now considered.

LANGUAGE ALLOCATION IN BILINGUAL CLASSROOMS

Introduction

Apart from teaching the curriculum in the first language or, as in submersion education, solely in the second language, there are a wide variety of possibilities in using two languages in the curriculum. One example is the immersion strategy where majority language children are educated through the medium of their second language, but where their first language is gradually used in the curriculum. Immersion education is considered in detail in Chapter 17.

The purpose of this section is to look at different dimensions of 'how and when' two languages can be (1) separated and (2) integrated in bilingual classrooms. The initial focus will be the **separation** of languages within the curriculum. For example, when two languages are assigned to different areas of the curriculum, the intention is usually to establish clear **boundaries** between the use of those languages in the curriculum. In the second part of this section, an examination will be made of the more integrated or concurrent use of two languages. For example, a teacher may repeat an explanation in a different language to clarify. The concluding part of this section will examine the problems and limitations of the concurrent use of two languages in the classroom.

There are different reasons for separating or sometimes integrating languages in bilingual classrooms (Faltis, 1997). **First**, if the purpose of bilingual education is to obtain language shift towards the majority language (e.g. transitional bilingual education), a brief and short-term dual use of a child's majority and minority languages may be allowed. When there is dual use and no strong boundaries between languages, the majority language is typically expected to develop as the minority language diminishes. **Second**, if the purpose of bilingual education is to maintain and develop the minority language, separation may be important via a distinct space and time for minority language usage across much of the curriculum. Clear boundaries for using the minority language, and separately using the majority language, are established (e.g. in developmental maintenance language education). Without boundaries and separation, the majority language may be increasingly used to the gradual exclusion of the minority language.

However, **thirdly**, if a strategic integration of languages in a class (e.g. where students are competent in both languages) gives higher student curriculum performance than language separation, a concurrent use of two languages may be valued. For example, if a strategy of the teacher orally transmitting a concept in Spanish followed by a written activity in English reinforced and enabled better assimilation of that concept, concurrent use of languages may be desirable for student achievement.

An example of a school situation where a decision about language methodology is necessary or desirable is a **mixed language classroom**. Where there is a mixture of, for example, Spanish first language speakers and English first language speakers in two way education, a clear policy and practice in language allocation is required. Where children in linguistically mixed classrooms have different levels of ability in the two languages, as well as different levels of ability in tackling the curriculum, a bilingual methodology may be essential. In Wales, a class may contain children who are relative beginners in Welsh (e.g. recent immigrants), those with some second language Welsh fluency, and native Welsh speakers. Some native Welsh speakers will be fluent in English, others may have more competence in Welsh than English. A school that aims to achieve a high standard of ability in both languages will need to consider the use and allocation of languages in classrooms and across the curriculum.

Language Separation

In the allocation of two languages in the classroom and in the curriculum, the need for **distinct separation and clear boundaries** between two languages has often been advocated. First, such separation has support from the sociolinguists who argue that, for a minority language to survive, it must have separate and distinct uses in society. In the discussion of diglossia, maintaining a relatively stable societal arrangement for the separate use of two languages was presented as important in minority language survival (see Chapter 3). Therefore, for a minority language to have purpose and strength, it must have a distinct language allocation in transmitting the curriculum (Williams, 2000).

Second, from child development research with bilinguals, it has often been argued that the 'one parent, one language' situation is one of the most effective patterns enabling childhood bilingualism to occur. If the mother speaks one language and the father another language, there is a distinct separation of languages. The child will therefore learn to speak one language to one parent, another language to the other parent. Such separation tends to result in the successful development of both languages within the very young child because there are distinct boundaries between the languages and a separate reception and production of language. Thus, an argument is that effective bilingual schools should find ways of mirroring language separation in such 'one parent, one language' homes by establishing **boundaries between languages**. What constitutes 'boundaries' will be examined in detail later.

Third, a concern in many minority language situations is the development of an **unstable codeswitching** among adults as well as children. Derogatory terms such as 'Spanglish' (for a mixture of Spanish and English) and 'Wenglish' (for a mixture of Welsh and English) highlight the concern of minority language preservationists about codemixing. The mixing of languages can be a half-way house, indicating a movement away from a minority language towards the majority language. Therefore, sociolinguists (see Chapter 3) have often argued for the importance of separation of languages and boundaries in use. The classroom experience can be a context for such separation. This is particularly to strengthen and maintain the purity and integrity of a minority language.

Having established three bases for language separation in the classroom and curriculum, we will now consider **how** languages can be separated. There are eight non-independent dimensions along which the separation of languages can occur in school settings. These will now be considered in turn:

Subject or Topic

In elementary schools and high schools, different curriculum areas may be taught in different languages. For example, Language, Arts, Social Studies, Religious Education, Art, Music and Physical Education may be taught through the minority language (e.g. Spanish in the USA; Filipino in the Philippines). Math, Science, Technology and Computer Studies may be taught through the majority language (e.g. English). Certain curriculum areas are reserved for one language, other curriculum areas for the second language. In kindergartens and elementary schools, the allocation may be by topic rather than subject. For example, a project on 'Conservation' may be through the minority language, a project on 'Weather' through the majority language.

The examples given so far reveal 'content sensitive' issues. That is, there is sometimes a call for arts and humanities culture to be relayed through the minority language, with Science and Technology relayed in an international majority language (see Rosenthal (1996) for a discussion of teaching Science to language minority students). Curriculum areas such as History and Geography are often regarded as best reflecting the heritage and culture of a language group. In contrast, Science and Technology may be seen as international, and dominated by the English language. The **danger** is that the minority language becomes associated with tradition and history rather than with Technology and Science. The minority language is thereby allocated a lower status and seen as much less relevant to modern existence. The danger may be that the minority language will be seen as irrelevant in computer communications, with a view that Science is white, western and mostly English in language.

Person
The use of two languages in a school may be separated according to person. Just as in some homes there is the 'one parent, one language' system, so different school staff may be identified with different languages. For example, there may be two teachers working in a team teaching situation. One teacher communicates with the children through the majority language, the other teacher through the children's minority language. There is a clear language boundary established by person. Alternatively, teachers' assistants, parents helping in the classroom, auxiliaries and paraprofessionals may function in the classroom as an alternative but separate language source for the children (e.g. grades K-2 in some US schools).

Time
A frequently used strategy in language allocation in schools is for classes to operate at different times in different languages. For example, in some dual language schools, one day may be through Spanish, the next day through English. Other schools alternate by half-days. The morning may be in Spanish, the afternoon in English, the next day reversing that situation. A third alternative is for different lessons to be allocated to different languages. This overlaps with the idea of separation by subject and topic.

   The separation of time need not be solely in terms of days, half-days or lessons. It may also be in terms of whole weeks or whole months or whole semesters. It also may valuably include a policy that varies by grade and age. For example, children may be taught through the minority language for the first two or three years of elementary education for 100% of time. Over Grades 3 to 7, an increasing amount of time may be allocated to the majority language inside the school.

Place
A lesser used means of language separation in the classroom is via different physical locations for different languages. For example, if there are two Science laboratories in the school, one may be labeled as a Spanish speaking laboratory, the other the English speaking laboratory. In immersion schools, students may have different classrooms for French and English lessons, paralleling the territorial principle (see Chapter 3). The children are expected to speak the language of that laboratory when entering it. The assumption is that a physical location provides enough cues and clues to prompt the child to adhere to a particular language in a

particular place. In reality, the teacher and other students may be more crucial in influencing the choice of language. Location is, however, a valuable 'extra' in encouraging language segregation.

A consideration of 'place' in language allocation needs to include all areas of the school. During morning and afternoon breaks, lunch-breaks, religious services and announcements, music and drama events, games and sports, the language balance of the school is affected. Sometimes teachers can allocate languages (e.g. in drama); other times, students have a dominant influence (e.g. in the playground). However, all informal events in the school create a language atmosphere, a language balance, and are summed to create the overall language experience of the school.

Medium of Activity

Another form of separation focuses on distinguishing between listening, speaking, reading and writing in the classroom. For example, the teacher may give an oral explanation of a concept in one language, with a follow-up discussion with the class in that same language. Then the teacher may ask the children to complete their written work in a second language. This sequence may be deliberately reversed in a second lesson. Another example would be when children read material through one language, and are then invited to write about it in the second language.

The aim of such a teaching strategy is to reinforce and strengthen learning by children. What is initially assimilated in one language is transferred and reinterpreted in a second language. By reprocessing the information in a different language, greater understanding may be achieved. However, this example shows that language separation soon links with a strategy to use both languages in the learning process. This idea of a rational, structured and sequenced use of two languages in learning is considered later — when the concurrent use of languages is examined.

One **danger** of 'different medium' separation is that one language may be used for oracy and another language for literacy. Where a minority language does not have a written script this may be a necessary boundary. Where a minority language does have written materials, the danger is that the minority language will be identified with oracy and the majority language with literacy. This has the potential effect of giving higher status and more functions to the majority language and its associated literacy. Hence, where this kind of 'medium separation tactic' is used, it is important for reversal to occur. For example, if oral explanations are given in one language with reading/writing in a different language, on the next day or next lesson, that situation should be reversed.

Curriculum Material

There are a variety of ways in which written, audio-visual and information technology curriculum material can be delivered in two languages, ensuring clear separation and non-duplication. Course materials may only be allocated in one language with the oral teaching in another language. This is separation 'across' curriculum material; there is also separation possible 'within' such material. For example, in elementary schools, dual language books (e.g. with English one side of the page and Spanish on the other, sharing the same pictures) may be useful in the early stages of biliteracy. Consideration of dual language books is given later in this section.

In high schools, reading material in History or Science may be as allocated by the teacher in both languages. However, duplication of information and ideas is not necessarily present. Rather, there can be a continuation and progression in themes and content. For example, a new topic may be introduced in one language by the student reading selected material. When a major sub-topic occurs, the teacher may require students to conduct their reading in a different language. Use of both languages helps understanding of the content while separation is occurring. The child does not have the choice of reading the English or the Spanish text, but needs to read both to gain a full comprehension of the topic. Again, it will be seen that language separation does not necessarily mean using two languages in isolation (or repeating the same content). A concern for separation involves policy and practice that includes varying use of **both** languages. The outcome is a classroom paradox; languages that are separated by function but are connected in an overall, holistic language and educational development policy.

Such a 'curriculum material separation' strategy tends to be used when, and only when both the child's languages are relatively secure, competent and well-developed. When this has occurred, the argument is that a child has to think more deeply about the material when moving between languages, comparing and contrasting, developing the theme of the material, assimilating and accommodating, transferring and sometimes translating in order to secure a concept and understanding.

Function

In schools and classes where there are bilingual children, there is often teaching in the majority language while the management of the classroom occurs in the minority language. For example, in US 'transitional bilingual education' schools with many Spanish speakers, the teacher may transmit the 'formal' subject matter in English, while conducting 'informal' episodes in Spanish. In this example, the stipulated curriculum is relayed in the majority language. However, when the teacher is organizing students, disciplining, talking informally with individual students or small groups, in short 'extra-explanation' episodes, a switch to the minority language is made.

Student

The previous seven dimensions have suggested that a school or a teacher may develop a policy about language allocation in a bilingual classroom. However, there is the real situation where students themselves help define the language that is being used in a classroom. For example, if a student addresses the teacher, it may not be in the language that the teacher has used to deliver the curriculum. To explain something with clarity, and for ease of communication, the student may switch to his or her preferred language. Students influence when and where languages are used, and affect boundary making. Thus separate dual language use can occur in the classroom by varying circumstance, student influence, and the formality or informality of particular events (e.g. students may feel at ease talking to teachers in their minority language in private or in classroom conversations).

Concurrent Uses of Languages in a Lesson

In many bilingual classrooms, the frequent **switching** between two or more languages is customary. The concurrent use of two languages in a bilingual classroom tends to be regular in practice, but rare as a predetermined teaching and learning strategy. Jacobson (1990) has argued that, on occasions, the integrated use of both languages rather than language separation can be of value in a lesson. Such a purposeful and structured use of both languages inside a lesson has certain problems that will be considered later. Four concurrent uses will now be considered (Jacobson, 1990).

Randomly Switching Languages

Bilingual individuals may switch languages both within sentences and across sentences. In many minority language groups, this is frequent both in the home and street as it is in the school. It is relatively rare for such switching to be stable across time. More often it is a half-way house, a sign of movement towards the majority language. For minority languages to survive as relatively distinct and standardized languages, few would argue for such a random practice to be encouraged in a bilingual classroom.

Translating

In some bilingual classrooms, teachers will repeat what they have previously said in another language. For example, the teacher may explain a concept in Spanish, and then repeat the same explanation in English. Everything is said twice for the benefit of children who are dominant in different languages. The danger is that the student will opt-out of listening when the teacher is transmitting in the weaker language. The student knows that the same content will be given in their preferred language and waits for that to occur. Such duplication appears to result in less efficiency, less language maintenance value and less likely achievement in the curriculum.

Previewing and Reviewing

One strategy in the concurrent use of languages in a classroom is to give the preview in the minority language and then the fuller review in the majority language. That is, a topic is introduced (or prior knowledge is established) in the child's minority language, for example, to give an initial understanding. Then, the subject matter is considered in depth in the majority language. This may be reversed. While an extension and reinforcement of ideas occurs by moving from one language to another, there is sometimes also unnecessary duplication and a slow momentum.

Purposeful Concurrent Usage

Jacobson has proposed a purposeful concurrent use of two languages (see Jacobson, 1990). The principles of what Jacobson calls the 'New Concurrent Approach' is that equal amounts of time are allocated to two languages, and teachers consciously initiate movement from one language to another. Such language movement inside a lesson occurs where there are discrete events and episodes with distinct goals for each language There must be a conscious and planned movement from one language to another in a regular and rational manner. Jacobson (1990) proposed this strategy to strengthen and develop both languages, and to reinforce taught concepts by being considered and processed in both languages. A use of both languages, it is suggested, contributes to a deeper understanding of the subject matter being studied.

Jacobson (1990) suggests a variety of **cues** that can trigger a switch from one language to another. Examples of such cues include:

- reinforcement of concepts;
- reviewing;
- capturing (and recapturing) student attention;
- praising and reprimanding students;
- change of topic;
- change in the stimulus material;
- change from formality to informality;
- to gain rapport;
- when there is fatigue.

The **amount of time** allocated to each language in the curriculum is important. Some kind of approximate balance (e.g. 50%/50%; or 67%/33%) between languages is needed, but more important is the purpose, manner and method in which the two languages are used. All four language abilities (understanding, speaking, reading, writing) may need fostering in both languages. To emphasize oracy in one language and literacy in another language may result in lopsided bilingualism.

Bilingual education involves more than the use of two languages across the curriculum. In bilingual education there should be a strategy to develop fully the four language abilities in both languages, not just in language lessons, but in other curricular areas and for all children of all ages and abilities. It is also important to use the minority language in the 'hidden curriculum' and not just for academic activities. Thus, staff may use the minority language for personal conversations, class announcements, on posters and wall displays, in praise and censure.

Translanguaging
Cen Williams' (1994) research on the development of language skills across the high school curriculum particularly examines the use of concurrent methodologies in 'strong' forms of bilingual education. He argues that the purposeful concurrent use of both languages in the classroom can be beneficial for the development of language skills in both languages, and also contributes to a deeper understanding of the subject matter being studied. He maintains that it is not the amount of time

allotted to each language in the lesson or the curriculum that is most significant, but rather the use made and the activities allocated to each language. The aim should be to **develop academic competence (CALP) in both languages** (see Chapter 8).

An example of the use of both languages in a lesson highlights a problematic sequence. The teacher introduces a topic in English, making some remarks in Spanish. Hand-outs and work sheets are in English. Class activities (e.g. teamwork) are carried out in the students' preferred language. The teacher interacts with the small groups and individual students in a random mixture of Spanish and English. The students complete the work sheet in English.

This type of situation is unlikely to develop students' academic competence in Spanish. The languages have an unequal status and use. To allow students to make progress in both languages, there needs to be **strategic classroom language planning**.

Cen Williams' (1994, 1996) high school research suggests that there are strategies that develop both languages successfully and also result in effective content learning. In particular he found '**translanguaging**' to work well. This term describes the hearing or reading of a lesson, a passage in a book or a section of work in one language and the development of the work (i.e. by discussion, writing a passage, completing a work sheet, conducting an experiment) in the other language. That is, the input and output are deliberately in a different language, and this is systematically varied. Thus 'translanguaging' is a more specific term than the general umbrella term 'concurrent use of two languages'. In 'translanguaging', the input (reading or listening) tends to be in one language, and the output (speaking or writing) in the other language.

For instance, a science work sheet in English is read by students. The teacher then initiates a discussion on the subject matter in Spanish, switching to English to highlight particular science terms. The students then do their written work in Spanish. Next lesson, the roles of the languages are reversed. In this example, the students need to understand the work to use the information successfully in another language.

Translanguaging has **four potential advantages**. Firstly, it may promote a deeper and **fuller understanding** of the subject matter. If the students have understood it in two languages, they have really understood it. It is possible, in a monolingual teaching situation, for students to answer questions or write an essay about a subject without fully understanding it. Processing for meaning may not have occurred. Whole sentences or paragraphs can be copied or adapted out of a text book or from dictation by the teacher without real understanding. It is less easy to do this with 'translanguaging'. To read and discuss a topic in one language, and then to write about it in another language, means that the subject matter has to be processed and 'digested'.

Secondly, 'translanguaging' may help students **develop skills in their weaker language**. Students might otherwise attempt the main part of the work in their stronger language and then undertake less challenging, related tasks in their weaker language. 'Translanguaging' attempts to develop academic language skills in both languages and **full bilingualism**.

Thirdly, the joint use of languages can facilitate **home–school cooperation**. If a child can communicate to a minority language parent in their usual medium, the parent can support the child in their school work.

Fourth, the integration of fluent English speakers and English learners (e.g. in US schools) of various levels of attainment is helped by 'translanguaging'. If English learners are integrated with first language English speakers, and if sensitive and strategic use is made of both languages in class, then the learners can **develop their second language ability concurrently with content learning**.

As is discussed in the limitations given below, there are potential problems in the complexity of managing, allocating and organizing such a use of two languages. However, the value of the idea is that the teacher plans the **strategic use** of two languages, thinks consciously about the use of two languages in the classroom, reflects and reviews what is happening, and attempts to cognitively stimulate students by a 'language provocative' and 'language diversified' lesson.

Issues and Limitations

In decisions about language separation and language allocation in a bilingual classroom, there are other ingredients and contexts that need taking into account before an effective dual language policy can be formulated.

First, the **aims of the school** in terms of language preservation and second language competence need to be examined carefully. School teachers are language planners, even if sub-consciously. Where a minority language is to be preserved in the children, then separation may be a central part of the policy. Where teachers are more enthusiastic about competence in the majority language (a second language), then different practices and outcomes in terms of language allocation will be desired. Less language boundaries may be desired. There may be a deliberate loosening of boundaries to ensure the development of the majority language.

Second, the **nature of the students** must be taken into account in any policy with regard to language boundaries and concurrent use. Different policies and practices may be required according to the age and grade level of the children (Romero & Parrino, 1994). If the children's language development is still at an early evolutionary stage, boundary setting will be more important. With older children, whose languages are relatively well developed, the concurrent use of two languages may be more viable and desirable. Older children may have more stability and separation in their language abilities.

Third, this suggests that a static policy with regard to boundaries and concurrent use within the school is less justifiable than a **progressive policy** that examines different uses across years and across grade levels. Early separation may be very important, later on in high school more concurrent use may be more defensible to enable conceptual clarity, depth of understanding and possibly to accelerate cognitive development.

Fourth, different dimensions of the school need different discussions about the separation and integration of languages (e.g. curriculum, whole school policies, classrooms, lessons). At what **level of organization** should separation occur? The discussion of language separation by curriculum material and medium of curriculum delivery showed that language separation is not a distinct issue from rational concurrent use. Language separation merges into a consideration of integrated use.

Fifth, the **language balance of the class** is often an important factor in a language separation decision. If all the children speak a minority or majority language, there may be ease in determining a language allocation. However, classes may be mixed, with differing balances of majority and minority language children. Who dominates numerically, linguistically and psychologically in the classroom? When the balance is tilted against language minority children, a clear separation with the curriculum balance towards the minority language may be desirable. Whether the children in a school are language minority children in a subtractive or additive situation will also impact on language allocation policies.

Sixth, where language minority children are in the numerical majority, a **slow change** rather than a sharp shift from language separation to concurrent use may be advisable.

Seventh, a school policy needs to take into account **'out of school exposure'** to the first and second language. Sometimes, an equal amount of time is advocated for two languages in the school, with half the curriculum in one language, the other half in a different language. If the child is surrounded by the majority language outside the school (e.g. street, screen and shop), then the balance may need to be more towards the minority language in school.

Eighth, the **replication and duplication** of content is a danger in bilingual classroom methodology. Where the same subject matter is repeated in a different language, some students will not concentrate or go 'off task'. Yet in many situations, where there is a mixture of different home and preferred languages in the classroom, for the sake of comprehension, a teacher may need to repeat information There are some multilingual classrooms (e.g. in New York, Toronto and London), with a considerable variety of languages represented among the children. This makes debates about concurrent use and language boundaries all the more difficult. One solution is the possibility of individualized learning via small groups (as occurs in progressive British and North American primary school practice). This may allow some language boundaries to be established, with different children addressed (e.g. by teachers aides) in their preferred language.

Ninth, the use of bilingual materials, particularly when they are built in a non-repetitive, non-parallel, but incremental, well sequenced and structured manner, can be valuable, particularly in high schools. However, the production and availability of materials in many minority languages is difficult to achieve. Funding may be difficult to secure for such separate minority language materials.

Tenth, in a concurrent and purposeful use of two languages in the classroom as advocated by Jacobson (1990), there is a danger of a unnatural, artificial, and highly complex language situation demanded of teachers. Where teachers are expected to manage the concurrent use of two languages in a classroom, it assumes a very high level of management skill, monitoring and reflection by such teachers. In reality, classrooms are busy, very fluid, often unpredictable places. Teachers have to react to the moment, to individual students who do not understand, with many situations being unplanned and unpredictable. Students themselves have an important influence on language use in the classroom, needing to communicate their understanding or lack of understanding in the most appropriate way. Classroom management of learning and behavior needs to be fluent, accepted by students and not abrupt and too unpredictable. Thus, language allocation in the classroom must fit naturally, predictably, fluently and flexibly into the complex management of the curriculum.

This completes a consideration of the concurrent use and separation of languages in the classroom. The chapter now moves on to focus on bilingual Deaf people and issues in their schooling.

BILINGUALISM, DEAF PEOPLE AND HEARING IMPAIRED PEOPLE

Introduction

About one in a 1000 people are born each year with varying degrees of hearing loss and they form a distinct minority. While Deaf people form a numeric minority of the total population, being a minority group refers to dimensions of power and status. Generally, Deaf people have much less power and prestige, lower recognition and leverage than majority groups in society. Deaf people have historically often been regarded as 'problems' within the education system, the social welfare system, among doctors and psychologists, and in the employment market. This is similar to most ethnic minority groups in the world.

There is a growing awareness that those who are deaf or have partial hearing are already, or can become, bilinguals. There is a also a current campaign for Deaf people to become bilingual through learning to sign first of all, followed by literacy in the language of the non-deaf (e.g. English in the USA, French in France). The aim of this section is to examine the relationship between bilingualism and Deaf people (Baker, 1999; Cline, 1997). We will find that there are many similarities between hearing bilinguals and current interests in the languages of Deaf communities throughout the world (Brelje, 1999).

Deaf Bilinguals

Deaf individuals can become bilingual through learning to sign first of all, followed by literacy in a language of the non-deaf. There are other forms of bilingualism among Deaf people: for example, those who learn to speak from hearing parents, followed by learning to sign. Others learn to sign first and then learn an oral form of the hearing language. Others learn to communicate by different means, by signs, speaking and writing — a Total Communication approach. Some Deaf people sign when in face-to-face communication, and use a written form (e.g. English) to communicate to members of the Deaf community via fax, textphone, computers and letters. The path from signing to majority language literacy is discussed later in this section.

For the moment, it is important to recognize that Deaf people (like many hearing bilinguals) form relatively **disadvantaged language minorities** and have certain things in common with hearing, language minority individuals and groups. Deaf people often have their own language **community**. Deaf individuals will typically wish to identify with the Deaf cultural community. Sometimes, they have been required to attempt to assimilate into the hearing community (Jankowski, 1997; Wrigley, 1996). Those with a hearing loss vary in their identification, sometimes identifying with Deaf people, other times with hearing people, with many possible variations.

Like most hearing bilinguals, Deaf people may use their two languages for **different functions and purposes**. For example, signing may be used to communicate with the Deaf community, while a spoken language or literacy in a majority language is used to communicate with the hearing community. Deaf people have too often been placed in **deficit types of education** that submerge them in the language and culture of hearers rather than an enrichment model where signing is allowed as the primary language.

Two Viewpoints about Deaf People

The **first viewpoint** is the **medical view** of deafness. Here deafness is defined as a defect or a handicap that distinguishes 'abnormal' deaf people from 'normal' hearing persons. Deafness is seen as a condition that needs to be remedied or cured as much as possible. Viewed as a disability, hearing aids and other devices that enhance hearing or the understanding of speech are recommended. Deaf people are expected to become as 'normal' as possible by avoiding purely visual methods of communication such as sign language, and learning spoken language as much as is viable.

One historical conception of Deaf people is that they live in a silent, and therefore deprived world. The following poem from William Wordsworth (1770–1850 – extracted from *The Excursion*, Book VII) sums up how hearing people have often conceived of deafness: a world that is silent, tragic and empty, unable to experience the stimulating and wonderful sounds of nature.

> … there, beneath
> A plain blue stone, a gentle Dalesman lies,
> From whom, in early childhood, was withdrawn
> The precious gift of hearing. He grew up
> From year to year in loneliness of soul;
> And this deep mountain-valley was to him
> Soundless, with all its streams. The bird of dawn
> Did never rouse this Cottager from sleep
> With startling summons; not for his delight
> The vernal cuckoo shouted; not for him
> Murmured the labouring bee.

This view that Deaf people inhabit a world that is silent and hollow is not a view shared by Deaf people themselves. Sound, or the lack of sound, is not an issue for

Deaf people unless they are told by hearing people that it is a problem. Sign language provides a natural form of communication.

To less aware people, sign language may seem primitive, rudimentary, and just a simple picture language whereas the spoken language is seen as the natural language for all in the community, including Deaf people. A central aim of education for the Deaf deriving from this viewpoint therefore becomes a mastery of spoken and eventually written language. Such education, and social pressures within the community, aim for the integration or **assimilation** of Deaf people with hearing people. Deaf people existing in separate communities, miming to each other, using sign-speech or having a Deaf culture is not entertained as wholesome or desirable. Thus such educators, professionals and policy-makers see themselves as helping Deaf people to overcome their 'handicap' and to live in the hearing world.

A **second viewpoint** is more in line with that increasingly expressed about hearing bilinguals: one of bilingualism, vitality as a linguistic and cultural minority community, and the need for an enriching dual language education (Baker, 1999; Cline 1997). Such a viewpoint commences with the assertion that Deaf people can do everything except hear. While there are differences between Deaf and hearing people, these are natural cultural differences, not deviations from a hearing norm. Thomas Gallaudet, the founder of the first Deaf school in the USA, argued that Deaf children cannot learn to speak or 'speech-read' well enough to use it as their primary means of communication. Signing for Deaf people is natural. As Veditz expressed in 1913, sign language is 'the noblest gift God has given to Deaf people' (quoted in Jankowski, 1997).

Thus, in this second viewpoint, deafness is regarded as a difference, a characteristic which distinguishes 'normal' Deaf people from 'normal' hearing people. Deaf people are regarded as owning sign language which is a full language in itself, grammatically complex and capable of expressing as much as any spoken language. Deaf people are regarded as a linguistic and cultural minority that needs preservation, enrichment and celebration.

Instead of emphasizing the deficiencies of Deaf people, their **abilities are emphasized**. A strong emphasis is placed on the use of vision as a positive, efficient and full communicative alternative to audible speaking and hearing. Sign language is thus not only equal to spoken language, but also the most natural language for people who are born deaf.

In Deaf **education**, the focus is increasingly on language development through signing, and later on bilingualism through literacy in the majority language. It is felt important that maximal language development occurs early on through signing. Early signing enables a focus on the subject matter of the curriculum (rather than learning to speak a majority language). Early use of signing in the classroom can enable Deaf people to perform relatively well in the curriculum. While there are currently few teachers fluent in sign, ideas about the importance of signing in education are gradually evolving.

In this viewpoint, Deaf people should form, where possible, a **cultural community** of their own. The Deaf have a common language in signing, a culture (see Ladd,

2001) and a set of needs that are distinct from the hearing community (Adams, 1997). The Deaf community is seen as an important vehicle for the socialization of Deaf and partially hearing people. Deaf adults can provide important role models for Deaf children, either as teachers or in the community. Thus, this second viewpoint supports bilingualism, a Deaf culture and the bilingual education of Deaf people.

Differences in Bilingual Goals

It is important to recognize that, among Deaf people and the hearing, there are not only different sub-groupings but also differences of opinion about the appropriate language of the Deaf, the education of the Deaf and their integration into mainstream speaking society. Such differences will now be briefly represented.

Hagemeyer (1992) suggests that there are **nine sub-populations among the deaf** in the USA. Such sub-dimensions refer to deaf culture and not to whether a person is also a member of Hispanic, native American, Asian or any other ethnic group that exists alongside being deaf. The nine groupings are as follows:

(1) Those who use sign language (e.g. American Sign Language — often represented as ASL) as their primary language.
(2) Those who can communicate both in ASL and English.
(3) Those mostly from the hearing impaired group who can communicate primarily through speech.
(4) Adults who became deaf later in life, who were not born deaf and may have acquired speech before deafness. Such people have the experience of hearing normally for a shorter or a longer period and may have speech patterns relatively well embedded before deafness occurred.
(5) The elderly who became hearing impaired or deaf later in life as the result of the aging process.
(6) Those who do not know either ASL nor English, but communicate through gestures, mime and their own signing system. Such people may have been denied access to a Deaf culture, to ASL and to education at an early age.
(7) Those who have residual hearing, perhaps describing themselves as hard of hearing, and who can hear with the use of various aids.
(8) Those people who are deaf and blind. An example is Helen Keller.
(9) Those people who have normal hearing, but because their parents, children, or other members of the family are deaf, they understand signing, or are fully conversant with Deaf culture and integrate with the Deaf community.

Sign Language

Deaf people share a common mode of language. Sign language can be a major marker in defining Deaf community membership. Through sign language, there is the possibility of establishing community culture, a sense of identity, shared meanings and understandings, and a way of life that is owned by the Deaf community.

Sign language, once a symbol of oppression, has become transformed into a **symbol of unity**.

> 'Sign language became the distinction that gave dignity to the Deaf community and transformed the "abnormal" into the "distinguished" by creating a reversal of the hierarchy ... and to define normality on their own terms.' (Jankowski, 1997, p. 44)

Sign language has allowed Deaf people to match the skills and abilities of hearing people: in communication, cognition and having an empowering community. Sign language has enabled Deaf people to create their own sense of 'normality'.

What is Sign Language?

Sign language is a fully developed, authentic language which allows its users to communicate the same, complete meaning as a spoken language. Sign language is not gesturing. Gesturing is relatively unsystematic, and is used in an *ad hoc* way to express a small number of basic expressions (e.g. pointing to something that is wanted). We all use non-verbal communication to add emphasis to our speech.

In contrast, signing is a very extensive, structurally complex, rule-bound, complete means of communication. Sign language can perform the same range of functions as a spoken language, and can be used to teach any aspect of the curriculum. As part of an ethnic awakening, sign language has increasingly been seen as the natural language of Deaf people.

There are a wide variety of sign systems in existence. To name but a few: American Sign Language, British Sign Language, Chinese Sign Language, Danish Sign Language, French Sign Language, Russian Sign Language and Thai Sign Language. However, many Deaf people do not use Sign Language. In the USA, for example, some have not learnt ASL because their parents were hearing people. Others have been to schools which taught them oralist (speaking) approaches (see later in this chapter). Other Deaf people prefer to use speech rather than sign language in their communities.

A breakthrough occurred in 1983 when the Swedish Government officially recognized Swedish Sign Language as a native language of Sweden. This was a crucial world precedent and a goal for Deaf communities in other countries to achieve political recognition as a distinct social group, rather than, as is sometimes the case, a scattering of individuals.

The Education of Deaf Students

There are a wide variety of approaches to the education of Deaf students and those who are hearing impaired (Powers *et al.*, 1999). These approaches range from minimal help to specially designed programs. At its worst, in mainstream 'hearing' education, the deaf may be regarded as having a serious mental as well as an auditory 'defect' and classified as remedial. In the history of schooling in most countries, there are plentiful examples of such an insensitive and uncivilized treatment.

In contrast, there are Special Schools and Units for Deaf students where, for example, the children are taught to thoroughly learn signing first of all, are given a full curriculum mostly through signing, and develop written and/or oral skills in the majority spoken language. Strong (1995) provides a review of nine programs in North America that use American Sign Language (ASL) and English in the classroom, and aim to promote a 'strong' version of bilingualism and biculturalism among Deaf people. English is usually taught as a second language (ESL) with varying emphasis on oracy and literacy in English.

There is considerable discussion, debate and development occurring in Deaf education (Knight & Swanwick, 1999; Powers *et al.*, 1999; Powers & Gregory, 1998). There is not total agreement as to preferred methods of approach: for example, using signing and literacy in the spoken language, a Total Communication approach, using Sign Supported English or Signed Exact English, the kind of sign language to use, whether to develop oral and/or written skills in the spoken majority language, policies of integration with hearing children and the development of relatively segregated Deaf communities.

One traditional approach has been to develop any residual hearing with the assistance of hearing aids and to develop speech reading skills and speech production among the deaf and the hearing impaired. For most of this century until the 1970s, this was the approach that dominated the education of deaf in North America and Europe. Such an approach was based on a belief:

- that Deaf children should integrate into mainstream society;
- that the curriculum could not be taught through sign language but required majority language proficiency;
- that signing as a language was insufficient for full intellectual development;
- that sign language was only a temporary crutch for those for whom the majority spoken language was essential;
- that achievement in the curriculum requires oracy and literacy in the majority language (e.g. English).

A **second approach** developed since the 1970s has been based on the philosophy of Total Communication. All modes of communication are regarded as appropriate for those who are deaf or partially hearing. Simultaneous communication is used that combines auditory input plus visual information, for example, via the use of signed English. However, a Total Communication approach is often assimilationist, aiming to enable Deaf people to communicate with hearing people.

A **third approach** concerns bilingualism for Deaf children through bilingual education (Knight & Swanwick, 1999). This recent initiative is contained in 12 suggestions that are mirrored in spoken bilingual education:

(1) That sign language should be the first language of all Deaf children and be regarded as their primary language.
(2) That sign language should be used to teach curriculum subjects such as science, humanities, social studies and mathematics.

(3) Sign language can be used to teach English or another majority language as a second language. Usually this will be to teach reading and writing skills in English rather than English oracy.

(4) The culture and language of the Deaf community are recognized and validated, with children learning that they belong to the culture of the Deaf. This approach tends to be favored by most but not all the Deaf community, but has not been favored by many politicians and education professionals who formulate policy and provision.

(5) Such bilingual education for Deaf students is partly based on the research and arguments for an enrichment form of bilingual education for hearing children:
   • bilingual education builds on a child's existing linguistic and intellectual resources;
   • concepts and knowledge developed in the first language transfer easily to the second language;
   • use of a children's heritage language gives pride and confidence in their culture and community;
   • a child's self-esteem and self-identity are boosted and not threatened by use of their first language;
   • school performance and curriculum attainment is raised when the first language is celebrated rather than devalued;
   • the lower achievement of minority language students and Deaf students needs to be addressed by enrichment forms (or 'strong forms') of bilingual education.

(6) Deaf children cannot acquire a spoken language easily or quickly because they have limited hearing abilities. If the curriculum is transmitted in the spoken language, they are being expected to learn the content of the curriculum using a level of language not yet acquired. This is analogous to minority language children being expected to operate in submersion education in the language of the majority they have yet to master.

(7) English or another majority language is developed through sign language. Often native sign language teachers will be employed in schools, where possible, to teach and to act as role models.

(8) The acquisition of a sign language should begin as early as possible, ideally soon after birth. Since about nine out of every ten Deaf children are born to hearing parents, this is often difficult, but with such parents being increasingly willing to sign and learn signing, the first language of such Deaf children can be sign language. Current thinking among the Deaf tends to suggest that early signing is preferable in most cases. Parents of Deaf children need to be aware of Deaf communities, of bilingual education for Deaf children, and to enhance their child's curriculum achievement, to expect signing as the medium of curriculum delivery plus literacy in the majority language.

(9) It is important to avoid language-delay in Deaf children, as has been found to occur when using auditory approaches and sometimes the Total Communication approach. Curriculum achievement will suffer if there is language delay.

(10) The supply of trained personnel in Deaf bilingual education, staff pre-service education programs, in-service education and certification and funding are often current challenges that are being faced by Deaf educators. These are practical problems to be overcome rather than problems of principles that are insurmountable.

(11) The parents of Deaf children need considerable emotional support, information and guidance to help their children become bilingual. In order for cognitive, linguistic, social and emotional development to occur among Deaf children, there needs to be a partnership between school and parents, and between school and community. While there is a considerable debate about the integration of Deaf children into a hearing society, (and their first loyalty being to the Deaf community), hearing parents of Deaf children need considerable support and sensitivity.

(12) The teaching situation in a bilingual Deaf education system may involve team teaching. The Deaf teacher may be a natural model for the acquisition of sign language with a hearing teacher acting as a model for the acquisition of proficiency in a majority language such as English or French. Ideally, both teachers should be bilingual models, being able to communicate in both sign language and the 'hearing' language. Also, both teachers in the team should have a knowledge of Deaf culture, Deaf differences and all the possibilities for Deaf children and adults.

In conclusion, this section on Deaf bilinguals has shown that there are **many similarities between hearing bilinguals and Deaf bilinguals**. Many of the justifications for retaining a minority language child's first language and for a 'strong' form of bilingual education for such children also hold for Deaf children. The argument that children from language minorities should become bicultural and culturally pluralistic also tends to hold for Deaf bilinguals. Language minorities are often the poor, low status, low power relations of majority language speakers. Even more so are the Deaf. Deaf bilinguals are often the poor relations of language minority bilinguals. A spoken minority language is often disdained and derided. Even more so is sign language. Achievement and status among Deaf children and adults are often only recognized and granted when speech monolingualism occurs.

When Deaf people come from language minority communities they form a minority of a minority. The examples of a Latino Deaf person in the USA, a Deaf Turk in Germany and a Deaf Bengali in England all represent individuals who are a minority within a minority. They are often the doubly underprivileged and the doubly despised. Where being a member of a language minority is joined by being Deaf, disempowerment, low status, discrimination and low self-esteem may be compounded. If many groups of bilinguals are underprivileged, even more so are Deaf bilinguals.

CONCLUSION

This chapter has highlighted some of the key elements in the schooling of bilinguals. The importance of developing the home language was initially stressed. Bilingual schooling appears an essential, but not by itself, a sufficient condition for the reproduction of the minority language in students. Such language development needs to occur across the curriculum, in Science as well as Language Arts, in Math and Technology as well as History and Geography. Language development needs to be joined by cultural development. Throughout the curriculum, in all areas and cross-curricular topics, the culture surrounding the minority language needs transmitting to give that language purpose, meaning and vitality.

The minority language is also secured in students if there are clear boundaries between it and the majority language in school. Separate functions for the two languages, and a clear demarcation in the classroom and curriculum are particularly important for younger children in the elementary school. Later on, when students' two languages are both well developed, the integration and concurrent use of two languages in the classroom may be considered as a means of reinforcement and reconceptualizing curriculum material.

The chapter ended by portraying the many parallels between Deaf bilinguals and hearing bilinguals. Views about Deaf people vary, with the medical view and a 'competent bilingual' view contrasted in this chapter. Both views link to different beliefs about the education of Deaf students. The discussion of different forms of bilingual education for Deaf students highlight this topic as an important area for discussion and debate.

KEY POINTS IN THE CHAPTER

- The first language development of minority language students benefits their all-round curriculum performance. Developing minority language cultural understanding and experience is an essential accompaniment to first language development.
- Such students may also be aided by a pedagogy that involves collaboration, the sharing of experiences to affirm their identity, and critical enquiry to understand power, inequality, justice, and local social and economic realities.
- The separation of two languages in classroom use can occur, for example, by setting boundaries through different allocation of subjects, teachers, time slots, place and type of curriculum material.
- Concurrent use of two languages may involve random switching to a more justifiable purposful use of each language. 'Translanguaging' involves varying the language of input and output in a lesson.
- Deaf people are frequently bilinguals, with sign language being a natural first language, plus literacy (and oracy) in a second 'hearing' language.
- The medical view of deafness as a problem and the need for assimilation of

Deaf people into mainstream society is contrasted to a bilingual/bicultural viewpoint which emphasizes their abilities, community and culture.
- Bilingual education for Deaf students mirrors this bilingual/bicultural viewpoint and reveals that many of the arguments for a 'strong' version of bilingual education hold for Deaf students.

SUGGESTED FURTHER READING

BAKER, C., 1999, Sign Language and the Deaf Community. In J.A. FISHMAN (ed.) *Handbook of Language and Ethnic Identity*. New York: Oxford University Press.

CENOZ, J. and GENESEE, F., 1998, Psycholinguistic perspectives on multilingualism and multilingual education. In J. CENOZ and F. GENESEE (eds) *Beyond Bilingualism: Multilingualism and Multilingual Education*. Clevedon: Multilingual Matters.

CLINE, T, 1997, Educating for bilingualism in different contexts: teaching the deaf and teaching children with English as an additional language. *Educational Review*, 49 (2), 151–158.

CUMMINS, J., 2000, *Language, Power and Pedagogy: Bilingual Children in the Crossfire*. Clevedon: Multilingual Matters.

FREEMAN, R., 1998, *Bilingual Education and Social Change*. Clevedon: Multilingual Matters.

GARCÍA, O. and BAKER, C. (eds.) 1995, *Policy and Practice in Bilingual Education: A Reader Extending the Foundations*. Clevedon: Multilingual Matters. (Section 3).

JACOBSON, R. 1990, Allocating two languages as a key feature of a bilingual methodology. In R. JACOBSON and C. FALTIS (eds) *Language Distribution Issues in Bilingual Schooling*. Clevedon: Multilingual Matters.

KNIGHT P. and SWANWICK, R., 1999, *The Care and Education of a Deaf Child*. Clevedon: Multilingual Matters.

MASHIE, S.N. 1995, *Educating Deaf Children Bilingually*. Washington, DC: Gallaudet University.

WILLIAMS, C., 2000, Welsh-medium and bilingual teaching in the further education sector. *International Journal of Bilingual Education and Bilingualism* 3 (2), 129–148.

WONG FILLMORE, L. and VALADEZ, C. 1986, Teaching bilingual learners. In M.C. WITTROCK (ed.) *Handbook of Research on Teaching* (3rd edn). New York: Macmillan.

STUDY ACTIVITIES

(1) Interview some parents about bilingual education (preferably gathering a variety of different viewpoints). Ask them what their preferences are for the use of the home language in school. Ask the parents if they want their children to be bilingual as a result of schooling. Ask parents what value and use they see in languages being taught or two languages being used as a medium of learning in school.

(2) Interview an administrator, a parent, a teacher and a principal about their attitudes to children's home languages in school. Find out what differences and what similarities there are between these different people. Try to explain the origins and the causes of the differences. Are there different majority and minority viewpoints? Can there be any integration of these varying viewpoints?

(3) Visit a school where there is a policy about the allocation of languages in the classroom. Try to locate a written school policy about language allocation and compare it with what you observe in one or more classrooms. Discuss your findings with a teacher. Chart the results of your observation and discussion

with a teacher on a poster to display to a small group. Compare your results with other members of the group.

(4) Visit a family with a deaf student and/or a school where there are deaf students. What are the goals in language development? What form of bilingualism exists? What are the attitudes and aspirations of the student and parents/teachers regarding language.

(5) Examine the differences between the education of Deaf people before and after the ethnic revival (see Baker, 1999). Discuss whether a 'Total Communication' approach is justified? Examine this from the viewpoints of the Hearing Community and the Deaf Community. Do you support the full integration of Deaf people into mainstream society or separate Deaf communities, and what part should education play in this preference?

Bilingual Schooling Issues: Underachievement, Assessment and Special Needs

Introduction

Explanations of Underachievement

Special Needs and Bilingual Education
The Frequency of Special Needs
in Bilingual Children
The Assessment and Placement
of Bilingual Children
The Alternative Causes of Special Needs
and Learning Difficulties in Children

Assessment and Bilingual Children

Conclusion

CHAPTER 14

Bilingual Schooling Issues: Underachievement, Assessment and Special Needs

INTRODUCTION

This chapter begins by examining some key themes in the education of bilinguals. underachievement is often found among language minorities, both in leaving school relatively early and in lower performance in the curriculum. The chapter examines the varying explanations for this, particularly whether bilingualism is a cause of such underachievement. This discussion extends into children with special needs, and the purpose and effectiveness of bilingual special education. The role of assessment in the identification, and particularly the mis-identification of bilingual children follows.

EXPLANATIONS OF UNDERACHIEVEMENT

There are frequent occasions when language minorities are found to underachieve or show high drop-out rates. Sometimes this is analyzed in research (see Chapter 12) but it is also a frequent topic of debate among teachers, educational psychologists, speech therapists, parents, students themselves and not least politicians (see Chapter 18).

When language minority children appear to exhibit underachievement in the classroom, what is the **explanation**? When first, second or third generation immigrant language minority children appear to fail in the classroom, where is the 'blame' popularly placed? When guest workers' children, indigenous minorities and distinct ethnic groups are shown statistically to have high drop-out rates, achieve less in examinations and tests or receive lower grades and averages, what is the cause?

First, the blame may be attributed to the child **being bilingual**. Bilingualism itself is often popularly seen as causing cognitive confusion. The explanation given is a picture of the bilingual brain with two engines working at half throttle, while the monolingual has one well tuned engine at full throttle. As Chapter 8 revealed, such an explanation is usually incorrect. Where two languages are well developed, then bilingualism is more likely to lead to cognitive advantages than disadvantages (see the 'three level house' diagram in Chapter 8). Only when both languages are poorly developed can 'blame' be attributed to bilingualism itself. Even then, the blame should not go to the victim, but to the societal circumstances that create under-developed languages.

Second, where underachievement exists, the reason may be given as **lack of exposure to the majority language**. In the US and England, a typical explanation for the underachievement of certain language minorities is insufficient exposure to English. Failure or below average performance is attributed to students having insufficiently developed English language competence to cope with the curriculum. Those who use Spanish or Bengali at home and in the neighborhood are perceived to struggle at school due to a lack of competence in the dominant, mainstream language. Thus submersion and transitional forms of bilingual education attempt to ensure a fast conversion to the majority language.

A fast conversion to the majority language stands the chance of doing more harm than good. It denies the child's skills in the home language, even denies the identity and self-respect of the child itself. Instead of building upon existing language proficiency and knowledge, the 'sink or swim' approach attempts to replace such language abilities. The high level of English used in the curriculum (e.g. in the USA) may also cause the child to show underachievement, with consequent demands for more of the same medicine (more English language lessons).

Bilingual education, when effectively implemented, is not the cause of underachievement; rather it is the cure. underachievement in majority language education (e.g. submersion and transitional bilingual education) may be combated by providing education through the medium of the minority language (e.g. two-way, developmental maintenance, heritage language programs). When the language minority child is allowed to operate in their heritage language in the curriculum, the evidence (see Chapter 10) suggests that success rather than failure results. Such success includes becoming fluent in the majority language (e.g. English). In the USA, Krashen's (1999) overview of research concludes that 'well-designed bilingual programs produce better academic English ... because they supply subject matter knowledge in the students' primary language, which makes the English the students hear and read much more comprehensible' (p. 7). Thus lack of exposure to English is a popular but improper explanation of underachievement. This explanation fails to note the advantages of education in the minority language for achievement. It inappropriately seeks an answer in increased majority language tuition rather than increased minority language education.

Third, when bilingual children exhibit underachievement, the attributed reason is sometimes a **mismatch between home and school**. Such a mismatch is seen as not just about language differences but also about dissimilarities in culture, values and beliefs (Delgado-Gaitan & Trueba, 1991). As an extreme, this tends to reflect a majority viewpoint that is assimilationist, imperialist and even oppressive. The child and family is expected to adjust to the system, not that the system should be pluralist and incorporate variety. For such an assimilationist viewpoint, the solution is in the home adjusting to mainstream language and culture to prepare the child for school. Past advice by some educational psychologists and speech therapists has been for language minority parents to raise their children in the majority, school language.

The alternative view is that, where practicable, the school system should be flexible enough to incorporate the home language and culture. A mismatch between home and school can be positively addressed by 'strong' forms of bilingual education for language minorities. By two-way, developmental maintenance and heritage language programs, through the inclusion of parents in the operation of the school, by involving parents as partners and participants in their child's education (e.g. paired reading schemes), the mismatch can become a merger.

Fourth, underachievement may be attributed to **socioeconomic factors** that surround a language minority group. Some typical circumstances are described by Trueba (1991).

> 'Many immigrant and refugee children have a life of poverty and rural isolation in crowded dwellings where they lack privacy, toilet and shower facilities, comfort, and basic medical attention. In some cases migrant life for children means abuse, malnutrition, poor health, ignorance and neglect. Uprooting a child from his/her land can lead to a life of stigma and low status.' (Trueba, 1991, p. 53)

Krashen (1999) reviewed drop-out rates in the USA among Hispanic young adults. He concludes that such young adults are more likely to drop-out (e.g. one in 12 non-Hispanic whites compared with one in five Hispanics). However, when Hispanic young adults have received bilingual education, there are lower drop-out rates. Drop-out seems connected with socioeconomic factors such as relative material poverty and the home print environment. When such factors are taken into account, Hispanic young adults have the same, or nearly the same drop-out rates as other groups (see Chapter 12).

Socioeconomic status is a broad umbrella term that rightly points to a definite cause of language minority underachievement. It provides an example of the importance of not blaming the victim, but analyzing societal features that contribute to underachievement. Such features may be economic deprivation, material circumstances and living conditions as well as psychological and social features as discrimination, racial prejudice, pessimism and immobilizing inferiority.

While **socioeconomic factors** are a strong explanation of language minority underachievement, two cautions must be sounded. Socioeconomic status does not explain why different language minorities of similar socioeconomic status may perform differently at school. In Chapter 18 we discuss the different ideologies or orientations that may vary between ethnic groups. Sociocultural factors within and between ethnic groups and not simply socioeconomic status are needed to begin to work out the equation of language minority achievement and underachievement.

This raises another issue. underachievement cannot be simply related to one of several causes. The equation of underachievement is going to be complex, involving a number of factors. Those factors will **interact** together and not be simple 'standalone' effects. For example, umbrella labels such as socioeconomic status need to be deconstructed into more definable predictors of underachievement (e.g. parents' attitude to education, literacy environments, material and emotional home conditions). Home factors will then interact with school factors providing an enormous number of different routes that may lead to school success or failure. The recipes of success and failure are many, with varying ingredients that interact together in complex ways. However, socioeconomic and sociocultural features are important ingredients in most equations of underachievement.

Fifth, part of the language minority underachievement equation is the **type of school** a child attends. This chapter and Chapter 10 highlight the different outcomes for language minority children in 'strong' compared with 'weak' forms of bilingual education. The same child will tend to attain more if placed in programs that use the heritage language as a medium of instruction than in programs which seek to replace the home language as quickly as possible. Therefore, when underachievement occurs in a language minority child or within a language minority group, the system of schooling needs scrutiny. A system that suppresses the home language is likely to be part of the explanation of individual and ethnic group underachievement where such problems exist (Cummins, 2000a).

Sixth, type of school is a broad heading under which there can exist superior and inferior submersion schools, outstanding and mediocre dual language and heritage language schools. Where underachievement exists, it is sometimes too simple to blame the type of school rather than digging deeper and locating more specific causes. Baker (1988, 1993) and Hornberger (1991) have listed some of the attributes that need examining to establish the **quality of education** for language minority children (e.g. the supply, ethnic origins and bilingualism of teachers, the commitment of teachers to bilingual education, the balance of language minority and language majority students in the classroom, the use and sequencing of the two languages across the curriculum over different grades, reward systems for enriching the minority language and culture, and appropriate curriculum resources). 'Strong' forms of bilingual education are not an instant guarantee of quality education. Diminishing and eradicating underachievement depends on the process of classroom activity, not just on a style of education.

Seventh, underachievement may be due to **real learning difficulties** and the need for some form of special education. It is important to make a distinction between real and apparent learning difficulties. Too often, bilingual children are labeled as having learning difficulties which are attributed to their bilingualism (Baca & Cervantes, 1998). As we have discussed in this section, the causes of apparent learning problems may be much less in the child and much more in the school or in the education system. The child is perceived as having learning difficulties when the problem may lie in the subtractive, assimilative system which itself creates negative attitudes and low motivation. In the 'sink or swim' approach, 'sinking' can be attributed to an unsympathetic system and to insensitive teaching methods rather than individual learning problems. Apart from system-generated and school-generated learning problems, there will be bilinguals with genuine learning difficulties (Cummins, 2000a). The essential beginning is to distinguish between real, genuine individual learning difficulties and problems which are caused by factors outside the individual.

Such a **distinction between the real and the apparent**, the system-generated and the remediable problems of the individual, focuses attention on alternatives. When underachievement exists, do we blame the victim, blame the teacher and the school, or blame the education system? When assessment, tests and examinations occur and show relatively low performance of language minority individuals and groups, will prejudices about bilingual children and ethnic groups be confirmed? Or can we use such assessment to reveal deficiencies in the architecture of the school system and the design of the curriculum rather than blame the child? As this section has revealed, underachievement tends to be blamed on the child and the language minority group. Often the explanation lies in factors outside of the individual. This discussion is now extended by examining bilinguals with special needs and bilingual special education.

SPECIAL NEEDS AND BILINGUAL EDUCATION

It is initially important to define who are the children with special needs who may need special education provision. Special needs includes those with exceptional gifted abilities (e.g. high IQ, outstanding musical or mathematical aptitude). However, the discussion of this topic more often revolves around those students with problems. **Categories of special need** which can be language-related vary from country to country but are likely to include the following areas: communication disorders, learning disabilities (e.g. dyslexia and developmental aphasia), severe subnormality in cognitive development, behavioral and emotional problems.

Certainly, some bilingual children do have special needs, and this includes children from 'elite' bilingual families (e.g. English–German) as well as from language minorities. However, none of these is caused by bilingualism. **Bilingualism** is not a direct cause of speech or language impairment, autism, dyslexia, developmental aphasia, severe subnormality in cognitive development, serious emotional disturbance or behavioral problems (e.g. see Cline & Frederickson (1999) on dyslexia in bilinguals). Being a member of a language minority may co-exist with such conditions, but is **not a cause** as will be illustrated later.

The Frequency of Special Needs in Bilingual Children

There is evidence in the USA that **bilingual children are over-represented** among those in need of special education (Harry, 1992; Gersten & Woodward, 1994; Baca & Cervantes, 1998). For example, Mercer's (1973) pioneering study found that Mexican-Americans were ten times more likely to be in special education than white Americans. Such over-representation is often due to biased assessment practices (see later). Over-representation is not the only scenario. Under-representation also occurs, particularly in states and districts where language minority students are a relatively small percentage of the population. Cline and Frederickson (1999) have shown that the identification of dyslexics who are also bilinguals is often overlooked.

Baca and Cervantes (1998) estimate that there are 1.2 million students from language minority backgrounds who are in need of special education in the USA, and of whom approximately three-quarters are Latinos. This immediately raises questions as to why language minority children may need special education. Why do bilingual children have special needs? Does bilingualism in some students lead to language and communication disorders (e.g. language delay)? One wrong response is that bilingualism leads to language and communication disorders (e.g. language delay). However, research does not attribute such disorders to bilingualism (Li Wei *et al.*, 1997). Rather, such beliefs derive from prejudice and ignorance of linguistic and cognitive research.

The communicative **differences** of bilingual children must be **distinguished from** communicative **disorders**. The failure to make this important distinction partly occurs because basic mistakes in assessment and categorization are made. The child is often assessed in a weaker, second language, thereby both language development and general cognitive development are measured inaccurately. For example, in Britain and the USA, immigrant children are sometimes assessed through the medium of English and on their English proficiency. Their level of language competence in Spanish, Vietnamese, Hmong, Korean, Cantonese, Turkish, Talagog or Panjabi, for example, is ignored.

The result is that such children are sometimes classed as having a 'language disability' and perhaps a 'learning disability'. Instead of being seen as developing bilinguals (i.e. children with a good command of their first language who are in the process of acquiring a second, majority language), they may be classed as of 'limited English proficiency' (LEP in the USA), or even as having general difficulties with learning. Their below-average test scores in the second language (e.g. English) are wrongly defined as a 'deficit' or 'disability' that can be remedied by some form of special education.

One particular language condition (language delay) has been particularly associated with bilingualism and illustrates how prejudice and misunderstanding can arise.

Language Delay

A particular pathology in children, 'language delay,' is often erroneously attributed to bilingualism. Language delay occurs when a child is very late in beginning to talk, or lags well behind peers in language development. Estimates of young children experiencing language delay vary from one in 20 to one in five of the child population. Such varying estimates partly reflect that some delays are brief and hardly noticeable. Others are more severe.

Language delay has a **variety of causes** (e.g. autism, severe subnormality, cerebral palsy, physical problems (e.g. cleft palate), psychological disturbance, emotional difficulties). However, in approximately two-thirds of all cases, the precise reason for language delay is not known (Li Wei *et al.*, 1997). Children who are medically normal, with no hearing loss, of normal IQ and memory, who are not socially deprived or emotionally disturbed, can be delayed in starting to speak, slow in development or have problems in expressing themselves well. In such cases, specialist, professional help needs to be sought. Speech therapists, clinical psychologists, educational psychologists, counselors or doctors may be able to give an expert diagnosis and suggest possible treatment of the problem. It is important that such professionals have an understanding of the nature of bilingualism in the clients they advise and treat.

Occasionally, well-meaning professionals make the diagnosis that bilingualism is the cause of language delay. If the causes are unknown, bilingualism might seem a likely cause. Raising children bilingually is widely believed to produce language delayed children. The evidence does not tend to support this belief (Li Wei *et al.*, 1997).

For the teacher, psychologist, speech therapist, counselor and parent, a practical decision has to be made in respect of language delayed bilingual children. Will the removal of one language improve, worsen or have no effect on such a child's language development? Given that the cause of the problem may be partially unknown, intuition and guesswork rather than 'science' often occurs as research in this area is still developing.

Let us assume the professional advice is to move from bilingualism to monolingualism. One issue immediately becomes **which language** to concentrate on if there is major diagnosed language delay. The danger is that parents, teachers and other professionals will want to accent the perceived importance of the majority language. In the USA, the advice is often that the child should have a solid diet of English (at home and particularly at school). The perceived language of school and success, employment and opportunity is the majority language. The advice often given is that the home, minority language should be replaced by the majority language.

Even when professionals accept that bilingualism is not the cause of a child's problem, moving from bilingualism to monolingualism is seen by some as a way to help improve the problem. The reasoning is usually that the 'extra demands' of bilingualism, if removed, will lighten the burden for the child. For example, if the child has an emotional problem or a language delay condition, for whatever cause, simplifying the language demands on the child may be seen as one way of solving or reducing the problem. The apparent complexity of a two language life is relieved by monolingualism. Is this the rational and suitable solution?

There are many occasions when changing from bilingualism to monolingualism will have no effect on language delay. For example, if the child seems slow to speak without an obvious cause, or seems low in self-esteem, dropping one language is unlikely to have any effect. On the contrary, the sudden change in schooling or family life may exacerbate the problem. The child may be further confused, even upset, if there is a dramatic change in the language of the school or family. If someone who has loved, cared for, or educated the child in one language (e.g. a minority language) suddenly only uses another language (e.g. the majority language), the emotional well-being of the child may well be negatively affected. The language used to express love and caring disappears. Simultaneously, and by association, the child may feel that the love and care is also not as before. Such an overnight switch may well have painful outcomes for the language delayed child. The mother tongue is denied, the language of the family is implicitly derided, and the communicative medium of the community is disparaged. The child may feel as if thrown from a secure boat into strange waters. **The solution in itself may exacerbate the problem**.

An alternative is that the **anchor language** is retained. The home language gives a sense of assurance and security amid stormy seas. Even if the child is slow in sailing in that language, with progress delayed, it is the boat known to the child. Being forced to switch to the majority language will not make the journey faster or less problematic. It is more important to learn to sail in a familiar boat (the home language) in minority language situations. Thus, in most cases, it is inappropriate to move from bilingualism to monolingualism.

However, it is dangerous to make this suggestion absolute and unequivocal. When there is language delay, there may be a few situations where maximal experience in one language is preferable. For example, where one language of a child is much securer and more well developed than another, it may be sensible to concentrate on developing the stronger language.

This does not mean that the chance of bilingualism is lost forever. If, or when, language delay disappears, the other language can be **reintroduced**. If a child with emotional problems and language delay really detests using (or even being spoken to) in a particular language, as part of a solution, the family may sensibly decide to accede to the child's preference. Again, once behavioral and language problems have been resolved, the 'dropped' language can be reintroduced, so long as it is immediately associated with pleasurable experiences.

Any temporary move from bilingualism to monolingualism should not be seen as the only solution needed. A focus on such a language change as the sole remedy to the child's problem is naïve and dangerous. For example, emotional problems causing language delay may require other rearrangements in the school or family's pattern of behavior. Language delay may require visits to a speech therapist for advice about language interaction between the child and significant adults. Temporary monolingualism should only be seen as one component in a package of attempted changes to solve the child's language problem. However, it is important to reiterate that, in the majority of cases, language delay will not be affected by retaining a bilingual approach.

The Assessment and Placement of Bilingual Children

Bilingual children are often over-represented in special needs education, and this is much due to biased assessment. Assessment can result in both cultural and linguistic bias, in the testing and the tester, in interpretation, discounting and omission (Usmani, 1999).

When bilingual children are assessed, it is important to keep three different aspects of their development distinct: (1) first language proficiency; (2) second language proficiency; and (3) the existence (or not) of a physical, learning or behavioral difficulty. This three-fold distinction enables a more accurate and fair assessment to be made with regard to special education. The child's level of functioning in a second language must not be seen as representing the child's level of language development. The child's development in the **first language** needs to be assessed (e.g. by observation if psychological and educational tests are not available) so as to paint a picture of proficiency rather than deficiency. The child's language proficiency is different from potential problems in an individual's capacities that require specialist treatment (e.g. hearing impairment, severely subnormal in 'IQ'). Neither the language and culture of the home, nor socioeconomic and ethnic differences should be considered as handicapping conditions in themselves. Social, cultural, family, educational and personal information needs to be collected to make a valid and reliable assessment and to make an accurate placement of the child in mainstream or special education. This is considered separately in the following section on the assessment of bilingual children.

The Example of the USA

In the USA, Public Law (94-142) gives the **right** to assessment that is not culturally discriminatory, to tests in the child's native language, to multi-dimensional 'all areas' assessment for all 'handicapped' students. The misdiagnosis of bilingual students for special education has led to court cases. Such court cases revealed how bilingual students were wrongly assessed as in need of special education (Maldonado, 1994). In some cases, teachers were unsure how to cope with a child whose English was relatively 'weak'. On this basis only, the teacher wanted special education for the 'Limited English Proficient' child.

In the USA, there is **legislation** to govern appropriate processes of assessment of those for whom English is an additional language. For example, the 1973 Californian case of *Diana* v. *The California State Board of Education* was based on nine Mexican-American parents who protested that their children (who were dominant in Spanish) were given an English language IQ test. The IQ test revealed 'normal' non-verbal IQ scores, but very low verbal IQ scores (as low as 30 for one child). As a result of this linguistically and culturally inappropriate IQ test, the Mexican-American children were placed in classes for the 'mentally retarded'. This case never went to court, but it established that testing should be conducted in a child's native language (and in English), and that non-verbal IQ tests were usually a fairer measurement of IQ than verbal tests (Valdés & Figueroa, 1994). As a result of this case, the collection of broader data on language minority children was required (rather than simple test data) to justify placement of such children in Special Education.

In 1975, Public Law 94-142, the Education for All Handicapped Children Act, federally mandated that all testing and assessment procedures should be non-discriminatory. 'Non-discriminatory' means using tests that are culturally and linguistically appropriate. Such testing procedures were only to be used by trained members of a **multidisciplinary** team. Apart from tests, teacher recommendations, observations of a child and other relevant information should create a multi-source file of evidence (Barona & Barona, 1992).

Such litigation and law has shown the importance of separating bilinguals with real learning difficulties from those bilinguals whose second language (e.g. English) proficiency is below 'native' average. The latter group should not be assessed as having learning difficulties and therefore in need of special education (Gersten & Woodward, 1994). The litigation also showed the wrongs done to bilingual students: **misidentification**, misplacement, misuse of tests and failure when allocated to special education.

Unfortunately, the fear of litigation by school districts can lead to an **over-referral** of bilingual students with a real need of special education. In the early 1980s, the trend in California, for example, was to assume that too many language minority students were in need of special education. When students did not appear to be benefiting from instruction in 'regular' classrooms, special education classes became the easy answer. Or, if teachers were unsure how to deal with a behavioral or learning problem, transfer to special education provision became an instant solution.

Towards the end of the 1980s, this had been reversed. The tendency moved to **under-estimating** the special needs of language minority children (Gersten & Woodward, 1994; Baca & Cervantes, 1998). Wrongful placement of children in special education (over-referral) made various administrators cautious of special education placement. A fear of legal action by parents and a realization that assessment devices often had low validity led administrators to be hesitant to place bilingual children in Special Education.

The see-saw between over- and under-referral to special education makes accurate assessment very important. The section on the assessment of bilingual children raises important issues about valid assessment of special need. However, accurate assessment and placement in different schools is not enough. The development of **effective instruction strategies** and an appropriate curriculum is crucial. So is the need to train teachers for bilingual students in special education. Educating the parents of special needs children is also a high priority.

Assessment will sometimes locate those who are bilingual *and* have a physical, neurological, learning, emotional, cognitive or behavioral difficulty. Such children may need some kind of special education or intervention. Estimates in the USA and other countries is typically that one in eight (approximately 12%) of language minority students will fit into this category. What form of Special Education should such children receive? Should such education be in their home language, where feasible, or in the majority language of the region? Or should such children be provided with education that uses both home and majority languages?

Bilingual Special Education

Special Education bilingual children can be served by a **variety** of institutional arrangements (Cloud, 1994). These include: Special Education schools (resident and non-resident), hospital-based education, residential homes, Special Education Units attached to mainstream schools, specially resourced classes in mainstream schools, withdrawal and pull-out programs (e.g. for extra speech and language help, behavioral management) and special help given by teachers, paraprofessionals or support staff in 'regular' classes. The extent to which such provision will be bilingual or monolingual will vary within and across such institutional arrangements. Such bilingual or monolingual provision will also depend on availability of provision (material and human), the type and degree of special education need or condition, proficiency in both languages, learning capacity, age, social and emotional maturity, degree of success in any previous education placements, and not least, the wishes of the parents and child.

When bilingual or language minority children have been assessed as having special needs, many educators argue that education solely in the dominant, majority language is needed. In the USA, the advice is sometimes given that Latino and other language minority children with special needs should be educated in monolingual, English language special schools. The argument is that such children are going to live in an English speaking society. When there is severe cognitive disability, it seems sensible that a child should be educated monolingually, in the minority or majority language. Such a child develops very slowly in one language.

Many special needs children will benefit considerably from **bilingual special education** rather than monolingual special education (Baca & Cervantes, 1998; Carrasquillo, 1990). One example is the recently arrived immigrant, special needs child. Placing such a child in a class where he or she doesn't speak the language of the classroom (e.g. English in the USA) will only increase failure and lower self-esteem. To be educated, the child preferably needs initial instruction mostly in the first language, with the chance to become as bilingual as possible. Most children with special needs are capable of developing in two languages. Many do not reach levels of proficiency in either language compared with peers in mainstream classrooms. Nevertheless, they reach satisfactory levels of proficiency in two languages according to their abilities. Becoming bilingual does not detract from achievement in other areas of the curriculum (e.g. mathematics and the creative arts). Canadian research tends to show that less able bilingual children share some of the cognitive advantages of bilingualism (Rueda, 1983). Just as their mathematical ability, literacy and scientific development may occur at a slower pace, so the two languages will develop with less speed. The size of vocabulary and accuracy of grammar may be less in both languages than the average bilingual child. Nevertheless, such children, acquiring two languages early, will usually be able to communicate in both languages, often as well as they would communicate in one language.

The movement of a bilingual student into special education often occurs after a conclusion is reached that the child's needs cannot be met by integration in a regular (i.e. non-special) classroom. This holds for those currently in bilingual education who may need special bilingual education because generally, **integration** is regarded as preferable to segregation. If children are placed in bilingual special education, it is important that they gain the benefits of those in other forms of bilingual education: dual language competence, biculturalism and multiculturalism, and other educational, cultural, self-identity and self-esteem benefits. These benefits have been discussed previously in this book.

One example not discussed so far is when children **fail** in a mainstream school due to their language proficiency not being sufficient to operate in the curriculum. For example, in the USA, some Spanish speaking children are in mainstream schools (a 'submersion' experience) and, although of normal ability, fail in the system (e.g. drop out of school, repeat grades, leave high school without a diploma) because their English proficiency is insufficiently developed to comprehend the increasingly complex curriculum.

This situation creates an apparent dilemma. By being placed in some form of **special education**, the child is possibly stigmatized as having a 'deficiency' and a 'language deficit'. Such special education may be a separate school (or a special unit within a larger school) that provides special ('remedial') education for bilingual children. Such schools and units may not foster bilingualism. Often, they will emphasize children becoming competent in the majority language (e.g. English in the USA). Such segregation may allow more attention to the second language but result in ghettoization of language minorities. While giving some sanctuary from sinking in second language submersion in a mainstream school, special education can be a retreat, marginalizing the child. Will such children in special education realize their potential across the curriculum? Will they have increased access to employment? Will their apparent failure be accepted and validated because they are associated with a remedial institution? Will there be decreased opportunities for success in school achievement, employment and self-enhancement?

The ideal for children in this dilemma may be neither mainstreaming nor special education. It is education which allows them to start and continue learning in their first language. The second language is nurtured as well — to ensure the development of bilinguals who can operate in mainstream society. In such schools, both languages are developed and used in the curriculum. Such schools avoid the 'remedial' or 'compensatory' associations of special education. Such schools celebrate the cultural and linguistic diversity of their students. In the USA, a movement towards inclusion and integration of special needs students can mean that they are placed in bilingual education along with their 'non special needs' peers.

Yet such bilingual education is sometimes in **danger** of being seen as a form of special education. Even when the 'language delayed' are separated from those who are in the early stages of learning the majority language (e.g. English in the USA), the danger is that the latter will still be assessed as in need of compensatory, remedial special education, including being allocated to bilingual education.

The Alternative Causes of Special Needs and Learning Difficulties in Children

The discussion of Special Education for bilingual children has suggested that one unfair assumption made about bilingual children who show learning difficulties is that bilingualism is the cause of those difficulties. Bilingualism is rarely a cause of learning difficulties. Learning difficulties are caused by a variety of possibilities, almost none of them aligned to bilingualism. Six examples of **causes outside the child** and his or her bilingualism follow. This list, which is not exhaustive or comprehensive, will indicate that bilingualism has nothing directly to do with many learning problems, either as a secondary or a primary cause.

(1)   Poverty and deprivation, child neglect and abuse, feelings of helplessness and desperation in the home, extended family and community may create personality, attitudinal and learning conditions that make assessment of learning difficulties more probable. Sometimes, such assessment will reflect prejudice, misjudgments and misperceptions about the child's home experiences. The learning problem may thus be in a **mismatch** between the culture, attitudes, expectations about education and values of the home and school. In Chapters 15 and 16 on literacy and biliteracy, this variation is examined with regard to local literacy and variations in ethnic group and social class uses of literacy. Different beliefs, culture, knowledge and cognitive approaches may be devalued with the child immediately labeled as of inferior intelligence, academically incompetent and of low potential.

(2)   The problem may be in the **standard of education**. A child may be struggling in the classroom due to poor teaching methods, a non-motivating, even hostile, classroom environment, a dearth of suitable teaching materials, or clashes with the teacher.

(3)   The school may be inhibiting or obstructing learning progress. If a child is being taught in a second language and the home language is ignored, then failure and perceived learning difficulties may result. One example is that of some Spanish speaking children in the USA. Such children are often placed in English-only classrooms on entry to school. They must sink or swim in English. Some swim; others sink and may be deemed to have a deficiency. By being assessed in their weaker second language (English) — rather than in their stronger home language (Spanish), such children are labeled as in need of special or remedial education. Thus the monolingual school system is itself responsible for learning failure. A school that promoted bilingualism would probably ensure learning success for the same child.

(4)   Another set of causes of learning difficulties are a lack of self-confidence, **low self-esteem**, a fear of failure and high anxiety in the classroom.

(5)   A fifth possibility is failure caused partly by interactions among children in the classroom. For example, where a group of children encourage each other to fool around, have a low motivation to succeed, or where there is bullying, hostility, social division, rather than cohesion among children in a classroom, the learning ethos may hinder the child's development.

(6) Another case is where there is a mismatch between the **gradient of learning** expected and the ability level of the child. Some children learn to read more slowly than others, still learning to read well, but after a longer period of time. Less able children can learn two languages within the (unknowable) limits of their ability. Other children experience specific learning difficulties (for example, dyslexia, neurological dysfunction, 'short-term memory' problems, poor physical coordination, problems in attention span or motivation). None of these specific learning difficulties or other language disorders are caused by bilingualism. At the same time, bilingual children will not escape from being included in this group. Bilingual families are no less likely to be affected than other families.

Almost the only occasion when a learning difficulty of a bilingual child is attached to bilingualism is the isolated case when a child enters the classroom with neither language sufficiently developed to cope with the particular language skills demanded by the curriculum. In such very rare cases where a child has simple conversational skills in two languages but cannot cope in the curriculum in either language, language may be related to learning difficulties.

ASSESSMENT AND BILINGUAL CHILDREN

The allocation of bilinguals to Special Education and the attribution of learning difficulties usually depends on some form of assessment. It is essential for any psychological and educational assessment of bilingual children to be fair, accurate and broad. Too often, tests given to bilingual children only serve to suggest their 'disabilities', supposed 'deficits' or lack of proficiency in a second language. Assessment can too easily legitimize the disabling of language minority students. Such students may come to be stigmatized by such tests, for example, because tests locate apparent weaknesses in the majority language and use monolingual scores as points of comparison. English language tests and IQ tests administered in the second language to US children are particular examples.

Yet for all the advice in legislation, all the discussions in academic literature and in research, bilinguals tend in many countries to be discriminated against in testing and assessment. Therefore, it is important to review the components of such bias, and more constructively, to suggest desirable practice. Ten overlapping and interacting issues in the assessment of bilingual children are now considered.

(1) The **temporary difficulties** faced by bilinguals must be distinguished from relatively more permanent difficulties that impede everyday functioning and learning. Brief language delays, temporary adjustment problems of immigrants and short-term stammering (stuttering) are examples of transient difficulties (Baker, 2000b). Dyslexia, hearing loss and neuroticism are examples where longer term problems may need treatment. This simple distinction hides different and complex dimensions. The means for distinguishing temporary and longer term problems follows.

(2) Diagnosis needs to go beyond a few, simple tests and engage a wide diversity of measurement and observation devices. Diagnosis needs to be extended over a time period and to avoid an instant conclusion and instantaneous remedy. **Observing** the child in different contexts (and not just in the classroom) will provide a more valid profile (language and behavior) of that child. The family and educational history of the child needs assembling. Parents and teachers need to be consulted, sometimes doctors, counselors, speech therapists and social workers as well. Samples of a child's natural communication need gathering, with the child in different roles and different situations (Hernandez, 1994).

An awareness or basic knowledge of a child's ethnic, cultural and linguistic background is important in fair assessment, but it may not be enough. To interpret test scores and classifications meaningfully and wisely and, in particular, to make decisions on the basis of assessment, requires a highly sensitive and sympathetic **understanding of a child's community, culture, family life and individual characteristics**. Children come to school with very differing home experiences, where different kinds of ability are cultivated and stressed. Such abilities prized by parents may be different from the abilities learned at school (Chamberlain & Medinos-Landurand, 1991).

For example, discovery learning and learning through play is not a part of all cultures. An investigative, questioning mode of thinking may not be encouraged within a culture. As reflected in parent–child relationships, adults provide authoritative knowledge that must be accepted and enacted by the child. Parents may teach literacy in a similar style, where the child is expected to memorize much or all of the Holy Book and repeat it without comprehension. Such family and community socialization practices have implications (1) for the type of assessment that reveals the strengths and weaknesses of the child; (2) for the importance of acquiring evidence about the culture of the child; and (3) for the process of assessment by the teacher, psychologist, speech therapist, counselor or other professional.

Test scores (e.g. on educational and psychometric tests) tend to be decontextualized and attenuated (Resnick & Resnick, 1992). An analogy helps to illustrate this important point. Test scores are like latitude and longitude. They provide points of reference on a map of human characteristics. As a standard measurement usable on all maps, they provide initial, rapid and instantly comparable information. But imagine the most beautiful place you know (e.g. a flower-enfolded, azure-colored lake set amid tall, green-sloped, ice-capped mountains). Does the expression of the latitude and longitude of that scene do justice to characterizing the personality and distinctiveness of that location? The attempted precision of the sextant needs to be joined by the full empathic exploration and evaluation of the character and qualities of the child.

Authentic language and behavior needs assessing rather than decomposed and decontextualized language skills. The levels of thinking and understanding of a child through both languages need assessing rather than superficial comprehension gleaned from a superficially 'scientific' test (e.g. with high test–retest reliability, and high correlations with similar tests). 'Inauthentic language' tests relate too often to a transmission style curriculum where obtaining the correct answer and 'teaching to the test' dominates teacher thinking and classroom activity. Such tests do not capture the communication abilities of the child, as for example, occur in the playground, on the street, at the family meal-table and in internal conversations when alone.

(3)   The choice of **assessors** for the child will affect the assessment. Whether the assessors are perceived to be from the same language group as the child will affect the child's performance (and possibly the diagnosis). The perceived age, social class, powerfulness and gender of the assessor(s) will affect how the child responds and possibly the assessment outcomes. The assessment process is not neutral. Who assesses, using what devices, under what conditions, all contribute to the judgment being made. An inappropriate assessor creates an increased risk of making two common, opposite judgmental errors concerning bilingual children: (1) generating a 'false positive', that is, diagnosing a problem when none is present; and (2) generating a 'false negative', that is, failing to locate a problem when one exists.

(4)   Children need assessing in their **stronger language**. Ideally children need assessing as bilinguals — in both their languages. The tests and assessment devices applied, and the language of communication used in assessment, should ideally be in the child's stronger language. An assessment based on tests of (and in) the child's weaker language may lead to a misdiagnosis, a false impression of the abilities of the child and a very partial and biased picture of the child. This sometimes occurs in the UK and the USA where bilingual children are tested in English, partly because of the availability of well regarded psychometric tests.

(5)   Parents and educators need to make sure the **language used** in the test is **appropriate** to the child. For example, a translation of the test (e.g. from English to Spanish) may produce inappropriate, stilted language. Also, the different varieties of Spanish, for example, may not be that used by the student. Chicano Spanish speaking parents will want the tests in Chicano or at least Mexican Spanish rather than the Cuban, Puerto Rican or Castilian variety of Spanish. Once Spanish speaking children have been in the USA for a time, their Spanish changes. English influences their way of speaking Spanish. So a test in 'standard' Spanish is inappropriate. A Spanish test may accept only one right answer, penalizing children for their bilingualism and their US Spanish. A monolingual standard of Spanish is inappropriate to such bilingual children.

Since there are language problems with tests (as outlined above and continued below), it is important to distinguish between a child's language profile and **performance profile** (Cummins, 1984a). The performance profile is more important as it attempts to portray a child's underlying cognitive abilities rather than just language abilities. A performance profile seeks to understand the overall potential of the child, not just their language proficiency. Cummins (1984a) has demonstrated this **distinction between a language profile and a**

performance profile on one frequently used IQ test in individual assessment — the Wechsler Intelligence Scale for Children: Revised (WISC-R). Bilingual children tend to score significantly higher on the Performance than the Verbal subtests. As Cummins (1984a, p. 30) suggests: 'The analysis of student performance on this test suggested that the majority of Verbal sub-tests were tapping ESL students' knowledge of the English language and North American culture in addition to, or instead of, verbal cognitive/academic ability'.

(6) There are times when a test or assessment device cannot be given in the child's stronger language. For example, appropriate bilingual professionals may not be available to join the assessment team, tests may not be available in the child's home language, and **translations** of tests may make those tests invalid and unreliable.

   Interpreters are sometimes necessary. Interpreters do have a valuable function. If trained in the linguistic, professional and rapport-making competences needed, they can make assessment more fair and accurate. Interpreters can also bring a possible bias into the assessment (i.e. 'heightening' or 'lowering' the assessment results through the interpretation they provide).

(7) There is a danger of focusing the assessment solely on the child. If the child is tested, the assumption is that the 'problem' lies within the child. At the same time, and sometimes instead, the **focus** needs to shift to **causes outside the child**. Is the problem in the school? Is the school failing the child by denying abilities in the first language and focusing on failures in the second (school) language? Is the school system denying a child's culture and ethnic character, thereby affecting the child's academic success and self-esteem? Is the curriculum delivered at a level that is beyond the child's comprehension or is culturally strange to the child? The remedy may be in a change to the school system and not to the child.

(8) The danger of assessment is that it will lead to the disablement rather than the **empowerment** of bilingual children (Cummins, 1984a, 1986b, 2000a). If the assessment separates children from powerful, dominant, mainstream groups in society, the child may become disabled. The assessment may lead to categorization in an inferior group of society and marginalization. Instead, assessment should work in the best, long-term interests of the child. Best interests does not only mean short-term educational remedies, but also long-term employment and wealth-sharing opportunities. The assessment should initiate advocating for the child, and not against the child.

(9) It is important to use the understanding of a child's **teachers** who have observed that child in a variety of learning environments over time. What do the child's teachers think is the root problem? What solutions and interventions do teachers suggest? Have the child's teachers a plan of action? A team of teachers, meeting regularly to discuss children with problems, is a valuable first attempt to assess and treat the child. Such a team can also be the school decision-maker for referral to other professionals (e.g. speech therapist, psychologist, counselor).

(10) Norm referenced **tests** are often used to assess the child (e.g. for entry into, or exit from a bilingual program). This means that the assessor can compare the child with other so called 'normal' children. The assessor can indicate how different the child is from the average. Many such tests are based on scores from 'native' language majority children. Thus, comparisons can be unfair for bilingual children. For example, tests of English language proficiency may have 'norms' (averages, and scores around the average) based on native speakers of English. This makes them biased against bilinguals and leads to the stereotyping of particular language and ethnic groups.

The **testing of bilinguals** has developed from the practice of testing **monolinguals**. Bilinguals are not the simple sum of two monolinguals but are a unique combination and integration of languages. The language configuration of bilinguals means that, for example, a bilingual's English language performance should not be compared with a monolingual's English language competence. A decathlete should not be compared with a 100 meter sprinter solely for speed of running. Monolingual norms are simply inappropriate for bilinguals (Grosjean, 1985). One example helps illustrate this point. Bilinguals use their languages in different contexts (domains). Thus they may have linguistic competence in varying curriculum areas, on different curriculum topics and on different language functions. Equal language facility in both languages is rare. Comparison on monolingual norms assumes such equal language facility across all domains, language functions and curriculum areas. This is unfair and inequitable.

Such norm referenced tests are often written by white, middle-class Anglo test producers. The test items often reflect their language style and **culture**. For example, the words used such as 'tennis racquet', 'snowman' and 'credit cards' may be unfamiliar to some immigrants who have never seen a snowman, played or watched tennis, or know about the culture of plastic money. Assessment items that reflect the unique learning experiences of language minority children will be excluded from a test for majority language or mainstream children. Such items will be highlighted by item analysis of an early draft of the test as 'unconnected' with the majority of the test items.

Such norm referenced tests are often 'pencil and paper' tests, sometimes involving multiple choice answers (one answer is chosen from a set of given answers). Such tests do not measure all the different aspects of language, of 'intelligence' or any curriculum subject. Spoken, conversational language and financial intelligence, for example, cannot be adequately measured by a simple pencil and paper test.

Some norm referenced tests report the results in **percentiles** (especially in the USA). Percentiles refer to the percentage of children below (and above) the child being tested. For example, being in the 40th percentile means that 39% of children score lower than the child being tested. Sixty percent of children of an age group score above the 40th percentile child. The child is in the 40th group from the bottom, all children being assumed to be divided into 100 equally sized groups. Percentiles are often used for entry and exit of students into bilingual programs in the USA. For example, a student may need to reach the 40th percentile on an English language test to be exited to a mainstream class. What 'percentile threshold' (e.g. 40th percentile) is used for entry or exit is essentially arbitrary, and liable to political rather than educationally derived decisions.

Norm referenced tests essentially compare one person against others. Is this important? Isn't the more important measurement about what a bilingual child can and cannot do in each curriculum subject? To say a child is in the 40th percentile in English doesn't tell the parent or the teacher what are a child's strengths and weaknesses, capabilities and needs in English. The alternative is assessment related directly to progress in each curriculum area.

Curriculum based assessment is called **criterion referenced testing**, and seeks to establish the relative mastery of a child in a curriculum area (Baker, 1995). It seeks to establish what a child can do, and what is the next area of a curriculum (e.g. reading) where progress can be made. A diagnosis may also be made, not necessarily of a fundamental psychological or learning problem, but of weaknesses that need remedial treatment to enable conceptual understanding (e.g. if a child has a problem in reading certain consonantal blends). Such criterion referenced assessment of bilingual students gives parents and teachers more usable and important information. It profiles for parents and teachers what a child can do in a subject (e.g. mathematics) and where development, or accelerated learning, should occur next. Such assessment enables an individualized program to be set for the child.

However, the sequences of learning that underpin a criterion referenced test may still reflect a **cultural mismatch** for the child. Criterion referenced assessment (usually, but not necessarily) assumes there is a relatively linear, step-by-step progression in a curriculum area (e.g. in learning to read, in number skills, in science). Such a progression may be culturally relative and culturally determined. As Cline (1993, p. 63) noted 'because of their different prior experiences, their learning hierarchy for a particular task may follow different steps or a different sequence (e.g. in relation to phonology and orthography in learning to read)'. Therefore, it is important to use curriculum assessment contexts and processes that are appropriate, comprehensible and meaningful to the bilingual child.

Solutions
Three solutions to the problems of testing bilinguals are provided by Valdés and Figueroa (1994). Their **first** solution is to attempt to minimize the potential harm of existing tests when given to bilingual individuals, by applying some of the guidelines given above. Their **second** solution is, temporarily, to ban all testing of bilinguals until more valid tests can be produced for bilingual populations. Their **third** alternative is that alternative approaches to testing and development be developed. This third option may be the one most favored by many teachers, educationalists and parents. It would, for example, bring in bilingual norms, more curriculum based assessment and portfolio type assessment, and a greater cultural and linguistic awareness of bilinguals.

Portfolio assessment that is developmental and which has width linguistically and contextually has become particularly popular. This is a collection over time of a sample of a child's unique growth (e.g. in both their languages). A student's port-folio will reveal advancing accomplishments in the form of authentic activities (possibly with staff observations included). A sense of ownership of the portfolio by the student is important to raise awareness of evolving accomplishments and a personal possession of progress.

However, this third solution is probably a new beginning but it is not enough. A **more radical solution** places change in assessment within (and not separate from) a change in expectations about the nature and behavior of bilingual students. This entails a shift in the politics and policy dimensions of the assessment of bilinguals. Merely changing tests may alleviate the symptoms of a problem, but not change the root cause. The root cause tends to be a bias against language minorities that is endemic in many societies and is substantiated by tests. By being biased against bilinguals in a cultural and linguistic form, and by a failure to incorporate an under-standing of the cognitive constitution of bilinguals, assessment confirms and perpetuates various discriminatory perceptions about language minority children.

Assessment thus sometimes serves by its nature and purpose, its form, use and outcomes to provide the evidence for **discrimination** and **prejudice** against language minorities (e.g. in the USA and Britain) to be perpetuated. Assessment results serve to marginalize and demotivate, to reveal underachievement and lower performance in language minority children. These results are often a reflection of the low status, inequitable treatment and poverty found among many language minorities. Assessment provides the data to make expectations about language minority students self-fulfilling and self-perpetuating. Changing assessment does not necessarily break into that cycle, unless it is a component of a wider reform movement.

Assessment must not in itself be blamed for bias against bilinguals. It is a conveyer and not a root cause of language minority discrimination and bias. Until there is authentic and genuine acceptance of cultural pluralism in a nation, a more widespread assent for multiculturalism, a minimizing of racism and prejudice against ethnic minorities, minor modifications in the assessment of bilinguals stand the chance of merely confirming the lower status and perceived 'deficiencies' of language minority children.

Too often the focus in assessing bilinguals is on their language competence (or on their 'limited proficiencies' as in the test-designated 'Limited English Proficient' students in the USA via tests such as the English Language Assessment Battery (LAB)). Rarely does the assessment of bilinguals in the education system focus on other important competences of a bilingual.

In the USA, the 1991 Secretary's Commission on Achieving Necessary Skills (SCANS) recommended that attention be given in high schools to work-related **competences**. For example, performance standards were called for in: interper-sonal skills (e.g. working in a team, negotiating, working well with people from culturally diverse backgrounds), interpreting and communicating information, thinking creatively, taking responsibility, sociability, self-management and integrity. These important 'life-skills' are regarded as 'essential accomplishments' for employment, self-respect and building a better world.

On some of these attributes, there is evidence to suggest that bilinguals may have advantages over monolinguals (e.g. negotiating, working well with people from culturally diverse backgrounds, interpreting and communicating information, thinking creatively). If the assessment of bilinguals focused more on these 'outside world' attributes and less on classroom linguistic skills in the majority language, a more affirmative and favorable, productive and constructive view of bilinguals might be promoted.

CONCLUSION

The chapter has attempted to indicate that underachievement and placement in special education is not a cause of bilingualism. The reasons for underachievement tend to reside in factors that surround bilinguals (e.g. their social and economic conditions) and are not an inevitable component of bilingualism. Traditional assessment in education often serves to misplace and misdiagnose bilinguals. Apparent rather than real difficulties are identified, with a depreciation of bilinguals' language and potential curriculum performance.

KEY POINTS IN THE CHAPTER

- underachievement in school is typically unfairly blamed on bilingualism. Lack of exposure to the majority language and a mismatch between the languages of home and school are often cited as causes of underachievement.
- The real causes of underachievement tend to lie in relative social and economic deprivation and exclusion, a school which rejects the home language and culture of the child, and occasionally real learning difficulties.
- Bilingual children are often over-represented in Special Education, being seen as having a language deficit. Paradoxically, they can also be under-represented when there is a fear of legal action for wrongful placement.
- Bilingualism has been associated with language and communication disorders (e.g. language delay). This is not supported by research.
- Special Education bilingual children are served by a variety of institutional arrangements including Special Education schools, Special Education Units attached to mainstream schools, specially resourced classes in mainstream schools, withdrawal and pull-out programs and special help given by teachers, paraprofessionals or support staff in 'regular' classes. Most special needs children will benefit from bilingual special education rather than monolingual special education.
- Assessment of bilingual children is enhanced when there is observation (in and out of the classroom) and not just testing, curriculum based assessment, a cultural and linguistic awareness of bilinguals, using appropriately trained assessors who seek to empower such children.

SUGGESTED FURTHER READING

BACA, L.M. and CERVANTES, H.T., 1998, *The Bilingual Special Education Interface* (3rd edn). Upper Saddle River, NJ: Prentice Hall.

CLINE, T. and FREDERICKSON, N., 1995, *Progress in Curriculum Related Assessment with Bilingual Pupils*. Clevedon: Multilingual Matters.

CUMMINS, J. 1984, *Bilingualism and Special Education: Issues in Assessment and Pedagogy*. Clevedon: Multilingual Matters.

CUMMINS, J., 2000, *Language, Power and Pedagogy: Bilingual Children in the Crossfire*. Clevedon: Multilingual Matters.

GARCÍA, O. and BAKER, C. (eds), 1995, *Policy and Practice in Bilingual Education: A Reader Extending the Foundations*. Clevedon: Multilingual Matters.

HAMAYAN, E.V. and DAMICO, J.S. (eds), 1991, *Limiting Bias in the Assessment of Bilingual Students*. Austin, TX: Pro-ed.

HARRY, B., 1992, *Cultural Diversity, Families and the Special Education System*. New York: Teachers College Press.

KEEL, P. (ed.), 1994, *Assessment in the Multi-Ethnic Primary Classroom*. Stoke on Trent (UK): Trentham Books.

LI WEI, MILLER, N. and DODD, B., 1997, Distinguishing communicative difference from language disorder in bilingual children. *Bilingual Family Newsletter* 14 (1), 3–4. Clevedon: Multilingual Matters.

VALDÉS, G. and FIGUEROA, R.A., 1994, *Bilingualism and Testing: A Special Case of Bias*. Norwood, NJ: Ablex Publishing Corporation.

STUDY ACTIVITIES

(1) Interview some parents or teachers with a bilingual student who has special needs (preferably gathering a variety of different viewpoints). Define the exact nature of those special needs. Find out the history of that student's education. Ask the parents or teachers what their preferences are for the use of languages in school and if they want their children to be bilingual as a result of schooling. Inquire about the value and use they see in languages for special needs children.

(2) Locate two students who are considered to have 'special needs'. Write a case study of each student, with contrasts and comparisons, to show the history of assessment and school placement. Evaluate the decisions made, indicating particular issues of practical importance.

(3) Find out about assessment practices in schools in your neighborhood. What practices exist at district and school level? What tests are used? How do assessment practices impact on bilingual students?

(4) Researching on two or three bilingual students, administer one or more assessment tests, tasks or other devices as allocated by your instructor. Analyze the results and profile the students (a) purely in terms of the test results, then (b) relating the test results to other qualitative information available on the students (e.g. interview the students).

Literacy in Minority Language and Multicultural Societies

Introduction

The Uses of Literacy in Bilingual and Multicultural Societies

Definitions of Literacy

Approaches to Literacy

Conclusion

Literacy in Minority Language and Multicultural Societies

INTRODUCTION

Throughout the world, literacy is regarded as a central foundation for personal and national development. Yet, as this chapter will show, what precisely is meant by literacy is neither simple nor uncontroversial. Literacy is variously said to cultivate values, norms of behavior and morals, create benign citizens, develop powers of thinking and reasoning, enculturate, emancipate and empower, provide enjoyment and emotional development, develop critical awareness, foster religious devotion, community development, and not least be central to academic success across the curriculum. The nature and future of language minorities is thus interwoven in their literacy practices.

In developed and developing countries, literacy is often associated with progress, civilization, social mobility and economic advancement. A classic, if disputed claim, is by Anderson (1966) who suggests that any society requires a 40% literacy rate for economic 'take off', a belief which is embedded in many literacy programs. Recently, literacy for information and communication technological use (e.g. the Internet) has been stressed.

Literacy levels in the population are frequently debated by governments (e.g. USA). A population literate in the majority language is perceived as helping secure national identity. Those without majority language literacy may be seen as unemployable, decreasing national productivity, causing underachievement at school, and working against national identity, social cohesion, common values and a shared morality (Street, 1995). Thus national issues and debates (e.g. unemployment, creation of wealth, school achievement, national identity) are often expressed under the guise of literacy deficits in a nation. Issues of poverty and unemployment, social unrest and immigrants are diverted into debates about low standards of literacy with the victim taking the blame. Literacy becomes a symbol and a perceived cause of many societal problems. Language minorities (e.g. immigrants in the USA) are frequently the victims who are allotted much blame.

The ability to read and write is often regarded as essential for personal survival, security and status in literate and less literate multilingual and multicultural societies. For those who fail to become literate, the consequences can be grievous and severe. Literacy impacts on people's daily lives in innumerable ways: social, cultural, economic, political and religious communication, for example. Where language minority members are relatively powerless and underprivileged, literacy is often regarded as a major key to self-advancement as well as community group and individual empowerment. If this is so, it is important to consider the **needs or uses for literacy** in students and adults in bilingual and multicultural societies.

In considering such needs and uses, it is important to note that literacy education for language minority students is often in a majority language (e.g. English language literacy in the USA; English in parts of Africa as an 'official' or international language). In contrast, where language minorities have access to bilingual education, literacy may be introduced in the home/minority language. In that case, literacy in the majority language (and hence biliteracy) will be developed later in the elementary school (e.g. around seven or eight years of age). This issue is considered in the next chapter. For the moment, the consideration of uses of literacy refers to literacy introduced in either the minority or majority language (or both languages developed in parallel).

THE USES OF LITERACY IN BILINGUAL AND MULTICULTURAL SOCIETIES

Heath (1980) defined seven contextualized uses of literacy based on her research in a working class community in Southeastern United States: instrumental (e.g. street signs), social-interactional (e.g. letters), news-related (e.g. newspapers), memory-supportive (e.g. address and telephone books), substitutes for oral messages (e.g. message for a child from parent), provision of a permanent record (e.g. birth certificates) and confirmation of attitudes (e.g. Bible, instructions). At a societal level, literacy can relate to a set of needs with widely differing perspectives:

Literacy is Needed for Survival

There are basic day-to-day uses of literacy. For example, a motorist needs to read road signs, a shopper needs to read instructions and labels on food packaging, the traveler needs to understand signs at bus stations, train stations and airports.

Literacy is Needed for Learning

Students need to be able to read text books, story books, laboratory manuals, examination sheets and tests for learning and assessment to take place.

Literacy is Needed for Citizenship

To complete bureaucratic forms, participate in local or regional government, vote, read local and national newspapers, read information that comes through the post or is on billboards, citizens need basic reading skills. To respond, react, complain and assert democratic rights, reading and writing are often valuable allies to speaking skills.

Literacy is Needed for Personal Relationships

Writing letters to friends and relatives who are no longer local, and sending seasonal greeting cards, are each aided by literacy.

Literacy is Needed for Personal Pleasure and Creativity

Being able to read gives students and adults access to magazines, novels, newspapers, comics, story books and non-fiction to be enjoyed in leisure time. Literacy enables the imagination to be stimulated, and creative instincts to be expressed.

Literacy is Needed for Employment

Many higher status and higher paid jobs require reading and writing skills.

Literacy is Needed for Community Development and Political Empowerment

Literacy can empower and liberate low-status, marginalized communities, emancipating those politically subjugated and despised.

Literacy is Needed to Empower the Mind

Wells and Chang-Wells (1992) suggest that literate thinking is 'the building up, metaphorically speaking, of a set of mental muscles that enable one effectively to tackle intellectual tasks that would otherwise be beyond one's powers' (p. 122). Literacy is seen as a mode of thinking, as a means of **reasoning**, reflecting and interacting with oneself. This is one foundation in individual empowerment.

The importance and usefulness of literacy for language minorities is revealed in public perceptions of those who are **illiterate**. Being unable to read and write is often regarded as shameful, embarrassing, indicating a deficiency, a symbol of low or marginal status, and in need of remediation in school or in adult classes. Reducing illiteracy is regarded as a key priority in UNESCO's aims, irrespective of country, continent, culture or caste.

Whether language minority children should first become literate in the majority language or in their minority language will be discussed later in this chapter. Also considered later will be whether majority language monoliteracy or biliteracy should be attempted. Before engaging in such discussions, it is important to explore the kind of literacy that language minority students and adults require. We start by considering **three contrasting definitions of literacy**. This provides an instant flavor of the keen debate about the nature and value of different kinds of literacy (Wiley, 1996a). The debate has important implications for bilingual students, as will be revealed.

DEFINITIONS OF LITERACY

The list of needs for literacy given above has already hinted that literacy plays different roles for different people. Compare two definitions of literacy. The first is a functional **definition** of, and skills approach to, literacy by UNESCO dating from 1962. A literate person is someone who

> 'has acquired the essential knowledge and skills which enable him to engage in all those activities in which literacy is required for effective functioning in his group and community and whose attainments in reading, writing and arithmetic make it possible for him to continue to use these skills towards his own and the community's developments.' (cited in Oxenham, 1980, p. 87)

In comparison, Hudelson (1994, p. 130) defines reading as

> 'a language process in which an individual constructs meaning through a transaction with written text that has been created by symbols that represent language. The transaction involves the reader's acting upon or interpreting the text, and the interpretation is influenced by the reader's past experiences, language background, and cultural framework, as well as the reader's purpose for reading'.

This is a definition that concentrates on reading as the construction of meaning, rather than on the skills of reading. While this definition only refers to reading, the idea extends to literacy in general.

The third **definition** derives from Wells and Chang-Wells (1992) who argue that 'To be literate is to have the disposition to engage appropriately with texts of different types in order to empower action, thinking, and feeling in the context of purposeful social activity' (p. 147). This definition deliberately allows for the possibility that different language minority communities attach a different value to different types of literacy.

Cultures differ from each other in their uses and purposes for literacy. For some cultures literacy is about promoting abstract thought, rationality, critical thinking, balanced and detached awareness, empathy and sensitivity. For other cultures literacy is about memorization, transmission of life stories revealing their heritage, values and morality, and centrally in certain religions, for the transmission of rules of religious and moral behavior. A Moslem for example, will be expected to read aloud from the *Qur'an*. Many Moslems are not expected to understand what they read, this being provided in their mother tongue. In some cultures, the mother is expected to read to her children and help them develop literacy skills, but she is not expected to read national newspapers or complete bureaucratic forms herself. The concept of literacy is therefore not single but plural, relative to a culture and creed, and not universal.

These three definitions (functional skills, construction of meaning, and sociocultural) will now be extended and explored by examining different educational approaches to literacy. These approaches, like the above definitions, are not necessarily discrete but overlap and can be combined in literacy learning. However, their emphases are different in the ways that they impact on students and approach literacy in minority language communities.

APPROACHES TO LITERACY

The Skills Approach

The concept of **functional literacy**, as in the UNESCO definition, appears to assume that literacy is the simple act of reading and writing. 'Acquiring essential knowledge and skills' refers to the ability to decode symbols on a page into sounds, followed by making meaning from those sounds. Reading is about saying the words on the page. Writing is about being able to spell correctly, and write in correct grammatical sentences. In both reading and writing, a literate person is able to understand and comprehend the printed word.

The assumption of this approach is that literacy is primarily a **technical skill**, neutral in its aims and universal across languages. The skills of reading and writing can be decomposed into vocabulary, grammar and composition. Teaching sounds and letters, phonics and standard language may be the important focus. Errors in reading and writing will also incur keen attention, alongside a concern with achieving scores on tests of reading and writing. Such tests tend to assess decomposed and decontextualized language skills, eliciting superficial comprehension rather than deeper language thinking and understanding. These reliable but 'inauthentic' tests tend to be used as templates for instruction. Measurement-led instruction promotes 'teaching to the test' and possibly decreases opportunities for developing higher order language and thinking skills.

Underneath the skills approach to literacy tends to be a belief that children need functional or 'useful' literacy only. Effective functioning implies that the student or adult will contribute in a collaborative, constructive and non-critical manner to the smooth running of the local and national community. **Functional literacy** is perceived as accepting the status quo, understanding and maintaining one's place in society, and being a faithful, contented citizen. This view is extended later in the book when the relationship between bilingualism and politics is considered.

Functional literacy does not mean reading print in 'quality' newspapers and books. Functional literacy is at a lower level: for example being able to read labels on tins and road signs, finding a number in a telephone directory. Among those who seem to be functionally literate, there will be those who are aliterate (who can read but don't), and those who manage to hide their illiteracy, as it is socially undesirable to be illiterate. Functional literacy may not be enough in advanced, technological societies. The populace constantly faces bureaucratic forms and written instructions which demand more advanced literacy skills. Functional literacy is unlikely to be enough to cope with such complex tasks.

It is important not to forget the amount of illiteracy and low levels of literacy in many countries. Criticism of the skills/functional approach must not hinder the necessity of all children of the 21st century becoming literate. Having the skills to read and write is an important asset for all minority language children – both in a majority and their minority language. However, the jury is still 'out' on the best route to acquiring reading and writing skills (Snow *et al.*, 1998). The next section will provide a contrast to the skills approach in terms of learning strategy.

The Whole Language Approach

The whole language approach to literacy is diametrically opposed to the concept of reading and writing as decoding and a series of separate skills. The whole language approach emphasizes learning to read and write naturally, for a **purpose**, for meaningful communication and for inherent pleasure (Whitmore & Crowell, 1994). Since Whole Language has been regarded as empowering and enlightening for down-trodden language minorities (compared with a functional approach to literacy), the style will be discussed in detail.

Generally, the whole language approach supports an holistic and integrated learning of reading, writing, spelling and oracy. The language used must have relevance and meaning to the language minority child. The use of language for communication is stressed; the operation rather than the form of language. With the whole language approach, students may be taught phonics contextually. That is, the students' attention is directed toward discreet parts of a text (e.g., letter sounds, digraphs) after they have explored the whole story or text. A Whole Language teacher uses a wide variety of texts and storybooks written to stimulate the imagination of children for their enjoyment and literacy development.

Whole language instruction treats reading and writing as reciprocal or mutually enhancing processes. Learning to read is also learning to write. A child learns to spell when learning to read. The more children read, the more their writing improves. Writing activities, like reading lessons have authentic purposes. A child writes for somebody in a particular situation and for a defined reason. Writing means reflecting on one's ideas and sharing meaning with others. This can be empowering for language minority students. Writing can be in partnership with others, involving drafting and redrafting. A child learns to write when they are writing for somebody with a meaning and a message.

Whole language teachers believe that constantly highlighting grammatical and spelling errors is soul-destroying for the child. Corrections concentrate on form and not function, on the medium and not the message. Students in whole language classrooms learn that conveying meaning is important in learning to write well. Efficient writing means making it comprehensible for an audience. As students receive feedback on their writings, through conferences with the teacher, in small groups and in pairs, they learn to make the corrections necessary to convey their desired messages effectively.

The philosophy of the whole language approach is that literacy instruction must be intellectually stimulating, personally relevant and enjoyable for the learner. This occurs when reading and writing involve real and natural events, not artificial stories, artificial sequences, rules of grammar and spelling, or stories that are not relevant to the child's experience. Reading and writing need to be interesting, relevant to the child's experience, allowing choice by the learner, giving children power and understanding of their world. Reading taught for its own sake is not fun. Going through a book of writing exercises following reading is not usually interesting or relevant to the child.

Children learn to read and write when there is a need to understand the **meaning** of a story, to chant a rhyme, to share the humor of a book. Writing is fun when it is **communication**. Part of a whole language approach is to stimulate the **creative imagination** and sheer enjoyment in reading. Much of what children and adults read is for leisure and pleasure, and while not politically neutral or morally objective, novels, magazines, comics and some poetry are designed to satisfy and stir the imagination. Literacy in the whole language approach is thus to develop aesthetic appreciation and interpersonal sensitivity which is a more empowering view of the language minority student than a functional approach.

Children need imaginative, vivid, interesting books that both relate to, and increase their experience, which make them laugh and stir their **imagination**. They need to feel that books are interesting, unstuffy, relevant to their world and their way of thinking. Children do not just need books on a library or classroom shelf. Magazines and newspapers, directories and posters, signs in the street, packages and labels are all reading material. Children writing to each other or to their grandparents in another country are forms of reading and writing centered round an authentic task. The rules of reading and writing are latently being taught.

The whole language approach is against basal readers in learning to read. Basal readers are reading books that use simplified vocabulary. There is often a set order in reading these books, moving from simple to more complex text in a gradually increasing gradient of difficulty. The learning of technical skills of reading are the prime aim of these books. Such graded series of readers entail a movement of smaller to larger skill elements, and a carefully controlled sequence of learning. The skills in a basal reading series exist not because this is how children learn to read, but partly because of the logistics of developing a series of lessons that can be taught sequentially, day after day, week after week, year after year. Students are typically tested for their ability to master each small component of the reading scheme, often before they are allowed to move on to the next component.

Such basal reading books tend to promote the ability to recognize rather than to comprehend, thus carrying a view of the language minority student that maintains subordination. The child may be able to read out loud to the teacher yet not understand the overt and covert meanings of the stories. Basal reading series typically tell teachers exactly what they should do and say while giving a lesson, seemingly giving a technology of teaching reading that is easily implemented in classrooms.

One alternative is the reading of '**real books**'. 'Real books' is a term used to describe books that entertain, sometimes inform, and assume that there should be much more than purely 'reading skills improvement' when children read books. At their best, they are laudable literature in themselves.

Ideally, 'real books' attempt to avoid the overwhelming white, middle-class, male perspectives that are manifestly and latently present in so much of traditional children's literature. Books need to challenge stereotyped gender roles, challenge traditional roles ascribed to mums and dads, and challenge the subservient portrayal of linguistic and cultural minorities. While reality has to be portrayed, understood and criticized by children, such children also need informing about alternatives. Reading needs to reflect and challenge contemporary reality, and pose different lifestyles and values. Ethnic minorities need to be presented, not in a restricted stereotyped social context, but outside their stereotype so as to challenge the status quo. For language minorities, this can become enlightening and empowering.

A whole language approach and attention to the skills of literacy are combined eclectically by many practicing teachers. There is an analogy with a musician. It is the overall musical performance that is important. Sometimes there is a need to practice scales, arpeggios, or trills as separate skills to improve the overall standard of musicianship. Accurately playing scales is not a musical performance. More important is the overall combination of accurate playing, interpretation of a musical score, creating an ambience with a piece of music and communicating with the listener. Similarly with reading and writing. Sometimes a teacher will concentrate on specific skills (e.g. irregular words, punctuation, spelling, grammar). Specific skills are not reading or writing. The overall activity needs to be the central focus.

A cautionary note with regard to language minority students needs sounding. The whole language approach has features that **overlap** with functional literacy. The child can still be viewed by the whole language approach as a relatively non-critical, monocultural, assimilated being. Literacy can be about socialization into customary, normative values and beliefs. Thus, the whole language approach can still result in an uncritical, accepting attitude by the child. For language minority children, especially in stigmatized, racist and prejudiced contexts, this may not always be empowering. What messages do whole language texts convey? Do they support assimilation rather than cultural diversity? Is whole language a vehicle for conveying a majority language meaning and message? We therefore move to further approaches to literacy to language minority students.

The Construction of Meaning Approach

A recent consideration of literacy (derived and elaborated from the Whole Language Approach) is constructivist. It emphasizes that readers bring their own meanings to text, that reading and writing is essentially a **construction and reconstruction of meaning**. Part of this consideration is that the meaning individuals give to a text depends on their culture, personal experiences and histories, personal understandings of the themes and tone of text, and the particular social context where reading occurs. As will be revealed later, this idea has implications for language minority children and adults, and for community development.

Readers bring **meaning** with them to texts. They make sense of a text from previously acquired knowledge. Without relevant background knowledge, readers may fail to construct much real meaning. For language minority students, this may accent their culture and not just that of the majority language. To help construct meaning, we need to know what kind of text it is. Is it a folk story or a real event?, Is it an advertisement that seeks to persuade, or a balanced report? It helps to know who has written the text, what is their background and beliefs.

Also, a reader's current knowledge, family background, social and economic lifestyle, and political orientation will all affect how the reader constructs meaning from the text. Different students of varying backgrounds will make **different inter-pretations** of the text. When there is a mismatch between the reader's knowledge and that which is assumed by the writer, the construction of meaning will be affected. This is the 'vicious circle' situation faced by many illiterate adults. They are denied access to certain kinds of knowledge and understanding of the world because they cannot read. Because they do not understand what is being taken for granted by writers of adult material, becoming literate as an adult is made difficult. Language minority groups, in particular, can be caught in this 'vicious circle' situa-tion. Trying to make sense out of texts from a different culture, with different cultural assumptions, makes predicting the storyline and understanding the text more difficult.

One role for teachers therefore is to **mediate** in the construction of meaning by learners who are becoming literate, helping them to construct meaning from text. A central idea in constructing meaning derives from the Russian psychologist, **Vygotsky** (1962). During the decade 1924–1934, he outlined the ways that teachers can intervene and arrange effective learning, by challenging and extending the child's current state of development. Meaning is constructed by the teacher moving from the present level of understanding of a child to a further level that is within the child's capability. This 'stretching' of the child is by locating the **zone of proximal development**. Vygotsky (1962) saw the zone of proximal development as the distance between a student's level of development as revealed when problem solving without adult help, and the level of potential development as determined by a student problem solving in collaboration with peers or teachers. The zone of proximal development is where new understandings are possible through collabo-rative interaction and inquiry.

To help children construct meaning from text, teachers need to be aware that literacy in classrooms exists in a **social context**, guided by culturally-bound ways of thinking. Bloome (1985) suggested that:

> 'when students are asked to read a story, they must do so in socially appropriate ways: silently or orally, individually, competitively, or co-operatively with other students, in a round-robin manner, etc. Students who read orally without error or who appropriately answer teacher questions may gain social status within the classroom. Students who read with error, give inappropriate answers, or who sit quietly, may be viewed as outcasts or non participants.' (p. 135)

In classrooms, students have to learn about the rules of behavior and expecta-tions for the different literacy events that teachers initiate. For example, there are do's and don't's, authoritative knowledge and culturally inappropriate responses.

The power relationships of the classroom (between student and teacher) shape language and literacy use. The social roles of students and teachers are taught and embedded in literacy events of the classroom. This theme of literacy and power relationships will be returned to when critical literacy is considered later.

Reading and writing occur in a particular context that considerably influences the process of learning to be literate. Reading and writing is often for someone or to someone. Even when reading silently to oneself there is an inner, reflective conversation where meaning is being created. The words that readers know, and the experience related to the words being read combine to form a context. This context allows students to guess the meaning of words they do not know and meanings that may be partly hidden.

The further reading and writing develops, the more text becomes socially and culturally embedded. The reading process within is shaped by the social forces from without. Dyson (1989) and Graves (1983) have shown how young writers develop and change through the influence of peers and teachers in school, as well as through experiences outside school such as the local community, political movements and ideological forces (e.g. religion).

Similarly, writing is not just a technical process of putting words down on paper with correct spellings and correct grammatical structure. Writing is **sharing meaning**. When students and adults write, they have an interpersonal purpose. They write in order to be read by an audience, to inform, persuade, influence or purely delight readers. In writing, there is an anticipation of a response or reaction from the audience. We write with some kind of understanding of the background, knowledge and culture of our readers. We use language in different ways to meet particular purposes. Newspaper editorials sometimes try to persuade. Cookery books try to inform and explain. Poets try to give deeper and fresh meanings. The effectiveness of writing depends on the writer being familiar with the conventions expected by readers. This all suggests that literacy is a social event and not a private, personal event. We often discuss our reading and writing with other people, making the social dimension of literacy even more prominent.

This leads to an argument that literacy is not just about information gathering and giving. It is also about developing thinking that is appropriate within a culture. Thus Wells and Chang-Wells (1992) conceive of literacy as 'a mode of thinking that deliberately makes use of language, whether spoken or written, as an instrument for its own development' (p. 123).

The Sociocultural Literacy Approach

A related and overlapping approach to the Construction of Meaning approach accents the **enculturation** aspect of literacy. For example, a language minority literacy program may be enthusiastic to ensure the child is fully socialized and enlightened in the heritage culture.

Sociocultural literacy is the ability to construct appropriate cultural meaning when reading. In theory, a person can be functionally literate but culturally illiterate (e.g. reading without meaning). In reading and writing, we bring not only previous experience, but also our values and beliefs enabling us to create meaning from what we read and insert understanding into what we write. A **cultural heritage** is discovered and internalized in reading. While reading and writing have certain observable, testable skills, beyond the skills of reading and writing is cultural literacy. For some people, such cultural literacy may lead to assimilation and integration (e.g. accepting the values and norms embedded in English language classics). Assimilationists may argue for a common literacy, transmitting the majority language culture to ensure assimilation of minority groups within the wider society.

An example of a majority assimilationist approach to cultural literacy is Hirsch's book (1988) *Cultural Literacy: What Every American Needs to Know*. In the Appendix to the book, Hirsch (1988) provides a list of 5000 items of what 'literate Americans know', or should know by the end of high school. The text box below lists the letter 'j' entries to provide a flavor of the 'desired cultural knowledge'. Such a list is intended as a 'reliable index of American literate culture' for 'effective national communication' and to 'insure domestic tranquility' (pp. xi and xii). Yet it mainly reflects male, North American, white, middle-class, Christian and classical culture. It is the culture of those in power and fails to represent adequately Latino, Asian or native Indian culture, for example.

Jack and Jill (rhyme), Jack and the Beanstalk (title), Jack be Nimble (text), Jack Frost, jack-of-all-trades – master of none, Andrew Jackson, Jesse Jackson, Stonewall Jackson, Jacksonian democracy, Jacksonville, Jack Sprat (text), Jacob and Esau, Jacobin, Jacob's Ladder (song,) Jakarta, Jamaica, Henry James, Jesse James, William James, Jamestown settlement, Janus, jargon, Jason and the Golden Fleece, Java, jazz, Thomas Jefferson, Jehovah, Jehovah's Witnesses, Dr. Jekyll and Mr. Hyde (title), je ne sais quoi, Jeremiah, Battle of Jericho, Jersey City, Jerusalem, Jesuits, Jesus Christ, jet stream, Jew, Jezebel, jihad, Jim Crow, jingoism, Joan of Arc, The Book of Job, Johannesburg, Gospel according to Saint John, John Birch Society, John Brown's Body (song), John Bull, John Doe, John Henry (song), Pope John Paul II, Andrew Johnson, Lyndon B. Johnson, Samuel Johnson, John the Baptist, Pope John XXIII, joie de vivre, Joint Chiefs of Staff, joint resolution, Jolly Roger, Jonah and the whale, John Paul Jones, Scott Joplin, Jordan, River Jordan, Joseph and his brothers, Chief Joseph, Saint Joseph, Joshua, Joshua Fit the Battle of Jericho (song,) journeyman, James Joyce, Judaism, Judas Iscariot, Judge not that ye be not judged, Judgment Day, Judgment of Paris, judicial branch, judicial review, Julius Caesar (title), Carl Jung, Juno (Hera), junta, Jupiter (planet), Jupiter (Zeus), justification by faith, justify the ways of God to men, juvenilia.

Adapted from Hirsch (1988, pp. 180–182)

In contrast, a cultural pluralist viewpoint will argue that national unity is not sacrificed by cultural literacy in the minority language or by multicultural literacy. Multicultural literacy is likely to give a wider view of the world, more windows on the world, a more colorful view of human history and custom, and a less narrow view of science and society.

Discussion of the **social and cultural context of literacy** raises the importance of **literacy in the mother tongue**. While the educational feasibility of this is discussed later, for the moment the educational argument is that literacy is most easily and most effectively learnt in the home language. The cultural argument is that mother tongue literacy gives access to the wealth of local and ethnic heritage contained in the literature. However, mother tongue literacy, while often culturally advantageous, is sometimes not without practical problems nor protests. Some native languages lack a grammar or an alphabet, have few educational materials for teaching purposes, plus a shortage of appropriate teachers and teacher training. Political objections include native language literacy being an impediment to national unity and immigrant assimilation, and the cost of maintaining a variety of indigenous and 'immigrant' languages in a region.

Where there is much variety of language cultures within a region, support for local literacies may be found. Street (1984, 1994) regards **local literacies** as literacy practices identified with local and regional cultures (as different from national culture). Such local literacies may be forgotten by international and national literacy campaigns (Hornberger, 1994) or there may be tensions between local and national/international literacy practice (Street, 1994). Local literacies (for examples, see Street, 1994), avoid the impoverishment of uniformity in literacy that is created by the dominance of English, for example. They make literacy relevant to people's lives, their local culture and community relationships.

The social and cultural context of literacy importantly includes the relationship between an **ethnic community** and literacy acquisition. What counts as reading differs between cultures, sub-cultures and ethnic groups. As Gregory (1993, 1994, 1996) demonstrates in studies of UK Asian and Chinese families, the purposes of reading, the resources provided by the home and the process of parents helping their children to read may differ from the purposes, resources and processes for literacy in the school. The school teaches reading for recreation and enjoyment; the family wants literacy for utilitarian purposes (e.g. avoiding unemployment and poverty, for trading and business transactions). The school literacy policy aims for a child-centered, individualized approach, with teacher as facilitator, partner and guide, allowing a wide choice of colorful attractive books. An ethnic group may, in contrast, provide literacy classes in Saturday schools, at the mosque or temple, sometimes with large numbers being tutored in the same class. In such out-of-school classes, the teacher may act as an authority and director. Learning the will of Allah, for example, may be the valued outcome. A treasured *Bible*, the *Qur'an* or other holy or highly valued book may be the focus of reading. At its best, the biliterate child becomes to appreciate and understand different cultures, differing traditions and viewpoints, leading to greater cultural sensitivity and inter-group tolerance.

Gregory (1993, 1994, 1996) further compares the style of literacy teaching in the home and school. In the schools she researched, the child is socialized gently into the 'literary club' via 'playing' with books in a relaxed atmosphere with little correction of mistakes. In ethnic Saturday schools, for example, children learn by rote, repeating letters, syllables and phrases until perfect. There is continuous practice, testing and correction of mistakes in a fairly strict and disciplined regime. Children may be given books only after they have proved their reading skills are worthy of such esteemed treasures. 'To have immediate access to books devalues both the book and the principle of hard work. Children must work their way towards knowledge slowly and the book is a reward for a child's conscious achievements. A love of books, therefore, comes after reading is learned and not as a necessary prerequisite for it' (Gregory, 1993, p. 57).

The **difference between school and ethnic group** literacy expectations and practices may be challenging for the child. The child is exposed to two literacy worlds, two versions of appropriate literacy behavior. The school, in particular, has a responsibility to defuse any tension, create a fusion and a harmony between the differences, such that both approaches are respected, prized and celebrated. If this is achieved, the bilingual student becomes not just biliterate but more deeply bicultural, with an expanded vision of literacy practices.

Research from the USA from Shirley Brice Heath (1986) showed how Chinese–US families, for example, tend towards parent controlled conversations that closely mirror the type of language behavior expected in many traditional classrooms. The parents asked children factual questions, evaluated their language, gave verbal correction and elaboration. Thus a certain form of literacy behavior and literacy use was established. Chinese–US families saw their role as complementing that of the school in literacy. Such parents saw themselves as active agents in their children's literacy development.

In contrast, Mexican–US parents often expected the extended family to share some of the responsibility for child-rearing. Such parents seldom expected conversations with their children while the parents were working. They relatively rarely asked questions of the children to assess their knowledge, understanding or attitudes. Older children within such families were expected to entertain the younger children. Younger children rarely interacted with just one adult, often being surrounded by a larger number of adults and children. However, young children grew up in a rich language environment, and although little conversation was directed specifically to them, they experienced the constant flow of language between adults, and between adults and other children. Children were taught to be respectful of adults, and typically not to initiate social conversations with adults. This cultural behavior is directly related to literacy expectations and uses. That is, literacy is not a separate cultural event, but mirrors in its form and function general **socialization** practices.

This concept of literacy tends to vary from the **expectations of school language** use in traditional classrooms. In such classrooms, it is not expected that children should interact only with other children. Much pupil–teacher interaction may be expected. Thus a difference may occur between patterns of language and literacy in the home and that expected in schools. For particular cultural and ethnic groups, this may make school a relatively more challenging and strange experience. The transition from the language and literacy of home to school may be more difficult for some language communities than for others. The school has the responsibility to effect harmonization, transition or preferably celebration of different literacy practices.

Heath (1986) identifies six genres of language use that are typically important for success in school.

(1) Adults engage in language activities with children that require children to label items, or adults frequently give the names of objects and ideas.

(2) Adults interpret what children have been saying, ask for explanations of what the child means or intends, and interpret classroom behavior.

(3) Children are expected to re-tell experiences or provide information that is known to adults. The listener may question the child so as to structure and 'scaffold' that information in particular ways.

(4) Children are expected to give performances to adults and their peers. The performance involves providing information or experiences that are new to the listener, or providing new interpretations of information that the listener already knows.

(5) Children provide a running narrative of events that are currently taking place or forecast what will occur in the future.

(6) Children recount stories that are familiar to them, that involve their imagination, some animation and a sequence of events towards a goal.

Heath (1986) refers to these six events as: label quests, meaning quests, recounts, accounts, event casts and stories.

While most of these patterns occur in the homes of children from all social classes and all ethnolinguistic groups, there are **differences between homes** in the frequency with which these dimensions occur. The effect is that children come to school with different degrees of familiarity with literacy linked behaviors.

In Shirley Brice Heath's (1982) research, certain pre-school children gained experience of books with their parents in a manner which paralleled that of interaction with teachers in elementary schools. The initiation–reply–evaluation sequence so often used by teachers was used by this particular group of parents. Such children were therefore prepared for the literacy culture of teachers in classrooms. Such children had also learnt to build book knowledge onto their own experience of the world and use it to structure and express that experience. Such children had implicitly learnt that literacy provides new dimensions of experience.

Such 'school-prepared' children had also been taught by their parents to 'listen and wait'. They had grown accustomed to listening to adults reading stories and waiting until the end before asking questions. Thus such children became used to using books in a way that they would experience for most of their schooling.

Shirley Brice Heath (1982, 1983) also described **communities** in the USA who had **different literacy practices**, important in themselves, but which did not match school-oriented literacy practices. Roadville children were members of working class, Christian parents who used literacy for Biblical and moral instruction. Fictional writing was rejected in favor of reading about real events that contained a moral message. The reading of a book in this community was a performance, rather than an interactive event. Books were used to inform and instruct a passive audience. 'Roadville adults do not extend either the context or the habits of literacy events beyond book reading. They do not, upon seeing an item or event in the real world, remind children of a similar event in a book and launch a running commentary on similarities and differences' (Heath, 1982, p. 61).

Thus Roadville children regarded a story as a real event containing accurate facts and as a lesson about being a good Christian. Fictional accounts of real events were regarded as lying. Reality and the truth were needed, not fiction. Thus Roadville children were socialized into a particular world view, a defined series of norms and beliefs, and specific beliefs about the uses (and 'to be avoided' uses) of literacy. Roadville children were encouraged and rewarded for telling stories that derived a moral message from real experience. While some may see such family training as failing to prepare the children for the literacy events of the school, another view is that the school fails to respond to the preferred literacy style of this type of community. A third view is that all children need to be exposed to the widest variety of 'cultures of literacy' and know what alternative uses exist for literacy.

Shirley Brice Heath (1982) concludes that literacy practices can only be understood and interpreted 'in relation to the larger sociocultural patterns which they may exemplify or reflect. For example, ethnography must describe literacy events in their sociocultural context, so we may come to understand how such patterns as time and space usage, care giving roles, and age and sex segregation are interdependent with the types and features of literacy events a community develops' (p. 74).

The Critical Literacy Approach

Literacy can work to **maintain the status quo**, to ensure that those with power and dominance in society influence, even control what the masses read and think. Propaganda, political pamphlets and newspapers and books can all be used to attempt to control the thinking and minds of the masses. Literacy can be conceived as an attempt through schooling and other formal and informal means of education to produce **hegemony** in society. Thus, those in power maintain control over those who could be subversive to social order, or democratically challenge their power base. Literacy can be used to instill certain preferred attitudes, beliefs and thoughts. Similarly, some religious traditions have deliberately used literacy to ensure that their members were, at the least, influenced by writings, at the worst, brainwashed. Careful selection by religious leaders and parents over what their children read, is an attempt to use literacy to control and contain the mind.

Graff (1979) has shown that in 19th century Canada, literacy was used for normative, **controlling purposes**. Illiterates were conceived as dangerous to the social stability, as alien to the dominant culture, representing a threat to the established order. Thus, an effort to increase literacy was a political move to maintain and further the position of the ruling elite. Since the elite realized that literacy could also lead to radical beliefs and ideas antagonistic to those in power, the teaching of literacy was carefully controlled.

Graff (1979) also attempted to show that literacy did not necessarily improve a person's chances of acquiring employment, wealth or power. Certain ethnic groups were disadvantaged, whatever their literacy rates, while others disproportionately obtained employment despite their relatively high illiteracy rates. For example, Irish Catholics in Canada did badly irrespective of being literate or illiterate. In comparison, English Protestants fared relatively better. Similarly, literate black people did relatively less well than other literate people. Whether literacy was an advantage or disadvantage depended on ethnicity. Being unemployed or in the worst paid jobs was a function more of ethnic background than of illiteracy.

Research also indicates that literacy tests used by companies when recruiting and selecting new staff are often unrelated to the literacy skills needed for doing the job (Street, 1995). Rather such tests have the effect of excluding certain ethnic and sociocultural groups. At a more macro level, this scenario relates to some governments blaming illiteracy in their country for high unemployment. This blames the victim and shifts the spotlight away from a lack of jobs to the unemployed's illiteracy (Street, 1995).

The style of literacy education that aims to control and contain tends to put **emphasis on reading skills** rather than comprehension, on being able to say the words and copy them down from a blackboard, with less emphasis on meaning and understanding. Students are not allowed to ask questions. Rather they are expected to read aloud large chunks of text that are subsequently corrected for pronunciation, stress and fluency.

Those with power and dominance in society also maintain their position by their view of what is '**correct language**'. Ethnic minorities with little political and economic power are often taught that their very patterns of speech and writing are inferior and deficient, and such language varieties are connected with their economic social and cultural deprivation. Such groups are expected to adopt standard majority language use (e.g. to speak 'proper' or 'correct' English).

This restricted form of literacy is still present in many schools in all continents of the world. The functional view of literacy, as evidenced in the UNESCO definition given earlier, often involves a kind of restricted literacy that, at its worst, can maintain oppression, a distance between elites and the subservient, and not focus on the empowering and 'critical consciousness' possibilities of literacy. This suggests that literacy education always has ideological roots (Street, 1984). Literacy can be used to maintain the status quo, a stable political structure, to avert subversion or activism among the masses. National literacy may promote integration of the masses and different ethnic groups. National literacy may attempt to promote unification and standardization of both language and culture.

In colonization and 'missionary' movements, a different kind of cultural standardization was sometimes attempted. For example, when literacy was brought by the missionaries to non-Christian areas of the world in the 19th century, the aim was to spread the Christian gospel, control the thinking, and influence the moral behavior of those who were assumed to be primitive and heathen. In literacy projects in developing countries in the 20th century, literacy has often been promoted for economic development. A literate work force has been considered essential for economic growth. Yet such programs were also used, consciously or subconsciously, to shore up the **established order** in a social system founded on injustice and inequality. Literacy in such programs has sometimes been used to condition the masses, to consolidate existing divisions of labor.

Literacy can be a tool of oppression; it can also be a **liberator** (Hornberger, 1994). It can be bar to opportunity; or a means of opening a door to empowerment. One way of attempting to **empower** people is through critical literacy. **Freire** (1970, 1973, 1985) and Freire and Macedo (1987) have argued for a literacy that makes oppressed communities socially and politically conscious about their subservient role and lowly status in society. The argument is that literacy must go well beyond the skills of reading and writing. It must make people aware of their sociocultural context and their political environment. This may occur through mother tongue literacy, multilingual literacy (and local/national/international **'multiple' literacies** of value in differing contexts) and local literacies (Street, 1984, 1995).

For language minority speakers, literacy for empowerment can be about stimulating language activism, the demand for language rights, self-determination and an equitable share of power. Freire's literacy education in Brazil's peasant communities and with other oppressed groups around the world assumes that when people become conscious about their subordinate role and inferior position in their community and society, they then become empowered to change their own lives, situations and communities.

Through literacy, one can understand political power and activity, which leads to collectively working together to change society, operating appropriately, being able to challenge and complain, to assert natural rights, and to demand equality of access, opportunity and treatment. Through **critical reflection** on texts, information and propaganda, minority language members can have a growing consciousness, an influence over their own lives and the institutions which serve them, and strive for more equality in society.

Freire (1970, 1973, 1985) argued that people acquiring literacy already have an understanding of their own social realities, enabling them to analyze the historical and social conditions which gave rise to their particular status, position and low power-base in society. Literacy instruction can draw on that understanding and make it conscious and explicit. Thus literacy teaching can become a direct political challenge to the hegemony of ruling capitalist states. Many adult literacy programs have been influenced by this 'critical literacy' ideology (Street, 1984).

In radical adult literacy programs, students create their own learning material rather than passively reading information and books that propagate a centralist, dominant perspective. Through creating their own books, (and the binding and distributing of them — for example poetry books), what it is to be literate is radically changed. Rather than reading becoming a passive exercise, literacy is seen as a production of ideas that need to be spread into the community. Students who had previously believed themselves to be failures in learning to read and write may come to recognize that it was the system that had failed them. Their illiteracy is then seen not as a personal problem but as a condition imposed or allowed by those in power.

Such a radical viewpoint about literacy needs to be seen in contrast to the 'whole language' approach in literacy development. Delpit (1988) argues that books within the whole language approach can be an uncritical celebration of stories and a transmission of accepted information. As such, the whole language movement may neglect issues of **power and social justice**, and maintain the status quo. What alternative is posed by the critical literacy movement?

At school level, the critical literacy approach is that learners should not just be invited to retell a story. They should be encouraged to offer their **own interpretation of text**. From the beginning, children should be encouraged to interpret and evaluate: Who is the writer? What is their perspective and bias? What kind of moral interpretation is made? What alternative interpretations and viewpoints are possible? Children will be encouraged not just to find the right answer to such questions, but to look critically at multiple viewpoints. Multicultural and multilingual children may be given diverse pieces of writing that reflect different cultural knowledge and attitudes. Differences in interpretation, and differences in experience and knowledge children bring to the text can be contrasted and compared.

This involves a change in traditional teacher and student roles in the classroom. Teachers become **facilitators** rather than transmitters of authoritative knowledge. Literacy development becomes a joint developmental and cooperative event between student and teacher rather than duplicating the dominant–subservient relationship that often occurs in classrooms and which mirrors political domination and subservience.

For example, rather than children being solely taught that Columbus discovered America and that Columbus was a hero whose arrival brought civilization and salvation to the indigenous population, teachers may invite students to search out other views about Columbus. Having read that Columbus initiated the slave trade, cut off the hands of any indigenous people who failed to bring him gold, and that the indigenous population suffered when Spanish rule was established, students might be asked to write their own critical versions of not only the life and contribution of Columbus, but also the way that Columbus is treated in many historical texts. Students would be encouraged by guided discovery methods to find that historical facts about Columbus have been selectively treated and interpreted by historians. More than one viewpoint is possible. One single viewpoint is both dangerous and biased, even if it is politically desired and comfortable.

Alma Flor Ada (1988a, 1988b) presents a critical literacy approach for classrooms based on Paulo Freire's work. She distinguishes four phases in the creative reading act.

The Descriptive Phase

In the descriptive phase, teachers will ask questions about text such as: What happened in a story? Who did what and why? This kind of phase exists in many classrooms, but in critical literacy, it must be extended beyond this stage. If reading stays at this phase, it tends to be passive, receptive and domesticating.

The Personal Interpretive Phase

Children will be asked if they have ever seen or experienced something like that portrayed in the story. What did you feel when you read the story? Did you like it? What kinds of emotion did you have? Does your family and community have similar experiences or stories? Ada points out that this process of personalization of stories may raise children's self-esteem. They are made to feel that their experiences and feelings are valued by the teacher and other students. It also enables children to learn that 'true learning occurs only when the information received is analyzed in the light of one's own experiences and emotions' (Ada, 1988a, p. 104).

The Critical Analysis Phase

The text is used to bring out broader social issues and generalizations. Students are asked, Is the text valid? What kind of experience or person is promoted by the story? Are there other ways in which the story could have been constructed? How and why would people of different cultures, social classes and gender have acted differently in the story? Students are invited to analyze, reflect and expand on the experiences of the story. Social implications are engaged and analyzed.

Creative Action Phase

Students are then challenged as to how their learning can be used to improve their lives or resolve issues and problems they face. Here the critical approach is transformed into constructive action. For example, students may decide to write letters to political figures, to those in their locality who have power, status and authority, or create a poster to try to persuade friends and neighbors. Students may compile a class newsletter or booklet that is given to other students in their school, or other schools, to sensitize people to the issues. They may write and circulate a petition in their neighborhood, write a play, or create poetry that tries to both analyze, and inform others, leading ultimately to empowerment and raised consciousness among language minorities.

Overview

Finally, in this consideration of critical literacy, it is valuable to contrast in more depth two relatively opposite approaches to highlight the classroom style of a critical literacy approach. The functional and critical approaches will now be compared for their representation in the classroom and the different ideology of each approach.

The functional view of literacy compared with the critical view of literacy is paralleled by two stereotypes of **literacy classrooms**. In one style, there is a lot of teacher talk, much student listening, closed and factual questions rather than open and stimulating questions, with silence and control very evident. The hidden curriculum is that teachers are implicitly teaching dependence upon authority, correct and convergent thinking, social control, passive involvement, neutral thinking and passive learning. Knowledge is posed as static, correct and inert, to be internalized and reproduced when necessary.

The critical literacy concept is that children should learn to search out different authorities often with differing viewpoints, ask questions and be willing to wonder, to depend on their own judgment, to think divergently and creatively, to work cooperatively and sociably, to avoid accepting knowledge and to question its source and motive, to analyze assumptions and biases, to consider multiple interpretations, tolerate uncertainty, to be actively involved in learning, and, if necessary, to be critical of social, economic and political issues in their own and their community's lives (Cummins, 2000b). Knowledge is seen as dynamic, ever changing, always relative, a catalyst for further inquiry and a catalyst for action. Cummins (1994) sums this up as follows:

- **In a Transmission Style**: Language is decomposed; knowledge is inert; learning is hierarchical, by internalization, moving from the simple to the complex. This may be connected to a **social control orientation** where curriculum topics are neutralized in respect to societal power relations and students are expected to be compliant and uncritical.
- **In a Critical Approach**: Language is meaningful; knowledge is catalytic, and there is a joint interactive construction of knowledge through critical enquiry within a student's zone of proximal development. This may be connected to a **social transformation orientation** where curriculum topics are focused on issues of relevant power relationships and students are enabled to become critical and empowered (Cummins, 2000b).

The literacy that is developed in classrooms varies considerably in reality and escapes neat classification into transmission and critical literacy orientations. However, the stereotyped positing of two opposites, while simple and sometimes extreme, reflects a key debate in literacy development in language minority children. The following table lists some of the practical characteristics of the transmission and critical classrooms.

CONCLUSION

This chapter has revealed that literacy in bilingual and multicultural societies is neither a simple nor a straightforward concept. While reading and writing initially seem easily understandable events, the different uses and definitions of literacy immediately spotlight complexity and controversy. The five different approaches to literacy discussed in this chapter highlight variations and contrasts to literacy education. Each approach has different expectations about bilingual children that pervade literacy policies, curriculum provision and classroom practices. One recent contrast is literacy in a majority language (e.g. English) with an accent on local, regional literacies perhaps leading to 'multiple literacies' with different uses of literacy in different contexts.

Schools are a powerful provider of literacy and help dictate what counts as proper language, correct ideas and appropriate knowledge to be transmitted though literacy practices. Superior forms of literacy, and the kinds of literacy required for success in education are school transmitted; other literacies are typically devalued (except religious literacies). Therefore, the self-esteem and identity of language minority children may be affected by which literacies are legitimated by the school, and which are ignored or despised.

One expectation of education is that children acquire literacy skills so they can function as 'good citizens' in a stable society. A contrasting expectation is that children should become empowered, even politically activated by becoming literate. Language minority children should be able to read, for example, to understand propaganda, and write to defend their community's interests or protest about injustice, discrimination and racism. They need to read the world and not just the word (Freire & Macedo, 1987). A different view is that reading and writing are for sheer pleasure and enjoyment, to celebrate, create and self-cultivate. Biliteracy may be particularly valuable for both empowerment and enjoyment approaches.

Functional Literacy/Transmission Classrooms

(1)   Literacy is getting the correct answers on worksheets, filling in blanks, circling appropriate answers.
(2)   Literacy is answering closed questions having read a story.
(3)   Literacy is reading words, sometimes without understanding their meaning.
(4)   Literacy is reading aloud to the teacher and the rest of the class, being perfect in pronunciation, intonation and accent.
(5)   Literacy is spelling words correctly, and writing in correct grammar.
(6)   Literacy is mechanically going through exercises, practicing skills, and giving correct answers on tests.
(7)   Literacy is learning to do but not necessarily to think.

Critical Literacy Classrooms

(1)   Literacy is seeing oneself as an active reader and writer.
(2)   Literacy involves enjoying reading, developing independent thoughts and judgments about reading and writing.
(3)   Literacy is sharing ideas, reflections, experiences and reactions with others in the classroom, both peers and teachers.
(4)   Literacy is gaining insights into oneself, one's life in the family and the community, into social and political control, the use of print and other mass media to inform, persuade and influence so as to maintain the status quo.
(5)   Literacy is about understanding the power relationships that lie behind reading and writing.
(6)   Literacy is about constructing and reconstructing meaning, critically examining the range of meanings in the story and outside the story.
(7)   Literacy is active writing for various purposes and audiences, often to influence and assert.
(8)   Literacy is about developing consciousness, increased self-reflection, increased reflection about status, power, wealth and privilege in society.
(9)   Literacy is about developing critical thinking habits, creative imagination, and posing alternatives, some of which may be radical.
(10) Literacy is about learning and interpreting the world, explaining, analyzing, arguing about and acting upon the world in which a person lives.

The importance of the five approaches lies in their varying proposals for the role, status and self-enhancement of bilingual children and adults. Does literacy produce cogs who aid the smooth running of a well oiled system? Does literacy produce students who are activated into asserting their rights to equality of power, purse and opportunity? A fundamental issue of literacy and biliteracy is thus political. When clarity is achieved in defining the intended uses of literacy for bilingual students, educational considerations such as approaches, methods and strategies become more rational.

KEY POINTS IN THE CHAPTER

- Literacy has many uses in bilingual, multicultural societies: for learning, citizenship, pleasure and employment for example.
- Cultures, sub-cultures and localities differ in their uses of literacy (e.g. religious groups, transmission of heritage values and beliefs).
- Five approaches to literacy comprise: the skills approach (functional literacy), the whole language approach, construction of meaning, sociocultural literacy and critical literacy.
- A transmission style to classroom literacy is contrasted to a critical approach where issues of power, status, equity and justice are addressed through a language minority perspective.

SUGGESTED FURTHER READING

CUMMINS, J., 2000, *Language, Power and Pedagogy: Bilingual Children in the Crossfire.* Clevedon: Multilingual Matters.
GARCÍA, O. and BAKER, C. (eds), 1995, *Policy and Practice in Bilingual Education: A Reader Extending the Foundations.* Clevedon: Multilingual Matters. (Section 3).
HEATH, S.B., 1983, *Ways with Words: Language, Life and Work in Communities and Classrooms.* Cambridge: Cambridge University Press.
HORNBERGER, N.H., 1994, Literacy and language planning. *Language and Education* 8 (1 & 2), 75–86.
WELLS, G. and CHANG-WELLS, G.L., 1992, *Constructing Knowledge Together: Classrooms as Centers of Inquiry and Literacy.* Portsmouth, NH: Heinemann.
WILEY, T.G., 1996, *Literacy and Language Diversity in the United States.* Center for Applied Linguistics and Delts Systems, McHenry, Illinois.
WHITMORE, K.F. and CROWELL, C.C., 1994, *Inventing a Classroom. Life in a Bilingual Whole Language Community.* York, ME: Stenhouse.

STUDY ACTIVITIES

(1) Observe two classrooms with different literacy programs for language minority children. How do the classrooms differ? What are the different beliefs and assumptions about literacy in the two classrooms?

(2) Design a short program to illustrate how critical literacy could be introduced to language minority students in Grades 5, 6 or 7.

CHAPTER 16

Literacy and Biliteracy in the Classroom

Introduction

**Classroom Processes Towards Literacy
in Bilingual and Multicultural Schools**
Literacy Strategies
Grouping and Assessment
Resources

Home and School Relationships

Biliteracy
The Development of Biliteracy

Conclusion

CHAPTER 16

Literacy and Biliteracy in the Classroom

INTRODUCTION

This chapter initially focuses on the more practical aspects of literacy and biliteracy in bilingual and multicultural schools. Teachers often adopt a varied and eclectic approach to literacy with bilinguals. Hence different classroom strategies are examined. A strategic approach by a teacher includes decisions about the grouping of children, resources to aid literacy development and importantly the key nature of home and school relationships. The second part of the chapter examines biliteracy and strategies that promote biliteracy in the classroom.

CLASSROOM PROCESSES TOWARDS LITERACY IN BILINGUAL AND MULTICULTURAL SCHOOLS

Many teachers use a broad, comprehensive and inclusive approach to literacy development. They do not solely focus on functional literacy nor on critical literacy, but attempt to develop the different kinds of literacy that were examined in the preceding chapter. Many teachers try to facilitate a **varied** use of reading and writing in their children, to develop independent readers and writers who are both skilled in language usage (this includes spelling and grammar) and who can also write creatively, critically, imaginatively, reflectively and for enjoyment. The multiple purposes of reading and writing are encouraged in many classrooms.

Literacy Strategies

In discussing strategies for second language literacy development, Hudelson (1994) lists various dimensions that are important. These will be considered under three headings: general, reading and writing. However, these should be seen as an integrated whole, not as separate.

General

(1) **Create a literate classroom environment**. Hudelson (1994) argues for a print-rich environment in the classroom to demonstrate the multiple functions of literacy. In the classroom, there could be charts, a content study area, attendance lists, menus, calendars, words of favorite songs, a classroom library containing books of varied genres and reading levels, information books to cover science, social studies and all other areas of the curriculum, a reading corner with comfortable chairs or pillows, a writing center or area containing a variety of sizes of paper and writing implements, and a display of children's original writing and published works. In all, an environment is needed where print is seen as varied, valuable and containing great vitality.

(2) **Encourage collaborative and cooperative learning**. Hudelson (1994) suggests that teachers should encourage children to learn with, and from, each other as well as to learn from the teacher. Children need to see each other as resources with a classroom as a workshop where learners work cooperatively together and independently on projects. Children need to be able to work on literacy events independently and interdependently, with the teacher attending to small groups and individuals to provide attention where it is needed.

(3) **Include literacy development as part of the content of other areas of the curriculum**. Literacy is achievable throughout the curriculum and through inter-disciplinary project work. For example, engaging one of the key crucial issues of the day may lend a critical perspective to literacy development. The study of racism, prejudice and supremacist attitudes may be undertaken in the critical literacy tradition. The aim is to make people more aware, more responsible and active citizens. Hudelson (1994) lists exemplar issues such as air pollution, water use, the destruction of the deserts, and the destruction of forests as typical areas for critical study. Such projects make learners active participants in their own literacy development, integrate oral with reading and writing development, promote interaction with others as central to literacy development, allow risk taking and initiative, requiring topics that are linguistically stimulating, intellectually challenging, rigorous and demanding so as to enable full literacy development.

Reading

(4) **Utilize predictable books**. One example of such books are the Big Books which contain relatively predictable stories in enlarged text that enable a larger group of children to read the text and see the pictures with the teacher. Hudelson (1994) provides an illustration of the way Big Books may be used with second language children to encourage literacy development, particularly focusing on the construction of meaning. Not necessarily in the sequence given below, teachers may use the following strategies with Big Books:

  A.   The teacher reads the Big Book to the child once or twice.

B.   The teacher may read the story to the child moving her hand to show the movement of the text.

C.   The children will be encouraged to read along as they see the words and hear the teacher pronounce the words.

D.   A teacher may stop at a predictable part of the story, close the book and ask the children what occurs next in the story. This focuses on the meaning of the story and encourages children to think of as many words as they can to make sense of the context of the overall story.

E.   The teacher may cover certain words or phrases in the text and ask children to guess what comes next. This prediction of missing words is important as 'good' readers tend to be good guessers when they cannot read a word.

F.   Teachers may cover up part of a word so that learners concentrate on partial clues within a word to guess what that word is, and then uncover its meaning.

G.   The teacher may focus the learner's attention on features of the text such as full stops, capital letters, other punctuation marks and particular groupings of letters (e.g. 'spr' as a consonantal blend).

(5) **Read aloud to children daily**. Children need experience of listening to fluent models of language production. Also reading aloud to children daily shares the literary heritage of varied cultures and simultaneously teaches that literature is one important way of understanding the world and making sense of everyday experience.

(6) **Organize responses of children to the literature they read**. Hudelson (1994) argues that children need time to respond to what they read, 'to construct meaning, to relate a story to their own lives, to comment on emotions and ideas that a piece has evoked' (p. 147). Such an activity recognizes that learners bring prior experiences with them to the books that they read and that they use those experiences to understand the meaning and to generalize from text. Such an activity teaches that learning is social and that reading is not a purely individual event but can be shared with others to engage multiple interpretations and varied meanings.

(7) **Include opportunities for self-selected reading**. Children need time to select their own reading material for pure enjoyment so as to learn that reading is not only a classroom and formal structured activity, but has value in itself. Thus access to a variety of interesting and stimulating books in both languages should be made available.

Writing

(8) **Utilize written personal narratives**. Learners and teachers can share their own personal stories, own experiences, own cultural events and their own constructs of the world. We all have stories we want to share which enable others to understand and appreciate us more, to come to terms with differences between students as well as similarities. It is valuable for students to

write stories on real events in their lives, with drafting, small and large group conferences to enable cooperation and participation, further editing with the help of the group and the teacher to produce a polished final document, and where the process is as important as the product. Children will learn to take into account others' understandings of their experiences, and different meanings that need to be accommodated in understanding an issue. Children will also learn that they have to write for an audience, so that the audience understands the text and not to produce a purely egocentric piece.

(9) **Utilize dialogic writing**. The use of dialogue journals is now customary in many classrooms. Teachers and learners have written conversations with each other, often focusing on personal matters. No correction of the learner's language is necessarily made, except that, when reading the teacher's response, the child will see a model of appropriate writing. Such a dialogue journal can also work between pairs of children. One child may be more fluent, the other child being lower down the developmental scale. Finding authentic reasons for writing a journal and carrying out a genuine dialogue will be essential to maintain interest and motivation.

(10) **Successful classrooms engage a variety of different purposes for writing**. Children may be asked to write to persuade, inform, query and question, to establish contact in relationships with other people, to express individuality and personal experience, to explore, to clarify and organize thinking, to reflect and raise consciousness, to exercise the imagination, to communicate information, to evaluate and appraise, to entertain, to provide a record of events, to give recipes and lists, to be poetic and humorous. As Willig (1990, p. 25) states:

> 'Writing is a key element in the search for meaning because it allows us to reflect on and to order our encounters with the world and the impact they make upon us. Equally important, we write to share thoughts and feelings with others through communications ranging from hastily written notes to formal, carefully argued essays on complex issues'.

Further Views about Writing

Smith (1982) argues that writing can be an extension and reflection of efforts to develop and express ourselves in the world around us, to make sense of the world and to impose order upon it. Writing can **communicate** with large numbers of people over an extended period of time. It can be **retrieved** by the author and the audience long after the message was created and can allow communication to take place without the presence of an audience.

For Wells and Chang-Wells (1992), the most important form of writing is when text is treated, not as a final representation of meaning that is given and self-evident, but as a tentative and provisional attempt to **capture current understanding**. This can provoke further attempts at understanding as the writer or some other reader interact with the text to interpret and reinterpret its meaning. Novels and philosophy, poetry and scientific reports, books about history and legal argument can all be engaged in this manner.

The writer and subsequent readers are constantly asking whether the text makes sense in relation to their own experience. In writing, one assesses what one knows already, what one needs to find out more about, what is unknown, what needs to be selected as relevant and pertinent, how to organize and express ideas in a form that is most appropriate for understanding by the intended audience. For Wells and Chang-Wells (1992), such a process in writing is **empowering**. It enables advances in intellectual, moral and affective understanding.

To be empowering, writing needs to be developed in a variety of types and uses. For example:

(1) **Instrumental uses in writing**. Writing for practical needs to manage and organize everyday life.
(2) **Social and interpersonal writing**. Writing to establish, build and maintain relationships with family, friends, neighbors and acquaintances far away.
(3) **Recreational writing**. Writing during leisure time for the pure enjoyment of being creative and imaginative.
(4) **Educational uses of writing**. Writing to educate oneself, writing essays and assignments to fulfill the requirements of courses in schools, colleges and universities.
(5) **Financial**. Writing to record numbers, often concerning money, salaries, expenditure and banking.
(6) **Environmental**. Writing for public consumption. Writing notices, posters and information that are to be read by members of the public.
(7) **Sending messages** when oral communication is not possible or when a written message (e.g. for legal purposes) is preferred.
(8) As an **aid to memory**. Writing down ideas, information and thoughts to preserve (for oneself and others) important information and ideas.
(9) **Autobiographical**. Writing a record of one's daily life as in self-reflective diaries so as to understand, order and organize oneself and one's experiences.
(10) **Creative**. Writing as a means of self-expression and imaginative contemplation.

Grouping and Assessment

A classroom approach using a broad and comprehensive strategy, may also use diverse grouping strategies in the development of literacy. Whole classwork, pair work, small group work, cooperative learning can all be used to good effect (Johnson, 1994). A diverse approach also means avoiding narrow standardized tests that purely reflect a skills approach to literacy (Edelsky, 1991). As Genesee and Hamayan (1994) argue, classroom based assessment needs to go much further than tests of inauthentic, decomposed language skills. Student portfolios, for example, are one important way that a teacher may gather information about the performance of their children in a classroom that may give a much fuller understanding of the strengths and weaknesses, and therefore the diagnostic attention needed to improve and develop a child's literacy.

Resources

As far as possible, the language resources of the classroom need to be **multilingual** partly to reflect the mother tongues of the children in the classroom, but also for the multilingual awareness of all children (Edwards, 1998). Sometimes it is difficult to find the quantity, quality and variety of reading materials in the mother tongues of children in bilingual classrooms. There are often problems importing books from other countries and problems in purchasing expensive books. Yet some schools do manage to collect excellent libraries of books in different languages (and multicultural books) via help from language communities, parents of children in the school and using minority language organizations who have contacts and a commitment to literacy development in children's mother tongues.

HOME AND SCHOOL RELATIONSHIPS

'**Parents as partners**' is as possible in the writing process as in reading. For example, parents may help compose books in their heritage language for use in the classroom. Children, teachers and parents may collaborate together to produce a multilingual book (e.g. starting school in different countries and cultures). Personal meaning, home and community culture, and classroom activity are joined in the promotion of biliteracy (Ada, 1995; Ada & Smith, 1998). As Hornberger (1990b) has shown, there can be different effective classroom strategies to make literacy tasks congruent with the community culture and values of the children. Use of first and second language texts, using students' community-based prior knowledge enables 'connect and transfer' to promote literacy and biliteracy.

A danger occurs when the school naively imposes its literacy practices on the home. With the best of intentions in promoting school-type reading practices in the home, the literacy practices of the school may be different from that of the home, as the research by Gregory (1993, 1994, 1996), considered in the preceding chapter, illustrates. Parents may be educated by the school about 'good reading habits' in their children, mirroring school literacy practices and school culture. This **assumes a deficit** in family literacy practices that may be unwarranted. As Auerbach (1989) has shown, marginalized language minority parents may be highly motivated towards literacy in their children. Literacy may be highly valued as a key to vocational and economic mobility. Plenty of books may be present in the home with plenty of encouragement and help given by parents within the traditions of their culture. Huss-Keeler (1997) found in research in the north of England that parents' interest in their child's literacy and helpfulness at home may be hidden to the teacher who sees non-attendance at parent–teacher meetings as indicative of parental disinterest.

Delgado-Gaitan (1990) argues that there is a great need for parents to become involved in their children's literacy development. She reports **three models of parental involvement** in children's education (see also Epstein's (1992) six types of partnership between family, community and school for a more elaborate typology).

The first, the **Family Influence Model** involves families attempting to provide the type of home learning environment most suited to cognitive and emotional development. Such parents believe that there is a body of information that children need to acquire for life skills. Teachers know this and teach it, and therefore parents need also to be partners in imparting such knowledge. Parents assume that there is a correct and right way to rear children (including literacy development) that can be learnt from books or child psychology experts, and that parents who apply this information will be successful as parents. Turning the situation round, the Family Influence Model also contains the idea of the school attempting to influence and change family life so that it fits the values and strategies of learning used by the school. The family is seen as a direct recipient of the school's influence, and the school–family collaboration establishes maximally effective environments for learning.

The **School Reform Model** operates where parents take more than an interest in the schooling of their children. Parents within this model try to change schools and make them more responsive to parents. Parents may place pressure on the schools to ensure that their values and standards are transmitted by the schools. Such parents know how to pressure and interact with schools, getting schools to change to be more responsive to student needs as perceived by parents. The assumption is that the school will accommodate parents' suggestions and influence. Such parents will attempt to become part of the power structure of the school by being on advisory committees, school governing committees or parent–teacher committees.

The **Cooperative Systems Model** moves one step further. Rather than collaboration as in the first model, and influence as in the second model, parents within the third model attempt to participate directly in school activities. For example parents may attend workshops in the school, help the teachers in the classroom, and become like paraprofessionals. Such parents see the home, school and community as interrelated and functioning as a whole. Parents play the roles of volunteer, paid employee, teacher at home, adult learner and helper.

Further explication of processes in teacher–parent relationships is given by Moll (1992). Luis Moll and his colleagues at the University of Arizona have used ethnographic studies of student communities to identify skills, knowledge, expertise and interests that Mexican **households** possess that can be used for the benefit of all in the classroom. For many language minority children and their families, the relationship between school and parents is limited and often non-existent. Moll shows how parents and other community members have much to give children in Latino classrooms. Such people can supplement the teacher, providing what Moll calls '**funds of knowledge**' that are 'cultural practices and bodies of knowledge and information that households use to survive, to get ahead or to thrive' (Moll, 1992, p. 21). Examples of funds of knowledge that could be used by schools include information about flowers, plants and trees, seeds, agriculture, water distribution and management, animal care and veterinary medicine, ranch economy, car and bike mechanics, carpentry, masonry, electrical wiring and appliances, fencing, folk remedies, herbal cures and natural medicines, midwifery, archaeology, biology and mathematics.

There are a variety of possible reasons for some parent–teacher relationships showing non-cooperation, a lack of understanding, a distance and even an antagonism between home and school cultures. Understanding such reasons helps explain why many language minority children fail in the system, have high drop-out rates and exhibit relatively low achievement.

Such language minority families may be socially and educationally isolated from the school. There is a knowledge gap between such families and the school that needs bridging (Pérez and Torres-Guzmán, 1996). If language minority parents are unable to speak the majority language of the teachers in the school, there may be an increased sense of helplessness and isolation. Such parents are reluctant or unable to discuss their children's progress with the teacher, unable or unwilling to go to parent–teacher meetings and other school events. While such parents may discuss problems about their children's schooling with one another, the issues and worries do not become resolved because there is a chasm between school and the home. Some parents may be intimidated by high status schools or feel that schools know best and should act unilaterally in dealing with their children.

In a case study of what can constructively be accomplished to empower such parents and resolve this problem, Delgado-Gaitan (1990) explains via an ethnographic study how parents were encouraged to organize themselves into a leadership group, and teach each other about how to communicate with schools. Through building awareness, followed by mobilization, motivation, and commitment, the attitudes and actions of a group of parents were changed. Over time, **parents** became convinced that they had the right, responsibility and power to deal with their children's academic and social concerns, and to foster strong relationships with the school for their children's greater achievement. Individual parents also began to realize that they had something to offer other parents, their children and the school. As parents became more involved, they felt more in control of their lives. They became empowered. 'Feelings of incompetence create isolation for parents. Those feelings must be replaced with a recognition of the ability to collaborate with others before active participation can occur' (Delgado-Gaitan, 1990, p. 158).

In this research study, the pre-school teacher included Mexican family activities in the classroom, and taught parents to be more conscious of their own interactions with their children. This teacher organized a parent committee that involved parents in decision-making activities in the kindergarten. She also incorporated the students' culture into the daily school curriculum. Therefore, she produced a culturally and educationally congruent education experience between the home and the school. Such a teacher became an important advocate of the power of parent–teacher cooperation.

Alma Flor Ada (1997) shows how classroom books are often 'foreign' to children, containing no similarities to their homes, communities and particularly to the lives they lead in minority language communities. She suggests effective ways that teachers can show acceptance and give status to children and their families, thus strengthening parent–child and parent–teacher interactions (Ada, 1995; Ada & Smith, 1998). For example, children may tape record interviews with their parents relating to the family experience (e.g. immigration, childhood memories, family names) and create family books, helping to break down communication barriers between school and home.

However, there are occasions when parents are a highly conservative, even a reactionary voice. For example, some parents may insist on skills achievement in the core curriculum. It is also important for conflicts between parents and teachers to be avoided, and cooperation sought for the benefit of the children. Teachers' professionalism and expertise need to be respected, as do parents' rights and interests in their children's socialization.

BILITERACY

In Chapters 3 and 4, we briefly discussed the importance of minority language literacy in the survival, reversal or enhancement of that language. At both the individual and the group level, minority language literacy gives that language increased functions and usage (and helps standardize that minority language). A minority language has a greater chance of survival when bureaucracy and books, newspapers and magazines, adverts and signposts are in that language. This may help to avoid the colonial situation where the majority language is used for all literacy purposes and the vernacular language is used purely for oral communication. Where oral communication is in the minority language and literacy is in the majority language, that minority language may have less chance of survival.

More positively, literacy in the minority language enables the attendant traditions and the culture to be accessed and reproduced. Reading literature in the minority language may be both for education and recreation, for instruction and for enjoyment. Whether literature is regarded as aiding moral teaching, of value as an art form, or as a form of vicarious experience, literacy is both an emancipator and an educator. As the UK Bullock Report (1975) stated:

> 'Literature brings the child into an encounter with language in its most complex and varied forms. Through these complexities are presented the thoughts, experiences, and feelings of people who exist outside and beyond the reader's awareness… It provides imaginative insights into what another person is feeling; it allows the contemplation of possible human experiences which the reader himself has not met.' (p. 125)

This quotation illustrates that literacy in the minority language is of value because it recreates the past in the present. It may both reinforce and extend the oral transmission of a minority culture. Minority language oracy without literacy can disempower the student. Literacy in the minority language not only provides a greater chance of survival at an individual and group level for that language. It also may encourage rootedness, self-esteem, the vision and world-view of one's heritage culture, self-identity and intellectual empathy.

Literacy enables access to language minority practices that help make sense of the world and hence affect the structure of human cognition (Wells, 1986). Biliteracy gives access to different and varied social and cultural worlds. Does this in turn lead to more diversified cognitive abilities, an increased ability to process and manipulate ideas and symbols? The research by Swain and Lapkin (1991a) points to first language literacy and then biliteracy as a strong source of cognitive and curriculum advantage for bilinguals.

The Development of Biliteracy

Given that literacy empowers, emancipates, enculturates, educates and can be an inherently enjoyable activity, there seems to be a strong argument for biliteracy. Pragmatically, most students from a minority language need to **function in the minority and majority language society**. This requires biliteracy rather than literacy only in the minority language.

In different minority language situations, the same question is often asked by parents and teachers. Is it better to be thoroughly literate in one language rather than attempt to be literate (or semi-literate) in two languages? Does literacy in one language interfere with becoming literate in a second language? Questions typically tend to be phrased in this negative way. The positive questions must also be asked. Does literacy in one language aid rather than impede literacy in a second language? Do the skills learnt in reading and writing one language transfer to reading and writing in a second language?

From **reviews** (Hornberger, 1989; Williams & Snipper, 1990; Krashen, 1996; McKay *et al.*, 1997; Edwards, 1998) and **research** (e.g. Lanauze & Snow, 1989; Torres, 1991; Hornberger, 1990b; Calero-Breckheimer & Goetz, 1993; Pérez & Torres-Guzmán, 1996), the evidence tends to reflect the positive rather than the negative questions.

Research has suggested that academic and linguistic skills in a minority language **transfer** relatively easily to the second language. Simply stated, a child who learns to read in Spanish at home or in school, does not have to start from the beginning when learning to read in English. Both in learning to read and in learning to write, 'language skills acquired in a first language can, at least if developed beyond a certain point in L1, be recruited at relatively early stages of L2 acquisition for relatively skilled performance in L2, thus shortcutting the normal developmental progression in L2' (Lanauze & Snow, 1989, p. 337).

When biliteracy is encouraged in minority language children, literacy skills and strategies from the first language appear to **transfer** to the second language (if using a similar writing system). While the vocabulary, grammar and orthography may be different, generalizable skills in decoding and reading strategies may easily transfer from first language literacy to second language literacy. Concepts and strategies (e.g. scanning, skimming, contextual guessing of words, skipping unknown words, tolerating ambiguity, reading for meaning, making inferences, monitoring, recognizing the structure of text, using previous learning, and using background knowledge about the text), and self-confidence in the Self as literate readily and easily transfer from first to second language literacy (Calero-Breckheimer & Goetz, 1993; Jiménez *et al.*, 1995). This is the idea found in the Common Underlying Proficiency or Dual Iceberg idea of Cummins and his Interdependence principle (see Chapter 8).

Transfer from first language to second language literacy is not unconditional and is likely to be contingent on the context of learning and the characteristics of the learner. The following factors may play an intervening role: (1) differences in the facilitating nature of the school, home and community environment (McKay *et al.*, 1997); (2) individual differences in language ability, language aptitude and language learning strategies; (3) individual differences in the analysis of their language (metalinguistic abilities); and (4) the inter-relationship between pairs of languages (e.g. Portuguese and Spanish compared with English and Chinese) – see McKay *et al.* (1997). (5) Reading ability in a second language is also partly dependent on the degree of proficiency in that second language (Lee & Schallert, 1997). Children literate in their first language still need to acquire the differences found in the second language (e.g. different sounds, vocabulary, grammatical structures), and these may need explicit instruction.

However, the view that reading ability in a second language is purely a function of proficiency in that second language is not generally supported by research (Calero-Breckheimer & Goetz, 1993). While the sounds of letters and decoding of words have a **separation** in learning to read in each language, the higher cognitive abilities and strategies required in making meaning from text are common to both languages. Overall reading competence in two languages does not operate separately.

When two languages have different writing systems (e.g. English, Chinese), 'general strategies, habits and attitudes, knowledge of text structure, rhetorical devices, sensorimotor skills, visual-perceptual training, cognitive functions, and many reading readiness skills transfer from L1 to L2 reading' (Ovando & Collier, 1998, p. 128).

This 'transfer' rather than 'separation' viewpoint has implications for the teaching of reading among language minority students. A '**separation**' view is that reading in the second language (e.g. English for language minority students in the USA) depends on the level of proficiency in the second language and not on first language reading ability. Therefore, students should be swiftly moved to education through the second language; maximal exposure is needed to literacy in the second (majority) language. Time spent reading in the minority language is time lost in learning to read in the majority language. In contrast, a '**transfer**' view argues for initial mastery of literacy in the minority language so that the cognitive skills and strategies needed for reading can be fully developed. Once well developed, these literacy skills and strategies transfer easily and readily to the second language.

One implication for teachers of the 'transfer' viewpoint is that repetition is to be avoided. For example, there is little point introducing the concept of metaphors in English lessons and then repeating exactly the same subject matter in Spanish lessons. **Coordination**, integration and synchronization are needed to ensure learning is cumulative and not repetitive.

An important intermediate factor is the **context** in which such language and literacy acquisition occurs. In Canadian immersion programs, for example, the context is additive. That is, the child's home language of English is not being replaced but is being added to by the acquisition of French. Evaluations of such immersion programs (see Chapter 11) show that literacy in French is acquired at no cost to literacy in English. In this additive, majority language context, a child may acquire literacy through the second language at no cost to literacy in the first language. In contrast, in a **subtractive environment**, the transfer of literacy skills between the two languages may be impeded. In such subtractive situations, literacy may more efficiently be acquired through the home, heritage, minority language. Literacy can be built up via the higher level of language skills in the home language rather than through the weaker majority language of English. When literacy is attempted through the second, majority language, the child's oracy skills in English may be insufficiently developed for such literacy acquisition to occur.

For teachers, this leaves the question of when to encourage biliteracy, given that there is some degree of literacy in one language. One model will be the **simultaneous** acquisition of biliteracy as well as bilingualism. Some bilingual children simultaneously learn to read and write in both languages. Other children will learn to read in their second language **before** they learn to read in their first (majority) language. An example is immersion education in Canada, where children learn to read in French before learning to read in English. Both these approaches will tend to result in successful biliteracy.

The third approach is where children acquire literacy in their first language, a minority language, and then **later** develop literacy skills in the majority language. This may, in some circumstances lead to monoliteracy in the majority language and not biliteracy. In a subtractive situation, minority (first) language literacy may become neglected. In Transitional Bilingual Education, for example, majority language literacy is promoted at the cost of minority language literacy. However, in Maintenance, Two-Way/Dual Language and Heritage Language education, this third approach tends to be additive, promoting literacy in both languages.

Simple answers about when to promote literacy in the second language are made difficult by other factors such as the educational and societal context and the age and ability of the child. Contrast the six-year-old just beginning to acquire pre-reading and pre-writing skills in the first language with an 18-year-old student, fluent in a first language. In the first case, biliteracy may best be delayed. In the latter case, oracy and literacy in the second language may be mutually reinforcing. Contexts will also vary. When a language minority child is constantly bombarded with majority language written material, from adverts to comics, computers to supermarkets, biliteracy may occur relatively easily. The accent in school can be on minority language literacy, but not exclusively. The opportunity for extending majority language literacy is often well served outside school. The preference with younger children may be to ensure first language literacy is relatively well established before introducing literacy in a second language. Such introduction may come in the middle years of elementary schooling (e.g. from seven years of age to 12 years of age depending on the level of literacy achieved in the first language).

CONCLUSION

This chapter has examined the various classroom strategies that may be valuable in classrooms where there is an accent on multiculturalism, biliteracy in majority and minority language children, and the empowerment of language minority students and their families. There are no 'best recipes' of approach; no 'right answers' to classroom processes towards literacy and biliteracy. Different aims and goals in schooling, and different political and educational demands, make the choice partly about 'how', but also about 'why' and 'for what purpose'.

Chapters 15 and 16 are founded on the importance of literacy and biliteracy in the empowerment of bilingual students and their communities. Taken together, these chapters have sought to show that classroom practicalities are not divorced from educational and political policies; that education provision cannot be separated from issues of power that affect the lives of bilinguals.

KEY POINTS IN THE CHAPTER

- Strategies in the classroom to promote biliteracy require cross-curriculum, collaborative and personalized approaches.
- Parents as partners in biliteracy development is important, including when local and family 'funds of knowledge' are utilized.
- When biliteracy is encouraged in minority language children, specific skills and strategies from the first language transfer to the second language.
- Some bilingual children simultaneously learn to read and write in both languages. Other children will learn to read in their first language before they learn to read in their second (majority) language. In immersion education this order is reversed. Both these approaches will tend to result in successful biliteracy. Contexts become important in the decision.

SUGGESTED FURTHER READING

DELGADO-GAITAN, C., 1990, *Literacy for Empowerment: The Role of Parents in Children's Education*. New York: Falmer Press.
EDWARDS, V., 1998, *The Power of Babel: Teaching and Learning in Multilingual Classrooms*. Stoke-on-Trent (UK): Trentham.
GREGORY, E., 1996, *Making Sense of a New World: Learning to Read in a Second Language*. London: Paul Chapman.
HORNBERGER, N.H., 1990, Creating successful learning contexts for bilingual literacy. *Teachers College Record* 92 (2), 212–29.
HUDELSON, S., 1994, Literacy development of second language children. In F. GENESEE (ed.) *Educating Second Language Children*. Cambridge: Cambridge University Press.
MULTILINGUAL RESOURCES FOR CHILDREN PROJECT, 1995, *Building Bridges: Multilingual Resources for Children*. Clevedon: Multilingual Matters.
PÉREZ, B. and TORRES-GUZMÁN, M.E., 1996, *Learning in Two Worlds. An Integrated Spanish/English Biliteracy Approach* (2nd edn). New York: Longman.

STUDY ACTIVITIES

(1) Visit a school where there is some attention to biliteracy. Make a case study (or a written or oral report) of one or more of the following:

(a) Discuss with the teacher the aims of such biliteracy. Does the teacher feel that biliteracy is possible or that literacy in one language is more important?

(b) What provision of reading matter in two languages is available in the classroom? How many books are there in different languages? Do any of the books have two or more languages within them? What is the style and content (e.g. type of stories) of the books? Are there differences (e.g. color, datedness, level of language) between books in the two languages?

(c) Observe and record how much time is spent on reading in classrooms in a school. How much time is allotted to each language?

(d) Ask teachers at what stage and ages reading in each language is introduced in their classrooms? What variations are there between teachers? To what level does oral and reading achievement in one language need to develop before the introduction of biliteracy? Does a child's interest and attitude have an influence on literacy and biliteracy?

(e) Ask a number of students their views on being able to read in two languages. Ask the students how much reading they do after school, and in what language or languages? What are their favorite books and what language is preferred?

(f) By interviewing, find examples of parent–teacher collaboration in the reading process. What kind of collaboration exists? How well do you feel it works? What improvements might be made? How are literacy practices different and similar in the home and school?

(2) Examine some dual language books (e.g. Spanish on one page, English on the opposite page). Ask some teachers and students their opinions about such books. Make a list of the pros and cons. Provide your own reasoned conclusion.

CHAPTER 17

Immersion
Classrooms

Introduction

Language Teaching and Learning
in the Immersion Classroom

Language Strategies in
Immersion Classrooms

Conclusion

CHAPTER 17

Immersion Classrooms

INTRODUCTION

When applied to language, 'immersion' was first used to describe intensive language programs for US troops about to go abroad in the Second World War. In the 1960s, 'immersion education' was coined to describe a new form of bilingual education (see Chapter 10). By today, immersion schooling occurs internationally: Australia, the Basque Country, Catalonia, Finland, Hungary, Hong Kong, Ireland, New Zealand, Singapore, South Africa and Wales, for example.

The structures of immersion education have become well established (see Chapters 10 and 11). But classroom strategies for learning and teaching that are indigenous to immersion education are still developing. In particular, language tactics are still evolving to ensure full dual language development and high achievement across the curriculum (Swain & Johnson, 1997).

This chapter considers the approach to language learning often taken in the immersion education programs. To begin with, here are two introductory points. First, it is important to repeat the distinction between teaching a language and teaching through a language. Language acquisition in the immersion programs is mostly through the second language being used as a medium of instruction in 50% to 100% of the curriculum (see Chapter 10).

Second, allied to the idea of language as a medium of instruction is the idea of **language across the curriculum** (Corson, 1990a). This is a view that language plays a central role across the curriculum. In all curriculum areas, students learn skills, knowledge, concepts and attitudes mostly through language. Thus, every curriculum area develops language competence. All subject areas, from music to mathematics, science to sport, contribute to the growth of a child's language. At the same time, mastery of a particular curriculum area is partly dependent on mastery of the language of that area. Obtaining fluency in the language of chemistry, psychology or mathematics, for example, is essential to understanding that subject.

LANGUAGE TEACHING AND LEARNING IN THE IMMERSION CLASSROOM

What are the main classroom features of successful immersion programs in the Basque Country, Catalonia and Wales, and elsewhere? First, the minimum time the second language needs to be used as a medium to ensure customary achievements levels is four to six years. Around the end of elementary schooling, immersion students show equal or higher performance in the curriculum compared with their mainstream peers. Second, the curriculum tends to be the same for immersion children as for their mainstream peers. Thus, immersion children can easily be compared with mainstream children for levels of achievement. Immersion students compared with mainstream students are neither more advantaged nor more disadvantaged by studying a common curriculum.

While immersion attempts to cultivate empathy for a student's **second language culture**, the immersion curriculum has hitherto tended not to have major distinctive components which differ from mainstream education, to develop such empathy and participation. For example in Canada, a known danger is that French becomes the language of school, and English the language of the playground, street and vocational success. The anglophone North American cultural influence is often so strong and persuasive that French immersion children are in danger of becoming passive rather than active bilinguals outside the school gates. The same occurs in many immersion schools in Wales where Welsh is the language of the classroom, but English is the peer 'prestige' language in the school yard and on the streets.

Third, it has been thought preferable to **separate languages in instruction** rather than to mix them during a single lesson (see Chapter 13). Thus immersion typically uses one language for one set of subjects; the other language for a separate set. When there is language mixing inside a lesson, students may wait for the explanation in their stronger language. Sustained periods of monolingual instruction will require students to attend to the language of instruction, thus both improving their language competences and acquiring subject matter simultaneously.

One residual problem is the language in which particular subjects are taught. For example, if mathematics and science, technology and computing are taught in the English language, will the hidden message be that English is of more value for scientific communication, for industrial and scientific vocations? Will English latently receive a special, reserved status? If the minority or second language is used for humanities, social studies, sport and art, is the hidden message that minority languages are only of value in such human and aesthetic pursuits? The choice of language medium for particular subjects may relegate or promote both the functions and the status of minority languages.

This raises the fourth issue. How much **time** should be devoted to the two languages within the curriculum? The typical recommendation is that a minimum of 50% of instruction should be in the second language. Thus, in French immersion in Canada, French medium teaching and learning may occur from 50% to 100% of the school week. As the graphs of Chapter 10 reveal, the amount of instruction in the

English language may increase as children become older. One factor in such a decision can be the amount of exposure to English a child receives outside school. Where a child's environment, home and street, media and community are English medium, for example, such saturation may imply that a smaller proportion of time needs to be spent on English in the school. At the same time, the public will usually require bilingual schools to show that children's majority language competences, particularly literacy, are not affected by bilingual education. Bilingual schools need to ensure that, through school instruction and school learning experiences, majority language proficiency and literacy is monitored and promoted (Rebuffot, 1993). Such majority language instruction may range from a minimum of 10% for seven-year-olds and older, to 70% or more for those in examination classes at secondary level schooling.

Fifth, immersion education has been built around the twin towers of teacher enthusiasm and parental commitment. Immersion **parents** have tended to be middle class, involved in school–teacher–parent committees, and take a sustained interest in their children's progress (see Holobow *et al.* (1991) for evidence that foreign language immersion in the USA is also successful with working-class children). For example, immersion education in Canada has, from its beginnings in Montreal in 1965 to the present, been powerfully promoted by parents (Baker & Jones, 1998). The first immersion classroom in 1965 owed much to parent initiation. Since then, the Canadian Parents for French organization has been a powerful pressure group for the recognition and dissemination, evolution and dispersion of immersion education. Such parents are frequently English-only speakers wanting bilingualism for their children. Parents have also been powerful advocates at the grassroots level for other 'strong' forms of bilingual education (e.g. both bilingual and English monolingual parents in Wales). Through localized pressure groups, schools which give native language medium teaching have successfully developed.

Teachers in immersion classrooms tend to have native or native-like proficiency in both the languages of the school. Such teachers are fully able to understand children speaking in their home language but speak to the children almost entirely in the immersion language. Teachers are thus important language models through their status and power role, identifying the immersion language with something of value and importance. Immersion teachers also provide the child with a model of pronunciation and style in the immersion language.

Immersion teachers are typically committed to bilingual education, enthusiastic about bilingualism in society, acting as bicultural and multicultural crusaders. Research in Wales by Roberts (1985) suggests the important nature of teacher commitment in immersion education. This commitment exists beyond teachers' interest in the education of children. In the equation of a successful bilingual school, such enthusiasm and commitment by headteachers and principals, teachers and auxiliary workers may be an important and often underestimated factor in success. There is a danger of seeing success in bilingual education as due to the system (e.g. immersion) and use of two languages in school. The commitment of bilingual teachers, and the special skills that a bilingual teacher uses beyond those required of a monolingual teacher, can too easily be underestimated in the equation of successful bilingual schooling.

Sixth, the immersion approach allows a relatively **homogeneous language classroom**. For example, in early total immersion, children will start from the same point. All are beginners without second language proficiency. This makes the task of the teacher less complex than in bilingual classes where there is a mixture of first and second language speakers. Initially, there will be no disparity of status due to some children being more proficient than others in the second language.

On a comparative education note, the term 'Immersion' is used in many countries across continents. In Finland and Canada, children are typically linguistically homogeneous at the start of schooling in not speaking the immersion language of the school. In contrast, there is sometimes a mixture of those who are fluent and those who are less fluent in the classroom language. For example, in an Irish immersion school, the classroom may be composed both of children whose home language is Irish and those whose home language is English but whose parents are keen for their children to be taught through the medium of Irish. The Irish and Welsh experiences tend to suggest that most children whose home language is English will cope successfully in minority language immersion classrooms. For such children, the language context is additive rather than subtractive. The danger is that the majority language of English, being the common denominator, will be the language used between students in the classroom, in the playground and certainly out of school. According to Lindholm (1990) 'To maintain an environment of educational and linguistic equity in the classroom, and to promote interactions among native and non-native English speakers, the most desirable ratio is 50% English speakers to 50% non-native English speakers' (p. 100). However, Lindholm (1990) suggests that little research has been conducted to determine the optimal classroom composition for successful bilingual education. A balance towards a greater proportion of minority language speakers may help to ensure that the 'common denominator' majority language does not always dominate in informal classroom and playground talk.

Seventh, immersion provides an **additive bilingual environment**. Students acquire a second language at no cost to their home language and culture. Such enrichment may be contrasted to subtractive bilingual environments where the home language is replaced by the second language. For example, where the home language is Spanish and the submersion approach is to replace Spanish by English, negative rather than positive effects may occur in school performance and self-esteem. This underlines that the term immersion education is best reserved for additive rather than subtractive environments. The term 'immersion education' is appropriate only when the home language is a majority language and the school is adding a second minority or majority language.

Eighth, most immersion teachers have to 'wear two hats': promoting achievement throughout the curriculum and ensuring second language proficiency. Such a dual task requires **immersion teacher training** (Bernhardt & Schrier, 1992; Björklund, 1997; Met & Lorenz, 1997). This has tended to be a weakness in countries using the immersion approach or a version of it. Both at the pre-service and professional development levels of education of teachers, the special needs of immersion teachers should be addressed. Methods in immersion classroom require induction into skills and techniques beyond those required in ordinary mainstream classrooms. Immersion teaching (and teacher training) methods are still evolving and are at a developmental stage.

In Finland, general teacher-training includes an introduction to the societal and individual features of bilingualism and bilingual education and centers such as the University of Vaasa have evolved a continuing education program for immersion teachers (Björklund, 1997). In the USA, the expertise is often found among teacher-training consultants rather than in colleges, with mentoring programs and videotapes also aiding professional development (Met & Lorenz, 1997).

LANGUAGE STRATEGIES IN IMMERSION CLASSROOMS

Immersion education is based on the idea that a first language is acquired relatively subconsciously. Children are unaware that they are learning a language in the home. Immersion attempts to replicate this process in the early years of schooling. The focus is on the content and not the form of the language. It is the task at hand that is central, not conscious language learning. In the early stages, there are no formal language learning classes, although simple elements of grammar such as verb endings may be taught informally. In the latter years of elementary schooling, formal consideration may be given to the rules of the language (e.g. grammar and syntax). The early stages of immersion tend to mirror the subconscious acquisition of learning of the first language. Only later will a child be made conscious of language as a system, to reinforce and promote communication.

Immersion also tends to assume that the earlier a language is taught the better. While teenagers and adults may learn a second language fluently and proficiently (see Chapter 5), research evidence tends to suggest that young children acquire authentic pronunciation better than adults (De Houwer, 1995). A young child is more plastic and malleable, with uncommitted areas in the left hemisphere of the brain. The argument for immersion schooling tends to be 'the earlier the better'.

In the first stages in Early Immersion classrooms, a teacher typically concentrates on listening and speaking skills. 'Oral skills are given more importance in kindergarten to Grade 3; reading and writing skills, even though started as early as Grade 1, are stressed in Grades 4 to 6' (Canadian Education Association, 1992). Students are not made to speak the immersion language with their teacher or with their peers in the initial stages. Children will initially speak their first language to each other and to their teacher, without any objection or reprimand. Immersion teachers do not force children to use the immersion language until they are naturally willing to do so. Early insistence on the immersion language may inhibit children and develop negative attitudes to that language and to education in general. Over the first two years, immersion children develop an understanding of the immersion language and begin to speak that language, particularly to the teacher.

In Canada, the most frequent grade in which English becomes part of the formal curriculum in Early Total French Immersion is Grade 3. Other practices include introducing English at an earlier grade or kindergarten and at Grade 4 (Canadian Education Association, 1992). While initially students will lag behind mainstream 'English' students in English language achievement, by Grade 5 or 6, Early Immersion students catch up and perform as well (Rebuffot, 1993).

In these early stages of Early Immersion, it is crucial that the teacher is comprehensible to the children. The teacher needs to be sympathetically aware of the level of a child's vocabulary and grammar, to deliver in the immersion language at a level the child can understand, and simultaneously be constantly pushing forward a child's competence in that language. The teacher will aim to push back the frontiers of a child's immersion language by ensuring that messages are both comprehensible and are slightly ahead of the learner's current level of mastery of the language.

The language used to communicate with the child at these early stages is often called **caretaker speech**. For the first year or two in immersion education, the vocabulary will be deliberately limited with a simplified presentation of grammar and syntax. The teacher may be repetitive in the words used and the ideas presented, with the same idea presented in two or more different ways. The teacher will deliberately speak slowly, giving the child more time to process the language input and understand the meaning. This tends to parallel the talk of mother to child (**motherese**) and **foreigner talk** (a person deliberately simplifying and slowing down so a foreigner can understand). During this caretaker stage, the teacher may be constantly questioning the child to ensure that understanding has occurred.

A teacher may also present the language to be used before a lesson topic is presented. When new words and new concepts are being introduced into a lesson, the teacher may spend some time in introducing the words and clarifying the concepts so that the language learner is prepared. Such teachers may also be sensitive to **non-verbal feedback** from students: questioning looks, losing concentration and glazed attention. Students will be encouraged to question the teacher for clarification and simplification when a misunderstanding has occurred. Such teaching strategies thus cover two different areas: the importance of comprehensible input and the importance of negotiating meaning. The worst case is when neither the teacher nor the student is aware that misunderstanding (or no understanding) has taken place. A more effective classroom is when students and teachers are negotiating meaning, ensuring that mutual understanding has occurred. Not only is the negotiation of meaning important in language development and in maximizing achievement throughout the curriculum, it is also important in aiding motivation of children within the classroom. Patronizing such children and oversimplifying are two of the dangers in this process. Therefore, constantly presenting students with ever challenging and advancing learning situations is important in classroom achievement.

Immersion classrooms need to have a particular view about **language errors**. Language errors are a usual and frequent part of the language learning process. Errors are not a symptom of failure. They are a natural part of learning. Errors are not permanent. With time and practice, they disappear. Therefore, immersion teachers are discouraged from over-correcting children's attempts to speak the immersion language. Just as parents are more likely to correct children's factual errors than their first language errors, the immersion teacher will tend to avoid constant correction of errors. Constant error correction may be self-defeating, even penalizing second language acquisition. Language accuracy tends to develop over time and with experience. Constant correction of error disrupts communication and content learning in the classroom (Met & Lorenz, 1997). When a child or several children constantly make the same errors, then appropriate but positive intervention may be of value.

In the early stages of immersion, there will be a natural **interlanguage** among children. A child may change the correct order in a sentence yet produce a perfectly comprehensible message. For example, faulty syntax may occur due to the influence of the first language on the second language. A child may put the pronoun or a preposition in the wrong order: as in 'go you and get it'. Interlanguage is not to be seen as error. Rather it indicates the linguistic creativity of students who are using their latent understanding of the first language to construct meaningful communication in the second language. Interlanguage is thus an intermediate, approximate and temporary system. It is a worthwhile attempt to communicate and therefore needs acceptance rather than condemnation. Seen as a halfway stage in-between monolingualism and being proficient in a second language, interlanguage becomes a stage in the journey and not a permanent rest point. However, Kowal and Swain (1997) indicate that a danger of immersion is that students reach native-like levels in reading and listening but not in writing and speaking. Once students are able to communicate their meaning to teachers and peers, there can be a lack of incentive for achieving native-like accuracy. Therefore, at later stages, intervention in error correction and more focus on form and not just content may be valuable. Encouraging students to be more analytical of the accuracy of their speech may be important if native-like performance is targeted.

Proficiency in the first language will contribute to proficiency in the second language. Concepts already attached to words in the first language will easily be **transferred** into the second language. The acquisition of literacy skills in the first language tends to facilitate the acquisition of literacy skills in the second language. However, not all aspects of a language will transfer. Rules of syntax and spelling may not lend themselves to transfer. The closer a language structure is to the second language structure, the greater the transfer there is likely to be between the two languages. For example, the transfer between English and Spanish is likely to be more than Arabic to English due to differences in syntax, symbols and direction of writing. However, the system of meanings, the conceptual map and skills that a person owns, may be readily transferable between languages.

The focus of immersion classrooms is typically on **real, authentic communication**, tasks, curriculum content and creative processes (e.g. Bernhardt, 1992; Dicks, 1992; Hall, 1993). However, as Harley (1991) has indicated, there is also a place for an analytical approach to the second and the first language in the classroom. An immersion classroom will not just enable children to acquire the second language in a subconscious, almost incidental manner. Towards the end of elementary education, the experiential approach may be joined by a meaning-based focus on the form of language. A child may at this point be encouraged to analyze their vocabulary and grammar. At this later stage, some lessons may have progress in the second language as their sole aim. After early sheltering with language, the development of vocabulary and grammar may be dealt with in a direct and systematic manner.

Snow (1990) provides a list of ten specific techniques that tend to be used by experienced and effective immersion teachers. This is a valuable summary of the discussion in this section.

(1) Providing plenty of contextual support for the language being used (e.g. by body language — plenty of gestures, facial expressions and acting).
(2) Deliberately giving more classroom directions and organizational advice to immersion students. For example, signaling the start and the end of different routines, more explicit directions with homework and assignments.
(3) Understanding where a child is at, thereby connecting the unfamiliar with the familiar, the known with the unknown. New material is linked directly and explicitly with the child's present knowledge and understanding.
(4) Extensive use of visual material. Using concrete objects to illustrate lessons, using pictures and audio-visual aids, giving the child plenty of hands-on manipulative activities to ensure all senses are used in the educational experience.
(5) Obtaining constant feedback as to the level of a student's understanding. Diagnosing the level of a student's language.
(6) Using plenty of repetition, summaries, restatement to ensure that students understand the directions of the teacher.
(7) The teacher being a role model for language emulation by the student.
(8) Indirect error correction rather than constantly faulting students. Teachers ensure that the corrections are built in to their language to make a quick and immediate impact.
(9) Using plenty of variety in both general learning tasks and in language learning tasks.
(10) Using frequent and varied methods to check the child's level of understanding.

CONCLUSION

Starting with one school, St Lambert near Montreal in September 1965, immersion methodology has spread from Canada to many countries of the world. Issues of language separation, culture in the curriculum, teaching styles and learning strategies, for example, have become researched in particular by Canadians. There is also a depth of teacher experience that has produced 'theories of practice' such that immersion methodology has become seasoned and refined.

KEY POINTS IN THE CHAPTER

- Immersion methodology attempts to ensure high levels of academic proficient language development in both languages, empathy for two or more cultures, and thus an additive experience.
- Language separation is preferred to the concurrent uses of language.
- Teacher enthusiasm and parental commitment are important ingredients in effective immersion approaches.
- Policies for when to introduce formal attention to the home language, comprehensible communication in the immersion language, plentiful feedback, attitude to language errors and interlanguage are needed in effective immersion classrooms.

SUGGESTED FURTHER READING

BERNHARDT, E.B. (ed.), 1992, *Life in Language Immersion Classrooms*. Clevedon: Multilingual Matters.

CALIFORNIA STATE DEPARTMENT OF EDUCATION, 1984, *Studies on Immersion Education. A Collection for United States Educators*. Sacramento, CA: California State Department of Education.

CLOUD, N., GENESEE, F. and HAMAYAN, E. V., 2000, *Dual Language Instruction: A Handbook for Enriched Education*. Boston: Heinle and Heinle.

HELLER, M., 1994, *Crosswords: Language, Education and Ethnicity in French Ontario*. New York: Mouton de Gruyter.

JOHNSON, R.K. and SWAIN, M., 1997, *Immersion Education: International Perspectives*. Cambridge: Cambridge University Press.

STUDY ACTIVITIES

(1) By reading, a visit to an immersion school, or looking at a video tape of immersion education (e.g. from the Ontario Institute of Studies in Education), write out a plan of a typical immersion classroom lesson. The plan should be in sufficient detail for a group of students to perform a dramatic sketch simulating the classroom sequence.

(2) Visit an 'immersion' (or similar) classroom, and by diagrams, pictures or photographs, portray the bilingual displays of the classroom. Capture in picture form, the wall displays, project work, activity corners, and other forms of display that attempt to provide an immersion classroom.

The Politics of Bilingualism

Introduction

Three Perspectives on Languages

US Language Orientations

The Advance of English

The Language Orientations of Different
Minority Groups

Assimilation

Pluralism

Eight Strategies for Linguistic and
Cultural Diversity

Assimilation and Immigrants

Maintaining Ethnic Identity

Equilibrium or Conflict?

Cummins' Theoretical Framework

Conclusion

CHAPTER 18

The Politics of Bilingualism

INTRODUCTION

Bilingualism not only exists within individuals, within their thinking systems, in the family and in the local community. Bilingualism is also directly and indirectly interwoven into the politics of a nation. Bilingualism is not only studied linguistically, psychologically and sociologically, it is also studied in relationship to **power and status structures** and **political systems** in society. The basis of this chapter is that bilingualism and bilingual education, whatever form it takes, cannot be properly understood unless connected to basic philosophies and politics in society. The activity of a bilingual classroom, and decisions about how to teach minority language children, are not based purely on educational preferences. Rather, calls for and against bilingual education are surrounded and underpinned by basic beliefs about minority languages and linguistic diversity, minority cultures and cultural diversity, immigration and immigrants, equality of opportunity and equality of outcomes, empowerment, affirmative action, the rights of individuals and the rights of language minority groups, assimilation and integration, desegregation and discrimination, pluralism and multiculturalism, diversity and discord, equality of recognition for minority groups and social cohesion.

Education has been conceived alternatively as part of the solution and part of the problem of achieving unity in diversity. For some people, bilingual education will facilitate national cohesion, cultural integration and enable different language communities to communicate with each other (e.g. Singapore). For other people, bilingual education will create language factions, national disunity, and cultural, economic and political disintegration (e.g. the 'Unz movement' in California and Arizona).

It is important for students, teachers and educational policy-makers to be aware of how their present and future activity not only concerns children in classrooms, but also fits into the overall **language policy** of a state or a nation. Teachers and education administrators are not only affected by political decisions and processes, they also deliver and implement those decisions and processes. Teachers are part of language paradoxes that are daily enacted and temporarily resolved in the classroom: ensuring equality of opportunity for all while celebrating distinctiveness and difference; ensuring diversity does not become discord; having a common purpose while encouraging colorful variety; developing the dignity of ethnicity and aiding national stability; making a student's life safe for and from ethnicity.

THREE PERSPECTIVES ON LANGUAGES

We begin by considering different assumptions and varying perspectives that are at the root of the politics of bilingualism and bilingual education. Ruiz (1984) proposed three basic orientations or perspectives about language around which people and groups vary: **language as a problem, language as a right and language as a resource**. These three different dispositions towards language planning may not exist at the conscious level. They may be embedded in the subconscious assumptions of planners and politicians. Such orientations are regarded as fundamental and related to a basic philosophy or ideology held by an individual.

Language as a Problem

Public discussions of bilingual education and languages in society often commence with the idea of language as causing complications and difficulties. This is well illustrated in the now-historical debates about the supposed **cognitive problems** of operating in two languages (see Chapters 7 and 8). Perceived problems are not limited to thinking. **Personality and social problems** such as split-identity, cultural dislocation, a poor self-image, low self-esteem and anomie are also sometimes attributed to bilinguals. At a group rather than an individual level, bilingualism is sometimes connected with the potential of national or regional disunity and inter-group conflict. Language is thus also viewed as a **political problem**.

Part of the 'language-as-problem' orientation is that perpetuating language minorities and language diversity may cause less integration, less cohesiveness, more antagonism and more conflict in society (see Parrillo, 1996). The perceived complication of minority languages is to be **solved by assimilation** into the majority language. Such an argument holds that the majority language (e.g. English) unifies the diversity. The ability of every citizen to communicate with ease in the nation's majority language is regarded as the common leveler. A strong nation is regarded as a unified nation. Unity within a nation is seen as synonymous with uniformity and similarity. The opposing argument is that it is possible to have national unity without uniformity. Diversity of languages and national unity can co-exist (e.g. Singapore, Luxembourg, Switzerland).

The co-existence of two or more languages is rarely a cause of tension, disunity, conflict or strife. Rather, the history of war suggests that economic, political and religious differences are prominent as causes. **Language, in and by itself, is seldom the cause of conflict**. Religious crusades and *jihads*, rivalries between different religions, rivalries between different political parties and economic aggression tend to be the instigators of strife (Otheguy, 1982).

In a internationally comparative research study on causes of civil strife, Fishman

(1989) found that language was not a cause. His analysis involved 130 countries with one outcome (dependent) variable namely civil strife (defined as the frequency, duration and intensity of conspiracy, internal war and turmoil). Predictor variables concerned measures of linguistic homogeneity/heterogeneity, social cultural, economic, demographic, geographic, historical and political measures. 'The widespread journalistic and popular political wisdom that linguistic heterogeneity *per se* is necessarily conducive to civil strife, has been shown, by our analysis, to be more myth than reality' (Fishman, 1989, p. 622). Rather, the causes of strife were found to be deprivation, authoritarian regimes and modernization.

A minority language is often connected with the **problems** of poverty, underachievement in school, minimal social and vocational mobility and with a lack of integration into the majority culture. In this perspective, the minority language is perceived as a partial cause of social, economic and educational problems, rather than an effect of such problems. This 'language is an obstacle' attitude is summed up in the phrase, 'If only they would speak English, their problems would be solved'. The minority language is thus seen as a handicap to be overcome by the school system. One resolution of the problem is regarded as the increased teaching of a majority language (e.g. English) at the expense of the home language. Developing bilingualism is an irrelevant or a secondary and less important aim of schooling. Thus submersion and transitional bilingual education aim to develop competent English language skills in minority language children as quickly as possible so they are on a par with English first language speakers in the mainstream classroom.

A **language problem** is sometimes perceived as **caused** by 'strong' forms of **bilingual education**. Such education, it is sometimes argued, will cause social unrest or disintegration in society. Fostering the minority language and ethnic differences might provoke conflict and disharmony. The response is generally that 'strong' forms of bilingual education will lead to better integration, harmony and social peace. As Otheguy (1982, p. 314) comments of the USA: 'Critics of bilingual education with a concern for civil order and social disharmony should also concern themselves with issues of poverty, unemployment, and racial discrimination rather than concentrate on the use of Spanish in schools. In pledges of allegiance, it is liberty and justice — not English — for all, that is to keep us indivisible'.

'Strong' forms of bilingual education should not be connected with the language problem orientation. Rather, the evidence suggests that developing bilingualism and biliteracy within a 'strong' bilingual education situation is educationally feasible and can lead to:

- higher achievement across the curriculum for minority language children;
- maintaining the home language and culture;
- fostering self-esteem, self-identity and a more positive attitude to schooling.

Such higher achievement may enable better usage of human resources in a country's economy and less wastage of talent. Higher self-esteem may also relate to increased social harmony and peace.

Within this 'problem' orientation, there not only exists the desire to remove differences between groups to achieve a common culture. There can be the desire for **intervention** to improve the position of language minorities. 'Whether the orientation is represented by malicious attitudes resolving to eradicate, invalidate, quarantine or inoculate, or comparatively benign ones concerned with remediation and "improvement", the central activity remains that of problem-solving' (Ruiz, 1984, p. 21).

Language as a Right

A different orientation to that of 'language as a problem' is thinking of language as a **basic, human right**. Just as there are often individual rights in choice of religion, so it is argued, there should be an individual right to choice of language, and to bilingual education (Cummins, 1999b). Just as there are attempts to eradicate discrimination based on color and creed, so people within this orientation will argue that language prejudice and discrimination need to be eradicated in a democratic society (May, 2001; Skutnabb-Kangas & Phillipson, 1994; Skutnabb-Kangas, 1999b).

Kloss (1977, 1998) makes a distinction between tolerance-oriented rights and promotion-oriented rights. At one level, language rights concern protection from discrimination. Many language minorities (e.g. Maori, Native Americans, Welsh) have suffered discrimination. For example, Welsh speaking children were formerly banned from speaking their language at school. If caught doing so, they would be wear a placard around their necks. At the end of the morning and afternoon, the child who last wore the placard was beaten with a cane. Discrimination can thus be present when people are forced to learn a language at school which is not their own, in competition with people who do not have to make this sometimes abrupt and forced adjustment. Such a discriminatory practice disadvantages language minorities while favoring those whose first language is international and prestigious (Kibbee, 1998).

At a promotion-oriented level, language rights are more positive and constructive, asserting the right to use a minority language freely, including in all official contexts. Such rights flourish particularly where there is relatively greater individual and group self-determination (Kibbee, 1998). However, language rights can sometimes be idealistic rather than realistic. If all majority and minority European languages were used in the European Parliament, translation and interpretation would be cost prohibitive. In South Africa, it is very expensive to produce the full range of educational resources (for different ages, curriculum areas, and ability levels) for the eleven official languages. Yet to privilege one or more languages over the others will be at cost to the speakers (e.g. less educational success) and the languages themselves (e.g. language shift).

A 'non-rights', *laissez-faire* approach to minority languages serves to strengthen the already powerful and prestigious languages. Therefore some form of linguistic rights becomes essential, at least in areas where a government has power. Governments typically have less power in economic activities, making rights in government-controlled areas even more important.

Such language rights may be derived from **personal**, legal and constitutional rights. Personal language rights will draw on individual liberties and the right to freedom of individual expression (May, 2001). It may also be argued that there are certain natural or moral language rights in **group** rather than individual terms. The rights of language groups may be expressed in terms of the importance of preservation of heritage language and culture communities and expressed as 'rights to protection' and 'rights to participation'. This includes rights to some form of self-determination. May (2001) argues the case for greater ethnocultural and ethnolinguistic self-determination and democracy as nation-states fragment.

A further level of language rights may be **international**, derived from pronouncements from organizations such as the United Nations, UNESCO, the Council of Europe and the European Community. Each of these four organizations has declared that minority language groups have the right to maintain their language. In the European Community, a directive (25th July 1977: 77/486/EEC) stated that Member States should promote the teaching of the mother tongue and the culture of the country of origin in the education of migrant workers' children. However, individual countries have generally ignored such international declarations. Particular international examples (e.g. Sámi in Norway, Kurds in Turkey, and Gikuyu speakers in Kenya) are portrayed in Skutnabb-Kangas and Phillipson (1994).

The kind of rights, apart from language rights, that ethnic groups may claim include: protection, membership of their ethnic group and separate existence, non-discrimination and equal treatment, education and information in their ethnic language, freedom to worship, freedom of belief, freedom of movement, employment, peaceful assembly and association, political representation and involvement, and administrative autonomy.

In the USA, the rights of the individual are a major part of democracy (Del Valle, 1998). As Trueba (1989, p. 103) suggests, 'American democracy has traditionally attached a very high value to the right to disagree and debate, and to enjoy individual and group cultural and linguistic freedom without jeopardizing the rights of others or our national unity'. In the USA, questions about language rights are not only discussed in college classrooms and language communities, and debated in government and federal legislatures. Language rights have a history of being tested in US courtrooms. This is significantly different from European experience where language rights have rarely been tried in law.

From the early 1920s to the present, there has been a continuous debate in **US courts of law** regarding the legal status of language minority rights. To gain short-term protection and a medium-term guarantee for minority languages, legal challenges have become an important part of the language rights movement in the USA. The legal battles are not just couched in minority language versus majority language contests. The test cases also concern children versus schools, parents versus school boards, state versus the federal authority (Ruiz, 1984). Whereas minority language activists among the Basques in Spain and the Welsh in Britain have been taken to court by the central government for their actions, US minority language activists have taken the central and regional government to court. Two connected examples will illustrate.

A crucial Supreme Court case in the USA was *Brown v. Board of Education* in 1954. Black children were deliberately segregated in southern schools. The Supreme Court ruled that equality in the US educational system was denied to such Black children due to segregation from their peers. Segregation denied equal educational opportunity through a critical part of the classroom: peer interaction. The Court decided that education must be made available to all children on equal terms, as guaranteed by the 14th Amendment. A segregationist doctrine of separate but equal education was inherently unequal.

A landmark in US bilingual education was a lawsuit. A court case was brought on behalf of Chinese students against the San Francisco School District in 1970. The case concerned whether or not non-English speaking students received equal educational opportunity when instructed in a language they could not understand. The failure to provide bilingual education was alleged to violate both the equal protection clause of the 14th Amendment and Title VI of the Civil Rights Act of 1964. The case, known as *Lau versus Nichols*, was rejected by the federal district court and a court of appeals, but was accepted by the Supreme Court in 1974. The verdict prohibited English submersion programs and resulted in nationwide 'Lau remedies'. Such remedies reflected a broadening of the goals of bilingual education to include the possible maintenance of minority language and culture. The Lau remedies created some expansion in the use of minority languages in schools, although they rarely resulted in true heritage language, enrichment or maintenance programs. For the purposes of this chapter, the Lau court case is symbolic of the dynamic and continuing contest to establish language rights in the USA particularly through testing the law in the courtroom (Lyons, 1990; Crawford, 1999).

Language rights are not only expressed in legal confrontations with the chance of being established in law. Language rights are often expressed at the **grassroots level** by protests and pressure groups, by local action and argument. For example, the *Kohanga Reo* (language nests) movement in New Zealand provides a grassroots instituted immersion pre-school experience for the Maori people (May, 1996). Beginning in 1982, these language nests offer a 'pre-school all-Maori language and culture environment for children from birth to school age, aimed at fostering complete development and growth within a context where only the Maori language is spoken and heard' (Corson, 1990a, p. 154).

One example of grass-roots expression of 'language as a right' is the recent Celtic (Ireland, Scotland and Wales) experience. In these countries, 'grassroots' created pre-school playgroups, 'mother and toddler' groups and adult language learning classes have been established so that the heritage languages can be preserved in both adult social interaction and especially in the young. Stronger activism and more insistent demands have led to the establishment of heritage language elementary schools, particularly in urban, mostly English speaking areas. Not without struggle, opposition and antagonistic bureaucracy, parents have obtained the right for education in the indigenous tongue. Such pressure groups have contained parents who speak the indigenous language, and those who speak only English, yet wish their children to be taught in the heritage language of the area.

In North American and British society, no formal recognition is usually made in politics or the legal system to categories or groups of people based on their culture, language or race. Rather the focus is on **individual rights**. The accent is on individual equality of opportunity, individual rewards based on individual merit. Policies of non-discrimination, for example, tend to be based on individual rather than group rights. Language minority groups will nevertheless argue for rewards and justice based on their existence as a definable group in society. Sometimes based on territorial rights, often based on ethnic identity, such **language group rights** have been regarded as a way of redressing injustices to language minorities. This may be a temporary step on the way to full individual citizenship rights as participative democracy tends to favor the equality of each individual rather than group privilege (Williams, 1998). Alternatively, language minorities may claim the right to some independent power, some measure of decision-making and some guarantee of self-determination. This is typically seen by the majority language group as a step on the road to self-determination, even apartheid (May, 1996).

When language group rights are obtained, 'what limited autonomy that is granted them is usually viewed with a great deal of suspicion, and often with outright opposition, because it may infringe on the individual rights of majority group members' (May, 1996, p. 153).

A note of **caution** about language rights needs sounding. Liberal words about individual rights can hide preferences for coercion and conformity (Skutnabb-Kangas, 1991). Stubbs (1991) talks of the experience in England with language minorities where government reports 'use a rhetoric of language entitlement and language rights, and of freedom and democracy... [which] makes the correct moral noises, but it has no legislative basis, and is therefore empty. There is talk of entitlement, but not of the discrimination which many children face; and talk of equality of opportunity, but not of equality of outcome' (pp. 220–221).

Similarly in the USA, when some school administrators hold a 'language as right' orientation, they tend to provide the legal minimum in support services for languages minority students.

Language as a Resource

An alternative orientation to 'language as a problem' and 'language as a right', is the idea of language as a **personal and national resource**. The recent movement in Britain and North America for increased second and foreign language fluency (e.g. in French) fits into this orientation (Dutcher, 1995). Under the general heading of 'language as a resource' also comes regarding minority and lesser used languages as a cultural and social resource. While languages may be viewed in terms of their economic bridge building potential, languages may also be supported for their ability to build social bridges across different groups, bridges for cross fertilization between cultures.

The recent trend in Europe and North America, for example, has been to expand **foreign language education**. Second language study is increasingly viewed as an essential resource to promote foreign trade and world influence. Thus, the paradox is that while bilingual education to support minority languages has tended to be undervalued in the USA, the current trend is to appreciate English speakers who learn a second language to ensure a continued major role for the USA in world politics and the world economy. There is a tendency to value the acquisition of languages while devaluing the language minorities who have them. While integration and assimilation is still the dominant ideology in US internal politics, external politics increasingly demand bilingual citizens (Kjolseth, 1983). Ovando (1990) describes US language policy as schizophrenic. 'On the one hand we encourage and promote the study of foreign languages for English monolinguals, at great cost and with great inefficiency. At the same time we destroy the linguistic gifts that children from non-English language backgrounds bring to our schools' (Ovando, 1990, p. 354).

It is ironic that many US and UK students spend time in school learning some of the very languages that children of immigrants are pressurized to forget. The politics of immigration serve to deny bilingualism; the politics of global trade serve increasingly to demand bilingualism. One result is that, along with the United Kingdom, the 'United States is a veritable cemetery of foreign languages, in that knowledge of mother tongues of hundreds of immigrant groups has rarely lasted past the third generation' (Portes & Hao, 1998, p. 269).

In the USA, the idea of language as a resource not only refers to the development of a second language in monolingual speakers. It also refers to the **preservation of languages** other than English. For example, children whose home language is Spanish or German, Italian or Mandarin, Greek or Japanese, Portuguese or French have a home language that can be utilized as a resource. One case is the Spanish speakers in the USA who together make the USA the fourth largest Spanish speaking country in the world. Just as water in the reservoir and oil in the oil field are preserved as basic resources and commodities, so a language such as Spanish, despite being difficult to measure and define as a resource, may be preserved for the common economic, social and cultural good. Suppression of language minorities, particularly by the school system, may be seen as economic, social and cultural wastage. Instead, such languages are a **natural resource** that can be exploited for cultural, spiritual and educational growth as well as for economic, commercial and political gain.

Within the 'language as a resource' orientation, there tends to be the assumption that linguistic diversity does not cause separation nor less integration in society. Rather, it is possible that **national unity and linguistic diversity can co-exist**. Unity and diversity are not necessarily incompatible. Tolerance and cooperation between groups may be as possible *with* linguistic diversity as they would be *unlikely* when such linguistic diversity is repressed.

A frequent debate concerns **which languages** are a resource? The favored languages tend to be those that are both international and particularly valuable in international trade. A lower place is given in the status rankings to minority languages that are small, regional and of less perceived value in the international marketplace. For example, in England, French has traditionally been placed in schools at the top of the first division. German, Spanish, Danish, Dutch, Modern Greek, Italian and Portuguese are the major European languages placed into the second division. Despite large numbers of mother tongue Bengali, Panjabi, Urdu, Gujerati, Hindi and Turkish speakers, the politics of English education relegates these languages to a lowly position in the school curriculum. Thus a caste system of languages has been created in England. The caste system is Eurocentric, culturally discriminatory and economically shortsighted, 'allowing languages already spoken in the home and community to be eroded, whilst starting from scratch to teach other languages in schools and colleges' (Stubbs, 1991, p. 225).

To **conclude**: while the three orientations have differences, they also share certain common aims: of national unity, of individual's rights, and of fluency in the majority language (e.g. English) being important to economic opportunities. The basic difference tends to be whether monolingualism in the majority language or full bilingualism should be encouraged as a means to achieving those ends. All three orientations connect language with politics, economics, society and culture. Each orientation recognizes that language is not simply a means of communication but is also connected with socialization into the local and wider society, as well as a powerful symbol of heritage and identity. The differences between the three orientations lie in the socialization and identity to be fostered: assimilation or pluralism, integration or separatism, monoculturalism or multiculturalism.

US LANGUAGE ORIENTATIONS

That the three orientations have common aims as well as vital differences is illustrated in the case of the USA. The USA has long been a willing receptacle of peoples of many languages: German, French, Polish, Italian, Greek, Welsh, Arabic, Chinese, Japanese and Spanish to name a few examples. Bull *et al.* (1992) portray the situation as follows:

> 'Cultural and linguistic differences have been a source of strength and controversy in the USA since its founding. Indeed, this country's founding and much subsequent US history can be seen as a continuing search for unity in diversity, for *e pluribus unum*, especially among its residents of European extraction. What could unite the New York Dutch, the Pennsylvania German, and the Virginia English; the Massachusetts Puritan, the Pennsylvania Quaker, the Maryland Catholic, and the Virginia Anglican; the Yankee trader, the northern farmer, and the southern plantation owner? How could the USA assimilate and capitalize upon its Norwegian, Irish, Russian, Italian, Polish, and Jewish immigrants? And more recently, what relationship could white Anglo majorities establish with formerly disenfranchised and economically marginalized African-American, Chinese, Japanese, Native American, and Latino minorities?' (Bull *et al.*, 1992, p. 1)

The receptacle of in-migration was transformed into a **melting pot** to assimilate and unify. The dream became an integrated United States with shared social, political and economic ideals. Quotes from two US Presidents illustrate this 'melting pot' attitude. Roosevelt in 1917 urged all immigrants to adopt the English language:

> 'It would be not merely a misfortune but a crime to perpetuate differences of language in this country… We should provide for every immigrant by day schools for the young, and night schools for the adult, the chance to learn English; and if after say five years he has not learned English, he should be sent back to the land from whence he came.' (quoted in Gonzalez, 1979)

President Reagan's view in the late 1980s was that it is 'absolutely wrong and against American concepts to have a bilingual education program that is now openly, admittedly dedicated to preserving their native language and never getting them adequate in English so they can go out into the job market and participate' (quoted in Crawford, 1999, p. 53; from the *Democrat Chronicle*, Rochester, 3 March, 1981, p. 2a). This melting pot attitude has continued with the English-only movement in the USA.

THE ADVANCE OF ENGLISH

Within the USA, basic differences in 'language orientation' are especially exemplified in the movement to make English the official rather than the *de facto* national language (Crawford, 1992a, 1992b, 1999; Dicker, 1996, 2000; Wiley & Lukes, 1996; McGroarty, 1997; Schmidt, 2000). The political debate over the place of English in the USA illustrates how languages can be alternatively seen as a problem, right or resource.

At the federal level, there is no reference to language in either the 1776 Declaration of Independence or the 1789 United States Constitution, the two founding documents of the USA. However, in the last 25 years in the USA, there have been proposals to add amendments to the Constitution that would name English as the official language. Called Official English or English-only legislation, considerable debate has been provoked.

In April 1981, Senator S.I. Hayakawa, a Californian Republican, proposed an English Language Amendment to the Constitution of the USA. This aimed at making English the official language of the USA so, he said, to develop further participative democracy and unification. The Amendment failed but it helped spawn the 'English-Only' or 'Official English' movement in the USA (which includes the 'US English' and the 'English First' organizations). US English was founded in 1983 by Senator Hayakawa and John Tanton who was particularly interested in restrictions on immigration and population control. By 1990 it was claimed that the membership of US English had grown to 400,000. In 1987, a more militant group – English First – joined US English in lobbying for the total supremacy of English in education, voting and administration.

Bilingual education was seen as promoting separate language communities, a division in US society, an indifference to English, and making English speakers, it was claimed, strangers in their own localities (Crawford, 1999). The solution for US English was through English language which would unite and harmonize. Learning English early in school, learning curriculum content through English would produce, it claimed, integrated US neighborhoods. Thus, US English's preferred immigrant is someone who learns English quickly as well as acquiring US customs and culture, acquires skills that are useful in the economic prosperity of the country, works hard and achieves the US dream. For Imoff (1990), bilingual education only serves to destroy rather than deliver that dream.

The movement for English as the proclaimed US national language has not been purely about English and national unity. Racism, bigotry, paranoia, xenophobia, white superiority and dominance have also been present. A Memorandum by Dr John Tanton, when Chairman of US English, revealed the darker side: 'As Whites see their power and control over their lives declining, will they simply go quietly into the night? Or will there be an explosion?' (quoted in Crawford, 1999, p. 68). This Memorandum went on further to pose perceived threats from Latinos: bribery as an accepted culture, Roman Catholicism as cultivating church authority rather than national authority, the non-use of birth control and fast population growth of Latinos, high drop-out rates in school and low educability. This hints at scapegoating, the displacement of fears about social, political and economic positioning onto language, and using English as a means of asserting cultural and economic superiority (Dicker, 2000).

While the debate about integration and pluralism will be examined later, there is little disagreement about certain desirable outcomes between the positions of the English-only group and the '**English-plus**' pro-bilingual response in the USA (e.g. children becoming fluent in English). The difference is in the route to its achievement. For the English-only group, English language skills are best acquired through English monolingual education. For the English-plus group, skills in the English language can be successfully fostered through 'strong' forms of bilingual education. Both groups appear to acknowledge that full English proficiency is important in opening doors to higher education, business, commerce and the occupational market. Full proficiency in the majority language will usually be equated to equality of educational and vocational opportunity.

As Chapter 11 shows, the evidence exists for support of 'strong' versions of bilingual education and hence for the 'English plus' position. Such evidence supports the use of the home minority language in the classroom at least until the end of elementary education and probably further. Achievement across the curriculum, achievement in subjects as diverse as science and history, mathematics and geography would not seem to suffer but be enhanced by 'strong' forms of bilingual education. Such achievement includes English (second) language competence. Research on the cognitive effects of bilingualism seems to support the ownership of two languages to enhance rather than impoverish intellectual functioning.

The **place of English** in the USA and much of the world is strong and becoming stronger. As a result of the emergence of the USA as the major economic power of the 20th century, and due to British colonization before the 20th century, the world

Certain states make reference to language in their Constitutions: New Mexico where English and Spanish are official languages; Hawaii where English and native Hawaiian are official languages; Colorado, Florida and Nebraska where English has been named as the official language. In 1988 Arizona passed an Amendment making English the official language. However, in 1998, the Arizona Supreme Court ruled out the Amendment as an infringement of the rights to free speech under the First Amendment of the Constitution. Many states have Resolutions or legislation declaring English as the official language. These include: Alabama, Alaska, Arizona, Arkansas, California, Georgia, Illinois, Indiana, Kansas, Kentucky, Mississippi, Missouri, Montana, Nebraska, New Hampshire, North Carolina, North Dakota, South Carolina, South Dakota, Tennessee, Virginia and Wyoming. New Mexico, Oregon and Washington have passed Resolutions in favor of English Plus. Further details can be found on James Crawford's WWW site: http://ourworld.compuserve.com/homepages/JWCRAWFORD/can-la.htm

status of English is not in doubt. Approximately 375 million people in the world speak English as a first language (Graddol, 1997). With English based Creoles and Pidgins, this rises to over 400 million speakers (Crystal, 1997). The number of English second language speakers is more contentious, with figures between 100 million and 400 million often quoted. Crystal's (1997) overview suggests 350 million and Graddol (1997) 375 million. The variations are due to guesses or estimates being required in many countries, and to the criteria for inclusion as a second language speaker (see Chapter 1) being variable — see Crystal (1995, 1997). The numbers who have learnt English as a foreign language also varies very widely with estimates ranging from 100 million to 1000 million depending on how much 'learning' has occurred. In all, Crystal's (1997) 'middle of the road' estimate is of a grand total of 1200–1500 million English speakers in the world.

Numbers of speakers is less important than the **prestigious domains and functions** that English dominates. 'English has a dominant position in science, technology, medicine, and computers; in research, books, periodicals, and software; in transnational business, trade, shipping, and aviation; in diplomacy and international organizations; in mass media entertainment, news agencies, and journalism; in youth culture and sport; in education systems, as the most widely learnt foreign language' (Phillipson, 1992, p. 6). Such a widespread use of English means that Anglo culture, Anglo institutions, and Anglo ways of thinking and communicating spread rapidly. English then tends to displace the domains and functions of other languages. In technology, communications, medicine, the Internet and entertainment, English has become the dominant world language and a major international communication link, for example, in politics, commerce, science, tourism and entertainment. Access to English means access to valued forms of knowledge and access to affluent and prestigious social and vocational positions.

Thus Gandhi (1927) accused **English** of being an intoxicating language, denationalizing a country such as India, and bringing mental slavery to Anglo forms of thinking and culture. He argued that English has been used in some multilingual societies to internally colonize, and to preserve the power of ruling elites. English has imposed linguistic uniformity that is culturally, intellectually, spiritually and emotional restricting. Other languages are then portrayed as confining, ethnocentric, divisive, alienating and anti-nationalistic. Asserting the dominance of English can become a means by which power elites justify exclusion and sustain inequality.

Yet it is not the language that is dominating but the people who use it. A language is not intrinsically dominating. No language is more suited to oppression, domination or imperialistm than another. It is the speakers of that language who are the oppressors, dominators and imperialists. Language can become the symbolic scapegoat for political and economic domination by people.

Also, as Davies (1996) warns, guilt about colonization and a desire to retreat to linguistic 'nature and innocence' should not prevent us in acknowledging that English gives access to personal status, modernization (e.g. technology, science), a global economy and international communication (Graddol, 1997; Graddol & Meinhof, 1999). Often students desire to learn English. For example, in the European Union, some 83% of pupils are reported to be learning English compared with 32% learning French and 16% learning German (Laitin, 1997).

However, advantages for individuals in the globalization of English need to be understood against the elitism and hegemony that is often attached to English (Pennycook, 1994; Wiley & Lukes, 1996; Dicker, 1996; McGroarty, 1997). Tollefson (1986) found that English in the Philippines was used as a means of 'creating and maintaining social divisions that serve an economy dominated by a small Philippine elite, and foreign economic interests' (p. 186). Thus while social psychology might view the role of English in the Philippines as 'instrumental motivation', at root there is a contest about political power and material wealth. There is nothing politically neutral about a language.

THE LANGUAGE ORIENTATIONS OF DIFFERENT MINORITY GROUPS

Alongside the immigrant languages in the USA is the existence of indigenous, native languages (e.g. Navajo — see Holm & Holm, 1990). Native Americans have been called 'strangers in their own country' as they are a minority with low power and status. Are there important differences between immigrant and indigenous language minorities, or differences between different immigrant minorities (e.g. the Chinese and the Mexican Americans) in language orientation? Ogbu (1978, 1983) made a distinction between 'castelike', 'immigrant' and 'autonomous' minority groups. (A minority group is defined in this book in terms of 'a minority of power' and not just by relative numerical size (Haberland, 1991).)

'**Autonomous**' minorities are not subordinate to the dominant majority group and have distinct separate identities. For example, some Jews in the USA often have a distinct racial, ethnic, religious, linguistic or cultural identity and are generally not politically or economically subordinate. Such autonomous minorities are unlikely to be characterized by disproportionate or persistent failure in school.

'**Castelike**' minorities tend to fill the least well paid jobs, are often given poor quality education, and are regarded as inferior by the dominant majority who sometimes negatively label them as 'culturally deprived', with 'limited English proficiency', with 'low innate intelligence' or pejoratively as 'bilinguals'. Ogbu (1978) classes Black Americans, Puerto Ricans, Mexican Americans, indigenous Indians and many Hispanic groups in the USA as 'castelike' minorities. The 'out-castes' of India and some of the Caribbean immigrants in England also share these characteristics. Such minorities may see themselves as relatively powerless, immobile in status and confined to subservience and domination. Most have been permanently and often involuntarily incorporated into the 'host' society. Such a group experience disproportionate failure at school. Failure at school confirms the low expectations they have of themselves and the negative attributions of majority groups. A sense of inferiority is joined by low levels of motivation to succeed in the wider society.

In the main, Ogbu's (1978) '**immigrant**' minorities have moved relatively willingly to the USA and may be relatively more motivated to succeed at school and seek prosperity. Cubans, Filipinos, Japanese and Koreans in the USA were included in this group (Ogbu, 1978). Another example is the Chinese immigrants who, as a generalization, are keen to succeed, positive about the opportunities in schooling and are relatively optimistic about improving their lot. Some 'immigrant' language minority individuals may arrive having been educated in the home country, and are literate and motivated to achieve.

'**Immigrant**' minorities tend to lack power, status and will often be low down on the occupational ladder. However, they do not necessarily perceive themselves in the same way as their dominant 'hosts'. 'As strangers, they can operate psychologically outside established definitions of social status and relations' (Ogbu, 1983, p. 169). Such 'immigrant' minorities may still suffer racial discrimination and hostility, yet are less intimidated and paralyzed by dominating majorities compared with 'castelike' minorities. Parents may have relatively strong aspirations for the success of their children in school and also expect vocational and social mobility in their offspring. Pride in ethnic identity is not lost but preserved by the parents, who see their reference group as back in the homeland or in the immigrant neighborhood.

One example of the influence of parents and the language community is given by Corson (1985, 1992). In Australia, 'Italian, Portuguese and Macedonian children from low-income backgrounds who had learned their English in school as a second language, out-performed their Anglo-Australian classmates from similar low-income backgrounds on a battery of language instruments and in school examinations, even though the latter spoke English as their mother tongue and were matched in non-verbal reasoning ability with the former' (Corson, 1992, p. 59). This example is important as it underlines the danger of simple statements about the expected performance of language minority children in mainstream education. The culture of the language community and the attitudes to schooling of parents may be examples of powerful influences on children's motivation to succeed in school.

There are many other factors contributing to the success of children than their type of minority group, including many 'success stories' from 'castelike minorities'.

Ogbu's (1978) distinction between 'autonomous, castelike and immigrant' minorities does not allow easy classification of different language minorities into these three groups. The criteria for classification are not precise enough nor are they validated by research studies. There is also the **danger** of stereotyping different language groups when there is much variability within such groups; sometimes more than the variability between the groups. However, the differences between 'castelike' and 'immigrant' minorities help explain why equally disadvantaged groups facing discrimination from the dominant majority perform differently at school. Poverty, poor quality schooling and powerlessness do not fully explain language minority failure in education. Beyond socioeconomic class and language differences, academic and economic success or failure may, in part, be due to cultural differences among language minorities. Castelike minorities seem locked into a system that perpetuates inequalities and discrimination. Other minorities attempt to escape the subtractive system which confines their participation in society and confirms their powerlessness. 'Immigrant' and autonomous minorities may show relatively less failure at school, partly explained by their different orientation to language. Language minority education ('strong' forms of bilingual education) therefore become highly important for castelike minorities to attempt to counteract the discrimination of the dominant minority and counteract the acceptance and internalization of that discrimination and economic deprivation.

The call for increased provision of 'strong' forms of bilingual education for 'castelike' and 'immigrant' minorities may not be welcomed by the dominant majority. Those with power and wealth may see such 'strong' forms of bilingual education as upsetting the status quo and usurping the power structure (Cummins, 1991a). The worry for the dominant majority may be that the 'castelike', the unemployed and those in poorly paid manual labor will be **empowered** by such education. The dominated may then begin to contest and threaten differences of rank, reward and rule. 'As the minority group is empowered through jobs, preferred status, professionalization, the majority becomes frightened. In an effort to regain control, it enforces monolingualism not only as an educational goal, but also as the most valuable educational approach' (O. García, 1991a, p. 5). When there is prosperity and liberal politics (e.g. the Civil Rights era), some empowerment of language minorities may be granted through 'strong' forms of bilingual education'.

When there is economic recession, less liberal politics and language minority self-assertiveness, 'strong' forms of bilingual education may be less favored by those in power. Dominant majorities at such times may wish to control access to the more prestigious jobs, preserve their power and wealth. This may result in hostility to 'strong' forms of bilingual education which threaten to give language minorities an increased share of power, wealth and status (O. García, 1991a).

The dominant majority often see minority language education as creating national disunity rather than unity, disintegration rather than integration. The frequent **criticism of bilingual education** is that it serves to promote differences rather than similarities, to separate rather than integrate. In England and in the USA, the majority public viewpoint tends to be for unity, integration and assimilation of immigrant, language minority communities. Indeed, the strongest arguments for bilingual education on cognitive and educational grounds may well fail unless a strong argument can be advanced for linguistic and cultural pluralism. Does bilingual education lead to greater or lesser tolerance, a common or a separate identity, a sense of anomie or an ability to belong to two cultures simultaneously? Are language minority children taught (rightly or wrongly) to be in conflict or at peace with the majority? Is bilingual education the arena for a power struggle between majority and minority? These questions are now tackled through examining the central debate on assimilation and pluralism.

ASSIMILATION

The social and political questions surrounding bilingual education tend to revolve around two contrasting ideological positions. 'At one extreme is **assimilation**, the belief that cultural groups should give up their "heritage" cultures and take on the host society's way of life. At the opposite pole is **multiculturalism**, the view that these groups should maintain their heritage cultures as much as possible' (Taylor, 1991, p. 1). In the US example, Schmidt (2000) talks of two camps: assimilationists and pluralists. 'Pluralists favor using the state to enhance the presence and status of minority languages in the United States, while assimilationists seek state policies that will ensure the status of English as the country's sole public language.' (p. 4).

The assimilationist viewpoint is pictured in the idea of a melting pot. Zangwill's play *'The Melting Pot'* (1914) introduced the idea of diverse immigrant elements being merged to make a new homogenized whole. 'Into the Crucible with you all! God is making the American'. The idea of the melting pot immediately throws up two different perspectives.

First, there is the idea that the final product, for example the US American, is made up by a contribution of all the cultural groups that enter the pot. The cultural groups melt together until the final product is a unique combination. No one ingredient dominates. Each cultural group makes its own contribution to the final taste. However, this is not the usual view associated with the melting pot. So second, the melting pot often means cultural groups giving up their heritage culture and adopting that of the host culture. In this second melting pot picture, cultural groups are expected to conform to the dominant national culture.

The rationale for this assimilationist perspective is that equality of opportunity, meritocracy and the **individual** having a chance of economic prosperity due to personal effort are each incompatible with the separate existence of different racial and cultural groups. When the emphasis is on individuality in terms of rights, freedom, effort and affluence, the argument for assimilation is that language **groups** should not have separate privileges and rights from the rest of society. Advantage and disadvantage associated with language minority groups is to be avoided so individual equality of opportunity can prevail.

'The assimilationist vision yearns for and insists upon a national community that is monolingual and monocultural, in which linguistic diversity does not threaten to engulf us in a babel of discordant sounds signifying a shredded social fabric. The pluralist vision, in contrast, understands the United States as an ethnically diverse and multilingual society with a tragic past of racialized ethnocultural domination, but standing now at a point of historic opportunity to realize – through a policy of multicultural and linguistic pluralism – the promise of its ongoing project of democratic equality. (Schmidt, 2000, p. 183)

Assimilationist ideology is an umbrella term under which a variety of types of assimilation may occur: cultural, structural, marital, identificational, attitudinal, behavioral, social and civic (Gordon, 1964). An important distinction is between **economic-structural** assimilation and **cultural** assimilation (Skutnabb-Kangas, 1977). Some immigrant and minority group members may wish to assimilate culturally into the mainstream society. Cultural assimilation refers to giving up a distinct cultural identity, adopting the mainstream language and culture. In general, language minorities will usually wish to avoid such cultural assimilation. However, economic-structural assimilation may be sought by language minorities. Such assimilation refers to equality of access, opportunities and treatment (Paulston, 1992b). For example, equal access to jobs, goods and services, equality in voting rights and privileges, equal opportunities and treatment in education, health care and social security, law and protection, may be desired by language minorities. Therefore, structural incorporation tends to be more desired and cultural assimilation more resisted (Schermerhorn, 1970; Paulston, 1992b).

Assimilation may be explicit, implied or concealed (Tosi, 1988). For example, **explicit assimilation** occurs when language minority children are required to take monolingual education solely in the majority language (e.g. submersion education in the USA). **Implied assimilation** is when such children are diagnosed as having 'special needs' and are offered compensatory forms of education (e.g. Sheltered English and Transitional Bilingual Education in the USA). **Concealed assimilation** may be found, for example, in some types of multicultural education program (see the next chapter) where language minorities may be instructed in racial harmony, national unity, and individual achievement using majority language criteria to gauge success. Such a program is designed to achieve hegemony and ethnic harmony (Tosi, 1988).

Since there are a **variety of forms of assimilation**, measuring the extent to which assimilation has occurred is going to be difficult. Is assimilation measured by segregation and integration in terms of housing of immigrants, for example, by their positions within the economic order, by the extent of intermarriage between different cultural groups or by the attitudes they exhibit? Assimilation is thus multidimensional and complex (Skutnabb-Kangas, 1991). Assimilation is neither easily defined nor easily quantified. Assimilationists may have mildly differing views. One example will illustrate.

A few assimilationists may accept that school students should maintain their home language and culture. However, they would argue that this is the **responsi-**

bility of the home and not the school (Porter, 1990). However, most assimilationists will argue that, if economic resources are scarce and school budgets are stretched, bilingual programs should not be supported, particularly if the costs are greater than regular mainstream programs (Secada, 1993).

PLURALISM

With the increased accent on **ethnicity** since the 1960s, the assumptions of assimilation were challenged and the 'new ethnicity' born (see Fishman, 1999). Ideologies that surround the terms **'integration'**, **'ethnic diversity'**, **'pluralism'** and **'multiculturalism'** (discussed in the next chapter) challenged the assimilationist philosophy. The picture of the melting pot has been contrasted with alternative images: the patchwork quilt, the tossed salad, the linguistic mosaic and the language garden. One popular metaphor is the salad bowl, with each ingredient separate and distinguishable, but contributing in a valuable and unique way to the whole. A different 'integration' metaphor, favored in Canada, is the linguistic mosaic, with different pieces joined together in one holistic arrangement.

A pluralist approach assumes that different language groups can live together in the same territory in relative harmony and without unjust domination of one group by another. An atmosphere of mutual understanding and tolerance is essential (Parrillo, 1996).

> 'Pluralists also argue that individual bilingualism is not only possible but desirable in that it facilitates cultural enrichment and cross-cultural understanding. By combating distrust and intolerance toward linguistic diversity, pluralists hope to create a climate of acceptance that will promote greater status equality between ethnolinguistic groups and therefore a higher level of national unity.' (Schmidt, 2000, p. 62/63)

Assimilationists argue that linguistic pluralism, rather than promoting harmony, leads to ethnic enclaves that cause inequalities between groups and particularly create ethnic conflict. For such people, linguistic assimilation provides the social, political, and economic integration necessary for equality of opportunity and political harmony.

In reality, there are often large status differences between languages in a society. Where one language is associated with power, wealth and prestige, the tendency of individuals is to choose this language of economic and social mobility. The economic dice is often so loaded against pluralism such that forced assimilation is a superfluous idea.

At another level of analysis, Schmidt (2000) argues that the root of the assimilation/pluralism issue is not language but identity, of which language is one component:

> 'ultimately the language policy debate in the United States is not about language as such but about what kind of political community we are and wish to be. It is, in short, centered in identity politics.' (p. 183)

Resolutions

In his detailed analysis, Schmidt (2000) suggests that apart from assimilation and pluralism, there are two other approaches to language policy: total domination by the language majority group and the exclusion of minority language (e.g. apartheid in the old South Africa), and confederation (as in Switzerland, Belgium and India – see Baker & Jones, 1998). In the context of the USA, Schmidt (2000) considers three language policy alternatives. He rejects the assimilationist argument as it ignores the legacy of racialized ethnic injustice and misconstrues the nature of relationships between individual identity, culture, the state, and equality of opportunity. He argues that the assimilationist argument also serves to maintain the privileged position of white, native English speakers.

While favoring a pluralist alternative, Schmidt (2000) finds obstacles to its complete acceptance. He argues that the kind of social integration that is envisioned by pluralism (i.e. individualist and voluntarist) is likely to perpetuate the very social inequalities between language groups that it seeks to overcome. He argues that a policy of linguistic pluralism is insufficient to achieve social and economic justice for language minority communities. Pluralists argue for individual choice in language and culture, but there is no equal choice as there is no equal starting-point or level playing field. Without an equal starting point, the context of choice for individuals is constrained by numerous unequal circumstances for which language minorities bear no responsibility. Thus Schmidt (2000) is pessimistic about the reality of outcomes for a pluralist position when there is free choice. The language of power in the USA is English, so individuals will typically choose English in pursuit of their own advantage. Social mobility and economic advance are pragmatically unlikely from a pluralist position, however strong the intellectual arguments.

> 'Assimilationists are unrealistic because their ideology posits a monocultural and monolingual country that does not exist in the real world; more importantly, a consequence of its unrealistic assumptions is the continued unjust subordination of language minority groups by the privileged Anglo, European-origin majority. Pluralists too are unrealistic in that they assume that an egalitarian society of multiple cultural communities can be achieved through a combination of individualistic rights-based free choice measures and moral exhortations to Anglos to respect linguistic and cultural diversity.' (Schmidt, 2000, p. 209)

In Quebec, the answer is to establish a separate language community. This is one rather unlikely alternative for the USA discussed by Schmidt (2000) – the establishment of non-English-dominant territories to reproduce themselves and flourish. Such language communities require territory of their own to withstand the strong pressure to shift to English in North America. Such a linguistic territory would give a minority language status and avoid marginalization and stigmatization. The USA already has such linguistic territories in the island commonwealth of Puerto Rico and in the American Indian reservations on the mainland. This would give regional autonomy to areas such as southern California, northern New Mexico and south Texas.

The establishing of non-English-dominant territories in the USA is seemingly not a politically viable option because most urbanized US areas have multiple groups of language minorities and thus a complex linguistic mosaic. Another alternative is an enhanced pluralist language policy in USA that aims for pluralistic integration – Schmidt's (2000) first-choice option that is also supported by May (2001) who argues for language minority group rights that retain within them the protection of individual liberties.

The two positions of assimilation and pluralism differ in such fundamental, ideological ways, that simple solutions and resolutions are impossible. When evidence for the maintenance of minority languages and cultures is produced, assimilationists are likely to argue that attitudes and behavior are still in the change process. That is, assimilationists will argue that, over time, people will move away from minority cultural maintenance and prefer the majority language and culture. Assimilationists tend to believe that bilingualism and biculturalism are temporary and transient, and lead to a preferable unifying monolingualism.

When evidence favors assimilation having taken place in society (e.g. by the second or third generation after in-migration), pluralists will tend to argue in two different ways. First, that the change towards assimilation has only occurred on certain dimensions (e.g. language rather than economic assimilation). Second, that sometimes the wheel turns full circle. Revival and resurrection in future generations may occur in response to repression and renouncement by previous generations.

The **difference between assimilationists and pluralists** is rooted in basic human ideologies and motives, making resolution all the more difficult. Any such resolution of the assimilation versus pluralism debate is also affected by the **economic reward system**. Both assimilation and pluralism can be promoted by the need to earn a living and the desire to acquire or increase affluence. Assimilation may be chosen to secure a job, to be vocationally successful and to achieve affluence. The minority language and culture may be left behind in order to prosper in the majority language community. At the same time, language planning can be used to ensure that there are jobs and promotion within the minority language community, as discussed in Chapter 4.

Resolution of the debate about assimilation versus pluralism must not be tightly stereotyped. The dominant group in society may, at times, not prefer assimilation. Minority groups may not be permitted to assimilate, thus keeping their members in poorly paid employment. Such a minority group is then exploited by the dominant group. The economic interests of the majority group can be served by **internal colonialism** rather than assimilation (e.g. economically isolating or manipulating an indigenous minority language group for majority group advantages).

Resolution is often pragmatic rather than philosophical. Often, being fluent in the majority language is an employment necessity, and this can promote assimilation. To obtain work and compete with members of the majority group, a minority language person typically has to function in the majority language. Bilinguals may also perceive that they can function economically both in their minority group and with the dominant group. That is, they have the ability to be economically viable in either language community and form a bridge between those two communities. However, as Chapter 20 will reveal, becoming bilingual by learning the majority language is no guarantee of economic improvement. Otheguy (1982, p. 306) provides a salutary warning from the US experience. 'English monolingualism has meant little in terms of economic advantages to most blacks and to the masses of poor descendants of poor European immigrants. Hispanics who now speak only English can often be found in as poor a state as when they first came. English monolingualism among immigrants tends to follow economic integration rather than cause it'.

Two opposing views – assimilation and pluralism – have so far been discussed. Edwards (1985) indicates that **middle positions** are possible. It is possible to participate in mainstream society and maintain one's minority language and culture. For many individuals, there will be both a degree of assimilation and a degree of preservation of one's heritage. Total assimilation and total isolation are less likely than some accommodation of the majority ideology within an overall ideology of pluralism; cultural maintenance within partial assimilation. Within multiculturalism and pluralism, an aggressive, militant pluralism may be seen as a threat to the social harmony of society. Instead, a more liberal pluralistic viewpoint may allow both membership of the wider community and an identification with the heritage cultural community.

EIGHT STRATEGIES FOR LINGUISTIC AND CULTURAL DIVERSITY

This analysis is widened by Tyack (1995) who suggests that there are eight strategies or solutions used to cope with ethnic, cultural or linguistic diversity in a country. This is based on a historical analysis of cultural diversity in the USA.

- **Discrimination**. For example, the segregation into separate schools and the denial of schooling to Chinese and Japanese immigrant children in California illustrate the most negative of reactions to linguistic and cultural diversity, and that is deliberate discrimination.
- **Separation**. Another form of segregation is to separate different language and cultural groups, sometimes with benign intent. For example, different provision is made for those of different linguistic and cultural origins. The aim is to provide appropriate education for different groups.
- **Assimilation**. The third strategy is to try and eradicate linguistic and cultural differences by assimilating immigrants into the same common characteristics. Or in the case of colonialization, to assimilate indigenous minority groups into the colonizer's language and culture. Attacks on bilingual education and a multicultural curriculum are often based on a fear that assimilation will not occur (or be resisted) through bilingual education.
- **Desegregation.** Desegregation attempts to secure full citizenship and educational rights for minority language and cultural groups. Equality of opportunity and equality of provision (e.g. in education) is attempted.

- **Ignore Differences**. Some believe that schools should act 'naturally' with regard to language and cultural minorities. As well as being color-blind, social-class-blind, gender-blind, schools should also be blind to linguistic and cultural differences among children. With the idealistic aim of treating everyone equally and without presuppositions, such neutrality is difficult to achieve and tends to ignore the differences in power, wealth and status between different language and cultural groups.
- **Compensation**. Another reaction to diversity is to give special help to ethnic, linguistic and cultural minorities. Compensatory education, remedial education, special tracks or streams and special reception centers for immigrants may each aim to give children a beneficial start, correct faulty socialization which children supposedly have received at home, or provide a fast transition into mainstream education.
- **Celebration**. Another strategy, particularly found in intercultural and multicultural education, is to celebrate ethnic, linguistic and cultural diversity. The differences between groups are appreciated, proclaimed and celebrated.
- **Preservation**. Another strategy is to maintain differences between the groups, believing that linguistic and cultural differences should be preserved in a positive way by detachment. Behind this idea is the concept of group as well as individual rights. The notion is that all groups have equal rights and such rights are best fostered by separate but equal treatment, preserving and not breaking down boundaries between groups.

These are not eight separate political or educational strategies. Rather, there is overlap and intermingling between the eight ideas. Nevertheless, they do suggest a variety of responses, a variety of motives, different perspectives and different wanted outcomes. For example, among the eight different responses there is a tension between:

- celebrating individual differences and celebrating group differences;
- a preference for individualism and personal freedoms and a preference for development that occurs through strong group membership;
- a desire for 'the common good' and universal equality of treatment for all people and a desire for local rights, local empowerment and minority group allegiance;
- solidarity at a national level, and solidarity in terms of an ethnic or linguistic group;
- social justice by equality of provision and social justice through diversity being celebrated and not eradicated.

ASSIMILATION AND IMMIGRANTS

The **debate** over assimilation and pluralism has recently sharpened (John Edwards, 1995; Takaki, 1993; Fishman, 1999; McKay & Wong, 2000). A re-emphasis on personal endeavor, individual striving for success, a lessening of reliance on welfare and collectives (e.g. positive discrimination for ethnic groups) has been joined by ethnic conflicts (e.g. in Bosnia, Croatia, Serbia and in the old USSR). This has led to increased arguments and disputes about the merits of assimilation and pluralism (Takaki, 1993). But such debates need placing in their historical context, particularly where immigrants are concerned.

The **expectation** was that immigrants into the USA, Canada, Germany and England, for example, would be pleased to have escaped political oppression or economic disadvantage and be jubilant to embrace equality of opportunity and personal freedom. The expectation was that an individual would be pleased to give up their past identity and make a commitment to a new national identity. Yet heritage culture and cultural identity have persisted, resisted and insisted. Assimilation has often not occurred. Is this deliberate or difficult, desired or unwelcome?

Assimilation may be sought by immigrants. Many wish to assimilate, but come to reside in segregated neighborhoods and segregated schools. Thus assimilation can be **prevented** by social and economic factors outside the wishes of the immigrants. Some groups of immigrants may wish to be categorized as US citizens, but are categorized and treated by mainstream society as different, separate and non-US. The conditions under which immigrants live may create the negative labels and social barriers that enforce non-integration. As Otheguy (1982, p. 312) remarks of the USA: 'Because of their experience with racism in this country, many Hispanics have long ago given up hope of disappearing as a distinct group'. The result may be the prevention of assimilation and integration with a consequent need to embrace some form of multiculturalism for survival, security, status and self-enhancement.

Veltman (2000) has shown empirically from US census data that US immigrants learn English quite rapidly, many adopting English as their primary and preferred language, even abandoning use of their mother tongue (e.g. Scandinavians, Germans), and rearing their children solely in English. This is the case for all language minorities although Spanish, Chinese and Greek immigrants are relatively more likely to maintain bilingualism. Thus repressive measures to assimilate immigrants or initiatives to promote English assimilation in schools are not needed. Immigration does not pose a threat to the dominance of English.

> 'The desire of immigrants in all minority language groups to learn English and make this language their own is sufficiently high to produce the kind of outcome that most Americans cherish, that is, that immigrants become English-speaking people. I unequivocally demonstrate that rates of language shift to English are so high that all minority languages are routinely abandoned, depriving the USA of one type of human resource that may be economically and politically desirable both to maintain and develop.' (Veltman, 2000, p. 58)

MAINTAINING ETHNIC IDENTITY

A different situation is where a language minority prefers not to assimilate culturally. Where an ethnic group wishes to maintain its cultural identity and a degree of enclosure (Schermerhorn, 1970), **boundaries** between it and the dominant majority may be essential to continued ethnic identity (Barth, 1966). Boundaries between the language minority group and the dominant group will aid the preservation of ethnic identity and help maintain the vitality of the heritage language. Establishing boundaries and ethnic identity rest on several criteria (Allardt, 1979; Allardt & Starck, 1981):

(1) Self-categorization as a distinct ethnic group.
(2) Common descent and ancestry, be it real or imagined.
(3) Owning specific cultural traits or exhibiting distinctive cultural patterns, of which language may be the strongest example.
(4) Well established social organization patterns for interacting within the group and separately with 'outsiders'.

Some of the members of an ethnic group will fulfill all these four criteria; every member must fulfill at least one of the four criteria to be a member of that ethnic group. These criteria highlight the difference between **self-categorization** and **categorization by others**, particularly categorization by the dominant group. Barth (1966) argued that such categorizations essentially define an ethnic group. 'The existence of an ethnic group always presupposes categorization, either self-categorization or categorization by others' (Allardt, 1979, p. 30).

Such categorizations are rarely stable and tend to change over time. Allardt (1979) argued that:

> 'Previously, it was majorities who mainly performed the categorization and labeling of minorities. The principal aim of categorization was exclusion: majorities acted in order to safeguard their material privileges or else to persecute minorities. The results were often severe patterns of discrimination. Of course, minorities also often defended themselves by defining their own criteria for inclusion and belonging. There has occurred a definite change in the present ethnic revival. It is now mainly the minority who categorizes... The problems in the fields of ethnic relations have, as it were, changed from problems of discrimination to problems of recognition.' (Allardt, 1979, p. 68)

Categorization by others will often use cultural and geographical criteria. Some categorizations are imposed upon a language minority (e.g. as having 'limited language proficiency') and at other times attributed less openly to that minority. Such categorizations from outside the group include negative remarks about non-assimilation and non-integration. Self-categorization may re-phrase outsider remarks as self-identity, ethnic awareness and self-recognition.

Ethnic identity can thus be created by imposed categorization from without, or by invoked categorization from within. Self-categorization can be achieved through promoting ethnic social institutions (e.g. law, mass media, religious units, entertainment, sport and cultural associations working in the heritage language). Ethnic community schools (heritage language education) plus the careful planning of the ethnic language in the curriculum may be major component in self-categorization (García, 1983). Mobilizing ethnic group members to agitate for language legitimacy and reform, working towards a defined idealized vision of the status of the language may also aid self-categorization (C.H. Williams, 1991b). This raises a fundamental debate of how to achieve ethnic identity and language rights: persuasion or agitation; reform or revolt? This debate is now considered.

Should minority language groups always be in a cooperative functional relationship with the majority language? Does non-violent conflict sometimes need to be present to achieve rights for a language community? The achievements of the Basques and the Welsh would both seem to suggest that **conflict** with the majority is one mechanism of achieving language rights. Such a conflict viewpoint will place more emphasis on group rights than on individual rights. To be Basque may conflict with being Spanish. To be Welsh can conflict with being British. To be Quebecois may conflict with being Canadian. In these circumstances, cultural pluralism may not always lead to order and the maintenance of majority language rules in society. Should language minority groups pursue equilibrium or conflict?

EQUILIBRIUM OR CONFLICT?

Paulston (1980, 1992b) presents two major paradigms to interpret bilingual education. In the **equilibrium paradigm**, the different wheels that create the clockwork mechanism of society interact relatively harmoniously. The school, the economic order, social mobility and social processes interlock and work relatively harmoniously together. Change in society occurs by gradual, slow and smooth evolution. Conflict and disharmony are to be avoided because they lead to a breakdown in the clockwork mechanism. Radically new components will cause the system to stop functioning smoothly. Individual components in the mechanism are relatively unimportant in themselves. It is the overall clockwork mechanism that is important.

When the clock goes wrong, the fault is not within the **system** itself. One or more components must be a problem and will need to be adjusted. With language minority groups and bilingual education, any apparent failure will not be due to the system, but will be due to those components themselves. That is, the problems lie with the minority language groups and within the form of the bilingual education system. The problem will not be the system as a whole nor the overall educational system. Any failure in language minority students may be attributed to their poor English proficiency rather than to the educational system. Individuals will be blamed – not the system. Since the system works through English language instruction, more English language is required by the language minorities. In turn, any disadvantage or poverty that exists in such groups can be solved by improving their achievement at school via greater competence in the majority language. Since the oil of the clockwork mechanism is English language proficiency, once this is in place, language minority students will have equality of opportunity in the educational and economic systems. Bilingual education must maintain equilibrium in society.

Genesee (1987) analyses the **Canadian immersion programs** through this equilibrium approach. Such immersion programs are regarded as giving the majority group in society — the English speaking Canadian children — the bilingual proficiency to maintain their socioeconomic dominance in Canada. Set against the protests from French Quebec about the status of the French language in Canada, immersion education may be seen as aiding the stability of the bilingual situation in Canada. More French–English bilinguals created by the immersion schools seems to answer some of the protests of the Quebec people. (This is not necessarily the view of Quebec people who sometimes believe that their right to French speaking jobs is threatened by such immersion students.) Thus Canadian immersion programs are seen to produce equilibrium in the Canadian language situation.

A different viewpoint to the 'clockwork mechanism' equilibrium perspective is the **conflict paradigm** (Paulston, 1980, 1992b). Such a paradigm holds that conflict is a natural and expected part of the relationship between unequal power groups in a complex society. Given differences in culture, values, the unequal allocation of resources and variations in power within society, then conflict, radical views and disruption can be expected. Such a viewpoint often argues that real change occurs more by conflict, protest, non-violent and sometimes non-peaceful action, and less through the mending of minor problems within a system. Formal education tends to reproduce the dominance of the ruling elite over the masses, reproduces economic, social and political inequalities, inequality of opportunity and inequality of outcome in society.

The picture of a clockwork mechanism is replaced by a picture of an operation on an unhealthy body. The removal of an organ, a painful injection, the replacement or addition of tissue by grafting or plastic **surgery** may be radical and initially disruptive, but perceived as important if the health of the whole body is to improve. Minority language groups may be allotted too little power, too few rewards, and be disadvantaged in resources and rights. Since schools may perpetuate that disadvantage and subordinate power position, such linguistic, cultural and educational discrimination will need radical surgery.

'Weak' forms of bilingual education tend to perpetuate inequalities experienced by language minorities (Skutnabb-Kangas, 1999). In consequence, within the conflict perspective, **bilingual education** should attempt to right such inequality and injustice by positive discrimination. Bilingual education should be interventionist, even clashing with dominant viewpoints. Bilingual education can serve to encourage social, economic and educational change and cultural pluralism (Rippberger, 1993). 'Strong' bilingual education can aid the status of minority languages and cultures, reduce the pulls and pushes towards assimilation, and aid the empowerment of minorities (Skutnabb-Kangas, 1999a). Yet the Canadian immersion program, a 'strong' form of bilingual education, can be analyzed in a different way.

The Canadian immersion programs have been analyzed through a conflict perspective and not just through the equilibrium approach (e.g. Heller, 1994). There are language tensions and conflicts in Canada. For example, many French first language speakers feel threatened by those bilinguals for whom French is a second language. Bilingual anglophones are seen to be accessing power, prestige and privilege that have hitherto been the preserve of bilingual francophones (e.g. by gaining positions in high status professions). With immersion schools, anglophones can gain the linguistic and cultural capital for increased social and economic mobility and for political power. 'Education is currently a major site of the struggle waged between anglophones and francophones, and within each group as well, over whether or not bilingualism should be valuable; and if so, whose property it should be. As such, it represents a struggle over the distribution of wealth and power' (Heller, 1994, p. 7). Bilingual education is thus not about unity or integration, in this perspective, nor is it neutral. Bilingual education is about gaining advantages, cultural, linguistic and social wealth, and dominance in Canadian society. As such, it produces conflict with the minority francophone community (e.g. in Ontario).

In the conflict paradigm, the problems exist within society as a whole, not simply in terms of 'individual deficiency' or 'educational provision'. The causes and determinants of minority language problems are **within society**, and not simply due to the characteristics of minority language children. Radical surgery is sometimes defended for the survival and stability of a healthy body. Long-term health sometimes requires the short-term pain of radical surgery.

Teachers and education administrators, policy-makers and college professors may sometimes be faced with a choice: oil the wheels of the system or be radical and attempt to change the system. Often, compromises are made by professionals: seeking evolution within relative stability; development within dominant perspectives. Within an overall desire for equilibrium, small conflicts about policy and provision among school staff, for example, may regularly occur.

There is also another combination: those for whom conflict is, and must be, perpetual. For particular types of language activists (e.g. in Wales and the Basque region), conflict can become the norm: an equilibrium of conflict. One form of conflict politics may be language minority militancy (Schermerhorn, 1970). Language militants may attempt to gain control over the dominant majority and gain some form of ascendancy.

How can schools contribute to oiling and developing the clockwork machine, or changing the sick body by interventions into the core curriculum? The role to be played by schools comes partly through cultural and language awareness courses (see the next chapter) and mostly in attempts to introduce multiculturalism and anti-racism into part or throughout the curriculum. The next chapter explores these latter possibilities. One answer to the question is given by Cummins (1996, 2000b).

CUMMINS' THEORETICAL FRAMEWORK FOR MINORITY STUDENT INTERVENTION AND EMPOWERMENT

Cummins (1996, 2000b) argues that relations of power are at the heart of schooling outcomes. No more so than for minority language children who often suffer devaluation of identity, added subordination and disempowerment in their schooling experience. He argues that much restructuring of schools in the last two decades has had little impact on the achievement levels of minority language students. The reason is we have failed to engage the core, essential issues such as securing a very positive student identity, creating strong school–parental partnerships and empowering children and raising their expectations.

Cummins' (1986b, 1996, 2000b) has developed a theoretical framework that directly relates to policy, provision and practice with language minority students. Behind the theory are two ideas that have been discussed in this book already. First, 'language minority students instructed through the minority language (for example, Spanish) for all or part of the school day perform as well in English academic skills as comparable students instructed totally through English' (1986b, p. 20). Teaching children through a second or minority language usually leads to the satisfactory development of English academic skills.

Instead, bilingual children in the USA, for example, are taught English with the covert aim being to create a socially cohesive society. There is a simultaneous rejection of the home language and culture. Such 'language replacement' creates failure followed by 'blaming the victim' and more intense efforts to eradicate language diversity in children (Cummins, 1996). A vicious circle is produced whereby the method (submersion education) of reducing the perceived threat of social disruption and division in itself produces outcomes (low achievement) that reinforce the myth of bilingual children as culturally and linguistically deprived.

The second idea is the **'interdependence hypothesis'**. This proposed that 'to the extent that instruction through a minority language is effective in developing academic proficiency in the minority language, transfer of this proficiency to the majority language will occur given adequate exposure and motivation to learn the language' (Cummins, 1986b, p. 20). Research by Verhoeven (1994), for example, suggests that there was positive transfer between languages in literacy skills, sound systems (phonology) and communication skills (pragmatics). As may be expected, there was little transfer in lexicon (vocabulary) and syntax (e.g. grammar). Underlying the surface characteristics of both languages is one common core of developed ability or 'academic proficiency'. Beneath two protrusions on the water lies the one iceberg.

The third statement concerns context. Community and school liaison, power and status relationships all need to be considered in schooling for language minority students. Cummins (2000b) suggests that power relationships are a key to understanding the position and interventions needed with language minority students. Power relationships range from collaborative to coercive. Where dominant–subordinate role expectations and relationships are found, culturally diverse students will typically be denied their identity and home language (Cummins, 1997). Collaborative approaches will enable and empower the student, amplifying their self-expression and identity, allocating power to the powerless (see Cummins, 2000b). This theme will be returned to later in this chapter.

Cummins' (1986b, 2000b) suggests that minority language students are **'empowered' or 'disabled'** by four major characteristics of schools.

(1) **The extent to which minority language students' home language and culture are incorporated into the school curriculum**. If a minority language child's

home language and culture are excluded, minimized or quickly reduced in school, there is the likelihood that the child may become academically 'disabled'. Where the school incorporates, encourages and gives status to the minority language, the chances of empowerment are increased. Apart from potential positive and negative cognitive effects, the inclusion of minority language and culture into the curriculum may have effects on personality (e.g. self-esteem), attitudes, social and emotional well-being. This point is important because it raises a question about why bilingual education which emphasizes the minority language is successful. Is it due to such education fostering cognitive and academic proficiency, as the interdependence hypothesis suggests? Or is it also due to students' cultural identity being secured and reinforced, thus enhancing self-confidence and self-esteem? Cummins (1986b, 2000b) sees minority students' language and culture existing on an **additive–subtractive dimension**. 'Educators who see their role as adding a second language and cultural affiliation to their students' repertoire are likely to empower students more than those who see their role as replacing or subtracting students' primary language and culture.' (p. 25)

(2) **The extent to which minority communities are encouraged to participate in their children's education**. Where parents are given power and status in the partial determination of their children's schooling, the empowerment of minority communities and children may result. When such communities and parents are kept relatively powerless, inferiority and lack of school progress may result. The growth of paired reading schemes is evidence of the power of a parent–teacher partnership. Parents listening to their children reading on a systematic basis tend to be effective agents of increased literacy.

As an illustration of the importance of community participation, Cummins (1996) cites the Pajaro Valley Family Literacy Project in a rural area surrounding Watsonville, California. Spanish speaking parents met once a month to discuss chosen books, write and discuss poems written by their children and themselves (Ada, 1988b). Books were related to prior experiences, critically analyzed and applied to everyday events. Parents read to their children – including television recordings of parents reading their children's stories. This gave children (and their parents) much pride in themselves, their growing literacy, their homes and heritage. Confidence in themselves and in the power of their own self-expression increased. The community's language, culture, and personal experiences were validated, celebrated and empowered.

Teachers are seen as being located on a dimension ranging from the **collaborative to the exclusionary**. Teachers at the collaborative end encourage parents of minority languages to participate in their children's academic progress through home activities or the involvement of parents in the classroom. Teachers at the exclusionary end maintain tight boundaries between themselves and parents (Cummins, 2000b). Collaboration with parents may be seen as irrelevant, unnecessary, unprofessional, even detrimental to children's progress.

(3) **The extent to which education promotes the inner desire for children to become active seekers of knowledge and not just passive receptacles**. Learning can be active, independent, internally motivated or passive, dependent and requiring external pulls and pushes. The **transmission** model of teaching views children as buckets into which knowledge is willingly or unwillingly poured and teacher-controlled 'legitimate facts' are placed in the 'bank' by students (Cummins, 2000b). The hidden curriculum of the 'banking' model may reinforce and symbolize the powerlessness of language minority students. There are those in control and those controlled. The alternative model is 'transformative' and requires **reciprocal interaction** involving:

> 'a genuine dialogue between student and teacher in both oral and written modalities, guidance and facilitation rather than control of student learning by the teacher, and the encouragement of student/student talk in a collaborative learning context. This model emphasizes the development of higher level cognitive skills rather than just factual recall, and meaningful language use by students rather than the correction of surface forms. Language use and development are consciously integrated with all curricular content rather than taught as isolated subjects, and tasks are presented to students in ways that generate intrinsic rather than extrinsic motivation.' (Cummins, 1986b, p. 28)

If the 'banking' model is allied to the **disablement** of minority language students, then the 'transformative' model is related to the **empowerment** of students. This latter model aims to give students more control over their own learning, with consequent potential positive effects for self-esteem, cooperation and motivation.

(4) **The extent to which the assessment of minority language students avoids locating problems in the student and seeks to find the root of the problem in the social and educational system or curriculum wherever possible**. Psychological and educational tests tend by their very nature to locate problems in the individual student (e.g. low IQ, low motivation, backwardness in reading). At worst, educational psychologists and teachers may test and observe a child until a problem can be found in that child to explain poor academic attainment. Such a testing ideology and procedure may fail to locate the root of the problem in the social, economic or educational system. The subtractive nature of transitional bilingual education, the transmission model used in the curriculum, the exclusionary orientation of the teacher towards parents and the community and the relative economic deprivation of minority children could each or jointly be the real origin of a minority language child's problem. Therefore assessment and diagnostic activity need to be **Advocacy rather than Legitimization oriented** (Cummins, 2000b). Advocacy means the assessor or diagnostician advocating for the child, by critically inspecting the social and educational context in which the child operates. This may involve comments about the power and status relationships between the dominant and dominated groups, at national, community, school and classroom level (Forhan & Scheraga, 2000).

Empowerment thus becomes an important concept in transforming the situations of many language minorities. 'Empowerment means the process of acquiring power, or the process of transition from lack of control to the acquisition of control over one's life and immediate environment' (Delgado-Gaitan & Trueba, 1991, p. 138). Empowerment means movement for minority language students from coercive, superior–inferior (subordinate) relationships, to collaborative relationships, power sharing and power creating, where the identities of minorities are affirmed and voiced. Thus for Cummins (1996), empowerment is 'the collaborative creation of power. Students whose schooling experiences reflect collaborative relations of power develop the ability, confidence and motivation to succeed academically. They participate competently in instruction as a result of having developed a secure sense of identity and the knowledge that their voices will be heard and respected in the classroom' (p. 15).

Empowerment can be furthered by education, but also needs to be realized in legal, social, cultural and particularly economic and political events. Delgado-Gaitan and Trueba (1991) argue for necessary sociocultural and political dimensions of empowerment to be added to the possibilities of empowerment through education. Empowerment also needs to include those language groups who generally receive minimal support and advocacy (e.g. Black English (Ebonics), Creole and Deaf People).

Empowerment and Pedagogy

When the focus is on the language minority group, and particularly when the focus is on the experience of individual bilinguals, differences in prosperity and economic opportunity, in power and pedagogic opportunity are evident. As a generalization, language minorities have less power and less chance of acquiring political power compared with language majorities. Such minorities are subservient to the majority who reproduce their dominance in particular classroom process (see below). This powerlessness is enacted, transmitted and reproduced in the **classroom** by the authority relationship of, for example, a majority language teacher and a submissive language minority student (Delpit, 1988, 1995).

If classrooms transmit and reinforce power relations and powerlessness, is this reversible? Is language minority powerlessness reproduced inside 'weak' forms of bilingual education? Can this be reversed by 'strong' forms of bilingual education? It is important to ask 'how' and 'why' language minority children are at a disadvantage in the classroom. Can there be **attempted reversal and empowerment**? Delpit's (1988, 1995) analyses the 'Culture of Power' in classrooms.

(1) The 'Culture of Power' is enacted in the classroom by:
   - teachers having power and dominance over students;
   - the curriculum (e.g. via text books) determining a legitimate world view; the curriculum taught may be restricted to a majority language viewpoint (e.g. white, US, English language) and taught as supreme, incontestable and 'correct';

- majority language educators define narrowly what constitutes approved forms of intelligent behavior; what is regarded as 'intelligent behavior' is formulated by the language majority; this is imposed on students from a language minority whose own forms of intelligent behavior are ignored;
- school leading to employment (or unemployment) and hence to economic status (or a lack of status).

(2) The 'Culture of Power' is embedded in ways of talking and writing, ways of dressing, manners and ways of interacting (e.g. compare 'upper', 'middle' and 'lower' or 'working' class children).

(3) Success in school and employment often requires acquiring or mimicking the culture of those in power. This is essentially upper and middle class culture. 'Children from other kinds of families operate within perfectly wonderful and viable cultures but not cultures that carry the codes or rules of power' (Delpit, 1988, p. 283). Language minority families have their own valid, well developed and valuable cultures already in place.

(4) Those outside of the 'Culture of Power' should be taught explicitly the rules and nature of that culture in order to become empowered. If styles of interaction, discourse patterns, manners and forms of dress, for example, are explained to a child, does this lead to the language minority child being empowered, or does this move such a child towards cultural separation?

Delpit (1995) has thus shown how in the USA power imbalances are paralleled in the classroom. Schools sometimes tolerate but do not embrace linguistic diversity, and often refuse to acknowledge the politics that surrounds bilingual education. Therefore, it becomes important to educate bilingual students to understand the politics of bilingual education and the culture of power.

CONCLUSION

Language planning and language shift are underpinned, both at a latent and a manifest level, by political beliefs and decisions. Underneath 'weak' and 'strong' forms of bilingual education lie different **views** about language communities, ethnic minorities and language itself. When language is viewed as a problem, there is often a call for assimilation and integration. Assimilationists will usually stress the majority language as the common leveler. When language is viewed as a right, the accent may vary between individual rights and language group rights. Such rights may be contested in law and expressed by political and grassroots movements.

Language may also be seen as a resource, a cultural and economic benefit, with a desire to maintain cultural and linguistic diversity. The political debate is often thus reduced to assimilation versus pluralism, integration versus multiculturalism. This debate relates directly to types of schooling: for example, submersion or heritage language; transitional bilingual education or dual-language education. 'Strong' forms of bilingual education may be seen as a form of reversing the powerlessness of those language minorities living within an assimilative and discriminatory political orientation. For language majorities, sensitization to language minorities may come through multicultural awareness. It is to multiculturalism we now turn.

KEY POINTS IN THE CHAPTER

- Three perspectives on languages depict variations among people: language as a problem, right or resource.
- The 'language as a problem' is currently a prevalent political and mass media viewpoint in the USA where the cultural assimilation of immigrants is sought, but not necessarily the economic assimilation.
- Language rights can be individual, group and international. In the USA, rights are tested in law courts.
- The place of English in the USA is frequently contested, with English-only groups asking for English as the sole official language and the removal of bilingual education.
- To maintain ethnic identity, boundaries are needed to remain a distinct group.
- A contrast between the equilibrium and conflict paradigms indicates basic political differences in language minority preferences and expectations.

SUGGESTED FURTHER READING

CRAWFORD, J., 1999, *Bilingual Education: History, Politics, Theory and Practice* (4th edn). Los Angeles: Bilingual Education Services.

CRAWFORD, J., 2000, *At War With Diversity*. Clevedon: Multilingual Matters.

CUMMINS, J., 2000a, *Language, Power and Pedagogy: Bilingual Children in the Crossfire*. Clevedon: Multilingual Matters.

DELPIT, L.D., 1995, *Other People's Children: Cultural Conflict in the Classroom*. New York: New York Press.

DICKER, S.J., 1996, Languages in America: A Pluralist View. Clevedon: Multilingual Matters.

GARCÍA, O. and BAKER, C. (eds), 1995, *Policy and Practice in Bilingual Education: A Reader Extending the Foundations*. Clevedon: Multilingual Matters. (Sections 1 and 4).

HALL, J.K. and EGGINGTON, W.G., 2000, *The Sociopolitics of English Language Teaching*. Clevedon: Multilingual Matters.

KIBBIE, D.A. (ed.), 1998 *Language Legislation and Linguistic Rights*. Amsterdam and Philadelphia: John Benjamins.

MAY, S., 1996, Indigenous language rights and education. In C. MODGIL, S. MODGIL and J. LYNCH (eds) *Education and Development: Tradition and Innovation* (Volume 1). London: Cassell.

McKAY, S.L. and WONG, S-L.C. (eds), 2000, *New Immigrants in the United States*. Cambridge: Cambridge University Press.

SCHMIDT, R., 2000, *Language Policy and Identity Policy in the United States*. Philadelphia: Temple University Press.

SKUTNABB-KANGAS, T., 1999, Education of minorities. In J.A. FISHMAN (ed.) *Handbook of Language and Ethnic Identity*. New York: Oxford University Press.

SKUTNABB-KANGAS, T. and PHILLIPSON, R. (eds), 1994, *Linguistic Human Rights*. New York: Mouton de Gruyter.

STUDY ACTIVITIES

(1) Among student groups, teachers in schools or in language communities, find out about different political viewpoints on language. Are there differences between different groups? Or are there more differences within those groups than between those groups?

(2) Interview two local politicians with differing viewpoints on bilingual education. Attempt to locate on what dimensions there are differences and similarities between these two politicians. Try to explain why there are differences.

(3) Follow a political controversy in current or previous newspapers. This controversy may concern languages in school or bilingual education or language minorities. Portray in words the varying political dimensions of the controversy. Does the controversy fit neatly into a two-way split (e.g. left-wing compared with right-wing viewpoints)? Or does the controversy have a number of different sides to it? Do you feel there are aspects of the controversy that are implicit rather than explicit?

(4) Follow one particular event regarding language in education. If possible, examine how that event is treated in two different languages (e.g. a Spanish newspaper and in an English language newspaper). What differences are there of interpretation and perception?

(5) Within a specific community, locate different interest groups and different sociocultural or socioeconomic groups of people. For example, compare working-class and middle-class viewpoints on bilingual education. How much do you think these varying viewpoints, if they exist, relate to home, social, economic, political and educational differences between the groups? Are there similarities as well as differences?

(6) Compose a short case study of a school with which you are familiar. Use Cummins' framework for describing and analyzing the school. Make a list of recommendations for how the school might raise its standards and quality through innovation and intervention with use of languages.

(7) Using a school you are familiar with, ask teachers and parents about school–home relationships. What forms of collaboration exist? What power relationships exist between teachers and parents? What part do parents play in literacy development?

CHAPTER 19

Multiculturalism and Anti-Racism

Introduction

The Nature of Multiculturalism

Multiculturalism in the School
Understandings
Values and Attitudes
Skills and Behaviors

**Anti-Racism and Prejudice
Reduction in the School**

Conclusion

Multiculturalism and Anti-Racism

INTRODUCTION

Bilingualism and diglossia co-exist with biculturalism and multiculturalism. Languages connected within an individual, and languages in contact in society, become fused with multiculturalism as a personal possession and as a focus in school. This chapter explores the idea of multiculturalism, and then the role that education can play in multiculturalism. The chapter is based on the notion that 'strong' bilingual education is usually multicultural through its students, staff and curriculum.

Multiculturalism has, as one foundation, the ideal of equal, harmonious, mutually tolerant existence of diverse languages, and of different religious, cultural and ethnic groups in a pluralist society. A multicultural viewpoint is partly based on the idea that an individual can successfully hold two or more **cultural identities**. It is possible to be Ukrainian and Canadian, Chinese and Malaysian, Mexican and North American. In a different sense, it is possible to be a Ukrainian-Canadian, a Chinese-Malaysian or a Mexican-North American, sometimes called the hyphenated variety. In this sense, identities are merged; the parts become a new whole. A redefined ethnicity creates a North American person who is not a replica of a Cuban in Cuba, Puerto Rican in Puerto Rico, Mexican in Mexico, nor a stereotypical white North American. Rather that person becomes a more or less integrated combination of parts of both.

Lynch (1992) suggests that there has been an historical **development of identity** from (1) the family group or tribe, through (2) the age of the city-state and single-state nationalism to (3) the present age of global rights and responsibilities and the internationalization of the lives of all inhabitants of this planet. He argues that 'we do not have to choose between local and ethnic loyalties, national citizenship and global community…and we are well on the way to recognizing three major levels of group affiliation: **local community membership**, by which is meant familial, ethnic, community or other cultural and social local groupings, including language, religion and ethnicity but not necessarily linked in the same geographic place at the same time; **national membership**, determined by birth or choice, but which may not be an exclusive membership; and **international membership**, which draws on the overlapping constellations which members of the world community have in common, regardless of the other two levels.' (pp. 16–17) The concept of international citizenship is part of the aims of multicultural education, considered later.

In England and the USA, movements towards multiculturalism have not tended to receive an official blessing nor central encouragement. Rather, an assimilationist viewpoint has continued (see Chapter 18). In contrast, in parts of Canada, Scandinavia and New Zealand for example, a relatively more multicultural approach has been taken, but with much **dispute and debate**. But what is multiculturalism, especially since the term tends to be used in a wide and ambiguous manner. What are the basic ideas of multiculturalism?

THE NATURE OF MULTICULTURALISM

The **basic beliefs of multiculturalists** include the following. Two languages and two cultures enable a person to have dual or multiple perspectives on society. Those who speak more than one language and own more than one culture are more sensitive and sympathetic, more likely to build cultural bridges than barricades and boundaries. Rather than being subtractive as in assimilation, multiculturalism bequeaths an additive person and process.

As an ideal, a person who is multicultural has more respect for other people and other cultures than the monocultural person who is stereotypically more culturally insular and introspective. At its worst, monoculturalism leads to a positive attitude to the dominant (host) culture and a negative attitude to the co-existence of minority cultures, especially immigrant cultures (e.g. Far Right movements in the UK). Pluralism and multiculturalism may lead to a positive attitude, not only to the host and minority cultures, but to the equal validity of all cultures. With multiculturalism at its best, out goes prejudice and racism; in comes empathy and sensitivity.

Research by Donald Taylor and his associates has found in both the USA and in Canada that different **public groups support multiculturalism** more than assimilation. For example, the research of Lambert and Taylor (1990) showed that nine different US groups all preferred multiculturalism to assimilation. The basic research question poses two alternatives:

> **Alternative A:** Cultural and racial minority groups should *give up* their traditional ways of life and take on the American way of life. (**Assimilationist**)

> **Alternative B:** Cultural and racial minority groups should *maintain* their ways of life as much as possible when they come to America. (**Multiculturalist**)

The debate is more complex than these two statements, with other alternatives and compromise positions being possible. (There is also the insensitive use of the word

'American'. Meant to imply US, it may be denigrating to those from South and Central America). Respondents are invited to respond by marking one number on the following seven-point scale:

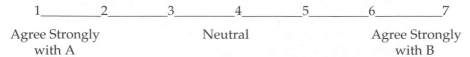

1_____2_____3_____4_____5_____6_____7

| Agree Strongly | Neutral | Agree Strongly |
| with A | | with B |

Attitudes to Assimilation and Multiculturism in US Ethnic Groups

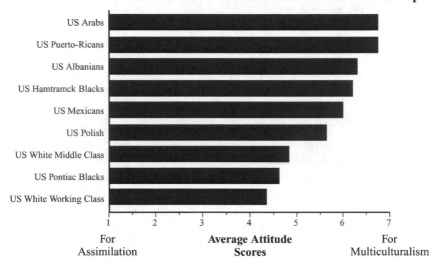

| For | Average Attitude | For |
| Assimilation | Scores | Multiculturalism |

Note: Hamtramck and Pontiac refer
to two different areas in Detroit, Michigan   (Adapted from Lambert & Taylor, 1990: page 136)

Support for multiculturalism is generally high among Arabs, Puerto-Ricans, Blacks, Mexicans, Albanians and Polish US citizens as the above graph reveals. Both white working class and white middle class US citizens favor multiculturalism more than assimilation, though less so than most other groups.

Thus Taylor (1991) is able to conclude over a series of studies that 'there is a strong endorsement for multiculturalism and an apparent rejection of assimilation' (p. 8). However, we need to ask whether such endorsement is a latent attitude or whether it results in positive action and behavior? Is the population saying it permits multiculturalism without being committed to it? Are there positive public attitudes but private skepticism? Is there interest in multiculturalism so long as it doesn't lead to involvement?

MULTICULTURALISM IN THE SCHOOL

Language minority groups are often the dominated in society. Those who have the power to make decisions about bilingual education usually come from the dominant group. The use of submersion and transitional forms of bilingual education has the tendency to perpetuate rather than alleviate the distance in power between the dominated and the dominating. Apart from requiring education through the dominant language (e.g. English in the USA), such educational programs seek to assimilate language minority groups. Not only is the language of such classrooms English, the majority culture will be transmitted. This may make minority language children feel less confident of their cultural background, their language community, their home values and beliefs, even less confident of themselves. Such an analysis provides one context for a discussion of multiculturalism in the classroom: a raising of **awareness of relationships** between different ethnic groups, and awareness of diverse cultures.

A second context for multicultural and anti-racist teaching is the response to in-migration, refugees, migrant workers, and the ever frequent crossing of national boundaries. If ethnically diverse populations are to co-exist peacefully within a nation, one educational activity is to promote **awareness of cultural diversity**. A classroom response has been to develop various programs to develop sensitivity and sympathy, understanding and awareness of diverse cultural groups. Such classroom programs are given different names with different emphases: multicultural education, multi-racial education, multi-ethnic education and intercultural education.

The aims of multicultural education are underpinned by political and ideological aims. The **assumptions of multicultural education** therefore include the following:

(1) There is a fundamental equality of all individuals and all minority groups irrespective of language and culture.

(2) In a democracy, there should be equality of opportunity irrespective of ethnic, cultural or linguistic origin.

(3) Any manifest or latent form of discrimination by the dominant power group against minorities requires elimination.

(4) A culturally diverse society should avoid racism and ethnocentrism.

(5) While generalizations about cultural behavior may be a natural part of humans making sense of their world, cultural stereotypes are to be avoided.

(6) Minority cultural groups in particular need awareness of their culture as a precondition and foundation for building on intercultural awareness.

(7) In mainstream monocultural education, language minority parents tend to be excluded from participation in their children's education. In multicultural education, parents should become partners.

(8) A pluralist integration is established by interaction and not a mosaic, by intermingling and a discovery of others to improve mutual understanding, break down stereotypes and prejudice, while increasing self-knowledge and self-esteem.

In its 'weak' sense, multicultural education focuses on the different beliefs, values, eating habits, cultural activities, dress and gestures (e.g. greetings and non-verbal reward systems) of varying ethnic groups. This form of 'cultural arti-fact' multicultural education attempts to extend the cultural vocabulary and cultural grammar of the individual child. The danger of such a 'window dressing' approach is that it divorces language from culture. A 'weak' form of multicultural education pays little or no attention to the home language of minority children. Since language and culture are inseparable, and since merely using a language is to impart its culture, a stronger form of multicultural education requires attention to the minority language that is part of the minority culture. This is sometimes attempted through language awareness programs (Hawkins, 1987; Baker & Jones, 1998). **Language Awareness programs** attempt to increase understanding, consciousness and sensitivity to the nature of language in everyday life. A program may include the following goals (Donmall, 1985):

(1) To make explicit a student's implicit knowledge of their first language or first languages.
(2) To develop skills in studying languages.
(3) To develop a perception and understanding of the nature and functions of language.
(4) To increase effectiveness in communication in the first, second and/or foreign languages.
(5) To give insights into the language learning process and thereby to aid the learning of the first language, second language and foreign languages.
(6) To develop an understanding among students of the richness of language variety within the class, school, community, region, nation and world. This may include discussing the variety of spoken and written forms of, for example, Spanish, Chinese, French, English, German throughout the world. This is to mitigate feelings of inferiority amongst those who speak a variety of a language (e.g. English as a second or third language).
(7) To foster better relations between ethnic groups by arousing students' aware-ness of the origins and characteristics of their own language and its place in the world.
(8) To help students overcome any feeling of dislocation between the language of the home, the language of the school, of text books and employment.
(9) To impart an understanding of the value of language as a crucial part of human life.
(10) To develop an understanding of bilingualism and biculturalism in the world.

Such a Language Awareness course is as important for majority language speakers as for language minorities.

The language aspects of multicultural education may be attempted by vicarious experience of minority languages through video recordings and live performances where the language and the culture are both presented in an authentic, inseparable way. Just as there is a **danger** of teaching about cultural diversity with sparse or no

Lynch (1992, pp. 42–43)) devised a set of working goals to guide **citizenship education** under the headings of: understandings, values and attitudes, skills and behaviors.

Understandings

- Understandings of the similarities and differences of human beings, their values, locations and styles of social and political life and the influence of these on individuals, groups, societies and the world community.
- Understandings of economic and environmental interdependence at local, national and international levels.
- Understandings of the varying ways in which pluralist democracies work.
- Understandings of the major human rights and responsibilities at the three levels and in social, cultural, economic and environmental spheres.
- Understandings of the varying ways in which pluralist democracies function.

Values and Attitudes

- Commitment to the values of human rights and pluralist democracy.
- Reciprocity, empathy and mutuality in all human affairs, whether cultural, social, economic, political or environmental.
- Willingness to participate in civic life at appropriate levels.
- Attitudes of openness to the cultures and ideas of others and mutuality in human relations.
- A strong commitment to gender and racial equality and willingness to fight socially and politically for them.
- A commitment to persuasion and dialogue as the major means to achieve social justice and change.
- Awareness of gender, cultural and national stereotyping and bias in their own culture and language and commitment to overcome them.

Skills and Behaviors

- Autonomous but socially responsible moral judgment and integrity, based on reflective and clarified values.
- Ability to accept the provisionality of human social and moral knowledge and the uncertainty which this implies.
- Responsible consumer and producer skills, responsive to the human and environmental rights of others.
- Engagement for human rights, justice and dignity.
- Ability to evaluate the economic, social, political and environmental decisions of others objectively.
- Interpersonal competence and the ability to make and maintain good human relationships.
- Ability to sustain dialogue within and across cultures.
- Communicative competence across a range of media and registers of language.
- Political literacy including the capacity for creative dissent, problem-solving, advocacy and creative conflict resolution.
- Decision-making, participatory and collaborative competences.
- Capacity for the development of satisfying and interactive human relations in different cultural contexts and across professional, personal and civic domains.

reference to the attendant language, so there is a danger of teaching a second language without immersion in the attendant culture.

In **Europe**, another variety or constituent of multicultural education is referred to as citizenship education. Citizenship education in Europe sometimes has much in common with the aims of multicultural and anti-racist education. However, it can also have assimilation aims and be linked with the education of immigrants (e.g. to take a citizenship examination).

The aims of a 'stronger' form of **multicultural education**, as is revealed in Lynch's (1992) list, have their basis partly in arousing awareness of, and sensitivity to, cultural diversity (Sleeter & Grant, 1987). Nieto (1999, p. xviii) defines 'Multicultural education as embedded in a sociopolitical context and as anti-racist and basic education for all students that permeates all areas of schooling, and that is characterized by a commitment to social justice and critical approaches to learning.'

The educational basis of a relatively 'strong' form of multicultural education is that all cultures are attempts to discover meaning. No one culture (including the umbrella idea of Western culture) has the monopoly of understanding. The **Postmodernist** view is that there is little or no transcendent truth, no ultimate reality outside of culture, no unalterable or fundamental qualities of women, ethnic groups or art. All meaning is socially constructed, with identities (and sense of identities) being socially constructed. In Postmodernism, all meanings are unstable, and none are neutral, but change through continuous negotiation and reconstruction. Given the temporary and constructed nature of all beliefs, there is much value in the sharing of different meanings across cultures. There is value in the meanings of those in a subordinate position (e.g. language minorities) just as there is in language majorities. The voices of the poor are as meaningful as the privileged; the understandings of the oppressed becomes as valid as the oppressor. Out of Postmodernist skepticism and uncertainty can develop new constructed meanings about the value of all languages and their attendant cultures.

Yet when the educational basis of multicultural education is discussed, **politics** is not very far away. In the USA, some 'liberals' have criticized multicultural education for being governed and manipulated from within a conservative education profession and by textbook companies and local and state education authorities (Olneck, 1993). As such, multicultural education was contained and controlled by those in power and posed little threat to the academic, cultural or bureaucratic establishments. Political **activists** in the USA have regarded multiculturalism as a key battleground for a reordering of politic relationships and power structures. Multiculturalism has therefore, sometimes become a call for the mobilization of those who wish to challenge ethnic inequalities and the established order. Thus multiculturalism symbolizes contests about whose values and ideology should be dominant in the curriculum, whose traditions and perspectives should be transmitted in the enculturation of students. For 'conservatives', the hidden agenda of multiculturalism is sometimes perceived as self-determination and autonomy rather than unity; the destabilization and undermining of society rather than equality; tribalization and separation rather than plurality.

Attempts to provide **multicultural education** vary widely (Ovando & McLaren, 2000). The term 'multicultural education' is very broad, ambiguous and diverse (May, 1999). It ranges from language and culture awareness programs for majority language children to the sharing of cultural experiences within a classroom containing a variety of ethnic groups. Multicultural education extends from the transmission of formal knowledge within a classroom, to the formal, hidden and pastoral curriculum each working towards mutual understanding, and to fighting against prejudice and racism. The range is from a timetabled, one lesson a week program to a radical reconstruction of both the whole curriculum and of relationships between schools and their communities (Coelho, 1998; Davidman & Davidman, 1994; Nieto, 1996). Multicultural education ranges at one end from scarce, token multicultural lessons to a political movement to secure equality of opportunity, combating underachievement, a political awareness of rights, debates about the reconstruction of society and a redress for current domination. Multicultural education can be about points of difference — dress and diet, language and religion. It may include lip-service to cultural diversity by a superficial 'saris, samosas, and steel bands' (clothes, food and music) approach. This may simply accentuate the differences, the colorful variations and the bizarre. The hidden message may then become the superiority of the dominant culture. At its worst, multicultural education may serve to reinforce and extend differences, often accidentally.

Nieto (1999) suggests that multicultural education will ultimately be judged by its success or otherwise in being allied to 'high quality' and 'high standards' education. While multicultural education may successfully increase cultural and social awareness and stimulate critical thinking skills, a **whole curriculum** approach must also show excellence in delivering basic skills, knowledge and understandings. Cummins (2000b) also argues for such an approach through 'transformative pedagogy' comprising: (1) education grounded in the lives of students which is (2) multicultural, anti-racist and pro-justice, (3) participatory and experiential, (4) academically rigorous with high standards of performance and (5) culturally sensitive. (6) Students should become critical in approach (7) enabling them to feel safe, significant and enthusiastic to share thoughts and feelings and (8) active in promoting social change and justice.

Multicultural education may require a reappraisal of the **whole curriculum** with an analysis of how seemingly neutral subjects like science and mathematics often solely use and perpetuate majority, dominant culture (Hodson, 1999). In the pictures of textbooks and the prose of the teacher, in the 'real life' problems to be tackled, the majority dominant culture may be represented and minority cultures ignored (Coelho, 1998).

While more subtle differences may exist in mathematics, science and technology, the more common and obvious examples of monoculturalism appear in the teaching of history and geography, literature and art, music and home economics (e.g. cookery), social studies and health education.

For example, Welsh children have been taught the **history** of England and Europe more than the history of Wales and the Celts. Mexican-American children

are taught US history, but not the history of Mexico, the annexation of Mexican territory or the role of Mexican-Americans in US history. Not only do many Mexicans in
the USA not know the history of their country of origin, they are often not taught
how their ethnic group has contributed to the development of the USA. The aim
thus becomes assimilation rather than awareness; dominance rather than diversity.
The fear and ignorance that tend to breed racism may unintentionally be perpe-
trated. Rather than celebrating ethnic identity and cultural diversity, a view of
cultural inequality may latently be conveyed. As Olneck (1993, p. 248) states:

> 'marginalized and subordinated groups are represented as voiceless objects,
> defined by their "apartness" and difference from, or by their inferior relation-
> ship to, those more central. In curricular representations, it is alleged, the
> perspectives from which history and experience occur, the actors deemed
> central, and the experiences, cultural expressions, and projects deemed valid
> and valuable are all those of dominant groups'.

One approach to 'multiculturalism throughout the curriculum' is through
content, showing that rationality is not the monopoly of any one culture, and that
understanding requires an interdependence of peoples. The 'discovery' of North
America can be taught from the perspective of native, indigenous peoples as well as
the invaders; the Crusades from a Muslim and Christian perspective; and heresies
from the viewpoint of heretics and 'believers'. In **curriculum** areas such as music
and art, there can be a genuine celebration of diversity (e.g. African, Caribbean,
Asian and different forms of Latino music; African art, Chinese and Japanese kites,
Islamic and Egyptian calligraphy).

In curriculum areas that systematically pursue a critical approach to understanding the world (e.g. nuclear physics), some cultures have been more fruitful
than others in explaining the world. However, the methods and approaches of
different cultures may all be worthwhile, as is competition between differing and
opposing ideas. For example, an understanding of the complexities of the solar
system have been better approximated by some cultures over the centuries. Yet an
understanding of the place of the individual within the solar system may be better
understood by, for example, an understanding of both eastern and western
theology and philosophy.

In **science and social science**, the danger is in teaching a male, white, western
view of the world. Instead, the world-wide origins of scientific discoveries, for
example, may be studied (e.g. paper, printing, gunpowder and the compass were
discovered by the Chinese and not by Europeans as is frequently taught). Science
and technology is constructed and relative. Different cultures have used science to
develop different knowledge and belief systems as Young (1987, p. 19) argues:

> 'Science is practice. There is no other science than the science that gets done. The
> science that exists is the record of the questions that it has occurred to scientists
> to ask, the proposals that get funded, the paths that get pursued and the results
> which lead…scientific journals and textbooks to publicize the work. …Nature

'answers' only the questions that get asked and pursued long enough to lead to results that enter the public domain. Whether or not they get asked, how far they get pursued, are matters for a given society, its educational system, its patronage system and its funding bodies.'

Another danger in multicultural education is in stereotyping 'Third World' situations as rural and rudimentary, famished and inferior. An alternative is in profiling black scientists, learning about inventions from China and India, and discovering the rapid recent changes in horticulture and forestry, soil science and social science in developing countries.

Alternative perspectives should not be included as an appendix to a mainstream view, isolating different perspectives from each other, and presenting a sanitized or expurgated version of history. Instead, there is a need to present integrated multiple perspectives, with the distinctive contributions of different cultural groups fairly represented, and the interdependence of different experiences faithfully told. For a school, this means avoiding the presentation of isolationist ideas in the curriculum (e.g. only a North American or Eurocentric view of the world) and avoiding cultural supremacist viewpoints (e.g. apartheid). In **religious education**, isolationism is sometimes taught. For example, a particular Christian fundamentalist or extreme Muslim viewpoint is taught with alternative viewpoints being forbidden. Similarly, supremacist viewpoints need to be avoided. An example is when Christianity is sometimes latently taught as superior to other world religions. This suggests that religious fundamentalism and cultural pluralism are incompatible.

Yet religion is a key element in multiculturalism. In Europe, **religion** has re-emerged as a social issue in relationships between different ethnic and language groups. With the relatively permanent settlement in Europe of 8 to 9 million immigrants from West and North West Africa, the Indian sub-continent and South East Asia, the mixing of Muslim (estimated at 6.5 million adherents in Europe), Buddhist, Hindu and Sikh with different Christian denominations has made religion a key element in debates about multiculturalism and multicultural education (Perotti, 1994; Ghuman, 1999).

ANTI-RACISM AND PREJUDICE REDUCTION IN THE SCHOOL

The psychological roots of racial prejudice and racial hostility are separate from the philosophical basis of multicultural education. However, as will be considered later, the reduction of anti-racism and prejudice are often included in a 'strong' version of multicultural education. There are multicultural programs and materials that do not include a study of racism or anti-racism. To learn, for example, about other cultures and ethnic groups is not to confront the racism that exists in one's own (and other) ethnic groups. Thus such multicultural education has been accused of leaving unaltered the racist fabric of society and failing to see racism as a causal need for multicultural education. When a study of **racism and anti-racism** is absent from a multicultural program, such a program can become a tranquilizer of action against racism, diverting resistance and confrontation of racism into harmless channels. Instead a form of anti-racist multiculturalism is possible (Todd, 1991). Such a program needs to include an analysis of the structural reasons (e.g. the institutionalization of racism, social stratification, discriminatory practices by government) why racism is perpetuated, and not just viewed as an attitude of individuals. Its proponents argue that rather than just engendering sympathy for the victims of racism, some sympathy is needed for the struggle to defeat racism, even when this means confrontation and non-violent direct action.

Rarely, if ever, does language diversity, in itself, cause poor **race relations**. While color of skin, creed and language often become the symbols and badges of racism, the roots of racism tend to lie in fear and misunderstanding, and in the unequal distribution of power and economic rewards. If the school is a witting or unwitting agent in the reproduction of social and economic differences in society, then schools may be perpetrators of racism. Multicultural education in school is therefore sometimes seen as a way of raising consciousness of racism both in the aggressor and the victim.

The danger of bilingual education is focusing on two languages rather than on many cultures. Creating bilingual students may not be enough to reverse the inequalities and injustices in society. A bilingual child may still be the victim of racism and may still be confined to dominated status unless the school system as a whole works to redress rather than reproduced inequalities (Attinasi, 1994).

> 'The crucial element in reversing language minority students' school failure is not the language of instruction but the extent to which educators work to reverse — rather than perpetuate — the subtle, and often not so subtle, institutionalized racism of the society as a whole. In other words, bilingual education becomes effective only when it becomes anti-racist education. Strong promotion of students' primary language can be an important component in empowering language minority students but it is certainly not sufficient in itself.' (Cummins, 1986a, p. 11)

It is a debated point as to the extent of the influence of school in **combating racism and reducing prejudice**. The preconceptions and attitudes of children and teachers, of politicians and policy-makers, the message of the hidden curriculum and the material of the formal curriculum may make difficult the winning of hearts and minds. So widespread, brutal and ingrained is racism in the school and street, that some argue for skill training rather than liberal education. Explicit racism may be combated in liberal education by a careful and conscious selection of teaching resources, the language of teaching, school organization and grouping in the classroom. Increased knowledge and greater understanding are sought as outcomes as are mutual tolerance and respect. For some, a more direct confrontational style with regard to racism is required. For example, through **roleplay**, white individuals may be confronted with their own racism and its consequences on others. Such roleplay will attempt to redress an inherent problem, in that some white people can never fully understand racism because they do not experience it.

A different viewpoint, pessimistic but with an element of reality, is that schools can do little to reconstruct power and racial relationships within society. This belief stems from the idea that multicultural education is a token and patronizing exercise. An alternative, radical view is that non-violent political activity is required amongst the victims of racism in school and particularly through political activity outside school. Such activity will attempt to reconstruct the power, dominance, political relationships in society and to seek to eradicate prejudice and fear, victimization and racial violence.

Such a radical view indicates that multicultural and anti-racist education can be neither value-free nor politically neutral. It aims at promoting equality of educational opportunity, the eradication of racial and cultural discrimination, and erasing racial dominance. Its danger is in being only for minorities and not for the enlightenment of majorities. In Britain, multicultural education may be provided in areas where ethnic minority children reside. It is often seen as irrelevant in all-white English-only schools.

At what point does preferring one's own language and culture become racist? If a minority language and culture, in protecting itself, wants to build strong boundaries between it and neighboring languages and cultures, is this ethnocentric and racist? Fishman (1991) argues that having security in self-identity may be a necessary precondition before accepting other languages and cultures. A language minority may need security within itself before becoming multicultural. Security and status in one's own language may be a necessary foundation for accepting other neighboring cultures and languages. However, if other languages and cultures are not accepted and respected, then there is the danger of incipient racism.

This relates also to the idea that a person can belong at different levels in the community. It is possible to be Jewish and British, Latino and North American, Irish and European. It is possible to be international and indigenous, a member of the local and the global village. However, there are times when belonging to two groups is seen as psychologically difficult. To be Welsh and British, Catalan and Spanish, may be difficult due to the incongruence, opposition and contested boundaries between two linked parts.

CONCLUSION

Among proponents of multicultural education, there are differences in preferred classroom style. There are those teachers who emphasize cultural folklore without the language; those who accent the superficially interesting without securing a sympathetic understanding; and those who want to provide all the colors and complexity of a multicultural world without a clear set of aims, goals, schemes, concepts and desired outcomes. Other teachers view multiculturalism as something that needs to exist throughout the curriculum, pervading every curriculum area. Through resource materials, the language of the classroom and seating and grouping arrangements, the ethos and atmosphere of the school becomes multicultural. For some, this relatively strong approach to multiculturalism will not be enough. In the widespread victimization and violence of racism, they see the mark of failure in multicultural education in school. Such an anti-racist movement requires not only direct intervention in all schools and by all teachers. It also requires changes in society and these will begin with political change. In this view-point, monocultural fundamentalism and racism cannot be combated through education alone.

A consideration of multiculturalism and anti-racism in the classroom highlights that politics, culture and language are inter-linked. Where minority languages and cultures exist, so does personal, group, regional and national politics. The political debate around both minority languages and bilingual education tends to center on assimilation versus integration, pluralism and diversity versus uniformity and standardization. Personal resolution of the debate often reflects compromise positions. It is possible to have harmonious national unity and a measure of diversity, to assimilate partially while retaining the heritage language and culture.

A discussion of bilingual education thus inevitably includes personal orientations and political objectives. The preference at a personal or political level for the melting pot or the language garden partly determines the kind of education system preferred for language minorities. This preference separates those who see language as a problem or as a resource. It separates those who require bilingual education to dissolve language and cultural differences from those who require bilingual education to celebrate diversity. There are those who see the classroom as a recipe for the integration of problematic, diverse ingredients. For others, pedagogy is a plan for maintaining the colorful diversity of resources in the language garden.

KEY POINTS IN THE CHAPTER

- Multiculturalism assumes that cultural diversity is preferable to a melting pot assimilationist ideology.
- For immigrant language minority groups, cultural identity may be a hyphenated variety (e.g. Cuban-American).
- Different multicultural programs operate in school, ranging from awareness raising, citizenship education (e.g. in Europeanization), to a reappraisal of how majority and minority cultures are portrayed in all areas of the curriculum.
- Combating anti-racism and generating a reduction in prejudice is also part of a multiculturalism educative process in school.

SUGGESTED FURTHER READING

DAVIDMAN, L. and DAVIDMAN, P.T., 1994, *Teaching with a Multicultural Perspective: A Practical Guide*. New York: Longman.

MAY, S. (ed.), 1999, *Critical Multiculturalism: Rethinking Multicultural and Antiracist Education*. London and Philadelphia: Falmer Press.

McKAY, S.L. and WONG, S-L.C. (eds), 2000, *New Immigrants in the United States*. Cambridge: Cambridge University Press.

NIETO, S., 1996, *Affirming Diversity: The Sociopolitical Context of Multicultural Education* (2nd edn). New York: Longman.

NIETO, S., 1999, *The Light in their Eyes: Creating Multicultural Learning Communities*. New York: Teachers College Press.

OVANDO, C.J. and McLAREN, P., 2000, *The Politics of Multiculturalism and Bilingual Education*. Boston: McGraw-Hill.

STUDY ACTIVITIES

(1) Visit a school with either multicultural students and/or with multicultural aims. What are the links in that school between multilingualism and multiculturalism? How is multiculturalism presented in the classroom and the school? Ask students how interested they are in learning about different cultures and different languages.

(2) Find out how to run a simple sociometric test. For example, ask children to nominate which two children they would invite to their party or which two children they most liked working with in the classroom. By placing the choices in a table or on a diagram, analyze the relationships between children. Are there cliques of children separated by different languages? Are the clusters of children separated along ethnic or ability lines? How does language appear to play a part in the friendships of the classroom, playground and street?

(3) As a group activity, create a collage with pictures and words as a decoration for your school or college. Using the theme of multiculturalism, present in pictures, words and symbols a theme of 'Multiculturalism For All'. Write a short explanation of the meaning of that collage.

CHAPTER 20

Bilingualism in the Modern World

Introduction

Occupational Bilingualism

Bilingualism and Tourism
Introduction
Raising the Profile of a Lesser Used Language
and Culture

Bilingualism and the Mass Media

**Information Technology
and Bilingualism**
Bilingualism and the Internet

Bilingualism and the Economy
Bilingualism as an Economic Advantage
Minority Languages and the Economy
Bilingualism and Economic Inequality

CHAPTER 20

Bilingualism in the Modern World

INTRODUCTION

This chapter takes a contemporary and **future look at bilingualism** and bilinguals. In the modern world, is a heritage (minority language) going to be an asset or an obstruction? For example, does tourism help sustain or dilute minority languages and their attendant cultures? Is bilingualism valuable for employment? Will bilinguals with two majority languages have a competitive advantage in developing global economies? Will the Internet and mass media ensure that English increasingly becomes the international language for global communication?

Forecasting the future is notoriously dangerous. However, current economic, political, social and cultural change is rapid, affecting all languages of the world. Therefore, five key modern themes are highlighted (employment, tourism, mass media, information technology and the economy) to show how languages within an individual and within society will be subject to fast moving tides of local and global development.

OCCUPATIONAL BILINGUALISM

The ownership of two languages has increasingly become seen as an asset as the 'communication world' gets smaller. As swift communication by phone and computer across great distances has become possible in recent decades, and as air travel has brought countries closer together, so the importance of bilingualism and multilingualism has been highlighted. As the amount of information available has dramatically increased, and the ease of delivering information round the world has quickened, so bilinguals, particularly those with 'English bilingualism', have become more important in the **employment market**. In tourism, marketing, retailing, airlines, public relations, banking, information and communications technology, accountancy, business consultancy, secretarial work, hotels, law and teaching, for example, bilingual and multilingual employees often have the competitive edge when applying for a post or for promotion. In the growing prevalence of screen-based labor, bilinguals are often marketable and seen as more multi-skilled.

There is often a marked contrast between bilingual professions that carry a high prestige, and professions where bilinguals are in jobs which symbolize the lower status of many language minority bilinguals. In this latter case, language minority members may speak two languages, yet be in lower status jobs, and be marginalized in their employment prospects and chances of sharing wealth. We will first consider bilingual professions that are prestigious.

An example of bilingual professions that are prestigious surround the **tourism and travel business**. Air hostesses, instructors on ski slopes in mainland Europe, those who conduct safaris in Africa, those who cater for sun seekers in the Mediterranean all prosper when they are bilingual or multilingual. To communicate with clients, to inform those being instructed, to satisfy those seeking rest and excitement, the use of two or more languages enhances job performance.

For bilinguals and multilinguals who are skilled in two or more languages, being an **interpreter** or **translator** is often a prestigious post. When politicians meet (e.g. European Commission, United Nations, on foreign visits) interpreters form the essential bridge. For example, when a US President meets the President of Russia, interpreters provide a smooth connection. Interpreting can also exist in a local language minority region.

In the highlands and islands of Scotland, translating facilities are available for those English-only speakers who need a translation when local government officials or elected community representatives are speaking Gaelic. Translating also can exist as a large-scale enterprise (e.g. in the United Nations and the European Union) where many documents have to be translated into official languages. Translation may also occur in language minority communities where, for example, a book or an article may be translated to or from the minority language.

Another example of a relatively prestigious bilingual profession is that of local **government officials** who deal with their communities. When enquiries are made about health, social benefit or local taxes, it is often important and necessary to have people who can use the language(s) of the local people. In many language minority situations, bilinguals in local government may have to deal with superiors and paper work in the majority language, but deal orally or in writing in the minority language with some or many of the local population.

Another example is when a local government official in Africa or India visits an indigenous ethnic group in a relatively remote part of the country. That local government official may need to talk in the dialect or local language of the people as well as talking to colleagues back in the town or city in a more widely used common language.

In the **caring professions** (e.g. counselors, therapists, psychologists, doctors, nurses, religious leaders), one issue of debate is the bilingual abilities of such professionals. Take, for example, the midwife. The midwife is present at that very special moment of a mother's experience. Communication with the midwife is not only important, it is also very emotional and precious. Can the midwife assist in the moment of pain and joy in the preferred language of the mother? If not, the mother will need to switch to using her second language.

When people visit a psychiatrist or counselor, it may be important for them to discuss and reveal the innermost depths of their being in the language of their choice. To switch to a second or third language because the professional is monolingual may be unsatisfactory. In the temple, mosque or church, it is often highly important that a religious leader conducts prayer or a funeral service in the language of the people. People may find praying in a second language unnatural, even awkward.

In language minority communities, the more prestigious jobs are sometimes filled by monolinguals and less prestigious posts by bilinguals. This may send a signal. Monolingualism symbolically connects with higher status employment, and bilingualism with lower status employment.

There are many times when the more prestigious professional (e.g. the consultant surgeon) only speaks the majority language, while the relatively less prestigious professional (e.g. the nurse on the hospital ward) is bilingual. This raises the occasional dilemma about whether it is more important to hire a monolingual who is more skilled at a profession, or a bilingual who is less skilled? (There will be many cases when bilinguals are as skilled or more skilled than the monolingual applicant for a post.)

This leads to the second part of this discussion about bilingual professions. In many **minority language situations**, those who are bilingual may be unemployed or in lower status jobs. A school is sometimes a good example. In a language minority community, many of the teachers may be monolingual in the majority language. Bilinguals are often in lower status jobs, for example, because they belong to underprivileged, marginalized ethnic minorities, sometimes underachieving in schools (e.g. USA). There is sometimes a vicious cycle of poverty, powerlessness, low expectations and lower motivation. Unemployment and lower status jobs become part of this cycle.

For example, in large cities in the USA, where there are large proportions of Spanish speakers, the **teachers** may be English language monolinguals. The cooks, cleaners, secretaries and janitors in the school may be the bilinguals. For students in the school, such a differentiation between monolinguals and bilinguals in the roles they play may send out messages. There is a hidden curriculum in employment patterns within the school. The students may acquire the idea subconsciously that monolingual English speakers are prestigious, relatively well paid and in relatively secure jobs. Those who speak Spanish as their home language and can cope in English as a second language tend to be allocated the lower class, more menial jobs. The role models in the school convey the message that to be bilingual is to be associated with less status and more poverty and disadvantage, less power and more subservience (McGroarty, 1990).

This discussion of bilingual professions has revealed the dual nature in the link between bilingualism and employment. In the first case there are those who can use their bilingualism as an advantage: to sell, to satisfy clients' needs, to succeed in providing a service. Bilingualism has an economic potential; it is an asset used by an individual for advancement. Bilingualism can become a **marketable ability** to bridge languages and cultures, securing trade and delivery of services.

In the second case, there are those people whose bilingual nature tends to mark them for the lower status, more marginalized and precarious employment. Such bilinguals may be allocated the poorest paid jobs in schools and shops. Bilingualism is attached to **low status jobs** that symbolize the least powerful, the least affluent and least prestigious sections in a society.

BILINGUALISM AND TOURISM

Introduction

Tourism has been a growing industry throughout the world in the 20th century. Increasing ease of travel and communications, more leisure time, earlier retirement, longer life and a greater disposable income have meant that vacations in other countries are part of the lifestyle of an increasing proportion of the population of many developed countries.

When people go on vacation, many are seemingly oblivious or indifferent to the indigenous language and culture of the region they are visiting especially if it is a minority language and culture. Travel inevitably involves the **contact of cultures and languages**. This can be a positive and enriching experience. Often, however, tourism is seen as the enemy of multiculturalism and multilingualism and especially of minority languages and cultures. It has been said that tourism ruins unspoilt rural areas with hotels, blocks of flats and marinas. Tourism can also pollute the cultural and linguistic environment. Tourists can be unaware of, and insensitive to cultural and linguistic diversity, expecting the language, food and other customs to be the same as at home. Too often, tourists wear 'blinkers', seeing only sun, sand and scenery and not being aware of the language and culture of the local inhabitants. Café signs in the South of France and Spain, 'English spoken here', 'English afternoon tea served', 'Fish and Chips Served Here' bear witness to expectations.

Mass tourism has contributed to the spread of the **English language** and Anglo culture throughout the world, at a cost to other languages and cultures. Mass tourism can also weaken the cultural, linguistic and economic structure of a region by its tendency to provide casual, seasonal employment and also a mass influx of temporary workers from other regions. Because of all these negative implications, tourism is often viewed with suspicion and contempt, especially by minority groups.

Tourism, however, is a growth industry. By 1996, throughout the European Union, nine million people were directly employed in the tourist industry, and it represented 5% of the GDP. Tourism is becoming increasingly important to the economy of many countries. In Europe, the European Union recently launched an action plan for cultural tourism. Fifty-three projects were launched throughout the European Community designed to foster long-term sustainable tourist development and to benefit the host languages and cultures.

Raising the Profile of a Lesser Used Language and Culture

Tourism can enhance awareness of bilingualism and biculturalism in two main ways. First, it gives those in the tourist industry the opportunity to introduce the local language(s) and culture(s) to visitors. This is especially important in minority language regions. Second, the tourist industry should be sensitive to visitors from other countries by being aware of their language needs and providing appropriate multilingual services.

Tourist areas often coincide with minority language regions. Tourists often wish to visit unspoilt rural areas, that are not over-developed and over-industrialized. These areas tend to be on the periphery, far from the urban centers of power and influence. Minority languages tend to be spoken in such areas. If we look at the regions where languages such as Welsh, Gaelic, Breton, Irish, Catalan, Basque and Frisian are spoken, they correspond with areas of considerable tourist activity.

Ideally, tourism should raise the profile of minority languages and cultures. The reality is, however, that the imbalance in power and prestige between majority and minority languages and cultures is reflected in the tourist industry. The lack of status of many minority languages in everyday life means that they may be more or less 'invisible' to the average tourist. Since the majority language of the country or region is more likely to be known and used by tourists, the tourist industry tends to operate in that language.

Also, the economic and power imbalance between minority and majority groups is often reflected in the fact that key positions in the tourist industry are often held by majority group members. Minority group members tend to be employed at the lower end of the scale, in jobs that are low status, not so well paid and often temporary or seasonal. This means that the economic benefits of tourism are not reaped by the minority community. Also, tourism is not structured in such a way as to bring economic benefits to more remote communities and areas of high unemployment.

If use is made of minority languages and cultures in tourist enterprises, this tends to follow an '**ethnic approach**', focusing on traditions, customs and cultural artifacts in a way that may portray them as 'quaint', 'archaic' or 'strange'. Whether we are talking about Breton embroidered costumes, Scottish tartan, Welsh harp music, Amish traditional dress, Native American rituals or Maori war dances, they may be presented as spectacles for gawking tourists rather than as part of real-life, contemporary living cultures.

Tourism need not militate against minority languages and cultures. Many visitors are interested in other languages and cultures and can be attracted by a more positive, distinctive and dignified image of a minority language and culture. However, to accomplish this, there is a need for a broad-based strategy. An important part of such a strategy would be the involvement of minority language speakers at a higher level in tourism. This could be accomplished by an attitude-building campaign, training in commerce and enterprise and financial incentives to set up new ventures. Another part of the strategy would be the central promotion by government and state tourist boards of minority language and culture in a positive and contemporary way. These types of strategies would ensure that minority language groups derive greater economic benefit from tourism, and that tourism itself is harnessed to promote and enhance the status of the minority language and culture, and reinforce its use in the community.

Tourism that actively promotes the host language and culture has been called 'cultural tourism'. With the growth of tourism throughout the world, more sophisticated and diverse strategies for boosting the tourist market have been devised. The importance of cultural tourism has been increasingly recognized.

BILINGUALISM AND THE MASS MEDIA

The 20th century has seen the rapid development of mass communications. There has been an explosion in the number and distribution of newspapers and magazines, but, more importantly, radio and television have become important vehicles of mass communication, in the form of news, information and entertainment. The majority of households in Western countries possess at least one television set, and to own a television is the ambition of many families in less economically advanced world countries.

Television (especially satellite television) has contributed to the creation of the global village – to the world-wide diffusion of important news, sport and culture. Television enables viewers to cross cultures. The development of satellite and cable technology has facilitated the transmission of programs world-wide. Television can contribute to multiculturalism, and to an empathy and insight into other cultures and lifestyles.

However, there is another side to television. The largest television industry in the world is in North America. It provides a mass of programs, mainly light entertainment and news. These programs transmit Anglo-American culture to other parts of the world. Anglo-American music, cultural practices and lifestyles may be seen as prestigious and important, and, by implication, the indigenous cultures of other countries may be disparaged as outmoded and backward.

The English language is also diffused throughout the world by the mass media. The wide use of subtitling (cheaper than dubbing) means that the English language is heard by audiences in many other countries and can be understood with the aid of the subtitles and the context. Since the advent of satellite television, more viewers have access to English language programs.

The widespread diffusion of the English language has had some beneficial effects. It has contributed to the development of bilingualism. It has provided a means for speakers of other languages to develop competence in English, as a useful language of international communication. In Scandinavian countries for instance, many English language films and other programs have traditionally been broadcast with subtitles. Only children's programs are dubbed. Motivation to learn English is usually high in Scandinavian countries, and television is one aid to competence. This is an additive bilingual situation, where the second language does not displace the first.

However, at the same time, the English language has penetrated, via television, into many majority languages. French and Japanese are two languages influenced by English via the mass media. This influx of borrowings from English has provoked anxiety among language purists in both Japan and France. The French government has taken steps to reduce the quantity of non-French language broadcasting on radio and television.

One positive development caused by the proliferation of international satellite and cable channels is that there is an increasing international market for programs. This, and the increasing use of subtitling, 'voice-overs' and dubbing, means that programs and films can be made in many lesser used languages. The cost can then be recouped by selling them on the international market.

On the other hand, when majority language mass media (e.g. English) enter minority language homes, the effect may be a **subtractive bilingual situation**. Minority language children in Britain and North America are exposed to the English language and Anglo-American culture from an early age. Minority language groups tend to be concerned about the potentially harmful effect on speakers of their language, especially young people and children, of the daily diet of majority language and culture. They are concerned that it further weakens the prestige and status of their own language and culture, further widening the gap between English (or another majority language) as the language of power, prestige, modern technology, fashion and entertainment and their own language, as an old-fashioned, outdated, despised and backward language of yesterday. There is also concern that watching majority language television may affect children's acquisition of their native language, and hasten language shift to the majority language.

During recent decades, there has been a concerted effort by many minority language groups to gain access to radio and particularly television. Minority language activists have seen **minority language radio and television** as vitally important to the maintenance of their language for the following reasons.

(1) Minority language media adds to the prestige and status of a language in the eyes of its speakers.
(2) Minority language media can add to a sense of unity and identity among its speakers.
(3) Minority language media helps to keep minority language speakers, especially children and young people, from the influence of majority language and culture. It acquaints them with their own heritage and culture and gives them pride in it.
(4) Minority language media can help disseminate a standard form of the language and also promotes new and technical vocabulary. Mass media can help the standardization of a minority language across a variety of registers.
(5) Minority language media can help the fluency of minority language speakers and can also help learners acquire the language.
(6) Minority language media creates well paid, high prestige jobs for minority language speakers. The radio and television industry can help boost the economy of minority language regions.

The value of minority language media in the maintenance of minority languages and the reversal of language shift has been disputed by Fishman (1991). Fishman argues that radio and television should not be hailed as the saviors of a minority language. He maintains that many minority language groups spend valuable resources in the lengthy and expensive task of establishing and maintaining minority language media, at the cost of more basic and fundamental issues such as the intergenerational transmission of the minority language. Fishman (1991a) suggests that the impact of majority language television, particularly English language television in the UK and North America, is so immense, that it cannot be countered by the much lesser influence of minority language.

However, there are benefits of minority language media in the prestige, maintenance and promotion of minority languages, cultures and economies. Siguán (1993) claims that Galician television has contributed greatly to the increase in **social prestige** of the language. In Catalonia, the two Catalan television channels, established in 1983 and 1989, are now watched by up to 40% of the population. In Wales, the establishment of a Welsh language television channel in 1982 led to the creation of many independent television companies in North Wales, which have boosted the **economy** of the area. Such minority language television is regarded as important in **standardizing** the language in a wide range of registers across the north and south of Wales. Welsh television has also been viewed as a major force in the creation and a maintenance of a sense of identity and unity among Welsh speakers.

INFORMATION TECHNOLOGY AND BILINGUALISM

With the rapid spread of technology and networked information has gone the rapid **spread of English**. The inherent danger is that minority languages, cultural diversity and therefore bilingualism come under threat. The information that transfers across the Internet highway tends mostly (but not exclusively) to be in English. Over 150 million people in the world are estimated to access the Internet in English. The language of digitized encyclopedias on CDs and the multiplicity of software tends also to be in English as does the language of games software.

Minority languages may seem in comparison to be part of tradition, of heritage and history, and may fail to attain the status and prestige of modern, high-prestige and high-profile international languages used by information technology. The danger lies in the identification of advanced technological society with the English language, and subsequently minority languages being identified only with home, religion and history. The danger is of a tiered information society: those who have the linguistic abilities to access information; those who cannot access new forms of communication and information as they are monolingual in a language not used in the information society.

Yet it is possible to harness technology to **aid minority language education**. For example, software can be displayed in or translated into the heritage language, and electronic mail and information exchange can be in that minority language. As more businesses begin to advertise using web pages, regional networks have developed using local languages on the Internet. It makes no sense advertising a shop in

Sweden if the main customers are local and not international. Also, as schools, colleges, universities, local government, libraries, record offices and local information agencies go on-line, their local pages are often in the regional language.

What is also important in preserving minority languages in a technological age is to ensure that there is appropriate **terminology** in the minority language. It is necessary to extend minority language vocabulary to embrace technological and computer terms in languages other than English. Such modernization aids the symbolic status of the language, particularly among the impressionable young. This ensures that information technology is a supporter and not a destroyer of bilingualism in children.

It is also possible to harness technology to aid minority language employment. The Information Superhighway makes residence in language minority rural areas more possible through improved speed and access in communications, and employment that allows people to **work at home**, using high speed computer links to receive and deliver services and products.

Bilingualism and the Internet

When students use communication technology, bilingual proficiency can be enhanced. Through the Internet, for example, **authentic language practice** is possible via purposeful and genuine activities (e.g. the use of electronic mail). There may be increased motivation to acquire a language via contact with real students in other countries and accessing authentic language sources to complete curriculum activity (e.g. a project on another country). Some examples follow.

Electronic mail and electronic conferencing are already one of the major Internet activities for language students, giving the feeling of the global village where barriers to communication (such as cost and the time of travel) are removed. There are increasing numbers of foreign language servers on the Internet accessible via 'sensitive maps' of sites in each country. They provide useful, relevant and topical information which is in a different language. Linguistic competence develops as a by-product of interest in the information.

By its nature, the Internet brings people speaking different languages into closer contact. By exchanging information with students in other countries, students can build increasing independence in language use, vary their language according to audience, and use language for real purposes. Students can take part in conversations and conferences over the Internet with native speakers, using not only written text but increasingly video and audio conferencing as well. Exchange visits can be reinforced with preparatory and follow-up Internet links, and there are possibilities of **virtual exchanges** and 'telepresence'.

The Internet provides teachers and learners with ready-to-use banks of multimedia resources: a wealth of video and audio recordings from all over the world, pictorial and written information, and activities generated by different language centers in different countries. Providers of information and training for language teachers can use the Internet to publicize events, courses, materials, services and a subscription-based, remote training, advice and information service.

World-Wide Web Sites for Bilinguals

1.   ERIC Clearinghouse on Languages and Linguistics
         http://www.cal.org/ericcll/
2.   National Clearinghouse for Bilingual Education (US)
         http://www.ncbe.gwu.edu/
3.   Office of Bilingual Education and Minority Languages (US)
         http://www.ed.gov/offices/OBEMLA/
4.   The Human Languages Page
         http://www.hardlink.com/~chambers/HLP/
         http://www.june29.com/HLP/
5.   Yahoo – Bilingual Education
         http://dir.yahoo.com/Education/Bilingual/
6.   Yahoo – Languages
         http://dir.yahoo.com/Social_Science/Linguistics_and_Human_Languages/
7.   Center for Applied Linguistics (US)
         http://www.cal.org/
8.   James Crawford's Language Policy Web Site and Emporium
         http://ourworld.compuserve.com/homepages/JWCRAWFORD/
9.   National Association for Bilingual Education
         http://www.nabe.org/
10. Foreign Language Resources on the Web
         http://www.itp.berkeley.edu/~thorne/HumanResources.html
11. Less Commonly Taught Languages
         http://carla.acad.umn.edu/lctl/lctl.html
12. Hobbes' Language World
         http://info.isoc.org/guest/zakon/languages/
13. Ethnologue Database
         http://www.sil.org/ethnologue/ethnologue.html
14. Welsh Language Board
         http://www.bwrdd-yr-iaith.org.uk/
15. Agora Language Marketplace
         http://agoralang.com/agora/
16. US Department of Education, Office of Civil Rights
         http://www.ed.gov/offices/OCR/
17. The MERCATOR Project (European Commission – which promotes the
     interests of the minority/regional languages and cultures within the Euro-
     pean Union).
         http://www.troc.es/mercator/index.htm
18. Language Policy Research Center (Israel)
         http://www.biu.ac.il:80/HU/lprc/
19. CILT (Centre for Information of Language Teaching and Research)
         http://www.cilt.org.uk/

World-Wide Web Sites for Bilinguals (*cont.*)

20. The Bilingual Families Web Page
     http://www.nethelp.no/cindy/biling-fam.html
21. Center for Advanced Research on Language Acquisition
     http://carla.acad.umn.edu/
22. OISE, University of Toronto, Second Language Education on the Web
     http://www.oise.utoronto.ca/~aweinrib/sle/
23. Kenji Hakuta's Home Page
     http://www.stanford.edu/~hakuta/
24. CAIT (Canadian Association of Immersion Teachers)
     http://www.educ.sfu.ca/acpi/
25. Centre for Language Immersion and Multilingualism
     http://www.uwasa.fi/hut/svenska/ImmLing.html
26. Center for Research on Education, Diversity & Excellence (CREDE)
     http://www.crede.ucsc.edu/
27. California Association for Bilingual Education
     http://www.bilingualeducation.org/
28 University of California Linguistic Minority Research Institute (UC LMRI)
     http://lmrinet.gse.ucsb.edu/
29. USC Center for Multilingual, Multicultural Research
     http://www-bcf.usc.edu/~cmmr/
30. Center for Language Minority Education
     http://www.clmer.csulb.edu/
31. Native American Languages
     http://www.mcn.net/~wleman/langlinks.htm
32. Multilingual Matters
     http://www.multilingual-matters.com/

BILINGUALISM AND THE ECONOMY

Bilingualism as an Economic Advantage

Among language minority groups, there is sometimes relatively high unemployment, low pay, poverty and powerlessness. Yet bilinguals have linguistic capital. Bilinguals typically have **marketable language skills** and intercultural knowledge. Bilinguals are often economically impoverished yet linguistically accomplished.

In an increasingly bilingual and multilingual world, with trade barriers being broken, with single markets in areas such as Europe growing, and with economic competition rapidly developing on a global scale, **competence in languages** is increasingly important. A US example is Southern Florida which has become a main center for South American business, and where Spanish language skills have become a bridge between the business cultures of the USA and Latin America (Fradd & Boswell, 1996). The growth of multinational corporations in Southern Florida has particularly increased with the emergence of markets in Latin America requiring Spanish, and not just English, as the language of trade. The growth of legal, financial and banking services in Miami is another example where bilinguals (Spanish and English) have distinct economic and employment advantages. It has been estimated that nearly half of the labor force in Florida requires some level of Spanish language skills in order to meet the needs of international business, tourism and Spanish language media enterprises (Fradd & Boswell, 1996).

Monica Heller (1999) suggests that, to gain advantage in the new global economy, bilinguals will need to adopt a different concept of their identity. The old politics of identity concern maintaining a heritage language and culture, conserving and protecting traditions, and perpetuating a well defined minority cultural identity. In contrast, Heller (1999) talks about a new pragmatic identity for language minorities, which allows them to take advantage of their multiple linguistic and cultural resources to participate in a global economy. The nature of the New World economy is an **ability to cross boundaries**, and bilinguals are skilled in such behavior. She suggests that it is not multilingualism and a hybrid dual language system that is valued in the new economy, but parallel monolingualisms.

In such a context, language minorities can act as **brokers** between different monolingual economic and political zones. However, this requires bilinguals to have linguistic resources that are sufficiently well developed to operate in either language group. From a Canadian context, Heller (1999) argues that 'minorities are now in a good position to market their linguistic capital' (p. 29). To do so, they have to move away from the politics of an ethnic authenticity and tradition towards a politics based on capital, globalization and a new international political and economic order. However, language minorities are often politically and economically marginalized, with litle chance of escape.

This immediately raises the question of **which languages** may be useful for economic advancement? In many countries of the world, it is English as a second or foreign language that has visible economic value. As Coulmas (1992) suggests,

> 'no Japanese businessman ever tries to operate on the American market without a sufficient command of English, whereas the reverse case, of American business people who expect to be able to do business in Japan without being proficient in Japanese, is not at all rare. On the one hand, this is a reflection of the arrogance of power, but on the other hand, it testifies to the fact that the opportunities for realizing the functional potential of English on the Japanese market are far better than those of realizing the functional potential of Japanese on the American market' (pp. 66–67).

As Willy Brandt, a former Chancellor of the old Federal Republic of Germany once said:

> 'If you wish to buy from us, you can talk any language you like, for we shall try to understand you. If you want to sell to us, then you must speak our language'.

Alongside the English language, the French, German, Japanese, Portuguese and Spanish languages have historically been regarded as important trading languages. However, in the future, this list of **modern languages for marketing and trading purposes** is likely to grow significantly. For example, Arabic and Bahasa Melayu, Mandarin and Cantonese, Swahili and Hausa, Bengali and Hindi/Urdu may each become increasingly valuable. Although the world is getting economically richer, the proportion of the wealth created and spent by Eastern countries may proportionally increase in relation to the West, and therefore positively affect the economic attractiveness of major eastern languages, and particularly the employability of bilinguals and multilinguals.

This scenario reflects the important half-truth of Coulmas (1992, p. 152) who suggests that

> 'in spite of the non-economic values attached to language, what prevails in matters of language is often that which is profitable'.

The other half of the truth is that language is also related to less tangible, measurable and affective characteristics such as the social, cultural and particularly religious value of a particular language.

The half-truth also hides the tension that can often exist between economic development and cultural reproduction. The economic value of a language may at times clash with preserving that language to reflect heritage, home values and historical traditions. Nevertheless, the economic value of language relates strongly to the prestige of that language and hence its chances of maintenance and reproduction.

In large businesses, as García and Otheguy (1994) reveal, we should be cautious in assuming that a modern foreign language is needed in top executives and top managers. In multinational corporations, for example, the tendency may not be to send executives with modern language qualifications abroad. Rather there will be local nationals within a country, working for that corporation, who are bilingual in both the regional or national language and an international language such as English. US corporations who run their operations abroad, and multinational organizations, may prefer locally-based executives because of their native-like fluency in the national languages, their thorough understanding of the cultures of that region, and their ability to communicate with customers and the work force as well as with international colleagues. Local nationals are often paid a lower salary than executives sent from, for example, the USA.

This indicates that large corporations and multinational companies are increasingly aware that international business requires the **use of regional and national languages**. To sell in Germany, Latin America, Japan, or the Pacific Basin, increasingly requires business people whose language and culture is congruent with that of the buyer. A congruent language is valuable for communication. Sometimes, there may be no other way to conduct trade (e.g. if the buyer does not speak English). Speaking the buyer's language also signals favorable attitudes to the buyer's ethnicity and culture. A competent understanding of the buyer's culture also signals respect for the buyer and their way of doing business.

In the Nuffield Languages Inquiry (2000) in the UK, it was admitted that

'English is not enough. We are fortunate to speak a global language but, in a smart and competitive world, exclusive reliance on English leaves the UK vulnerable and dependent on the linguistic competence and the goodwill of others ... Young people from the UK are at a growing disadvantage in the recruitment market. The UK workforce suffers from a chronic shortage of people at all levels with usable language skills ... Mobility of employment is in danger of becoming the preserve of people from other countries' (p. 6).

García and Otheguy (1994) found in their research, that **smaller and medium-sized businesses** often require executives and managers who are capable of speaking in languages other than English or other majority languages. To have the edge over competitors, the language of business is important, and where it is congruent with the language of the area for business, a competitive edge is added. Those who insist that English should be the international medium of business may be selling themselves short, economically, socially and personally.

This reflects a paradox. While English is often accepted as the international language in multinational companies and international trade, the massive spread of English during this century has led to a reaction, rather like adjusting a balance, with a few national and regional groups wishing to assert their local identity through a retention of their heritage language and culture. This has occurred in France and the UK, for example. An increased accent on national and regional languages in the face of international trade, has led to buying from those who are willing to speak the language and culture of the region rather than imposing their own language on the buyer. Nevertheless, the competitive edge has often more to do with prices, lowest quotations, and the lowest bid rather than language preference.

Minority Languages and the Economy

In suggesting that bilingualism has economic advantages, the only languages to be highlighted so far have been majority languages. English, German, French and Arabic, for example, are relatively prestigious majority languages. What is the place of minority languages in the economy? Will bilinguals from language minorities have no economic advantage, no valuable trading language in their minority language, no chance, due to their bilingualism, of getting out of the poverty trap that many experience?

In Europe, for example, the move from regional and state economies to a single European market policy, interlocking business structures in different European countries, encouraging mobility in businesses across European countries may leave a distinction between core and periphery, between those in important urban business areas and those in **rural peripheries** (e.g. rural areas in Ireland, Wales and Scotland). Since many indigenous minority languages in Europe are found in regions that are relatively sparsely populated, economically underdeveloped, with poorer rural road and transport systems, there is a danger that there will growing inequality between core and periphery.

In the economic restructuring that has occurred in the last 60 years, increased competition has led to the need for more efficiency to maintain profit. Industries and services have frequently had to 'automate, emigrate or evaporate'. Emigration of industries has been to countries such as Taiwan, Mexico, Brazil and Singapore, where wages, and therefore production costs, are relatively low. Such outside investment may sometimes offer work and wages to language minority members, but may also have negative consequences for language minorities.

One negative consequence is that the investment may not reach a language minority. For example, where such minorities live in rural areas (e.g. Irish and Welsh speakers), economic growth may be in the urban 'core' rather than the rural periphery. Alternatively, the higher grade jobs may be in relatively affluent city areas, and the lower grade, poorly paid work in the more remote areas.

A different scenario is when a peripheral area attracts **inward investment** (e.g. factories are located in remoter areas). The tendency is for the local language minorities to provide relatively cheap workers, while the better paid (language majority) managers either operate from their far-away city headquarters or move into the periphery language community. In both cases (given below), the managers may have a negative effect on language maintenance:

(1)   By working from city headquarters, there is a geographical separation of majority language manager and minority language proletariat that represents a status, and a social, cultural, economic and power division. Such a division has prestige consequences for the majority and minority language. Each language is identified with greater or lesser affluence, higher and lower status, more or less power.

(2)   By living in the language minority community, a manager who does not learn the local language evokes a class distinction. The manager speaks the majority language; the workers the minority language. One is a higher socioeconomic class; the other a lower socioeconomic class. There is a **social class division**, and a separation or fracture within the social class structure of the community (Morris, 1992). Social tensions may result that lead to divisions along both social class and language dimensions. As Morris (1992) found in her research, one solution is language minority managers who are able to operate across social classes inside their language group.

For language minorities, it seems essential that, through entrepreneurial activity, enterprise and risk-taking, they develop small and medium-sized businesses. Such businesses, sometimes located in rural areas, sometimes producing goods for export, sometimes using ease of communications (e.g. via computers) to deliver services, are essential for local languages to be preserved. **Language minority businesses** need to be networked where possible, within a region and increasingly internationally.

The absence of community-based, ethnically-based businesses increases the risk of the emigration of more able, more skilled and more entrepreneurial people away from the area, hence leaving the language itself in peril. A language community without economic activity is in danger of starving the language of one essential support mechanism. An **economically wealthy language** has a higher probability of being a healthy language. An economically impoverished language is placed at risk.

While language communities are not necessarily internally integrated, (having their own inner power and status struggles, differences and divisions), such language communities need to generate their own **local economies** and to be able to market their products and services beyond the region. In Gwynedd, North Wales, for example, there are two examples of economic language planning. First, new businesses located in language minority communities are initially subsidized, professionally advised and developed. Second, many jobs now demand bilingual applicants. The ability to use Welsh and English is regarded as essential for employment in teaching, many administrative jobs, local authority services, secretarial and clerical posts. Thus the Welsh language is given a vital economic foundation.

Some minority language businesses (e.g. local radio and television stations) create language-related economic activity that, in itself, spawns secondary economic activity to support such businesses (e.g. catering services, translation services, music and drama activities).

In many countries of the world, there are examples of language communities who are immigrant rather than indigenous who, through fast food (e.g. the Chinese restaurants) and the clothes trade (e.g. various Asian groups) maintain their language via ethnic industries. The language is supported by businesses where factory workers, shop workers and managers work partly or mainly through their heritage language.

Another success story is the development of the Cuban enclave economy in **Miami** which shows the possibility of a minority language economy developing in a region. Following the influx of Cubans into Miami in the 1960s, a Cuban enclave economy developed. Based on sufficient capital, a capable labor force, a ready market for products and a sufficient Cuban population to support Cuban-owned businesses, economic success of the enclave soon resulted.

This eastern area of the USA also demonstrates the vital nature of languages other than English for thriving international trade. Boswell's (1998) research shows that in Florida, bilinguals (Spanish/English) have an income advantage over monolingual English speakers of, on average, 2000 dollars. Such bilinguals have an average income advantage of 7000 to 8000 dollars over those who are monolingual in Spanish. This is partly because Florida is a major focus of trade with Latin America (about one-third of all US trade) and the Caribbean (approximately half of US trade). Exports from Florida to Latin American countries grew from six billion dollars in 1985 to close to 24 billion dollars by 1997 and are likely to increase (Boswell, 1998). Languages in addition to English have become important and influential in this economic growth.

This raises an issue about those language minorities who are often located in inner-city, **urban, immigrant communities**. As already expressed at the start of this section, such families and language communities are often surrounded by poverty, deprivation, unemployment and inequality of opportunity to acquire wealth. García and Otheguy (1994) provide an analysis of the economic possibilities of such urban language communities, particularly in the USA. The ability to speak a minority language can be crucial in gaining access to such an ethnic business. If everyone else in the organization speaks Spanish or Cantonese, to gain employment requires knowledge of that language.

A minority language may also be valuable at the customer interface. García and Otheguy (1994) relate an example.

> 'As the burgers and fries popped over the counter at the usual speed on the line with the Spanish-speaking employee, the line with the English-speaking employee was moving slowly, creating inefficiencies caused by her difficulty in communicating with the Spanish-speaking customers' (p. 110).

The problem with many ethnic businesses is the level of status, salary and conditions that such businesses provide for their employees. Often the jobs available are of lower status with a lower salary, making advancement not always easy or possible. García and Otheguy (1994) found that in US businesses, the demand for bilingual workers was not usually at the top executive levels. Rather, the need for bilinguals was for the lower and middle ranges of occupation. For example, US businesses required bilingual secretaries, clerks, shop floor assistants, rather than bilingual managers and executives. Waldman's (1994) US research found that the five most needed language abilities required were: telephone; customer contact or relations; translation and interpretation; word processing and correspondence. Spanish was the language most required by companies, followed by German, French and Japanese.

However, smaller companies indicated that language skills are of value in their higher positions. In small companies, the language of the whole work force may be the minority language. Thus cohesion and an integrated purpose is attained when managers speak the same language as those whom they manage.

Bilingualism and Economic Inequality

In the economic recession years of the 1980s, divisions between the rich and the poor tended to increase. In the USA, for example, African Americans and Latinos tended to find that the quality of their employment, the chance of finding a job if unemployed, opportunities for upward mobility and the value of wages as against inflation were all made more difficult in the recession. Among Latinos, who showed a population growth in the 1980s and 1990s in the USA, the movement of jobs away from urban areas to suburban areas (for service-oriented and goods-producing industries) made the finding of jobs and moving above the poverty line increasingly difficult. As Morales and Bonilla (1993, p. 11) suggest:

'Latinos entering the labor market in the last decade have encountered difficult conditions. For many, the outcome has been unstable employment, diminished job opportunities, and extreme impoverishment. Latinos in the USA display several distinct characteristics: high rates of immigration and reproduction, low levels of education, high rates of urbanization, concentration in low-paying jobs, and high levels of poverty.'

Historically, antagonism towards immigrants (particularly in times of economic recession) is typically directed at newcomers who are blamed for taking away jobs from long-standing citizens. Immigrants are then blamed for economic and social ills in society. However, US research tends to show the opposite (Dicker, 1998). Immigrants tend to stimulate and benefit the economy and their effect on job displacement is very small (less than 1%). Immigrants tend to have a stimulating effect on the economy by (a) opening as many new businesses as non-immigrants, (b) keeping businesses from relocating outside the country by providing inexpensive labor, which (c) keeps down the costs of goods and services. Indeed a 1997 United States National Academy of Sciences Panel found that immigrants add approximately 10 million dollars per year to the country's economic output such that 'the vast majority of Americans are enjoying a healthier economy as a result of the increased supply of labor and lower prices that result from immigration' (James P. Smith, the Panel's Chairperson, quoted in Dicker, 1998, p. 286).

While there are ethnic group differences, the overall picture is of low wage employment among language minority members, relatively fewer opportunities for promotion and upward mobility, low vocational expectations and motivation, more economically disenfranchised communities and hence a possible economic poverty trap. However, it is not an inevitable condition of language minorities that they are economically deprived, impoverished or that they lack entrepreneurial enterprise. In the USA, poverty and inequality are not equally shared by all Latinos. Morales and Bonilla (1993) suggest that Puerto Rican, Mexican and Dominican language groups in the USA appear to share a greater burden of poverty. US Central and South Americans, and particularly US Cubans, exhibit less poverty than other Latinos.

A research study by García (1995) found that the salaries earned by different Latino groups in the USA did not have a simple connection with their being bilingual or English monolinguals. While Mexican and Puerto Rican bilinguals in the USA earned on average $4000 and $3200, respectively, less than those who were monolingual English speakers, the Cuban-American bilinguals showed a different pattern in earnings. Cuban-Americans tended to earn almost $1000 more than the average English language monolingual. Because Cuban-Americans may have reached a higher level of education, be regarded as political allies of Americans and enemies of Castro's Cuba, and because Cuban-Americans in areas such as Dade County have created their own businesses to serve the local ethnic community and to trade in areas such as Latin America, Spanish-English speakers in this group have gained socioeconomic power. García (1995) concludes that her findings:

'demonstrate that speaking only English does not always make a difference in the achievement of economic prosperity, and that bilingualism, rather than monolingualism, is a useful commodity in some communities, including the Latino one.' (p. 157)

To conclude: with the Spanish-speaking population of the USA rapidly growing, and with Spanish an important trading language in Latin America and elsewhere, there is a possibility that Spanish may be of increasing economic value inside the USA and for marketing abroad. Therefore, it seems economically valuable in the next century to be bilingual. For some individuals, this is to gain employment and try to avoid poverty. For others, bilingualism may be of value to work locally for international and multinational corporations. For yet others, who wish to travel abroad to do their trade, languages also become increasingly important.

The concept that speaking English is all one needs, whether in Europe or the USA, is naive. While English is often at the leading edge of economic modernization and technological development, selling and marketing, tailoring products and services to suit local markets requires local languages. The importance of knowledge of languages other than English in economics and foreign trade was acknowledged by the USA in a report accompanying the formulation of the Foreign Language Assistance for National Security Act of 1983.

'It is precisely this combination of foreign language ability and business expertise … that is now needed and will be required even more in the future by US companies if they are to compete successfully in these (Asian, the Middle East, Eastern Europe) markets.' (John McDougall, Executive Vice President of the Ford Motor Company)

Moving from a minority language to a majority language for perceived economic purposes may not reap the expected rewards. There is no guarantee that those who become linguistically assimilated (e.g. speak English-only) in countries like the USA will gain employment. The evidence from García and Otheguy (1994) and Morales and Bonilla (1993) confirms that the ability to speak English does not give equal access to jobs and wealth. Linguistic assimilation does not mean incorporation into the economic structure of the country. If there is a growth of ethnic businesses (e.g. in urban areas), and a development of language minority businesses in peripheral, rural areas, then bilingualism rather than English monolingualism may become more economically valuable.

KEY POINTS IN THE CHAPTER

- In a world economy and ease of international communications, bilinguals and multilinguals are increasingly required in many occupations.
- The growth of tourism has potential economic benefits for many minority languages, but is allied to the rapid spread of English and preference for historical culture than contemporary living culture.

- Minority language mass media and use in information technology is required for the status of a language but is often in competition with the dominant anglophone mass media.
- Minority language groups are often identified with relatively high unemployment, low pay, poverty and powerlessness. However, local niche economies, working from home, and community initiatives can support and sustain a language minority.
- Bilingualism can be more valuable than majority language monolingualism, giving a competitive edge for an increasing number of vocations.

SUGGESTED FURTHER READING

COULMAS, F., 1992, *Language and Economy*. Oxford: Blackwell.
CUMMINS, J. and SAYERS, D., 1996, Multicultural education and technology: Promise and pitfalls. *Multicultural Education* 3 (3), 4–10.
GARCíA, O., 1995, Spanish language loss as a determinant of income among Latinos in the United States: Implications for language policy in schools. In J.W. TOLLEFSON (ed.) *Power and Inequality in Language Education*. Cambridge: Cambridge University Press.
GARCíA, O. and OTHEGUY, R., 1994, The value of speaking a LOTE in US Business. *Annals of the American Academy of Political and Social Science* 532, 99–122.
HALL, J.K. and EGGINGTON, W.G., 2000, *The Sociopolitics of English Language Teaching*. Clevedon: Multilingual Matters.
LAVER, J. and ROUKENS, J., 1996, The global information society and Europe's linguistic and cultural heritage. In C. HOFFMANN (ed.) *Language, Culture and Communication in Contemporary Europe*. Clevedon: Multilingual Matters.

STUDY ACTIVITIES

(1) Carry out a survey in your locality and find out how many different jobs use bilingual skills. Alternatively, analyze job advertisements in local papers for language skills required.

(2) Survey the employment and unemployment pattern of people from local language minorities.

(3) How much (1) provision and (2) use is made of different languages on terrestrial, cable and satellite television received by a sample of people in local language minorities. Also, what languages do they use with IT (e.g. use of the World Wide Web).

(4) Make a poster or handout advertising the sites available for using a minority language on the Internet.

(5) In a small discussion or focus group, examine a selection of the dualisms or dimensions presented below. These attempt to sum up some of the debates and important dimensions of thinking in this book. Regard this as a 'summative' question that requires other chapters of the book to be considered and integrated.

  (i) Briefly state what are the different viewpoints alluded to in those dualisms/ dimensions you have chosen.

  (ii) Indicate how these dualisms/dimensions relate to different views of bilingualism, bilingual education and multicultural education. What are the implications for the kind of language and cultural approach adopted in a school?

(a) Linguistic compared with the Sociocultural/Sociolinguistic view of bilinguals.
(b) Individual compared with Group analysis of bilingualism/diglossia.
(c) Skills compared with Competences
(d) Fractional compared with a Holistic view of bilinguals.
(e) Subtractive compared with an Additive view of bilinguals.
(f) Preservationists compared with Modernizers.
(g) The Rights (individual and group) view compared with the Empowerment view.
(h) Assimilationist compared with the Pluralist view.
(i) The Functional view compared with the Conflict view.
(j) The deprivation, remedial, problem, disabled view of bilinguals compared with the resource, beneficial, colorful, talent view of bilinguals.

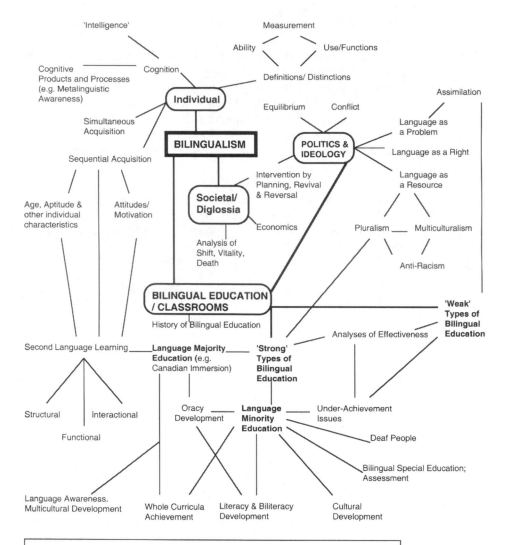

'Intelligence'

Measurement

Ability   Use/Functions

Cognitive
Products and Processes   Cognition
(e.g. Metalinguistic
Awareness)

Definitions/ Distinctions

Assimilation

Individual

Simultaneous
Acquisition

Equilibrium   Conflict

Language as
a Problem

BILINGUALISM

**POLITICS &
IDEOLOGY**

Language as a Right

Sequential Acquisition

Intervention by
Planning, Revival
& Reversal

Language as
a Resource

Age, Aptitude &
other individual
characteristics

Attitudes/
Motivation

**Societal/
Diglossia**

Pluralism   Multiculturalism

Economics

Analysis of
Shift, Vitality,
Death

Anti-Racism

**BILINGUAL EDUCATION
/ CLASSROOMS**

'Weak'
Types of
Bilingual
Education

History of Bilingual Education

Analyses of Effectiveness

Second Language Learning

**Language Majority
Education** (e.g.
Canadian Immersion)

'Strong'
Types of
Bilingual
Education

Structural   Interactional

Oracy
Development

**Language
Minority
Education**

Under-Achievement
Issues

Functional

Deaf People

Bilingual Special Education;
Assessment

Language Awareness.
Multicultural Development

Whole Curricula
Achievement

Literacy & Biliteracy
Development

Cultural
Development

Notes: 1. A Conceptual Map needs to be multidimensional not two dimensional.
2. For simplicity, some connections are missing (e.g. Education and Cognition;
Language Majority Education & Cultural Development).
3. This is one of many possible maps; it is a schema for this book only.
4. Extensions by further divisions and sub-divisions will enlarge the map (e.g. Integrative
and Instrumental Motivation as branches from Attitudes/ Motivation).

A Conceptual Map of the Book

Bibliography

ACAC, 1993, *Developing a Curriculum Cymreig*. Cardiff: ACAC.

ADA, A.F., 1995, Fostering the home–school connection. In J. FREDERICKSON (ed.), *Reclaiming Our Voices: Bilingual Education, Critical Pedagogy and Praxis*. Ontario, CA: California Association for Bilingual Education.

ADA, A.F., 1997, Mother-tongue literacy as a bridge between home and school cultures. In J.V. TINAJERO & ALMA FLOR ADA, (eds), *The Power of Two Languages: Literacy and Biliteracy for Spanish Speaking Students*. New York: Macmillan/McGraw-Hill.

ADA, A.F., 1988a, Creative reading: A relevant methodology for language minority children. In L.M. MALAVE (ed.), *NABE '87. Theory, Research and Application: Selected Papers*. Buffalo: State University of New York.

ADA, A.F., 1988b, The Pajaro Valley experience: Working with Spanish-speaking parents. In T. SKUTNABB-KANGAS & J. CUMMINS (eds), *Minority Education: From Shame to Struggle*. Clevedon: Multilingual Matters.

ADA, A.F. & SMITH, N.J., 1998, Fostering the home–school connection for Latinos. In M.L. GONZALEZ, A. HUERTA-MACIAS & J.V. TINAJERO (eds), *Educating Latino Students: A Guide to Successful Practice*. Lancaster, Pennsylvania: Technomatic.

ADAMS, J.W., 1997, *You and Your Deaf Child* (2nd edn). Washington, DC: Gallaudet University Press.

AFOLAYAN, A., 1995, Aspects of bilingual education in Nigeria. In B.M. JONES & P. GHUMAN (eds), *Bilingualism, Education and Identity*. Cardiff: University of Wales Press.

AGER, D.E., 1997, *Language, Community and the State*. Exeter: Intellect Books.

AITCHISON, J., 1991, *Language Change: Progress or Decay*. Cambridge: Cambridge University Press.

ALLADINA, S. & EDWARDS, V., 1991, *Multilingualism in the British Isles*. London: Longman.

ALLARDT, E., 1979, Implications of the ethnic revival in modern, industrialized society. A comparative study of the linguistic minorities in Western Europe. *Commentationes Scientiarum Socialium* 12. Helsinki: Societas Scientiarum Fennica.

ALLARDT, E. & STARCK, C., 1981, *Sprakgranser och Samhallsstruktur*. Stockholm: Almquist and Wiksell.

ALLEN, P. *et al.*, 1989, Restoring the balance: A response to Hammerly. *Canadian Modern Language Review* 45 (4), 770–776.

AMERICAN PSYCHOLOGICAL ASSOCIATION, 1982, Review of Department of Education report entitled: '*Effectiveness of Bilingual Education: A Review of Literature*', Letter to Congressional Hispanic Caucus, April 22nd.

ANDERSEN, R., 1983, Introduction: A language acquisition interpretation of pidginization and creolization. In R. ANDERSEN (ed.), *Pidginization and Creolization as Language Acquisition*. Rowley, MA: Newbury House.

ANDERSON, C.A., 1966, Literacy and schooling on the development threshold. In C.A. ANDERSON & M. BOWMAN (eds), *Education and Economic Development*. London: Frank Cass.

ANDERSON, J., 1995, *Learning and Memory*. New York: John Wiley.

439

ANDERSSON, T. & BOYER, M., 1970, *Bilingual Schooling in the United States* (2 volumes). Austin, TX: Southwest Educational Laboratory.

ANDRES, F., 1990, Language relations in multilingual Switzerland. *Multilingua* 9 (1), 11–45.

APPEL, R. & MUYSKEN, P., 1987, *Language Contact and Bilingualism*. London: Edward Arnold.

ARIAS, M. & CASANOVA, U. (eds), 1993, *Bilingual Education: Politics, Practice, Research*. Chicago: National Society for the Study of Education/University of Chicago Press.

ARNAU, J., 1997, Immersion education in Catalonia. In J. CUMMINS & D. CORSON (eds), *Bilingual Education*. Volume 5 of the *Encyclopedia of Language and Education*. Dordrecht: Kluwer.

ARNBERG, L., 1981, Bilingual education of young children in England and Wales. University of Linkoping, Sweden, Department of Education.

ARNBERG, L., 1987, *Raising Children Bilingually: The Pre-School Years*. Clevedon: Multilingual Matters.

ARNBERG, L. & ARNBERG, P., 1992, Language awareness and language separation in the young bilingual child. In R.J. HARRIS (ed.), *Cognitive Processing in Bilinguals*. Amsterdam: North-Holland.

ARTIGAL, J.M., 1991, *The Catalan Immersion Program: A European Point of View*. Norwood, NJ: Ablex.

ARTIGAL, J.M., 1993, Catalan and Basque immersion programmes. In H. BAETENS BEARDSMORE (ed.), *European Models of Bilingual Education*. Clevedon: Multilingual Matters.

ARTIGAL, J.M., 1997, Plurilingual education in Catalonia. In R. JOHNSON & M. SWAIN (eds), *Immersion Education: International Perspectives*. Cambridge: Cambridge University Press.

ASHER, R.E. & SIMPSON, J.M.Y. (eds), 1994, *The Encyclopedia of Language and Linguistics*. 10 Volumes. Oxford: Pergamon.

ATTINASI, J.J., 1994, Racism, language variety and urban US minorities: Issues in bilingualism and bidialectalism. In S. GREGORY & R. SANJEK (eds), *Race*. New Jersey: Rutgers University Press.

ATTINASI, J.J., 1998, English Only for California children and the aftermath of Proposition 227. *Education* 119 (2), 263–283.

AUERBACH, E.R., 1989, Toward a social-contextual approach to family literacy. *Harvard Educational Review* 59 (2), 165–181.

AUGUST, D. & HAKUTA, K., 1997, *Improving Schooling for Language-Minority Children*. Washington, DC: National Academy Press.

AUGUST, D. & HAKUTA, K., 1998, *Educating Language-Minority Children*. Washington, DC: National Academy Press.

BACA, L.M. & CERVANTES, H.T., 1998, *The Bilingual Special Education Interface* (3rd edn). Upper Saddle River, NJ: Prentice Hall.

BACHI, R., 1956, A statistical analysis of the revival of Hebrew in Israel. *Scripta Hierosolymitana* 3, 179–247.

BACHMAN, L.F., 1990, *Fundamental Considerations in Language Testing*. Oxford: Oxford University Press.

BAETENS BEARDSMORE, H., 1986, *Bilingualism: Basic Principles*. Clevedon: Multilingual Matters.

BAETENS BEARDSMORE, H., 1993, The European school model. In H. BAETENS BEARDSMORE (ed.), *European Models of Bilingual Education*. Clevedon: Multilingual Matters.

BAETENS BEARDSMORE, H., 1999, Language policy and bilingual education in Brunei Darussalam. *Bulletin Des Seances* (Academie Royale Des Sciences D'Outre-Mer) 45 (4), 507–523.

BAETENS BEARDSMORE, H. (ed.), 1993, *European Models of Bilingual Education*. Clevedon: Multilingual Matters.

BAETENS BEARDSMORE H. & LeBRUN, N., 1991, Trilingual education in the Grand Duchy of Luxembourg. In O. GARCÍA (ed.), *Bilingual Education: Focusschrift in Honor of Joshua A. Fishman*. Amsterdam/Philadelphia: John Benjamins.

BAETENS BEARDSMORE, H. & SWAIN, M., 1985, Designing bilingual education: Aspects of immersion and 'European School' models. *Journal of Multilingual and Multicultural Development* 6 (1), 1–15.

BAETENS BEARDSMORE, H. & VAN BEECK, H., 1984, Multilingual television supply and language shift in Brussels. *International Journal of the Sociology of Language* 48, 65–79.

BAKER, C., 1985, *Aspects of Bilingualism in Wales*. Clevedon: Multilingual Matters.

BAKER, C., 1988, *Key Issues in Bilingualism and Bilingual Education*. Clevedon: Multilingual Matters.

BAKER, C., 1990, The effectiveness of bilingual education. *Journal of Multilingual and Multicultural Development* 11 (4), 269–277.

BAKER, C., 1992, *Attitudes and Language.* Clevedon: Multilingual Matters.

BAKER, C., 1993, Bilingual education in Wales. In H. BAETENS BEARDSMORE (ed.), *European Typologies of Bilingual Education.* Clevedon: Multilingual Matters.

BAKER, C., 1995, Bilingual education and assessment. In B.M. JONES & P. GHUMAN (eds), *Bilingualism, Education and Identity.* Cardiff: University of Wales Press.

BAKER, C., 1999, Sign language and the deaf community. In J.A. FISHMAN (ed.), *Handbook of Language and Ethnic Identity.* New York: Oxford University Press.

BAKER, C. 2000a, *A Parents' and Teachers' Guide to Bilingualism* (2nd edn). Clevedon: Multilingual Matters.

BAKER, C., 2000b, *The Care and Education of Young Bilinguals: An Introduction for Professionals.* Clevedon: Multilingual Matters.

BAKER, C., 2000c, Three perspectives on bilingual education policy in Wales: Bilingual education as language planning, bilingual education as pedagogy and bilingual education as politics. In R. DAUGHERTY, R. PHILLIPS & G. REES (eds), *Education Policy in Wales: Explorations in Devolved Governance.* Cardiff: University of Wales Press.

BAKER C. & HINDE J., 1984, Language background classification. *Journal of Multilingual and Multicultural Development* 5 (1), 43–56.

BAKER C. & JONES, S.P., 1998, *Encyclopedia of Bilingualism and Bilingual Education.* Clevedon: Multilingual Matters.

BAKER, K., 1987, Comment on Willig's 'A meta analysis of selected studies of bilingual education'. *Review of Educational Research* 57 (3), 351–362.

BAKER, K., 1992, Ramirez et al.: Misled by bad theory. *Bilingual Research Journal* 16 (1&2), 63–89.

BAKER, K.A. & de KANTER, A.A., 1981, *Effectiveness of Bilingual Education: A Review of Literature.* Washington, DC: Office of Planning, Budget and Evaluation, US Department of Education.

BAKER, K.A. & de KANTER, A.A., 1983, *Bilingual Education.* Lexington, MA: Lexington Books.

BALKAN, L., 1970, *Les Effets du Bilingualisme Français: Anglais sur les Aptitudes Intellectuelles.* Brussels: Aimav.

BARONA, M.S. & BARONA, A., 1992, Assessment of bilingual preschool children. In R.V. PADILLA & A.H. BENAVIDES (eds), *Critical Perspectives on Bilingual Education Research.* Tempe, AZ: Bilingual Press.

BARTH, F., 1966, *Models of Social Organization* (Occasional Paper No. 23). London: Royal Anthropological Institute.

BEL, A., 1993, Some results of the immersion programme in Catalonia. *Notícies del SEDEC/Newsletter of the Servei d'Ensenyament del Catalonia.*

BENTON, R.A., 1991, 'Tomorrow's schools' and the revitalization of Maori. In O. GARCÍA (ed.), *Bilingual Education: Focusschrift in Honor of Joshua A. Fishman.* Amsterdam/Philadelphia: John Benjamins.

BENYON, J. & TOOHEY, K., 1991, Heritage language education in British Columbia: Policy and programs. *Canadian Modern Language Review* 47 (4), 606–616.

BEN-ZEEV, S., 1977a, The influence of bilingualism on cognitive strategy and cognitive development. *Child Development* 48, 1009–1018.

BEN-ZEEV, S., 1977b, The effect of bilingualism in children from Spanish–English low economic neighborhoods on cognitive development and cognitive strategy. *Working Papers on Bilingualism* 14, 83–122.

BERLINER, D.C., 1988, Meta-comments: A discussion of critiques of L.M. Dunn's monograph 'Bilingual Hispanic Children on the US Mainland'. *Hispanic Journal of Behavioral Sciences* 10 (3), 273–300.

BERNHARDT, E.B. (ed.), 1992, *Life in Language Immersion Classrooms.* Clevedon: Multilingual Matters.

BERNHARDT, E.B. & SCHRIER, L., 1992, The development of immersion teachers. In E.B. BERNHARDT (ed.), *Life in Language Immersion Classrooms.* Clevedon: Multilingual Matters.

BERTHOLD, M., 1992, An Australian experiment in French immersion. *Canadian Modern Language Review* 49 (1), 112–125.

BERTHOLD, M., 1995, *Rising to the Bilingual Challenge: Ten Years of Queensland Secondary School Immersion.* Canberra: National Languages and Literacy Unit of Australia.

BIALYSTOK, E., 1987a, Influences of bilingualism on metalinguistic development. *Second Language Research* 3 (2), 154–166.

BIALYSTOK, E., 1987b, Words as things: Development of word concept by bilingual children. *Studies in Second Language Learning* 9, 133–140.

BIALYSTOK, E., 1988, Levels of bilingualism and levels of linguistic awareness. *Developmental Psychology* 24 (4), 560–567.

BIALYSTOK, E., 1992, Selective attention in cognitive processing: The bilingual edge. In R.J. HARRIS (ed.), *Cognitive Processing in Bilinguals*. Amsterdam: North-Holland.

BIALYSTOK, E., 1997, Effects of bilingualism and biliteracy on children's emerging concepts of print. *Developmental Psychology* 33 (3), 429–440.

BIALYSTOK, E. (ed.), 1991, *Language Processing in Bilingual Children*. Cambridge: Cambridge University Press.

BIALYSTOK, E. & CODD, J., 1997, Cardinal limits: Evidence from language awareness and bilingualism for developing concepts of number. *Cognitive Development* 12 (1), 85–106.

BIALYSTOK, E. & HERMAN, J., 1997, Does bilingualism matter for early literacy? *Bilingualism: Language and Cognition* 2 (1), 35–44.

BIALYSTOK, E. & MAJUMDER, S., 1999, The relationship between bilingualism and the development of cognitive processes in problem solving. *Applied Psycholinguistics* 19, 1, 69–85.

BIALYSTOK, E. & RYAN, E.B., 1985, Toward a definition of metalinguistic skill. *Merrill-Palmer Quarterly* 31 (3), 229–251.

BILD, E. & SWAIN, M., 1989, Minority language students in a French immersion programme: Their French proficiency. *Journal of Multilingual and Multicultural Development* 10 (3), 255–274.

BJÖRKLUND, S., 1997, Immersion in Finland in the 1990s: A state of development and expansion. In R.K. JOHNSON & M. SWAIN, 1997, *Immersion Education: International Perspectives*. Cambridge: Cambridge University Press.

BJÖRKLUND, S. & SUNI, I., 2000, The role of English as L3 in a Swedish immersion program in Finland. In J. CENOZ & U. JESSNER (eds), *English in Europe: The Acquisition of a Third Language*. Clevedon: Multilingual Matters.

BLACHFORD, D.RU., 1997, Bilingual education in China. In J. CUMMINS & D. CORSON (eds), *Bilingual Education*. Volume 5 of the *Encyclopedia of Language and Education*. Dordrecht: Kluwer.

BLOOME, D., 1985, Reading as a social process. *Language Arts* 62, 134–142.

BLOOMFIELD L., 1933, *Language*. New York: Holt.

BOSWELL, T.D., 1998, Implications of demographic changes in Florida's public school population. In S.H. FRADD & O. LEE (eds), *Creating Florida's Multilingual Global Work Force: Educational Policies and Practices for Students Learning English as a New Language*. Tallahassee, Florida: Florida Department of Education.

BOURDIEU, P., 1991, *Language and Symbolic Power*. Cambridge: Polity Press.

BOYD, S. & LATOMAA, S., 1999, Fishman's theory of diglossia and bilingualism in the light of language maintenance and shift in the Nordic Region. In G. EXTRA & L. VERHOEVEN (eds), *Bilingualism and Migration*. Berlin & New York: Mouton de Gruyter.

BOYLE, E.R., 1990, Is there a bilingual answer for Hong Kong? *Evaluation and Research in Education* 4 (3), 117–127.

BRAINE, M.D., 1987, Acquiring and processing first and second languages. In P. HOMEL, M. PALIJ & D. AARONSON (eds), *Childhood Bilingualism: Aspects of Linguistic, Cognitive and Social Development*. Hillsdale, NJ: Lawrence Erlbaum.

BRELJE, H.W. (ed.), 1999, *Global Perspectives on the Education of the Deaf in Selected Countries*. Hillsboro, OR: Butte Publications.

BRIGHT, W. (ed.), 1992, *The International Encyclopedia of Linguistics*. Oxford: Oxford University Press.

BRISK, M.E., 1998, *Bilingual Education: From Compensatory to Quality Schooling*. Mahwah, NY: Lawrence Erlbaum.

BROWN, D. (ed.), 1997, *Education Policy and Language Learning for a Multilingual Society*. Durban: University of Natal.

BRUCK, M., LAMBERT, W.E. & TUCKER, G.R., 1976, Cognitive consequences of bilingual schooling: The St Lambert Project through Grade 6. Unpublished Manuscript. Department of Psychology, McGill University.

BULL, B.L., FRUEHLING, R.T. & CHATTERGY, V., 1992, *The Ethics of Multicultural and Bilingual Education*. New York: Teachers College Press.

BULLOCK REPORT (DEPARTMENT OF EDUCATION AND SCIENCE), 1975, *A Language for Life*. London: HMSO.

BULWER, J., 1995, European Schools: Languages for all? *Journal of Multilingual and Multicultural Development* 16 (6), 459–475.

BUTTS, R.F., 1980, *The Revival of Civic Learning*. Bloomington, IN: Phi Delta Kappa.

BYRAM, M., 1998, Cultural identities in multilingual classrooms. In J. CENOZ & F. GENESEE (eds), *Beyond Bilingualism: Multilingualism and Multilingual Education*. Clevedon: Multilingual Matters.

CALDWELL, J. & BERTHOLD, M., 1995, Aspects of bilingual education in Australia. In B.M. JONES & P.S.S. GHUMAN (eds), *Bilingualism, Education and Identity*. Cardiff: University of Wales Press.

CALERO-BRECKHEIMER, A. & GOETZ, E.T., 1993, Reading strategies of biliterate children for English and Spanish texts. *Reading Psychology* 14, 177–204.

CALIFORNIA STATE DEPARTMENT OF EDUCATION, 1984, *Studies on Immersion Education. A Collection for United States Educators*. Sacramento, CA: California State Department of Education.

CALIFORNIA STATE DEPARTMENT OF EDUCATION, 1989, *Foreign Language Framework*. Sacramento, CA: California State Department of Education.

CAMPBELL, R. & SAIS, E., 1995, Accelerated metalinguistic (phonological) awareness in bilingual children. *British Journal of Developmental Psychology* 13 (1), 61–68.

CANADIAN EDUCATION ASSOCIATION, 1991, *Heritage Language Programs in Canadian School Boards*. Toronto: Canadian Education Association.

CANADIAN EDUCATION ASSOCIATION, 1992, *French Immersion Today*. Toronto: Canadian Education Association.

CANALE, M., 1983, On some dimensions of language proficiency. In J.W. OLLER (ed.), *Issues in Language Testing Research*. Rowley, MA: Newbury House.

CANALE, M., 1984, On some theoretical frameworks for language proficiency. In C. RIVERA (ed.), *Language Proficiency and Academic Achievement*. Clevedon: Multilingual Matters.

CANALE, M. & SWAIN, M., 1980, Theoretical bases of communicative approaches to second language teaching and testing. *Applied Linguistics* 1, 1–47.

CANTONI, G. (ed.), 1996, *Stabilizing Indigenous Languages*. Flagstaff: Northern Arizona University.

CAREY, S.T., 1991, The culture of literacy in majority and minority language schools. *Canadian Modern Language Review* 47 (5), 950–976.

CARLISLE, J.F. *et al.*, 1999 Relationship of metalinguistic capabilities and reading achievement for children who are becoming bilingual. *Applied Psycholinguistics* 20 (4), 459–478.

CARRASQUILLO, A.L., 1990, Bilingual special education: The important connection. In A.L. CARRASQUILLO & R.E. BAECHER (eds), *Teaching the Bilingual Special Education Student*. Norwood, NJ: Ablex.

CARRASQUILLO, A.L. & RODRIGUEZ, V., 1996, *Language Minority Students in the Mainstream Classroom*. Clevedon: Multilingual Matters.

CARROLL, B., 1980, *Testing Communicative Performance*. Oxford: Pergamon Press.

CARROLL, J.B., 1968, The psychology of language testing. In A. DAVIES (ed.), *Language Testing Symposium. A Psycholinguistic Perspective*. Oxford: Oxford University Press.

CARTER, T.P. & CHATFIELD, M.L., 1986, Effective bilingual schools: Implications for policy and practice. *American Journal of Education* 95 (1), 200–232.

CASANOVA, U., 1991, Bilingual education: Politics or pedagogy? In O. GARCÍA (ed.), *Bilingual Education: Focusschrift in Honor of Joshua A. Fishman*. Amsterdam/Philadelphia: John Benjamins.

CASANOVA, U., 1992, Shifts in bilingual education policy and the knowledge base. In R.V. PADILLA & A.H. BENAVIDES (eds), *Critical Perspectives on Bilingual Education Research*. Tempe, AZ: Bilingual Press.

CASANOVA, U. & ARIAS M.B., 1993, Contextualizing bilingual education. In B. ARIAS & U. CASANOVA (eds), *Bilingual Education: Politics, Research and Practice*. Berkeley, CA: McCutchan.

CAZABON, M., LAMBERT, W. & HALL, G., 1993, *Two-Way Bilingual Education: A Progress Report on the Amigos Program*. Santa Cruz, CA: National Center for Research on Cultural Diversity and Second Language Learning.

CAZDEN, C.B., 1992, *Language Minority Education in the United States: Implications of the Ramirez Report*. Santa Cruz, CA: National Center for Research on Cultural Diversity and Second Language Learning.

CAZDEN, C.B. & SNOW, C.E., 1990a, Preface to C.B. CAZDEN & C.E. SNOW (eds), *English Plus: Issues in Bilingual Education*. London: Sage.

CAZDEN, C.B. & SNOW, C.E. (eds), 1990b, *English Plus: Issues in Bilingual Education*. (*The Annals of the American Academy of Political and Social Science* Vol. 508). London: Sage.

CENOZ J., 1998, Multilingual education in the Basque Country. In J. CENOZ & F. GENESEE (eds), *Beyond Bilingualism: Multilingualism and Multilingual Education*. Clevedon: Multilingual Matters.

CENOZ, J., 2000, Research on multilingual acquisition. In J. CENOZ & U. JESSNER (eds), *English in Europe: The Acquisition of a Third Language*. Clevedon: Multilingual Matters.

CENOZ J. & GENESEE, F., 1998, Psycholinguistic perspectives on multilingualism and multilingual education. In J. CENOZ & F. GENESEE (eds), *Beyond Bilingualism: Multilingualism and Multilingual Education*. Clevedon: Multilingual Matters.

CENOZ, J. & JESSNER. U. (eds), 2000, *English in Europe: The Acquisition of a Third Language*. Clevedon: Multilingual Matters.

CENOZ, J. & PERALES, J., 1997, Minority language learning in the administration: Data from the Basque Country. *Journal of Multilingual and Multicultural Development* 18 (4), 261–270.

CENOZ, J. & VALENCIA, J.F., 1994, Additive trilingualism: Evidence from the Basque Country. *Applied Linguistics* 15, 195–207.

CHAMBERLAIN, P. & MEDEIROS-LANDURAND, P., 1991, Practical considerations for the assessment of LEP students with special needs. In E.V. HAMAYAN & J.S. DAMICO (eds), *Limiting Bias in the Assessment of Bilingual Students*. Austin, TX: Pro-Ed.

CHAMOT, A.U., 1999, *The Learning Strategies Handbook*. White Plains, NY: Longman.

CHOMSKY, N., 1965, *Aspects of the Theory of Syntax*. Cambridge, MA: MIT Press.

CHRISTIAN, D., 1994, *Two-Way Bilingual Education: Students Learning Through Two Languages*. Santa Cruz, CA: National Center for Research on Cultural Diversity and Second Language Learning.

CHRISTIAN, D. *et al.*, 1997, *Profiles in Two-Way Immersion Education: Students Learning Through Two Languages*. Washington DC: Center for Applied Linguistics.

CLAPHAM, C. & CORSON, D. (eds), 1997, *Language Testing and Assessment*. Volume 7 of the *Encyclopedia of Language and Education*. Dordrecht: Kluwer.

CLARKSON, P.C., 1992, Language and mathematics: A comparison of bilingual and monolingual students of mathematics. *Educational Studies in Mathematics* 23, 417–429.

CLARKSON, P.C. & GALBRAITH, P., 1992, Bilingualism and mathematics learning: Another perspective. *Journal for Research in Mathematics Education* 23 (1), 34–44.

CLINE, T., 1993, Educational assessment of bilingual pupils: Getting the context right. *Educational and Child Psychology* 10 (4), 59–68.

CLINE, T., 1997, Educating for bilingualism in different contexts: Teaching the deaf and teaching children with English as an additional language. *Educational Review* 49 (2), 151–158.

CLINE, T. & FREDERICKSON, N., 1999, Identification and assessment of dyslexia in bi/multilingual children. *International Journal of Bilingual Education and Bilingualism* 2 (2), 81–93.

CLINE, T. & FREDERICKSON, N. (eds), 1995, *Progress in Curriculum Related Assessment with Bilingual Pupils*. Clevedon: Multilingual Matters.

CLINE, T. & FREDERICKSON, N. (eds), 1996, *Curriculum Related Assessment. Cummins and Bilingual Children*. Clevedon: Multilingual Matters.

CLOUD, N., 1994, Special education needs of second language children. In F. GENESEE (ed.), *Educating Second Language Children*. Cambridge: Cambridge University Press.

CLOUD, N., GENESEE, F. & HAMAYAN, E.V., 2000, *Dual Language Instruction: A Handbook for Enriched Education*. Boston: Heinle & Heinle.

CLYNE, M., 1988, Bilingual education: What can we learn from the past? *Australian Journal of Education* 32 (1), 95–114.

CLYNE, M., 1991, Bilingual education for all. An Australian pilot study and its implications. In O. GARCÍA (ed.), *Bilingual Education: Focusschrift in Honor of Joshua A. Fishman*. Amsterdam/Philadelphia: John Benjamins.

CLYNE, M., 1995, *The German Language in a Changing Europe*. Cambridge: Cambridge University Press.

CLYNE, M., 1997, Some of the things trilinguals do. *International Journal of Bilingualism* 1 (2), 95–116.

COELHO, E., 1998, *Teaching and Learning in Multicultural Schools*. Clevedon: Multilingual Matters.

COLLEGE FOR CONTINUING EDUCATION, 1992, *Bilingual Considerations in the Education of Deaf Students: ASL and English*. Washington, DC: Gallaudet University.

COLLIER, V.P., 1989, How long? A synthesis of research on academic achievement in a second language. *TESOL Quarterly* 23 (3), 509–531.

COLLIER, V.P., 1992, A synthesis of studies examining long-term language minority student data on academic achievement. *Bilingual Research Journal* 16 (1&2), 187–212.

COLLIER, V.P., 1995a, Acquiring a second language for school. *Directions in Language and Education* 1 (4), 1–12. (National Clearinghouse for Bilingual Education).

COLLIER, V.P., 1995b, *Promoting Academic Success for ESL Students: Understanding Second Language Acquisition For School*. Elizabeth, NJ: New Jersey Teachers of English to Speakers of Other Languages-Bilingual Educators.

COMMITTEE ON EDUCATION AND LABOR, 1983, *Foreign Language Assistance for National Security Act of 1983 Report*. (United States House of Representatives 98th. Congress). Washington DC: GPO.

COMRIE, B., 1987, *The World's Major Languages*. London: Routledge.

CONKLIN, N. & LOURIE, M., 1983, *A Host of Tongues*. New York: The Free Press.

COOK, V.J., 1991, *Second Language Learning and Language Teaching*. London: Edward Arnold.

COOK, V.J., 1992, Evidence for multicompetence. *Language Learning* 42 (4), 557–591.

COOPER, R.L., 1989, *Language Planning and Social Change*. Cambridge: Cambridge University Press.

CORDER, S., 1967, The significance of learners' errors. *International Review of Applied Linguistics* 5, 161–170.

CORSON, D., 1985, *The Lexical Bar*. Oxford: Pergamon.

CORSON, D., 1990a, *Language Policy Across the Curriculum*. Clevedon: Multilingual Matters.

CORSON, D., 1990b, Three curriculum and organizational responses to cultural pluralism in New Zealand schooling. *Language, Culture and Curriculum* 3 (3), 213–225.

CORSON, D., 1992, Bilingual education policy and social justice. *Journal of Education Policy* 7 (1), 45–69.

COULMAS, F., 1992, *Language and Economy*. Oxford: Blackwell.

COULMAS, F. (ed.), 1997, *The Handbook of Sociolinguistics*. Oxford: Blackwell.

CRAWFORD, J., 1992, *Hold Your Tongue: Bilingualism and the Politics of 'English Only'*. Reading, MA: Addison-Wesley.

CRAWFORD, J., 1995, Endangered native American Languages: What is to be done and why? *Bilingual Research Journal* 19 (1), 17–38.

CRAWFORD, J., 1997, The campaign against Proposition 227: A post mortem. *Bilingual Research Journal* 21 (1).

CRAWFORD, J., 1999, *Bilingual Education: History, Politics, Theory and Practice* (4th edn). Los Angeles: Bilingual Educational Services.

CRAWFORD, J. (ed.), 1992b, *Language Loyalties: A Source Book on the Official English Controversy*. Chicago: University of Chicago Press.

CROMDAL, J., 1999, Childhood bilingualism and metalinguistic skills: Analysis and control in young Swedish–English bilinguals. *Applied Psycholinguistics* 20 (1), 1–20.

CRYSTAL, D., 1995, *The Cambridge Encyclopedia of the English Language*. Cambridge: Cambridge University Press.

CRYSTAL, D., 1997, *English as a Global Language*. Cambridge: Cambridge University Press.

CRYSTAL, D., 2000, *Language Death*. Cambridge: Cambridge University Press.

CUMMINS, J., 1975, Cognitive factors associated with intermediate levels of bilingual skills. Unpublished manuscript, Educational Research Centre, St Patrick's College, Dublin.

CUMMINS, J., 1976, The influence of bilingualism on cognitive growth: A synthesis of research findings and explanatory hypotheses. *Working Papers on Bilingualism* 9, 1–43.

CUMMINS, J., 1977, Cognitive factors associated with the attainment of intermediate levels of bilingual skills. *Modern Language Journal* 61, 3–12.

CUMMINS, J., 1978, Metalinguistic development of children in bilingual education programs: Data from Irish and Canadian Ukrainian–English programs. In M. PARADIS (ed.), *Aspects of Bilingualism*. Columbia: Hornbeam Press.

CUMMINS, J., 1979, Cognitive/academic language proficiency, linguistic interdependence, the optimum age question. *Working Papers on Bilingualism*, 19, 121–129.

CUMMINS, J., 1980a, The construct of language proficiency in bilingual education. In J.E. ALATIS (ed.), *Georgetown University Round Table on Languages and Linguistics 1980*. Washington, DC: Georgetown University Press.

CUMMINS, J., 1980b, The entry and exit fallacy in bilingual education. *NABE Journal* 4 (3), 25–59.

CUMMINS, J., 1981a, *Bilingualism and Minority Language Children*. Ontario: Ontario Institute for Studies in Education.

CUMMINS, J., 1981b, The role of primary language development in promoting educational success for language minority students. In CALIFORNIA STATE DEPARTMENT OF EDUCATION (ed.), *Schooling and Language Minority Students. A Theoretical Framework*. Los Angeles: California State Department of Education.

CUMMINS, J., 1983a, *Heritage Language Education: A Literature Review*. Ontario: Ministry of Education.

CUMMINS, J., 1983b, Language proficiency, biliteracy and French immersion. *Canadian Journal of Education* 8 (2), 117–138.

CUMMINS, J., 1984a, *Bilingualism and Special Education: Issues in Assessment and Pedagogy*. Clevedon: Multilingual Matters.

CUMMINS, J., 1984b, Wanted: A theoretical framework for relating language proficiency to academic achievement among bilingual students. In C. RIVERA (ed.), *Language Proficiency and Academic Achievement*. Clevedon: Multilingual Matters.

CUMMINS, J., 1986a, Bilingual education and anti-racist education. *Interracial Books for Children Bulletin* 17 (3&4), 9–12.

CUMMINS, J., 1986b, Empowering minority students: A framework for intervention. *Harvard Educational Review* 56 (1), 18–36.

CUMMINS, J., 1989, Language and literacy acquisition. *Journal of Multilingual and Multicultural Development* 10 (1), 17–31.

CUMMINS, J., 1991a, The politics of paranoia: Reflections on the bilingual education debate. In O. GARCÍA (ed.), *Bilingual Education: Focusschrift in Honor of Joshua A. Fishman (Volume 1)*. Amsterdam/Philadelphia: John Benjamins.

CUMMINS, J., 1991b, The development of bilingual proficiency from home to school: A longitudinal study of Portuguese-speaking children. *Journal of Education* 173 (2), 85–98.

CUMMINS, J., 1992a, Heritage language teaching in Canadian schools. *Journal of Curriculum Studies* 24 (3), 281–286.

CUMMINS, J., 1992b, Bilingual education and English immersion: The Ramirez Report in theoretical perspective. *Bilingual Research Journal* 16 (1&2), 91–104.

CUMMINS, J., 1992c, Empowerment through biliteracy. In J.V. TINAJERO & A.F. ADA (eds), *The Power of Two Languages: Literacy and Biliteracy for Spanish-speaking Students*. New York: McGraw-Hill.

CUMMINS, J., 1993, The research base for heritage language promotion. In M. DANESI, K. McLEOD & S. MORRIS (eds), *Heritage Languages and Education: The Canadian Experience*. Oakville: Mosaic Press.

CUMMINS, J., 1994, Knowledge, power and identity in teaching English as a second language. In F. GENESEE (ed.), *Educating Second Language Children*. Cambridge: Cambridge University Press.

CUMMINS, J., 1996, *Negotiating Identities: Education for Empowerment in a Diverse Society*. Ontario, CA: California Association for Bilingual Education.

CUMMINS, J., 1997, Cultural and linguistic diversity in education: A mainstream issue? *Educational Review* 49 (2), 105–114.

CUMMINS, J., 1999a, Alternative paradigms in bilingual education research: Does theory have a place? *Educational Researcher* 28 (7), 26–32 (plus p. 41).

CUMMINS, J., 1999b, The ethics of Doublethink: Language rights and the bilingual education debate. *TESOL Journal* 8 (3), 13–17.

CUMMINS, J. 2000a, *Language, Power and Pedagogy: Bilingual Children in the Crossfire*. Clevedon: Multilingual Matters.

CUMMINS, J. 2000b, Putting language proficiency in its place: responding to critiques of the conversational/academic language distinction. In J. CENOZ & U. JESSNER (eds), *English in Europe: The Acquisition of a Third Language*. Clevedon: Multilingual Matters.

CUMMINS, J. & CORSON, D. (eds), 1997, *Bilingual Education*. Volume 5 of the *Encyclopedia of Language and Education*. Dordrecht: Kluwer.

CUMMINS, J. & DANESI, M., 1990, *Heritage Languages. The Development and Denial of Canada's*

Linguistic Resources. Toronto: Our Schools/Ourselves Education Foundation and Garamond Press.

CUMMINS, J. & GULUTSAN, M., 1974, Some effects of bilingualism on cognitive functioning. In S. CAREY (ed.), *Bilingualism, Biculturalism and Education*. Edmonton: University of Alberta Press.

CUMMINS, J. & MULCAHY, R., 1978, Orientation to language in Ukrainian–English bilingual children. *Child Development* 49, 1239–1242.

CUMMINS, J. & SAYERS, D., 1996, Multicultural education and technology: Promise and pitfalls. *Multicultural Education* 3 (3), 4–10.

CUMMINS, J. & SWAIN, M., 1986, *Bilingualism in Education*. New York: Longman.

CZIKO, G.A., 1992, The evaluation of bilingual education: From necessity and probability to possibility. *Educational Researcher* 21 (2), 10–15.

DANESI, M., 1991, Revisiting the research findings on heritage language learning: Three interpretive frames. *Canadian Modern Language Review* 47 (4), 650–659.

DANESI, M., McLEOD, K. & MORRIS, S. (eds), 1993 *Heritage Languages and Education: The Canadian Experience*. Oakville: Mosaic Press.

DANOFF, M.N., COLES, G.J., McLAUGHLIN, D.H. & REYNOLDS, D.J., 1977, *Evaluation of the Impact of ESEA Title VII Spanish/English Bilingual Education Programs Volume 1*. Palo Alto, CA: American Institutes for Research.

DANOFF, M.N., COLES, G.J., McLAUGHLIN, D.H. & REYNOLDS, D.J., 1978, *Evaluation of the Impact of ESEA Title VII Spanish/English Bilingual Education Programs Volume 3*. Palo Alto, CA: American Institutes for Research.

DARCY, N.T., 1953, A review of the literature on the effects of bilingualism upon the measurement of intelligence. *Journal of Genetic Psychology* 82, 21–57.

DAVIDMAN, L. & DAVIDMAN, P.T., 1994, *Teaching with a Multicultural Perspective: A Practical Guide*. New York: Longman.

DAVIES, A., 1996, Review Article: Ironising the myth of linguicism. *Journal of Multilingual and Multicultural Development* 17 (6), 485–496.

DAWE, L.C., 1982, The influence of a bilingual child's first language competence on reasoning in mathematics. Unpublished PhD dissertation, University of Cambridge.

DAWE L.C., 1983, Bilingualism and mathematical reasoning in English as a second language. *Educational Studies in Mathematics* 14 (1), 325–353.

DE HOUWER, A., 1990, *The Acquisition of Two Languages from Birth: A Case Study*. New York: Cambridge University Press.

DE HOUWER, A., 1995, Bilingual language acquisition. In P. FLETCHER & B. MACWHINNEY (eds), *The Handbook of Child Language*. Oxford: Blackwell.

DEL VALLE, S., 1998, Bilingual education for Puerto Ricans in New York City. *Harvard Educational Review* 68 (2), 193–217.

DELGADO-GAITAN, C., 1990, *Literacy for Empowerment: The Role of Parents in Children's Education*. New York: Falmer.

DELGADO-GAITAN, C. & TRUEBA, H., 1991, *Crossing Cultural Borders: Education for Immigrant Families in America*. New York: Falmer.

DELPIT, L.D., 1988, The silenced dialogue: Power and pedagogy in educating other people's children. *Harvard Educational Review* 58 (3), 280–298.

DELPIT, L.D., 1995, *Other People's Children: Cultural Conflict in the Classroom*. New York; New York Press.

DEPARTMENT OF EDUCATION and SCIENCE, 1985, *Education for All* (Swann Report). London: HMSO.

DEPARTMENT OF EDUCATION and SCIENCE AND THE WELSH OFFICE, 1990, *Welsh in the National Curriculum (No. 2)*. London: HMSO.

DEUCHAR, M., & QUAY, S., 1999, Language choice in the earliest utterances: A case study with methodological implications. *Journal of Child Language* 26 (2), 461–475.

DEVILLAR, R.A., FALTIS, C.J. & CUMMINS, J.P. (eds), 1994, *Cultural Diversity in Schools: From Rhetoric to Practice*. Albany, NY: State University of New York Press.

DEWAELE, J-M., 2000, Three years old and three first languages. *Bilingual Family Newsletter* 17 (2), 4–5.

DIAZ, R.M., 1985, Bilingual cognitive development: Addressing three gaps in current research. *Child Development* 56, 1376–1388.

DIAZ, R.M. & KLINGER, C., 1991, Towards an explanatory model of the interaction between bilingualism and cognitive development. In E. BIALYSTOK (ed.), *Language Processing in Bilingual Children*. Cambridge: Cambridge University Press.

DICKER, S.J., 1996, *Languages in America: A Pluralist View*. Clevedon: Multilingual Matters.

DICKER, S.J., 1998, Adaptation and assimilation: US business responses to linguistic diversity in the workplace. *Journal of Multilingual and Multicultural Development* 19 (4), 282–302.

DICKER, S.J., 2000, Official English and bilingual education: The controversy over language pluralism in US society. In J.K. HALL & W.G. EGGINGTON (eds), *The Sociopolitics of English Language Teaching*. Clevedon: Multilingual Matters.

DICKS, J.E., 1992, Analytic and experiential features of three French immersion programs: Early, middle and late. *Canadian Modern Language Review* 49 (1), 37–60.

DIEBOLD, A.R., 1964, Incipient bilingualism. In D. HYMES *et al.* (eds), *Language in Culture and Society*. New York: Harper and Row.

DI PIETRO, R., 1977, Code-switching as a verbal strategy among bilinguals. In F. ECKMAN (ed.), *Current Themes in Linguistics*. Washington, DC: Hemisphere Publishing.

DIXON, R.M., 1997, *The Rise and Fall of Languages*. Cambridge: Cambridge University Press.

DOGANCAY-AKTUNA, S., 1997, Language planning. In N. HORNBERGER & D. CORSON (eds), 1997, *Research Methods in Language and Education*. Volume 8 of the *Encyclopedia of Language and Education*. Dordrecht: Kluwer.

DOLSON, D.P. & MEYER, J., 1992, Longitudinal study of three program models for language-minority students: A critical examination of reported findings. *Bilingual Research Journal* 16 (1&2), 105–157.

DONALDSON, M., 1978, *Children's Minds*. Glasgow: Fontana/Collins.

DONMALL, B.G., 1985, *Language Awareness. Report to the National Congress on Languages in Education*. London: CILT.

DÖPKE, S., 1992, *One Parent–One Language: An Interactional Approach*. Amsterdam: John Benjamins.

DORIAN, N.C., 1981, *Language Death: The Life Cycle of a Scottish Gaelic Dialect*. Philadelphia: University of Pennsylvania Press.

DORIAN, N.C., 1998, Western language ideologies and small-language prospects. In L.A. GRENOBLE & L.J. WHALEY, *Endangered Languages: Current Issues and Future Prospects*. Cambridge: Cambridge University Press.

DORIAN, N.C., 1989 (ed.), *Investigating Obsolescence: Studies in Language Contraction and Death*. Cambridge: Cambridge University Press.

DÖRNYEI, Z., 1994, Motivation and motivating in the second language classroom. *The Modern Language Journal* 78 (3), 273–284.

DÖRNYEI, Z., 1998, Motivation in second and foreign language teaching. *Language Teaching* 31, 3, 117–135.

DÖRNYEI, Z. & CSIZER, K., 1998, Ten Commandments for motivating language learners: Results of an empirical study. *Language Teaching Research* 2 (3), 203–229.

DÖRNYEI, Z. & SCOTT, M.L., 1997, Communication strategies in a second language: Definitions and taxonomies (Review Article). *Language Learning* 47 (1), 173–210.

DOSANJH, J.S. & GHUMAN, P.A., 1996, *Child-Rearing in Ethnic Minorities*. Clevedon: Multilingual Matters.

DOYLE, A., CHAMPAGNE, M. & SEGALOWITZ, N., 1978, Some issues on the assessment of linguistic consequences of early bilingualism. In M. PARADIS (ed.), *Aspects of Bilingualism*. Columbia: Hornbeam Press.

DUFF, P.A., 1991, Innovation in foreign language education: An evaluation of three Hungarian–English dual-language schools. *Journal of Multilingual and Multicultural Development* 12 (6), 459–476.

DULAY, H.C. & BURT, M.K., 1973, Should we teach children syntax? *Language Learning* 23, 245–258.

DULAY, H.C. & BURT, M.K., 1974, Errors and strategies in child second language acquisition. *TESOL Quarterly* 8, 129–136.

DULAY, H.C. & BURT, M.K., 1977, Remarks on creativity in language acquisition. In M. BURT, H. DULAY & M. FINOCCHIARO (eds), *Viewpoints on English as a Second Language*. New York: Regents.

DULAY, H.C. & BURT, M.K., 1978, *Why Bilingual Education? A Summary of Research Findings* (2nd edn). San Francisco, CA: Bloomsbury West.

DULAY, H.C. & BURT, M.K., 1979, Bilingual education: A close look at its effects. *Focus*, No. 1.

DUNCAN, S.E. & DE AVILA, E.A., 1979, Bilingualism and cognition: Some recent findings. *NABE Journal* 4 (1), 15–50.

DUQUETTE, G., 1999, *Vivre et enseigner en milieu minoritaire*. Sudbury, Ontario: Presses de l'Université Laurentienne.

DUTCHER, N., 1995, *The Use of First and Second Languages in Education: A Review of International Experience*. Washington, DC: World Bank.

DUTCHER, N., 1996, *Overview of Foreign Language Education in the United States*. NCBE Resources Collection Series, No.6 Spring 1996. Washington, DC: National Clearinghouse for Bilingual Education.

DYSON, A., 1989, *The Multiple Worlds of Child Writers: A Study of Friends Learning to Write*. New York: Teachers College Press.

EASTMAN, C.M., 1983, *Language Planning: An Introduction*. San Francisco: Chandler and Sharp.

EASTMAN, C.M., 1992, Codeswitching as an urban language, contact phenomenon. *Journal of Multilingual and Multicultural Development* 13 (1&2), 1–17.

ECHEVARRIA, J. & GRAVES, A., 1998, *Sheltered Content Instruction*. Boston: Allyn & Bacon.

ECHEVARRIA, J., VOGT, M, & SHORT, D., 2000, *Making Content Comprehensible for English Language Learners: The SIOP Model*. Boston, MA: Allyn and Bacon.

ECIS (See European Council of International Schools).

EDELSKY, C., 1991, *With Literacy and Justice for All: Rethinking the Social in Language and Education*. London: Falmer.

EDELSKY, C. *et al.*, 1983, Semilingualism and language deficit. *Applied Linguistics* 4 (1), 1–22.

EDWARDS, J., 1981, The context of bilingual education. *Journal of Multilingual and Multicultural Development* 2 (1), 25–44.

EDWARDS, J., 1985, *Language, Society and Identity*. Oxford: Blackwell.

EDWARDS, J., 1994a, *Multilingualism*. London: Routledge.

EDWARDS, J., 1994b, Parochialism and intercourse: Metaphors for mobility. *Journal of Multilingual and Multicultural Development* 15 (2&3), 171–178.

EDWARDS, J., 1994c, Ethnolinguistic pluralism and its discontents. *International Journal of the Sociology of Language* 110, 5–85.

EDWARDS, V., 1995a, Community language teaching in the UK: Ten years on. *Child Language Teaching and Therapy* 11 (1), 50–60.

EDWARDS, V., 1995b, *Reading in Multilingual Classrooms*. Reading: University of Reading.

EDWARDS, V., 1995c, *Speaking and Listening in Multilingual Classrooms*. Reading: University of Reading.

EDWARDS, V., 1995d, *Writing in Multilingual Classrooms*. Reading: University of Reading.

EDWARDS, V., 1996, *The Other Languages: A Guide to Multilingual Classrooms*. Reading: Reading and Language Information Centre.

EDWARDS, V., 1998, *The Power of Babel: Teaching and Learning in Multilingual Classrooms*. Stoke-on-Trent: Trentham.

EDWARDS, V. (ed.), 1995, *Building Bridges: Multilingual Resources for Children*. Clevedon: Multilingual Matters.

EDWARDS, V. & REDFERN, A., 1992, *The World in a Classroom: Language in Education in Britain and Canada*. Clevedon: Multilingual Matters.

EDWARDS, V. & REHORICK, S., 1990, Learning environments in immersion and non-immersion classrooms: Are they different? *The Canadian Modern Language Review* 46 (3), 469–493.

EDWARDS, V. & WALKER, S., 1996, Some status issues in the translation of children's books. *Journal of Multilingual and Multicultural Development* 17 (5), 339–348.

ELLIS, N., 1992, Linguistic relativity revisited: The bilingual word-length effect in working memory during counting, remembering numbers and mental calculation. In R.J. HARRIS (ed.), *Cognitive Processing in Bilinguals*. Amsterdam: North-Holland.

ELLIS, N. & SCHMIDT, R., 1997, Morphology and longer distance dependencies. *Studies in Second Language Acquisition* 19, 145–171.

ELLIS, R., 1985, *Understanding Second Language Acquisition*. Oxford: Oxford University Press.

ELLIS, R., 1997, *SLA Research and Language Teaching*. Oxford: Oxford University Press.

EPSTEIN, J., 1992, *School and Family Partnerships*. Baltimore: Center on Families, Communities, Schools and Children's Learning (John Hopkins University).

ERICKSON, F., 1987, Transformation and school success: The politics and culture of educational achievement. *Anthropology and Education Quarterly* 18 (4), 335–356.

EUROPEAN COMMISSION, 1996, *Euromosaic: The Production and Reproduction of the Minority*

Language Groups in the European Union. Luxembourg: Office for Official Publications of the European Communities.

EUROPEAN COUNCIL OF INTERNATIONAL SCHOOLS, 1998, *The ECIS International Schools Directory*. Saxmundham, Suffolk: John Catt Educational Ltd.

EVANS, G.L., 2000, Dwy iaith o'r diwrnod cyntaf: Bilingual from the beginning. *Bilingual Family Newsletter* 17 (2), 1–2.

FABBRO, F., 1999, *The Neurolinguistics of Bilingualism: An Introduction*. Hove: Psychology Press.

FALTIS, C.J., 1993a, *Joinfostering: Adapting Teaching Strategies for the Multilingual Classroom*. New York: Macmillan.

FALTIS, C.J., 1993b, Critical issues in the use of sheltered content teaching in high school bilingual programs. *Peabody Journal of Education* 69 (1), 136–151.

FALTIS, C.J., 1997, *Joinfostering: Adapting Teaching for the Multilingual Classroom* (2nd edn). Upper Saddle River, NJ: Prentice Hall.

FALTIS, C.J. & HUDELSON, S.J., 1998, *Bilingual Education in Elementary and Secondary School Communities*. Boston: Allyn & Bacon.

FANTINI, A., 1985, *Language Acquisition of a Bilingual Child: A Sociolinguistic Perspective*. San Diego: College Hill Press.

FERGUSON, C., 1959, Diglossia. *Word* 15, 325–340.

FERGUSON, C.A., HOUGHTON, C. & WELLS, M.H., 1977, Bilingual education: An international perspective. In B. SPOLSKY & R. COOPER (eds), *Frontiers of Bilingual Education*. Rowley, MA: Newbury House.

FEUERVERGER, G., 1994, A multilingual literacy intervention for minority language students. *Language and Education* 8 (3), 123–146.

FEUERVERGER, G., 1997, 'On the edges of the map': A study of heritage language teachers in Toronto. *Teacher and Teacher Education* 13 (1), 39–53.

FIGUROA, P., 1984, Minority pupil progress. In M. CRAFT (ed.), *Education and Cultural Pluralism*. London: Falmer Press.

FISHMAN, J.A., 1965, Who speaks what language to whom and when? *La Linguistique* 67–68.

FISHMAN, J.A., 1971, The sociology of language. In J. FISHMAN (ed.), *Advances in the Sociology of Language, Volume 1*. The Hague: Mouton.

FISHMAN, J.A., 1972, *The Sociology of Language*. Rowley, MA: Newbury House.

FISHMAN, J.A., 1976, *Bilingual Education. An International Sociological Perspective*. Rowley, MA: Newbury House.

FISHMAN, J.A., 1977, The social science perspective. In CENTER FOR APPLIED LINGUISTICS (ed.), *Bilingual Education: Current Perspectives*. Arlington, VA: CAL.

FISHMAN, J.A., 1980, Bilingualism and biculturalism as individual and as societal phenomena. *Journal of Multilingual and Multicultural Development* 1, 3–15.

FISHMAN, J.A., 1989, *Language and Ethnicity in Minority Sociolinguistic Perspective*. Clevedon: Multilingual Matters.

FISHMAN, J.A., 1990, What is reversing language shift (RLS) and how can it succeed? *Journal of Multilingual and Multicultural Development* 11 (1&2), 5–36.

FISHMAN, J.A., 1991, *Reversing Language Shift*. Clevedon: Multilingual Matters.

FISHMAN, J.A., 1993, Reversing language shift: Successes, failures, doubts and dilemmas. In E.H. JAHR (ed.), *Language Conflict and Language Planning*. New York: Mouton de Gruyter.

FISHMAN, J.A., 2000a, Conclusions: From theory to practice (and vice versa). In J.A. FISHMAN (ed.), *Can Threatened Languages be Saved?* Clevedon: Multilingual Matters.

FISHMAN, J.A., 2000b, Why is it so hard to save a threatened language? In J.A. FISHMAN (ed.), *Can Threatened Languages be Saved?* Clevedon: Multilingual Matters.

FISHMAN, J.A. (ed.), 1999, *Handbook of Language and Ethnic Identity*. New York: Oxford University Press.

FISHMAN, J.A. (ed.), 2000c, *Can Threatened Languages be Saved?* Clevedon: Multilingual Matters.

FITZGERALD, J., 1993, Views on bilingualism in the United States: A selective historical review. *Bilingual Research Journal* 17 (1&2), 35–56.

FITZPATRICK, F., 1987, *The Open Door: The Bradford Bilingual Project*. Clevedon: Multilingual Matters.

FORHAN, L.E. & SCHERAGA, M., 2000, Becoming sociopolitically active. In J.K. HALL & W.G. EGGINGTON (eds), *The Sociopolitics of English Language Teaching*. Clevedon: Multilingual Matters.

FRADD, S.H. & BOSWELL, T.D., 1996, Spanish as an economic resource in metropolitan Miami. *Bilingual Research Journal* 20 (2), 283–337.

FREDERICKSON, N. & CLINE, T., 1990, *Curriculum Related Assessment with Bilingual Children*. London: University College London.

FREDERICKSON, N. & CLINE, T., 1996, The development of a model of curriculum related assessment. In CLINE, T. & FREDERICKSON, N. (eds), 1996, *Curriculum Related Assessment. Cummins and Bilingual Children*. Clevedon: Multilingual Matters.

FREEMAN, R., 1995, Equal educational opportunity for language minority students: From policy to practice at Oyster Bilingual School. *Issues in Applied Linguistics* 6 (1), 39–63.

FREEMAN, R., 1998, *Bilingual Education and Social Change*. Clevedon: Multilingual Matters.

FRIERE, P., 1970, *Pedagogy of the Oppressed*. New York: Seabury Press/Continuum.

FRIERE, P., 1973, *Education for Critical Consciousness*. New York: Continuum.

FRIERE, P., 1985, *The Politics of Education*. South Hadley, MA: Bergin and Garvey.

FRIERE, P. & MACEDO, D., 1987, *Literacy: Reading the Word and the World*. South Hadley, MA: Bergin and Garvey.

FROMM, E., 1970, Age regression with unexpected reappearance of a repressed childhood language. *International Journal of Clinical and Experimental Hypnosis* 18, 79–88.

FULIGNI, A.J., 1997, The academic achievement of adolescents from immigrant families: The roles of family background, attitudes, and behavior. *Child Development* 68 (2), 351.

GAARDER, A.B., 1977, *Bilingual Schooling and the Survival of Spanish in the United States*. Rowley, MA: Newbury House.

GAL, S., 1979, *Language Shift: Social Determinants of Linguistic Change in Bilingual Austria*. New York: Academic Press.

GALAMBOS, S.J. & HAKUTA, K., 1988, Subject-specific and task-specific characteristics of metalinguistic awareness in bilingual children. *Applied Psycholinguistics* 9, 141–162.

GÁNDARA, P. *et al.*, 2000, *The Initial Impact of Proposition 227 on the Instruction of English Learners*. University of California, Davis: UC Linguistic Minority Research Institute.

GANDHI, M., 1927 (English edition, 1949), *The Story of My Experiments with Truth*. London: Cape.

GARCÍA, E., 1983, *Early Childhood Bilingualism*. Albuquerque: University of New Mexico Press.

GARCÍA, E.E., 1988, Effective schooling for Hispanics. *Urban Education Review* 67 (2), 462–473.

GARCÍA, E.E., 1991, Effective instruction for language minority students: The teacher. *Journal of Education* 173 (2), 130–141.

GARCÍA, O., 1983, Sociolinguistics and language planning in bilingual education for Hispanics in the United States. *International Journal of the Sociology of Language* 44, 43–54.

GARCÍA, O., 1988, *The Education of Biliterate and Bicultural Children in Ethnic Schools in the United States*. Essays by Spencer Fellows of the National Academy of Education, Vol. 4, pp. 19–78.

GARCÍA, O., 1991a, Latinos and bilingual education in the United States: Their role as objects and subjects. *New Language Planning Newsletter* 6 (2), 3–5.

GARCÍA, O. (ed.), 1991b, *Bilingual Education: Focusschrift in Honor of Joshua A. Fishman*. Amsterdam/Philadelphia: John Benjamins.

GARCÍA, O., 1992a, Societal multilingualism in a multicultural world in transition. In H. BYRNE (ed.), *Languages for a Multicultural World in Transition*. Illinois: National Textbook Company.

GARCÍA, O., 1992b, Societal bilingualism and multilingualism (mimeo). New York: City University of New York.

GARCÍA, O., 1992c, For it is in giving that we receive: A history of language policy in the United States. Paper presented to a conference 'American Pluralism: Toward a History of the Discussion', State University of New York at Stonybrook, June 7th 1992.

GARCÍA, O., 1993, Understanding the societal role of the teacher in transitional bilingual classrooms: Lessons from sociology of language. In K. ZONDAG (ed.), *Bilingual Education in Friesland: Facts and Prospects*. Leewarden: Gemeens Chappelijk Centrum voor Onderwijsbegeleiding in Friesland.

GARCÍA, O., 1995, Spanish language loss as a determinant of income among Latinos in the United States: Implications for language policy in schools. In J.W. TOLLEFSON (ed.), *Power and Inequality in Language Education*. Cambridge: Cambridge University Press.

GARCÍA, O., 1997, Bilingual education. In F. COULMAS (ed.), *The Handbook of Sociolinguistics*. Oxford: Blackwell.

GARCÍA, O. & BAKER, C. (eds), 1995, *Policy and Practice in Bilingual Education: A Reader Extending the Foundations*. Clevedon: Multilingual Matters.

GARCÍA, O. & FISHMAN, J.A. (eds), 1997, *The Multilingual Apple: Languages in the United States*. New York: Mouton de Gruyter.

GARCÍA, O. & OTHEGUY, R., 1985, The masters of survival send their children to school: Bilingual education in the ethnic schools of Miami. *Bilingual Review* 12 (1&2), 3–19.

GARCÍA, O. & OTHEGUY, R., 1988, The language situation of Cuban Americans. In S.L. McKAY & S.C. WONG (eds), *Language Diversity: Problem or Resource?* New York: Newbury House.

GARCÍA, O. & OTHEGUY, R., 1994, The value of speaking a LOTE in US business. *Annals of the American Academy of Political and Social Science* 532, 99–122.

GARCÍA, R. & DIAZ, C.F., 1992, The status and use of Spanish and English among Hispanic youth in Dade County (Miami) Florida: A sociolinguistic study. *Language and Education* 6 (1), 13–32.

GARDNER, H., 1984, *Frames of Mind: The Theory of Multiple Intelligences*. London: Heinemann.

GARDNER, N., 2000, *Basque in Education in the Basque Autonomous Community*. Vitoria-Gasteiz: Euskal Autonomi Erkidegoko Administrazioa.

GARDNER, R.C., 1985, *Social Psychology and Second Language Learning*. London: Edward Arnold.

GARDNER, R.C., LALONDE, R.N. & MACPHERSON, J., 1986, Social factors in second language attrition. *Language Learning* 35 (4), 519–540.

GARDNER, R.C., LALONDE, R.N. & PIERSON, R., 1983, The socio-educational model of second language acquisition: An investigation using LISREL causal modeling. *Journal of Language and Social Psychology* 2, 51–65.

GARDNER, R.C. & LAMBERT, W.E., 1972, *Attitudes and Motivation in Second Language Learning*. Rowley, MA: Newbury House.

GEARY, D., CORMIER, P., GOGGIN, J., ESTRADA, P. & LUNN, M., 1993, Mental arithmetic: A componential analysis of speed-of-processing across monolingual, weak bilingual and strong bilingual adults. *International Journal of Psychology* 28 (2), 185–201.

GENERAL ACCOUNTING OFFICE, 1987, *Bilingual Education. A New Look at the Research Evidence*. Washington, DC: General Accounting Office.

GENESEE, F., 1976, The role of intelligence in second language learning. *Language Learning* 26, 267–280.

GENESEE, F., 1978, Second language learning and language attitudes. *Working Papers on Bilingualism* 16, 19–42.

GENESEE, F., 1983, Bilingual education of majority-language children: The immersion experiments in review. *Applied Psycholinguistics* 4, 1–46.

GENESEE, F., 1984, Historical and theoretical foundations of immersion education. In CALIFORNIA STATE DEPARTMENT OF EDUCATION (eds), *Studies on Immersion Education: A Collection for United States Educators*. California: California State Department of Education.

GENESEE, F., 1987, *Learning Through Two Languages*. Cambridge, MA: Newbury House.

GENESEE, F., 1998, A case study of multilingual education in Canada. In J. CENOZ & F. GENESEE (eds), *Beyond Bilingualism: Multilingualism and Multilingual Education*. Clevedon: Multilingual Matters.

GENESEE, F. (ed.), 1994, *Educating Second Language Children*. Cambridge: Cambridge University Press.

GENESEE, F. (ed.), 1999, *Program Alternatives for Linguistically Diverse Students*. Santa Cruz: Center for Research on Education, Diversity & Excellence, University of California.

GENESEE, F., BOIVIN, I. & NICOLADIS, E., 1996, Talking with strangers: A study of bilingual children's communicative competence. *Applied Psycholinguistics* 17 (4), 427–442.

GENESEE, F. & GÁNDARA, P., 1999, Bilingual education programs: A cross national perspective. *Journal of Social Issues* 55 (4), 665–685.

GENESEE, F. & HAMAYAN, E., 1980, Individual differences in young second language learners. *Applied Psycholinguistics* 1, 95–110.

GENESEE, F. & HAMAYAN, E., 1994, Classroom-based assessment. In F. GENESEE (ed.), *Educating Second Language Children*. Cambridge: Cambridge University Press.

GENESEE, F. & LAMBERT, W.E., 1983, Trilingual education for majority language children. *Child Development* 54, 105–114.

GENESEE, F., TUCKER, G.R. & LAMBERT, W.E., 1975, Communication skills in bilingual children. *Child Development* 46, 1010–1014.

GERSTEN, R. & WOODWARD, J., 1994, The language minority student and special education: Issues, trends and paradoxes. *Exceptional Children* 60 (4), 310–322.

GHUMAN, P.S., 1993, *Coping with Two Cultures*. Clevedon: Multilingual Matters.

GHUMAN, P.S., 1994, *Asian Teachers in British Schools*. Clevedon: Multilingual Matters.

GHUMAN, P.S., 1999, *Asian Adolescents in the West*. Leicester: British Psychological Society.

GILES, H., BOURHIS, R. & TAYLOR, D., 1977, Towards a theory of language in ethnic group relations. In H. GILES (ed.), *Language, Ethnicity and Intergroup Relations*. London: Academic Press.

GILES, H. & BYRNE, J.L., 1982, An intergroup approach to second language acquisition. *Journal of Multilingual and Multicultural Development* 3 (1), 17–40.

GILES, H. & COUPLAND, N., 1991, *Language: Contexts and Consequences*. Milton Keynes: Open University Press.

GLASS, G.V., McGAW, B. & SMITH, M.L., 1981, *Meta-analysis in Social Research*. Beverly Hills: Sage.

GLIKSMAN, L., 1976, Second language acquisition: The effects of student attitudes on classroom behavior. Unpublished MA thesis, University of Western Ontario.

GLIKSMAN, L., 1981, Improving the prediction of behaviours associated with second language acquisition. Unpublished PhD thesis, University of Western Ontario.

GOMEZTORTOSA, E., MARTIN, E.M., GAVIRIA, M., CHARBEL, F. & AUSMAN, J., 1995, Selective deficit of one language in a bilingual patient following surgery in the left perisylvian area. *Brain and Language* 48 (3), 320–325.

GONZALEZ, J.M., 1979, Coming of age in bilingual/bicultural education: A historical perspective. In H.T. TRUEBA & C. BARNETT-MIZRAHI (eds), *Bilingual Multicultural Education and the Professional: From Theory to Practice*. Rowley, MA: Newbury House.

GOPINATHAN, S. *et al.*, 1998, *Language, Society and Education in Singapore: Issues and Trends* (2nd edn). Singapore: Times Academic Press.

GORDON, M.M., 1964, *Assimilation in American Life: The Role of Race, Religion and National Origins*. New York: Oxford University Press.

GRADDOL, D., 1997, *The Future of English?* London: British Council.

GRADDOL, D. & MEINHOF, U.H. (eds), 1999, *English in a Changing World*. AILA Review 13. Oxford: Catchline (The English Trading Company).

GRAFF, H.J., 1979, *The Literacy Myth: Literacy and Social Structure in the 19th Century City*. New York: Academic Press.

GRAVELLE, M., 1996, *Supporting Bilingual Learners in Schools*. Stoke-on-Trent: Trentham.

GRAVES, D.H., 1983, *Writing: Teachers and Children at Work*. London: Heinemann.

GREEN, D.W., 1998, Bilingualism and Thought. *Psychologica Belgica* 38 (3/4), 251–276.

GREENE, J., 1998, *A Meta-Analysis of the Effectiveness of Bilingual Education*. Claremont, CA: Tomas Rivera Policy Institute.

GREGORY, E., 1993, Sweet and sour: Learning to read in a British and Chinese school. *English in Education* 27 (3), 53–59.

GREGORY, E., 1994, Cultural assumptions and early years' pedagogy: The effect of the home culture on minority children's interpretation of reading in school. *Language, Culture and Curriculum* 7 (2), 111–124.

GREGORY, E., 1996, *Making Sense of a New World: Learning to Read in a Second Language*. Paul Chapman, London.

GRENOBLE, L.A. & WHALEY, L.J., 1998, Toward a typology of language endangerment. In L.A. GRENOBLE & L.J. WHALEY, *Endangered Languages: Current Issues and Future Prospects*. Cambridge: Cambridge University Press.

GRIFFITHS, M., 1986, Introduction. In M. GRIFFITHS (ed.), *The Welsh Language in Education*. Cardiff: Welsh Joint Education Council.

GRIMES, B.F., 1996, *Ethnologue – Languages of the World* (13th edn). Texas: The Summer Institute of Linguistics. (http://www.sil.org/ethnologue/ethnologue.html).

GROSJEAN, F., 1982, *Life with Two Languages*. Cambridge, MA: Harvard University Press.

GROSJEAN, F., 1985, The bilingual as a competent but specific speaker-hearer. *Journal of Multilingual and Multicultural Development* 6 (6), 467–477.

GROSJEAN, F., 1992, Another view of bilingualism. *Cognitive Processing in Bilinguals* 83, 51–62.

GROSJEAN, F., 1994, Individual bilingualism. In R.E. ASHER & J.M. SIMPSON (eds), *The Encyclopedia of Language and Linguistics* (Volume 3). Oxford: Pergamon.

GUILFORD, J.P., 1982, Cognitive psychology's ambiguities: Some suggested remedies. *Psychological Review* 89, 48–59.

GUPTA, A.F., 1997, When mother-tongue education is not preferred. *Journal of Multilingual and Multicultural Development* 18 (6), 496–506.

HABERLAND, H., 1991, Reflections about minority languages in the European Community. In F. COULMAS (ed.), *A Language Policy for the European Community*. New York: Mouton de Gruyter.

HAGEMEYER, A., 1992, *The Red Notebook*. Silver Spring, MD: National Association of the Deaf.

HAKUTA, K., 1986, *Mirror of Language. The Debate on Bilingualism*. New York: Basic Books.

HAKUTA, K., 1999, *A Critical Period for Second Language Acquisition? A Status Review*. National Center for Early Development and Learning. Chapel Hill: University of North Carolina. (See also http://www.stanford.edu/~hakuta/).

HAKUTA, K., BUTLER, Y.G. & WITT, D., 2000, *How Long does it take English Learners to Attain Proficiency?* University of California Linguistic Minority Research Institute Policy Report 2000–1 (See also http://lmrinet.ucsb.edu/resdissem.html).

HAKUTA, K. & D'ANDREA, D., 1992, Some properties of bilingual maintenance and loss in Mexican background high-school students. *Applied Linguistics* 13 (1), 72–99.

HALL, J.K. & EGGINGTON, W.G. (eds), 2000, *The Sociopolitics of English Language Teaching*. Clevedon: Multilingual Matters.

HALL, K., 1993, Process writing in French immersion. *Canadian Modern Language Review* 49 (2), 255–274.

HALLIDAY, M.A.K., 1973, *Explorations in the Functions of Language*. London: Edward Arnold.

HALLINGER, P. & MURPHY, J.F., 1986, The social context of effective schools. *American Journal of Education*, May, 328–355.

HAMAYAN E.V. & DAMICO, J.S. (eds), 1991, *Limiting Bias in the Assessment of Bilingual Students*. Austin, TX: Pro-Ed.

HAMERS, J.F. & BLANC, M.H.A., 1982, Towards a social-psychological model of bilingual development. *Journal of Language and Social Psychology* 1 (1), 29–49.

HAMERS, J.F. & BLANC, M., 1983, Bilinguality in the young child: A social psychological model. In P.H. NELDE (ed.), *Theory, Methods and Models of Contact Linguistics*. Bonn: Dümmler.

HAMERS J.F. & BLANC, M.H.A., 2000, *Bilinguality and Bilingualism* (2nd edn). Cambridge: Cambridge University Press

HAMMERLY, H., 1988, French immersion (does it work?) and the development of the bilingual proficiency report. *Canadian Modern Language Review* 45 (3), 567–578.

HANSEGÅRD, N.E., 1975, Tvåspråkighet eller halvspråkighet? Aldus, Series 253, Stockholm, 3rd edn.

HARDING, E. & RILEY, P., 1987, *The Bilingual Family: A Handbook for Parents*. New York: Cambridge University Press.

HARLEY, B., 1986, *Age in Second Language Acquisition*. Clevedon: Multilingual Matters.

HARLEY, B., 1991, Directions in immersion research. *Journal of Multilingual and Multicultural Development* 12 (1&2), 9–19.

HARLEY, B., 1994, After immersion: Maintaining the momentum. *Journal of Multilingual and Multicultural Development* 15 (2&3), 229–244.

HARLEY, B. *et al.*, 1987, *The Development of Bilingual Proficiency. Final Report* (3 volumes). Toronto: Ontario Institute for Studies in Education.

HARLEY, B. *et al.*, 1990, *The Development of Second Language Proficiency*. Cambridge: Cambridge University Press.

HARRIS, J., 1984, *Spoken Irish in Primary Schools. An Analysis of Achievement*. Dublin: Instituid Teangeolaiochta Eireann.

HARRIS, J. & MURTAGH, L., 1999, *Teaching and Learning Irish in Primary School: A Review of Research and Development*. Dublin: Instituid Teangeolaiochta Eireann.

HARRIS, R.J. (ed.), 1992, *Cognitive Processing in Bilinguals*. Amsterdam: North-Holland.

HARRISON, D. & MARMEN, L., 1994, *Languages in Canada*. Ottawa: Statistics Canada.

HARRY, B., 1992, *Cultural Diversity, Families and the Special Education System: Communication and Empowerment*. New York: Teachers College Press.

HART, D., LAPKIN, S. & SWAIN, M., 1987, Communicative language tests: Perks and perils. *Evaluation and Research in Education* 1 (2), 83–94.

HARTMAN, D. & HENDERSON, J. (eds), 1994, *Aboriginal Languages in Education*. Alice Springs, Australia: IAD Press.

HAWKINS, E., 1987, *Awareness of Language: An Introduction*. New York: Cambridge University Press.

HEATH, S.B., 1980, The functions and uses of literacy. *Journal of Communication* 30 (1), 123–133.

HEATH, S.B., 1982, What no bedtime story means: Narrative skills at home and school. *Language in Society* 11, 49–78.

HEATH, S.B., 1983, *Ways with Words: Language, Life and Work in Communities and Classrooms*. Cambridge: Cambridge University Press.

HEATH, S.B., 1986, Sociocultural contexts of language development. OFFICE OF BILINGUAL AND BICULTURAL EDUCATION (eds), *Beyond Language: Social and Cultural Factors in Schooling Language Minority Students*. Los Angeles: California State University, Evaluation, Dissemination and Assessment Center.

HELLER, M., 1992, The politics of codeswitching and language choice. *Journal of Multilingual and Multicultural Development* 13, 123–142.

HELLER, M., 1994, *Crosswords: Language Education and Ethnicity in French Ontario*. Berlin and New York: Mouton de Gruyter.

HELLER, M., 1999, *Linguistic Minorities and Modernity: A Sociolinguistic Ethnography*. New York: Longman.

HELOT, C., 1988, Bringing up children in English, French and Irish: Two case studies. *Language, Culture and Curriculum* 1 (3), 281–287.

HEREDIA, R. & McLAUGHLIN, B., 1992, Bilingual memory revisited. In R.J. HARRIS (ed.), *Cognitive Processing in Bilinguals*. Amsterdam: North-Holland.

HERNANDEZ, R.D., 1994, Reducing bias in the assessment of culturally and linguistically diverse populations. *Journal of Educational Issues of Language Minority Students* 14, 269–300.

HERNÁNDEZ-CHÁVEZ, E., BURT, M. & DULAY, H., 1978, Language dominance and proficiency testing: Some general considerations. *NABE Journal* 3 (1), 41–54.

HICKEY, T., 1997, *Early Immersion Education in Ireland: Na Naíonraí*. Dublin: Institiuid Teangeolaiochta Eireann.

HICKEY, T., 1999, Parents and early immersion: Reciprocity between home and immersion pre-school. *International Journal of Bilingual Education and Bilingualism* 2 (2), 94–113.

HIRSCH, E.D., 1988, *Cultural Literacy: What Every American Needs to Know*. New York: Vintage Books.

HODSON, D., 1999, Critical multiculturalism in science and technology education. In S. MAY (ed.), *Critical Multiculturalism: Rethinking Multicultural and Antiracist Education*. London & Philadelphia: Falmer Press.

HOFFMANN, C., 1985, Language acquisition in two trilingual children. *Journal of Multilingual and Multicultural Development* 6 (6), 479–495.

HOFFMANN, C., 1991, *An Introduction to Bilingualism*. London: Longman.

HOFFMANN, C., 1998, Luxembourg and the European Schools. In J. CENOZ & F. GENESEE (eds), *Beyond Bilingualism: Multilingualism and Multilingual Education*. Clevedon: Multilingual Matters.

HOLM, A. & HOLM, W., 1990, Rock Point, A Navajo way to go to school. In C.B. CAZDEN & C.E. SNOW (eds), *The Annals of the American Academy of Political and Social Science*, Vol. 508, 170–184.

HOLM, A. & HOLM, W., 1995, Navajo language education: Retrospect and prospects. *Bilingual Research Journal* 19 (1), 141–167.

HOLOBOW, N.E., GENESEE, F. & LAMBERT, W.E., 1991, The effectiveness of a foreign language immersion program for children from different ethnic and social class backgrounds. *Applied Psycholinguistics* 12 (2), 179–198.

HOLT, D.D., 1993, *Cooperative Learning: A Response to Linguistic and Cultural Diversity*. McHenry, IL: Center for Applied Linguistics and Delta Systems.

HORNBERGER, N.H., 1988, *Bilingual Education and Language Maintenance: A Southern Peruvian Quechua Case*. Dordrecht, Holland: Foris.

HORNBERGER, N.H., 1989, Continua of biliteracy. *Review of Educational Research* 59 (3), 271–296.

HORNBERGER, N.H., 1990a, Teacher Quechua use in bilingual and non-bilingual classrooms of Puno, Peru. In R. JACOBSON & C. FALTIS (eds), *Language Distribution Issues in Bilingual Schooling*. Clevedon: Multilingual Matters.

HORNBERGER, N.H., 1990b, Creating successful learning contexts for bilingual literacy. *Teachers College Record* 92 (2), 212–229.

HORNBERGER, N.H., 1991, Extending enrichment bilingual education: Revisiting typologies and redirecting policy. In O. GARCÍA (ed.), *Bilingual Education: Focusschrift in Honor of Joshua A. Fishman (Vol. 1)*. Amsterdam/Philadelphia: John Benjamins.

HORNBERGER, N.H., 1994, Literacy and language planning. *Language and Education* 8 (1&2), 75–86.

HORNBERGER, N.H. & CORSON, D. (eds), 1997, *Research Methods in Language and Education*. Volume 8 of the *Encyclopedia of Language and Education*. Dordrecht: Kluwer.

HORNBERGER, N.H., HARSCH, L. & EVANS, B., 1999, Language education of language minority students in the United States (The Six Nations Education Research Project: The United States). *Working Papers in Educational Linguistics* 15 (1), 1–92.

HOUSEN, A. & BAETENS BEARDSMORE, H., 1987, Curricular & extra-curricular factors in multilingual education. *SSLA* 9, 83–102.

HOWE, M.A.J., 1997, *IQ in Question: The Truth about Intelligence*. London: Sage.

HUANG, G.G., 1995, Self-reported biliteracy and self-esteem: A study of Mexican American 8th graders. *Applied Psycholinguistics* 16, 271–291.

HUDDY, L. & SEARS, D.O., 1990, Qualified public support for bilingual education: Some policy implications. In C.B. CAZDEN & C.E. SNOW (eds), *The Annals of the American Academy of Political and Social Science, Volume 508*, 119–134.

HUDDY, L. & SEARS, D.O., 1995, Opposition to bilingual education: Prejudice or the defense of realistic interests? *Social Psychology Quarterly* 58 (2), 133–143.

HUDELSON, S., 1994, Literacy development of second language children. In F. GENESEE (ed.), *Educating Second Language Children*. Cambridge: Cambridge University Press.

HUDSON, L., 1966, *Contrary Imaginations. A Psychological Study of the English Schoolboy*. Harmondsworth, Middlesex: Penguin.

HUDSON, L., 1968, *Frames of Mind*. Harmondsworth, Middlesex: Penguin.

HUFFINES, M.L., 1991, Pennsylvania German: 'Do they love it in their hearts?' In J.R. DOW (ed.), *Language and Ethnicity. Focusschrift in Honor of Joshua Fishman*. Amsterdam/Philadelphia: John Benjamins.

HUMMEL, K.M., 1993, Bilingual memory research: From storage to processing issues. *Applied Psycholinguistics* 14, 267–284.

HUNTER, J.E., SCHMIDT, F.L. & JACKSON, G.B., 1982, *Meta-analysis: Cumulating Research Findings Across Studies*. Beverly Hills, CA: Sage.

HURD, M., 1993, Minority language children and French immersion: Additive multilingualism or subtractive semi-lingualism. *Canadian Modern Language Review* 49 (3), 514–525.

HUSBAND, C. & KHAN, V.S., 1982, The viability of ethnolinguistic vitality: Some creative doubts. *Journal of Multilingual and Multicultural Development* 3 (3), 193–205.

HUSS-KEELER, R.L., 1997, Teacher perception of ethnic and linguistic minority parental involvement and its relationship to children's language and literacy learning: A case study. *Teacher and Teacher Education* 13 (2), 171–182.

HYMES, D., 1972a, On communicative competence. In J. PRIDE & J. HOLMES (eds), *Sociolinguistics*. London: Penguin.

HYMES, D., 1972b, Models of interaction of language and social life. In J.J. GUMPERZ & D. HYMES (eds), *Directions in Sociolinguistics: The Ethnography of Communication*. New York: Holt, Rinehart and Winston.

IANCO-WORRALL, A.D., 1972, Bilingualism and cognitive development. *Child Development* 43, 1390–1400.

IATCU, T., 2000, Teaching English as a third language to Hungarian–Romanian bilinguals. In J. CENOZ & U. JESSNER. *English in Europe: The Acquisition of a Third Language*. Clevedon: Multilingual Matters.

IMEDADZE, N., 1960, On the psychological nature of early bilingualism (in Russian) *Voprosy Psikhologii* 6, 60–68.

IMOFF, G., 1990, The position of US English on bilingual education. In C.B. CAZDEN & C.E. SNOW (eds), *The Annals of the American Academy of Political and Social Science, Vol. 508*, 48–61. London: Sage.

ISAACS, E., 1976, *Greek Children in Sydney*. Canberra: Australian National University Press.

JACOBSON, R., 1990, Allocating two languages as a key feature of a bilingual methodology. In R. JACOBSON & C. FALTIS (eds), *Language Distribution Issues in Bilingual Schooling*. Clevedon: Multilingual Matters.

JACOBSON, R. & FALTIS, C., 1990, *Language Distribution Issues in Bilingual Schooling*. Clevedon: Multilingual Matters.

JACQUES, K. & HAMLIN, J., 1992, PAT scores of children in bilingual and monolingual New Zealand primary classrooms. *Delta (NZ)* 46, 21–30.

JANKOWSKI, K.A., 1997, *Deaf Empowerment: Emergence, Struggle and Rhetoric*. Washington, DC: Gallaudet University Press.

JIMÉNEZ, R.T., GARCÍA, G.E. & PEARSON, P.D., 1995, Three children, two languages and strategic reading: Case studies in bilingual/monolingual reading. *American Educational Research Journal* 32 (1), 67–97.

JOHNSON, D.M., 1994, Grouping strategies for second language learners. In F. GENESEE (ed.), *Educating Second Language Children*. Cambridge: Cambridge University Press.

JOHNSON, R.K. & SWAIN, M., 1994, From core to content: Bridging the L2 proficiency gap in late immersion. *Language and Education* 8, 211–229.

JOHNSON, R.K. & SWAIN, M., 1997, *Immersion Education: International Perspectives*. Cambridge: Cambridge University Press.

JONES, G.M., 1997, Immersion Programs in Brunei. In J. CUMMINS & D. CORSON (eds), *Bilingual Education*. Volume 5 of the *Encyclopedia of Language and Education*. Dordrecht: Kluwer.

JONES, G.M. MARTIN, P.W. & OZÓG, A.C.K., 1993, Multilingualism and bilingual education in Brunei Darussalem. In G.M. JONES & A.C.K. OZÓG (eds), *Bilingualism and National Development*. Clevedon: Multilingual Matters.

JONES, G.M. & OZÓG, A.C.K. (eds), 1993, *Bilingualism and National Development*. Clevedon: Multilingual Matters.

JONES, W.R., 1959, *Bilingualism and Intelligence*. Cardiff: University of Wales Press.

JONES, W.R., 1966, *Bilingualism in Welsh Education*. Cardiff: University of Wales Press.

JONG, E. de, 1986, *The Bilingual Experience: A Book for Parents*. New York: Cambridge University Press.

KAPLAN, R.B. & BALDAUF, R.B., 1997. *Language Planning from Practice to Theory*. Clevedon: Multilingual Matters.

KARDASH, C.A. *et al.*, 1988, Bilingual referents in cognitive processing. *Contemporary Educational Psychology* 13, 45–57.

KARNIOL, R., 1992, Stuttering out of bilingualism. *First Language* 12, 255–283.

KATZNER, K., 1995, *The Languages of the World*. London: Routledge.

KAUR, S. & MILLS, R., 1993, Children as interpreters. In R.W. MILLS & J. MILLS (eds), *Bilingualism in the Primary School*. London: Routledge.

KEATLEY, C.W., 1992, History of bilingualism research in cognitive psychology. In R.J. HARRIS (ed.), *Cognitive Processing in Bilinguals*. Amsterdam: North-Holland.

KEEL, P. (ed.), 1994, *Assessment in the Multi-Ethnic Primary Classroom*. Stoke-on-Trent: Trentham.

KESSLER, C. & QUINN, M.E., 1982, Cognitive development in bilingual environments. In B. HARTFORD, A. VALDMAN & C.R. FOSTER (eds), *Issues in International Bilingual Education. The Role of the Vernacular*. New York: Plenum Press.

KEYSER, R. & BROWN, J., 1981, *Heritage Language Survey Results*. Toronto, Canada: Research Department, Metropolitan Separate School Board.

KIBBEE, D.A., 1998, Presentation: Realism and idealism in language conflicts and their resolution. In D.A. KIBBEE (ed.), *Language Legislation and Linguistic Rights*. Amsterdam & Philadelphia: John Benjamins.

KING, K., 2000, *Language Revitalization: Processes and Products*. Clevedon: Multilingual Matters.

KJOLSETH, R., 1983, Cultural politics of bilingualism. *Sociolinguistics Today* 20 (4), 40–48.

KLEIN, E.C., 1995, Second versus third language learning: Is there a difference? *Language Learning* 45, 419–465.

KLINE, P., 1983, *Personality Measurement and Theory*. London: Hutchinson.

KLOSS, H., 1977, *The American Bilingual Tradition*. Rowley, MA: Newbury House.

KLOSS, H., 1998, *The American Bilingual Tradition*. McHenry, IL: Center for Applied Linguistics and Delta Systems.

KNIGHT P. & SWANWICK, R., 1999, *The Care and Education of a Deaf Child*. Clevedon: Multilingual Matters.

KOLERS, P., 1963, Interlingual word association. *Journal of Verbal Learning and Verbal Behavior* 2, 291–300.

KOWAL, M. & SWAIN, M., 1997, From semantic to syntactic processing: How can we promote it in the immersion classroom? In In R.K. JOHNSON & M. SWAIN, *Immersion Education: International Perspectives*. Cambridge: Cambridge University Press.

KOZOL, J., 1985, *Illiterate America*. New York: Doubleday.

KRASHEN, S., 1977, The monitor model for second language performance. In M. BURT, H. DULAY & M. FINOCCHIAO (eds), *Viewpoints on English as a Second Language*. New York: Regents.

KRASHEN, S., 1981, *Second Language Acquisition and Second Language Learning*. Oxford: Pergamon Press.

KRASHEN, S., 1982, *Principles and Practices of Second Language Acquisition*. Oxford: Pergamon Press.

KRASHEN, S., 1985, *The Input Hypothesis: Issues and Implications*. London: Longman.

KRASHEN, S., 1996, *Under Attack: The Case Against Bilingual Education*. Culver City, CA: Language Education Associates.

KRASHEN, S., 1999, *Condemned Without a Trial: Bogus Arguments Against Bilingual Education*. Portsmouth, NH: Heinemann.

KRASHEN, S. & TERRELL, T., 1983, *The Natural Approach: Language Acquisition in the Classroom*. Oxford: Pergamon.

KRASHEN, S., TSE, L., McQUILLAN, J., 1998, *Heritage Language Development*. Culver City, CA.: Language Education Associates.

KRAUSS, M., 1992, The world's languages in crisis. *Language* 68, 6–10.

KRAUSS, M., 1995, Language loss in Alaska, the United States and the World. *Frame of Reference* (Alaska Humanities Forum) 6 (1), 2–5.

KYLE, J.G., 1988, *Sign Language: The Study of Deaf People and their Language*. Cambridge: Cambridge University Press.

KYLE, J.G. (ed.), 1987, *Sign and School*. Clevedon: Multilingual Matters.

LADD, P., 2001, *Understanding Deaf Culture*. Clevedon: Multilingual Matters.

LADO, R., 1961, *Language Testing*. New York: McGraw Hill.

LADO, R., 1964, *Language Teaching: A Scientific Approach*. New York: McGraw-Hill.

LAITIN, D.D., 1997, The cultural identities of a European State. *Politics and Society* 25 (3), 277–302.

LAM, T.C., 1992, Review of practices and problems in the evaluation of bilingual education. *Review of Educational Research* 62 (2), 181–203.

LAMBERT, W.E., 1974, Culture and language as factors in learning and education. In F.E. ABOUD & R.D. MEADE (eds), *Cultural Factors in Learning and Education*. 5th Western Washington Symposium on Learning, Bellingham, Washington.

LAMBERT, W.E., 1980, The social psychology of language. In H. GILES, W.P. ROBINSON & P.M. SMITH (eds), *Language: Social Psychological Perspectives*. Oxford: Pergamon.

LAMBERT, W.E. & CAZABON, M., 1994, *Students' Views of the Amigos Program*. Santa Cruz, CA: National Center for Research on Cultural Diversity and Second Language Learning.

LAMBERT, W.E. & TAYLOR, D.M., 1990, *Coping with Cultural and Racial Diversity in Urban America*. New York: Praeger.

LAMBERT, W.E. & TUCKER, R., 1972, *Bilingual Education of Children. The St Lambert Experiment*. Rowley, MA: Newbury House.

LAMENDELLA, J., 1979, The neurofunctional basis of pattern practice. *TESOL Quarterly* 13, 5–13.

LANAUZE, M. & SNOW, C., 1989, The relation between first- and second-language writing skills. *Linguistics and Education* 1, 323–339.

LANDRY, R., ALLARD, R. & THéBERGE, R., 1991, School and family French ambiance and the bilingual development of Francophone Western Canadians. *Canadian Modern Language Review* 47 (5), 878–915.

LANZA, E., 1992, Can bilingual two-year-olds code-switch? *Journal of Child Language* 19, 633–658.

LANZA, E., 1997, *Language Mixing in Infant Bilingualism: A Sociolinguistic Perspective*. Oxford: Oxford University Press.

LAPKIN, S., HARLEY, B. & TAYLOR, S., 1993, Research directions for core French in Canada. *Canadian Modern Language Review* 49 (3), 476–513.

LAPKIN, S., SWAIN, M. & SHAPSON, S., 1990, French immersion research agenda for the 90s. *Canadian Modern Language Review* 46 (4), 638–674.

LASAGABASTER, D., 2000, Three languages and three linguistic models in the Basque Country. In J. CENOZ & U. JESSNER. *English in Europe: The Acquisition of a Third Language*. Clevedon: Multilingual Matters.

LAURÉN, C., 1994, Cultural and anthropological aspects of immersion. In *Language Immersion: Teaching and Second Language Acquisition: From Canada to Europe. Second European Conference 1994, Vaasa Finland*, Issue 192, pp. 21–26.

LAURÉN, C., 1997, Swedish immersion programs in Finland. In J. CUMMINS & D. CORSON (eds), *Bilingual Education*. Volume 5 of the *Encyclopedia of Language and Education*. Dordrecht: Kluwer.

LAURÉN, U., 1991, A creativity index for studying the free written production for bilinguals. *International Journal of Applied Linguistics* 1 (2), 198–208.

LAURIE, S.S., 1890, *Lectures on Language and Linguistic Method in School*. Cambridge: Cambridge University Press.

LAVER, J. & ROUKENS, J., 1996, The global information society and Europe's linguistic and cultural heritage. In C. HOFFMANN (ed.), *Language, Culture and Communication in Contemporary Europe*. Clevedon: Multilingual Matters.

LEBLANC, R., 1992, Second language retention. *Language and Society* 37, 35–36.

LEBRUN, N. & BAETENS BEARDSMORE, H., 1993, Trilingual education in the Grand Duchy of Luxembourg. In H. BAETENS BEARDSMORE (ed.), *European Models of Bilingual Education*. Clevedon: Multilingual Matters.

LEE, J-W., & SCHALLERT, D.L., 1997, The relative contribution of L2 Language proficiency and L1 reading ability to L2 reading performance: A test of the threshold hypothesis in an EFL context. *TESOL Quarterly* 31 (4), 713–739.

LEMAN, J., 1993, The bicultural programmes in the Dutch-language school system in Brussels. In H. BAETENS BEARDSMORE (ed.), *European Models of Bilingual Education*. Clevedon: Multilingual Matters.

LENNEBERG, E., 1967, *Biological Foundations of Language*. New York: Wiley.

LEOPOLD, W.F., 1939–1949, *Speech Development of a Bilingual Child. A Linguists' Record* (4 volumes). Evanston, IL: Northwestern University Press.

LESSOW-HURLEY, J., 1996, *The Foundations of Dual Language Instruction* (2nd edn). New York: Longman.

LEWIS, E.G., 1977, Bilingualism and bilingual education: The ancient world of the Renaissance. In B. SPOLSKY & R.L. COOPER (eds), *Frontiers of Bilingual Education*. Rowley, MA: Newbury House.

LEWIS, E.G., 1981, *Bilingualism and Bilingual Education*. Oxford: Pergamon.

LI WEI, MILLER, N. & DODD, B., 1997, Distinguishing communicative difference from language disorder in bilingual children. *Bilingual Family Newsletter* 14 (1), 3–4.

LI WEI, MILROY, L. & PON SIN CHING, 1992, A two-step sociolinguistic analysis of codeswitching and language choice: The example of a bilingual Chinese community in Britain. *International Journal of Applied Linguistics* 2 (1), 63–86.

LIN, J., 1997, Policies and practices of bilingual education for the minorities in China. *Journal of Multilingual and Multicultural Development* 18 (3), 193–205.

LINDHOLM, K.J., 1987, *Directory of Bilingual Education Programs* (Monograph No. 8). Los Angeles: University of Southern California, Center for Language Education and Research.

LINDHOLM, K.J., 1990, Bilingual immersion education: Criteria for program development. In A.M. PADILLA, H.H. FAIRCHILD & C.M. VALADEZ (eds), *Bilingual Education: Issues and Strategies*. London: Sage.

LINDHOLM, K.J., 1991, Theoretical assumptions and empirical evidence for academic achievement in two languages. *Hispanic Journal of Behavioral Sciences* 13 (1), 3–17. Also in A.M. PADILLA (ed.), 1995, *Hispanic Psychology: Critical Issues in Theory and Research*. Thousand Oaks, CA: Sage.

LINDHOLM, K.J., 1994, Promoting positive cross-cultural attitudes and perceived competence in culturally and linguistically diverse classrooms. In R.A. DEVILLAR, C. FALTIS & J. CUMMINS (eds), *Cultural Diversity in Schools: From Rhetoric to Practice*. Albany, NY: State University of New York Press.

LINDHOLM, K.J. & ACLAN, Z., 1991, Bilingual proficiency as a bridge to academic achievement: Results from bilingual/immersion programs. *Journal of Education* 173 (2), 99–113.

LINDHOLM-LEARY, K.J., 2000, *Biliteracy for Global Society: An Idea Book on Dual Language Education*. Washington, DC: NCBE (see: http://www.ncbe.gwu.edu/).

LINDHOLM-LEARY, K.J., 2001, *Dual Language Education*. Clevedon: Multilingual Matters.

LINGUISTIC MINORITIES PROJECT, 1985, *The Other Languages of England*. London: Routledge and Kegan Paul.

LITTLEBEAR, R., 1999, Some rare and radical ideas for keeping indigenous languages alive. In J. REYHNER *et al.*, *Revitalizing Indigenous Languages*. Flagstaff, AZ: Northern Arizona University.

LONG, M., 1985, Input and second language acquisition theory. In S. GASS & C. MADDEN (eds), *Input in Second Language Acquisition*. Rowley, MA: Newbury House.

LOWE, P., 1983, The oral interview: Origins, applications, pitfalls and implications. *Die Unterrichtspraxis* 16, 230–244.

LUCAS, T., HENZE, R. & DONATO, R., 1990, Promoting the success of Latino language-minority students: An exploratory study of six High Schools. *Harvard Educational Review* 60 (3), 315–340.

LUKMANI, Y.M., 1972, Motivation to learn and learning proficiency. *Language Learning* 22, 261–273.

LYNCH, J., 1992, *Education for Citizenship in a Multicultural Society*. New York: Cassell.

LYON, J., 1996, *Becoming Bilingual: Language Acquisition in a Bilingual Community*. Clevedon: Multilingual Matters.

LYONS, J.J., 1990, The past and future directions of Federal bilingual-education policy. In C.B. CAZDEN & C.E. SNOW (eds), *Annals of the American Academy of Political and Social Science*, Vol. 508, 119–134. London: Sage.

MACÍAS R.F. *et al.*, 1998, *Summary Report of the Survey of States' Limited English Proficient Students*. Washington, DC: National Clearinghouse for Bilingual Education.

MACÍAS R.F., 2000, The flowering of America: Linguistic diversity in the United States. In S.L. McKAY & S-L.C. WONG (eds), *New Immigrants in the United States*. Cambridge: Cambridge University Press.

MACKEY, W.F., 1965, *Language Teaching Analysis*. London: Longman.

MACKEY, W.F., 1970, A typology of bilingual education. *Foreign Language Annals* 3, 596–608.

MACKEY, W.F., 1978, The importation of bilingual education models. In J. ALATIS (ed.), *Georgetown University Roundtable: International Dimensions of Education*. Washington, DC: Georgetown University Press.

MACKEY, W.F., 1991, Language diversity, language policy and the sovereign state. *History of European Ideas* 13, 51–61.

MACNAB, G.L., 1979, Cognition and bilingualism: A reanalysis of studies. *Linguistics* 17, 231–255.

MACNAMARA, J., 1966, *Bilingualism and Primary Education, A Study of Irish Experience*. Edinburgh: Edinburgh University Press.

MACNAMARA, J., 1969, How can one measure the extent of a person's bilingual proficiency. In L.G. KELLY (ed.), *Description and Measurement of Bilingualism* (pp. 80–119). Toronto: University of Toronto Press.

MACNEIL, M.M., 1994, Immersion programmes employed in Gaelic-medium units in Scotland. *Journal of Multilingual and Multicultural Development* 15 (2&3), 245–252.

MACSWAN, J., 2000, The threshold hypothesis, semilingualism, and other contributions to a deficit view of linguistic minorities. *Hispanic Journal of Behavioral Sciences* 22 (1), 3–45.

MÄGISTE, E., 1984, Learning a third language. *Journal of Multilingual and Multicultural Development* 5 (5), 415–421.

MAHER, J., 1997, Linguistic minorities and education in Japan. *Educational Review* 49 (2), 115–127.

MALAKOFF, M., 1992, Translation ability: A natural bilingual and metalinguistic skill. In R.J. HARRIS (ed.), *Cognitive Processing in Bilinguals*. Amsterdam: North-Holland.

MALAKOFF, M. & HAKUTA, K., 1990, History of language minority education in the United States. In A.M. PADILLA, H.H. FAIRCHILD & C.M. VALADEZ (eds), *Bilingual Education Issues and Strategies*. London: Sage.

MALDONADO, J.A., 1994, Bilingual special education: Specific learning disabilities in language and reading. *Journal of Educational Issues of Language Minority Students* 14, 127–147.

MALHERBE, E.C., 1946, *The Bilingual School*. London: Longman.

MANZER, K., 1993, Canadian immersion: Alive and working well in Finland. *Language and Society* 44, 16–17.

MAR-MOLINERO, C., 1987, The teaching of Catalan in Catalonia. *Journal of Multilingual and Multicultural Development* 10 (4), 307–326.

MARTIN, D., 1997, Towards a new multilingual language policy in South Africa. *Educational Review* 49, 2, 129–139.

MARTIN-JONES, M., 2000, Bilingual classroom interaction: A review of recent research. *Language Teaching* 33 (1), 1–9.

MARTIN-JONES, M. & ROMAINE, S., 1986, Semilingualism: A half baked theory of communicative competence. *Applied Linguistics* 7 (1), 26–38.

MÄSCH, N., 1994, The German model of bilingual education. In R. KHOO, U. KREHER & R. WONG (eds), *Towards Global Multilingualism: European Models and Asian Realities*. Clevedon: Multilingual Matters.

MASHIE, S.N., 1995, *Educating Deaf Children Bilingually*. Washington, DC: Gallaudet University.

MATSUMI, N., 1994, Process of words memory in second language acquisition: A test of bilingual dual coding model. *Japanese Journal of Psychology* 64 (6), 460–468.

MATTHEWS, T., 1979, *An Investigation Into the Effects of Background Characteristics and Special Language Services on the Reading Achievement and English Fluency of Bilingual Students*. Seattle, WA: Seattle Public Schools, Department of Planning.

MAY, S., 1996, Indigenous language rights and education. In C. MODGIL, S. MODGIL & J. LYNCH (eds), *Education and Development: Tradition and Innovation* (Volume 1). London: Cassell.

MAY, S., 1999, Critical multiculturalism and cultural difference. In S. MAY (ed.), *Critical Multiculturalism: Rethinking Multicultural and Antiracist Education*. London & Philadelphia: Falmer Press.

MAY, S., 2001, *Language and Minority Rights*. London: Longman.

McCARTY, T.L., 1997, American Indian, Alaska Native, and Native Hawaiian bilingual education. In J. CUMMINS & D. CORSON (eds), *Bilingual Education*. Volume 5 of the *Encyclopedia of Language and Education*. Dordrecht: Kluwer.

McCARTY, T.L. & WATAHOMIGIE, L.J., 1999, Indigenous community-based language education in the USA. In S. MAY (ed.), *Indigenous Community-Based Education*. Clevedon: Multilingual Matters.

McCONNELL, B., 1980, Effectiveness of individualized bilingual instruction for migrant students. Unpublished PhD dissertation, Washington State University.

McCRACKEN, W., 1991, *Deaf-Ability Not Disability*. Clevedon: Multilingual Matters.

McGAW, B., 1988, Meta-analysis. In J.P. KEEVES (ed.), *Educational Research, Methodology and Measurement*. New York: Pergamon.

McGROARTY, M., 1990, Bilingualism in the workplace. *Annals of the American Academy of Political and Social Science* 511, 159–179.

McGROARTY, M., 1992, The societal context of bilingual education. *Educational Researcher* 21 (2), 7–9.

McGROARTY, M., 1997, Language policy in the USA: National values, local loyalties, pragmatic pressures. In W. EGGINGTON & H. WREN (eds), *Language Policy: Dominant English, Pluralist Challenges*. Philadelphia: John Benjamins.

McGROARTY, M.E. & FALTIS, C., 1991, *Languages in School and Society: Policy and Pedagogy*. Berlin/New York: Mouton de Gruyter.

McKAY, P. et al., 1997, *The Bilingual Interface Project Report*. Department of Employment, Education, Training and Youth Affairs, Canberra.

McKAY, S., 1988, Weighing educational alternatives. In S.L. McKAY & S.C. WONG (eds), *Language Diversity: Problem or Resource?* New York: Newbury House.

McKAY, S.L. & HORNBERGER, N.H. (eds), 1996, *Sociolinguistics and Language Teaching*. Cambridge: Cambridge University Press.

McKAY, S.L. & WONG, S-L.C. (eds), 2000, *New Immigrants in the United States*. Cambridge: Cambridge University Press.

McLAREN, P., 1988, Culture or canon? Critical pedagogy and the politics of literacy. *Harvard Educational Review* 58, 211–234.

McLAUGHLIN, B., 1987, *Theories of Second-Language Learning*. London: Edward Arnold.

McLAUGHLIN, T & McLAUGHLIN, D., 2000, Reversing Navajo language shift, revisited. In J.A. FISHMAN, (ed.), *Can Threatened Languages be Saved?* Clevedon: Multilingual Matters.

McMAHON, A.M., 1994, *Understanding Language Change*. Cambridge: Cambridge University Press.

McQUILLAN, J. & TSE, L., 1995, Child language brokering in linguistic minority communities: Effects on cultural interaction, cognition and literacy. *Language and Education* 9 (3), 195–215.

McQUILLAN, J. & TSE, L., 1996, Does research matter? An analysis of media opinion on bilingual education, 1984–1994. *Bilingual Research Journal* 20 (1), 1–27.

MERCER, J.R., 1973, *Labeling the Mentally Retarded*. Berkeley, CA: University of California Press.

MET, M., 1998, Curriculum decision-making in content-based language teaching. In J. CENOZ & F. GENESEE (eds), *Beyond Bilingualism: Multilingualism and Multilingual Education*. Clevedon: Multilingual Matters.

MET, M. & LORENZ, E.B., 1997, Lessons from US immersion programs: Two decades of experience. In R.K. JOHNSON & M. SWAIN, 1997, *Immersion Education: International Perspectives*. Cambridge: Cambridge University Press.

MEYER, M.M. & FIENBERG, S.E., 1992, *Assessing Evaluation Studies: The Case of Bilingual Education Strategies*. Washington, DC: National Academy Press.

MILLER-NOMELAND, M., 1993, *Kendall Demonstration Elementary School: Deaf Studies Curriculum Guide*. Washington, DC: Gallaudet University.

MILLS, R.W. & MILLS, J. (eds), 1993, *Bilingualism in the Primary School: A Handbook for Teachers*. London: Routledge.

MITCHELL, D.E., DESTINO, T., KARAM, R.T. & COLÓN-MUÑIZ, A., 1999, Changes in educational policy: The politics of bilingual education. *Educational Policy* 13 (1), 86–103.

MITCHELL, R. & MYLES, F., 1998, *Second-Language Learning Theories*. London: Arnold.

MOHANTY, A.K., 1994, *Bilingualism in a Multilingual Society: Psycho-Social and Pedagogical Implications*. Mysore, India: Central Institute of Indian Languages.

MOLL, L.C., 1992, Bilingual classroom studies and community analysis. *Educational Researcher* 21 (2), 20–24.

MORALES, R. & BONILLA, F., 1993, *Latinos in a Changing US Economy*. London: Sage.

MORISON, S.H., 1990, A Spanish–English dual-language program in New York City. In C.B. CAZDEN & C.E. SNOW (eds), *The Annals of the American Academy of Political and Social Science*, Vol. 508, 160–169. London: Sage.

MORRIS, D., 1992, The effects of economic changes on Gwynedd society. In L. DAFIS (ed.), *Lesser Used Languages: Assimilating Newcomers*. Carmarthen, Wales: Joint Working Party on Bilingualism in Dyfed.

MOSELEY, C. & ASHER, R.E., 1994, *Atlas of the World's Languages*. London: Routledge.

MULTILINGUAL RESOURCES FOR CHILDREN PROJECT, 1995, *Building Bridges: Multilingual Resources for Children*. Clevedon: Multilingual Matters.

MUÑOZ, C., 2000, Bilingualism and trilingualism in school students in Catalonia. In J. CENOZ & U. JESSNER. *English in Europe: The Acquisition of a Third Language*. Clevedon: Multilingual Matters.

MYERS-SCOTTON, C., 1972, *Choosing a Lingua Franca in an African Capital*. Edmonton, Champaign (IL): Linguistic Research.

MYERS SCOTTON, C., 1983, The negotiation of identities in conversation: A theory of markedness and code choice. *International Journal of the Sociology of Language* 44, 115–136.

MYERS SCOTTON, C., 1991, Making ethnicity salient in codeswitching. In J.R. DOW (ed.), *Language and Ethnicity. Focusschrift in Honor of Joshua Fishman*. Amsterdam/Philadelphia: John Benjamins.

MYERS-SCOTTON, C., 1992, Comparing codeswitching and borrowing. *Journal of Multilingual and Multicultural Development* 13 (1&2), 19–39.

MYERS-SCOTTON, C., 1993, *Duelling Languages: Grammatical Structure in Codeswitching*. Oxford, New York: Oxford University Press.

MYERS-SCOTTON, C., 1997, Code-switching. In F. COULMAS (ed.), *The Handbook of Sociolinguistics*. Oxford: Blackwell.

MYERS SCOTTON, C. & URY, W., 1977, Bilingual strategies: The social functions of code-switching. *Linguistics* 193, 5–20.

NAIMAN, N., FROHLICH, M. & TODESCO, A., 1975, The good second language learner. *TESL Talk* 6, 58–75.

NÁÑEZ, J.E., PADILLA, R.V. & MÁEZ, B.L., 1992, Biliguality, intelligence and cognitive information processing. In R.V. PADILLA & A.H. BENAVIDES (eds), *Critical Perspectives on Bilingual Education Research*. Tempe, AZ: Bilingual Press.

NELDE, P.H., LABRIE, N. & WILLIAMS, C.H., 1992, The principles of territorality and personality in the solution of linguistic conflicts. *Journal of Multilingual and Multicultural Development* 13 (5), 387–406.

NETTLE, D. & ROMAINE, S., 2000, *Vanishing Voices: The Extinction of the World's Languages*. Oxford: Oxford University Press.

NEUFELD, G.G., 1974, A theoretical perspective on the relationship of bilingualism and thought: Revisited. *Working Papers on Bilingualism*, No. 2, 125–129.

NICOLADIS, E., 1998, First clues to the existence of two input languages: Pragmatic and lexical differentiation in a bilingual child. *Bilingualism: Language and Cognition* 1, 105–116.

NICOLADIS, E. & GENESEE, F., 1996, Word awareness in second language learners and bilingual children. *Language Awareness* 5 (2), 80–90.

NICOLADIS, E. & GENESEE, F., 1997, Language development in preschool bilingual children. *Journal of Speech-Language Pathology and Audiology* 21 (4), 258–270.

NICOLADIS, E. & SECCO, G., 2000, The role of a child's productive vocabulary in the language choice of a bilingual family. *First Language* 20 (58), 3–28.

NIETO, S., 1996, *Affirming Diversity. The Sociopolitical Context of Multicultural Education* (2nd edn). New York, London: Longman.

NIETO, S., 1999, *The Light in their Eyes: Creating Multicultural Learning Communities*. New York: Teachers College Press.

NUFFIELD FOUNDATION, 2000, *Languages: The Next Generation: The Final Report and Recommendations of The Nuffield Languages Inquiry*. London: The Nuffield Foundation.

Ó GLIASÁIN, M., 1996, *The Language Question in the Census of the Population*. Dublin: Linguistics Institute of Ireland.

Ó RIAGÁIN, P., 1992, *Language Maintenance and Language Shift as Strategies of Social Reproduction*. Dublin: The Linguistics Institute of Ireland.

Ó RIAGÁIN, P., 2000, Irish language production and reproduction 1981–1996. In J.A. FISHMAN, (ed.), *Can Threatened Languages be Saved?* Clevedon: Multilingual Matters.

O'MALLEY, J., & CHAMOT, A., 1990, *Learning Strategies in Second Language Acquisition*. Cambridge: Cambridge University Press.

OBLER, L., 1983, Knowledge in neurolinguistics: The case of bilingualism. *Language Learning* 33 (5), 159–191.

OCEI, 1993, *Censo Indígena de Venezuela*. Caracas: Oficina Central de Estadística e Informática.

OCHS, T., 1993, 'Why can't we speak Tagalog?' The problematic status of multilingualism in the International School. *Journal of Multilingual and Multicultural Development* 14 (6), 447–462.

OGBU, J., 1978, *Minority Education and Caste: The American System in Cross-Cultural Perspective*. New York: Academic Press.

OGBU, J., 1983, Minority status and schooling in plural societies. *Comparative Education Review* 27 (2), 168–190.

OKA, Hideo, 1994, Studies on bilingualism and their implication in Japan. In R. MICHAEL BOSTWICK (ed.), *Immersion Education International Symposium Report on Second Language Acquisition through Content Based Study: An Introduction to Immersion Education*. Numazu, Japan: Katoh Gakuen.

OLLER, J.W., 1979, *Language Tests at School*. London: Longman.

OLLER, J.W., 1982, Evaluation and testing. In B. HARTFORD, A. VALDMAN & C. FOSTER (eds), *Issues in International Bilingual Education*. New York: Plenum Press.

OLLER, J.W. & PERKINS, K., 1978, A further comment on language proficiency as a source of variance in certain affective measures. *Language Learning* 28, 417–423.

OLLER, J.W. & PERKINS, K., 1980, *Research in Language Testing*. Rowley, MA: Newbury House.

OLNECK, M.R., 1993, Terms of inclusion: Has multiculturalism redefined equality in American education? *American Journal of Education* 101 (3), 234–260.

ORELLANA, M.F., EK, L. & HERNÁNDEZ, A., 1999, Bilingual education in an immigrant community: Proposition 227 in California. *International Journal of Bilingual Education and Bilingualism* 2 (2), 114–130.

OTHEGUY, R., 1982, Thinking about bilingual education: A critical appraisal. *Harvard Educational Review* 52 (3), 301–314.

OTHEGUY, R. & OTTO, R., 1980, The myth of static maintenance in bilingual education. *Modern Language Journal* 64 (3), 350–356.

OVANDO, C.J., 1990, Essay review: Politics and pedagogy: The case of bilingual education. *Harvard Educational Review* 60 (3), 341–356.

OVANDO, C.J. & COLLIER, V.P., 1998, *Bilingual and ESL Classrooms. Teaching in Multicultural Contexts*. Boston: McGraw-Hill.

OVANDO, C.J. & McLAREN, P., 2000, *The Politics of Multiculturalism and Bilingual Education*. Boston: McGraw-Hill.

OXENHAM, J., 1980, *Literacy: Writing, Reading and Social Organization*. London: Routledge and Kegan Paul.

OXFORD, R.L., 1990, *Language Learning Strategies: What Every Teacher Should Know*. Boston: Heinle and Heinle.

OXFORD, R.L., 1993, Individual differences among your students: Why a single method can't work. *Journal of Intensive English Studies* 7, 27–42.

OXFORD, R.L., 1994, *Language Learning Strategies: An Update*. ERIC Digest. Washington, DC: ERIC Clearinghouse on Languages and Linguistics.

PADILLA, A.M., 1991, English Only vs. bilingual education: Ensuring a language-competent society. *Journal of Education* 173 (2), 38–51.

PADILLA, A.M. & SUNG, H., 1992, A theoretical and pedagogical framework for bilingual education based on principles from educational psychology. In R.V. PADILLA & A.H. BENAVIDES (eds), *Critical Perspectives on Bilingual Education Research*. Tempe, AZ: Bilingual Press.

PADILLA, R.V. & BENAVIDES, A.H. (eds), 1992, *Critical Perspectives on Bilingual Education Research*. Tempe, AZ: Bilingual Press.

PAIVIO, A., 1986, *Mental Representations: A Dual Coding Approach*. Oxford: Oxford University Press.

PAIVIO, A., 1991, Mental representations in bilinguals. In A.G. REYNOLDS (ed.), *Bilingualism, Multiculturalism and Second Language Learning*. Hillsdale, NJ: Lawrence Erlbaum.

PAIVIO, A. & DESROCHERS, A., 1980, A dual-coding approach to bilingual memory. *Canadian Journal of Psychology* 34, 390–401.

PAKIR, A., 1994, Making bilingualism work: Developments in bilingual education in ASEAN. In R. KHOO, U. KREHER & R. WONG (eds), *Towards Global Multilingualism: European Models and Asian Realities*. Clevedon: Multilingual Matters.

PARADIS, M., 2000, The neurolinguistics of bilingualism in the next decades. *Brain and Language* 71, 178–180.

PARRILLO, V.N., 1996, *Diversity in America*. Thousand Oaks CA: Pine Forge Press.

PATTANAYAK, D.P., 1988, Monolingual myopia and the petals of the Indian lotus. In T. SKUTNABB-KANGAS & J. CUMMINS (eds), *Minority Education: From Shame to Struggle*. Clevedon: Multilingual Matters.

PAULSTON, C.B., 1980, *Bilingual Education: Theories and Issues*. Rowley, MA: Newbury House.

PAULSTON, C.B., 1992a, *Linguistic and Communicative Competence*. Clevedon: Multilingual Matters.

PAULSTON, C.B., 1992b, *Sociolinguistic Perspectives on Bilingual Education*. Clevedon: Multilingual Matters.

PAULSTON, C.B., 1994, *Linguistic Minorities in Multilingual Settings*. Amsterdam/Philadelphia: John Benjamins.

PAULSTON, C.B., 1997, Language policies and language rights. *Annual Review of Anthropology* 26, 73–85.

PAULSTON, C.B. (ed.), 1988, *International Handbook of Bilingualism and Bilingual Education*. New York: Greenwood.

PAULSTON, C.B., CHEE CHIN, P. & CONNERTY, M.C., 1993, Language regenesis: A conceptual overview of language revival, revitalisation and reversal. *Journal of Multilingual and Multicultural Development* 14 (4), 275–286.

PAVLENKO, A., 1999, New approaches to concepts in bilingual memory. *Bilingualism: Language and Cognition* 2 (3), 209–230.

PAVLENKO, A., 2000, What's in a concept? *Bilingualism: Language and Cognition* 3 (1), 31–36.

PEAL, E. & LAMBERT, W.E., 1962, The relationship of bilingualism to intelligence. *Psychological Monographs* 76 (27), 1–23.

PEDERSEN, R.N., 1992, *One Europe: 100 Nations*. Clevedon: Channel View Books.

PELLERANO, C. & FRADD, S.H., 1998, *Coral Way Elementary School: A Success Story in Bilingualism and Biliteracy* (http://www.ncbe.gwu.edu/ncbepubs/discover/03coral.htm).

PENNYCOOK, A., 1994, *The Cultural Politics of English as an International Language*. New York: Longman.

PÉREZ, B. & TORRES-GUZMÁN, M., 1996, *Learning in Two Worlds: An Integrated Spanish/English Biliteracy Approach* (2nd edn). New York: Longman.

PERLMANN, J., 1990, Historical legacies: 1840–1920. In C.B. CAZDEN & C.E. SNOW (eds), *English Plus: Issues in Bilingual Education*. London: Sage.

PEROTTI, A., 1994, *The Case for Intercultural Education*. Strasbourg: Council of Europe Press.

PHILLIPSON, R., 1992, *Linguistic Imperialism*. Oxford: Oxford University Press.

PINTNER, R. & ARSENIAN, S., 1937, The relation of bilingualism to verbal intelligence and school adjustment. *Journal of Educational Research* 31, 255–263.

POHL, J., 1965, Bilingualismes. *Revue Roumaine de Linguistique* 10, 343–349.

POPLACK, S. & MEECHAN, M., 1998, Introduction: How languages fit together in codeswitching. *International Journal of Bilingualism* 2 (2), 127–138.

POPLACK, S., SANKOFF, D. & MILLER, C., 1988, The social correlates and linguistic processes of lexical borrowing and assimilation. *Linguistics* 26, 47–104.

PORTER, R., 1990, *Forked Tongue: The Politics of Bilingual Education*. New York: Basic Books.

PORTES, A. & HAO, L., 1998, E pluribus unum: Bilingualism and loss of language in the second generation. *Sociology of Education* 71 (October), 269–294.

POWERS, S. & GREGORY, S., 1998, *The Educational Achievements of Deaf Children*. London: Department for Education and Employment.

POWERS, S., GREGORY, S. *et al.*, 1999, *A Review of Good Practice in Deaf Education*. London: Royal National Institute for Deaf People.

PRICE, E., 1985, Schools Council Bilingual Education Project (Primary Schools) 1968–1977: An assessment. In C.J. DODSON (ed.), *Bilingual Education: Evaluation, Assessment and Methodology*. Cardiff: University of Wales Press.

PUCCI, S., 1994, Supporting Spanish language literacy: Latino children and free reading resources in schools. *Bilingual Research Journal* 18 (1&2), 67–82.

PUCCI, S., 2000, Spanish language literacy maintenance: Central Americans in Los Angeles. *Southwest Journal of Linguistics* 20, 2.

PURKEY, S.C. & SMITH, M.S., 1983, Effective schools: A review. *Elementary School Journal* 86 (4), 427–452.

QUAY, S., 1994, Language choice in early bilingual development. Unpublished PhD, University of Cambridge.

QUEZADA, M., WILEY, T.G. & RAMIREZ, J.D., 1999, How the reform agenda shortchanges English learners. *Educational Leadership* 57 (4), 57–61.

RAMÍREZ, A.G., 1985, *Bilingualism Through Schooling: Cross Cultural Education for Minority and Majority Students*. Albany: State University of New York Press.

RAMÍREZ, J.D., 1992, Executive summary. *Bilingual Research Journal* 16, (1&2), 1–62.

RAMÍREZ, J.D. & MERINO, B.J., 1990, Classroom talk in English immersion, early-exit and late-exit transitional bilingual education programs. In R. JACOBSON & C. FALTIS (eds), *Language Distribution Issues in Bilingual Schooling*. Clevedon: Multilingual Matters.

RAMÍREZ, J.D., YUEN, S.D. & RAMEY, D.R., 1991, *Final Report: Longitudinal Study of Structured English Immersion Strategy, Early-exit and Late-exit Programs for Language-minority Children. Report Submitted to the US Department of Education*. San Mateo, CA: Aguirre International.

RANSDELL, S.E. & FISCHLER, I., 1987, Memory in a monolingual mode: When are bilinguals at a disadvantage. *Journal of Memory and Language* 26, 392–405.

RANSDELL, S.E. & FISCHLER, I., 1989, Effects of concreteness and task context on recall of prose among bilingual and monolingual speakers. *Journal of Memory and Language* 28, 278–291.

REBUFFOT, J., 1993, *Le Point sur L'Immersion au Canada*. Anjou, Quebec: Centre éducatif et Culturel.

REID, S., 1993, *Lament for a Nation: The Life and Death of Canada's Bilingual Dream*. Vancouver: Arsenal Pulp Press.

RESNICK, L.B. & RESNICK, D.P., 1992, Assessing the thinking curriculum: New tools for educational reform. In B.R. GIFFORD & M.C. O'CONNOR (eds), *Changing Assessments: Alternative Views of Aptitude, Achievement and Instruction*. Boston: Kluwer.

RESNICK, M.C., 1993, ESL and language planning in Puerto Rican education. *TESOL Quarterly* 27 (2), 259–275.

REYHNER, J. & TENNANT, E., 1995, Maintaining and renewing native languages. *Bilingual Research Journal* 19 (2), 279–304.

REYNOLDS, A.G., 1991, The cognitive consequences of bilingualism. In A.G. REYNOLDS (ed.), *Bilingualism, Multiculturalism and Second Language Learning*. Hillsdale, NJ: Lawrence Erlbaum.

REYNOLDS, D., BELLIN, W., AB IEUAN, R., 1998, *A Competitive Edge: Why Welsh Medium Schools Perform Better*. Cardiff: Institute of Welsh Affairs.

REYNOLDS, P., 1971, *A Primer in Theory Construction*. Indianapolis: Bobbs-Meirill.

RHEE, J., 1999, Theories of citizenship and their role in the bilingual education debate. *Columbia Journal of Law and Social Problems* 33 (1), 33–83.

RICCIARDELLI, L.A., 1992, Creativity and bilingualism. *Journal of Creative Behavior* 26 (4), 242–254.

RICCIARDELLI, L.A., 1993, Two components of metalinguistic awareness. *Applied Psycholinguistics* 14 (3), 349–367.

RICENTO, T. & BURNABY, B., 1998, *Language and Politics in the United States and Canada: Myths and Realities*. Mahwah, NJ: L. Erlbaum.

RICHARDS, J.C. & ROGERS, T.S., 1986, *Approaches and Methods in Language Teaching*. Cambridge: Cambridge University Press.

RILEY, R.W., 1998, *Helping All Children Learn English*. Washington, DC: US Department of Education.

RINGBOM, H., 1985, *Foreign Language Learning and Bilingualism*. Turku: Abo Akademi.

RIPPBERGER, S.J., 1993, Ideological shifts in bilingual education: Mexico and the United States. *Comparative Education Review* 37 (1), 50–61.

RIVERA, C. (ed.), 1984, *Language Proficiency and Academic Achievement*. Clevedon: Multilingual Matters.

ROBERTS, C., 1985, Teaching and learning commitment in bilingual schools. Unpublished PhD thesis, University of Wales.

ROBERTS, C., 1987, Political conflict over bilingual initiatives: A case study. *Journal of Multilingual and Multicultural Development* 8 (4), 311–322.

ROBERTS, G., 1994, Nurse/patient communication within a bilingual health care setting. *British Journal of Nursing* 3 (2), 60–67.

ROBINSON, C.D.W., 1996, *Language Use in Rural Development: An African Perspective*. New York: Mouton de Gruyter.

ROBSON, A., 1995, The assessment of bilingual children. In M.K. VERMA, K.P. CORRIGAN & S. FIRTH. (eds), *Working with Bilingual Children*. Clevedon: Multilingual Matters.

ROMAINE, S., 1995, *Bilingualism* (2nd edn). Oxford: Basil Blackwell.

ROMAINE, S., 2000, *Language in Society: An Introduction to Sociolinguistics* (2nd edn). Oxford: Oxford University Press.

ROMERO, M. & PARRINO, A., 1994, Planned Alternation of Languages (PAL): Language use and distribution in bilingual classrooms. *Journal of Educational Issues of Language Minority Students* 13, 137–161.

RONJAT, J., 1913, *Le developpement du langage observe chez un enfant bilingue*. Paris: Champion.

ROSENTHAL, J., 1996, *Teaching Science to Language Minority Students: Theory and Practice*. Clevedon: Multilingual Matters.

ROSENTHAL, R., 1966, *Experimenter Effects in Behavioral Research*. New York: Appleton-Century-Crofts.

ROSIER, P. & HOLM, W., 1980, *The Rock Point Experience: A Longitudinal Study of a Navajo School Program*. Washington, DC: Center for Applied Linguistics.

ROSSELL, C.H., 1992, Nothing matters?: A critique of the Ramirez *et al.* longitudinal study of instructional programs for language-minority children. *Bilingual Research Journal* 16 (1&2), 159–186.

ROSSELL, C.H. & BAKER, K., 1996, The educational effectiveness of bilingual education. *Research in the Teaching of English* 30 (1), 7–74.

RUBAGUMYA, C.M., 1990, *Language in Education in Africa*. Clevedon: Multilingual Matters.

RUBAGUMYA, C.M. (ed.), 1994, *Teaching and Researching Language in African Classrooms*. Clevedon: Multilingual Matters.

RUBIN, J., 1975. What the good language learner can teach us. *TESOL Quarterly*, 9, 41–51.

RUBIN, J., 1977, Attitudes toward language planning. In C.C. ELERT *et al.* (eds), *Dialectology and Sociolinguistics*. UMEA: UMEA Studies in the Humanities 12.

RUEDA, R., 1983, Metalinguistic awareness in monolingual and bilingual mildly retarded children. *NABE Journal* 8, 55–68.

RUHLEN, M., 1991, *A Guide to the World's Languages*. London: Edward Arnold (Hodder Stoughton).

RUIZ, R., 1984, Orientations in language planning. *NABE Journal* 8 (2), 15–34.

SAER, D.J., 1922, An inquiry into the effect of bilingualism upon the intelligence of young children. *Journal of Experimental Pedagogy* 6, 232–240 and 266–274.

SAER, D.J., 1923, The effects of bilingualism on intelligence. *British Journal of Psychology* 14, 25–38.

SAER, D.J., SMITH, F. & HUGHES, J., 1924, *The Bilingual Problem*. Wrexham: Hughes and Son.

SAIF, P.S. & SHELDON, M.E., 1969, *An Investigation of the Experimental French Program at Bedford Park and Allenby Public Schools*. Toronto: Toronto Board of Education.

SANKOFF, G., 1972, Language use in multilingual societies. In J.B. PRIDE & J. HOLMES (eds), *Sociolinguistics: Selected Readings*. Harmondsworth: Penguin.

SAUNDERS, G., 1988, *Bilingual Children: From Birth to Teens*. Clevedon: Multilingual Matters.

SCHERMERHORN, R.A., 1970, *Comparative Ethnic Relations*. New York: Random House.

SCHINKE-LLANO, L., 1989, Early childhood bilingualism: In search of explanation. *Studies in Second Language Acquisition (SSLA)* 11 (3), 223–240.

SCHLOSSMAN, S., 1983, Is there an American tradition of bilingual education? *American Journal of Education* 91, 139–186.

SCHMIDT, R., 2000, *Language Policy and Identity Policy in the United States*. Philadelphia: Temple University Press.

SCHUMANN, J., 1978, *The Pidginization Process: A Model for Second Language Acquisition*. Rowley, MA: Newbury House.

SEARS, C., 1998, *Second Language Students in Mainstream Classrooms*. Clevedon: Multilingual Matters.

SECADA, W.G., 1991, Degree of bilingualism and arithmetic problem solving in Hispanic First Graders. *Elementary School Journal* 92 (2), 213–231.

SECADA, W.G., 1993, The political context of bilingual education in the United States. In B. ARIAS & U. CASANOVA (eds), *Bilingual Education: Politics, Research and Practice.* Berkeley, CA: McCutchan.

SECRETARY'S COMMISSION ON ACHIEVING NECESSARY SKILLS (SCANS), 1991, *What Work Requires of Schools. A SCANS Report for America 2000.* Washington, DC: US Department of Labor.

SELINKER, L., SWAIN, M. & DUMAS, G., 1975, The interlanguage hypothesis extended to children. *Language Learning* 25, 139–152.

SHARWOOD SMITH, M.A., 1989, Crosslinguistic influence in language loss. In K. HYLTENSTAM & L.K. OBLER (eds), *Bilingualism Across the Lifespan: Aspects of Acquisition, Maturity and Loss.* Cambridge: Cambridge University Press.

SHOHAMY, E., 1983, The stability of the oral proficiency trait on the oral interview speaking test. *Language Learning* 33, 527–540.

SHOHAMY, E., 1997, *Critical Language Testing and Beyond.* Plenary Paper presented at the American Association of Applied Linguistics (AAAL), Orlando, March 1997.

SHOHAMY, E., 1999, Unity and diversity in language policy. Paper presented at the AILA Conference, Tokyo, August 1999.

SHOHAMY, E., 2000, *The Power of Tests: A Critical Perspective on the Uses and Consequences of Language Tests.* London: Longman.

SIEGEL, J., 1996, *Vernacular Education in the South Pacific: A Report of AusAID.* New England, Australia: University of New England.

SIEGEL, J., 1997, Formal vs. non-formal vernacular education: The education reform in Papua New Guinea. *Journal of Multilingual and Multicultural Development* 18 (3), 206–222.

SIERRA, J. & OLAZIREGI, I., 1989, *EIFE 2. Influence of Factors on the Learning of Basque.* Gasteiz, Spain: Central Publications Service of the Basque Government.

SIGUÁN, M., 1993, *Multilingual Spain.* Amsterdam: Swets and Zeitlinger.

SIGUÁN, M. & MACKEY, W.F., 1987, *Education and Bilingualism.* London: Kogan Page.

SINGLETON, D., 1989, *Language Acquisition: The Age Factor.* Clevedon: Multilingual Matters.

SKEHAN, P., 1986, Where does language aptitude come from? In P.M. MEARA (ed.), *Spoken Language.* London: CILT.

SKEHAN, P., 1988, Language testing. *Language Teaching*, 21 (January) 1–13 and (October) 211–22.

SKEHAN, P., 1998, *A Cognitive Approach to Language Learning.* Oxford: Oxford University Press

SKINNER, B.F., 1957, *Verbal Behavior.* New York, Appleton-Century-Crofts.

SKUTNABB-KANGAS, T., 1977, Language in the process of cultural assimilation and structural incorporation of linguistic minorities. In C.C. ELERT *et al.* (eds), *Dialectology and Sociolinguistics.* UMEA: UMEA Studies in the Humanities.

SKUTNABB-KANGAS, T., 1981, *Bilingualism or Not: The Education of Minorities.* Clevedon: Multilingual Matters.

SKUTNABB-KANGAS, T., 1991, Swedish strategies to prevent integration and national ethnic minorities. In O. GARCÍA (ed.), *Bilingual Education: Focusschrift in Honor of Joshua A. Fishman.* Amsterdam/Philadelphia: John Benjamins.

SKUTNABB-KANGAS, T., 1999a, Education of minorities. In J.A. FISHMAN (ed.), *Handbook of Language and Ethnic Identity.* New York: Oxford University Press.

SKUTNABB-KANGAS, T., 1999b, Linguistic human rights – Are you naive, or what? *TESOL Journal* 8 (3), 6–12.

SKUTNABB-KANGAS, T., 2000, *Linguistic Genocide in Education – Or Worldwide Diversity and Human Rights?* Mahwah, NJ: Erlbaum.

SKUTNABB-KANGAS, T. & CUMMINS, J. (eds), 1988, *Minority Education: From Shame to Struggle.* Clevedon: Multilingual Matters.

SKUTNABB-KANGAS, T. & PHILLIPSON, R., 1989, 'Mother tongue': The theoretical and sociopolitical construction of a concept. In U. AMMON (ed.), *Status and Function of Languages and Language Variety.* New York: W. de Gruyter.

SKUTNABB-KANGAS, T. & PHILLIPSON, R. (eds), 1994, *Linguistic Human Rights: Overcoming Linguistic Discrimination.* Berlin: Mouton de Gruyter.

SKUTNABB-KANGAS, T. & TOUKOMAA, P., 1976, *Teaching Migrant Children Mother Tongue and Learning the Language of the Host Country in the Context of the Socio-Cultural Situation of the Migrant Family.* Tampere, Finland: Tukimuksia Research Reports.

SLEETER, C.E. & GRANT, C.A., 1987, An analysis of multicultural education in the United States. *Harvard Educational Review* 57 (4), 421–444.

SMITH, D.J. & TOMLINSON, S., 1989, *The School Effect*. London: Policy Studies Institute.

SMITH, F., 1923, Bilingualism and mental development. *British Journal of Psychology* 13, 271–282.

SMITH, F., 1982, *Writing and the Writer*. London: Heinemann.

SMOLICZ, J.J., 1994, *Australian Diversity*. University of Adelaide: Centre for International Studies and Multicultural Education.

SNOW, C.E., BURNS, M.S. & GRIFFIN, P., 1998, *Preventing Reading Difficulties in Young Children*. Washington, DC: National Academy Press.

SNOW, C.E. & HOEFNAGEL-HÖHLE, M., 1978, The critical period for language acquisition: Evidence from second language learning. *Child Development* 49, 1114–1128.

SNOW, M.A., 1990, Instructional methodology in immersion foreign language education. In A.M. PADILLA, H.H. FAIRCHILD & C.M. VALADEZ (eds), *Foreign Language Education: Issues and Strategies*. London: Sage.

SPOLSKY, B., 1989a, Maori bilingual education and language revitalization. *Journal of Multilingual and Multicultural Development* 10 (2), 89–106.

SPOLSKY, B., 1989b, Review of '*Key Issues in Bilingualism and Bilingual Education*'. *Applied Linguistics* 10 (4), 449–451.

SPOLSKY, B., 1989c, *Conditions for Second Language Learning*. Oxford: Oxford University Press.

SPOLSKY, B., 1998, *Sociolinguistics*. Oxford: Oxford University Press.

SPOLSKY, B. & COOPER, R. (eds), 1977, *Frontiers of Bilingual Education*. Rowley, MA: Newbury House.

SPOLSKY, B. & SHOHAMY, E., 1999, *The Languages of Israel: Policy, Ideology and Practice*. Clevedon: Multilingual Matters.

SRIDHAR, K.K., 1996, Societal multilingualism. In S.L. McKAY, & N.H. HORNBERGER, 1996, *Sociolinguistics and Language Teaching*. Cambridge: Cambridge University Press.

STERN, II.II., 1984, A quiet language revolution: Second language teaching in Canadian contexts: Achievements and new directions. *Canadian Modern Language Review* 40 (5), 506–524.

STERN, H.H., 1992, *Issues and Options in Language Teaching*. Oxford: Oxford University Press.

STERNBERG, R.J., 1985, *Beyond IQ: A Triarchic Theory of Human Intelligence*. Cambridge: Cambridge University Press.

STERNBERG, R.J., 1988, *The Triarchic Mind: A New Theory of Human Intelligence*. New York: Viking.

STOTZ, D. & ANDRES, F., 1990, Problems in developing bilingual education programs in Switzerland. *Multilingua* 9 (1), 113–136.

STREET, B.V., 1984, *Literacy in Theory and Practice*. Cambridge: Cambridge University Press.

STREET, B.V., 1994, What is meant by local literacies. *Language and Education* 8 (1&2), 9–17.

STREET, B.V., 1995, *Social Literacies: Critical Approaches to Literacy in Development, Ethnography and Education*. Longman, New York & London.

STRONG, M., 1995, A review of bilingual/bicultural programs for deaf children in North America. *American Annals of the Deaf* 140 (2), 84–94.

STUBBS, M., 1991, Educational language planning in England and Wales: Multicultural rhetoric and assimilationist assumptions. In F. COULMAS (ed.), *A Language Policy for the European Community*. New York: Mouton de Gruyter. Also in O. GARCÍA & C. BAKER (eds), 1995, *Policy and Practice in Bilingual Education: A Reader Extending the Foundations*. Clevedon: Multilingual Matters.

SWAIN, M., 1972, Bilingualism as a first language. Unpublished PhD dissertation, University of California, Irvine.

SWAIN, M., 1985, Communicative competence: Some roles of comprehensible input and comprehensible output in its development. In S. GASS & C. MADDEN (eds), *Input in Second Language Acquisition*. Rowley, MA: Newbury House.

SWAIN, M., 1986, Communicative competence: Some roles of comprehensible input and comprehensible output in its development. In J. CUMMINS & M. SWAIN, 1986, *Bilingualism in Education*. New York: Longman.

SWAIN, M., 1993, The output hypothesis: Just speaking and writing aren't enough. *Canadian Modern Language Review* 50, 158–164.

SWAIN, M., 1997, French immersion programs in Canada. In J. CUMMINS & D. CORSON (eds), *Bilingual Education*. Volume 5 of the *Encyclopedia of Language and Education*. Dordrecht: Kluwer.

SWAIN, M. & LAPKIN, S., 1982, *Evaluating Bilingual Education: A Canadian Case Study*. Clevedon: Multilingual Matters.

SWAIN, M. & LAPKIN, S., 1991a, Additive bilingualism and French immersion education: The roles of language proficiency and literacy. In A.G. REYNOLDS (ed.), *Bilingualism, Multiculturalism and Second Language Learning*. Hillsdale, NJ: Lawrence Erlbaum.

SWAIN, M. & LAPKIN, S., 1991b, Heritage language children in an English–French bilingual program. *Canadian Modern Languages Review* 47 (4), 635–641.

SWAIN, M., LAPKIN, S., ROWEN, N. & HART, D., 1990, The role of mother tongue literacy in third language learning. *Language, Culture and Curriculum* 3 (1), 65–81.

SWAIN, M. & JOHNSON, R.K., 1997, Immersion education: A category within bilingual education. In R.K. JOHNSON & M. SWAIN, *Immersion Education: International Perspectives*. Cambridge: Cambridge University Press.

SWAN, D., 1996, *A Singular Pluralism: The European Schools 1984–1994*. Dublin: Institute of Public Administration.

TAKAKI, R., 1993, Multiculturalism: Battleground or meeting ground? *Annals of the American Academy of Political and Social Science* 530, 109–121.

TANSLEY, P. & CRAFT, A., 1984, Mother tongue teaching and support: A Schools Council enquiry. *Journal of Multilingual and Multicultural Development* 5 (5), 367–384.

TARONE, E., 1980, Communication strategies, foreigner talk and repair in interlanguage. *Language Learning* 30, 417–431.

TAYLOR, D.M., 1991, The social psychology of racial and cultural diversity. In A.G. REYNOLDS (ed.), *Bilingualism, Multiculturalism and Second Language Learning*. Hillsdale, NJ: Lawrence Erlbaum.

TAYLOR, D.M., CRAGO, M.B. & McALPINE, L., 1993, Education in Aboriginal communities: Dilemmas around empowerment. *Canadian Journal of Native Education* 20 (1), 176–183.

THOMAS, J., 1988, The role played by metalinguistic awareness in second and third language learning. *Journal of Multilingual and Multicultural Development* 9, 235–247.

THOMAS, W.P., 1992, An analysis of the research methodology of the Ramirez Report. *Bilingual Research Journal* 16 (1&2), 213–245.

THOMAS, W.P. & COLLIER, V.P., 1995, *Language Minority Student Achievement and Program Effectiveness. Research Summary*. Fairfax, VA: George Mason University.

THOMAS, W.P. & COLLIER, V.P., 1997, *School Effectiveness for Language Minority Students*. Washington, DC: National Clearinghouse for Bilingual Education.

THOMAS, W.P., COLLIER, V.P. & ABBOTT, M., 1993, Academic achievement through Japanese, Spanish or French: The first two years of partial immersion. *Modern Language Journal* 77 (2), 170–179.

THOMPSON, L., 2000, *Young Bilingual Learners in Nursery School*. Clevedon: Multilingual Matters.

TIKUNOFF, W.J., 1983, *Compatibility of the SBIF Features With Other Research Instruction of LEP Students*. San Francisco: Far West Laboratory.

TODD, R., 1991, *Education in a Multicultural Society*. London: Cassell.

TOLLEFSON, J., 1986, Language planning and the radical left in the Philippines. *Language Problems and Language Planning* 10 (2), 177–189.

TOLLEFSON, J.W., 1991, *Planning Language, Planning Inequality*. London: Longman.

TOLLEFSON, J.W. (ed.), 1995, *Power and Inequality in Language Education*. Cambridge: Cambridge University Press.

TOMLINSON, S., 1986, Ethnicity and educational achievement. In S. MODGIL, G. VERMA, K. MALLICK & C. MODGIL (eds), *Multicultural Education. The Interminable Debate*. London: Falmer.

TORRANCE, E.P., 1974a, *Torrance Tests of Creative Thinking: Directions Manual and Scoring Guide*. Lexington, MA: Ginn.

TORRANCE, E.P., 1974b, *Torrance Tests of Creative Thinking: Norms-Technical Manual*. Lexington, MA: Ginn.

TORRES, G., 1991, Active teaching and learning in the bilingual classroom: The child as an active subject in learning to write. In O. GARCÍA (ed.), *Bilingual Education: Focusschrift in Honor of Joshua A. Fishman*. Amsterdam/Philadelphia: John Benjamins.

TOSI, A., 1983, *Immigration and Bilingual Education*. Oxford: Pergamon.

TOSI, A., 1988, The jewel in the crown of the modern prince: The new approach to bilingualism in multicultural education in England. In T. SKUTNABB-KANGAS & J. CUMMINS (eds), *Minority Education: From Shame to Struggle*. Clevedon: Multilingual Matters.

TOSI, A., 1991, High-status and low-status bilingualism in Europe. *Journal of Education* 173 (2), 21–37.

TOSI, A. & LEUNG, C., 1999, *Rethinking Language Education: From a Monolingual to a Multilingual Perspective*. London: CILT.

TOUKOMAA, P. & SKUTNABB-KANGAS, T., 1977, *The Intensive Teaching of the Mother Tongue to Migrant Children at Pre-school Age* (Research Report No. 26). Department of Sociology and Social Psychology, University of Tampere.

TREFFERS-DALLER, J., 1992, French–Dutch codeswitching in Brussels: Social factors explaining its disappearance. *Journal of Multilingual and Multicultural Development* 13 (1&2), 143–156.

TREFFERS-DALLER, J., 1994, *Mixing Two Languages: French–Dutch Contact in a Comparative Perspective*. Berlin/New York: Mouton de Gruyter.

TROIKE, R.C., 1978, Research evidence for the effectiveness of bilingual education. *NABE Journal* 3 (1), 13–24.

TRUEBA, H.T., 1988, Culturally based explanations of minority students' academic achievement. *Anthropological and Education Quarterly* 19, 270–287.

TRUEBA, H.T., 1989, *Raising Silent Voices: Educating the Linguistic Minorities for the 21st Century*. New York: Newbury House.

TRUEBA, H.T., 1991, The role of culture in bilingual instruction. In O. GARCÍA (ed.), *Bilingual Education: Focusschrift in Honor of Joshua A. Fishman (Volume 1)*. Amsterdam/Philadelphia: John Benjamins.

TSE, L., 1995, Language brokering among Latino adolescents: Prevalence, attitudes, and school performance. *Hispanic Journal of Behavioral Sciences* 17 (2), 180–193.

TSE, L., 1996a, Language brokering in linguistic minority communities: The case of Chinese- and Vietnamese-American students. *Bilingual Research Journal* 20 (3&4), 485–498.

TSE, L., 1996b, Who decides?: The effects of language brokering on home–school communication. *Journal of Educational Issues of Language Minority Students* 16, 225–234.

TUCKER, G.R. and d'ANGLEJAN, A., 1972, An approach to bilingual education: The St Lambert Experiment. In M. SWAIN (ed.), *Bilingual Schooling: Some Experiences in Canada and the United States*. Ontario: Ontario Institute for Studies in Education Symposium Series No. 1.

TUNMER, W.E. & HERRIMAN, M.L., 1984, The development of metalinguistic awareness: A conceptual overview. In W.E. TUNMER, C. PRATT & M.L. HERRIMAN (eds), *Metalinguistic Awareness in Children*. Berlin: Springer-Verlag.

TUNMER, W.E. & MYHILL, M.E., 1984, Metalinguistic awareness and bilingualism. In W.E. TUNMER, C. PRATT & M.L. HERRIMAN (eds), *Metalinguistic Awareness in Children*. Berlin: Springer-Verlag.

TUNMER, W.E., PRATT, C. & HARRIMAN, M.L. (eds), 1984, *Metalinguistic Awareness in Children: Theory, Research and Implications*. Berlin: Springer-Verlag.

TYACK, D., 1995, Schooling and social diversity: Historical reflections. In W.D. HAWLEY & A.W. JACKSON (eds), *Toward a Common Destiny: Improving Race and Ethnic Relations in America*. San Francisco: Jossey-Bass.

UNITED NATIONS EDUCATIONAL, SCIENTIFIC AND CULTURAL ORGANIZATION (UNESCO) 1953, *The Use of Vernacular Languages in Education*. Paris: UNESCO.

UNITED NATIONS EDUCATIONAL, SCIENTIFIC AND CULTURAL ORGANIZATION (UNESCO) 1991, *World Education Report 1991*. Paris: UNESCO.

UNITED STATES DEPARTMENT OF EDUCATION, 1992, *The Condition of Bilingual Education in the Nation: A Report to the Congress and the President*. Washington, DC: Department of Education.

US BUREAU OF THE CENSUS, 1992, *Population Projections of the United States, by Age, Sex, Race, and Hispanic Origin: 1992 to 2050*. Washington DC: US Government Printing Office.

US BUREAU OF THE CENSUS, 1996, *The Official Statistics; IDB Data Access-Display Mode*. Washington DC: US Government Printing Office. (http://www.census.gov/ftp/pub/ipc/www/idbprint.html).

USMANI, K., 1999, The Influence of Racism and Cultural Bias in the Assessment of Bilingual Children. *Educational and Child Psychology* 16 (3), 44–54.

VAID, J. & HALL, D.G., 1991, Neuropsychological perspectives on bilingualism: Right, left and center. In A.G. REYNOLDS (ed.), *Bilingualism, Multiculturalism and Second Language Learning*. Hillsdale, NJ: Lawrence Erlbaum.

VALDÉS, G., 1995, The teaching of minority languages as academic subjects: Pedagogical and theoretical challenges. *The Modern Language Journal* 79 (3), 299–328.

VALDÉS, G., 1997, Dual language immersion programs: A cautionary note concerning the education of language-minority students. *Harvard Educational Review* 67 (3), 391–428.

VALDÉS, G., 1998, The world outside and inside school: Language and immigrant children. *Educational Researcher* 27 (6), 4–18.

VALDÉS, G. & FIGUEROA, R.A., 1994, *Bilingualism and Testing: A Special Case of Bias*. Norwood, NJ: Ablex.

VALDÉS-FALLIS, G., 1976, Social interaction and code-switching patterns: A case study of Spanish/English alternation. In G. KELLER et al. (eds), *Bilingualism in the Bicentennial and Beyond*. New York: Bilingual Press.

VAN EK, J.A., 1986, *Objectives for Foreign Language Learning. Volume I: Scope*. Strasbourg: Council of Europe.

VAN EK, J.A., 1987, *Objectives for Foreign Language Learning. Volume II: Levels*. Strasbourg: Council of Europe.

VELTMAN, C., 2000, The American linguistic mosaic: Understanding language shift in the United States. In S.L. McKAY & S-L.C. WONG (eds), *New Immigrants in the United States*. Cambridge: Cambridge University Press.

VERDOODT, A.F., 1996, The demography of language. In F. COULMAS (ed.), *The Handbook of Sociolinguistics*. Oxford: Blackwell.

VERHOEVEN, L.T., 1994, Transfer in bilingual development: The linguistic interdependence hypothesis revisited. *Language Learning* 44 (3), 381–415.

VERMA, M.K., CORROGAN, K.P. & FIRTH, S. (eds), 1995, *Working With Bilingual Children*. Clevedon: Multilingual Matters.

VOLTERRA, V. & TAESCHNER, T., 1978, The acquisition and development of language by bilingual children. *Journal of Language* 5, 311–326.

VON GLEICH, U. & SUNY, W.W., 1994, Changes in language use and attitudes of Quechua–Spanish bilinguals in Peru. In P. COLE, G. HERMON & M.D. MARTIN (eds), *Language in the Andes*. Newark, DE: University of Delaware.

VON GLEICH, U. & WÖLCK, W., 1994, Changes in language use and attitudes of Quechua–Spanish Bilingual in Peru. In P. COLE, G. HERMON & M.D. MARTIN (eds), *Language in the Andes*. Newark, DE: University of Delaware.

VYGOTSKY, L.S., 1962, *Thought and Language*. Cambridge, MA: MIT Press.

WAGGONER, D., 1988, Language minorities in the United States in the 1980s. In S.L. McKAY & S.C. WONG (eds), *Language Diversity: Problem or Resource?* New York: Newbury House.

WAGGONER, D., 1998, Ethnic and linguistic minorities in the United States. *Numbers and Needs* 8 (2), 1–4.

WAGNER, S.T., 1980, The historical background of bilingualism and biculturalism in the United States. In M. RIDGE (ed.), *The New Bilingualism*. Los Angeles: University of Southern California Press.

WALDMAN, I., 1994, Bilingual administrative support personnel in United States corporations. *The Modern Language Journal* 78 (3), 327–338.

WEINREICH, U., 1970, *Languages in Contact: Findings and Problems*. The Hague: Mouton.

WELLS, G., 1986, *The Meaning Makers: Children Learning Language and Using Language to Learn*. London: Heinemann.

WELLS, G. & CHANG-WELLS, G.L., 1992, *Constructing Knowledge Together: Classrooms as Centers of Inquiry and Literacy*. Portsmouth, NH: Heinemann.

WELSH LANGUAGE BOARD, 1998, *Priorities in Language Planning*. Cardiff: Welsh Language Board.

WELSH LANGUAGE BOARD, 1999, *A Strategy for the Welsh Language: Targets for 2000–2005*. Cardiff: Welsh Language Board.

WESCHE, M.B., 1993, French immersion graduates at university and beyond: What difference has it made? In J.M. ALATIS (ed.), *The Georgetown Roundtable on Languages and Linguistics 1992*. Washington, DC: Georgetown University Press.

WHITMORE, K.F. & CROWELL, C.C., 1994, *Inventing a Classroom. Life in a Bilingual Whole Language Community*. York, ME: Stenhouse.

WILEY, T.G., 1996a, *Literacy and Language Diversity in the United States*. McHenry, IL: Center for Applied Linguistics and Delts Systems.

WILEY, T.G., 1996b, Language planning and policy. In S.L. McKAY, & N.H. HORNBERGER (eds), 1996, *Sociolinguistics and Language Teaching*. Cambridge: Cambridge University Press.

WILEY, T.G., 1999, Proposition 227: California restricts the educational choices for language minority children. *The Bilingual Family Newsletter* 16 (2) 1–7.

WILEY, T.G. & LUKES, M., 1996, English-Only and Standard English ideologies in the US. *TESOL Quarterly* 30 (3), 511–535.

WILLIAMS, C., 1994, Arfarniad o Ddulliau Dysgu ac Addysgu yng Nghyd-destun Addysg Uwchradd Ddwyieithog. Unpublished PhD thesis. Bangor: University of Wales.

WILLIAMS, C., 1996, Secondary education: Teaching in the bilingual situation. In C. WILLIAMS, G. LEWIS & C. BAKER (eds), *The Language Policy: Taking Stock*. Llangefni (Wales): CAI.

WILLIAMS, C., 2000, Welsh-medium and bilingual teaching in the further education sector. *International Journal of Bilingual Education and Bilingualism* 3 (2), 129–148.

WILLIAMS, C.H., 1991a, Language planning and social change: Ecological speculations. In D.F. MARSHALL (ed.), *Language Planning, Volume III*. Philadelphia: John Benjamins BV.

WILLIAMS, C.H., 1991b, *The Cultural Rights of Minorities: Recognition and Implementation* (Discussion Papers in Geolinguistics No. 18). Staffordshire: Staffordshire Polytechnic.

WILLIAMS, C.H., 1996, Geography and contact linguistics. In H. GOEBL, P.H. NELDE & Z.S.W. WÖLCK, W. (eds), *Contact Linguistics: An International Handbook of Contemporary Research*, Vol. 1. Berlin, New York: Walter de Gruyter.

WILLIAMS, C.H., 1998, Introduction: Respecting the citizens – Reflections on language policy in Canada and the United States. In T. RICENTO & B. BURNABY (eds), *Language and Politics in the Unites States and Canada: Myths and Realities*. Mahwah, NJ: Erlbaum.

WILLIAMS, C.H., 1999, The communal defence of threatened environments and identities. *Geografski vestnik* 71, 105–120.

WILLIAMS, G., 1992, *Sociolinguistics: A Sociological Critique*. London: Routledge.

WILLIAMS, J.D. & SNIPPER, G.C., 1990, *Literacy and Bilingualism*. New York: Longman.

WILLIAMS, M. & BURDEN, R., 1997, *Psychology for Language Teachers*. Cambridge: Cambridge University Press.

WILLIG, A.C., 1981/82, The effectiveness of bilingual education: Review of a report. *NABE Journal* 6 (2&3), 1–19.

WILLIG, A.C., 1985, A meta-analysis of selected studies on the effectiveness of bilingual education. *Review of Educational Research* 55 (3), 269–317.

WILLIG, A.C. & RAMIREZ, J.D., 1993, The evaluation of bilingual education. In B. ARIAS & U. CASANOVA (eds), *Bilingual Education: Politics, Research and Practice*. Berkeley, CA: McCutchan.

WILLIG, C.J., 1990, *Children's Concepts and the Primary Curriculum*. London: Paul Chapman.

WINSLER, A. *et al.*, 1999, When learning a second language does not mean losing the first: Bilingual language development in low-income, Spanish-speaking children attending bilingual preschool. *Child Development* 70 (2), 349–362.

WITKIN, H.A. *et al.*, 1962, *Psychological Differentiation*. New York: John Wiley.

WITKIN, H.A. *et al.*, 1971, *A Manual for the Embedded Figures Test*. Palo Alto, CA: Consulting Psychologists Press.

WONG FILLMORE, L., 1979, Individual differences in second language acquisition. In C. FILLMORE, D. KEMPLER & W. WANG (eds), *Individual Differences in Language Ability and Language Behavior*. New York: Academic Press.

WONG FILLMORE, L., 1982, Instructional language as linguistic input: Second language learning in classrooms. In L. WILKINSON (ed.), *Communicating in the Classroom*. New York: Academic Press.

WONG FILLMORE, L., 1991a, When losing a second language means losing the first. *Early Childhood Research Quarterly* 6, 323–346.

WONG FILLMORE, L., 1991b, Second-language learning in children: A model of language learning in social context. In E. BIALYSTOK (ed.), *Language Processing in Bilingual Children*. Cambridge: Cambridge University Press.

WONG FILLMORE, L. & VALADEZ, C., 1986, Teaching bilingual learners. In M.C. WITTROCK (ed.), *Handbook of Research on Teaching* (3rd edn). New York: Macmillan.

WORLD BANK, 1982, *The Use of First and Second Languages in Primary Education: Selected Case Studies* (World Bank Staff Working Paper No. 504). Washington, DC: World Bank.

WRIGLEY, O., 1996, *The Politics of Deafness*. Washington, DC: Gallaudet University Press.

WURM, S.A. (ed.), 1996, *Atlas of the World's Languages in Danger of Disappearing*. Paris: UNESCO Publishing.

YATIM, A.M., 1988, Some factors affecting bilingualism amongst trainee teachers in Malaysia. Unpublished PhD thesis, University of Wales.

YOUNG, R.M., 1987, Interpreting the production of science. In D. GILL & L. LEVIDOV (eds), *Anti-Racist Science Teaching*. London: Free Association Books.

YTSMA, J., 2000, Trilingual Primary Education in Friesland. In J. CENOZ & U. JESSNER. *English in Europe: The Acquisition of a Third Language*. Clevedon: Multilingual Matters.

YUKAWA, E., 1997, *L1 Japanese Attrition and Regaining: Three Case Studies of Two Early Bilingual Children*. Stockholm: Centre for Research on Bilingualism, Stockholm University.

ZANGWILL, I., 1909, *The Melting Pot*. London: Heinemann.

ZAPPERT, L.T. & CRUZ, B.R., 1977, *Bilingual Education: An Appraisal of Empirical Research*. Berkeley, CA: Bay Area Bilingual Education League.

ZELASKO, N. & ANTUNEZ, B., 2000, *If Your Child Learns in Two Languages*. Washington, DC: National Clearinghouse for Bilingual Education (see: http://www.ncbe.gwu.edu/).

ZENTELLA, A.C., 1988, The language situation of the Puerto Ricans. In S.L. McKAY & S.C. WONG (eds), *Language Diversity: Problem or Recourse*. New York: Newbury House.

ZENTELLA, A.C., 1997, *Growing Up Bilingual*. Malden, MA: Blackwell.

ZOBL, H., 1993, Prior linguistic knowledge and the conservation of the learning procedure. In S.M. GASS & L. SELINKER (eds), *Language Transfer in Language Learning*. Amsterdam/Philadelphia: John Benjamins.

ZONDAG, K., 1991, Bilingual education in Friesland from the innovator's point of view. In O. GARCÍA (ed.), *Bilingual Education: Focusschrift in Honor of Joshua A. Fishman*. Amsterdam/Philadelphia: John Benjamins.

Index

Authors

A.C.A.C., 272
Ab Ieuan, R., 208
Abbott, M., 218
Aclan, Z., 218
Ada, F., 336, 337, 347, 349, 395
Adams, J., 287
Afolayan, A., 222
Aitchison, J., 44, 59
Allard, R., 115
Allardt, E., 48, 390
Allen, P., 235
American Psychological Association, 247
Andersen, R., 115
Anderson, C.A. 319
Anderson, J., 129
Andersson, T., 183
Andres, F., 45, 208
Arias, M., 183, 266
Arnau, J., 233
Arnberg, L., 108, 148
Arsenian, S., 139
Artigal, J. M., 208, 229
Asher, R., 49
Attinasi, J., 252, 412
Auerbach, E.R., 347
August, D., 195, 232, 239, 242, 248, 253, 254, 255, 256, 261, 263, 266

Baca, L.M., 299, 301, 305, 306, 317
Bachi, R., 98
Bachman, L.F., 36, 37, 38, 39, 40
Baetens Beardsmore, H., 5, 16, 29, 71, 131, 222, 223, 224, 225, 226, 242
Baker, C., xiii, ix, 13, 14, 16, 20, 22, 29, 35, 41, 56, 70, 71, 77, 87, 88, 90, 95, 96, 107, 108, 122, 123, 146, 153, 160, 186, 201, 208, 212, 218,

223, 226, 229, 243, 261, 266, 284, 286, 293, 294, 299, 309, 314, 317, 340, 359, 399, 406
Baker, K., 245, 246, 247, 248, 249, 250, 256
Baldauf, R., 55
Balkan, L., 147, 155
Barona, A., 305
Barona, M.S., 305
Barth, F., 390
Bel, A., 207, 229
Bellin, W., 208
Benavides, A.H., 161
Benyon, J., 209
Ben-Zeev, S., 147, 149, 151, 153
Berliner, D.C., 231
Bernhardt E.B., 360, 363, 365
Berthold, M., 208
Bialystok, E., 150, 151, 152, 153, 155, 156, 161, 167
Bild, E., 271
Björklund, S., 100, 360, 361
Blachford, D., 208
Blanc, M., 115
Bloome, D., 327
Bloomfield L., 6, 15, 28
Bonilla, F., 433, 434, 435
Boswell, T., 427, 428, 432
Bourdieu, P., 83
Bourhis, R., 68, 70, 72
Boyd, S., 46
Boyer, M., 183
Boyle, E., 229
Braine, M., 98
Brelje, H., 284
Bright, W., 49
Brisk, M., 195, 255
Brown, D., 208

474

Brown, J., 230
Bull, B., 375
Bullock Report (Department of Education and Science), 350
Bulwer, J., 223
Burden, R., 124
Burns, M., 324
Burt, M., 118,
Butler, Y., 174
Byram, M., 270
Byrne, J., 115, 116

Caldwell, J., 208
Calero-Breckheimer, A., 351, 352
California State Department of Education, 111, 112, 233, 365
Campbell, R. 150
Canadian Education Association, 205, 240, 361, 362
Canale, M., 37
Cantoni, G., 208, 211, 212
Carey, S., 236
Carlisle, J., 150, 153
Carrasquillo, A., 197, 306
Carroll, B., 5
Carroll, J., 36
Carter, T., 261
Casanova, U., 183, 187, 266
Cazabon, M., 218
Cazden, C., 192, 250, 266
Cenoz, J., 100, 208, 224, 225, 226, 271, 272, 293
Cervantes, H., 299, 301, 305, 306, 317
Chamberlain, P., 310
Chamot, A., 128
Chang-Wells, G., 321, 322, 328, 340, 342, 343
Chatfield, M., 261
Chattergy, V., 375
Chomsky, N., 118, 129
Christian, D., 215, 217, 218
Clapham, C., 20, 31, 40
Clarkson, P., 166, 167
Cline, T., 33, 176, 178, 179, 180, 284, 286, 293, 300, 301, 314, 317
Cloud, N., 306, 365
Clyne, M., 99
Codd, J., 150, 151
Coelho, E., 409
Collier, V., 218, 257, 258, 259, 261,352
Colón-Muñiz, A., 199
Conklin, N., 59, 62, 66, 68
Cook, V., 9
Cooper, R., 53, 55, 57, 59
Corder, S., 119

Corson, D., 20, 31, 40, 201, 226, 232, 242, 357, 372, 380
Coulmas, F., 66, 84, 428, 429, 436
Coupland, N., 84, 116
Crago, M., 239
Crawford, J., 183, 186, 187, 188, 201, 211, 226, 252, 255, 266, 372, 376, 377, 399
Cromdal, J., 150
Crowell, C., 324, 340
Cruz, B., 232, 247
Crystal, D., 49, 51, 52, 84, 378
Csizer, K., 125
Cummins, J., 6, 11, 88, 119, 122, 141, 146, 147, 153, 155, 156, 164, 165, 166, 167, 168, 169, 170, 171, 172, 173, 174, 175, 178, 180, 201, 209, 226, 232, 238, 239, 240, 241, 242, 243, 250, 256, 261, 271, 272, 293, 299, 300, 311, 312, 317, 338, 340, 370, 381, 393, 394, 395, 396, 397, 399, 409, 412, 436
Cziko, G., 249, 261

d'Andrea, D., 92, 173
d'Anglejan, A., 205
Damico, J., 317
Danesi, M., 226, 238, 240, 241, 243
Danoff, M., 229, 230
Darcy, N., 136
Davidman, L., 409, 414
Davidman, P., 409, 414
Davies, A., 379
Dawe, L., 166, 167
De Avila, E., 155, 166
De Groot, A., 161
De Houwer, A., 90, 91, 107, 361
De Kanter, A., 245, 246, 247, 248, 250, 256
Del Valle, S., 371
Delgado-Gaitan, C., 298, 347, 349, 354, 397
Delpit, L., 335, 397, 398, 399
Department of Education & Science & the Welsh Office, 34
Desrochers, A., 144
Destino, T., 199
Deuchar, M., 91
DeWaele, J-M., 99
Di Pietro, R., 103
Diaz, C., 60
Diaz, R., 141, 156, 159
Dicker, S., 376, 377, 379, 399, 434
Dicks, J., 363
Diebold, A., 6
Dixon, R., 44, 59
Dodd, B., 301, 302, 307
Dogancay-Aktuna, S., 55

Dolson, D., 14, 250
Donaldson, M., 150
Donato, R., 261, 264, 266
Donmall, B., 406
Döpke, S., 108
Dorian, N., 63, 64
Dörnyei, Z., 123, 125
Dosanjh, J., 95
Doyle, A., 148
Dulay, H., 118, 127, 232, 247
Duncan, S., 155, 166
Duquette, G., 238
Dutcher, N., 232, 238, 241, 243, 373
Dyson, A., 328

Eastman, C., 101
Echevarría, J., 197, 198
ECIS, 223
Edelsky, C.,178, 346
Edwards, J., 64, 66, 232, 387, 388
Edwards, V., 95, 240, 347, 351, 352
Eggington, W., 399, 436
Ellis, N., 129, 150
Ellis, R., 4, 122, 133
Epstein, J., 347
European Commission, 22
Evans, G., 55

Fabbro, F., 142, 143, 161
Faltis, C., 197, 198, 274
Fantini, A., 89, 108
Ferguson, C., 44, 193
Fienberg, S., 250
Figueroa, R., 3, 31, 40, 137, 138, 159, 161, 304, 314, 317
Fischler, I., 150, 160
Fishman J., 7, 12, 13, 44, 45, 46, 47, 66, 72, 73, 74, 75, 76, 77, 78, 79, 81, 82, 83, 84, 192, 209, 368, 369, 384, 388, 413, 424
Fitzgerald, J., 183
Fitzpatrick, F., 229, 230
Forhan, L., 396
Fradd, S., 186, 427, 428
Frederickson, N., 33, 176, 178, 179, 180, 300, 301, 317
Freeman, R., 220, 271, 293
Friere, P., 335, 339
Fruehling, R., 375

Gaarder, A., 59
Gal, S., 63
Galambos, S., 150, 152, 153
Galbraith, P., 167

Gándara, P., 212, 214, 233, 236, 252
Gandhi, M., 378
García, E., 89
García, O., ix, 52, 53, 184, 194, 199, 201, 209, 212, 218, 226, 243, 266, 293, 317, 340, 381, 390, 399, 429, 430, 433, 434, 435, 436
Gardner, H., 137
Gardner, N., 208, 224
Gardner, R., 115, 123
Geary, D., 150
General Accounting Office, 254
Genesee, F., 91, 92, 100, 107, 122, 153, 154, 155, 156, 201, 212, 214, 224, 226, 233, 234, 236, 271, 272, 293, 346, 359, 365, 319
Gersten, R., 300, 305
Ghuman, P., 95, 411
Giles, H., 68, 70, 72, 84, 115, 116
Glass, G., 247
Gliksman, L., 124
Goetz, E., 351, 352
Gonzalez, J., 376
Gordon, M., 383
Graddol, D., 378, 379
Graff, H., 333
Grant, C., 408
Graves, A., 197, 198
Graves, D., 328
Greene, J., 250, 256
Gregory, E., 330, 347, 354
Gregory, S., 288, 289
Grenoble, L., 50, 63
Griffin, P., 324
Grimes, B., 49
Grosjean, F., 7, 8, 33, 101, 144, 313
Guilford, J., 137
Gulutsan, M., 147, 156
Gupta, A., 240

Haberland, H., 379
Hagemeyer, A., 287
Hakuta, K., 89, 92, 98, 150, 152, 153, 159, 169, 173, 174, 183, 187, 195, 232, 239, 242, 248, 253, 254, 255, 256, 261, 263, 266
Hall, D., 143
Hall, G., 218
Hall, J., 399, 436
Hall, K., 363
Halliday, M., 38
Hamayan, E., 155, 317, 346, 365
Hamers, J., 115
Hamlin, J., 208
Hammerly, H., 235
Hansegård, N., 9

Hao, L., 374
Harding, E., 108
Harley, B., 97, 171, 236, 363
Harris, J., 34, 208
Harris, R., 150
Harry, B., 301, 317
Hart, D., 32
Hartman, D., 208
Hawkins, E., 406
Heath, S.B., 320, 331, 332, 333, 340
Heller, M., 102, 236, 238, 243, 365, 392, 393, 428
Henderson, J., 208
Henze, R., 261, 264, 266
Herman, J., 150, 161
Hernandez, R., 310
Hernandez-Chavez, E., 11
Herriman, M., 150
Hickey, T., 233, 235, 237
Hinde J., 13, 20-2
Hirsch, E., 329
Hodson, D., 409
Hoefnagel-Höhle, M., 171
Hoffmann, C., 16, 99, 223, 225
Holm, A., 209, 211, 247, 379
Holm, W., 209, 211, 247, 379
Holobow, N., 359
Holt, D., 271
Hornberger, N., 20, 40, 55, 66, 72, 186, 192,
    195, 214, 229, 299, 330, 340, 347, 351, 354
Houghton, C., 193
Housen, A., 131, 223, 224
Howe, M., 137
Huddy, L., 256, 257
Hudelson, S., 197, 198, 322, 342, 343, 344, 354
Hudson, L., 144
Huffines, M., 55
Hughes, J., 136
Hummel, K., 150
Hunter, J., 247
Hurd, M., 271
Husband, C., 72
Huss-Keeler, R., 347
Hymes, D., 13, 37, 119

Ianco-Worrall, A., 148, 151
Iatcu, T., 100
Imedadze, N., 156
Imoff, G., 377
Isaacs, E., 135

Jacobson, R., 279, 280, 283, 293
Jacques, K., 282
Jankowski, K., 285, 286, 288

Jessner, U.,100, 224
Jimenez, R., 351
Johnson, D., 346
Johnson, R., 207, 226, 233, 235, 236, 243, 357, 365
Jones, G., 222, 233
Jones, S.P., viii, xi, 14, 16, 41, 56, 87, 90, 95,
    96, 153, 160, 186, 212, 218, 223, 359, 406
Jones, W.R., 138, 140

Kaplan, R., 55
Karam, R., 199
Kardash, C., 150
Kaur, S., 104, 105
Keatley, C., 150
Keel, P., 317
Kessler, C., 166
Keyser, R., 230
Khan, V., 72
Kibbee, D., 370, 399
King, K., 72
Kjolseth, R., 374
Klein, E., 271
Kline, P., 30
Klinger, C., 156
Kloss, H., 183, 370
Knight, P., 289, 293
Kolers, P., 144
Kowal, M., 363
Krashen, S., 87, 113, 121, 122, 128, 133, 208,
    210, 246, 250, 251, 262, 297, 351
Krauss, M., 50
Kroll, J., 161

Labrie, N., 47
Ladd, P., 286
Lado, R., 5, 36, 118
Laitin, D., 379
Lambert, W.E., 58, 114, 123, 131, 140, 141,
    142, 204, 218, 271, 359, 403, 404
Lanauze, M., 351
Landry, R., 115
Lanza, E., 90, 91, 92, 108
Lapkin, S., 32, 229, 230, 233, 234, 238, 271, 351
Lasagabaster, D., 100, 224
Latomaa, S., 46
Laurén, C., 208, 233
Laurén, U., 146, 147
Laurie, S., 135, 136
Laver, J., 436
Leblanc, R., 200
Lebrun, N., 225
Lee, J-W., 352
Leopold, W., 89, 148

Lewis, E.G., 1802
Li Wei, 14, 301, 302, 370
Lin, J., 208
Lindholm, K., 212, 218, 360
Lindholm-Leary, K., 212, 214, 215, 218, 219, 220, 226, 266
Linguistic Minorities Project, 28
Littlebear, R., 48
Lorenz, E., 360, 361, 363
Lourie, M., 59, 62, 66, 68
Lowe, G., 32,
Lucas, T., 261, 264, 266
Lukes, M., 376, 379
Lukmani, Y., 124
Lynch, J., 402, 407, 408
Lyon, J., 89, 108
Lyons, J., 183, 187, 372

Macedo, D., 335, 339
Macías, R., 24, 189
Mackey, W.F., 5, 49, 115, 182, 192, 193
MacNab, G., 141, 158
Macnamara, J., 5, 229, 230
MacNeil, M., 208
MacSwan, J., 9
Mägiste, E., 271
Maher, J., 182, 208
Majumder, S., 150, 153
Malakoff, M., 105, 183
Maldonado, J., 304
Malherbe, E., 229
Manzer, K., 208
Martin, D., 282
Martin, P., 222
Martin-Jones, M., 104, 171, 178
Mäsch, N., 222
Mashie, S., 293
Matsumi, N., 144
Matthews, T., 230
May, S., 50, 51, 370, 371, 372, 373, 386, 399, 409, 414
McAlpine, L., 239
McCarty, T., 211, 212, 226
McConnell, B., 230
McGaw, B., 247
McGroarty, M., 376, 379, 419
McKay, S., 66, 197, 351, 352, 388, 399, 414
McLaren, P., 409, 415
McLaughlin, B., 129, 133
McLaughlin, D., 209, 211, 212
McLaughlin, T., 209, 211, 212
McLeod, K., 226
McMahon, A., 44, 59

McQuillan J., 105, 253
Medeiros-Landurand, P., 310
Meechan, M., 101
Meinhof, U., 379
Mercer, J., 301
Merino, B., 199, 249
Met, M., 222, 270, 271, 360, 361, 363
Meyer, J., 214
Meyer, M., 250
Miller, C., 180
Miller, N., 301, 302, 317
Mills, R., 104, 105
Milroy, L., 14
Mitchell, D., 199
Mitchell, R., 133
Mohanty, A., 154
Moll, L., 348
Morales R., 433, 434, 435
Morison, S., 212
Morris, D., 431
Morris, S., 226
Moseley, C., 49
Mulcahy, R., 166
Multilingual Resources for Children Project, 354
Muñoz, C., 100
Murtagh, L., 34, 208
Myers Scotton, C., 101, 102, 103
Myhill, M., 151
Myles, F., 133

Naiman, N., 128
Náñez, J., 136
Nelde, P., 47
Nettle, D., 48, 49, 51, 66, 84
Neufeld, G., 156
Nicoladis, E., 90, 91, 92, 107, 153, 156
Nieto, S., 408, 409, 415
Nuffield Languages Inquiry, 430

Ó Gliasáin, M., 24
Ó Riagáin, P., 82
O'Malley, J., 128
Ochs, T., 223
Ogbu, J., 379, 380, 381
Oka, H., 208
Olaziregi, I., 208, 229
Oller, J., 5, 11, 12, 37, 122, 169
Olneck, M., 408, 410
Otheguy, R., 192, 193, 212, 218, 368, 369, 387, 389, 429, 430, 433, 435, 436
Otto, R., 192, 193
Ovando, C., 352, 374, 409, 415

Oxenham, J., 322
Oxford, R., 128
Ozóg, A., 222

Padilla, A., 150
Padilla, R., 161
Paivio, A., 144
Pakir, A., 222
Parrillo, V., 368, 384
Parrino, A., 282
Paulston, C., 37, 47, 61, 66, 82, 84, 183, 383, 391, 392
Pavadis, M., 142, 143
Pavlenko, A., 150
Peal, E., 140, 141, 142
Pellerano, C., 186
Pennycook, A., 379
Pereles, J., 208
Pérez, B., 349, 351, 354
Perkins, K., 11, 122
Perlmann, J., 183
Perotti, A., 411
Phillipson, R., 370, 371, 378, 399
Pintner, R., 139
Pon Sin Ching, 14
Poplack, S., 101, 180
Porter, R., 384
Portes, A., 374
Powers, S., 288, 289
Price, E., 229
Pucci, S., 78

Quay, S., 91
Quezada, M., 252
Quinn, M., 166

Ramírez, J.D., 199, 248, 249, 250, 252
Ransdell, S., 150, 160
Rebuffot, J., 204, 205, 359, 362
Redfem, A., 240
Reid, S., 47
Resnick, D., 310
Resnick, L., 310
Resnick, M., 64
Reyhner, J., 209, 211
Reynolds, A., 140, 157
Reynolds, D., 208
Rhee, J., 187
Ricciardelli, L., 146, 147, 150, 152
Riley, P., 108
Riley, R., 220f, 252
Ringbom, H., 271
Rippberger, S., 392

Rivera, C., 178, 180
Roberts, C., 237, 359
Roberts, G., 102
Robinson, C., 71
Robson, A., 175, 176, 178
Rodriguez, V., 197
Romaine, S., 16, 44, 48, 49, 51, 59, 66, 84, 89, 101, 104, 107, 171, 178
Romero, M., 282
Ronjat, J., 88
Rosenthal, J., 275
Rosenthal, R., 159
Rosier, P., 247
Rossell, C., 250, 256
Roukens, J., 436
Rubin, J., 128
Rueda, R., 159, 306
Ruiz, R., 368, 370, 371
Ryan, E., 150

Saer, D., 136, 138, 229
Saif, P., 271
Sais, E., 150
Sankoff, D., 102
Saunders, G., 108
Sayers, D., 436
Schallert, D., 352
Scheraga, M., 396
Schermerhorn, R., 200, 383, 389, 393
Schinke-Llano, L., 89
Schlossman, S., 183
Schmidt, F., 376
Schmidt, R., 129, 183, 187, 382, 383, 384, 385, 386, 399
Schrier, L., 360
Schumann, J., 115, 127
Scott, M., 125
Sears, C., 223, 226
Sears, D., 256, 257
Secada, W., 175, 384
Secco, G., 92
Selinker, L., 235
Sharwood Smith, M., 101
Sheldon, M., 271
Shohamy, E., 32, 36, 40, 58, 71, 95, 96, 174
Siegel, J., 208
Sierra, J., 208, 229
Siguán, M., 115, 424
Singleton, D., 97
Skehan, P., 32, 122, 133
Skinner, B., 117
Skutnabb-Kangas, T., 6, 9, 11, 16, 30, 66, 166, 197, 198, 370, 371, 373, 383, 392, 399

Sleeter, C., 408
Smith, F., 136, 230, 345
Smith, N., 347, 349
Snipper, J., 351
Snow, C.E., 171, 192, 266, 324, 351
Snow, M.A., 364
Spolsky, B., 56, 58, 64, 66, 71, 95, 96, 114, 133, 208
Sridhar, K., 46
Starck, C., 390
Stern, H.H., 3, 233
Sternberg, R.J., 157, 158
Stotz, D., 208
Street, B., 319, 330, 334, 335
Strong, M., 289
Stubbs, M., 48, 373, 375
Sung, H., 150
Suni, I., 100
Swain, M., 32, 37, 130, 131, 148, 207, 223, 226, 229, 230, 233, 234, 235, 236, 243, 271, 351, 357, 363, 365
Swan, D., 223, 224, 226
Swanwick, R., 289, 293

Taeschner, T., 90
Takaki, R., 388, 389
Taylor, D., 68, 7072, 239, 382, 403, 404
Tennant, E., 209, 211
Terrell, T., 121, 128, 133
Théberge, R., 115
Thomas, J., 271
Thomas, W., 218, 250, 259, 261
Thompson, L., 87
Todd, R., 412
Tollefson, J., 116, 379
Toohey, K.,, 209
Torrance, E., 145
Torres, G., 351
Torres-Guzmán, M., 349, 351, 354
Tosi, A., 223, 224, 383
Toukomaa, P., 11, 166
Treffers-Daller, J., 102
Troike, R., 232, 247
Trueba, H., 298, 371, 379
Tse, L., 104, 105, 106, 253
Tucker, G., 204, 205
Tunmer, W., 150, 151
Tyack, D., 387

United Nations Educational, Scientific and Cultural Organization (UNESCO), 33, 49, 270, 322
United States Department of Education, 250

Ury, W., 103
Usmani, K., 304

Vaid, J., 143
Valadez, C., 293
Valdés, G., 3, 31, 40, 137, 138, 159, 161, 195, 255, 304, 314, 317
Valdés-Fallis, G., 104
Valencia, J., 271
van Beeck, H., 71
van Ek, J., 113, 130
Veltman, C., 389
Verhoeven, L., 272, 394
Volterra, V., 90
Von Gleich, U., 62
Vygotsky, L., 156, 327

Waggoner, D., 189
Wagner, S., 196
Waldman, L., 433
Watahomigie, L., 211, 226
Wells, G., 321, 322, 328, 340, 342, 343, 350
Wells, M., 193
Welsh Language Board 55, 57
Wesche, M., 236
Whaley, L., 50, 63
Whitmore, K., 324, 340
Wiley, T., 9, 10, 55, 170, 171, 178, 180, 252, 321, 340, 376, 379
Wiliams, Cen, 275, 280, 281, 293
Williams, G., 45, 82, 116
Williams, J., 351
Williams, M., 124
Willig, A., 247, 248, 250, 251, 256
Willig, C., 345
Winsler, A., 87
Witkin, H., 154, 155
Witt, D., 174
Wölck, W., 62
Wong Fillmore, L., 92, 93, 120, 171, 293
Wong, S-L.C., 388, 399, 414
Woodward, J, 300, 305
Wurm, S., 49, 50

Yatim, A., 124
Young, R., 410
Ytsma, J., 100
Yukawa, E., 89

Zangwill, O., 382
Zappert, L., 232, 247
Zentella, A., 59, 265
Zobl, H., 271

Subject Index

Academic Language Competence, 11
Accommodation theory, 115f
Acculturation, 115
Acquisition planning, 56f
Additive bilingualism, 58, 114f, 353, 360, 395
Adult language learning, 95
Age, 97
Anti-racism, 402f, 411f
Anxiety, 127
Aptitude, 122f
Arizona, 252, 264
Assessment, 19, 177, 304f, 309f, 346f, 396
Assimilation, 110, 187, 192, 196, 198, 368, 382f, 388f, 402f
Asymmetrical principle, 47
Attitudes, 53, 103, 123f, 235, 238, 407
Audiolingualism, 117f
Australia, 208
Austria, 63
Autonomous minorities, 379f

Balance theory, 135, 163f
Balanced bilinguals, 7, 141, 158
Basques, 192, 208, 229, 358
Belgium, 27
BICS, 169f
Bilingual Education Act, 186f, 190, 191
Biliteracy, 342f, 350f
Boundaries, 47f, 63f, 91, 92, 216, 273f, 389f
Brain, 142f
Brunei, 222

California, 111, 233, 251f, 264
CALP, 169f, 281
Canada, 27, 204f, 229, 230, 233f, 357f, 391f
Caretaker speech, 362
Castelike minorities, 380f
Catalan, 208, 358
Census, 19, 22, 24f
Childhood bilingualism, 86f
Chinese, 14
Circumstantial bilingualism, 3
Civil Rights, 185, 370f
Codeswitching, 100f, 275
Cognition (see Thinking)
Common underlying proficiency, 165f
Communicative language, 31, 119, 222, 363
Communicative sensitivity, 153f
Community, 43, 72, 82, 88, 332, 402
Comprehensible language input, 121
Comprehensible language output, 131
Concurrent language use, 279f

Conflict paradigm, 392f
Connectionism, 129
Constructivism, 222, 326f
Context embedded communication, 170f
Context reduced communication, 170f
Context, 12, 29, 86, 113f, 115f, 124, 126, 139, 157, 255, 262, 276f, 327, 353
Contrastive analysis, 118
Conversational fluency, 11
Coral Way Elementary School, 218
Corpus language planning, 55f
Courts, 185, 190f, 304, 371, 372
Creative thinking, 144f
Criterion referenced testing, 33, 35, 314
Critical literacy, 333f, 338, 339
Crosslinguistic influence, 101
Cuban, 46, 186, 218, 432
Cultural pluralism, 73, 193, 384f
Culture, 74, 75, 112, 115, 272f, 313, 322, 329, 387f, 397f, 402f, 420f

Deaf bilinguals, 284f, 288f
Developmental Independence hypothesis, 169
Developmental maintenance education, 187, 208f, 209, 218, 238f
Diglossia, 44f
Divergent thinking, 144f
Domains, 12, 27, 378
'Double Semilingualism', 9
Drop-out, 262
Dual coding model, 142f
Dual language education, 212f, 259

Economy and bilingualism, 69, 79, 80, 111, 241, 386, 427f, 430f, 433f
Effectiveness of bilingual education, 229f, 245f
Elective bilingualism, 3
Elementary & Secondary Education Act (ESEA), 186f, 190, 191
Employment, 113, 417f
Empowerment, 312, 321, 335, 381, 393f, 396, 397
Endangered languages, 48f
England, 229, 230, 297
English language, 92, 94, 95, 184, 239, 246f, 261, 376f, 420, 422, 424
English-only movement, 219, 376f
Enrichment bilingual education, 192f
Equilibrium paradigm, 391f
ESL, 195f

Ethnic community schools, 187, 208f
Ethnic identity, 116, 384f, 389f
European schools, 223f
Expert overviews, 254f

Field dependency / independency, 154f
Finland, 68, 208, 360
Foreign language teaching, 199, 374
Fractional view of bilinguals, 7
Functional literacy approach, 323f
Functions of language, 3, 12
Funds of knowledge, 348

Gaelic, 63
Germany, 222
Graded Intergenerational Disruption Scale
    (GIDS), 75f

Hearing impaired people, 284f
Hebrew, 95, 96, 98, 99
Heritage language education, 208f, 238f
Holistic view of bilinguals, 8
Home (see Parents),
Hong Kong, 229

Identity, 51, 69, 402f
Immersion bilingual education, 167, 204f,
    217, 357f, 391f
Immigrants, 48, 60f, 70, 98, 171, 183f, 233f,
    375f, 380f, 388f, 433
Individual bilingualism, 2f
Individual differences, 121f, 127f
Information processing, 129
Information technology, 424f
Inputs, 117f
Instrumental motivation, 123f
Integrative motivation, 123f
'Intelligence'/IQ, 136f, 304, 312
Interdependence, 119, 394
Intergenerational language transmission,
    78, 81, 93
Inter-language marriage, 70
Interlanguage, 363
International schools, 223
Internet, 425f
Interpreters, 104f, 312, 418
Ireland, 182, 208, 229, 235, 360, 372
Israel, 95, 96, 98, 99

Japan, 182

Language ability, 3, 4f, 24, 122
Language achievement, 4

Language acquisition, 87f, 93f, 110f, 114,
    118, 129
Language allocation, 269f, 273f
Language as a problem, 368f
Language as a resource, 373f
Language as a right, 370f
Language awareness, 406f
Language background, 13, 20
Language balance, 30
Language borrowing, 101
Language choice, 13
Language competence, 4, 36f, 130
Language death, 48f, 63f
Language delay, 301f
Language diversity, 51, 53, 374
Language dominance, 30
Language errors, 362
Language Garden analogy, 52f
Language learning, 87, 94f, 114
Language loss, 59f, 92
Language maintenance, 58f
Language performance, 311
Language planning, 50, 52f, 55f, 75
Language proficiency, 4, 28, 33, 215
Language reproduction (see
    Intergenerational language transmission)
Language revitalization, 68f
Language revival / reversal, 72f, 75f
Language rights, 370f
Language separation, 216, 273f
Language shift, 47f, 54f, 58f, 68f
Language skills, 4
Language status, 68f
Language vitality, 68f
Lateralization, 143
Lau (remedies), 186, 188, 190, 191, 372
Law, 182, 190f, 304, 371f
Learner processes, 129f
Learning difficulties, 299f, 308f
Learning styles, 128f
Limited English Proficiency (LEP), 5, 8
Literacy, 5, 319f, 342f
Local literacies, 330
Luxembourg, 225

Mainstream bilingual education, 199f
Maintenance bilingual education, 192, 209
Malaysia, 124
Maori, 372
Mass media, 71, 422f
Measurement, 18
Meta analysis, 247, 248, 250
Metalinguistic awareness, 148f, 150f

Mexicans, 410
Motivation, 123f
Multiculturalism, 384, 402f
Multilingualism, 99f

Native Americans, 51, 183f, 208, 211f, 427
Navajo, 64, 208, 211, 247, 379
Networks, 43
Neurolinguistics, 142f
New Zealand, 208, 372
Nigeria, 222
Norm referenced tests, 33, 314

One parent families, 90
Oracy, 5, 32
Oral interview, 32
Outputs, 130f

Papua New Guinea, 208
Parents, 87f, 210, 263, 297f, 310, 332, 347f,
    359, 384, 394f
Pennsylvania Amish/German, 48, 54, 70
Personality principle, 47f
Peru, 229
Politics, 36, 116, 367f, 408
Postmodernism, 408
Power, 36, 51, 74, 112, 116, 336, 367f
Prejudice reduction, 411f
Processes, 150, 249
Productive language skills, 5
Proposition 227, 251f
Public opinion, 227, 251f
Puerto Ricans, 64
Pull-out classes, 197f

Quebec, 385
Quechua, 62

Racism, 411f
Receptive language skills, 5
Religion, 71, 411
Reversing language shift, 73f
Rights, 370f
Riley, Richard, 220f, 252
Rurality, 71, 430

Scotland, 63, 372
SDAIE, 197f
Segregationist education, 198
'Semilingualism', 9
Separate underlying proficiency, 164f
Separatist education, 200f
Sequential bilingualism, 87

Sheltered English, 195, 197f
Sign language, 287f
Simultaneous bilingualism, 87f
Singapore, 222
Situation (see Context)
Societal bilingualism, 2, 44f, 115
Sociocultural literacy, 328f
Socioeconomic / sociocultural class, 178,
    298, 431
Sociolinguistics, 44f
South Africa, 80, 208, 229
Spanish, 26, 208, 307, 308
Special education, 306f
Special needs, 300f, 308f
Status language planning, 55f, 68
Structural approach, 118f
Structured immersion, 195f
Study activities, x, 16, 40, 66, 84, 108, 133,
    161, 180, 202, 227, 243, 266, 293, 317, 340,
    355, 365, 399, 415, 436
Submersion, 195f, 207, 217
Subtractive bilingualism, 58, 114f, 353, 395,
    423
Surface fluency, 169f
Switzerland, 45, 208

Territorial principle, 47f
Testing, 10, 39, 138f, 313
Thinking, 6, 112, 136f, 163f, 259
Thresholds, 147, 155, 166f, 169f
Title VII funds, 187
Total Communication, 284, 289
Tourism, 418f, 420f
Transfer, 101, 210, 351, 352, 363
Transitional bilingual education, 198f, 217,
    219, 245f
Translanguaging, 280f
Trilingual education, 225, 271
Trilingualism, 98f, 225, 271
Two way language education-see Dual
    language education,
Typology of bilingual education, 192f

Ulpan, 95f
Underachievement, 296f
United States, 19, 24f, 92, 94, 98, 111, 120,
    174, 182f, 229f, 245f, 297f, 304f, 320, 369f,
    375f, 432

Venezuela, 26

Wales, 46, 47, 57, 70, 182, 192, 208, 229, 237,
    272, 358, 360, 372

Whole curriculum approach, 409
Whole language, 324f
Withdrawal classes, 197f
Word association, 30

World Wide Web, 425f
Writing, 344f

Zone of Proximal Development, 327